Under the editorship of

WILLIAM L. LANGER

COOLIDGE PROFESSOR OF HISTORY
HARVARD UNIVERSITY

The *French* REVOLUTION

AS TOLD BY CONTEMPORARIES

BY E. L. HIGGINS

ARKANSAS STATE TEACHERS COLLEGE

COOPER SQUARE
PUBLISHERS, INC.
NEW YORK 1975

COPYRIGHT 1938 by E. L. Higgins
Reprinted by permission of Houghton Mifflin Company
Published 1975 by Cooper Square Publishers, Inc.
59 Fourth Avenue, New York, N. Y. 10003

Printed in the United States of America
by Sentry Press, Inc., New York, N. Y. 10013

Library of Congress Cataloging in Publication Data

Higgins, Earl Leroy, ed, and tr.
The French Revolution as told by contemporaries. *New York,*
~~Reprint of the 1938 ed. published by Houghton Mifflin,~~ *Cooper Square*
~~Boston.~~ *Publishers, Inc.,*
  ~~Bibliography: p.~~ *1975.*
  1. France—History—Revolution, 1789-1799—Personal
narratives. 1. Title. ~~Apr 23, 1975~~
DC145.H53   1974   944.04   74-79396
ISBN 0-8154-0492-1

463p. 23cm.

DC
145
H53
1974

Editor's Introduction

THE great conflict of ideas and interests, the tragic clash of forceful personalities, the international struggles which together make the French Revolution have oft been recounted, and by some of the foremost historians of modern times. Yet even now there is nothing approaching a consensus of opinion on many of the basic aspects of this great overturn. It is, in fact, most unlikely that there will ever be one generally accepted account of it. Each generation will continue the effort to unearth new material and each generation will proceed to put its own interpretation on the constantly growing mass of evidence. Under the circumstances, knowledge of the sources, always important, is indispensable for an understanding of the course of events. But the sources, apart from their number, are widely scattered and in many instances almost inaccessible. Mr. Higgins' book therefore should prove to be of genuine value to the student. He has made a very discriminating selection from a wide body of material, much of it not easily available and a good deal of it not hitherto translated. Most of the fundamental forces and outstanding events are well represented in his collection and in all cases he has taken pains to adduce variant views of the matters discussed. Louis XVI appeared very differently to courtiers like Fersen and to popular agitators like Marat, and the same would hold true of all the leading actors. By presenting several estimates of the same person or several accounts of the same thing, Mr. Higgins has enabled the student not only to recognize differences of view, but also to recapture some of the uncertainty and excitement of great affairs as they transpire. Even those who have read widely in the history of the Revolution are sure to find fresh enjoyment in this volume. For here, after all, is the raw material from which later narratives have been shaped. With the sources so conveniently and so ably collated, every reader may remake this epochal history for himself.

WILLIAM L. LANGER

Preface

THE object of this volume is to present the French Revolution through the medium of contemporaries and as a connected narrative. Hitherto, source books have been made up of isolated extracts and have lacked continuity.

Very few of the numerous memoirs and collections of documents have been translated into English. Of these few, some are out of print. Even those in French are often difficult to obtain; for example, La Fayette's *Mémoires*, which were published a hundred years ago.

Through a readable narrative made up of primary sources one becomes familiar with the individuals in the Revolution who have told their own stories and the field of memoir literature is opened for further exploration. It has been possible to obtain some knowledge of these authors without the embarrassment of the repetitions, trivialities, and personalities often found in memoirs.

Out of the wealth of material dealing with the Revolution, it has been difficult to make selections. In general, the most interesting passages and the best-known authors have been chosen. Both sides have been given, and royalist vies with revolutionist in denouncing his enemies. The views are often contradictory, as when Barras and Bonaparte make opposite representations in regard to the latter's services on the 13th Vendémiaire. The reader learns to distinguish prejudices, propaganda, and distortions, and to discount violences, denunciations, and partisan bitterness. He also learns to distrust the written word and seek his own interpretation.

In reading a contemporary account, one notices a quaintness, a vividness, and a freshness that carry the reader back to the period with which it deals. One becomes less abstract, less didactic, and perhaps less prejudiced in reading the words of the protagonists in a great historical drama.

I wish to acknowledge my indebtedness to P. F. Collier & Son Company for permission to use extracts from Mme. Campan's *Memoirs of Marie Antoinette* (*Memoirs of the Courts of Europe*) and from Fersen's *Diary and Correspondence* (*Versailles Memoirs*); to Longmans, Green & Company for extracts from Miles's *Correspondence on the French Revolution, 1789–1817*; to Professor Frederick B. Artz of Oberlin College and Miss Ora Blackmun for suggestions and corrections; to Professor William L. Langer of Harvard University for his assistance and editorship; and to my wife, who has greatly aided in the translating and in the preparation of the manuscript.

Contents

Introduction

Weber, I, 75–79.[1]

THE French Revolution has been vast and prolonged; there has been a complexity of events and people; many passions, dangerous though noble, terrible though infamous, have here displayed their enthusiasm or frenzy and have here waged battle or made common cause. Therefore, in abandoning themselves to speculation or metaphysics, thirty different writers might assign thirty different causes for this shock which the world has experienced, and each render his explanation plausible.

The truth is that there are numerous causes of which one may say, "Without that the Revolution would not have happened"; but there is not one which could be put forward as the sole cause of the Revolution.

I have watched events with all the attention of which my mind is capable; I have read what has been printed; I have meditated over a number of manuscript memoirs, from which I have been permitted to draw information; and, seeking always to fix upon simple ideas, I have been constrained to recognize three primary and immediate causes of the French Revolution: the disorder in the finances, the disposition of mind, and the war in America.

If order had reigned in the treasury; if the equilibrium between expenditure and receipts had been perfect; then the ideas of independence, which filled all minds, would have been vented in private circles, in academic sessions, or in a few parliamentary remonstrances; would have given way to peaceful practices; would have been checked by a reciprocal restraint; would even have entered into a new order of submission, in being applied to the common weal by the new administrative corps which arose everywhere and remained under the control of the king.

If the general disposition of mind had been, under Louis XVI, what it had been under Louis XIV, or even under half the reign of Louis XV, the disorder of the finances would not have led to any political catastrophe. The void in the treasury might have been filled with more or less promptitude; a suppression of salaries might have been decreed; investigations, more or less severe, instituted; a few administrators might have been disturbed and punished; but no one would have dreamed of organizing an insurrection against the king.

Finally, if, in this combination of circumstances, there had been no war in America; and there had been sixteen millions less in the national debt; then the disposition of mind would not have suddenly carried theories of peaceful independence to the convulsions and excesses of an actual revolt.

[1] Weber was the foster brother of Marie Antoinette. See the Bibliography for notes on Weber and other contemporaries.

To have prevented the French Revolution, then, one of these three things was necessary: to arrange the finances, to control the trend of thought, or to abandon the American insurgents. By avoiding one of these three causes of disturbance, the other two would have been rendered powerless. Instead, all three were united when they were most potent. A Leopold, a Frederick, a Gustavus might still have found a way to triumph over these; but Louis XVI was born to be the father of a submissive people, and not to be the master of rebellious subjects; the Providence which had destined him to be a great example, had given him the constancy of martyrs rather than the courage of heroes, the confiding purity of angels rather than the suspicious wisdom of mortals; and, in the crisis into which he found himself thrown, no one could make up for the action, the will, and the character of the master.

This last consideration is painful to express, but impossible to dissimulate. The character of the unfortunate Louis XVI, and the variance between his particular virtues and the requirements of events, have obviously contributed so much to the success of the Revolution, that I ought perhaps to present them here as a fourth primary cause, after the three which I have already given. But beyond that, in my opinion, there are no circumstances or persons that do not belong to the multitude of secondary causes. Things were inevitable, names almost immaterial; lacking one personage, another would have come forward. Whenever, in a great state, the sources of the public treasury have dried up; when the old restraints of rank and subordination are broken down, and there is no firm hand to impose new ones immediately, then it must be expected that vices, passions, and even virtues will enter into a fermentation whose effects will be incalculable. Then men of stern probity will desire to profit by the moment to introduce rigorous justice throughout; while others, either incapable of understanding, or resolved to proscribe this justice, will at one time declare open war upon it, and at another appear to range themselves in its train, in order to clothe their crimes with its name. There will be enthusiasts, dangerous by the very purity of their intentions, and corrupt beings who will willingly cause public misfortune to further their personal interests. There will be youth, avid for novelties, drunk with presumption, and disdaining the experience of centuries; old men, bowed down by the yoke of routine, and understanding nothing except that which exists no longer; men who believe themselves placed in wisdom, as in nature, between these two ages, and who would reconcile the past, the present, and the future, will persuade nowhere and displease everywhere. One will see those ambitious for power and for riches seize, some without discernment and others without scruple, all means of satiating the passion which torments them. Into this tumult, already so terrible, the discontented, the vindictive, the envious, the ingrate will throw themselves. At first, they will all belong to the classes superior in rank, in fortune, or in education. Soon each will devote all his efforts to move what one calls the brute mass of society, in order to detach some portion of it, and use it against his rivals. Once put into movement, this mass will overwhelm everything, men and projects, opposition and counsel, enemies and leaders.

That is a general description of the French Revolution; it is that of every revolution which breaks out in like circumstances and with like principles.

I. The Monarchy

THE GOVERNMENT OF 1789. (Mme. de Staël, 26.)

THE last years of Louis XV, it cannot be repeated too often, had discouraged the government; and, unless a warlike king could have directed the imagination of the French towards conquests, nothing could distract the different classes of the state from the important demands that all believed they had the right to make. The nobles were tired of being merely courtiers; the higher clergy desired additional influence in affairs; the *parlements* had too much or too little political strength to be contented with being only judges; and the nation, which included the writers, the capitalists, the great merchants, a great number of proprietors, and a crowd of individuals in the administration, the nation impatiently compared the government of England, where talent could rise to anything, with that of France, where one was nothing except by favor or birth. Thus all speech and action, all virtue and all passions, all sentiments and all vanities, the popular mind and the fashion tended equally to the same end.

THE DESIRE FOR A CONSTITUTION IN 1789. (Mme. de Staël, 78.)

Les Maximes de droit public français, published in 1775 by a magistrate of the *parlement* of Paris, accord entirely with those which have been proclaimed by the Constituent Assembly on the necessity of the balance of powers, of the consent of the nation to subsidies, of its participation in legislative acts, and of the responsibility of ministers. There is not a page in which the author does not recall the contract existing between the people and the kings, and it is on the facts of history that he bases it.

Other reputable men in the French magistrature declare that there were constitutional laws in France, but that they had fallen into disuse. Some say that they had not been in force since Richelieu, others say since Charles V, others since Philip the Fair, and others, finally, since Charlemagne. Assuredly it matters little whether such laws existed, if they have been forgotten for so many centuries. But it is easy to terminate the discussion. If there are fundamental laws, if it is true that they contain all the rights assured to the English nation, then the friends of liberty are in accord with the partisans of the old order of things; and yet the negotiation of an agreement would, it seems to me, be very difficult.

ABUSES OF POWER. (*Jefferson, I, 86, Autobiography.*)

Nor should we wonder at this pressure [for a fixed constitution] when we consider the monstrous abuses of power under which this people were ground to powder; when we pass in review the weight of their taxes, and the inequality of their distribution; the oppressions of the tithes, the *tailles*,[1] the *corvées*,[2] the *gabelles*,[3] the farms and the barriers; the shackles on commerce by monopolies; on industry by guilds and corporations; on the freedom of conscience, of thought, and of speech; on the freedom of the press by censorship, and of the person by *lettres de cachet*;[4] the cruelty of the criminal code generally; the atrocities of the rack; the venality of judges, and their partiality to the rich; the monopoly of military honors by the *noblesse*; the enormous expenses of the queen, the princes, and the court; the prodigalities of pensions; and the riches, luxury, indolence, and immorality of the clergy. Surely, under such a mass of misrule and oppression, a people might justly press for thorough reformation, and even might dismount their roughshod riders, and leave them to walk on their own legs.

NO GENERAL POSITIVE LAW. (*Extract from a speech of Lally-Tollendal to the National Assembly, July 15, 1789.*)

You have no law to protect your individual safety and liberty from arbitrary attacks ... and, during the reign of a king whose justice is known and whose probity is respected by all Europe, ministers have caused your magistrates to be torn from the sanctuary of the laws by armed satellites. In the preceding reign, all the magistrates in the kingdom were dragged from their seats and from their homes, and scattered by exile, some on the tops of mountains, others in the slough of marshes, all in situations more obnoxious than the most horrible of prisons. Go back still farther and you will find a hundred thousand *lettres de cachet* issued on account of paltry theological squabbles; and farther still and you see as many sanguinary commissions as arbitrary imprisonments; nay, you will find no spot on which you can repose till you come to the reign of your good Henri IV.

You have no law which establishes the liberty of the press ... and up to this time your thoughts have been enslaved, your wishes chained; the cry of your hearts under oppression has been stifled, sometimes by the despotism of individuals, at others by the still more terrible despotism of bodies.

You have not, or at least you no longer have, a law requiring your consent to taxes ... and, for two centuries past, you have been burdened with more than three or four hundred millions of taxes without having consented to a single one.

You have no law which establishes the responsibility of all the ministers of the executive power ... and the creators of those sanguinary commissioners, the issuers of those arbitrary orders, the dilapidators of the public exchequer, the violators of the sanctuary of public justice, those who have imposed upon the virtues of one king, those who have flattered the passions of another, those

[1] Property taxes.   [2] Taxes payable in labor.
[3] Salt taxes.   [4] Sealed letters for arbitrary arrest.

who brought disasters upon the nation, have been called to no account — have undergone no punishment.

Lastly, you have no general, positive, written law, no diploma at once royal and national, no great charter, upon which rests a fixed and invariable order, from which each learns how much of his liberty and property he ought to sacrifice for the sake of preserving the rest, which ensures all rights, which defines all powers. On the contrary, the system of your government has varied from reign to reign, frequently from ministry to ministry; it has depended on the age and the character of one man. In minorities, under a weak prince, the royal authority, which is of importance to the prosperity and the dignity of the nation, has been indecently degraded, either by the great, who with one hand shook the throne and with the other crushed the people, or by bodies which at one time seized with temerity what at another they had defended with courage. Under haughty princes who had flattered, under virtuous princes who were deluded, this same authority has been carried beyond all bounds. Neither have your secondary powers, as you call them, been better defined or fixed. Sometimes the *parlements* have laid it down as a principle that they could not interfere in affairs of state; at others, they have insisted that it was their prerogative to discuss them as representatives of the nation. On the one hand were seen proclamations making known the will of the king, on the other decrees in which the king's officers forbade, in the king's name, the execution of the king's orders. Among the courts the like discord prevails; they quarrel about their origin, their functions; they mutually launch anathemas at each other by their decrees.

THE PARLEMENTS. (*Besenval, I, 351*.)

Since originally nothing is written in France, nothing is undeniably established. The legislative power which, in fact, resides in the person of the king, because he has two hundred thousand men at his orders, has sometimes denied the right of remonstrance to the *parlement*; but the public outcry has always forced the rendering of it — more especially as the prince has means, acknowledged though violent, to make himself obeyed. When the *parlement* resists obstinately, after a certain number of royal commands, to register his edicts, he holds what is called a *lit de justice*; that is to say, he goes to the *parlement*, accompanied by princes, peers, and a few notables, the latter to form his retinue. There in his presence he makes them strike out of the registers the resolutions contrary to his will and register the edict that he desires.

(*Young, 321–322*.)

The *parlement* of Rouen passed an *arrêt* [1] against killing calves; it was a preposterous one, and opposed by the administration; but it had full force; and had a butcher dared to offend against it, he would have found, by the rigor of his punishment, who was his master. Inoculation was favored by the court in Louis XV's time; but the *parlement* of Paris passed an *arrêt* against it, much more effective in prohibiting, than the favor of the court in encouraging, the

[1] A decree or decision.

practice. Instances are innumerable, and I may remark, that the bigotry, ignorance, false principles, and tyranny of these bodies were generally conspicuous; and that the court (taxation excepted) never had a dispute with a *parlement* but the *parlement* was sure to be wrong. Their constitution, in respect to the administration of justice, was so truly rotten, that the members sat as judges, even in causes of private property in which they were themselves the parties, and have, in this capacity, been guilty of oppressions and cruelties which the crown has rarely dared to attempt.

LETTRES DE CACHET. (*Mme. de Staël, 148–149.*)

The *lettres de cachet* permitted the royal and consequently the ministerial power to exile, to deport, or to imprison for his entire life, without trial, any man whatever. Such power, wherever it exists, constitutes despotism. It ought to have been abolished on the day that the deputies of the French nation met. . . .

The supreme authority of the king permitted him to protect, by *lettres de cachet*, a noble from the action of the law, when he had committed a crime. The Comte de Charolais was a striking example in the last century, and many others of the same kind could be cited. However, by a singular contrast, the relatives of a noble lost none of their prestige when he incurred the penalty of death, while the family of a man of the third estate was dishonored if the tribunals condemned him to the degrading punishment of the gallows, from which nobles alone were exempt.

(*Young, 60.*)

Take the road to Lourdes [Gascony], where is a castle on a rock, garrisoned for the mere purpose of keeping state prisoners, sent hither by *lettres de cachet*. Seven or eight are known to be here at present; thirty have been here at a time; and many for life — torn by the relentless hand of jealous tyranny from the bosom of domestic comfort; from wives, children, friends, and hurried for crimes unknown to themselves — more probably for virtues — to languish in this detested abode of misery — and die of despair. Oh, liberty! liberty! — and yet this is the mildest government of any considerable country in Europe, our own excepted.

THE PROVINCES AND THE INTENDANTS. (*Mme. de Staël, 41–42.*)

The provinces last united to the crown, such as Languedoc, Burgundy, Brittany, etc., were called *pays d'états*, because they had reserved the right to be administered by an assembly composed of the three orders of the province. The king fixed the sum total that he required, but the estates made the assessment. These provinces persisted in the refusal of certain taxes, from which they pretended to be exempt by agreements made with the crown. From that came the inequalities in the system of impositions, the multiple opportunities for smuggling between one province and another, and the establishment of customs duties in the interior.

The *pays d'états* enjoyed great advantages: not only did they pay less, but the sum exacted was assessed by the proprietors who knew the local interests, and were actively concerned. The roads and public establishments were much better cared for, and the taxpayers were treated with much more consideration. The king had never admitted that the estates possessed the right of consenting to imposts; but they conducted themselves as if they had this right in reality. They did not refuse the money asked of them; but they called their contributions *a free gift*. Upon the whole, their administration was preferable to that of other provinces, which were much more numerous and no less merited the interest of the government.

Intendants were named by the king to govern the thirty-two generalities of the kingdom; they did not encounter obstacles except in the *pays d'états*, and sometimes on the part of one of the twelve provincial *parlements* (the *parlement* of Paris was the thirteenth); but, in the greater part of the generalities administered by an intendant, this agent of government alone disposed of the interests of an entire province. He had under his orders an army of employees of the public treasury, detested by the people. These employees tormented them one by one to extort from them taxes disproportionate to their means; and when one wrote to the minister of finances to complain of the vexations of the intendant or of the sub-delegate, it was to this same intendant that the minister sent the complaints, since the supreme authority communicated with the provinces only through them.

FINANCIAL POLICIES OF THE MINISTERS. (*D'Argenson, II, 30–34.*)

These tyrants of ministers think they can stimulate industry and change people's ways by necessitating the payment of large subsidies. For a long time I have heard this cruel idea advocated. It is founded on the idleness which is believed to exist on lands that are tax-exempt (which results only from facility in fraud), and the toil in the districts subject to the heaviest taxes. They do not see that this stimulus has already gone beyond its purpose and has become troublesome, and that labor is discouraged when the increase in taxes is greater than the increase in the profits of labor. . . .

The Cardinal [Fleury] is still praised for imitating the Romans in the Capitol, who threw bread out of the window to prove that they had some left, when in reality it was lacking. . . .

Since here one laughs at the most serious things, there is an epigram current about the cardinal. Of this I remember only the outline. France is a sick man who during a period of three hundred years has been treated by three doctors clothed in red. The first (Richelieu) bled him, the second (Mazarin) dosed him, the third (Fleury) has put him on a diet.

FINANCIAL TYRANNY IN THE PROVINCES. (*D'Argenson, II, 23–27.*)

The real evil which undermines this kingdom and cannot fail to bring its ruin, is that they are too blind here to the decay of the provinces. . . . There is a present certitude that distress is prevalent to an unheard-of degree. At the moment I write, in the midst of peace, with the probability of a harvest, if not abundant, at least passable, men are dying around us of poverty as thick as flies, and are eating grass. The provinces of Maine, Angoumois, Touraine, Haut-Poitou, Périgord, Orléanais, and Berry are the most maltreated; it approaches the neighborhood of Versailles. It is beginning to be recognized, though the impression be but momentary.

I have long perceived the danger that menaces us, and I was perhaps the first to give the alarm on returning from a trip to my lands nearly two years ago. I have said and still think that this condition is not a matter of temporary circumstances, and if a bad year makes the evil more apparent, it will be further advanced than one would think. I have proposed elsewhere means of restoring activity to our fields, and of rescuing them from the financial tyranny that exhausts them, but the moment is unfavorable to innovations. . . .

M. Orry [the controller-general] has faith only in the reports of financiers, who naturally are interested in hiding the truth from him. He thinks the intendants who speak to him more frankly are like parish priests and charitable women whose unrestrained sympathies exaggerate the scenes of misery. Moreover, he has disgusted all his intendants, no voice is lifted between the throne and the people, and the kingdom is oppressed with taxes like a conquered territory. The only aim is the collection of the current year's taxes, without thinking of what the inhabitant can pay the year after.

It is true that our reasoners are at fault; there have been no marked famines, or at most only semi-annually in certain provinces, with satisfactory harvests in others. But everywhere one realizes the dearth of money and of means to buy provisions. With this poverty, grain and provisions rise in price, and labor is no longer employed. Nevertheless, the taxes are rigorously exacted, and the *taille* raised extremely high. . . .

Normandy, that excellent country, succumbs under the weight of taxes and under the exactions of the farmers-general;[1] the farmers are ruined and have disappeared. I know persons who are reduced to using valets to make their excellent lands produce.

THE TAXES. (*Mme. de Staël, 39–40.*)

. . . the most numerous class of the state was weighed down with tithes (*dîmes*) and feudal dues, from which the Revolution delivered it; the *gabelles* and imposts which certain provinces endured, and from which others were freed, the inequality of assessment, founded on the exemptions of the nobles and clergy, all concurred to render the situation of the people infinitely less happy than it is now. Each year the intendants forced the sale of the remaining possessions of the poverty-stricken, because many taxpayers found it impossible to pay the taxes demanded of them; in no other state in Europe were the people treated in a manner so revolting.

THE CORVÉE AND THE TAILLE. (*D'Argenson, III, 290–292.*)

A zeal for fine roads had laid hold of the ministry and the provincial intendants. No sooner had the latter perceived this avenue of authority and useful-

---

[1] Financiers who contracted to collect taxes.

ness open to them than they threw themselves into it headlong. It is a new *taille* to crush the people. It is estimated that during the year a fourth of the laborers work a fourth of their time in the *corvées*, where they must provide for their own nourishment, and with what? Their horses, oxen, and mules are requisitioned, and without any consideration....

Every day I am informed of horrible new injustices in the provinces. According to what my neighbors tell me the population has decreased more than a third in ten years. The statute-labor on the highways is the most horrible *taille* that has ever been borne. The inhabitants have taken the course of retiring to the small towns. There are a number of villages which have been abandoned by everybody. I have several parishes that owe me three years' *taille*. But a constant succession of seizures goes on by which the *taille* collectors are enriched and are in a position to advance money. Much is owed to them through attachments, without the said collectors losing thereby. Quite the reverse is true. These poor subjects are treated in a worse fashion than if they were under an enemy requisition. My parish, which was ruined by hail this summer and expected a reduction of the *taille*, has been given instead a *minot* (thirty-nine liters) more of salt. Sainte-Maure, a large place, but one contributing more to the *corvée*, has been extremely favored; its *taille* has been diminished six hundred livres without rhyme or reason.

ABUSES IN THE LEVYING OF TAXES. (*Young, 314.*)

The abuses attending the levy of taxes were heavy and universal. The kingdom was parcelled into generalities, with an intendant at the head of each, into whose hands the whole power of the crown was delegated for everything except the military authority; but particularly for all affairs of finance. The generalities were subdivided into *elections*, at the head of which was a sub-delegate, appointed by the intendant. The rolls of the *taille, capitation*,[1] *ving-tièmes*,[2] and other taxes, were distributed among districts, parishes, and individuals, at the pleasure of the intendant, who could exempt, change, add, or diminish, at pleasure. Such an enormous power, constantly acting, and from which no man was free, might in the nature of things degenerate in many cases into absolute tyranny. It must be obvious that the friends, acquaintances, and dependents of the intendant, and of his sub-delegates, and the friends of these friends, to a long chain of dependence, might be favored in taxation, at the expense of their miserable neighbors; and that noblemen, in favor at court, to whose protection the intendant himself would naturally look up, could find little difficulty in throwing much of the weight of their taxes on others, without a similar support. Instances, and even gross ones, have been reported to me in many parts of the kingdom, that make me shudder at the oppression to which numbers must have been condemned, by the undue favors granted to such crooked influence. But, without recurring to such cases, what must have been the state of the poor people paying such heavy taxes, from which the nobility and clergy were exempted? A cruel aggravation of their misery, to see those who could best afford to pay, exempted because able!

[1] Poll-tax.
[2] An income tax varying from eleven to twenty per cent.

THE COURT. (*D'Argenson, V, 349–351.*)

The court! The court! In that single word lies all the nation's misfortune. The court has become the national senate. The lowest *valet de chambre* of Versailles is a senator; the *femmes de chambre* are part of the government. If they do not command, they at least prevent the execution of laws and regulations, and through special exceptions there are no longer any laws, regulations, or authorities. It will be even worse when it is a question of reforms in the state, and when those reforms are imperative. Every minister trembles before some valet; and how much truer this is when a favorite has great influence, when the master is too kind and too weak to deal with those about him....

It is the court that corrupts the morals of the nation by its luxury, its extravagance, its artificial manners, its ignorance, and its intrigue in place of emulation. All places, positions, and grades in the army go to the courtiers through favoritism; hence there is no longer any attempt to rise by merit.

In the finances everything is sold; all the money of the provinces goes to Paris never to return; all the people go there to make fortunes by intrigue....

Justice cannot be administered with integrity; the judges fear the grandees, and base their hopes only upon favor. In short, the king no longer reigns, and disregards even the virtues that he has.

Those are the fruits of the establishment by Louis XIV of a capital at Versailles expressly for the court. He was still powerful and gave authority to his ministers. But these are not supported under Louis XV, who distrusts them and prefers his courtiers and favorite. There is, as a result, anarchy and an oligarchy of satraps. Favor means influence, and the possession of favor is more important than the rights of authority.

(*Miot de Mélito, I, 7–8.*)

Prior to those times of disturbance and revolution, when the court was the whole state, three principal personages divided it among them, and each exercised a more or less decisive influence: the queen, Monsieur (afterwards Louis XVIII), and the Comte d'Artois (afterwards Charles X); but the queen's party had always been the strongest. The queen's domination was chiefly exercised through her influence over the mind of her husband, a man of pure life and good intention, but whose qualities were injured by weakness of character and temperament which rendered him incapable of forming and adhering to any resolution; and this although he was capable of profound dissimulation, the fruit of the evil education which was given to the princes of the House of Bourbon, and which was partially the cause of their misfortunes.

THE COMTE D'ARTOIS. (*Miot de Mélito, I, 8–9.*)

The Comte d'Artois, who put no restraint upon his passions, indulged to excess in gambling and profligacy. While he was the intimate companion of the young men of the court, who were led by his example, he was at the same time duped and robbed by old debauchees, who took advantage of his inexperience. For the rest, he meddled but little with the administration of affairs except for money wherewith to pay his debts, which amounted to an enormous sum at the epoch of the first Assembly of Notables. He did not begin to take part in public affairs until the beginning of the year 1787, when, by declaring himself against any concession to the ideas of the times, and by supporting M. de Calonne, he exhibited opinions and took a line contrary to those adopted or followed by his brother.

THE COMTE DE PROVENCE. (*Miot de Mélito, I, 9.*)

Monsieur was a clever man, but he was held to be pedantic. He was disliked in the queen's circle, where he was nicknamed "Hortensius." Being repulsed by that clique, which, according to him, did not do justice to his merit, he made one for himself, more intimate and less restrained; formed relations and had love affairs in which the intellectual rather than the emotional side of his character was, it was said, engaged. The resentment which he cherished against the queen, and the natural bent of his mind, led to his appearing in the Assembly of Notables as the chief of the liberal party, and to his being regarded as belonging to the sect of philosophers. Henceforth he stood high in the opinion of the public, and if he had had sufficient courage and real attachment to the new ideas to put himself at the head of the movement which was beginning, he would probably have been able to prevent some of its excesses. But it seems that he aimed rather at rendering himself formidable to the queen, who had scorned and ridiculed him, than at achieving a more serious sort of distinction; when he had gratified his private revenge he withdrew from the stage on which he had made a brief appearance and hid himself from all observers.

THE QUEEN'S PARTY. (*Miot de Mélito, I, 10–11.*)

The queen's party, composed of a number of amiable and clever men and women, but who had no real importance based upon superior ability or the *éclat* of great services rendered to the country, held exclusive domination at court, disposed of all patronage, and succumbed, so to speak, under the mere weight of favor, wealth, and honors. But just as the circle which the queen had formed around herself was calculated to secure to her all the enjoyments of intimate friendship in private life and the satisfaction of making those whom she loved happy, it was also likely to become fatal to her peace so soon as the eye of the public should penetrate it. This was exactly what happened at the moment when the imperative needs of the social condition of the country turned men's minds towards projects of improvement, the demand for which became increasingly evident with each rent in the veil which covered so much prodigality. When the crisis came, the queen found no one among her intimates who could aid or sustain her. Her friends had no credit with the outside world; they enjoyed no public esteem; they were objects either of hatred or of envy; and their own safety being seriously menaced, what could they do but escape from the country?

They neither could nor would give her any but bad advice, for they themselves must have been the first to suffer by wise counsels. It was impossible

for them to snatch her away from the brink of the precipice to which they
had led her, and they soon found their only resource in flight.

MARIE ANTOINETTE. (*Weber, I, 25–26.*)

Nature, as Mme. de Polignac said, had formed Marie Antoinette to occupy
a throne. A royal stature, a noble beauty, a manner of holding her head,
difficult to describe, inspired respect. Her features, without being regular,
had that which is better, an infinite charm. The fairness of her complexion
embellished them and gave a dazzling radiance to her face. The most winning
manners were added to so many charms; and in this first flower of her youth,
the elegance and vivacity of her movements, the open and naïve expression
of kindness of heart and naturalness of mind, were particularly pleasing to
the French of that time. She charmed her husband, the king [Louis XV]
and his family, the court and the town, the great and the small, all ranks,
all sexes, and all ages.

(*Besenval, II, 309.*)

The queen is far from lacking intellect, but her education has been negative
so far as instruction is concerned. Except for novels, she has never opened a
book, and does not even seek the ideas that society can give; as soon as a
subject takes a serious turn, a look of boredom comes over her face and chills
the conversation. Her conversation is desultory, intermittent, and flutters
from object to object. Being without natural gaiety, she amuses herself with
the day's idle story, with little liberties cleverly toned down, and above all
with the scandal that is found at court; that is what pleases her. Accommodating, unexacting, but without depth of feeling, except for her intimacy
with Mme. de Polignac she knew, it might be said, nothing of friendship; for
the Abbé de Vermont and M. d'Esterhazy cannot be used as examples. She
created them both, and considers them as her work, her dependents, rather
than as her friends.

THE QUEEN'S DISLIKE OF ETIQUETTE. (*Rivarol, 314–315.*)

The breaking down of etiquette is another source of objections against the
queen. By that, they say, she has lessened the consideration and respect of
the people for her. It is certain that this princess, always more feminine than
regal, has yielded too much to the charms of private life. Monarchs are
actors condemned never to leave the stage. A queen who has to live and die
on a real throne ought not to desire the enjoyment of that fictitious and tran-
sient empire which grace and beauty give to ordinary women, and which
make them queens of the moment.

(*Lafont-d'Ausonne; Saint-Edme, II, 189.*)

At Trianon, Marie Antoinette received and invited only a small number of
chosen people. . . . For a week all customs and, as it were, all reminders of

Versailles were renounced. One retired early; one arose almost at the same moment as the sun. One enjoyed with delight the balm and perfume of spring mornings. One drank pure milk and ate fresh eggs in the farmhouse or in the dairy. One breakfasted under the trees on stretches of green lawn. One made garlands, one embroidered *en cercle*, one wore out a village distaff, one made at least some thread. Promenades in the shade came to suspend these employments; and, after dinner, which at times took place in the mill and most often in the thatched cottage of the queen, one danced some rustic steps to the modest sounds of the mandolin and the tambourine. All the court could not be admitted to these innocent and restrained pleasures. Turbulent pride complained of preferences; envy agitated its vipers.

(*Mme. de Staël, 25–26.*)

The Queen of France, Marie Antoinette, was one of the most amiable and gracious persons who had ever been on the throne. There was nothing to prevent her keeping the love of the French, for she had done nothing to lose it. The personal character of the queen and king were thus worthy of attachment; but the arbitrary nature of the French government, as the centuries had made it, accorded so badly with the spirit of the times that even the virtues of the princes disappeared in the vast ensemble of abuses by which they were surrounded. When people feel the need of a political reform, the private qualities of the monarch do not suffice to arrest the force of this impulsion. An unhappy chance placed the reign of Louis XVI in an epoch in which great talents and great inspirations were necessary to struggle with the spirit of the century, or to make (which would have been better) a reasonable compromise with that spirit.

LOUIS XVI. (*Marmontel, III, 293.*)

Louis XVI, raised to the throne at the age of twenty, brought to it a feeling very precious when moderate, and very dangerous when excessive, the distrust of his own powers. The vice of his education had been the very reverse of that which is usually imputed to the education of princes: he had been too much intimidated; and while his elder brother, the Duc de Bourgogne, was living, he had been taught to feel too sensibly, on the side of the intellect, the superiority which that truly premature prince had over him.

(*Mme. Roland, 263.*)

Louis XVI was not exactly the man they were interested in painting in order to discredit him. He was neither the stupid imbecile that they presented for the disdain of the people, nor the fine, judicious, virtuous man that his friends described. Nature had made him an ordinary man, who would have done well in some obscure station. He was ruined in being educated for the throne, and lost through mediocrity in a difficult period when he could have been saved only through genius and strength. An ordinary mind, brought up near the throne and taught from infancy to dissemble, acquires many advantages for dealing with people; the art of letting each see only what is suitable for him to see is for it only a habit to which practice gives an appearance of cleverness: one would have to be an idiot to appear stupid in such a situation. Louis XVI had, moreover, a good memory and much activity; he never remained idle, and read a great deal. He knew well the various treaties made by France with the neighboring powers, and he was the best geographer in his kingdom. The knowledge of names, the exact application to the faces of the court personages to whom they belonged, of anecdotes personal to them, had been extended by him to all the individuals who appeared in some manner in the Revolution. But Louis XVI, without elevation of soul, without boldness of mind, without strength of character, still had his ideas narrowed and his sentiments perverted, so to say, by religious prejudices and jesuitical principles.... If he had been born two centuries earlier, and if he had had a reasonable wife, he would have made no more noise in the world than many other princes of his race who have passed across the stage without having done much good or much harm.

II. *Classes and Privileges*

WEALTH OF THE CLERGY. (*Bouillé, 44–45.*)

THE clergy in France formed in the state an order which had conserved the right to regulate the contributions which it had to pay, making assessments and collections; it had even refused to give the government an evaluation of its wealth, which was not known until the Revolution, and which was found to amount to one hundred and eighty millions of revenue. It had not been obligated to the state for a long time, except in the paying of ten million *décimes* [one million francs]. The other contributions that the government asked of it, and which it accorded, were called *free gifts*. . . . If at the time of the Assembly of Notables in 1787, the clergy had not obstinately refused to pay its debts, as was then proposed, by giving up its seignorial rights and hunting privileges, by alienating even some vacant benefices, as the Cardinal de Richelieu had forced them to do at the Assembly of Notables in 1626, and by paying like other landowners of the kingdom the two *vingtièmes* or a tenth of its revenue and a poll-tax that could not be evaluated at less than three or four millions, it would have contributed from twenty-one to twenty-two millions to the expenses of the state. In 1710 the clergy had, with the sum of twenty-four millions, bought itself off from paying the poll-tax.

INEQUALITIES IN THE CLERGY. (*Ferrières, II, 52–54.*)

. . . there were dioceses which contained fifteen hundred square leagues, and others which contained only twenty; parishes which were ten leagues in circumference, and others which had scarcely fifteen families. Among the priests there were some whose allowances scarcely reached seven hundred livres; while in their neighborhood were benefices of ten and twelve thousand livres income, possessed by ecclesiastics who performed no function in the cult and who, residing elsewhere, carried away the revenue of these benefices, dissipating it in luxury, debauchery, and lavish expenditure. . . . Inasmuch as the appointment of bishops had been concentrated in the hands of the king, or rather in the hands of the ministers, too often the choice fell, not upon him who possessed the most apostolic virtues, but upon him whose family enjoyed the greatest influence. What evils have not resulted from this! Most of the bishops, incapable of fulfilling their duties, entered upon them with insuperable distaste. This distaste extended even to the places where they were to exercise their functions, and had become so general that the small number of prelates who remained were cited as models. The same abuses reigned in the selection of the grand vicars: all thought more of soliciting favors than of deserving them. Totally abandoned by those who were supposed to administer them, the dioceses remained in the hands of obscure secretaries.

THE FRENCH CLERGY'S CONDUCT. (*Young, 327–328.*)

The clergy in France have been supposed, by many persons in England, to merit their fate from their peculiar profligacy. But the idea is not accurate: that so large a body of men, possessed of very great revenues, should be free from vice, would be improbable, or rather impossible; but they preserved, what is not always preserved in England, an exterior decency of behavior. One did not find among them poachers or fox-hunters, who, having spent the morning scampering after hounds, dedicate the evening to the bottle, and reel from inebriety to the pulpit. Such advertisements were never seen in France, as I have heard of in England: *Wanted a curacy in a good sporting country, where the duty is light and the neighborhood convivial.*

THE TITHE. (*Young, 319–320.*)

In regard to the oppressions of the clergy, as to tithes, I must do that body a justice, to which a claim cannot be laid in England. Though the ecclesiastical tenth was levied in France more severely than in Italy, yet was it never exacted with such horrid greediness as is at present the disgrace of England. When taken in kind, no such thing was known in any part of France, where I made inquiries, as a tenth; it was always a twelfth, or a thirteenth, or even a twentieth of the produce.... Such mildness, in the levy of this odious tax, is absolutely unknown in England. But mild as it was, the burthen to people groaning under so many other oppressions, united to render their situation so bad that no change could be for the worse.

(*Dumont, 55.*)

"Tithes," said the Archbishop of Aix, in a whining tone, "that voluntary offering of the devout faithful..."

"Tithes," interrupted the Duc de La Rochefoucauld, in his quiet and modest way, which rendered the hit more piquant, "that voluntary offering of the devout faithful, concerning which there are now forty thousand lawsuits in the kingdom."

A DESIRE FOR RELIGIOUS REFORM. (*Mme. de Staël, 22.*)

The majority of the French, in the eighteenth century, desired the suppression of the feudal régime, the establishment of English institutions, and above all, religious tolerance. The influence of the clergy on temporal affairs revolted everybody; and as true religious sentiment is that which most avoids intrigues and power, there was no longer any faith in those who used religion to influence the affairs of this world. Some writers, and Voltaire above all, deserve to be blamed for not having respected Christianity in attacking superstition; but the circumstances in which Voltaire lived must not be forgotten: he was born at the end of the century of Louis XIV, and the atrocious injustices suffered by the Protestants struck his imagination while he was yet a child.

(*Thibaudeau, I, 61–62.*)

For two centuries the way had been prepared for a great religious reform in Europe.

For more than fifty years philosophy had brought it to people's minds. Excepting a very small number of writers who had professed atheism, or rather had endowed matter with intelligence and deified nature, most of the philosophers had attacked only fanaticism, intolerance, and popery. The ceremonies of the cult were no longer, one might say, anything but a spectacle, one dispensed with it without remorse, one practiced it through habit or through hypocrisy. High society, and even the court, gave the example, and incredulity or indifference spread through all classes. Voltaire had made proselytes in all the courts of Europe. The great Frederick, Catherine the Great, and nearly all the little princes of Germany corresponded with him, with Diderot, and with D'Alembert, loudly proclaiming their love of tolerance and their contempt of superstition. The precepts and dignity of thrones were humbled before the philosophers, whose lessons they received and propagated.

A PRIEST DEFENDS THE PHILOSOPHERS. (Morellet, II, 351–352.)

M. de Voltaire is accused of having disseminated principles of scepticism in his writings; it is not for us to condemn him or absolve him; but whether this imputation is well or badly founded, it is none the less true that this celebrated man equalled Corneille and Racine in his tragedies, that he wrote the most beautiful epic poem in our language, that he embellished philosophic virtues and ethics with the charms of an original, piquant, and persuasive style, and above all, that he was in Europe the apostle of tolerance, acting thus as the benefactor of humanity. It is on account of all these things that we regard him as the foremost man of letters of his nation and his time; we believe that we can give him this praise without being suspected of impiety by the religious who are not blinded by passion. I well understand that the theologian believes it to be to the interest of religion that all people who are suspected of some freedom of thought should have neither talents, merits, nor virtue; but, since it has pleased God to make it thus, would it not be more reasonable to submit to the dispositions of a Providence that knows better than we the means of sustaining the faith against the attacks of the sceptical? The religion established in the world by rude and uncultivated men will doubtless be preserved through the same means, and its enemies cannot destroy the work of God. In supposing, then, that the V's, the D's, and the B's, and the H's[1] are guilty of some originality of thought, let them

[1] Probably refers to Voltaire, Diderot, Beccaria, and Holbach.

be praised according to their talents; and let us praise them without scruple and without remorse, as we praise the Platos, the Ciceros, the Homers, and the Vergils. A time will come when all these great geniuses will be harassed as were the others and praised where they were not. *Laudantur ubi non sunt, cruciantur ubi sunt.*

THE CLERGY AND ITS OPPONENTS. (*Ségur, I, 24–25.*)

The clergy, proud of its influence and its riches, was far from believing its existence menaced; but it was irritated by the boldness of the philosophers and, although part of its members in taking too great a part in social affairs participated to some extent in the new inclinations, not limiting themselves to attacking licentiousness, they strove vainly to repel the verities which the disappearance of the darkness [of ignorance] rendered palpable to all eyes, and persisted in having respect for the old puerile superstitions struck down by the torch of reason and the light attacks of ridicule.

However, since everyone was influenced by the atmosphere of his century, this same clergy had softened the austerities which had rendered the reign of Louis XIV so sad; it let fall into desuetude the edicts of persecution against the Protestants (cause of so much shame and injury to France) and its furious disputes on Jansenius and Molina.[1]

JANSENISTS AND PROTESTANTS. (*Morellet, I, 32–33.*)

While we were in the Sorbonne, the quarrel of the Jansenists with the Archbishop of Beaumont, who wished to have the sacraments denied to the dying who could not produce proof of confession to an approved priest, was raging hotly; the *parlement* was in pursuit of the priests and vicars who refused the last sacrament for lack of proof, and the archbishop suspended those who administered it. Naturally this raised in the schools the question of religious and civil liberty.

A more important problem helped to revive the same question. The Protestants in Languedoc were accused of agitating for the liberty of their cult. In the meantime they married outside the Church, had their children baptized by priests who consented not to mention the religion of the parents, complained bitterly of being excluded from employment, and demanded equal citizenship with their neighbors.

We occupied ourselves a great deal with all that; and, carried away by the spirit of philosophy which had begun to take wing in the great work of Montesquieu and in the *Encyclopédie*, the most hardy of us did not waver between the two opinions and, ignoring false prudence and the prejudices of the school, declared for civil liberty in endeavoring to distinguish it from religious tolerance.

[1] Cornelius Jansen, a Dutch theologian, held certain views on divine grace, free will, and predestination, as did also the Spanish Jesuit Molina.

THE NOBILITY. (Bouillé, 50–52.)

The nobility had undergone still greater changes; it had lost, not only its ancient splendor, but almost its existence, and had entirely decayed. There had been in France nearly eighty thousand noble families. (This was not surprising since four thousand civil charges gave nobility or transmitted it, and since the king daily accorded patents of nobility, these being so profuse during the War of the Succession that they were sold at two thousand *écus tournois.*[1]) Included in this numerous nobility were about a thousand families whose origin dated from the earliest times of the monarchy. Among these there were scarcely two or three hundred who had escaped poverty and misfortune. There could still be found at court a few great names which brought to mind the noted personages who had made them illustrious, but which too often were brought into disrepute by the vices of those who had inherited them. There were a few families in the provinces who had continued to exist and command respect, in conserving the patrimonies of their fathers in spite of the limits put to the entail previously perpetual in the nobility, or in repairing ancestral fortunes by alliances with plebeian families. The remainder of this ancient nobility languished in poverty, and resembled those ancient oaks mutilated by time, where nothing remains except the ravaged trunks. No longer convoked either for military service or for the provincial or national assemblies, they had lost their ancient hierarchy. If honorary titles remained to some illustrious or ancient families, they were also held by a multitude of newly created nobles who had acquired by their riches the right to assume them arbitrarily. The greater part of the large estates that conferred titles had become the appanages of financiers, wholesale merchants, or their descendants. The fiefs were for the most part in the hands of the bourgeois of the towns. The nobility, in short, were not distinguishable from the other classes of citizens, except by the arbitrary favors of the court, and by exemptions from imposts, less useful to them than onerous to the state and shocking to the people. They had conserved nothing of their ancient dignity and consideration; they retained only the hate and jealousy of the plebeians. Such was the situation of the nobility of the kingdom, if I except Brittany and a few *provinces d'état* in which they had retained honorary prerogatives.

(Ferrières, I, 2–3.)

People were so tired of the court and the ministers that the greater part of the nobles were what has since been called democrats; a denomination, however, which is not exact; for they did not desire to put the government in the hands of the people; they desired only to retire it from the ministerial oligarchy in whose hands it was concentrated.

SUPERFICIALITY OF THE NOBLES. (Ségur, I, 24.)

The heads of the old noble families, believing themselves as unshakable as the monarchy, slept without fear upon a volcano. The exercise of their

[1] An *écu tournois* was worth about forty-three cents.

charges; royal promotions, favors, or rebuffs; and the nomination or dismissal of ministers, were the sole objects of their attention, the motives of their movements, and the subjects of their conversations. Indifferent to the real affairs of state as to their own, they allowed themselves to be governed, some by the intendants of the provinces, others by their own intendants; but they regarded with a chagrined and scornful eye the changes in costumes which were being introduced, the abandonment of liveries, the vogue of dress-coats and English styles.

(*Mme. de Staël, 43–44.*)

The great nobles in France were not very well informed, because they had nothing to gain by being so. Grace in conversation, which would please at court, was the surest means of arriving at honors. This superficial education was one cause of the downfall of the nobles: they could no longer fight against the intelligence of the third estate; they should have tried to surpass it. The great lords would have by degrees gained supremacy in the primary assemblies through their knowledge of administration, as formerly they had acquired it by their swords; and the public mind would have been prepared for the establishment of free institutions in France.

CONTRADICTORY IDEAS OF THE NOBLES. (*Mme. de Staël, 26.*)

The party of the aristocrats, that is to say, the privileged, are persuaded that a king of firmer character would have been able to prevent the Revolution. They forget that they themselves were the first to begin, courageously and rightly, the attack upon the royal power; and what resistance could this power oppose to them, since the nation was then on their side? Ought they to complain of having been the stronger against the king and the weaker against the people? That was inevitable.

(*Ségur, I, 62–63.*)

Nourished on the principles of a military monarchy, reared in the pride of a privileged nobility, in the prestige of the court, and in maxims of piety, while, on the other hand, carried away by the license of the century, by a gallantry in which we gloried; inspired to liberty by the writing of philosophers, and by the orations of *parlements*; instead of having a particular aim and decided principles, we wished to enjoy at the same time the favors of the court, the pleasures of the city, the approbation of the clergy, the affection of the people, the applause of the philosophers, the renown given by literary success, the favor of the ladies, and the esteem of worthy men; so that a young French courtier, animated with the desire for renown which distinguishes superior men from the vulgar, thought, spoke, and acted by turns like an inhabitant of Athens, of Rome, of Lutetia, like a paladin, a crusader, a courtier, like a follower of Plato, of Socrates, or of Epicurus.

THE ARMY. (*Vaublanc, 80.*)

The factious began from this time to speak of his [Louis XVI's] character in such a fashion as to show that they founded their hopes upon his weakness. Hitherto it had not been the factious, but the innovators and the restive, already impatient of all authority. In the army they were made discontented by all the wearisome minutiae of which I have spoken, and by changes entirely opposed to those ideas of liberty and equality that the government itself was beginning to proclaim. The regulation that prescribed proofs of nobility for a sub-lieutenancy alienated many and gave support to the pratings of the declaimers.

(*Ségur, I, 66.*)

The regiments were filled by enlistment only, so that instead of seeing the younger sons of all classes called to the colors by conscription and by a general law, there were only young men who had decided to enroll because of some disorderliness or because of indolence. There was no prospect of advancement, and there was nothing more rare than for soldiers and non-commissioned officers to become officers. The small number of these who happened to be promoted, had obtained promotion only after long years of service. The name given them indicates their rareness: they were called *officiers de fortune*. Nobles alone had the right to enter the service as sub-lieutenants.

THE CAPITAINERIES. (*Barère, I, 249.*)

The chase, in the eyes of the kings of France, was a great prerogative, and a social institution.

The hunting code contained regulations, provisions, and hierarchies that would have been ridiculous had it not been of immemorial usage in France and one of the most ancient rights of feudalism, one of its usurpations.

There has been, in the history of France, such and such a king, under whose reign a man could be killed with more impunity than a boar or a stag. From this originated the ancient *capitaineries*, with gamekeepers as ferocious as their masters, possessing the right of life and death over men found within the confines of these museums of animals and wild beasts designed for the amusement of princes. . . .

These *capitaineries* were so necessary and so important that orders were given to maintain enough wild beasts to occupy several hunting parties at the same time. Game abounded everywhere, feeding at the expense of landholders, and the boars in collaboration with the stags devoured all crops without indemnity.

It was well known that of all the *capitaineries*, the one whose régime was most severe and most murderous on account of the barbarous impunity of the gamekeepers, was the *capitainerie* of Grosbois, belonging, with the vast forest of Sénart, to the brother of the king, the Comte de Provence, called at court, Monsieur.

(*Young, 316–317.*)

The *capitaineries* were a dreadful scourge on all the occupiers of land. By this term is to be understood the paramountship of certain districts, granted by the king to the princes of the blood, by which they were put in possession of the property of all game, even on lands not belonging to them; and, what is very singular, on manors granted long before to individuals; so that the erecting of a district into a *capitainerie* was an annihilation of all manorial rights to game within it. This was a trifling business in comparison to other circumstances; for, in speaking of the preservation of game in these *capitaineries*, there must be understood whole droves of wild boars, and herds of deer not confined by any wall or pale, but wandering at pleasure over the whole country, to the destruction of crops, and to the peopling of the galleys by the wretched peasants who presumed to kill them in order to save food which was to support their helpless children. The game in the *capitainerie* of Montceau, in four parishes only, did mischief to the amount of 184,263 livres per annum. No wonder then that we should find the people asking, "We loudly solicit the destruction of the *capitaineries* and of every sort of game." And what are we to think of demanding, as a favor, the permission "to gather their grain, to mow their meadows, and to remove the stubble regardless of partridges and other game"? Now, an English reader will scarcely understand it without being told that there were numerous edicts for preserving game which prohibited weeding and hoeing, lest the young partridges should be disturbed; steeping the seed, lest it should injure the game; fertilizing with night soil, lest the flavor of the partridges should be injured by feeding on the corn so produced; mowing hay, etc., before a certain time, so late as to spoil many crops; and taking away the stubble, which would deprive the birds of shelter. The tyranny exercised in these *capitaineries*, which extended over four hundred leagues of country, was so great that many *cahiers* demanded the utter suppression of them.

FEUDAL GRIEVANCES. (*Young, 317–319.*)

Nothing can exceed the complaints made in the *cahiers* under this head. They speak of the dispensation of justice in the manorial courts, as comprising every species of despotism: the districts indeterminate — appeals endless — irreconcilable to liberty and prosperity — and irrevocably proscribed in the opinion of the public — augmenting litigations — favoring every species of chicane — ruining the parties — not only by enormous expenses on the most petty objects, but by a dreadful loss of time. The judges [are] commonly ignorant pretenders, who hold their courts in cabarets, and are absolutely dependent on the seigneurs, in consequence of their feudal powers. . . .

In passing through many French provinces, I was struck with the various and heavy complaints of the farmers and the little proprietors of the feudal grievances, with the weight of which their industry was burdened; but I could not then conceive of the multiplicity of the shackles which kept them poor and depressed. I understood it better afterwards, from the conversation and complaints of some of the *grands seigneurs*, as the Revolution advanced;

and I then learned that the principal rental of many estates consisted in services and feudal tenures, by the baneful influence of which the industry of the people was almost exterminated.

THE BOURGEOISIE. (*Bouillé, 52–54.*)

... that which the clergy and the nobility had lost in consideration, in riches, and in power, had been acquired by the third estate since the reign of Henri IV and since the last meeting of the States-General in 1614. France had founded colonies in America; she had established a maritime commerce; she had created manufactures; she had, so to say, rendered all Europe and part of the world tributary to her industry. The immense riches brought to the kingdom were distributed only to the plebeians, the prejudices of the nobles excluding them from commerce and from all the mechanical and liberal arts. Even this increase in wealth, in augmenting the currency, had contributed to their impoverishment, and that of proprietors in general. But the cities were considerably enlarged: commercial centers were established, such as Lyon, Nantes, Bordeaux, and Marseille, becoming as important and as rich as the capitals of some neighboring states. Paris had increased in a terrific manner; and while the nobles were quitting their estates to ruin themselves there, the plebeians were piling up wealth by means of their industry. All the little provincial towns had become more or less commercial; almost all had manufactures or some particular commercial product. All were peopled with *petits bourgeois*, who were richer and more industrious than the nobles, and who had found the way, themselves or their fathers, to enrich themselves in the administration or in the leasing of the fiefs and lands of the great lords and nobles, or even in their service, when they could not take part in greater speculations. They had received, in general, an education which had become more necessary to them than to the nobles, of which some, by their birth and by their wealth, obtained the leading places in the state without merit and without talents, while the others were destined to languish as subalterns in the army. Thus at Paris and in the large cities the bourgeoisie was superior in riches, in talents, and in personal merit. In the provincial towns it had the same superiority over the country nobility; it felt this superiority and yet was humiliated everywhere; it found itself excluded by the military regulations from places in the army; it was, in some manner, from the higher clergy, by the selection of bishops from among the higher nobles, and of grand vicars in general from among the nobles; it was from some chapters of the cathedral. The high magistracy rejected it likewise, and most of the sovereign courts admitted only nobles to their company.

THE PEASANTS. (*Jefferson, IX, 313–327.*)

The plains [of Champagne] are in corn, the hills in vineyard, but the wine [is] not good. There are a few apple trees, but none of any other kind, and no inclosures. No cattle, sheep, or swine; fine mules.

Few châteaux; no farmhouses, all the people being gathered in villages. Are they thus collected by that dogma of their religion, which makes them believe that to keep the Creator in good humor with his own works they must mumble a Mass every day? Certain it is that they are less happy and less virtuous in villages than they would be insulated with their families on the grounds they cultivate. The people are illy clothed. Perhaps they have put on their worst clothes at this moment, as it is raining. But I observe women and children carrying heavy burdens, and laboring with the hoe. This is an unequivocal indication of extreme poverty. Men, in a civilized country, never expose their wives and children to labor above their force and sex, as long as their own labor can protect them from it. I see few beggars. Probably this is the effect of a police. . . .

The people of Burgundy and Beaujolais are well clothed, and have the appearance of being well fed. But they experience all the oppressions which result from the nature of the general government, and from that of their particular tenures, and of the seignorial government to which they are subject. . . .

There are few châteaux in this province [Dauphiné]. The people, too, are mostly gathered into villages. There are, however, some scattering farmhouses. These are made either of mud, or of round stone and mud. They make inclosures also, in both those ways. Day laborers receive sixteen or eighteen sous the day and feed themselves. Those by the year receive, men three louis, women half that, and are fed. They rarely eat meat; a single hog salted being the year's stock for a family. But they have plenty of cheese, eggs, potatoes, and other vegetables, and walnut oil with their salad. . . .

[Aix] The wages of a laboring man are one hundred and fifty livres the year, a woman's sixty to sixty-six livres and fed. Their bread is half wheat, half rye, made once in three or four weeks, to prevent too great a consumption. In the morning they eat bread with an anchovy, or an onion. Their dinner, in the middle of the day, is bread, soup, and vegetables. Their supper the same. With their vegetables they have always oil and vinegar. The oil costs about eight sous the pound. They drink what is called *piquette*. This is made after the grapes are pressed, by pouring hot water on the pumice. On Sunday they have meat and wine. Their wood for building comes mostly from the Alps, down the Durance and Rhône. A stick of pine, fifty feet long, girting six feet three inches at one end, and three feet three inches at the other, costs, delivered here, from fifty-four to sixty livres.

LESS MISERY THAN EXPECTED. (Extract from a letter of Jefferson to La Fayette, Nice, April 11, 1787.)

In the great cities, I go to see what travellers think alone worthy of being seen; but I make a job of it, and generally gulp it all down in a day. On the other hand, I am never satiated with rambling through the fields and farms, examining the culture and cultivators, with a degree of curiosity which makes some take me for a fool, and others to be much wiser than I am. I have been pleased to find among the people a less degree of physical misery than I had expected. They are generally well clothed, and have plenty of food, not animal indeed, but vegetable, which is as wholesome. Perhaps they are overworked, the excess of the rent required by the landlord obliging them to too many hours of labor in order to produce that and wherewith to feed and clothe themselves. The soil of Champagne and Burgundy I have found more universally good than I had expected, and as I could not help making a comparison with England, I found that comparison more unfavorable to the latter than is generally admitted. The soil, the climate, and the productions are superior to those of England, and the husbandry as good . . . the southern provinces . . . afford a singular spectacle. Calculating on the poverty of their soil, and their climate by its latitude only, they should have been the poorest in France. On the contrary they are the richest, from one fortuitous circumstance. Spurs or ramifications of high mountains, making down from the Alps, and, as it were, reticulating these provinces, give to the valleys the protection of a particular inclosure to each, and the benefit of a general stagnation of the northern winds produced by the whole of them, and thus countervail the advantage of several degrees of latitude. From the first olive fields of Pierrelatte, to the *orangeries* of Hières, has been continued rapture to me.

POITOU UNIMPROVED. (*Young, 72.*)

Poitou, from what I see of it, is an unimproved, poor, and ugly country. It seems to want communication, demand, and activity of all kinds; nor does it, on the average, yield the half of what it might. The lower part of the province is much richer and better.

PROSPERITY IN BÉARN. (*Young, 61.*)

Take a road to Monein, and come presently to a scene which was so new to me in France, that I could hardly believe my own eyes. A succession of many well-built, tight, and comfortable farming cottages, built of stone, and covered with tiles, each having its little garden, inclosed by clipt thorn hedges, and young trees nursed up with so much care, that nothing but the fostering attention of the owner could effect anything like it. To every house belongs a farm, perfectly well inclosed, with grass borders mown and neatly kept around the cornfields, with gates to pass from one inclosure to another. The men are all dressed with red caps, like the highlanders of Scotland. There are some parts of England (where small yeomen still remain) that resemble this country of Béarn; but we have very little that is equal to what I have seen in this ride of twelve miles from Pau to Monein. It is all in the hands of little proprietors, without the farms being so small as to occasion a vicious and miserable population. An air of neatness, warmth, and comfort breathes over the whole. It is visible in their new-built houses and stables; in their little gardens; in their hedges; in the courts before their doors; even in their coops for their poultry, and the sties for their hogs. A peasant does not think of rendering his pig comfortable if his own happiness hangs by the thread of a nine-year lease. We are now in Béarn, within a few miles of the cradle of Henry IV. Do they inherit these blessings from that good prince? The benignant genius of that good monarch seems to reign still over the country; each peasant has the fowl in the pot.

PROSPERITY NEXT TO WRETCHEDNESS IN LANGUEDOC. (*Young, 54.*)

From Gange to the mountain of rough ground which I crossed, the ride has been the most interesting which I have taken in France; the efforts of industry the most vigorous; the animation the most lively. An activity has been here, that has swept away all the difficulties before it, and has clothed the very rocks with verdure. It would be a disgrace to common sense to ask the cause; the enjoyment of property must have done it. Give a man the secure possession of a bleak rock, and he will turn it into a garden; give him a nine-year lease of a garden, and he will turn it into a desert. To Mondardier over a rough mountain covered with box and lavender; it is a beggarly village, with an *auberge* that made me almost shrink. Some cut-throat figures were eating black bread, whose visages had so much of the galleys that I thought I heard their chains rattle. I looked at their legs, and could not but imagine they had no business to be free. There is a species of countenance here so horribly bad, that it is impossible to be mistaken in one's reading. I was quite alone, and absolutely without arms. Till this moment, I had not dreamt of carrying pistols: I should now have been better satisfied, if I had had them. The master of the *auberge*, who seemed first cousin to his guests, procured for me some wretched bread with difficulty, but it was not black. — No meat, no eggs, no legumes, and execrable wine: no corn for my mule; no hay; no straw; no grass: the loaf fortunately was large; I took a piece, and sliced the rest for my four-footed Spanish friend, who ate it thankfully, but the *aubergiste* growled.

FRANCE BETTER THAN SPAIN. (*Young, 43.*)

From the natural and miserable roads of Catalonia, you tread at once on a noble causeway, made with all the solidity and magnificence that distinguishes the highways of France. Instead of beds of torrents you have well-built bridges; and from a country wild, desert, and poor, we found ourselves in the midst of cultivation and improvement. Every other circumstance spoke the same language, and told us by signs not to be mistaken, and some great and operating cause worked an effect too clear to be misunderstood. The more one sees, the more I believe we shall be led to think that there is but one all-powerful cause that instigates mankind, and that is government! — Others form exceptions, and give shades of difference and distinction, but this acts with permanent and universal force. The present instance is remarkable; for Roussillon is in fact a part of Spain; the inhabitants are Spaniards in language and customs; but they are under a French government.

POVERTY IN GUYENNE. (*Young, 27.*)

Pass Payrac, and meet many beggars, which we had not done before. All the country, girls and women, are without shoes and stockings; and the ploughmen at their work have neither sabots nor feet to their stockings. This is a poverty that strikes at the root of national prosperity; a large consumption among the poor being of more consequence than among the rich: the wealth of a nation lies in its circulation and consumption; and the case of poor people abstaining from the use of manufactures of leather and wool ought to be considered as an evil of the first magnitude. It reminded me of the misery of Ireland.

THE MÉTAYERS. (*Young, 18.*)

To La Ferté Lowendahl,[1] a dead flat of hungry sandy gravel, with much heath. The poor people, who cultivate the soil here, are *métayers*, that is, men who hire the land without ability to stock it; the proprietor is forced to provide cattle and seed, and he and his tenant divide the produce; a miserable system, that perpetuates poverty and excludes instruction.

BRITTANY. (*Young, 123–125.*)

My entry into Bretagne gives me an idea of its being a miserable province....

To Combourg, the country has a savage aspect; husbandry not much further advanced, at least in skill, than among the Hurons, which appears incredible amidst inclosures; the people almost as wild as their country, and their town of Combourg one of the most brutal filthy places that can be seen; mud houses, no windows, and a pavement so broken as to impede all passengers, but ease none — yet here is a château, and inhabited ...

To Montauban. The poor people seem poor indeed; the children terribly ragged ... as to shoes and stockings, they are luxuries. A beautiful girl of six or seven years playing with a stick, and smiling under such a bundle of rags as made my heart ache to see her: they did not beg, and when I gave them anything seemed more surprised than obliged. One-third of what I have seen of this province seems uncultivated, and nearly all of it in misery. What have kings, and ministers, and parliaments, and states, to answer for their prejudices, seeing millions of hands that would be industrious, idle and starving, through the execrable maxims of despotism, or the equally detestable prejudices of a feudal nobility?

CHAMPAGNE NEAR VERDUN. (*Young, 197–198.*)

Walking up a long hill to ease my mare, I was joined by a poor woman, who complained of the times, and that it was a sad country; demanding her reasons, she said her husband had but a morsel of land, one cow, and a poor little horse, yet they had a *franchar* (forty-two pounds) of wheat, and three chickens, to pay as a quit-rent to one seigneur; and four *franchar* of oats, one chicken, and one sou to pay to another, besides very heavy *tailles* and other taxes. She had seven children, and the cow's milk helped to make the soup. But why, instead of a horse, do you not keep another cow? Oh, her husband could not carry his produce so well without a horse; and asses are little used in the country. It was said, at present, that something was to be done by some great folks for such poor ones, but she did not know who nor how, but God send us better, for the *tailles* and dues are crushing us. This woman, at no great dis-

[1] La Ferté-Saint-Aubin near Orléans.

tance, might have been taken for sixty or seventy, her figure was so bent, and her face so furrowed and hardened by labor, but she said she was only twenty-eight. An Englishman who has not travelled, cannot imagine the figure made by infinitely the greater part of the countrywomen in France; it speaks, at first sight, hard and severe labor: I am inclined to think that they work harder than the men, and this, united with the more miserable labor of bringing a new race of slaves into the world, destroys absolutely all symmetry of person and every feminine appearance. To what are we to attribute this difference in the manners of the lower people in the two kingdoms? To government.

III. The Influence of Philosophy

AN ANTI-MONARCHICAL WIND. (D'Argenson, V, 346–347.)

A PHILOSOPHICAL wind is blowing from England; one hears the murmur of the words *liberty* and *republicanism;* they are already in people's minds, and we know how public opinion rules the world. The times of adoration have passed; the name of master, so dear to our ancestors, sounds unpleasant to our ears. For aught one knows there is a new conception of government in certain heads that will emerge in battle array at the first occasion. Perhaps the revolution will be accomplished with less opposition than one thinks; there will be no need of princes of the blood, great lords, or religious fanaticism; all will be accomplished by acclamation, as in the election of popes at times. Today all classes are discontented: the military disbanded by the peace; the clergy offended in its privileges; the *parlements,* corporate bodies, provincial governments, debased in their functions; the lower classes crushed by taxes, and racked by misery; the financiers alone triumphant and reviving the reign of the Jews. Combustible matters everywhere. A riot might become a revolt, and a revolt a complete revolution; bringing real tribunes of the people, consuls, and commissaries; and depriving the king and his ministers of their excessive power for harm.

PHILOSOPHY UNDERMINES THE GOVERNMENT. (Journal de Maëstricht, June 12, 1778; Mirecourt, I, 63–64.)

The origin of the evil must be looked for in the spirit of revolt and irreligion caused by the flood of infamous writings which circulate not only in the upper classes, but descend today even to the dwellings of the people.

From top to bottom of the social body, in the palace as in the cottage, imbecile ragamuffins, whom a wise government would do well to have whipped in the public square, set themselves up for philosophers and cultivate blasphemy.

During a voyage which the director of the *Journal de Maëstricht* made last year in France, he saw the *Analyse de Bayle*[1] in the hands of the servants of M. le Duc de S——. They read passages aloud in the middle of the antechamber.

Elsewhere a flock of peddlers, unwatched by the police, disseminate in the country districts the infectious writings of Voltaire, of the materialist Diderot,

---

[1] A profoundly irreligious book by François de Marsy, expelled from the college of Jesuits for his depravity. (Note of the journalist.)

of the dangerous misanthrope of Geneva [Rousseau], and those of Helvétius, the most fanatical of the unbelievers and the most ignoble apostle of pleasure.

All these books do not preach the disdain of religion and of right customs alone; they preach revolt against the royal authority and sap the base of all the conservative principles of the state.

TRUE PHILOSOPHY NOT TO BLAME. (Weber, I, 80–81.)

It is only recalling a verity that all the world must have observed to say that each century of our history in modern times has been dominated by a certain state of mind; that after the century of the crusades came successively that of chivalry, that of the renaissance of letters and of religious sects, that of polished literature, of grandeur, of politeness, and of the fine arts, and finally, that of the exact sciences, of philosophy, of political economy, of daring thought, and independent beliefs.

To anathematize indiscriminately the spirit of the past century and to execrate the very name of philosophy because the men who devastated France called themselves philosophers would be like traducing religion because the assassins of Saint Bartholomew had a poignard in one hand and a crucifix in the other.

That which is just, reasonable, and salutary is to honor true philosophy, were it only because it is the most determined enemy of the false; to tear the mask from the criminal and the fanatic who wish to cover their extravagance or their infamy; to encourage the study of natural laws which lead always to their Author, and of social laws which lead always to peace; but to bar the road to sedition, while giving freedom to thought; to discern the benefits and abuses of that which, good in itself, can become disastrous through a wrong application; and above all to recall ceaselessly to men the need they have of moderation and of avoiding excesses of all kinds, because all excess brings, with the evils which it itself produces, evils of the excess which is provoked in opposing it.

TRADITION DISCREDITED. (Mme. de Staël, 97.)

The light of philosophy, that is to say the valuation of things according to reason and not according to custom, had made such progress in Europe that the possessors of privileges, kings, nobles, or priests, were the first to make excuses for the abusive advantages that they enjoyed. They strongly desired to retain them, but they pretended to be indifferent to them, and the most adroit flattered themselves that they had quieted public opinion enough to prevent its disputing with them that which they had the air of discrediting.

THE PHILOSOPHERS NOT INTENTIONALLY SUBVERSIVE. (Weber, I, 110.)

People have exaggerated in saying that these philosophers intended at that time the subversion of society and the overturning of thrones. They did this without knowing it. Those of that epoch wanted to be the preceptors and not the destroyers of kings. In fact, Montesquieu, if he had brought forth only his work on the Romans and his *Spirit of the Laws*; Beccaria, in writing his *Trea-*

tise on Crimes and Punishments; Voltaire, in refuting Machiavelli and defending Calas, Sirven, and Lally; Rousseau, in pleading the cause of nature, of ethics, and of the Scriptures; and the authors of the *Encyclopédie*, whenever they respected religious principles, merited perhaps the indulgence of the powers of the earth.

GENERAL DISSATISFACTION. *(Ségur, I, 20–21.)*

The *parlements* made remonstrances, the priests sermons, the philosophers books, the young courtiers epigrams. Each, feeling that the administration was in bad hands, set at defiance a government which no longer inspired either confidence or respect. The barriers of authority, worn out and crumbling, no longer opposed any real obstacle to private ambitions which, seizing their chance, hastened with different views towards the same goal.

The old nobles, ashamed of being ruled by a low-born favorite and inglorious ministers, regretted the times of feudalism and their power as it had been before Richelieu. The clergy remembered with bitterness its influence under the reign of Mme. de Maintenon. The great corps of magistrates opposed to arbitrary power and the dilapidation of the finances a resistance which gave them popularity.

Everything seemed to breathe the spirit of the League and the Fronde,[1] and since, when public spirit is aroused, it needs a rallying sign, a sort of standard, this was furnished by the philosophers. The words *liberty, property,* and *equality* were pronounced. These magic words resounded far and wide, and were at first repeated enthusiastically by the very people who later attributed to them all their misfortunes.

No one dreamed of a revolution, although it was rapidly taking place in people's minds. Montesquieu had brought into the light of day the ancient rights of peoples so long buried in obscurity. Mature men studied and envied the laws of England. The young people were enamored with horses, jockeys, boots, and English jackets.

INFLUENCE OF THE ENGLISH PHILOSOPHERS. *(Weber, I, 81–83.)*

Voltaire plumed himself, all his life, upon having first introduced to his compatriots the great geniuses and profound philosophers that glorified England. He would have had nothing but thanks due him if he had limited himself to familiarizing France with Shakespeare invoking in the eternal mover of the heavens his hope, his stay, and his guide; with Bacon pronouncing that a little philosophy dispels religion, but that much philosophy restores it; and with Newton, that is to say, the greatest genius that has ever existed, inclining profoundly each time he heard pronounced the name of God. Even Locke, in spite of the delicate questions that he never feared to fathom; Locke, who had been a friend of order as well as of liberty; Locke, who died a Christian as well as a philosopher, could be regarded as belonging to all the human species whose cause he pleaded. Bourdaloue had said at the same time as Locke, and he said it to Louis XIV in the chapel of Versailles: "Kings were

[1] Rebellions against the court.

made for the people, and not the people for kings." Massillon, repeating the same maxim to the young Louis XV, had added, "It is we who have given you the crown." Bossuet and Fénélon had said even more.

But unhappily the country of Shakespeare, of Bacon, of Locke, and of Newton was also that of Tyndal, of Woolston, of Toland, of Shaftesbury, and of Bolingbroke; and Voltaire, who had sipped all the poisons of these last, soon returned to inundate France with them in publishing his *Lettres philosophiques*. It was difficult to conceive, towards the end of the last century, of the inconsequence of Bayle, or of that of all the men who were energetic in revealing the abuses of philosophy, and who incited them most effectively by their perfidious scepticism. One saw Montesquieu, perhaps more inconsistent yet, without even veiling his contradictions under the appearance of doubt, extol Christianity in the *Spirit of the Laws*, ridicule it in the *Lettres persanes*,[1] and in this last work give the first signal for all the attacks which have since multiplied against religion with a rancor as baneful as they are scandalous.

INFLUENCE OF THE CLASSICS. (*Mme. Roland, 113–121.*)

It is beyond question that our character and opinions are much influenced by our situation; but one would say that the education that I received and the ideas that I acquired by study or from other people all combined to inspire me with republican enthusiasm in causing me to sense the ridiculousness or injustice of a multitude of privileges and distinctions. Thus, in my reading, I became enamored with the reformers of inequality; I was Agis and Cleomenes in Sparta; I was the Gracchi in Rome; and, like Cornelia, I should have reproached my sons for my being known only as the mother-in-law of Scipio. I retired with the people to the Aventine Mount, and I voted for the tribunes. Today, since experience has taught me to weigh all with impartiality, I see in the enterprises of the Gracchi and in the conduct of the tribunes wrongs and evils which had not enough impressed me. . . .

I well desire to point out that in this multitude of books,[2] which chance or circumstances had caused to pass through my hands and of which I have vaguely indicated those first called to my mind by places or persons, there was not yet any Rousseau: it is because I did in truth read him too late, and a good thing it was for me; he would have made me mad; I should have never read anything else: perhaps he would only too well have, so to speak, fortified my weaknesses.

THE ENCYCLOPEDIE. (*D'Argenson, IV, 63–65; V, 125.*)

A great storm is rising against the *Dictionnaire encyclopédique*,[3] and this storm originates among the Jesuits, there having been a quarrel this winter between

---

[1] These contradictions are explained by the dates of the two works. Montesquieu respected at an advanced age the religious principles that he had attacked in a youthful work. (Berville and Barrière.)

[2] By Diderot, D'Alembert, Raynal, Holbach, Voltaire, etc.

[3] An analytical dictionary of the sciences, arts, and trades, by a society of men of letters, arranged by Diderot and D'Alembert; forming in its beginning twenty-eight volumes, in folio; 1751–1772. *The Universal Dictionary* and *Journal de Trévoux*, so called because printed at the printing office of the principality of Dombes, of which Trévoux was the chief town, were begun in 1701 and 1704. (Littré.)

the authors of this work and the journals of Trévoux. The Jesuits are Italians; they lay distant plans for vengeance. But what can be contrived against the authors of this grand and useful enterprise? The accusation of impiety is brought against them. Hence the attack upon the Sorbonne thesis of one of them, the Abbé de Prades, for a mere trifle. . . .

The Abbé de Prades has been condemned for his famous Sorbonne thesis. He will be obliged to retract. . . . He is accused of affectation, of having affected to cram his thesis with hazardous propositions intended to scandalize, and of giving them a background of materialism and irreligion corresponding to the mode of the philosophers of the century, to that philosophic liking of today for natural religion. Woe to him who speaks of it henceforth! The *parlement* thinks of using coercion, and suggests having the first offender flogged. My friend D'Alembert is one of the leading suspects. The *Dictionnaire encyclopédique* is in danger of attack and prohibition. It is the lair, they say, of the impious group. Here is a frightful storm that menaces the best writers of the century, and is going to subject them anew to the Jesuits.

The author [D'Alembert] is one of my best friends; certain items of this work [*Mélanges de littérature, d'histoire, et de philosophie*] were even composed at my estate at Segrez; the passages translated from Tacitus are among this number . . .

His essay on *Gens de lettres* seemed to me the most outstanding of this group, not counting the introduction to the *Encyclopédie*, which was already known to the public.

In this the author depicts himself as he is, free, poor, truthful, ingenious, happy, in short, and working for the happiness of others.

(Marmontel, II, 51–52.)

The years I passed at Versailles were those in which the spirit of philosophy was in its greatest activity. D'Alembert and Diderot had hoisted its standard in the immense laboratory of the *Encyclopédie*, and all who were most distinguished among men of letters were there rallied round them. Voltaire, on his return from Berlin, from which place he had chased the unhappy Arnaud, and where he could not remain himself, had retired to Geneva; and from thence he blew that spirit of liberty, of innovation, and of independence that has since made such progress. In his spite against the king he has been guilty of imprudences; but they were guilty of a much greater who obliged him to remain in a land of liberty, when he would fain have returned to his country. The king's answer, "Let him remain where he is," was not sufficiently deliberate. His attacks were not such as could there be prevented. Versailles, where he would have been less bold than in Switzerland or Geneva, was the place of exile they should have given him. The priests should have opened to him that magnificent prison: it was thus that Cardinal Richelieu acted towards the first nobility.

VOLTAIRE. (Ségur, I, 166–167.)

Voltaire, the prince of poets, the patriarch of philosophers, the glory of his century and of France, had been for many years exiled from his country. The

French all delighted in reading his works, and practically none of them had ever seen him. His contemporaries were for him, if one may speak thus, like a sort of posterity. Admiration for his versatile genius was, in many people, a species of cult and of adoration; his writings adorned all the libraries; his name occupied all minds; and his features were not to be seen. His spirit dominated, directed, and modified all the thought of his time; but except for a small number of men who had been admitted into his philosophical sanctuary at Ferney, he reigned for the rest of his fellow citizens as an invisible power.

Never perhaps did any mortal operate as great changes as he in the manners of his century. Never did any reformer fight and vanquish, without appearing in the *mêlée*, more enemies who believed themselves invincible, more errors consecrated by time, more prejudices rooted in old beliefs.

(Marmontel, III, 217–218.)

Voltaire, whom I had just seen expire, had sought glory by all the roads that are open to genius, and had deserved it by immense labors and brilliant successes. But on all these roads he had encountered Envy, and all the furies by whom she is escorted. Never did a man of letters bear so much outrage, without any other crime than great talents and the ardor of signalizing them. Those who envied him fancied they could be his rivals by showing themselves his enemies; those whom in his way he trod under his feet still insulted him as they lay. The combat was not always worthy of him; and he had more insects to crush than serpents to strangle. But he never could either disdain or provoke offense: the vilest of his assailants have been branded with his hand: the arm of ridicule was the instrument of his vengeance, and he wielded it most fearfully and cruelly. But the greatest of blessings, repose, was unknown to him. It is true that Envy at last appeared tired of the pursuit, and began to spare him on the brink of the grave.

VOLTAIRE'S IDEAS ON LAW. (Voltaire, XXXI, 897–899.)

No ecclesiastical law should have any force except it have the express sanction of the government. It is by this means that Athens and Rome were freed from religious quarrels.

These quarrels are the portion of barbarous nations, or those that have become barbarous.

Magistrates alone should have power to allow or prohibit work on feast days, because it is not the business of priests to forbid men to cultivate their fields.

Everything which concerns marriages should depend solely on the magistrates, and priests should limit themselves to the august function of blessing them.

Lending at interest should be purely a concern of the civil law, since it alone has charge of commerce.

All ecclesiastics should be subject in all cases to the government, because they are subjects of the state.

One should never be so shamefully ridiculous as to pay foreign priests the first year's revenue of land which citizens have given to native priests.

No priest should ever have the power to take from a citizen the least prerogative under the pretext that the citizen is a sinner, because the priest is a sinner and ought to pray for sinners instead of judging them.

Magistrates, laborers, and priests should bear the expenses of the state equally, because they belong to the state equally.

There should be but one weight, one measure, one custom.

The punishment of criminals should be useful. A hanged man is good for nothing, but a man condemned to hard labor still serves the country, and is a living lesson.

All law should be clear, uniform, and precise; to interpret it is almost always to corrupt it.

Nothing should be counted infamous except vice.

Taxes should never be anything but proportional.

Law should never be in contradiction to usage; for if the custom is good the law is worth nothing.

VOLTAIRE ON TOLERANCE. (*Voltaire, XXIII, 72–110.*)

Cast your eyes on the other hemisphere. See Carolina, of which wise Locke was the lawmaker; seven families suffice for the establishment of a public worship approved by law: this liberty has produced no disorder. God forbid us citing this as an example for France to imitate! It is given only to show that unlimited tolerance has not been followed by the slightest dissension; but that which is very useful and good in a new colony is not suitable in an old monarchy.

What shall we say of the primitives who have been called *Quakers* in derision and who, with usages that are perhaps ridiculous, have been so virtuous and have so unavailingly taught peace to the rest of mankind? There are a hundred thousand of them in Pennsylvania; discord and controversy are unknown in the home they have made for themselves; and the very name of their city of Philadelphia, which constantly reminds them that men are brothers, is the object-lesson and shame of peoples who do not yet know tolerance.

After all, this tolerance has never brought civil war; intolerance has covered the earth with carnage. Let us judge now between these two rivals, between the mother who desires her son killed, and the mother who gives him up provided he lives.

I do not speak here of the interests of nations; and in respecting, as I should, theology, I consider in this regard only the physical and moral good of society. I beg all impartial readers to weigh these verities, to rectify them, and to extend them. Attentive readers who communicate their thoughts always go further than the author . . .

What! Is each citizen to be permitted to believe and to think that which his reason rightly or wrongly dictates? He should indeed, provided that he does not disturb the public order; for it is not contingent on man to believe or not to believe; but it is contingent on him to respect the usages of his country; and if you say that it is a crime not to believe in the dominant religion, you accuse then yourself the first Christians, your ancestors, and you justify those whom you accuse of having martyred them.

You reply that there is a great difference, that all religions are the work of men, and that the Apostolic Roman Catholic Church is alone the work of God. But in good faith, ought our religion because it is divine reign through hate, violence, exiles, usurpation of property, prisons, tortures, murders, and thanksgivings to God for these murders? The more the Christian religion is divine, the less it pertains to man to require it; if God made it, God will sustain it without you. You know that intolerance produces only hypocrites or rebels; what distressing alternatives! In short, do you want to sustain through executioners the religion of a God whom executioners have put to death and who taught only gentleness and patience?

VOLTAIRE'S BELIEF IN RIDICULE. (*Letter to M. Bertrand, a Swiss cleric, January 8, 1764.*)

I shall not cease, my dear sir, in spite of the complaints of your priests and the clamors of ours, to preach tolerance from the roof-tops, as long as persecution does not cease. The advances of reason are slow; the roots of prejudices are deep. Doubtless I shall not see the fruits of my efforts, but they will be seeds that perhaps will sprout some day.

You do not find, my dear friend, that pleasantry is suited to grave matters. We French are gay; the Swiss are more serious. In the charming country of Vaud, which inspires joy, might not gravity be the result of government? Remember that nothing is more effective in crushing superstition than covering it with ridicule. I do not confuse it with religion, my dear philosopher. The former is the object of foolishness and pride; the latter is dictated by wisdom and reason. The first has always produced turmoil and war; the latter maintains union and peace. My friend Jean Jacques [Rousseau] does not like comedies, and you do not want to be amused by innocent pleasantries. In spite of your seriousness, however, I love you tenderly.

ROUSSEAU. (*D'Argenson, V, 123–124.*)

I have read the discourse of Rousseau at Geneva that has just carried off the prize of the Academy of Dijon [*Discourse on Inequality Among Men*]. . . .

I likewise competed for the same prize through a dissertation that I believed erudite and reasonable; but the Academy in public session declared that the content of dissertations of this sort was not of the kind admitted, thus recognizing, very unphilosophically in my opinion, a natural inequality among men.

Rousseau gets into a passion and goes to extremes in all of his philosophical views. In his first work he disapproves of the sciences, in the second he affirms that we do not even have music in France. How can he be so insensible to the beautiful French music, so noble, so simple, so touching? Finally he disapproves of all civilization, and sends us back to live in the woods like savages and horses. . . .

He ought to expect much criticism. King Stanislas is working on a refutation under the name of the Chevalier de Solignac, head of his Academy of Lunéville. . . .

What he [Rousseau] says against luxury is admirable; only he is too austere.

He is a philosopher who, to be independent, left M. Dupin, the farmer-general, and lives fifth floor, copying music at six sous a roll.

(*Marmontel, III, 10–11.*)

"What a man!" exclaimed I; "and he fancies himself kind-hearted!" Diderot replied: "He should be so, for he was born with sensibility, and, at a distance, he loves every human being. He only hates those who approach him, because his vanity induces him to think that they are all envious of him; that they flatter him but to injure him; and that even those who pretend to love him share in the conspiracy. This is his disease. Interesting on account of his misfortunes, his talents, and a fund of kindness and rectitude that his heart cherishes, he would have friends, if he believed in friendship. As it is, he will never have any, or they will love him singly; for he will always distrust them. This fatal mistrust, this light and prompt facility, not only of suspecting, but of believing of his friends all that is most atrocious, most mean, and most infamous; of attributing to them baseness and perfidy, without any other proof than the dreams of an ardent and somber imagination, whose vapors cloud his disordered brain, and whose malignant influence sours and poisons his gentlest affections; in short, this delirium of a melancholy and timid mind, made savage by misfortune, was most truly the disease of Rousseau, and the torment of his soul."

ORIGIN OF ROUSSEAU'S PHILOSOPHY. (*Marmontel, II, 261–262.*)

I will now tell you the fact, in its simplicity, such as Diderot related it to me, and such as I related it to Voltaire.

"I was" — it is Diderot who speaks — "I was a prisoner at Vincennes; Rousseau came to see me there. He made me his Aristarchus, as he has said himself. One day, as we were walking together, he told me that the Dijon Academy had just proposed an interesting question, and that he was desirous of treating it. This question was: *Has the re-establishment of arts and sciences contributed to the improvement of morals?* 'Which side will you take?' I asked. 'The affirmative,' he answered. ''Tis the ass's bridge,' said I; 'all ordinary talents will take that road; and you will find there only common ideas, whereas the contrary side presents a new, rich, and fertile field for philosophy and for eloquence.' 'You are right,' returned he, after a moment's reflection, 'and I'll take your advice.'" "Thus, from that moment," added I, "his part and his mask were decided."

"You do not astonish me," said Voltaire; "that man is factitious from head to foot; he is so in his mind and in his soul. But it is in vain for him to play now the stoic and now the cynic; he will eternally belie himself, and his mask will stifle him."

ROUSSEAU'S BACK-TO-NATURE IDEAS. (*Rousseau, VII, 1–18.*)

All is good on coming from the hands of the Maker; all degenerates in the hands of man. He forces one country to nourish the products of another and one tree to bear the fruit of another; he mixes and confounds the climates, the elements, and seasons; he mutilates his horse and his slave; he upsets everything, he disfigures everything, he loves deformity and monsters; he desires nothing to be as nature made it, not even man; he must be trained for him like a riding-horse; he must be given the proper contour, like a tree in his garden.

Without that, everything would be worse yet, and our species does not want to be half made over. In the state things are, a man left to himself from birth would be, compared to the others, the most grotesque of all. Prejudices, authority, necessity, examples, and all the social institutions in which we are submerged would suppress his naturalness, and put nothing in its place. It would be like a young tree that grows by chance in the middle of a road, and that passers-by soon kill by knocking it in all directions and bending it down in various ways....

In the natural order, men being all equal, their vocation is to be men, and whoever is well trained for that can fill any position. That my pupil be destined to the sword, the church, or the bar matters little. Life as a human being comes before the vocation desired by his parents. Life is the trade I wish him to learn. On leaving my hands he will be, I admit, neither magistrate, soldier, nor priest; he will be first a man; all that a man ought to be he can be as well as another, and in whatever place chance may put him he will always be able to fill it. *Occupavi te, fortuna, atque cepi, omnesque aditus tuos interclusi, ut ad me aspirare non posses.* ...

All our wisdom consists in servile prejudices; all our usages are subjection, restriction, and constraint. Civilized man is born, lives, and dies in slavery; at birth he is sewed in swaddling clothes; at death he is nailed in a coffin; as long as he keeps the human form he is enchained by our institutions.

It is said that many midwives pretend, in kneading the heads of newborn infants, to give them more conventional forms: and it is allowed to be done! Our heads are badly fashioned by the Author of our being! They must be refashioned without by midwives and within by philosophers! The Caribs are happier than we by half.

(Letter of Voltaire to Rousseau, August 30, 1755.)

I have received, Monsieur, your book against the human race; I thank you for it. You please men when you tell them the truth about themselves, but you do not reform them. One could not paint in stronger colors the horrors of human society, in which our ignorance and our weakness promise us so many consolations.

There has never been so much talent employed in trying to make us beasts: in reading your book one desires to go about on all fours. However, as it has been more than sixty years since I lost the habit, I feel that unfortunately it is impossible for me to resume it, and I leave this natural allurement to those more worthy of it than you and I.

Neither can I take ship to go seek out the savages of Canada: first, because the maladies with which I am overwhelmed keep me close to the greatest physicians of Europe, and I should not find the same succor among the

Missouris; secondly, because war is going on in that country, and the example of our nations has caused the savages to be almost as bad as we are.

I limit myself to being a peaceful savage in the solitude that I have chosen near your native country, where you ought to be.

I agree with you that literature and science have sometimes caused much harm. The enemies of Tasso made of his life a tissue of misfortunes; those of Galileo had him groaning in prisons, at seventy years of age, for having known the movement of the earth, and, what is more shameful, made him retract. As soon as your friends had begun the *Dictionnaire encyclopédique*, those who dared to be their rivals treated them as deists, atheists, and even as Jansenists. . . .

If anyone ought to complain about literature, it is I, since it has caused me to be persecuted everywhere; but one must love it in spite of the abuse made of it, as it is necessary to love the society whose pleasures are corrupted by wicked men; as it is necessary to love one's country whatever injustices are endured there; as it is necessary to love and serve the Supreme Being in spite of the superstitions and fanaticism which so often dishonor His cult.

M. Chappuis informs me that your health is very bad; you should come and restore it in your native air, enjoy liberty, drink with me the milk of our cows, and browse on our herbs.

I am very philosophically and with the greatest esteem, etc.

THE SOCIAL CONTRACT. (*Rousseau, II, 4-24.*)

Man is born free and is everywhere in chains. One believes himself the master of others, which does not prevent his being more of a slave than they. How has this come about? I do not know. What can render it legitimate? I believe I can solve that problem.

If I only considered force and its effects, I should say: As long as a people is forced to obey, and it obeys, it does well; as soon as it can throw off the yoke, and it throws it off, it does better yet; for recovering its liberty by the same right by which it was taken from it, either it is justified in recovering it, or it was unjust to take it away. But the social order is a sacred right, which serves as a base for all the others. However, this right does not come from nature; it is, then, founded on conventions. . . .

I conjecture that men arrive at that point where the obstacles that oppose their conservation in the natural state successfully resist the forces that each individual can employ to maintain himself in that state. Then this primitive state can no longer exist; and the human species will perish if it does not change its manner of existence.

But, since men cannot engender new forces, but only unite and direct those which exist, they have no other means of self-preservation than to form by aggregation a sum total of their forces that can prevail over the resistance, put them under a single direction, and make them act in concert.

This union of forces cannot take place except through the co-operation of many: but the force and liberty of each man being the first instruments of his preservation, how can he engage them without prejudice to himself and without neglecting himself? This difficulty found in my subject can be stated in these terms:

"To find a form of association which defends and protects with the whole common force the person and goods of each member, and in which each uniting himself with all still obeys only himself and remains as free as before." Such is the problem to which the social contract gives the solution. . . .

If one thus subtracts from the social pact everything but its essence, one will find that it reduces itself to the following terms: *Each of us puts his person and all his power under the supreme direction of the general will; and we receive into the group each member as an indivisible part of the whole.*

Immediately, in the place of the particular person of each contracting party, this act of association produces a moral and collective corps composed of as many members as the assembly has voices, which receives from this act its unity, its common *self*, its existence, and its will.

This public person which is formed by the union of all the others took formerly the name of *City*, and takes now that of *Republic*, or of *Body Politic*, which is called by its members *State* when it is passive, *Sovereign* when it is active, and *Power* when comparing it to others. As to its members, they take collectively the name of *People*, and call themselves in particular *Citizens*, as participants in the sovereign authority, and *Subjects*, as submitting to the laws of the state. But these terms often overlap, and are used for one another; it suffices to be able to distinguish them when they are used with all preciseness.

MONTESQUIEU ON THE SEPARATION OF THE POWERS. (*Montesquieu, I,* 216–217.)

When the legislative and executive powers are united in the same person, or in the same body of magistrates, there can be no liberty; because apprehensions may arise lest the same monarch or senate should enact tyrannical laws to execute them in a tyrannical manner.

Again there is no liberty if the power of judging be not separated from the legislative and executive powers. Were it joined with the legislature, the life and liberty of the subject would be exposed to arbitrary control; for the judge would be then the legislator. Were it joined to the executive power, the judge might behave with all the violence of an oppressor.

There would be an end of everything were the same man or the same body, whether of the nobles or of the people, to exercise those three powers, that of enacting the laws, that of executing the public resolutions, and that of judging the crimes or differences of individuals.

Most kingdoms of Europe enjoy a moderate government because the prince who is invested with the two first powers leaves the third to his subjects. In Turkey, where these three powers are united in the sultan's person, the subjects groan under the weight of the most frightful oppression.

In the republics of Italy, where these three powers are united, there is less liberty than in our monarchies. Hence their government is obliged to have recourse to as violent methods for its support as even that of the Turks; witness the state inquisitors (at Venice), and the lion's mouth into which every informer may at all hours throw his written accusations.

What a situation must the poor subjects be in, under those republics! The same body of magistrates are possessed, as executors of the laws, of the whole power they have given themselves in quality of legislators. They may plunder the state by their general determination, and as they have likewise the judiciary power in their hands, every private citizen may be ruined by their particular decisions.

The whole power is here united in one body; and though there is no external pomp that indicates a despotic sway, yet the people feel the effects of it every moment.

Hence it is that many of the princes of Europe, whose aim has been levelled at arbitrary power, have constantly set out with uniting in their own persons all the branches of magistracy, and all the great offices of the state.

DIDEROT. (*Morellet, I, 29–30.*)

The conversation of Diderot, an extraordinary man whose talent could be no more denied than his wrongs, had great power and great charm; his discourse was animated, sincere, subtle without obscurity, varied in form, vivid with imagination, fecund in ideas, and ingenious in arousing them in others. One would allow himself to be carried along for hours on end as on a gentle limpid river, bordered by rich countrysides ornate with beautiful habitations.

... there has never been a man more complacent, more indulgent than Diderot; he lends and gives understanding to others. He feels a desire to make converts, not precisely to atheism, but to philosophy and reason. It is true that if religion and deism barred his path he would not stop or alter his course; but I have never seen him show any zeal in inspiring ideas of this kind; he defends them good-humoredly, and shows no animosity towards those who do not agree with them.

QUESNAY. (*Marmontel, II, 31–32.*)

Quesnay, very incommodiously lodged in Mme. de Pompadour's entresol, was occupied from morning till night only with political and rural economy. He thought he had reduced his system to calculations and axioms, whose evidence was irresistible; and, as he was forming a school, he was pleased to give himself the pains of explaining his new doctrine to me, in order to make me a disciple and a proselyte. I, who thought of making him my mediator with Mme. de Pompadour, applied my whole powers of mind to understand the truths which he thought so evident, but in which I could only discover vagueness and obscurity. To pretend to comprehend what I really did not was above my powers. But I listened with patient docility; and left him the hope of finally enlightening me, and of instilling his doctrine. This would have been enough to gain me his good will. I did more, I used to applaud a labor that I really found estimable; for it tended to render agriculture commendable, in a country where it was too much disdained, and to turn a variety of valuable minds to this study. I had even an opportunity of flattering him in this sensible part, which he afforded me.

PHILOSOPHY AND CONDUCT. (*Ségur, I, 146–147.*)

Never has one seen a greater contrast in opinions, tastes, and manners; in the midst of academies one applauded the maxims of philanthropy, diatribes against vainglory, and hopes of eternal peace; but, on going forth, one would agitate, intrigue, and declaim to influence the government to war. Each endeavored to surpass the others in luxury, while speaking of republicanism and preaching equality. At court there had never been more magnificence and vanity nor less power. One censured the Versailles authorities and paid court to those of the *Encyclopédie.*

We preferred a word of praise from D'Alembert or Diderot to the most signal favor of a prince. Gallantry, ambition, and philosophy were all intermingled and confounded; prelates left their dioceses to solicit ministries; priests composed verses and licentious tales.

The court applauded the republican maxims of Brutus; monarchs prepared to embrace the cause of a people revolting against its king; in fine, one spoke of independence in army camps, of democracy in aristocratic homes, of philosophy in ballrooms, of metaphysics in boudoirs.

THE SALONS. (*Ségur, I, 149–150.*)

As a matter of fact, one found then at the Hôtel de La Rochefoucauld, at D'Alembert's, and at Mme. Geoffrin's, the most distinguished philosophers and men of letters, and that spirit of liberty which was to change the face of the world in enlightening it, and unfortunately also undermine all its bases in wishing to give it new ones.

In the reunions which took place at the Maréchale de Luxembourg's, at La Vallière's, and at the Hôtel de Choiseul, one saw reproduced all that the reign of Louis XV had offered in personages conspicuous by their rank, their urbanity, and their gallantry. At Mme. Deffant's one was certain to encounter the most renowned foreigners, drawn by curiosity to know the France, old and new, which at home they vilified ponderously and accused of frivolity, but which at the same time was, is, and will be the object of their jealousy.

THE MARIAGE DE FIGARO. (*Mme. Campan, 181–182.*)

Beaumarchais had long possessed a reputation in certain circles in Paris for his wit and musical talents, and at the theaters for dramas more or less indifferent, when his *Barbier de Séville* procured him a higher position among dramatic writers. His *Mémoires* against M. Goësman had amused Paris by the ridicule they threw upon a *parlement* which was disliked; and his admission to an intimacy with M. de Maurepas procured him a degree of influence over important affairs. He then became ambitious of influencing public opinion by a kind of drama in which established manners and customs should be held up to popular derision and the ridicule of the new philosophers. After several years of prosperity the minds of the French had become more generally critical; and when Beaumarchais had finished his monstrous but diverting *Mariage de Figaro*, all people of any consequence were eager for the gratification of hearing it read, the censors having decided that it should not be performed. These readings of *Figaro* grew so numerous that people were daily heard to say, "I have been (or I am going to be) at the reading of Beaumarchais's play." The desire to see it performed became universal; an expression that he had the art to use compelled, as it were, the approbation of the nobility, or of persons in power, who aimed at ranking among the magnanimous; he made his Figaro say that "none but little minds dreaded little books."

LIBERTY AND EQUALITY PRAISED BUT DENIED. (Mme. Campan, 155.)

There was no class of persons that did not heartily approve of the support given openly by the French government to the cause of American independence. The constitution planned for the new nation was digested at Paris, and while liberty, equality, and the rights of men were commented upon by the Condorcets, Baillys, Mirabeaus, etc., the minister Ségur published the king's edict, which, by repealing that of the 1st of November, 1750, declared all officers not noble by four generations incapable of filling the rank of captain, and denied all military rank to the *roturiers*, excepting sons of the Chevaliers de Saint-Louis. The injustice and absurdity of this law was no doubt a secondary cause of the Revolution.

IV. *The Reforms of Turgot and Necker*

THE DEATH OF LOUIS XV. (*Besenval, I, 289–292.*)

THE king was taken ill the 28th of April, 1774, at the Petit Trianon, during one of those trips lasting two or three days, with which he constantly tried to mitigate the uselessness of his life and escape the idleness and boredom which followed him everywhere. . . .

The people, overwhelmed with taxes to amend the depredation of the finances dissipated in luxury and swallowed up by the cupidity of the favorite and the attendant intriguers, and, moreover, indignant at the disorderly life of this prince, regarded his death as the only means of deliverance from oppression, and expressed themselves about it loudly in the streets.

(*Mme. Campan, 57.*)

The dauphin was with the dauphiness. They were expecting together the intelligence of the death of Louis XV. A dreadful noise, absolutely like thunder, was heard in the outer apartment; it was the crowd of courtiers who were deserting the dead sovereign's antechamber to come and do homage to the new power of Louis XVI. This extraordinary tumult informed Marie Antoinette and her husband that they were called to the throne; and, by a spontaneous movement, which deeply affected those around them, they threw themselves on their knees; both, pouring forth a flood of tears, exclaimed: "O God! guide us, protect us; we are too young to reign."

THE LAST PROCESSION. (*Besenval, I, 307–308.*)

The corpse was conducted two days later to Saint-Denis, the convoy resembling the conveyance of a burden which one is anxious to be rid of rather than the last services rendered a monarch. Since the king had died of a contagious disease [smallpox], it was not possible to observe the ceremonies and many ruinous absurdities which were practiced on like occasions. The coffin was put into a large carriage; another carried the Duc d'Ayen and the Duc d'Aumont; a third the grand-almoner and the *curé* of Versailles. A score of pages and half a hundred mounted grooms, carrying torches, without being in black any more than the carriages, composed the cortège, which departed at a fast trot at eight o'clock in the evening, and arrived at Saint-Denis at eleven o'clock, among the jeers of the curious who bordered the road, and

who, favored by the darkness, gave rein to mockery, the dominant characteristic of the nation. They did not stop at that: epitaphs, placards, and verses
were lavished to dishonor the memory of the deceased king.

THE CORONATION. (*Mme. Campan, 88–89.*)

The coronation took place at Reims, with all the accustomed pomp. At
this period the people's love for Louis XVI burst forth in transports not to be
mistaken for party demonstrations or idle curiosity. He replied to this enthusiasm by marks of confidence worthy of a people happy in being governed by a good king; he took a pleasure in repeatedly walking without
guards in the midst of the crowd which pressed around him, and called down
blessings on his head. I remarked the impression made at this time by an
observation of Louis XVI. On the day of his coronation he put his hand up
to his head, at the moment of the crown being placed upon it, and said,
"It pinches me." Henri III had exclaimed, "It pricks me." Those who were
near the king were struck with the similarity between these two exclamations,
though not of a class likely to be blinded by the superstitious fears of ignorance.

THE ACCESSION OF LOUIS XVI. (*Morellet, I, 229–231.*)

If the entire reign of Louis XVI is taken into consideration, the sinister
predictions of which I speak have been only too well justified; but these fears
could have anticipated nothing of that which we have seen since. And as for
the early years of his reign, the fact is that they were better for the nation than
the most brilliant of the reign of Louis XV; the government of the new
monarch was milder and wiser; science, art, and social relations were already
making excellent progress; everything tended towards betterment, and one
cannot too greatly deplore the upheaval which, to reform some abuses which
would gradually have corrected themselves, has plunged a great people into
an abyss of evil.

The new king called to his side M. de Maurepas, honoring him with full
confidence. It is pretended that he hesitated between him and M. de Machault.
The latter was in reality an octogenarian, but still vigorous, and survived his
rival to perish in prison at the age of ninety, ulcerated and in want, a cruelty
unknown to savage nations, and examples of which are only too numerous in
the history of our misfortunes.

M. de Maurepas had constantly shown sympathy and esteem for M. Turgot,
who saw him rather often. An Abbé de Véry, full of admiration for the virtue
and talents of M. Turgot, was the intimate friend and familiar of Mme. de
Maurepas; he had some influence even over the mind of the old man, who,
in spite of the disdain he affected for philosophy, and the fear he had of
the philosopher, feeling sure that he could halt him when he wished, called
him to the ministry. For the first two months he was minister of the navy,
and then minister of finances, when the Abbé Terray was removed.

MAUREPAS. (*Ségur, I, 228.*)

The sole aim of this unconcerned old man was to pass tranquilly the little time he had yet to live; he wished, so to speak, to be free from all cares by having the king carry on a day by day government. Reluctant in tolerating any ideas of reform that might cause complaint and cabals, or extended plans of campaign where great success could be purchased by great risks, he would have liked to play the terrible game of war without hazarding too much; in short, he wanted to parade and not to fight.

His indecision clogged deliberations; petty intrigues occupied him more than important affairs of state. He never considered the gravest matters except jokingly, and the scepter that had been confided to him seemed nothing but a toy calculated to amuse his second childhood.

MAUREPAS RECALLS THE PARLEMENTS. (*Ségur, I, 37–38.*)

At the moment M. de Maurepas was named, the quarrel between the old *parlements* that had been dismissed and those that had replaced them seemed to be the only sign of an approaching storm. M. de Maurepas hastened to extinguish this fire which alarmed him. He recalled the disgraced *parlements*; their exile had been an act of tyranny; their recall should not have been a triumph for them: it was. Their power was unconditionally restored and this victory of the high magistracy over authority encouraged the spirit of resistance and innovation. An unjust harshness had, by repression, engendered a spirit of independence; an act of justice feebly done gave it a new impulse.

THE REFORMS OF LOUIS XVI. (*Bouillé, 59–61.*)

Frenchmen! what sacrifices did he not make, if not for your happiness, at least to please you and satisfy you? Ah! if they are effaced from your memory, I will retrace them for you. At his accession to the throne, you ardently desired the re-establishment of the *parlements* that Louis XV had been forced to destroy; he re-established them. He chose for ministers the men believed to be the wisest and most upright, and who had reputations for probity or talent, and he followed this principle constantly throughout his entire reign; if he was mistaken in his choice, he was misled by public opinion. He abolished the *corvée* and servitude in some of your provinces; he changed the ancient penal code which still recalled the ignorance and barbarity of your fathers; he made a trial of provincial administrations, which he wished to extend to the whole of France in order to establish economy in the collection and destroy arbitrariness in the assessment and levying of public taxes; he destroyed the abuse of *lettres de cachet*, of which precedent necessitated the modern use; he emptied the state prisons, which soon enclosed none but the men dangerous to society and detained by the principles of humanity and justice; and he put, to say no more, M. de Malesherbes, the wisest of Frenchmen, at the head of the state police, which he only abandoned contrary to the wishes and instances of the king. Forever occupied with the assuagement and the happiness of his people, he assembled the notables of the kingdom to find the means, and you have seen with what ardor he desired the destruction of the *gabelle* and others of the more burdensome taxes; it was not his fault that this great object was not accomplished.

He conserved the purest manners in the midst of a most corrupt court, a gentle and intelligent piety in the midst of irreligion and atheism, and a personal economy in the midst of the most extravagant luxury.

(*Weber, I, 126–127.*)

Louis XVI seemed to have made himself solely responsible in regard to public affairs; and while he preserved the greater part of Europe from the scourge of war, and sent his armies to triumph in the New World, to the interior of his kingdom he brought all the blessings of peace. He founded or remodelled hospitals, made prisons more humane, honored and encouraged agriculture, built canals, drained marshes, constructed bridges, abolished servitude, established schools for the people, reformed criminal law, suppressed torture, equalized the assessment of taxes by lightening the burden of his more oppressed subjects, imposed upon himself severe retrenchments, and submitted accounts everywhere to equitable laws.

(*Vaublanc, 123.*)

The actions of this prince had been entirely praiseworthy since the beginning of his reign; he had abolished *corvées* and torture, established a number of provincial assemblies as an experiment to test their usefulness, abolished mortmain, recalled the *parlements*, which resumed their functions to the universal joy of France, gave an example of the greatest personal economy, suppressed several *corps d'élite* that served the splendor of the throne, and undertook a maritime war after having contracted a close alliance that assured the co-operation of the naval forces of Spain and Holland.

THE KING AT CHERBOURG (1786). (*Dumas, I, 126–127.*)

Louis XVI, who devoted his attention with an enlightened ardor to everything that concerned the increase and the improvement of his navy, had particularly at heart the formation of the port of Cherbourg, which was to be one of the most glorious monuments of his reign. He desired to judge for himself of the state of the works, of what had already been done, and to encourage the undertaking with his presence.... It was a grand sight.... the king embarked on board the fire-ship, which was commanded by Commodore Albert de Rions, one of our most celebrated naval officers ... M. de Rions asked Louis XVI what should be the name of the ship, to which His Majesty replied, "Let it be called the *Patriot*," and this name was fixed to the stern in the presence of the king, who gave orders to put to sea.... The wind having freshened, the admiral represented to the king that it was time to tack, because if he proceeded any farther he could not promise to return to Cherbourg. "Never mind," said the king, who was much pleased with this trip; "we shall be well received in some English port."

TURGOT'S REFORMS. (*Marmontel, III, 304–305.*)

Although, in two years, by means of reduction and economy, he had considerably diminished the mass of debt with which the treasury was charged, it was still thought that he treated as a chronic disease the exhaustion and ruin of the finances and of credit. The prudence of his regimen, his means of amelioration, the encouragement and the relief which he gave to agriculture, the liberty he restored to commerce and to industry, promised only slow successes, and only tardy resources, while there were urgent demands for which it was requisite to provide.

His system of liberty for all kinds of commerce admitted in its extent neither of restriction nor limit; and, with respect to the object of the first necessity, when even this absolute liberty should only have been attended with momentary dangers, the risk of suffering the chief resource of life to dry up from a whole people was not a risk to run without inquietude. The perseverance of Turgot to subject the commerce of grain to no kind of restriction too much resembled obstinacy. It was by this that his credit in the opinion of the king received a mortal wound.

(Weber, I, 136–137.)

Turgot, commended to the choice of Louis XVI by his genius, virtue, and the benedictions of a populous province in which he had been intendant, brought to the administration of finances a spirit of justice and a plan of universal beneficence. "There are only M. Turgot and I who love the people," said Louis XVI; and for love of the people they abolished together the dues on grain, the encumbrances that hindered commerce, the restrictions on the grain trade, and finally the *corvées*. Partisans of the abuses became alarmed. They aroused the people against the law that was to nourish the people. A fictitious famine was produced in the midst of abundance. Revolts broke out in the capital and neighboring provinces. The storehouses were broken into, and the grain and flour strewn over the highways or thrown into the river. All the bakehouses were pillaged, and at Paris there was talk of marching on Versailles. . . . It required a *lit de justice* and express commands to force the *parlement* to register the suppression of *corvées* and the abolition of taxes on industry.

TURGOT'S SLOWNESS. (*Morellet, I, 15–16.*)

The mind of M. Turgot was exceedingly active; but when he began to work, and it was a question of writing things out and carrying them into execution, he was slow and dilatory. He was slow because he wished to give to everything the degree of perfection he desired, even to *minutiae*, and because he could never accept help, being dissatisfied with everything he had not done himself. He was dilatory also, losing time in arranging his desk and trimming his pens; not that he did not think profoundly while pottering about, but mere thinking did not advance him in his work.

These things that I describe, the never being satisfied and the meticulousness in regard to his own work that caused him to consume valuable time, have been very noticeable in the whole course of his ministry and probably contributed to bringing about his retirement.

OPPOSITION TO TURGOT. (*Marmontel, III, 300–301.*)

The new minister felt strongly that a diminution in the expenditure, economy in the employment of the revenues, and in the expenses of collecting them, the abolition of all privileges burdensome to commerce and to agriculture, and a more equal distribution of the taxes on all classes were the true remedies that should be applied to the state's deep wound, and a king who breathed only justice and love for his people was easily persuaded of it. But soon Maurepas, seeing how much the esteem and confidence which Turgot inspired in the young king exceeded the bounds he wished to prescribe to them, was jealous of his own work, and eagerly hastened to destroy it.

In a country where so many people live by abuses and disorder, a man whom favor cannot bend, nor indulgence corrupt, must necessarily have for his enemies all those he dissatisfied and all those he threatened. Turgot had too much boldness and candor in his character to stoop to the intrigues of a court: he was accused of severe obstinacy and want of address; and ridicule, which, with us, degrades everything, having once attacked him, Maurepas felt that he could easily overthrow him. He began by listening to, and by encouraging with a smile, the malice of the courtiers.

TURGOT'S FALL. (*Weber, I, 137–139.*)

The *parlement* resolved the re-establishment of the *corvées* and the dismissal of the controller-general. The prime minister began to be jealous of the ascendancy that the sagacity and integrity of Turgot gave him in the heart of his virtuous master. The king was brought to fear that serious troubles would occur. He was told that Turgot did good badly. The young prince, not daring to assume responsibility for his plans, sacrificed the minister of his heart. But Turgot had been allowed to begin the execution of plans which he was not allowed to finish. The economics of business were deranged. The burden was again thrown upon the people whom he had relieved, because there had not been time enough to repair the deficiencies in the revenue. His successor, appointed by the Comte de Maurepas, entered upon the office of controller-general; saying naïvely that he knew nothing about finances and had to learn before taking charge.

CLUGNY AND TABOUREAU. (*Marmontel, III, 307.*)

Turgot was dismissed (May, 1776), and the administration of the finances was confided to Clugny, who seemed to have come there only to spoil and plunder with his companions and his mistresses, and who died in the ministry after four or five years of an impudent pillage of which the king only was ignorant.

Taboureau took his place, and, like an honest man, he soon confessed himself incapable of fulfilling it. They had given him for an assistant, under the title of director of the royal treasury, a man whose superiority he himself recognized. His modesty honored his retreat. And Necker succeeded him as controller-general of the finances.

FRANCE AIDS THE AMERICANS. *(Ségur, I, 102–104.)*

At this period, liberty, dormant in the civilized world for so many centuries, awoke in another hemisphere and struggled gloriously against an antiquated domination armed with the most redoubtable forces.

In vain had England, proud of her power, her numerous fleets, and her riches, hired and sent forty thousand men to America to stifle this liberty in its cradle.

The courage of these new republicans drew to them throughout Europe the esteem and good wishes of friends of justice and humanity. The younger generation, by a singular contrast, brought up in the midst of monarchies to admire great literary geniuses and the heroes of Greece and Rome, carried to the point of enthusiasm the sympathy inspired in them by the American insurrection.

The French government, which desired to weaken the power of England, was gradually influenced by this liberal opinion declared with such vivacity. It even gave in secret, or allowed to be given through the medium of commerce, arms, munitions, and money to the Americans. . . .

The veil with which they were covered became daily more transparent: soon were seen arriving in Paris the American representatives, Silas Deane and Arthur Lee. Shortly afterward, the celebrated Benjamin Franklin came to join them. It would be difficult to describe the warmth and partiality with which they were received in France, in an ancient monarchy, these envoys of a people in insurrection against its monarch.

Nothing could be more astonishing than the contrast of the luxury of our capital, of the elegance of our manners, of the magnificence of Versailles, of all those remaining traces of the proud monarchy of Louis XIV, and of the polite but superb hauteur of our great nobles, with the almost rustic *habille-ments*, the simple but proud deportment, the frank and unguarded language, the undressed and powderless hair, in short, with that antique bearing which seemed to transport within our walls, to the atmosphere of the softened and submissive civilization of the seventeenth century, sages contemporary with Plato, or republicans of the time of Cato and Fabius.

This unexpected spectacle ravished us all the more for being new and coming at the precise time when literature and philosophy spread among us all a desire for reforms, a penchant for innovations, and the germ of an ardent love for liberty.

(Weber, I, 121.)

. . . September 4, 1778, the *parlement* of Rouen sent its resignation to the king after remonstrances in which it had dared to paraphrase this famous verse:

"L'injustice à la fin produit l'indépendance."

This was precisely the year in which the Anglo-American colonies, after having declared themselves independent of their mother country and their sovereign, got the King of France to ally himself with them in a treaty that soon kindled war in the four corners of the globe, and created with peace a state of affairs still more disastrous than the war itself.

Joseph II, being at Versailles, had been asked his opinion of the projects of the American insurgents. "I beg to be excused," he had replied; "it is my business to be royalist." This expressed in a single phrase all there was to say and all there was to do, or rather not do, in this important and dangerous situation.

RESULT OF THE AMERICAN WAR. (*Weber, I, 128–129.*)

All these warriors in the prime of life who had run to fight in the New World had departed Frenchmen and returned Americans. They had only been in search of perils and military glory: they brought back systems and patriotic enthusiasm. They returned to the midst of a court, bearing on their breasts the wounds received in the cause of liberty, and on their coats the external sign of a republican decoration. La Fayette, who had made himself the ally of the Americans before his king, who with the ardor and prodigality of all great passions, but with a secretiveness and perseverance incomprehensible at his age, had armed a vessel for the American cause, had loaded it with munitions of all kinds to the value of nearly a million, and had stolen away from his family to take ship without anyone having penetrated his secret; La Fayette, who had commanded an army of insurgents, who had conquered with them, whom the United States had adopted as a citizen, and whom Washington had called son for six years; La Fayette returned to his native country, full of the burning desire and vain illusions of an exotic liberty, which, transplanted into France, would there produce fruits so different from those he expected. He had, it was said, in his back cabinet, at Paris, a cardboard mounted in a brilliant frame, and divided into two columns: in one could be read the Declaration of Rights proclaimed by the Anglo-Americans: the other was blank, and appeared to await the same declaration by the French.

NECKER'S BORROWINGS. (*Ségur, I, 232.*)

M. Necker had, by simple expedients, given to the government immense resources for sustaining the costs of the war without increasing the taxes, even on the contrary lightening their weight; he had filled the treasury by annuities, the interest of which was to be paid by means of reforms and economy in the expenditures for luxuries and court.

It was good business, but bad politics. He did not know the power and number of the persons, great and small, interested in the abuses. He learned it only too soon to his sorrow. Private interests were victorious over the common good. The state was sacrificed to the court, economy to luxury, wisdom to vanity.

THE COMPTE RENDU. (Ségur, I, 228–229.)

... M. Necker, who ably administered the finances, took a step that was considered important and useful by some, dangerous and detrimental by others: he printed and published the financial report that he had rendered the king.

This innovation, without precedent in France, produced there a kind of mental revolution. Hitherto the nation, a stranger to its own affairs, had remained in complete ignorance of its income, its expenditures, its debts, the extent of its needs, and the extent of its resources. It was for all the French, even among the educated classes, the veritable *arcanum imperii* [imperial mystery].

This appeal to public opinion was an appeal for liberty: as soon as the public had satisfied its curiosity on these important points that had always been hidden from its eyes, it discussed, praised, censured, and passed judgment.

The nation, awakened on the principal point of its interests, was not slow in believing or recalling that in regard to accounts and taxes it ought not be reduced to the sole duty of settling and paying, and that it had the right to examine, grant, or refuse the burdens imposed upon it.

This opinion, quickly formed, became more and more manifest until some years after it burst forth with unexpected violence.

THE COURT AND THE MINISTRY. (Extract from a letter of Mercy to Kaunitz, December 22, 1780.)

I strongly insisted upon the future supplanting of M. de Maurepas. After lengthy discussions, the queen said to me, "Could a subject be found as agreeable to me as this one? Search for me; I have no one to rely upon but you." This apparently important proposal, although made in good faith, is none the less illusory, and can be confided only to the wisdom and penetration of Your Highness, since, in case of a quite possible bad choice, it would be very easy to accuse me of bad judgment or of negligence.

But my position near the queen is such that although urged continually by her to tell her what I think, and given indications of the most consistent confidence, I find myself perpetually frustrated by her companions, made necessary to her by an immoderate desire for frivolity, and who by their importunities can always obtain any absurdity and almost entirely destroy what little good I try to accomplish.

THE FALL OF NECKER IN 1781. (Mme. de Staël, 48–54.)

The second-class courtiers declared against M. Necker. The great lords, having no inquietude whatever as to their positions or their fortunes, were in general more independent in their views than that obscure swarm which hangs to favor in order to obtain some new gift on each new occasion. M. Necker made some retrenchments in the king's household; in the sum allotted to pensions, in the financial charges, and in the gratuities accorded to people of the court on these charges. This economic system was not at all agreeable to all those people who had formed the habit of being paid by the government, and of following the profession of solicitation as a means of livelihood. . . .

But the partisans of the princes and the financiers were actively opposed to him. A memoir which he presented to the king in regard to the establishment of provincial assemblies had been indiscreetly published, and the *parlements* had noted that M. Necker gave as one of the reasons for this institution, the weight of opinion which it might lend against the *parlements* themselves if they acted as ambitious corporations, and not according to the national desire. This was enough to cause these magistrates, jealous of their contested political authority, boldly to call M. Necker an innovator. But of all the innovations, that which the courtiers and financiers detested most was economy. Such enemies, however, would not have been able to overthrow a minister for whom the nation evinced more attachment than it had ever shown for anyone else since the administration of Sully and Colbert if the Comte de Maurepas had not dexterously seized upon the means of overthrowing him. . . .

M. de Maurepas caused it to be secretly circulated that it would please the king to attack his minister. . . . M. Necker was content . . . to require a sign of the sovereign's favor which would discourage the libellers; he desired that they be removed from the household of Monseigneur le Comte d'Artois, in which they held posts, and that he be accorded entrance to the council of state, from which he had been dislodged on the pretext that he professed the Protestant religion, although his presence there was eminently useful. . . .

M. Necker offered his resignation if the conditions he asked were not accorded. M. de Maurepas, who had urged him to take this step, foresaw with certitude the result: for the feebler monarchs are, the more faithful they are to maxims of firmness taught them from infancy, and of which one of the first is that a king ought never refuse to accept a resignation, nor agree to the conditions that a public functionary demands for the continuation of his services.

The next day M. Necker returned from Versailles, having ceased to be minister.

FLEURY AND THE FINANCES. (*Weber, I, 148.*)

Joly de Fleury, such was his name, offered a ministry that was ashamed of being one: he had scarcely taken up the burden than he was already crushed by it. He had at least either the good faith or address to let it be known that he lived on what his predecessor had left in reserve; but he did not have the ability to replace what he spent. He established a third *vingtième* without opposition from the *parlement* of Paris, where he had, to his advantage, two brothers and a nephew. In spite of the unopposed fraternal registering, the tax could never be entirely collected, which seemed to justify completely the assertion of the Abbé Terray as well as the system of M. Necker. In default of a tax, he attempted a loan which was not even half subscribed. He saw that he could not go on, and asked to resign.

D'ORMESSON'S MINISTRY. (*Weber, I, 149–150.*)

He was succeeded by another magistrate, the worthy bearer of a name revered in the annals of justice and virtue; but among all the things required for the administration of the finances, he had only the scrupulousness and disinterestedness of an Aristides, transmitted to him by his ancestors from generation to generation. His zealous energy equalled his purity of heart and, in other things, as well as in some phases of his new ministry, his talent was recognized; but he was too young to be controller-general, and his task was too complicated. ... He made a grave mistake: the government meddled in the payments of the discounting bank. It was believed that it was going bankrupt. All Paris was in the Rue Vivienne. The government withdrew; the uneasiness increased; the ministry that had been caught off guard resigned. M. de Calonne, intendant of Flanders, and M. de Meilhan, intendant of Hainault, were put forth by the public and their friends; the king chose the first.

CALONNE. (*Marmontel, III, 339–340.*)

[Calonne], believing himself at the source of inexhaustible riches, without calculating either the wants or the expenses that awaited them; intoxicated with his own prosperity, in which he imagined he saw that of the state; disdaining all foresight, neglecting all economy as unworthy of a powerful king; persuaded that the first art of a man in place is the art of pleasing; resigning to favor the care of his fortune, and thinking only of rendering himself agreeable to those who study to be feared in order to be bought, he suddenly saw himself encompassed by praise and vainglory. Nothing was talked of but the graces of his reception, and the charms of his language. It was to paint his character that the expression of *formes élégantes* was borrowed from the arts; and that new word, *l'obligeance,* appeared to be invented for him. It was said that the ministry of finance had never been filled with so much gracefulness, ease, and dignity. The facility with which he transacted business astonished everyone, and the gaiety with which he treated it, however important it might be, made him admired as a man of prodigious talent. Even those, in short, who dared to doubt whether he were the best of ministers were forced to acknowledge that he was the most charming.

THE IMPOSSIBLE WILL BE DONE. (*Weber, I, 300–301.*)

Shortly after the termination of the war, when France, victorious, pacified, exhalted, appeared to have attained the highest degree of prosperity, the queen believed she might ask for the execution of one of the articles of her marriage contract, in which it was stipulated that she should be given a special establishment. ... The Queen of France discovered the Château of Saint-Cloud, which belonged to the House of Orléans, and desired to acquire it. The wholesome air of this beautiful spot, so essential to the health of the precious pledges that she had given to the state, its charming position between Paris and Versailles, the custom that had made it a kind of public garden for the Parisians, and the pleasure of finding herself there on holidays when crowds gathered, in the midst of her subjects like a mother in the midst of a cherished family, determined the preference that Marie Antoinette gave to Saint-Cloud in making it her habitation. However, she wished to know, before making this acquisition, if the state of the finances permitted it. How can one believe that the queen should have been on guard against the alluring assurances of a minister who, to the few requests she made of him, replied always with a manner so delicate and so amiable, "If that which Your Majesty desires is possible, it is done; if it is impossible, it will be done." Was it for Marie Antoinette to contest the assertions of the minister of finances, and to verify whether there was or was not a deficit?

The acquisition of Saint-Cloud was concluded for six million *livres tournois*.

CALONNE AND THE DEFICIT. (*Weber, I, 151–153.*)

He took the oath as controller-general in the month of November, 1783.

In December, 1783, a month after the conclusion of peace, a hundred millions were borrowed on life-annuities to pay off the expenses of the war.

In December, 1784, one hundred and twenty-five millions were borrowed...

In December, 1785, eighty millions were borrowed, payable in ten years, to finish the payment of all the war debts, to pay back debts in the different departments, and to maintain that abundance of funds so necessary to the success of useful operations.

In September, 1786, thirty millions were borrowed by the city of Paris to be deposited in the coffers of the king.

In February, 1787, after another borrowing of fifty millions by the bank of discount, also to be deposited in the coffers of the king, there was an Assembly of Notables chosen from among the three orders of the kingdom, and two eventualities were suddenly revealed to the nation: one, that since the year 1776 public loans had mounted to a billion six hundred and forty-six millions; and the other, that there existed now in the revenue an annual deficit, reckoned by the minister at one hundred and twelve, and soon carried by the Notables to one hundred and forty millions. ...

There was scarcely six years' time between the *compte rendu* of M. Necker, which in the midst of war had shown a surplus of ten millions in the receipts, and the *compte rendu* of M. de Calonne, which in the fourth year of peace presented a deficit of one hundred and forty millions in the same receipts, augmented by another eighty after the issuing of the first account.

There were only fourteen months between the edict in which M. de Calonne had spoken to the nation of the abundance of funds, and the discourse in which he announced a frightful insufficiency! The minister turned public opinion against him. The *parlements*, which made it their duty to serve as its mouthpiece, drew up the most vigorous remonstrances. They refused to register his new edicts; and each time that they were on this account the object of persecution by the court, the people arranged for them the honors of a triumph.

With such a state of mind, M. de Calonne judged that there was nothing more to obtain through the *parlements*. He was still able, however, to make the two indirect loans of which I have spoken, one in the name of the city of Paris, and the other through the bank of discount; then he resolved to execute his great plan for a general amelioration, and to execute it through an Assembly of Notables.

THE DIAMOND NECKLACE AFFAIR. *(Besenval, II, 162.)*

Boehmer is a famous jeweller who sold to the queen, some years ago, ear-drops that possessed great value and beauty, due as much to the size and purity of the stones as to their being perfectly matched. In association with several colleagues, he had assembled a necklace which yielded in no way to the pendants, and for which he demanded one million six hundred thousand francs. This necklace attracted a great deal of attention, and it was said that the queen was going to buy it. I spoke to her about it. She replied to me that, whatever desire she might have for the diamonds, and however beautiful the necklace might be, it was too dear for their means and for her to allow the king to give it to her, all the more since he had just acquired Rambouillet and Saint-Cloud, an expenditure perhaps too large for the present state of the finances; she added that she did not want to be taxed with augmenting the embarrassment by a whim.

THE CARDINAL DE ROHAN DECIDES TO BUY THE NECKLACE FOR THE QUEEN. *(Mme. de La Motte, 58–59.)*

The queen, as much through obstinacy as through love of adornment, passionately desiring the acquisition of the necklace ... the cardinal,[1] forever deluding himself with the idea of some day or other being prime minister, and consequently in a position to re-establish his shattered fortunes, found no sacrifice too dear when it was a question of satisfying the fantasies of the one from whom he expected his elevation and his fortune ... he contracted to procure the necklace for the queen.

THE QUEEN'S NAME FORGED. *(Mme. de La Motte, 72–76.)*

... with the first overtures that he [Rohan] had made, the jewellers had appeared disposed to make personal arrangements. But, when it was a question of making the final dispositions, they spoke in a manner to make him understand only too clearly that they suspected him of wishing to buy these diamonds to make some money on them.... [They demanded that the queen evidence her approval.] I decided that *as a matter of form* it was necessary to *show* the jewellers something that they would take to be the approval of the queen ... after dinner I took him [Villette] apart ... it appeared to him as it had to me that ... it mattered little by whose hand the approval was written, since the jewellers would not know the writing; but he added, " ... you do not suspect the risk that one runs in counterfeiting signatures. It is an act which the law ranges with a number of crimes under the denomination of crimes of forgery; doubtless you will not advise me to commit a crime; but

---

[1] The Cardinal de Rohan, Bishop of Strasbourg, grand-almoner of France, "a man who united much exterior elegance with many mental graces, and even attainments, but without restraint in his passions or conduct, easy in his manners, spending extravagantly, full of thoughtlessness and frivolity." (Besenval, II, 39–41.)

here is what we can do.... Firstly, I shall not change my writing at all; secondly, I shall give to the queen the inaccurate title of *Antoinette de France*;[1] the note being presented by the cardinal, they will not examine it and you will promise me to burn it in my presence when the jewellers are paid, and that will be an end of the business." I gave him my word of honor and he signed the note according to our agreement.

THE JEWELLERS SHOW THE NOTE TO BRETEUIL. (*Mme. de La Motte, 89-91*.)

As supreme head of the *haute police*, one can conceive that, with the aid of fifty thousand spies in his pay, few things were hidden from him [Breteuil]; he had been informed long since of the negotiation for the necklace, and he had hoped to turn it to account in consummating the downfall of the cardinal... The Baron de Breteuil... moved heaven and earth to make the jewellers uneasy... The jewellers, intimidated, rendered to the minister an exact account of all that had passed; since in the number of circumstances that of the signature *Antoinette de France* was the most striking, M. de Breteuil seized upon it with avidity, and... pressed them to present a memoir to Her Majesty who, on reading the first line, cried: "What are these people talking about? I believe they have lost their heads!"

ROHAN ARRESTED. (*Besenval, II, 163-165*.)

On Ascension Day in the year 1785, all the court was assembled in the cabinet of the king; the Cardinal de Rohan, in surplice and camail, awaited His Majesty, who was going to mass, to which the grand-almoner's charge called him. The king summoned him to his inner cabinet, where he was a little astonished to find the queen also. The king demanded an explanation concerning the necklace which he was to have procured for the queen. "Ah, Sire!" cried the cardinal, "I see too late that I have been tricked!" "But," said the queen, "even if you were so easily deceived, you should not have mistaken my writing, which you surely know." Without replying to her, the cardinal, addressing himself to the king, protested his innocence... His Majesty said to him, "I warn you that you are going to be arrested." "Ah, Sire!" cried the cardinal, "I will always obey the orders of Your Majesty; but deign to spare me the mortification of being arrested in my pontifical robes, before the eyes of the whole court." "It must be done," rejoined the king. The cardinal desired to insist, but the king left him brusquely. I have heard all these details from the queen...

ROHAN ACCUSES LA MOTTE. (*Mme. de La Motte, 100, note*.)

This base subterfuge was not in the soul of the cardinal, but Cagliostro[2]

---

[1] The correct form would have been *Antoinette d'Autriche*.

[2] "The Comte de Cagliostro is one of those beings who appear from time to time, unknown people who pass as being adept, dabbling in medicine, alchemy, and sometimes in magic, marvellous in everything, whose extraordinary adventures are always exaggerated by the public, and who, after having ruined the foolish, end their exploits in the pillory... The Cardinal de Rohan had known him at Strasbourg, and bestowed upon him so much friendship, and so much confidence, that Cagliostro, having come to Paris, remained with him." (Besenval, II, 161-162.)

had him so well indoctrinated that, at the moment the king had him arrested, he said like a parrot, "I was tricked by a woman named Valois de La Motte, who they say has left the country"; he believed it, and hoped that because of the instructions that he had given us we would not be found.

THE QUEEN DISCREDITED. (*Besenval, II, 171.*)

The Palais teemed with people, and joy was universal when it was known that the cardinal was declared innocent.[1]   The judges were applauded and given such a hearty welcome that they had difficulty in passing through the crowd, so strong was the hate against the opposite party, so deep rooted were the animosities against the queen and the court!

[1] Mme. de La Motte was branded, whipped, and imprisoned, but shortly afterwards allowed to escape.

V. Bankruptcy and the Notables

THE STATE OF THE FINANCES. (*Rabaut Saint-Étienne, 6–7.*)

THE apparent facility . . . with which the people seemed to pay such weighty imposts encouraged the invention of new ones. The expenditures of the court were arbitrary, and the substance of the people had been dissipated for a long time in ostentatious frivolities. The throne was besieged by a multitude of avaricious men and interested women, on whom was lavished, under various pretexts, the wealth of the state. Ruinous wars, undertaken thoughtlessly, and often for the sole advantage of a few individuals, had added, during two reigns, to the general distress. Disastrous loans had gradually created an immense debt; and the nation, frightened at the situation of the finances, saw only the discouraging prospect of bankruptcy.

(*Besenval, II, 230.*)

It was nevertheless extraordinary to see the king ready to declare bankruptcy at a time when France was so flourishing, the population at the highest level, agriculture and industry highly developed, and Paris overflowing with money. Such is the inevitable consequence of a bad administration which is without principles and without consistency, of depredations of all kinds, and of a weak government that offers no rallying-point. I also strongly believe that the evil was made greater than it was; for to show that ruin was inevitable, whatever resources remained, was enough to indicate that it was necessary to engage a capable man who would restore credit.

THE ASSEMBLY OF NOTABLES. (*Extract from a letter of Jefferson to John Jay, Paris, January 9, 1787.*)

You will have seen in the public papers that the king has called an Assembly of the Notables of this country. This has not been done for one hundred and sixty years past. Of course, it calls up all the attention of the people. The objects of this assembly are not named: several are conjectured. The tolerating the Protestant religion; removing all the internal custom-houses to the frontier; equalizing the *gabelles* on salt through the kingdom; the sale of the king's domains, to raise money; or, finally, the effecting this necessary end by some other means, are talked of. But in truth, nothing is known about it. This government practices secrecy so systematically that it never publishes its purposes or its proceedings sooner or more extensively than necessary.

(*Bouillé, 43–44.*)

The Notables were then convoked for January 29, 1787; I was elected to this assembly: it had not met since 1626, in the reign of Louis XIII; but Cardinal Richelieu was then in charge of the kingdom: he directed all its movements; he utilized it to serve his projects and support his operations. It was quite different this time. The opening of this assembly had been delayed until the 22nd of February; M. de Vergennes died during this interval, and M. de Calonne lost his support. Another inconvenience of this delay was that it gave the Notables and the public time to recover from their first astonishment, and gave the intriguers means of preparing their expedients to hinder the execution of the government's projects. The Notables, composed of the most distinguished persons in the clergy, nobility, magistracy, and municipal bodies of the principal cities, would naturally be opposed to the destruction of the abuses by which they profited. There was, then, only a beginning of the enthusiastic movement which might have brought them to make the great sacrifices expected of them. They had time to understand the matters which were to be considered in this assembly, and to prepare and combine their opposition. However, most of the nobles, representatives of the cities, and councillors attached to the government, whose creatures they were, were well intentioned. They formed a considerable part of this gathering, and would have carried the rest with them if the intrigues of the Archbishop of Toulouse, since Cardinal de Loménie [Brienne], a notable who wished to become minister, supported by the other ministers, by the queen herself, and seconded by the members of the clergy and of the magistracy, had not dispelled the good dispositions of the assembly. It only occupied itself then in destroying the minister who had evoked it; and he, abandoned by the king, was disgraced and forced to quit the kingdom, in the fear of being delivered over to the vengeance of the *parlements* and the fury of the people.

(*Extract from a letter of Jefferson to John Jay, Paris, February 23, 1787.*)

The assembly met yesterday; the king, in a short but affectionate speech, informed them of his wish to consult with them on the plans he had digested, and on the general good of his people, and his desire to imitate the head of his family, Henry IV, whose memory is so dear to the nation. The *garde des sceaux* then spoke about twenty minutes, chiefly in compliment to the orders present. The controller-general, in a speech of about an hour, opened the budget, and enlarged on the several subjects which will be under deliberation. He explained the situation of the finances at his accession to office, the expenses which their arrangement had rendered necessary, their present state, with the improvements made in them, the several plans which had been proposed for their further improvement, a change in the form of some of their taxes, the removal of the interior custom-houses to the frontiers, and the institution of provincial assemblies. The assembly was then divided into committees, with a prince of the blood at the head of each. In this form, they are to discuss separately the subjects which will be submitted to them. Their decision will be reported by two members to the minister, who, on view of the separate decisions of all the committees, will make such changes in his plans as will best accommodate them to their views, without too much departing from his own, and will then submit them to the vote (but I believe not to the debate) of the general assembly, which will be convened for this purpose one day in every week, and will vote individually.

THE FALL OF CALONNE. (Bailly, I, 2–4.)

The need of money rendered the government feeble and dependent. The governed had therefore an enormous advantage, which I presumed they would know how to make use of. This assembly of five hundred of the most distinguished citizens of all classes, occupied with the most important affairs of the state, could not fail to bring about great reforms. This assembly, this reunion, was a symbol of that of the nation; they were citizens deliberating less upon the affairs of state than upon their own interests: for a number of years the best minds had meditated on political economy; and the assembly, convoked to give advice and information regarding the administration of the kingdom, would naturally direct all thoughts to this point and direct the attention of the entire nation to it. . . .

The Assembly of Notables produced no other effect than to bring the evil into greater prominence and make known the urgent necessity of curative measures. Nothing else could have been expected; they had the right to advise, but no authority. This assembly began to attack the ministers, and M. de Calonne was put out of office by the same men he had chosen and convoked. One of these men, the Archbishop of Toulouse (M. de Loménie-Brienne), with a reputation for talent and ambition, was put in his place. This choice was greatly applauded.

BRIENNE. (Weber, I, 168–169.)

A week later the real minister showed himself; it was Brienne, Archbishop of Toulouse. The Abbé de Vermont was indebted to this prelate for having been sent to Vienna, by the Duc de Choiseul, as instructor of the young archduchess destined to become Queen of France. He seized this opportunity of serving his benefactor through the queen, whose intimate confidence he possessed. . . . The queen spoke; the king was persuaded. Both believed, not without reason, that it was nothing less than a question of public welfare; and as regarded the means of remedying the evil, both were influenced by popular prejudices.

BRIENNE'S POLICY. (Marmontel, IV, 3–5.)

In the wreck of Calonne, he [Brienne] seemed to have collected all that could be saved: the edicts of the stamp duty and of the land tax, which he presented to the parlement, were the edicts of Calonne. He might have made the authority of the Notables his support; and, between the two great rocks of the States-General and of bankruptcy, he had the powerful means of reducing that assembly to recognize the necessity of the taxes. He only dissolved it. Nothing was there decreed or concluded.

He heard the cry of the nation that demanded Necker's recall, and, had he solicited it himself of the king, such a solicitation would have honored him; he would thereby have confirmed himself in the eminent place that he occupied; he would have relieved himself from the burden of the finances; he would have secured his own repose, inspired blessings on his elevation, covered with a veil of dignity his indecent fortune, concealed at his ease his idle incapacity, in a word, he would have conducted himself like a skilful and an honest man; he had not the courage to do it. That fatal fear of being effaced, of being surpassed, deprived him of this courage. In vain did his friends entreat him to call to his aid the man whom the public voice invoked; he answered, "The king and queen will not consent to it." "It depends on you," said Montmorin to him, "to persuade the queen that Necker is necessary to you, and I will undertake to persuade the king of it." Brienne, thus closely pressed, answered, "I can do without him." Thus empires perish.

THE STAMP DUTY AND THE LAND TAX. (*Marmontel, IV, 6–9.*)

To gain the public favor, he began by desiring to establish provincial assemblies; and in rendering them elective and dependent on the people, he did that lightly and inconsiderately which would have required the most serious reflection. Despotic as he was, he wanted to give himself the appearance of popularity, and to pass for a republican. He supported this part very ill.

After having dismissed the Notables, he sent to the *parlement* his two edicts of the stamp duty and the land tax, as if they were necessarily to pass at first view, without any difficulty. . . .

The *parlement* of Paris demanded that the state of the finances should be communicated to it; this demand was reasonable. In order to regulate the amount and the duration of the subsidies according to the exigencies of the state, the *parlement* ought to know what those exigencies were: the right of remonstrance implied the right of examining; and unless the minister required from it the obedience of a slave, he could not refuse to enlighten it on its duties. This was what Brienne would not listen to. He did not perceive that it was more necessary than ever that there should be in the name of the people a form of deliberation and of acceptance for taxes, and that if the government disputed the right of the *parlement,* as it then stood, to record and consent to edicts, the nation would give itself representatives who would be less manageable. It was this that the minister and the *parlement* should both have foreseen, and united to prevent.

To remove the difficulty, Brienne advised the king to hold a *lit de justice* at Versailles, where, by express command, the edict of the stamp duty and that of the land tax were registered; this old child was a stranger to the age he lived in.

BRIENNE'S CONCESSIONS. (*Besenval, II, 250.*)

Previous to this *lit de justice*, the Archbishop of Toulouse had announced great reforms in the departments as well as in the king's household, which should bring more than the forty millions promised to the Notables. And, as in this operation one never knew where to begin except in the departments and benefits of the king, it was with these that the archbishop occupied himself, in adding some retrenchments in the charges of the court, and even of the crown, which was unprecedented; hoping thereby to pacify the *parlement*, as if such paltry economies could take the place of prompt and substantial improvements, and give the general satisfaction that would be produced by profitable retrenchments in important things, as well as in the establishment and preferences of the king.

REFORMS IN THE ROYAL HOUSEHOLD. (*Fersen, 68.*)

It was the day of the closing of the Assembly of the Notables, and I am very glad to have seen that ceremony. It was very imposing, and will probably never be seen again in our day. The results of that assembly are great reforms in the households of the princes; but most of them bear only on abuses and on the old ostentatious splendor, which is scarcely noticed and was of no use except to absorb enormous sums. The Comte d'Artois has already returned four hundred thousand francs from his household to the king. The reform in the queen's stable amounts to two hundred and· fifty thousand francs; in short, it seems that they have taken a firm resolution to correct abuses as much as possible. The king has already reduced his packs of boar-hounds and wolf-hounds; all the falcons and the emoluments of the grand falconer are to be suppressed, so they tell me. There is much else, but I cannot remember it. They talk of a diminution of two-fifths of all pensions above ten thousand francs; but that is not certain.

THE PARLEMENT REFUSES TO REGISTER THE EDICTS. (*Weber, I, 178–179.*)

The moment was not slow in coming when the *parlements* were to break their silence and throw off their respectfulness. The princes and peers received from the king the order to go to the *parlement* of Paris for the registering of the edicts deliberated by the Notables. The establishment of provincial assemblies and the regulation of the trade in grain passed without difficulty. But, in regard to the suppression of *corvées*, commissioners were named; and as soon as the edict of the stamp duty appeared, the *parlement* declared "that it was impossible for it to believe in the necessity of the duty before having itself verified the deficit and seen the state of receipts and expenditure, as well as the estimate of the economies and improvements that His Majesty had announced"; and it petitioned the king to communicate to it all this information.

The king refused to the *parlement* communications that were useless, to say the least, recalled to it the nature of its functions, and ordered it to register the edict of the stamp duty. The *parlement* reiterated its supplications, received a third order which it repulsed with a third refusal; and suddenly accusing itself of a usurpation almost immemorial; abjuring in a day, to overturn the state, the pretensions that it had harbored for centuries as a means of agitation; and branding with the name of error that which it had called up to now the constitutive principles of *parlements*, it placed in its remonstrances this unexpected declaration, which, brought forth in the midst of a general effervescence, was to have such terrible consequences: "The nation alone, in States-General assembled, can give the necessary consent to a permanent tax. The *parlement* has not the power to give this consent, still less that of attesting it when nothing establishes it. Charged by the sovereign to announce his will to the people, it has never been charged by the latter to replace them."

THE PARLEMENT EXILED. *(Mallet du Pan, I, 146–147.)*

The *parlement* has been banished to Troyes; the *lettres de cachet* for each member were conveyed by the officers of the French guards at three o'clock in the morning: they were ordered to leave Paris during the day, and to report themselves in Troyes within four days....

Monsieur went with a large suite to register the taxes at the *chambre des comptes*, and the Comte d'Artois to do the same at the *cour des aides*. It was nine o'clock. Monsieur entered the *chambre des comptes*, by the small street of Sainte-Anne, and was greeted with some applause. The Comte d'Artois arrived a quarter of an hour afterwards at the Cour du Mai. Eight or ten thousand people were assembled, filling the large hall, the corridor, the court, the square, and the approaches.... The prince ascended the great staircase through the crowd, and proceeded to the Sainte-Chapelle to receive the deputation of the *cour des aides*, who went to meet him, and attended him to the bench in front of the large staircase. When he reached this place, the crowd pressed around him, and there was considerable hissing, hooting, and even groaning. The prince's guards flourished their drawn swords in order to open a passage and disperse the people, and the Prince d'Hénin, captain of His Highness's guards, called out to the French and Swiss guards, "Below there! Ready arms!" At this motion of drawn swords, and at this signal, the crowd poured along the staircase and the corridors in inconceivable dismay. I myself was carried over the balustrade.

DISORDER IN THE FINANCES. *(Weber, I, 185.)*

Meanwhile, all credit was impaired. The state of the finances deteriorated from day to day. Not only were the subsidies necessary to provide for the acknowledged deficit not established, but this deficit increased on all sides as a result of the distrust and instability, the decrease in funds, the hindrances to commerce, the stagnation of the currency, the terrors of ignorance, the manoeuvers of stock jobbing, and the intrigues of ambition.

BRIENNE UNABLE TO MEET THE SITUATION. *(Young, 92.)*

The feeling of everybody seems to be that the archbishop [Brienne] will not be able to do anything towards exonerating the state from the burden of its present situation; some think that he has not the inclination; others that he has not the courage; others that he has not the ability. By some he is thought to be attentive only to his own interest; and by others, that the finances are too much deranged to be within the power of any system to recover, short of the States-General of the kingdom; and that it is impossible for such an assembly to meet without a revolution in the government ensuing. All seem to think that something extraordinary will happen; and a bankruptcy is an idea not at all uncommon. But who is there that will have the courage to make it.

A REVOLUTION PREDICTED. (*Young, 97–98.*)

One opinion pervaded the whole company, that they are on the verge of some great revolution in the government; that everything points to it; the confusion in the finances great; with a deficit impossible to provide for without the States-General of the kingdom, yet no ideas formed of what would be the consequence of their meeting: no minister existing, or to be looked to in or out of power, with such decisive talents as to promise any other remedy than palliative ones: a prince on the throne, with excellent dispositions, but without the resources of a mind that could govern in such a moment without ministers: a court buried in pleasure and dissipation, and adding to the distress, instead of endeavoring to be placed in a more independent situation: a great ferment amongst all ranks of men, who are eager for some change, without knowing what to look to, or to hope for: and a strong leaven of liberty, increasing every hour since the American Revolution; altogether form a combination of circumstances that promise e'er long to ferment into motion if some master hand, of very superior talents, and inflexible courage, is not found at the helm to guide events, instead of being driven by them. It is very remarkable that such conversation never occurs, but bankruptcy is a topic: the curious question on which is, *Would a bankruptcy occasion a civil war and the total overthrow of the government?* The answers that I have received to this question appear to be just: such a measure, conducted by a man of abilities, vigor, and firmness, would certainly not occasion either one or the other. But the same measure attempted by a man of a different character might possibly do both. All agree that the States of the kingdom cannot assemble without more liberty being the consequence; but I meet with so few men that have any just ideas of freedom that I question much the species of this new liberty that is to arise. They know not how to value the privileges of the people: as to the nobility and the clergy, if a revolution added anything to their scale, I think it would do more mischief than good.

BESENVAL WARNS THE QUEEN. (*Besenval, II, 260–261.*)

In these circumstances, and shortly before the removal of the *parlement*, the queen took my arm for a *tête-à-tête* promenade in her Trianon gardens, where she spoke to me of the state of affairs.... I remarked to the queen that it was useless for her to flatter herself that she could pacify the *parlement*; that the more one temporized the more audacious it would become; that it was high time the king showed himself the master, and that he showed it by authoritative actions, lacking which he would have *to remove his crown perhaps never again to replace it upon his head;* that I was certain that, seeing the state of public opinion, this course would have great results; that I feared it; but that it would be better to risk everything than be degraded. "Ah!" cried the queen, "what great misfortune M. de Calonne has brought upon this country with the Notables!"

THE PARLEMENT RECALLED. (*Marmontel, IV, 10.*)

Scarcely was the *parlement* arrived at Troyes when Brienne, in conferring with the keeper of the seals, recollected, as by accident, that the presence of that court would be necessary to him for his loans in the month of November. "If I had thought of that sooner," exclaimed he, "I should not have exiled it; I must recall it instantly"; and his emissaries were immediately put into action. (I am indebted to the keeper of the seals for these details.)

THE KING YIELDS TO THE PARLEMENT. (*Weber, I, 187–188.*)

The king temporarily withdrew the two fiscal edicts that had been voted by the Notables, and statesmen believed his authority compromised from this moment. The *parlement* of Paris registered provisionally the continuation of the two *vingtièmes*, with more exactitude in their collection, and the *parlements* in the provinces reproached it with having violated the principles that it had just professed. "You are as wise as Charles V," said the *parlement* to the king, who had been dragged into such dangerous imprudence. "I am content with your obedience," replied the king to the *parlement* which, even in registering the *vingtièmes*, had just repeated that it persisted in all its resolutions. However that may be, the *parlement* on its return to Paris was given its vacation, and there was really temporary tranquillity.

THE PARLEMENT AND THE LETTRES DE CACHET. (*Weber, I, 194–197.*)

Without doubt it was impossible for the king to allow the continuance of the act by which the *parlement* had just discredited a loan indispensable to the conservation of the state, and no sensible person would have been surprised to learn the next day that the king had sent for the great deputation of the *parlement* with its registers. But the *premier ministre*, who seemed determined to appear severe and remain inactive, lightly committed himself to that odious tyranny which punishes independent voting in a deliberative body constituted by law. He used *lettres de cachet* to carry off two magistrates whom he imprisoned in two strong castles. A third order of the same nature exiled the Duc d'Orléans to his Rainci estate, and this punishment increased the hate that this prince had already vowed long since against the court....

For four months all France resounded with remonstrances, resolutions, and cries of every kind imperiously demanding the revocation of the prince's exile, the liberation of the imprisoned magistrates, the abolition of *lettres de cachet*; and already some wishes were being expressed for the destruction of the Bastille and the other prisons of state.

THE DEFICIT BECOMES KNOWN. (*Weber, I, 198.*)

Towards the month of April, 1788, the government, faithful to the engagement that it had made to render an annual account of the finances, announced that it was going to publish the amount of receipts and expenditures of the current year. The result of the reckoning had already leaked out to the public. The disproportion between the regular revenue and the total expenditures of this year was sixty millions.

THE COUR PLÉNIÈRE. (*Weber, I, 215–216.*)

Foreign no doubt to the practices of the last few centuries, it was not, however, an innovation either in the annals or in the civil law of the French monarchy. The king merely re-established that high tribunal of former times, that *cour plénière* which two French monarchs, one called "the Wise," had defined as "the council of vassals and barons, the court of the baronage and peerage, the universal *parlement*, the high jurisdiction of France, the sole image of sovereign majesty, the ancient source of all justice in the kingdom, and the principal council of kings."

The basis of this *cour plénière* was to be composed of the chancellor or keeper of the seals of France and the entire main chamber of the *parlement* of Paris, in which seats were held by the princes of the blood, the peers of the kingdom, the grand officers of the crown, prelates, marshals of France, governors of provinces, other personages of like qualifications, the councillors of state or masters of petitions, two magistrates of the *chambre des comptes* of Paris, two of the *cour des aides*, and a deputy of each provincial *parlement*. All membership in the *cour plénière* was irrevocable and for life. They were to be presided over by the king, in his absence by the chancellor or the keeper of the seals, and, in case of their default, by the first president or other presidents of the *parlement* of Paris. The regular sessions were to be held in the main chamber of the said *parlement*, and the sessions were to last from December 1 to April 1.

All these explanations given, all these edicts read and registered by the express command of the king, the keeper of the seals announced a fifth and last law, which adjourned all the *parlements* of the kingdom until the new order was established; a measure which, two years later, was to be imitated, not for reform, but to abolish all these courts. This last law announced, the king resumed his discourse. He declared that all his desires related to the happiness of his subjects, and that the more moderate those desires, the more firmly they would be executed. He ordered those who were to be members of the *cour plénière* to remain at Versailles, the others to retire, and the *lit de justice* was at an end.

THE MAGISTRATES REFUSE TO ATTEND THE COUR PLÉNIÈRE. (*Weber, I, 220–221.*)

The magistrates, retained at Versailles by the order of the king to compose the *cour plénière*, wandered in the streets of the town or in the corridors of the château, without ever entering the chamber prepared for their sessions. It was necessary to dismiss them to their homes, to have time to devise a course of procedure. Everywhere people lampooned and scoffed at this unhappy *cour plénière*, dead before it was born.

THE CLERGY ASKED FOR A LOAN. *(Weber, I, 224–225.)*

Meanwhile the need of money, the original cause of all these disorders, had induced the archbishop-minister to convoke in Paris a special assembly of the clergy. He hoped to obtain from the corps to which he belonged a momentary subsidy, and he wanted the clergy to revive credit by a solemn approval of the establishment of provincial administrations and equality of assessment. The Baron de Breteuil, secretary of state, and the virtuous M. Lambert, controller-general of finances, presented themselves before the assembly in the character of commissaries of the king, asking the modest succor of a million eight hundred thousand livres for the year 1788, and a like sum for the following year.... Opposition was raised, which was triumphant next day by a large majority.... It was decreed that before deliberating on any gift the clergy, as the first order of the state, should make representations to the king in regard to the *cour plénière* and the existing condition of public affairs.

REBELLION IN DAUPHINÉ. *(Weber, I, 229–231.)*

On May 11, three days after the publication of the new edicts, a great part of the nobility of Dauphiné, being assembled at Grenoble, had named three deputies to go to the king to demand the revocation of his edicts, the re-establishment of the local assembly of Dauphiné, and the convocation of the States-General of the kingdom.... The Duc de Tonnerre, commandant, distributed to all members of the *parlement lettres de cachet*, which exiled each magistrate to his particular residence.... All the bells of Grenoble rang the tocsin, all the populace divided itself into various mobs ... the main body of the rebels hastened to the dwelling of the commandant, and, in spite of a guard of three hundred men armed with balls and bayonets, entered the court. Now the Duc de Tonnerre shows himself at the windows, harangues, throws down money, and promises to support the wishes of the people in regard to the government. The order is given to force in the doors. While they labor here, the inhabitants of the faubourgs, and thousands of mountaineers summoned from their habitations on the heights by the tocsin, come armed with variegated weapons to besiege the rear of the house of the commandant situated upon the rampart. After discharging their musketry, to which there is little reply, they escalade the parapet, possess themselves of the garden; the house is forced on all sides. Wine flows in the cellars; furniture flies from the windows; the commandant is surrounded, seized by the collar; the ax is raised over his head; turned aside by an officer, it rises again and rests suspended, until the duke has signed the capitulation that is dictated to him. He engages himself then to regard the *lettres de cachet* as null and void, to order the *parlement* to remain, the concierge of the *palais* to turn over the keys, and the troops to return to their barracks: one cannot conceive why they left them.

THE STATES-GENERAL CONVOKED AND THE COUR PLÉNIÈRE SUSPENDED. (Weber, I, 247.)

On August 8, 1788, appeared a decision of the council which announced the convocation of the States-General, fixed their opening for May 1, 1789, and suspended until that date the establishment of the *cour plénière*.

From this day forth, no human action could prevent the meeting of the States-General, except perhaps a foreign war, with the king at the head of his army.

THE FALL OF BRIENNE. (Bailly, I, 4–5.)

He did not have what his reputation had promised: he forgot the rôle that he had played in the Assembly [of Notables]; he did not see that the enormity of the evil, the necessity of a remedy, and the attention paid by all to public things called for inevitable reform in the administration, and caused the States-General to be needed. If he had had them convoked at once, he would have at one and the same time acquired a claim to public gratitude and made a clever political stroke. It was not wise to leave the people time in which to reflect upon their condition, and the nation to know its needs, its rights, and its forces. The States-General assembled then would have made great reforms; but they would not have dared nor have been able to change everything. These reforms were feared, and it was thought desirable to avoid uniting a nation that might remember that it is sovereign and a master to give orders. Palliatives were tried which increased the evil instead of curing it; and it was left to the *parlement* of Paris to have the honor of asking for the States-General. This demand of the *parlement*, although it may since have repented of having made it, should not be forgotten. When liberty has been recovered, and a régime of law founded, it is just to remember all that helped prepare this new order of things. The archbishop [Brienne] hesitated for more than a year on the holding of the States-General, promising ceaselessly and delaying always what the state of affairs and the disposition of the public rendered indispensable. He left two entire years for the citizens to think thereon, to be enlightened by a multitude of writings, to form plans, and to arrive in force at this redoubtable assembly. He essayed fiscal decrees which were refused; he caused M. le Comte d'Artois to be badly received, hooted, and almost in danger at the *cour des aides*. This scene was the first struggle of physical force against the power of opinion, the trial of the forces of a great people against the force of one man. Finally M. de Brienne was replaced by M. Necker, and either because things were so far advanced that they could no longer be dissimulated, or because the genius and principles of M. Necker inspired him, he occupied himself seriously with the convocation of the States-General. It was announced in the month of November, 1788.

THE SECOND ASSEMBLY OF NOTABLES. (Morellet, I, 339–340.)

Towards the end of 1788, the movements which were brewing the French Revolution were already making themselves forcibly felt.

The Assembly of Notables, convoked in February of the preceding year, had begun the mental agitation. In the month of April, the Archbishop of Sens [Brienne] had succeeded M. de Calonne. The 23rd of August, 1788, he had yielded the ministry to M. Necker. The latter had convoked the Notables anew in October. The new assembly's main subject of discussion had been the form to be given to the States-General promised by the king.

Ought they to follow the plan of 1614, by which the deputies of the nobility, clergy, and commons took part in almost equal numbers? Or would they give the commons a double number of deputies, equal in number to the deputies of both clergy and nobility?

The discussion of this question occupied the second Assembly of Notables, and its debates, disseminated to the public and followed by the clubs which began to multiply and become more inflammable, created in the entire nation, and especially in the capital, an agitation which it was soon impossible to control.

As soon as the hare was started, a multitude of pursuers took up the hue and cry. Numerous writers treated the question in various manners and with opposite convictions.

THE QUESTION OF THE ORDERS. (*Extract from a letter of Jefferson to Cutting, Paris, August 23, 1788.*)

The interesting question now is how the States-General shall be composed. There are three opinions. (1) To place the three estates, clergy, noblesse, and commons, in three different houses. The clergy would probably like this, and some of the nobility; but it has no partisans out of those orders. (2) To put the clergy and noblesse into one house, and the commons into another. The noblesse will be generally for this. (3) To put the three orders into one house, and make the commons the majority of that house. This reunites the greatest number of partisans, and I suspect it is well patronized in the ministry, who, I am persuaded, are proceeding *bona fide* to improve the constitution of their country. As to the opposition which the English expect from the personal character of the king, it proves they do not know what his personal character is. He is the honestest man in his kingdom, and the most regular and economical. He has no foible which will enlist him against the good of his people; and whatever constitution will promote this he will befriend. But he will not befriend it obstinately: he has given repeated proofs of a readiness to sacrifice his opinion to the wish of the nation. I believe he will consider the opinion of the States-General as the best evidence of what will please and profit the nation, and will conform to it. All the characters at court may not be of this disposition, and from thence may, possibly, arise representations capable of leading the king astray; but upon a full view of all circumstances, I have sanguine hopes that such a constitution will be established here as will regenerate the energy of the nation, cover its friends, and make its enemies tremble.

THE CONVOCATION OF THE STATES-GENERAL. (Bailly, I, 5–7.)

M. Necker obtained from the king the double representation of the third estate. It was entirely just. It is not with the awakening of reason that ancient privileges and absurd prejudices should be appealed to. The prejudices are destined to disappear, the privileges are only conventions which cannot be perpetual in society, and are alienations which a growing nation has always the right to retract. At the very least, twenty-four million men opposed to two hundred thousand should have half the votes; and an enlightened posterity will scarcely believe that this has been so difficult to prove and to establish. All that was set forth in a number of writings published by Target. M. Rabaut Saint-Étienne showed that the third estate was the nation minus the clergy and the nobility; M. l'Abbé Siéyès, that the third estate was the nation itself and ought to be in possession of all its rights. It is thus and with such weapons that they made ready for the States-General and for recovering the rights of the nation and the third estate. But if these rights have been obtained, it should not be forgotten that it is due to both M. Necker and the king, to the minister who proposed it and to the king who consented to it: both have made possible the regeneration of the realm. It has been too often forgotten.... Since we are speaking of causes of the regeneration, the first cause was the character of Louis XVI; with a king less good, and with ministers more adroit, there would have been no revolution.

NOBLES, THIRD ESTATE, AND THE PARLEMENT. (Fersen, 69–70.)

Affairs in this country are not in a more tranquil state than they are in Sweden; on the contrary, minds are furiously excited; but with what a difference! Here we have a patient with a good constitution and in all the vigor of his age, for whom we need only a good physician; but the question is to find one. There appears to be a great schism between the nobles and the third estate; the latter wants to be represented in greater numbers and to have more influence in the States-General than it has hitherto had. The *parlements*, which used to be united with the nobles, have been abandoned by them in consequence of a late decree of the *parlement* of Paris abolishing feudal rights, which demands no less than the English constitution. There were two parties in the chamber on that occasion; all the old members were against the resolution, but the young ones carried it. They say also that the provincial *parlements* are not all of one opinion, and that several are contrary to the decree of that of Paris. So here is disunion among the great bodies of the kingdom; it remains to be seen what will result for the king. But in any case, it seems to me that things will go better than was thought at first, and that France will recover in Europe the great influence that she ought to have there....

The fermentation of minds is general; nothing is talked of but the constitution; the women, especially, are mixed up in the matter, and you know, as I do, the influence they have in this country. It is all a delirium; everyone is an administrator and talks of nothing but "progress"; in the antechambers the lackeys are busy reading political pamphlets, ten or a dozen of which appear daily; I do not see how the printing offices suffice for them all; they are the fashion of the moment, however, and you know, as I do, the empire that that has here.

UNPROPITIOUS CONDITIONS. *(Fersen, 70.)*

We are having a very severe winter, freezing for three weeks; the cold has been up to thirteen degrees and at midday two, three, and four degrees. For a week past there has been four inches of snow in the streets of Paris and the roofs are covered. The river is frozen, which hampers the provisioning of Paris, so that they fear a famine; it is also feared in the provinces. There is very little wheat, and what there is they cannot grind because of the lack of water, for there has been no rain since August.

(Bailly, I, 7.)

In the winter of 1788–1789, which was so disastrous and so difficult to endure on account of the severe cold, and the lack of grain and flour, which was occasioned by the terrible hail of the 13th July preceding, and which already began to be felt, preparation was made for the convocation of the States-General.

VI. *The States-General*

THE ELECTIONS TO THE STATES-GENERAL. (*Extract from a letter of Jefferson to Thomas Paine, Paris, March 17, 1789.*)

[THE] meeting of the States is to be at Versailles on the 27th of April. This country is entirely occupied in its elections, which go on quietly and well. The Duc d'Orléans is elected for Villers-Cotterets. The Prince de Condé has lost the election he aimed at; nor is it certain he can be elected anywhere. We have no news from Auvergne, whither the Marquis de La Fayette is gone. In general, all the men of influence in the country are gone into the several provinces to get their friends elected, or be elected themselves.... a tumult arose in Bretagne, in which four or five lives were lost. They are now quieter, and this is the only instance of a life lost as yet in this revolution.... The Duc d'Orléans has given instructions to his proxies in the bailiwicks, which would be deemed bold in England, and are reasonably beyond the reach of an Englishman, who, slumbering under a kind of half reformation in politics and religion, is not excited by anything he sees or feels, to question the remains of prejudice.

(*Boissy-d'Anglas; Dumouriez, II, 413–414.*)

Noble and discredited by his vices, Mirabeau could not be elected, either by the third estate, which did not care for nobles, or by the nobility, which did not care to put its confidence in men without morality. He was obliged to go to Marseille to set on foot and merit an election by a factious group; but that in itself was the cause of his being debarred from the ministry and of the opposition which he experienced for a long time among the wiser of the commons.

The court saw him only as an agitator, the nobility only as a turncoat, and the majority of the third estate only as an ambitious man without scruples, whom it was both discreditable and dangerous to employ ...

(*Bouillé, 74–75.*)

The States-General ... was composed, as regards the clergy, of lesser propertyless ecclesiastics, opposed to the smaller number of higher clergy; there were to be found, in the nobility, men who were bold, adroit, and enterprising, fitted to corrupt and divide it; lastly, the representation of the Third was

doubled, and this order was filled with that species of men, so numerous and
so dangerous in France, who lived by their talents, their wits, and their industry, and who owed their existence to credulity and human weakness. A
multitude of lawyers, of procurators, of lesser magistrates, of practitioners,
of doctors, of artists, of obscure authors, and of men without condition or
property represented or believed they represented the French people and
stimulated all the passions already in fermentation.

CAHIERS DRAWN UP. (Marmontel, IV, 77-78.)

Our functions [as electors] were not confined to the election of deputies,
we had likewise to form their instructions for complaints, petitions, and demands; and every grievance gave rise to fresh declamation. The indefinite
words of equality, liberty, and the sovereignty of the people resounded in
our ears; each heard them, and each interpreted them as his fancy directed.
In the regulations of the police, in the money edicts, in the gradations of authority, on which order and public tranquillity rest, there was nothing in which
some character of tyranny was not found; and a ridiculous importance was
attributed to the minutest details. I will cite but one example of it.

The subject was the wall and the gates of Paris, which were denounced as
calculated only to confine beasts, and as most offensive to men. "I have seen,"
said one of the orators to us, "yes, citizens, I have seen at the gate Saint-
Victor, on one of the pillars, in sculpture, will you believe it? I have seen the
enormous head of a lion, open-jawed, and vomiting chains, with which he
threatened the passengers. Is it possible to imagine a more fearful emblem of
despotism and of slavery?"

(Larevellière-Lépeaux, I, 60-61.)

I had trouble enough at first in making my good villagers understand that
the States-General could not occupy itself with details peculiar to their commune; they understood at last that they must concern themselves, for the
moment, with what was of universal interest and with general reforms such
as the abolition of all privileges, dîmes, feudal dues, obligationless livings,
religious orders of both sexes, gabelles, etc. They eagerly seized upon my
proposal to demand that priests be chosen by the parishioners, that the
celibacy of priests be abolished, that all cults be given equal freedom, and,
lastly, to assure the success of these changes, prevent new abuses, and regulate
the expenses of the nation, that there be a yearly assembly of representatives,
etc.

(Young, 341-342.)

Here are a few of the ameliorations demanded: to have the trial by jury,
and the habeas corpus of England; to deliberate by head and not by order,
demanded by the nobility themselves; to declare all taxes illegal and suppressed — but to grant them anew for a year; to abolish forever the capitaineries; to establish a separate national discounting bank inaccessible to the

influence of the executive power; that all the intendants should be suppressed; that no treaties of commerce should be made but with the consent of the States; that the orders of begging monks be suppressed; that *all* monks be suppressed, and their goods and estates sold; that tithes be forever suppressed; that all feudal rights, duties, payments, and services be abolished; that salaries be paid to the deputies; that the permanence of the National Assembly is a necessary part of its existence; that the Bastille be demolished; that the duties of *aides* on wine, brandy, tobacco, salt, leather, paper, iron, oil, and soap be suppressed; that the *apanages* be abolished; that the domains of the king be alienated ... that the pay of soldiers be augmented; that the kingdom be divided into districts, and the elections proportioned to the population and to contributions; that all citizens paying a determinate quota of taxes vote in the parochial assemblies; that it is indispensable in the States-General to consult the Rights of Man; that the deputies shall accept of no place, pension, grace, or favor.

ARRIVAL OF THE DEPUTIES. (*Ferrières, I, 6.*)

Accordingly as the deputies arrived in Paris, the different parties inspired them with their friendships, their hates, and their interests. A general disquietude seemed to be in the air: it was a vague desire for change. The French had been until now under the constraint of a strict and vigilant police, which repressed all their movements and thwarted all their ideas. Unacquainted with political combinations and having no basic conceptions of the social contract, the rights of the nation, the rights of the monarch, or of those of individuals or various classes of citizens, they exaggerated everything, preferring error to truth in that it was more grandiloquent. They gave themselves over to an intemperance of words and ideas that would have made one believe that this people had suddenly awakened from a long enchantment and just recovered the faculty of speaking and thinking.

(*Miot de Mélito, I, 11–12.*)

The courtier's last hope was that the obstacles would become so entirely insurmountable as to render the meeting of the States impossible, and for that end they all schemed. As a result of this system, the deputies arriving at Versailles — and particularly those of the third estate — far from being made welcome by the court, were offended by sarcasms and jests from the queen's circle and that of the Comte d'Artois. The language, the manners, even the names of these newcomers were turned into ridicule, and the very men who were destined to shine soon afterwards by their superior talent and by their impressive speeches, and to dictate to the throne and to this heedless court, were at first regarded as provincials whom the fine ladies and gentlemen of Paris and Versailles might mystify with impunity. An obsolete ceremonial, forms of etiquette that had fallen into disuse since greater freedom had penetrated into the atmosphere of the court, were revived, and thus, between the other two orders and the deputies of the third estate, a line of demarcation, as marked as it was humiliating, was drawn.

A RIOT IN PARIS. (*Jefferson, I, 89–90, Autobiography.*)

Hitherto no acts of popular violence had been produced by the struggle for political reformation. Little riots, on ordinary incidents, had taken place as at other times, in different parts of the kingdom, in which some lives, perhaps a dozen or twenty, had been lost; but in the month of April, a more serious one occurred in Paris, unconnected, indeed, with the revolutionary principle, but making part of the history of the day. The Faubourg Saint-Antoine is a quarter of the city inhabited entirely by the class of day laborers and journeymen in every line. A rumor was spread among them that a great paper manufacturer, of the name of Reveillon, had proposed, on some occasion, that their wages should be lowered to fifteen sous a day. Inflamed at once into rage, and without inquiring into its truth, they flew to his house in vast numbers, destroyed everything in it, and in his magazines and workshops, without secreting, however, a pin's worth to themselves, and were continuing this work of devastation when the regular troops were called in. Admonitions being disregarded, they were of necessity fired on, and a regular action ensued, in which about one hundred of them were killed, before the rest would disperse. There had rarely passed a year without such a riot in some part or other of the kingdom; and this is distinguished only as contemporary with the Revolution, although not produced by it.

THE OPENING OF THE STATES-GENERAL. (*Miot de Mélito, I, 12–14.*)

It was in the midst of this agitation that the opening of the States-General took place. I was present, as a spectator, at the ceremony which preceded it on the previous day. In the long procession winding through the wide streets of Versailles, the public remarked with dislike those distinctions of rank and of costume which divided into three separate classes the men on whom our fate was about to depend, and who ought to have possessed equal rights. It was mortifying to see the gold-embroidered cloaks of the noble deputies, the plumes on their caps, the episcopal purple proudly displayed by the clergy, while a humble cloak of black woolen stuff and a plain round cap, a strange costume revived from the feudal ages, marked the deputies of the third estate. Nevertheless, their firm demeanor, their steady gait, their expression of mingled dissatisfaction and confidence drew all eyes upon them, and they were received with hearty salutations not offered to the other orders. There was a crowd of courtiers round the princes, but they passed on amid silence. The king's countenance expressed neither emotion nor interest. He advanced, as usual, without dignity, and seemed to be merely accomplishing some duty of etiquette. Monsieur, who walked with difficulty, was serious and thoughtful; he seemed to be thoroughly impressed with the importance of the day's proceedings. The Comte d'Artois, casting disdainful glances right and left on the crowd lining the streets, showed evident signs of vexation and ill humor. The queen, with anxious brow and close-shut lips, made vain endeavors to hide her uneasiness and to impart a look of satisfaction to her noble and majestic countenance; but the weight at her heart, full of anxiety and bitter thoughts, made her unable to maintain it.

THE FIRST SESSION (MAY 5, 1789). (Morris, I, 304.)

... the different members are brought in and placed, one bailiwick after the other. When M. Necker comes in, he is loudly and repeatedly clapped, and so is the Duc d'Orléans, also a bishop who has long lived in his diocese and preached there what his profession enjoins. Another bishop, who preached yesterday a sermon, which I did not hear, is applauded.... An old man, who refused to dress in the costume prescribed for the Third, and who appears in his farmer's habit, receives a long and loud plaudit. M. de Mirabeau is hissed, though not very loudly. The king at length arrives, and takes his seat, the queen on his left, two steps lower than himself. He makes a short speech, very proper, and well spoken, or rather read.

THE KING'S SPEECH.

Gentlemen:

The day long desired by my heart has come at last, and I find myself in the midst of representatives of the nation over which I have the honor of reigning. A long interval has intervened since the last meetings of the States-General, and although the convocation of these assemblies appears to have fallen into disuse, I have not hesitated to re-establish a usage from which the nation can draw renewed strength, and which can discover to the nation a new source of prosperity. The indebtedness of the state, already immense at my accession to the throne, has become yet greater under my reign: a war, expensive but honorable, has been the cause; the increased taxation necessitated by it has caused unequal assessment to be more noticeable.

A general disquietude, an overzealous desire for innovation, has taken possession of all minds, and would end in misleading public opinion entirely, if one had not hastened to counteract it by a reunion of wise and moderate counsel. In relying upon this, gentlemen, I have called you, and I see with gratitude that it has been justified already by the disposition shown by the first two orders to renounce their privileges. The hope I have conceived of seeing all the orders, inspired by a common sentiment, co-operate with me for the general good will be realized. I have already ordered considerable retrenchments in expenditures; you will present to me in this regard additional ideas which I will cordially welcome. But, in spite of the resources offered by strict economy, I fear, gentlemen, that my subjects cannot be relieved as promptly as I would desire.

I will submit to you the exact state of the finances; and when you have examined it, I am in advance assured that you will propose most efficacious means of establishing a permanent system and of strengthening public confidence. There is a state of agitation; but an assembly of representatives of the nation will listen no doubt only to the counselling of wisdom and of prudence. You will have apprehended, gentlemen, that this has not been done on several recent occasions; the dominant spirit of your deliberations will respond to the veritable sentiments of a generous nation whose love for its kings has always been the distinctive characteristic: I will remember nothing else.

I know the authority and the power of a just king in the midst of a faithful people attached at all times to the principles of the monarchy; they have made the glory and eminence of France; I owe it sustenance and I will give it constantly. All that one can expect from the most sincere interest in the public welfare, all that one can demand of a sovereign, the first friend of his people, you can, you must expect from my sentiments. Gentlemen, may a happy accord reign over this assembly, and this epoch become forever memorable for the welfare and prosperity of the kingdom! It is the wish of my heart, it is the most ardent of my desires, it is, in short, what I expect as a reward for my good intentions and my love for my people.

THE KING'S SPEECH WELL RECEIVED. (*Morris, I, 304–305.*)

The tone and manner [of the speech] have all the *fierté* which can be desired in, or expected from, the blood of the Bourbons. He is interrupted in the reading by acclamations so warm and of such lively affection that the tears start from my eyes in spite of myself. The queen weeps, or seems to weep, but not one voice is heard to wish her well. . . . After the king has spoken, he takes off his hat, and when he puts it on again, his nobles imitate the example. Some of the Third do the same; but by degrees they, one after the other, take them off again. The king takes off his hat. The queen seems to think it wrong, and a conversation seems to pass, in which the king tells her he chooses to do it. . . . The nobles uncover by degrees, so that if the ceremonial requires these manoeuvers, the troops are not yet properly drilled.

After the king's speech, and the coverings and uncoverings, the keeper of the seals makes one much longer; but it is delivered in a very ungraceful manner, and so indistinctly that nothing can be judged of it by me until it is in print. When he has done M. Necker arises. He tries to play the orator, but he plays it very ill. The audience salute him with a long and loud plaudit. Animated by their approbation, he falls into action and emphasis; but a bad accent and ungraceful manner destroy much of the effect which ought to follow from a composition written by M. Necker, and spoken by M. Necker. He presently asks the king's leave to employ a clerk, which being granted, the clerk proceeds in the lecture. It is very long. It contains much information, and many things very fine, but it is too long, has many repetitions, and too much compliment, and what the French call *emphase*. The plaudits were long, loud, and incessant. These will convince the king and queen of the national sentiment, and tend to prevent the effects of the intrigue against the present administration, at least for a while. After this speech is over, the king rises to depart, and receives a long and affecting "Long live the King!" The queen rises, and, to my great satisfaction, she hears for the first time in several mouths the sound of "Long live the Queen!" She makes a low courtesy, and this produces a louder acclamation, and that a lower courtesy.

THE COMMONS DISSATISFIED WITH NECKER'S SPEECH. (*Rabaut Saint-Étienne, 73–74.*)

The first two orders, who knew the inclinations of the court, showed no dissatisfaction in regard to the speech of M. Necker, however much they may have hated him; but the deputies of the commons **received it** with the greatest coldness. Seated on their remote benches and with a silence conformable to the severity of their costume, they expected at each moment the words which would correspond to the exalted ideas which they held and which they have since carried out. *Equality* and *liberty*: these two words were already the rallying signs of the French. The people and their representatives had already been led by the current of events to desire a general reform, which the council did not promise them, but which the mistakes of the court and the first two orders accelerated.

THE THIRD ESTATE REFUSES TO ORGANIZE. (*Rabaut Saint-Étienne, 74–75.*)

From this moment the struggle began. That very evening the deputies of the commons, assembled by provinces, agreed that they would meet in the hall of the States-General, which they regarded as the national chamber, and that they would there await the other orders to deliberate in common. They never abandoned this plan. In fact, how would it have benefited the third estate to have half the votes in the States-General if, by the division into three chambers, it really had only a third? The next day the first two orders assembled, each in a separate chamber, and the commons repaired to the national chamber. There they waited in vain for the clergy and the nobility; and, regarding themselves only as unauthorized deputies, whose powers were not yet verified, they concerned themselves only with the order of their assembling, without permitting themselves any deliberation. In the other two chambers they began to occupy themselves with the verification of powers, each in its own order. It was thus tacitly announced that they would not unite with the deputies of the third estate.

NEGOTIATIONS BETWEEN THE ORDERS. (*Rivarol, 12.*)

The nobility ... declared itself constituted the 11th of May, after having verified its powers. But the clergy proceeded more mildly; it suspended the verification of its powers, regarded itself as unconstituted, and offered its mediation to the other two orders. Commissaries were appointed in the three chambers to concert upon a plan of conciliation. His Majesty himself had one drawn up, under the title of *overture*, and sent it to the States-General.

This plan of conciliation produced only contestations, meetings of commissaries, addresses to the king, deputations, and nothing decisive. Days went by, and the task of restoring France was not begun. Some motions on the dearness of grain and the misery of the people, on the validity of certain elections, on the police regulations, etc., consumed entire weeks.

ARGUMENTS ON THE VERIFICATION OF POWERS. (*Procès-verbal sur la vérification des pouvoirs, 8–9.*)

The gentlemen of the nobility, having insisted on the respect due to the ancient usages, recalled that in 1614 the verification of powers was executed by order, and expressed the fear that the verification of powers in common would bring about a vote by head in a general assembly.

It was declared several times by the gentlemen of the commons that they were solely charged with conferring on the verification of powers; that the reasons which made necessary this verification in common were decisive in themselves, and independent of the form of expressing opinion which would be adopted in the States-General; since, even in case one voted by order, it would be equally important to all to know the powers of all the deputies of all classes, who, in each chamber, pretended to have the right to hinder the effect of the deliberations in the others.

Entering next upon the question of usages, the gentlemen of the commons remarked that if in 1614 the powers were verified separately, that was only a provisory examination and purely matter-of-fact; but that on all contested powers the final decision had been delegated to the king's council.

(Dumont, 70–71.)

It was a great blunder of the government to leave this question unsettled. If the king had ordered the union of all three, he would have had the third estate for him; and had he ordered the separation, he would have been supported by the nobility and the clergy. The States-General would certainly not have begun their proceedings by an act of disobedience towards the king, then considered as the provisional legislator. But in coming to no decision on the subject, he opened the lists to the combatants, and the royal authority was destined to become the prey of the victors.

PARIS IN A TURMOIL. (Rivarol, 13–15.)

While the commons, intrenched in the force of their inertia, by their attitude and their numbers embarrassed the deputies of the nobility and the clergy, public opinion in the capital took a very lively trend. The crowding of curious Parisians to Versailles was incessant. But the nobility and clergy, concerned only with their particular interests, closed their chambers to the assiduousness of the Parisians. The hall of the commons, open to the whole nation, allowed an association, so to speak, with its work and its spirit, and the effects of this popularity were soon perceptible. The capital, aroused, fermented; the Palais-Royal became the hotbed of inflammatory ideas and formed another assembly of the commons which, by the vivacity of its deliberations, the perpetuity of its sessions, and the number of its members, surpassed the assembly at Versailles. These new commons made motion upon motion, resolution upon resolution; they had their president and their orators: *solemque suum, sua sidera norunt.* And they not only already rivalled the official commons, they soon fraternized with them. One saw their deputies arrive at Versailles, and these deputies were received and given a hearing. The court, astonished at seeing this parhelion of the States-General, could cry like Pentheus, "I see two Thebes and two suns!"

(Young, 153–154.)

The business going forward at present in the pamphlet shops of Paris is incredible.... This spirit of reading political tracts, they say, spreads into the provinces, so that all the presses of France are equally employed. Nineteen-twentieths of these productions are in favor of liberty, and commonly violent against the clergy and the nobility; I have today bespoke many of this description that have reputation, but enquiring for such as had appeared on the other side of the question, to my astonishment I find there are but two or three that have merit enough to be known. Is it not wonderful that while the press teems with the most levelling and even seditious principles, that if put in execution would overturn the monarchy, nothing in reply appears, and not the least step is taken by the court to restrain this extreme licentiousness of publication? It is easy to conceive the spirit that must thus be raised among the people. But the coffee-houses in the Palais-Royal present yet more singular and astonishing spectacles; they are not only crowded within, but other expectant crowds are at the doors and windows, listening *à gorge déployée* to certain orators, who from chairs or tables harangue each his little audience; the eagerness with which they are heard and the thunder of applause they receive for every sentiment of more than common hardiness or violence against the present government cannot easily be imagined. I am all amazement at the ministry permitting such nests and hotbeds of sedition and revolt, which disseminate amongst the people, every hour, principles that by and by must be opposed with vigor, and therefore it seems little short of madness to allow the propagation at present.

THE COMMONS SUMMON THE NOBLES TO JOIN THEM. (*Bailly, I, 126–129.*)

The assembly had no other resort than to summon the two privileged chambers to the hall of the States for the ratification of powers in common. Consequently he [Siéyès] proposed the following resolution:

"The assembly of the commons, deliberating on the overture of conciliation proposed by the commissioners of the king, has deemed it incumbent on it to take at the same time into consideration the resolution which the nobility have hastened to adopt respecting the same overture.

"It has been seen that the nobility, notwithstanding the acquiescence at first professed, soon introduced a modification which retracts it almost entirely, and that consequently their resolution on this subject cannot be considered as any other than a positive refusal.

"From this consideration, and because the nobility have not desisted from their preceding deliberations, in opposition to every plan of reunion, the deputies of the commons conceive that it has become absolutely useless to bestow any further attention on an expedient which can no longer be called conciliatory, since it has been rejected by one of the parties to be conciliated.

"In this state of things, which replaces the deputies of the commons in their original position, the assembly judges that it can no longer wait inactive for the privileged classes without sinning against the nation, which has doubtless a right to require a better use of its time.

"It is of the opinion that it is an urgent duty for the representatives of the nation, to whatever class of citizens they belong, to form themselves, without further delay, into an active assembly, capable of commencing and fulfilling the object of their mission. The assembly directs the commissioners who attended the various conferences, called conciliatory, to draw up a report of the long and vain efforts of the deputies of the commons to bring back the classes of the privileged to true principles; it takes upon itself the exposition of the motives which oblige it to pass from a state of expectation to a state of action; finally, it resolves that this report and these motives shall be printed at the head of the present deliberation.

"But, since it is not possible to form themselves into an active assembly without previously recognizing those who have a right to compose it — that is to say, those who are qualified to vote as representatives of the nation — the same deputies of the commons deem it their duty to make a last trial with the clergy and the nobility, who claim the same quality, but have nevertheless refused up to the present moment to make themselves recognized.

"Moreover, the assembly, having an interest in certifying the refusal of these two classes of deputies, in case they should persist in their determination to remain unknown, deems it indispensable to send a last invitation, which shall be conveyed to them by deputies charged to read it before them, and to leave a copy of it in the following terms:

"'Gentlemen, we are commissioned by the deputies of the commons of France to apprise you that they can no longer delay the fulfilment of the obligation imposed on all the representatives of the nation. It is assuredly time that those who claim this quality should make themselves known by a common verification of their powers, and begin at length to attend to the national interest, which alone, and to the exclusion of all private interests, presents itself as a grand aim to which all the deputies ought to tend by one general effort. In consequence, and from the necessity which the representatives of the nation are under to proceed to business, the deputies of the commons entreat you anew, gentlemen, and their duty enjoins them to address to you, as well individually as collectively, a last summons to come to the hall of the States, to attend, concur in, and submit, like themselves, to the common verification of powers. We are at the same time directed to inform you that the general call of all the bailiwicks convoked will take place in an hour, that the assembly will immediately proceed to the verification, and that such as do not appear will be declared defaulters.' "

NAMING THE NATIONAL ASSEMBLY. (Bailly, I, 147.)

One debated the great question of deciding in what manner and under what form the assembly should constitute itself; some wished it to declare itself the *Nation*; M. de Mirabeau proposed the denomination of *Representatives of the French People*. M. Mounier proposed the constitution of a *Lawful Assembly of the Representatives of the Greater Part of the Nation Acting in the Absence of the Minor Part*; M. Pison du Garland, *The Active and Lawful Assembly of the Representatives of the French Nation*; M. Barère de Vieuzac, deputy of Bigorre, *The Representatives of the Much Greater Part of the French in the National Assembly*. Messieurs Target, Biauzat, and Rabaut Saint-Étienne likewise proposed plans of constitution more or less similar to the first; others, *The Representatives of Almost the Whole of the French People*; another, *The Representatives of Twenty-Four Million Men*; and finally M. de Grand, the denomination of *National Assembly*.

THE NATIONAL ASSEMBLY CONSTITUTES ITSELF. (*Bailly, I, 158–161.*)

A *yes* and *no* vote was taken by roll call, and the motion of the Abbe Siéyès was adopted by a large majority. Here is the resolution that was adopted and which is the first constitutional act:

"The Assembly, deliberating after the verification of powers, ascertains that it is already composed of representatives sent directly by ninety-six hundredths, at least, of the nation. Such a mass of deputation could not remain inactive on account of the deputies of certain bailiwicks, or of certain classes of citizens; for the absent, *who have been called*, cannot prevent those present from exercising the plenitude of their rights, especially when the exercise of those rights is an urgent, an imperative duty.

"Moreover, as it belongs only to the verified representatives to concur in the national will, and as all the verified representatives are to be admitted into this Assembly, it is further indispensable to conclude that it belongs to it, and to it alone, to interpret and to represent the general will of the nation.

"There cannot exist any veto, any negative power, between the throne and the Assembly.

"The Assembly therefore declares that the general labor of the national restoration can and ought to be begun by the deputies present, and that they ought to prosecute it without interruption and without impediment.

"The denomination of *National Assembly* is the only one suitable to the Assembly in the present state of things, as well because the members who compose it are the only representatives legitimately and publicly known and verified, as because they are sent by nearly the whole of the nation; and lastly because, the representation being one and indivisible, none of the deputies, for whatever order or class he has been elected, has the right to exercise those functions separately from this Assembly.

"The Assembly will never relinquish the hope of collecting in its bosom all the deputies who are now absent; it will not cease to call them to fulfill the obligation imposed upon them to concur in the holding of the States-General. At whatever moment the absent deputies present themselves during the session that is about to be opened, it declares beforehand that it will be ready to receive them, and to share with them, after the verification of their powers, the series of important labors which are to accomplish the regeneration of France.

"The National Assembly decrees that the reasons for the present resolution be immediately drawn up, to be presented to the king and to the nation."

This resolution agreed upon, the Assembly voted to apprise the king of it in a respectful address, and the room resounded with repeated cries of "Long live the King!"

THE HALL CLOSED TO THE DEPUTIES. (*Bailly, I, 181.*)

For several days they had been announcing to us a royal session, but it was only a rumor in Versailles, without other basis. I sent to the hall and learned that it was surrounded by French guards. I was informed of a notice conceived in these terms: *By Order of the King.* I no longer doubted that it was indeed question of a royal session. "The king having resolved to hold a royal session of the States-General on the 22nd of June, the preparations to be made in the three halls which serve for the meetings of the orders require that these meetings be suspended until after the holding of the said session. His Majesty will make known by a new proclamation the hour at which he will meet on Monday the Assembly of the States."

THE DEPUTIES GO TO THE TENNIS COURT. (Bailly, I, 187.)

In the avenue we encountered a great number of deputies: all were of the opinion that the Assembly should meet for deliberation in this delicate situation, and should consequently search for a suitable place. M. Guillotin proposed the Tennis Court: they resolved to betake themselves there. I walked at the head of this concourse of deputies; and, fearing that some political reason would close the entrance to us, I asked five or six deputies to go ahead of us and take possession of it. The master of the Tennis Court received us gladly, and hastened to procure for us all the conveniences he could; having no guard, I asked two deputies to place themselves at the door to prevent the entrance of strangers.

THE TENNIS COURT OATH. (Bailly, I, 189–192.)

Another member had the idea of the oath; there instantly arose a general cry of approbation; and, after a rather short discussion, the Assembly decreed the following resolution, so simple yet so firm:

"The National Assembly, considering itself called to establish the constitution of the kingdom, to operate the regeneration of the public order, and to maintain the true principles of the monarchy, can in no way be prevented from continuing its deliberations in whatever place it may be forced to establish itself; and wherever its members foregather, there is the National Assembly.

"Be it resolved that all members of this Assembly immediately take solemn oath never to separate, and to reassemble wherever circumstances require, until the constitution of the kingdom is established and fixed upon firm foundations; and that the said oath being taken, all members in general, and each in particular, shall confirm by their signatures this irrevocable resolution." . . .

This resolution is still one of the monuments to the wisdom of the National Assembly. It assured its safety, it protected the interests of France, and made certain the establishment of the constitution not yet begun. There was beyond any doubt a desire and project to divide this Assembly, grown too redoubtable; this was being prepared for, and it was indubitably with the intention of making a great change in the ministry, and of striking a blow at the Assembly, that they brought in troops in rather large numbers around Paris and Versailles. It is evident that the action which the Assembly had just taken made division impossible. If the order had been given, it would not have been carried out. . . .

Soon after the taking of the oath, they proceeded with the roll call of the bailiwicks, sénéchaussées, provinces, and cities; and each of the members present, in responding to the roll call, came to the desk and signed. A single person, M. Martin d'Auch, had the temerity to add to his signature the word opposed.

Instantly a great tumult arose; great distress was felt by the Assembly at this lack of unanimity in the resolution; distress yielded to indignation, and fury took possession of the greater part of the members of the Assembly.

THE CLERGY JOINS THE THIRD ESTATE. (Bailly, I, 199.)

[On the second day following the Tennis Court oath] the majority of the clergy met in the choir of the church. Soon its deputation was announced, led by M. l'Évêque de Chartres, and in which I saw with pleasure that worthy Abbé d'Abbecourt, who had played an important part in this useful and decisive proceeding, and who had lost his fortune with such calmness and resignation. M. l'Évêque de Chartres said: "Gentlemen, the majority of the order of the clergy having taken the resolution to unite for the verification of powers, we come to announce it to you, and to ask of you a place in the Assembly."

TWO NOBLES JOIN THE THIRD ESTATE. (Bailly, I, 202–203.)

... soon after this important reunion, we saw enter M. le Marquis de Blacons and M. le Comte Antoine d'Agoust, members of the nobility of Dauphiné, deputies of the three orders of that province; and M. de Blacons said: "Gentlemen, the majority of the clergy having surmounted all the difficulties presented by our instructions, we come to submit to you the verification of our powers and ask for the communication of yours." These gentlemen, the first of the nobles to join us, were a precious conquest; they received great applause, and took places in the seats of the nobility.

THE KING ADDRESSES THE ORDERS IN A ROYAL SESSION.

Gentlemen:

I believed I was doing everything in my power for the good of my people when I had taken the resolution to call you together; when I had surmounted all the difficulties with which your convocation was surrounded; when I anticipated, so to speak, the wishes of the nation, in showing in advance what I wished to do for its welfare. It seemed as if you had only to complete my work, and the nation awaited with impatience the moment when, by the concurrence of the beneficent views of its sovereign and the enlightened zeal of its representatives, it would enjoy the prosperity that this co-operation would procure for it.

The States-General have been in session for nearly two months, and they have not yet been able to come to an agreement on the preliminaries of their operations ... I owe it to the common welfare of my kingdom, I owe it to myself, to end these deplorable divisions. It is with this resolution, gentlemen, that I assemble you once more around me; it is as the common father of all my subjects, it is as the defender of the laws of my kingdom, that I come to recall their true spirit and check the inroads that may have been made upon them.

But, gentlemen, after having clearly established the respective rights of the different orders, I expect of the patriotic zeal of the first two orders, I expect of their attachment to my person, I expect of the knowledge they have of the pressing evils of the state, that, in things which concern the general welfare, they will be the first to propose a *rapprochement* of ideas and sentiments which I regard as necessary in the present crisis, and which should insure the safety of the state. . . .

I have desired also, gentlemen, to put before your eyes the different benefits that I accord to my people. There is no intention of circumscribing your zeal in the circle which I am going to trace, for I shall adopt with pleasure any other ideas for the public good that may be proposed by the States-General. I can say, without misapprehension, that never has king done as much for any nation; but what other could have better merited it by its sentiments than the French nation? I am not afraid to say that those who, by exaggerated pretensions or unseasonable difficulties, still retard the effect of my paternal intentions will be unworthy of the name of Frenchmen.

DECLARATION OF THE KING'S INTENTIONS.

I. No new impost shall be established, no old one prolonged beyond the term fixed by law, without the consent of the representatives of the nation. . . .

III. Since loans may necessitate an increase of imposts, none shall be made without the consent of the States-General . . .

IX. When the formal dispositions announced by the clergy and the nobility, of renouncing their pecuniary privileges, shall have been realized by their deliberations, the intention of the king is to sanction them, and to allow no longer any sort of privileges or distinctions in the payment of monetary contributions.

X. The king desires that, to consecrate a disposition so important, the very name of *taille* be abolished in his kingdom . . .

XII. All rights, without exception, shall be constantly respected, and His Majesty expressly includes under the name of rights, *tithes, quit-rents, annuities, feudal, and seignorial rights*, and in general all the rights and prerogatives, useful or honorary, attached to lands and fiefs, or appertaining to persons.

XIII. The first two orders of the state shall continue to enjoy exemption from personal charges; but the king will sanction the States-General's occupying itself with the means of converting these kinds of charges into pecuniary contributions, and then subjecting all orders of the state to them equally. . . .

XV. The king, desiring to assure the personal liberty of all citizens in a substantial and lasting manner, invites the States-General to search for and propose to him the most suitable means of reconciling the abolition of the warrants known as *lettres de cachet*, with the maintaining of public safety . . .

XVII. There shall be established, in the different provinces or generalities of the kingdom, provincial States with two-tenths of their members chosen from the clergy, including bishops, three-tenths from the nobility, and five-tenths from the third estate. . . .

XIX. The deputies of these provincial States will deliberate in common on all affairs, following the usage observed in the provincial assemblies which these States will replace. . . .

XXV. The States-General will occupy itself with the project long since conceived by His Majesty, of removing the custom-houses to the frontiers of the kingdom, in order to allow national and foreign merchandise complete freedom of circulation within the interior.

XXVI. His Majesty desires that the deplorable effects of the tax on salt and the importance of this revenue be carefully discussed, and that, in any substitution, means of at least lightening the burden be proposed. . . .

XXX. His Majesty desires that the use of the *corvée* for the building and upkeep of roads be entirely and forever abolished in his kingdom. . . .

XXXII. His Majesty will keep the States-General constantly informed of the regulations being made by him for the restriction of the *capitaineries* . . .

LOUIS COMMANDS THE ORDERS TO SIT SEPARATELY. (Bailly, I, 213–215.)

"You have just heard, gentlemen, the result of my dispositions and views; they are conformable to the sincere desire I have to promote the public welfare; and if, by a fatality far from my thought, you abandon me in such a noble enterprise, I will alone work the prosperity of my people, I will consider myself alone their true representative; and knowing your *cahiers*, knowing the perfect accord which exists between the general desire of the nation and my beneficent intentions, I shall have all the confidence that such a rare harmony must inspire; I shall proceed to the goal I desire to attain, with all the courage and firmness that it inspires in me.

"Reflect, gentlemen, that none of your projects, none of your dispositions, can have the force of law without my special approbation. I am thus the natural guarantee of your respective rights, and all the orders of the state can rely upon my equitable impartiality. All defiance on your part would be a great injustice. Up to the present it is I who have done everything for the well-being of my people, and it is rare perhaps for the only ambition of a sovereign to be the inducing of his subjects to agree to accept his beneficences.

"I order you, gentlemen, to separate at once and betake yourselves tomorrow morning, each to the chamber assigned to your order, there to resume your sessions. I consequently order the grand master of ceremonies to have the halls made ready." And the king retired.

Unhappy prince, into what have you been led, and how you have been deceived! After the departure of the king, all of the nobility and part of the clergy retired; the commons remained in their place, quietly and in silence. The grand master of ceremonies came up to me and said, "Monsieur, you have heard the order of the king?" I replied to him, "Monsieur, the Assembly adjourned until after the royal session; I cannot dismiss it until it has deliberated." "Is that your reply, and can I report it to the king?" "Yes, Monsieur." And I added to my colleagues who were around me, "I believe that the nation in assembly cannot receive orders." It has been said and repeated that I made this response to M. de Brezé. The official response to his message is that which I have just reported. I respected the king too much to make such a reply; I knew too well the consideration that a president owes to the Assembly to engage it thus without its consent. It was for it to weigh, to know, and to declare its rights. As a matter of fact, Mirabeau spoke out and, declaiming against the grand master of ceremonies, said about what has since been repeated, "Go tell those who sent you that the force of bayonets has no power against the will of the nation." There has been much praise of this response, which is not one, but an apostrophe which he should not have made, which he did not have the right to make, since it is for the president alone to speak, and which was at the same time out of place and out of measure. Moderation demands that one reply only to what is said. Had anyone spoken of bayonets, had force been appealed to, had a single menace escaped the mouth of M. de Brezé? No. He recalled, as was his duty, an order of the king. Did the king have the right to give this order? The Assembly, in continuing the session, decided not; and I, in declaring that the Assembly could not separate before having deliberated, had conserved its rights and dignity; and I remained within the bounds which an Assembly and its president ought always to observe.

THE THIRD ESTATE IN REBELLION. (Rabaut Saint-Étienne, 90–91.)

When the grand master of ceremonies had retired, deliberation began. M. Camus, crying out against the despotism of this *lit de justice*, called a royal session, an attack on the liberty of the States-General, put a motion before the Assembly to persist in its resolutions, which no authority could annul. Several members supported him with equal force; and the Abbé Siéyès, in the midst of the general indignation, coldly summed it up: "Gentlemen," he said, "you are today what you were yesterday." The Assembly decreed that it persisted in its resolutions. However, since this despotic act, inspired in the king, was sufficient announcement that the court would not stop there, since the personal liberty of the deputies could be violated, and since already rumors of it had spread, the National Assembly declared the persons of all deputies inviolable; that all who dared make an attempt on their liberty were infamous, traitors to the country, and guilty of a capital crime, and reserved to itself the right to prosecute all who might be authors or executors of like orders.

LIBERAL NOBLES JOIN THE THIRD. (Extract from a letter of Jefferson to John Jay, Paris, June 24, 1789.)

This day (the 25th) forty-eight of the nobles have joined the *Tiers*. Among these is the Duc d'Orléans. The Marquis de La Fayette could not be of the number, being restrained by his instructions. He is writing to his constituents to change his instructions or to accept his resignation. There are with the *Tiers* now one hundred and sixty-four members of the clergy, so that the common chamber consists of upwards of eight hundred members. The minority of the clergy, however, call themselves the chamber of the clergy, and pretend to go on with business.

THE DISAFFECTION OF THE TROOPS CAUSES THE KING TO YIELD. (Extract from a letter of Jefferson to John Jay, Paris, June 29, 1789.)

I have before mentioned . . . the ferment into which the proceedings at the *séance royale* of the 23rd had thrown the people. The soldiery was also affected by it. It began in the French guards, extended to those of every other denomination (except the Swiss), and even to the bodyguards of the king. They began to quit their barracks, to assemble in squads, to declare they would defend the life of the king, but would not cut the throats of their fellow citizens. ... Similar accounts came in from the troops in other parts of the kingdom, as well from those which had not heard of the *séance royale*, as those which had, and gave good reason to apprehend that the soldiery, in general, would side with their fathers and brothers, rather than with their officers. The operation of this medicine, at Versailles, was as sudden as it was powerful. The alarm there was so complete that in the afternoon of the 27th the king wrote a letter to the president of the clergy, the Cardinal de La Rochefoucauld, in these words:

"My Cousin:
Wholly engaged in promoting the general good of the kingdom, and desirous, above all things, that the Assembly of the States-General should apply themselves to objects of general interest, after the voluntary acceptance by your order of my declaration of the 23rd of the present month, I pass my word that my faithful clergy will, without delay, unite themselves with the other two orders, to hasten the accomplishment of my paternal views. Those, whose powers are too limited, may decline voting until new powers are procured. This will be a new mark of attachment which my clergy will give me. I pray God, my Cousin, to have you in His holy keeping. LOUIS."

A like letter was written to the Duc de Luxembourg, president of the *noblesse*. The two chambers entered into debate on the question, whether they should obey the letter of the king. There was considerable opposition; when notes written by the Comte d'Artois to sundry members, and handed about among the rest, decided the matter, and they went in a body and took their seats with the *Tiers*, and thus rendered the union of the orders in one chamber complete. As soon as this was known to the people of Versailles, they assembled about the palace, demanded the king and queen, who came and showed themselves in a balcony. They rent the skies with cries of "*Vive le roi!*" — "*Vive la reine!*" They called for the dauphin, who was also produced, and was the subject of new acclamations. After feasting themselves and the royal family with this tumultuary reconciliation, they went to the house of M. Necker and M. de Montmorin, with shouts of thankfulness and affection. Similar emotions of joy took place in Paris, and at this moment the triumph of the *Tiers* is considered as complete.

THE DUC D'ORLÉANS REFUSES THE PRESIDENCY. (*Bailly, I, 276.*)

I announced that, in the election of the president, M. le Duc d'Orléans had received the great plurality of votes, 553 out of the 660 that voted. The choice was loudly applauded. I at once yielded him the chair, and he said: "Gentlemen, if I believed I could well fill the place for which you have named me, I should take it with pleasure. But, gentlemen, I should be unworthy of your kindness if I were to accept, knowing how little I am fitted to it. Accept then, gentlemen, my refusal and see in this refusal only the indubitable proof that I will always sacrifice my personal interests to the good of the state."

The sole act of his presidency was to order that the Assembly organize itself at once into committees, and, on a new ballot, a plurality of 700 votes out of 793 named M. l'Archevêque de Vienne.

VII. The Fall of the Bastille

WITHIN the Assembly, matters went on well. But it was soon observed that troops, and particularly the foreign troops, were on their march towards Paris, from various quarters, and that this was against the opinion of M. Necker. The king was probably advised to this, under the pretext of preserving peace in Paris and Versailles, and saw nothing else in the measure. That his advisers are supposed to have had in view, when he should be secured and inspirited by the presence of the troops, to take advantage of some favorable moment, and surprise him into an act of authority for establishing the declaration of the 23rd of June, and perhaps dispersing the States-General, is probable. The Maréchal de Broglie was appointed to command all the troops within the Isle of France, a high-flying aristocrat, cool and capable of everything. Some of the French guards were soon arrested under other pretexts, but, in reality, on account of their dispositions in favor of the national cause. The people of Paris forced the prison, released them, and sent a deputation to the States-General, to solicit a pardon. The States, by a most moderate and prudent *arrêté*, recommended these prisoners to the king, and peace to the people of Paris. Addresses came in to them from several of the great cities, expressing sincere allegiance to the king, but a determined resolution to support the States-General.

MIRABEAU AND THE TROOPS. (*Mounier, 11.*)

While Paris was surrounded with troops, the Comte de Mirabeau, being with M. Duroveray of Geneva, in the court of the Menus at Versailles, approached MM. Bergasse, de La Fayette, Duport, and myself. He asked us to go into one of the offices with him: he imparted his resolution to have the Assembly demand the removal of the troops.... The Comte de Mirabeau, after having spoken of the necessity of obstructing whatever projects the court might have, spoke as follows: "Gentlemen, I encountered yesterday M. le Duc d'Orléans, to whom I said, 'Monseigneur, you cannot deny that we may soon have Louis XVII instead of Louis XVI; and if this were not the case you would be at least lieutenant-general of the kingdom.' The Duc d'Orléans replied to me, gentlemen, in a very amiable manner."

I reflected upon these expressions of the Comte de Mirabeau; and after the king had replied that he had never intended to impair the liberty of the Assembly, and that if it still had the least uneasiness in regard to the presence of the troops he was willing to transfer it to Soissons, I resolved to combat any new resolution on this subject. I wished to prevent a struggle between the royal authority and the Assembly, which appeared to me equally dangerous to both; I imparted my resolution to many of the deputies. The Comte de Mirabeau, who had made vain efforts to prevent them from being satisfied with the king's response, did not lose hope of continuing the combat. He was working on a second address. He called me into one of the offices, where I found him with MM. Buzot and Robespierre. He tried to make me abandon my projected opposition. I persisted in maintaining it; I told him that I was excessively alarmed by all the manoeuvers employed at Paris to cause defection in the troops, that the first address appeared sufficient for proving to the government that our eyes were open to their designs, that several phrases which it contained were extremely likely to stir up the soldiers, that a second address would increase the danger, and that in this situation an ambitious prince appearing in the midst of the army, after having distributed money and diatribes, could seize the throne. He responded, "But simple fellow that you are, I am as much attached to the royalty as you; but what difference will it make if we have Louis XVII instead of Louis XVI, and what need have we of a baby to govern us?" . . . I said that if I knew of a man who had the design of profiting by circumstances to take the throne, and I foresaw a probability of success, I would make it a duty to poignard him. The Comte de Mirabeau suddenly changed tone and countenance, and endeavored to make me believe that he had not meant literally everything that he had said.

ACTIVITIES OF THE ASSEMBLY. (*Ferrières, I, 80.*)

Calm, apparently, in the midst of the different movements taking place around it, the National Assembly continued its work. The excessive price of grain deserved all its solicitude. Bread, although of the very worst quality, was selling at four sous a pound. The Assembly established a committee on provisions. This committee set to work; but obscured by the shadows increasingly cast around it, it could not adopt any plan. Necker submitted a memoir; in this he discussed the above considerations, and the considerable expenditures made by the government for provisions. When they asked the minister for the proofs of his calculations, he replied that he would communicate them to the king, and refused the elucidations necessary to the action of the committee.

THE COUNTER-REVOLUTIONISTS DESIRE TO DISSOLVE THE ASSEMBLY. (*Mme. de Staël, 122.*)

M. Necker was not ignorant of the real reason for bringing up the troops, although they desired to hide it from him. The intention of the court was to assemble at Compiègne all members of the three orders who had not favored the policy of innovation, and there have them consent quickly to the imposts and loans which it needed, in order to then dismiss them. As such a project could not be seconded by M. Necker, they planned to dismiss him as soon as the military force was gathered. Fifty warnings a day informed him of his situation, and it was impossible for him to doubt it; but having seen the violent effect produced, on the 23rd of June, by the rumors of his dismissal, he had decided not to expose the public to a new shock; for what he dreaded most in the world was to obtain a personal triumph at the expense of the authority of the king.

THE DISMISSAL OF NECKER. (Bailly, I, 323–324.)

Another person arriving from Paris informed us of the dismissal of M. Necker. I would not believe it at first; but one of my friends, dropping in, cited a man who had read it to him, and I could no longer doubt it. I was dismayed by this unexpected event, so dangerous in the present state of finances and so appalling as to the sequel seemingly announced by this act of authority.

M. Necker received on Saturday the 11th, while at dinner, a note from the king which ordered him to depart at once. He said nothing during the dinner, got into a carriage soon afterwards with Mme. Necker, under pretext of a drive, and took the road to Saint-Ouen, whence he departed at midnight, after having written to his daughter to warn her himself of the event and of his departure. He then took the road to Brussels.

PARIS AFTER NECKER'S DISMISSAL. (Rivarol, 43–44.)

At the first news of the departure of M. Necker, Paris was dismayed, the Palais-Royal trembled, the Bourse closed, theater performances were suspended (observe that this was done by the order of the States-General of the Palais-Royal), and ten thousand armed brigands ran riot through the streets. An alarming day was succeeded by a still more frightful night, since to the affliction of having lost M. Necker was joined the fear inspired by these brigands.

The tocsin sounded on all sides; several houses began to be pillaged. The merchants did not dare to open their stores, workshops were deserted, and the city was already uninhabitable, when the bourgeois, to defend themselves, suddenly took up arms, instead of having recourse to the king, the born defender of the state, who could not refuse his troops to the cities, and from whom the cities could not refuse to accept the troops. By this general insurrection, Paris, from being uninhabitable, became inaccessible.

THE COMMITTEE OF ELECTORS FORMED. (Ferrières, I, 102.)

However, the electors and municipal officers assembled at the Hôtel de Ville. Some were agents of the Revolution and forwarned of the designs of the revolutionists; others, unacquainted with these manoeuvers, were frightened by an uprising that seemed to menace people and property. The tocsin sounded in all the churches; night approached; a troop of brigands, armed with sabers and muskets, and carrying lighted torches, ran through the streets threatening to burn the principal buildings: these movements had the intention of putting fear into the souls of the bourgeois, and of authorizing the nomination of a committee capable of giving system to the momentary insurrection of the populace. This committee was formed with fourteen electors, and several municipal officers, known to be attached to Necker and the Orléans party. M. de Flesselles was named president; his liaisons with the court rendered him suspect; they promised themselves to supervise his measures and spy upon his actions.

CAMILLE DESMOULINS AROUSES THE MOB. (*Desmoulins in Le Vieux Cordelier, No. 5.*)

It was half-past two; I came to sound out the people. My anger against the despots was turned into despair. I did not think the gatherings of people, although deeply moved or dismayed, sufficiently disposed to insurrection. Three young men appeared to me inspired with a more impetuous courage; they went hand in hand. I saw that they had come to the Palais-Royal with the same design as I; some passive citizens followed them. "Gentlemen," I said to them, "here is the beginning of a civic throng; one of us must do his duty, and mount a table to harangue the people." — "Get up here." — "I am willing." Immediately I was carried upon the table rather than allowed to mount it. Scarcely was I upon it than I saw myself surrounded by an immense crowd. Here is my short harangue, which I shall never forget.

"Citizens! there is not a moment to lose. I come from Versailles; M. Necker is dismissed: this dismissal is the tocsin of a Saint Bartholomew for patriots: this evening all the Swiss and German battalions will sally forth from the Champ-de-Mars to cut our throats. We have only one resource, to fly to arms, and wear cockades for the recognition of one another."

I had tears in my eyes, and spoke with a power that I have never been able to regain, or describe. My motion was received with unending applause. I continued, "What colors will you have?" Someone cried, "Choose!" "Will you have green, the color of hope, or the blue of Cincinnatus, color of American liberty and democracy?" Some voices were raised, "Green, the color of hope!" At that I cried, "Friends! the signal is given: there are spies and satellites of the police watching me. At least I will not fall into their hands alive." Then, drawing two pistols from my pocket, I said, "Let all citizens imitate me!" I descended stifled in embraces; some pressed me to their hearts; others bathed me with their tears: a citizen of Toulouse, fearing for my life, wished never to abandon me. Meanwhile they had brought me a green ribbon. I put it first in my hat, then distributed it among those who surrounded me.

THE INSURRECTION OF JULY 12. (*Besenval, II, 362.*)

The insurrection of the 12th took on an alarming character. Fearing that the different posts of cavalry destined to maintain tranquillity in the faubourgs were insufficient, or that, provoked beyond a certain point, they would depart from the express instructions that had been given them, I sent them an order to betake themselves to the Place Louis XV....

(*Bailly, I, 327.*)

[The people had gone] to Curtius', and there had taken possession of the busts of M. Necker and of M. le Duc d'Orléans; it is pretended that at that time they believed the latter exiled also. These busts, covered with crape, were carried in triumph; the people cried, "Hats off!" In the Rue Saint-Martin, a detachment of the watch was engaged to accompany this parade for the purpose of maintaining order; it went from the Rue Saint-Honoré as far as the Place Vendôme. There they found a detachment of the Royal Germans . . .

(*Morris, I, 317.*)

[In] the Place Louis XV, I observe the people, to the number of perhaps one hundred, picking up stones, and, looking back, find that the cavalry are returning. Stop at the angle to see the fray if any. The people take post among the stones, which lie scattered about the whole place, being there hewn for the bridge now building. The officer at the head of this party is saluted by a stone, and immediately turns his horse in a menacing manner towards the assailant. But his adversaries are posted on ground where cavalry cannot act. He pursues his route, therefore, and the pace is soon increased to a gallop, amid a shower of stones. One of the soldiers is either knocked from his horse, or the horse falls under him. He is taken prisoner and at first ill treated. They had fired several pistols, but without effect. Probably they were not even charged with ball. A party of Swiss guards are posted in the Champs-Élysées with cannon.

THE EVENTS OF JULY 13. (*Morris, I, 318.*)

. . . the Hôtel de Force is forced, and all the prisoners out. . . . my coachman tells me he cannot bring my carriage, having already been stopped and turned back. In fact, the city of Paris is in as fine a tumult as anyone could wish. They are getting arms wherever they can find any. Seize sixty barrels of powder on the Seine. Break into the Monastery of Saint-Lazare and find a store of grain, which the holy brotherhood had laid in. Immediately it is put into carts and sent to the market, and on every cart a friar. The *garde-meuble* of the king is attacked, and the arms are delivered up, to prevent worse consequences. These, however, are more curious than useful. But the detail of the variety of this day's deeds would be endless.

(*Fournier l'Américain, 11–12.*)

The people deliberated on the formation of the citizens into a national armed corps and on the selection of a chief. It was upon me that the choice fell. We immediately put ourselves into a state of permanent military service, and each of us was already cognizant of the duties, with all that they implied, imposed upon us in the quality of defenders of liberty, considering that our task was that of putting ourselves in perpetual opposition to despotism and all its satellites.

I sallied forth from the Palais-Royal at the head of my brothers in arms. The unique confidence that is inspired by the sentiment of liberty made us consider ourselves as being in arms. As yet we had nothing but clubs, ancient swords, pruning-hooks, pitchforks, spades, etc., but from this very moment patrols were put in action. We entered the Rue Saint-Honoré, and arriving before the gate of the Oratoire, we arrested a cavalier carrying packets to the troops encamped at Saint-Denis. I had these packets seized and we carried them to the Hôtel de Ville.

THE ASSEMBLY PLACES THE RESPONSIBILITY UPON THE MINISTERS.

Therefore, the National Assembly, interpreter of the sentiments of the nation, declares that M. Necker, and likewise the other ministers who have just been dismissed, take with them its esteem and its regrets.

Resolved, that, through fear of the disastrous consequences that the response of the king may entail, it will not cease to insist upon the withdrawal of the troops extraordinarily assembled near Paris and Versailles, and on the establishment of bourgeois guards.

Resolved anew, that there can exist no intermediary between the king and the National Assembly.

Resolved, that the ministers and the civil and military authorities are responsible for every enterprise contrary to the rights of the nation and the decrees of the Assembly.

Resolved, that the present ministers and councils of His Majesty, of whatever rank or state they may be, or whatever functions they may have, are personally responsible for the present calamities and for all those that may follow.

PARIS ON JULY 14. (Extract from a letter of Jefferson to John Jay, Paris, July 19, 1789.)

On the 14th, they [the committee of electors] sent one of their members (M. de Corny, whom we knew in America) to the Hôtel des Invalides, to ask arms for their bourgeois guard. He was followed by, or he found there, a great mob. The governor of the Invalides came out, and represented the impossibility of his delivering arms without the orders of those from whom he received them. De Corny advised the people then to retire, and retired himself; and the people took possession of the arms. It was remarkable that not only the Invalides themselves made no opposition, but that a body of five thousand foreign troops, encamped within four hundred yards, never stirred.

(Marmontel, IV, 201.)

The people then, in the presence of the troops of the Champ-de-Mars, ransacked with full license the Hôtel des Invalides. Twenty-eight thousand muskets were found there in the vaults of the dome; and with this booty, and the cannon of the esplanade drawn through Paris in triumph, the conquerors returned to the Hôtel de Ville. There they learned that the governor of the

Bastille, the Marquis de Launay, summoned in his turn to furnish arms and ammunition, had answered that he had none. A general cry was instantly heard from every corner of the square, "Let's go and attack the Bastille!"

(*Dusaulx, 332–333.*)

The first who advanced against the Bastille went there only to demand munitions and arms; they were threatened; they swore to triumph or die.

The crowd increased with every moment; it was augmented by citizens of every age and condition; officers, soldiers, firemen; women and priests; the greater part without arms and confusedly assembled.

One saw hastening thither even country people. One saw foreigners and warriors craving danger, warriors recently arrived from the various parts of the globe; some the evening before or even that very day, who had fought in two worlds, and had already contributed to several revolutions.

A young Greek, subject of the Grand Turk, there observed our enthusiasm and came back a Frenchman.

A number, as soon as they learned of the attack on the Bastille, went there for various motives; some, it is said, in the hope of pillage, but they were swept away. Others went there only to succor the wounded, or to save from the fury of the assailants relatives, friends, or those from whom they had, during their captivity, received consolations; so that humanity, gratitude, and filial piety were exercised at the risk of death.

THE ATTACK ON THE BASTILLE. (*Marmontel, IV, 202–206.*)

This resolution appeared to be sudden and unexpected among the people. But it was premeditated in the council of the chiefs of the Revolution. The Bastille, as a state prison, had always been odious on account of the iniquitous use to which the despotism of ministers had applied it under preceding reigns; and, as a fortress, it was formidable, particularly to those populous and mutinous faubourgs which its walls commanded, and which, in their riots, saw themselves under fire of the cannon of its towers. To agitate these multitudes at its will, and make them act boldly, the republican faction then ardently desired that they might be rid of this imposing object. Honest men, even the most peaceful and most enlightened, wished too that the Bastille might be destroyed, because they hated the despotism of which it was the bulwark; and in this wish they consulted their personal security more than their real safety; for the despotism of license is a thousand times more dreadful than that of authority, and the unbridled populace is the most cruel of tyrants. The Bastille, then, should not have been destroyed, but its keys should have been deposited in the sanctuary of the laws.

The court thought it impregnable; it would have been so, or its attack and siege would have cost rivers of blood had it been defended; but the man to whom it was confided, the Marquis de Launay, would not, or dared not, or could not use the means he had of rendering its resistance murderous; and this populace, that so vilely assassinated him, owed him thanks and praises.

De Launay had expected to intimidate the crowd; but it is evident that he

wished to spare it. He had fifteen pieces of cannon on the towers; and whatever calumny may have said, to palliate the crime of his assassination, not
one single cannon shot was fired from these towers. There were besides, in
the interior of the castle, three cannon loaded with case shot, pointed in
front of the drawbridge. These would have made great slaughter at the
moment when the people came pouring in crowds into the first court; he
fired but one, and that but once. He was provided with firearms of every
kind, with six hundred musketoons, twelve rampart muskets carrying balls of a
pound and a half, and four hundred *biscaïens*. He had procured from the
arsenal abundance of ammunition, bullets, fifteen thousand cartridges, and
twenty thousand pounds of powder. In fine, he had collected on the two
towers of the drawbridge a mass of stones and broken iron, in order to crush
the besiegers if they should advance to the foot of the walls. But in all these
preparations to sustain a siege, he had forgotten provisions; and shut up in
his castle with eighty Invalides [pensioners], thirty-two Swiss soldiers, and his
staff, all the store he had on the day of the attack consisted of two sacks of
flour and a little rice; a proof that all the rest was only to inspire terror.

The small number of Swiss soldiers that had been sent to him were sure
men and well disposed to defend themselves; the Invalides were not so, and
he must have known that; but at least he ought not to have exposed them to
the fear of hunger. Too inferior to his situation, and in that stupor with
which the presence of danger strikes a weak mind, he looked on it with a
steadfast but troubled eye; and rather motionless with astonishment than
with resolution. Unhappily, not a man in the council supplied the foresight
that he wanted.

THE BASTILLE FALLS. (*Marmontel, IV, 206–210.*)

"The Bastille," said the brave Élie to me, "was not taken by main strength.
It surrendered even before it was attacked. It surrendered on the promise
I gave upon the honor of a French officer, and on the part of the people, that
not a man should be hurt if the fortress surrendered." This is the simple fact,
and such as Élie attests it to me. The following details of it are written as
he dictates.

The forecourts of the Bastille had been abandoned. Some determined men
having dared to break the chains of the drawbridge which barred the entrance
into the first court, the people rushed in there in crowds; and deaf to the voice
of the soldiers who, from the tops of the towers, forbore to fire on them, and
cried out to them to retire, they persisted in advancing towards the walls of
the castle. It was then that they were fired upon by the soldiers; and being
put to flight, they saved themselves under the covert of the forecourts. One
killed and a few wounded spread terror even to the Hôtel de Ville; multitudes came to demand urgently, in the name of the people, that deputations
might be resorted to, in order to stop the carnage. Two of these deputations
arrived, one by the arsenal, and the other by the side of the Faubourg Saint-
Antoine. "Advance!" cried the Invalides to them from the tops of the towers.
"We will not fire on you; advance with your flag. The governor is going down,
the castle bridge will be let down in order to introduce you, and we will give

hostages." The white flag was already hoisted on the towers, and the soldiers held their arms inverted in sign of peace. But neither of the deputations dared to advance so far as the last forecourt. At the same time, the crowd was pressing towards the drawbridge and firing from all sides. The besieged then had reason to think that these appearances of deputation were but a trick to surprise them; and after having cried in vain to the people not to advance, they found themselves obliged to fire in their turn.

The people, repulsed a second time, and furious at seeing some of their own body fall under the fire of the fortress, took that revenge in which it usually indulges. The barracks and shops of the forecourt were pillaged; the house of the governor was delivered to the flames. The firing of one cannon, loaded with case shot, and a discharge of musketry had driven back this crowd of robbers and incendiaries; when, at the head of a dozen brave citizens, Élie, advancing to the very edge of the ditch, cried out to the besieged to surrender, promising that not a man should be hurt. He then perceived a hand extended through an opening in a part of the drawbridge and presenting to him a note. This note was received by means of a plank that was held over the ditch; it was written in these words:

"We have twenty thousand pounds of powder. We will blow up the castle if you do not accept our capitulation.

DE LAUNAY."

Élie, after having read the note, cried out that he accepted it; and on the part of the fort, all hostilities ceased. However, De Launay, before he gave himself up to the people, wished that the capitulation should be ratified and signed at the Hôtel de Ville, and that, to secure his own safety and that of his soldiers, an imposing guard should receive and protect them. But the unfortunate Invalides, thinking to hasten their deliverance, did violence to the governor by crying out from the court, "The Bastille surrenders!"

It was then that De Launay, seizing the match of a cannon, threatened to go and set fire to the powder magazine; and perhaps he was firmly resolved to do it. The sentinels who guarded the magazine presented to him their bayonets; and in spite of himself, without further precaution or delay, he saw himself forced to surrender.

THE SURRENDER. (*Memoir Drawn Up by the Soldiers and Non-commissioned Officers of the Garrison.*)

It was then that M. de Launay asked the garrison what course should be followed, that he saw no other than to blow himself up rather than to expose himself to having his throat cut by the people, from the fury of which they could not escape; that they must remount the towers, continue to fight, and blow themselves up rather than surrender.

The soldiers replied that it was impossible to fight any longer, that they would resign themselves to everything rather than destroy such a great number of citizens, that it was best to put the drummer on the towers to beat the recall, hoist a white flag, and capitulate. The governor, having no flag, gave them a white handkerchief. Rouf and Roulard mounted the towers, circuited the platform three times with the drummer beating the recall, all of which lasted about a quarter of an hour; the people keeping up a continual fire without paying any attention to the flag or the recall.

A quarter of an hour after the Invalides and the drummer had descended, the besiegers, seeing that there was no longer any firing from any side of the Bastille, advanced, while firing, to the interior bridge, crying out, "Lower the bridge!" The Swiss officer spoke to them through a sort of loophole near the drawbridge, and asked to march out with the honors of war; they replied, "No." The said officer wrote out the capitulation and passed it through the hole, saying that they desired to render themselves and lay down their arms, on condition of a promise not to massacre the troop; there was a cry of, "Lower your bridge; nothing will happen to you!"

(Marmontel, IV, 211–213.)

The little drawbridge of the fort being first opened, Élie entered with his companions, all brave and honorable men, and fully determined to keep his word. On seeing him, the governor went up to him, embraced him, and presented him with his sword, with the keys of the Bastille.

"I refused his sword," said Élie to me, "and took only the keys." His companions received the staff and the officers of the garrison with the same cordiality, swearing to serve them as a guard and defense; but they swore in vain.

As soon as the great bridge was let down (and it is not known by what hand that was done) the people rushed into the court of the castle and, full of fury, seized on the troop of Invalides. The Swiss who were dressed only in linen frocks escaped among the crowd, all the rest were arrested. Élie and the honest men who had entered with him exerted all their efforts to tear from the hands of the people the victims which they themselves had delivered to it. Ferocity held obstinately attached to its prey. Several of these soldiers, whose lives had been promised them, were assassinated; others were dragged like slaves through the streets of Paris. Twenty-two were brought to the Grève, and, after humiliations and inhuman treatment, they had the affliction of seeing two of their comrades hanged. When they were presented at the Hôtel de Ville, a furious madman said to them: "You deserve to be hanged; and you shall be so presently." Fortunately the French guards interceded for their pardon; the people suffered itself to be persuaded. But it was without pity for the officers of the garrison. De Launay, torn from the arms of those who wished to save him, had his head cut off under the walls of the Hôtel de Ville. In the midst of his assassins, he defended his life with the courage of despair; but he fell under their number. De Losme-Salbray, his major, was murdered in the same manner. The adjutant, Mirai, had been so, near the Bastille. Pernon, an old lieutenant of the Invalides, was assassinated on the wharf Saint-Paul, as he was going to the hall. Another lieutenant, Caron, was covered with wounds. The head of the Marquis de Launay was carried about Paris by this same populace that he would have crushed had he not been moved to pity.

Such were the exploits of those who have since been called the heroes and conquerors of the Bastille. On the 14th of July, 1789, about eleven o'clock in the morning, the people had assembled before it; at forty minutes after four it had surrendered. At half an hour after six the head of the governor was carried in triumph to the Palais-Royal. Among the number of the conquerors, which has been said to amount to eight hundred, many people have been mentioned who had not even approached the castle.

THE KING INFORMED OF THE FALL OF THE BASTILLE. (Weber, I, 385.)

When M. de Liancourt had made known to the king the total defection of his guards, the taking of the Bastille, the massacres that had taken place, and the rising of two hundred thousand men, after a few moments' silence the king said, "It is then a revolt." "No, Sire," replied the duke. "It is a revolution."

The king, seeing then that the time for action had passed, and that it would take rivers of blood to suppress a sedition so vast, decided to renounce the project he had conceived of maintaining against the factious, by force of arms, his authority, and the laws of the state. He resolved to put an end to the massacres that were staining the capital with blood, and of which one could not foresee the end, by withdrawing his troops and abandoning himself to the torrent which was sweeping all before it.

(Extract from a letter of Jefferson to John Jay, Paris, July 19, 1789.)

... he [the king] went, about eleven o'clock, accompanied by his brothers, to the States-General, and there read them a speech, in which he asked their interposition to re-establish order. Though this be couched in terms of some caution, yet the manner in which it was delivered made it evident that it was meant as a surrender at discretion. He returned to the château afoot, accompanied by the States. They sent off a deputation, the Marquis de La Fayette at their head, to quiet Paris.

LA FAYETTE MADE COMMANDER OF THE NATIONAL GUARD. (Procès-verbal des Électeurs, I, 459.)

At the moment when the National Assembly prepared to leave, every voice united to proclaim M. le Marquis de La Fayette commandant of the Paris militia.

M. le Marquis de La Fayette, accepting this honor with every sign of respect and gratitude, drew his sword and took the oath to sacrifice his life for the preservation of that precious liberty, the defense of which they had been pleased to confide to him.

At the same instant, every voice also proclaimed M. Bailly provost of merchants. A voice was heard: "No, not provost of merchants, but mayor of Paris." And in acclamation all those present repeated, "Yes, mayor of Paris!"

M. Bailly was leaning on the desk, his eyes bathed in tears, and his heart so moved that, in his expressions of gratitude, it was only heard that he was not worthy of so great an honor, nor capable of bearing such a burden.

LOUIS' LETTER RECALLING NECKER.

I have been deceived in regard to you. My principles have been violated. I am at last enlightened. Return, return, Monsieur, without delay to resume your right to my confidence, which you shall have henceforth. **You know my heart.** Together with my whole nation, I await you, and I most sincerely share its impatience. Upon which, I pray God, Monsieur, that until your return He will have you in His holy keeping.

LOUIS

THE PRINCES EMIGRATE. (*Révolutions de Paris, No. 2.*)

However, it was during the night between Thursday and Friday that the lady of Polignac and the princes Lambesc and De Vaudemont departed at last; likewise the Comte de Vaudreuil, the Sieurs Barentin and Broglie, De Ville-deuil, Berthier, Foulon, De La Vauguyon, etc., etc., left Versailles; it was on this same night that the Prince de Condé, having assembled two hundred armed men at Chantilly, finally sought safety in flight towards two o'clock in the morning. The rendezvous of the cabal was at Brussels, and on all sides the conspirators withdrew from us, seized with fright, and with despair in their souls; the heads carried on pikes had spread terror and alarm; they took the road under various disguises; the women wore men's clothing, the men dressed themselves as valets, as artisans, and some as poor farmers. M. le Comte d'Artois himself followed their example, and then the capital became tranquil; the camp at Saint-Denis withdrew; their precipitate flight made them abandon some equipages that were brought to the capital; in short, the cause of the nation, of humanity, and of justice appeared to have the better of it at last. Certain individuals, almost negligible and unworthy of being free, who had until then been doubtful of success, were converted, and declared themselves with us; such were the greater part of the officers and sergeants of the guards who presented themselves to the committee of the Hôtel de Ville, to offer their services to the nation, and who were thanked as they should have been.

THE DESTRUCTION OF THE BASTILLE ORDERED.

The permanent committee established at the Hôtel de Ville, provisionally authorized until the establishment of a regular municipality, and democrati-cally elected by the citizens of the districts,

Has ordered that the Bastille be demolished without loss of time after a visit by the two architects charged with directing the operation of the demolition under the command of M. le Marquis de La Salle, charged with the measures necessary to prevent accidents.

And for the notification of the present order, four electors will betake them-selves to the Bastille. Two deputies of the National Assembly now present at the Hôtel de Ville will be invited to accompany them.

And the present order shall be read, published, and posted.

VERGUE, ROUEN, SAGERET, Sheriffs
ETHYS DE CORNY, Public Prosecutor
BOUCHER, FAUCHET, TASSIN, DU VEYRIER,
NYON, BANCAL DES ISSARTS, DE LEUTRE,
LEGRAND DE SAINT-RENÉ, JEANNIN, Electors
VEYTARD, Recorder

THE KING DECIDES TO GO TO PARIS. (*Bailly, II, 44–45.*)

The Archbishop of Vienne returned to the Assembly, bringing a letter of the king's recalling M. Necker. The Assembly, moved by this communication and full of esteem for the minister, ordered added to the letter of the king a letter of its own to testify to its esteem, its regrets, and its hopes for his return. They decreed a deputation to the king to thank him for the dismissal of the ministers. It was about to depart when they learned that the king would go to Paris on the morrow and that he asked the Assembly to make this resolve known to his good city of Paris. A deputation of twelve members to Paris was at once named. Moreover, they decreed that the king be entreated to permit a numerous deputation to accompany him at the time of his entry into Paris. They had the double motive of honoring the king, and of surrounding him with representations of the nation when he had no other guard. This precaution was not offensive to the city of Paris. The fidelity of its inhabitants was well known; but it was not unnecessary in times of trouble, when it was impossible to pretend that there were not brigands mingled with the honest citizens.

LOUIS RECONQUERED BY HIS PEOPLE. (*Bailly, II, 58.*)

The king arrived [at the gates of Paris]. I presented the keys to him and said: "Sire, I bring to Your Majesty the keys of your good city of Paris; they are the same that were presented to Henri IV. He had reconquered his people; now the people have reconquered their king."

(*Dumont, 124.*)

When M. Bailly told him that Henri IV had conquered his people, but the people had now conquered their king, he turned around and said to the Prince de Beauvau, "Perhaps I had better not hear that." The Prince de Beauvau made a sign in reply, and the orator proceeded.

(*Bailly, II, 60–64.*)

The march ran by the Place Louis XV, the Rue Saint-Honoré, the Rue du Roule, and the quays up to the Hôtel de Ville; the way was bordered on two sides by a hedge of national guards, almost everywhere in three and sometimes in four ranks, armed with muskets, swords, pikes, lances, scythes, clubs, etc.; one saw women, monks, and Capuchins with muskets on their shoulders. It has been estimated that there were two hundred thousand men in arms.... I believe this an exaggeration....

When the king passed at the Place Louis XV, a carbine shot, coming from the neighborhood of the Palais-Bourbon, killed a woman not far from his carriage. We have reason to believe that this misfortune was an accident, but it appeared extraordinary....

Having arrived first at the Hôtel de Ville, they proposed that I present to the king the cockade of three colors that the Parisians had adopted since the Revolution as a means of recognizing one another. I did not know how the king would take it, and if there was not something improper in this proposition; however, it seemed to me that I ought to present the cockade, and that the king ought not to refuse it.

When the king descended from the carriage, I walked near him, preceding him by a few steps, and presented it to him, in saying, "Sire, I have the honor to offer Your Majesty the sign distinctive of the French." The king took it with a good grace and put it in his hat.

(*Rivarol, 54–55.*)

M. Lally-Tollendal, the deputy of whom we have already spoken, also harangued His Majesty; but his apostrophes were for the audience. "Behold him," he cried, "behold this king!" and continued in this vein a long and pathetic paraphrase of the *Ecce homo!* for the same circumstances induce the same expressions.

Finally His Majesty, crushed by the weight of such a day, expressed the desire to retire: he had approved everything, sanctioned everything; the cup was drained, and the Revolution consummated; they could not oppose his desire, and before midnight the King of France was free to return to Versailles.

DISORDERS FOLLOWING THE FALL OF THE BASTILLE. (*Weber, I, 400–402.*)

The royal authority found itself paralyzed everywhere at the same time. Each parish had its municipality and its own national guard, each independent of the others. There was formed thus, suddenly, in the heart of a vast monarchy, forty-four thousand republics....

M. Necker returned to Versailles in the midst of this general combustion. En route he was a witness of conflagrations that destroyed the châteaux of Burgundy and Franche-Comté, and devastations of all sorts carried on with impunity to the shame and scandal of France. There was no longer any government in all its vast extent; the last trace of it was effaced.

(*Ferrières, I, 178–179.*)

One hundred and fifty châteaux in Franche-Comté, Mâconnais, and Beaujolais were already burned! The conflagration threatened to consume all the estates.... Shall I speak of murders, of atrocities committed against the nobles?... M. de Baras, cut into pieces before his wife... M. de Montesson, shot after having seen his father-in-law's throat cut! A nobleman, paralyzed, abandoned on a funeral-pile! Another whose feet they burned to make him give up his title deeds! The unfortunate M. de Belsunce, massacred at Caen! Mme. de Berthilac, forced, the ax over her head, to give up her land! Mme. la Princesse de Listenois, constrained to the same sacrifice, with a scythe at her neck, and her two daughters fainting at her feet! The Marquis de Tremand, an infirm old man, chased at night from his château, hunted from city to city, arriving at Bâle, almost dying, with his broken-hearted daughters! The Comte de Montessu and his wife, with pistols at their heads for three hours, and asking for death as a favor, taken from their carriage to be thrown into a pond! The Baron de Mont-Justin, suspended in a well, and hearing the question deliberated as to whether he should be allowed to fall or made to perish in another manner!... Alsace, Champagne, and Dauphiné a prey to the fury of a troop of brigands sent from Paris; and to authorize these sanguinary atrocities, deputies of the commons wrote to their bailiwicks that the nobles wished to blow up the hall of the Assembly at a time when there was no one present but the commons! They told the peasants that the nobles were against the king; they sent supposed orders to burn the châteaux, to massacre the nobles.... These odious means prepared the session of the 4th of August. It was while surrounded by the bodies of nobles massacred in the light of the flames that devoured their châteaux that the Assembly pronounced the decrees violating the sacred rights of legitimate property!

FOULON AND BERTHIER PUT TO DEATH. (*Rivarol, 63–64.*)

M. Foulon, old in business affairs, and known for his talents, was the father-in-law of M. Berthier, intendant of Paris. He was delivered by the peasants of his estate to the Parisian populace. He was accused, without proof, of having said at one time in his life that *the people could eat hay.*

This proverbial phrase would not have brought him to his death if he had not been made one of the ephemeral ministers who succeeded M. Necker. That was his real crime. It has been observed that this same people, which is always moved to pity by the passion of Jesus Christ, tried to inflict it on this unfortunate minister, as if derision and impiety added to vengeance. He was given a crown of thorns, and when, overcome by tortures and fatigue, he asked to drink, they offered him vinegar. His head, paraded through the streets of Paris, was carried that same day to his son-in-law, who was approaching Paris in the midst of a mob of peasants and bourgeois in arms. Forced to kiss the ensanguined head, M. Berthier was soon massacred under the windows of this Hôtel de Ville which was vainly demanding his pardon of the tigers it could no longer master. The soldier who tore out the heart of M. Berthier, as a bleeding offer to MM. Bailly and La Fayette, proved to these *modern sages* that the people imbibe liberty, like strong liquors, only to become intoxicated and enraged.

THE ASSEMBLY REFUSES TO PUNISH THE MURDER OF FOULON AND OTHERS. (*Ferrières, I, 162.*)

...I will say to my contemporaries, I will say to posterity, that the National Assembly authorized these murders and these conflagrations; that a member of that Assembly (the young Barnave) dared to say in the tribune, "Is then this blood so pure that one should so regret spilling it?" When Lally-Tollendal, painfully affected by the misfortunes which desolated his unhappy country, proposed, invoked with prayers even, mild but efficacious means of remedying them, the Assembly eluded and soon refused these means with opinionated perseverance, and only adopted them when it was sure that by the most culpable intriguing it had rendered them useless. Vainly did Lally cry,

"I absolve my conscience of the misfortunes that will result from your refusal and I wash my hands of the blood that will flow!" Cries of fury arose from all sides. A deputy rushed up to Lally and angrily accused him of abusing his popularity. Mirabeau reproached him for yielding to his feelings when it was only a question of reasoning. "Nations must have victims," added Mirabeau with a ferocious look. "One should harden his heart to individual suffering; only at that price can one be a citizen!"

LA FAYETTE RESIGNS COMMAND OF THE NATIONAL GUARD. (*Bailly, II, 129–134.*)

I received this morning the following letter from M. de La Fayette: "Monsieur, entrusted by popular confidence with the military command of the capital, I have not ceased to maintain that in the present circumstances this confidence, to be useful, must be universal. I have not ceased informing the people that the more intensely I was devoted to their interests the more incapable I was of purchasing their favor by unjustifiable complaisance. You know, Monsieur, that of the two men who perished yesterday, one was placed under guard, the other had been brought in by our troops, and both were destined, by civil law, to submit to a regular trial; it was the means of satisfying justice, of knowing the accomplices, and of fulfilling the solemn engagements given by all the citizens to the National Assembly and the king.

"The people did not listen to my advice; and the day on which it loses the confidence promised to me, I must, as I told them in advance, resign a post in which I can no longer be useful."

He had at the same time written a circular letter to the districts to inform them of the resignation that he had rendered me, and to beg that he be replaced as soon as possible. . . .

M. de La Fayette came that evening. He brought a number of resolutions from the districts which, immediately and with emphasis, returned him his resignation. . . .

Finally, a large number of resolutions having arrived at the Assembly in the presence of M. de La Fayette, he could not resist any longer, and consented to resume the command; thus the resignation was offered and withdrawn on the same day.

VIII. *Feudalism Abolished*

ANARCHY AND DISSATISFACTION CAUSE THE ASSEMBLY TO ACT. (*Weber, I, 404.*)

To PLEASE this monarchical people by whose turbulence it was not a little disquieted, the Assembly announced that before beginning to work on the constitution it would proclaim a declaration of the rights of man; that is to say, instead of writing a useful work, it would amuse itself by making a dangerous preface.

As this declaration contained propositions that were metaphysical and vague, and the people had become bored with the two weeks' discussion of them, the National Assembly, burning to show its zeal, finally took action *en masse* during the session, on the evening of August 4.

(*Bailly, II, 212–213.*)

During the evening M. Target read a draft of the proclamation intended to stop the pillaging and burning of the châteaux, and require the payment of taxes, rents, and feudal dues, which were no longer being paid voluntarily.

This proclamation was the occasion of a majestic deliberation and a scene that was veritably grand, absorbingly interesting, and forever memorable. It was declared that both the refusal to pay feudal dues and the burning of title deeds resulted from hatred of the feudal régime with its burden upon the peasants.

THE VICOMTE DE NOAILLES PROPOSES TO ABOLISH FEUDAL RIGHTS.

How can one hope, gentlemen, to calm the agitation in the provinces, assure public liberty, and confirm proprietors in their true rights without knowing the cause of the insurrection manifesting itself in the interior of the kingdom? And how can it be remedied without applying the remedy to the malady which causes it?

The *communautés* have made demands, but not for a constitution. The demand for a constitution came from the bailiwicks. What then have they demanded? That excises be suppressed; that sub-delegates be abolished; that feudal rights be lightened or changed.

The *communautés* have seen their representatives occupy themselves for three months or more with what we call and what is in effect the common weal. The common weal appears to be what they desire above all else and most ardently hope to obtain.

In spite of the disagreements among the representatives of the nation, the country districts saw nothing but their own agents who were working for their happiness, and powerful personages who opposed it. What was the result? They thought it necessary to resist authority by force of arms, and today they know no rein. As a result the kingdom vacillates between two alternatives, the destruction of society and a governmental system which will be the admiration of all Europe.

How can this government be established? By calming the people. How can this be realized? By showing the people that no one opposes them except where conservatism is necessary. To bring about this extremely necessary quiet, I propose an announcement declaring that the representatives of the nation have decided the impost shall be paid by every individual in the kingdom in proportion to his income; that all public burdens will in the future be equally supported by all; that all feudal rights be redeemable by the *communautés* in money or exchangeable at a fairly estimated price; and that the seignioral *corvées*, mortmains, and other personal servitudes be abolished without compensation.

THE DUC D'AGUILLON SECONDS NOAILLES.

Gentlemen, everyone is lamenting the scenes of horror here in France. The agitation of the people in support of liberty when culpable ministers wished to rob us of it is an obstacle to this same liberty when the views of the government, as at present, seem to accord with the desire for public well-being.

Not only are there brigands who, arms in hand, wish to enrich themselves by these calamities; in several provinces the entire people have leagued together to destroy châteaux, ravage estates, and, above all, seize upon charter-rooms where titles to feudal property are deposited. In short, they seek to throw off the yoke which has weighed upon them for so many centuries; and it must be avowed, gentlemen, that the uprising, although culpable, for all violent aggression is such, has an excuse in the vexations visited upon the people. Those proprietors of fiefs, the feudal lords, are very rarely guilty of the excesses concerning which their vassals complain; but their stewards are often pitiless, and the unhappy tiller of the soil, subjected to the barbarous remnants of feudal laws which still exist in France, bewails the constraint of which he is the victim. These rights, it cannot be denied, are a sort of property, and all property is sacred; but they are onerous for the people, and everyone admits that it puts a continual burden upon them. . . .

I do not doubt that, far from denying this truth, the proprietors of fiefs and seignioral estates are disposed to make a sacrifice of their rights in the name of justice. They have already renounced their privileges and their pecuniary exemptions. At this moment, one cannot demand their renunciation, pure and simple, of feudal rights; these rights are their property; they are the sole fortune of many individuals, and equity forbids exacting the abolition of any property without according a just indemnity to the proprietor who sacrifices his rights to the public good.

On account of these important considerations, gentlemen, and to make the people feel that you are efficaciously occupying yourselves with its dearest interests, I desire that the National Assembly declare that imposts be supported equally by all citizens in proportion to their means, and that henceforth all feudal rights of fiefs and seignioral estates be redeemable by the vassals of these same fiefs and lands, if they so desire; and that the re-embursement be fixed by the Assembly at a certain proportion. In my opinion this proportion ought to be one to thirty ...

THE ASSEMBLY ABOLISHES THE FEUDAL SYSTEM.

ARTICLE I. The National Assembly completely abolishes the feudal system. It decrees that, in the rights and dues that are feudal as well as rental, those which maintain real or personal mortmain and personal servitude, and those which pertain to them, shall be abolished without compensation. All others are declared redeemable, and the amount and manner of redemption shall be fixed by the National Assembly. Of the said rights, those which are not suppressed by this decree shall continue to be collected until indemnified.

II. The exclusive right to pigeon-houses and dove-cotes is abolished. The pigeons shall be kept shut up at periods decided upon by the communities; during this time they shall be regarded as game, and everyone shall have the right to kill them on his own land.

III. The exclusive right of chase and open warrens is likewise abolished, and every proprietor has the right to destroy, or have destroyed on his own land, all kinds of game; provided that he conform to the police laws which may be made relative to public safety. All *capitaineries*, even royal ones, and all hunting reserves, under whatever denomination they may be, are likewise abolished, but the personal pleasures of the king shall be provided for by means compatible with the respect due to property and liberty. The president (of the Assembly) shall be charged with asking the king to recall those banished and sent to the galleys for the mere act of hunting, to release prisoners at present detained, and to suppress prosecutions now taking place.

IV. All manorial courts are suppressed without compensation; nevertheless, the officials of these courts shall continue their functions until the National Assembly shall have provided for the establishment of a new judicial order.

V. Tithes of every kind and the dues substituted for them, under whatever name they are known or collected, even when compounded for, whether possessed by secular or regular bodies, beneficed clergy, people concerned with building churches or with mortmain, or even the Order of Malta or other religious or military orders, including those tithes which have been abandoned to the laity in substitution and in option on suitable allowances, are abolished, subject to the provision of other means for the expenses of the divine cult, for the support of the priests, for the relief of the poor, for the repairing and reconstructing of churches and parsonages, and all the establishments, seminaries, schools, hospitals, societies, etc., the support of which is at present affected. However, until this has been provided, and the former possessors have begun to enjoy this compensation, the National Assembly orders that the said tithes continue to be collected according to the laws and in the accustomed manner.

As to the other tithes, of whatever nature they may be, these shall be redeemable in the manner which shall be decided upon by the Assembly; and until this has been regulated, the National Assembly orders that the collection of them shall continue.

VI. All perpetual ground rents, either in kind or in money, of whatever species or of whatever origin, or to whomever due, whether mortmain, domains, *apanages*, or pertaining to the Order of Malta, shall be redeemable.

VII. The sale of judicial and municipal offices is hereby abolished. Justice shall be rendered gratuitously. However, the incumbents of these offices shall continue to exercise their functions and to receive their emoluments, until compensation has been provided by the Assembly.

VIII. The surplice fees of country priests are suppressed, and shall cease to be paid as soon as an increase in the proper salaries and living allowances of the curates shall have been provided; and arrangement shall be made to regulate the position of the priests in the cities.

IX. Pecuniary privileges, real or personal, in regard to taxes are forever abolished. Taxes shall be levied on all citizens and property in the same manner and form, and ways shall be devised for the collection of proportional taxes on all property, even for the last six months of the current year.

X. Public liberty and a national constitution being more advantageous to the provinces than privileges which prevent the unification of the kingdom, it is hereby decreed that all special privileges in provinces, principalities, districts, cantons, cities, and communities, either pecuniary or of any other nature, are abolished forever, and shall remain incorporated in the law common to all the French.

XI. All citizens, without distinction of birth, can be admitted to all positions and dignities, whether ecclesiastical, civil, or military, and no useful profession shall be considered derogatory.

XII. In the future no money shall be sent for any reason whatever to the court at Rome, to the vice-legation of Avignon, or to the nunciature of Lucerne. The clergy shall look to their bishops for the provision of benefices and dispensations. These shall be accorded gratuitously, in spite of all reservations, expectancies, and monthly distributions, all the churches of France having the right to the same liberty.

XIII. *Déports*, rights of *côte-morte, dépouilles, vacat*, rights of quit-rents, Peter's pence, and others of like kind established in favor of bishops, archdeacons, archpriests, chapters, *curés primitifs*, and other clergy, under whatever name they may be, are abolished; but a suitable provision shall be made for the endowment of archdeacons and archpriests who are not already sufficiently endowed.

XIV. Plurality of benefices shall not be allowed in the future when the revenues of the benefice or benefices which one possesses exceed three thousand livres. Nor shall one be permitted to possess several pensions from benefices, or a pension and a benefice, if the income from things of this kind already possessed exceeds the sum of three thousand livres.

XV. When the National Assembly has received a report on the state of pensions, dispensations, and emoluments, it will, in concert with the king, begin the suppression of those which have not been merited, and the reduction of those which are excessive, deciding upon a sum which the king can in the future dispose of for this purpose.

XVI. The National Assembly decrees that a medal shall be struck in memory of the eventful and important deliberations which have taken place for the benefit of France, and that a *Te Deum* of thanksgiving shall be chanted in all the parishes and churches of the kingdom.

XVII. The National Assembly solemnly proclaims Louis XVI the *Restorer of French Liberty.*

XVIII. The National Assembly shall go in a body to the king to present to His Majesty the decree just formulated, to offer him the homage of a most respectful gratitude, and to beg that he permit the *Te Deum* to be chanted in his chapel, and that he himself be present at this.

XIX. The National Assembly shall occupy itself, immediately after the constitution, with the formulation of laws necessary for the development of the principles established by the present decree, which decree shall immediately be dispatched by the deputies to all provinces together with the decree of the 10th of this month, there to be printed, read from parish pulpits, and posted everywhere thought necessary.

THE ASSEMBLY CONCERNED WITH RIGHTS RATHER THAN DUTIES.
(*Rivarol, 84.*)

The National Assembly had been elected to make a constitution, not a revolution. Thus far our deputies had done nothing but destroy. Now they yielded to the temptation of placing a declaration of the rights of man at the head of the constitution; may they not repent of it! Princes, who hear always of their rights and privileges and never of their duties, are in general a bad species of men. Does the National Assembly want to make us into so many princes? Are not passions already too strong in the human heart? Ought a legislative assembly pander to the enviousness which does not want one man to be worth more or possess more than another?

(*Dumont, 139–141.*)

The idea was American, and there was scarcely a member who did not consider such a declaration an indispensable preliminary. I well remember the long debate on the subject, which lasted several weeks, as a period of mortal ennui. There were silly disputes about words, much metaphysical trash, and dreadfully tedious prosing. The Assembly had converted itself into a Sorbonne, and each apprentice in the art of legislation was trying his yet unfledged wings upon such puerilities. After the rejection of several models, a committee of five members was appointed to present a new one. Mirabeau, one of the five, undertook the work with his usual generosity, but imposed its execution upon his friends. He set about the task, and there were he, Duroveray, Clavière, and I writing, disputing, adding, striking out, and exhausting both time and patience upon this ridiculous subject. At length we produced our piece of patchwork, our mosaic of pretended natural rights which never existed.... *Men are born free and equal!* that is not true. They are not born free;

on the contrary, they are born in a state of weakness and necessary dependence. *Equal!* how are they so, or how can they be so? If by equality is understood equality of fortune, of talents, of virtue, of industry, or of rank, then the falsehood is manifest. It would require volumes of argument to give any reasonable meaning to that equality proclaimed without exception. In a word, my opinion against the declaration of the rights of man was so strongly formed that this time it influenced that of our little committee. Mirabeau, on presenting the project, even ventured to make some objections to it, and proposed to defer the declaration of rights until the constitution should be completed. "I can safely predict," said he, in his bold and energetic style, "that any declaration of rights anterior to the constitution will prove but the almanac of a single year!"

(*Bailly, I, 314.*)

Then M. de La Fayette read a project for the declaration of the rights of man. This declaration had the fault of not always being clear and precise enough; of having in anticipation mingled the rights of the citizen, which are assured to him by the constitution, with those of man, which are given to him by nature; but the principles were very good, and in a moment everybody was occupied with this declaration, M. de La Fayette having had the honor of presenting it first. M. de Lally-Tollendal, who had the floor after him, said some opportune words: "M. de La Fayette speaks of the liberty for which he has fought." This speech made an impression and was enthusiastically applauded.

THE DECLARATION OF THE RIGHTS OF MAN.

The representatives of the French people, constituted as a National Assembly, considering that ignorance, forgetfulness, or contempt of the rights of man are the sole causes of public misfortunes and the corruption of governments, have resolved to set forth in a solemn declaration the natural, inalienable, and sacred rights of man, in order that this declaration, constantly before all members of the social body, may recall to them at all times their rights and duties; in order that the acts of the legislative power and of the executive power, being at each instant open to comparison with the aims of all political institutions, may be more respected; and in order that the demands of citizens, founded henceforth on simple and incontestable principles, shall tend always to the maintenance of the constitution and the happiness of all.

Accordingly, the National Assembly accepts and declares, in the presence and under the auspices of the Supreme Being, the following rights of man and of the citizen:

Article I. Men are born and remain free and equal in rights. Social distinctions can be founded only upon common utility.

II. The purpose of all political association is the safeguarding of the natural and imprescriptible rights of man. These rights are liberty, property, security, and resistance to oppression.

III. The principle of all sovereignty resides essentially in the nation. No body, no individual, can exercise any authority which does not expressly emanate from it.

IV. Liberty consists in freedom to do all that does not harm others. Thus the exercise of the natural rights of each man has no other limits than those which assure other members of society the enjoyment of these same rights. These limits can be determined only by law.

V. The law has the right to forbid only those actions which are harmful to society. All that is not forbidden by law cannot be prevented; and no one can be constrained to do what it does not command.

VI. The law is the expression of the general will. All citizens have the right to assist personally, or through their representatives, in its formation. It ought to be the same for all, whether it protects or whether it punishes. All citizens, being equal in its eyes, are equally admissible to all dignities, places, and public positions according to their capacity, and without other distinctions than those of their virtues and talents.

VII. No man can be accused, arrested, or detained except in cases determined by the law, and according to the forms that it has prescribed. Those who solicit, expedite, or execute arbitrary orders, or have them executed, should be punished; but every citizen, summoned or seized by virtue of the law, ought to obey instantly. He renders himself culpable by resistance.

VIII. The law should establish only those punishments which are strictly and evidently necessary; and no one can be punished except by virtue of a law established and promulgated previous to the offense and legally applied.

IX. As every man is presumed innocent until he has been declared guilty, when it is deemed indispensable to make an arrest, all severity not necessary for making sure of the person should be rigorously repressed by law.

X. No one should be disturbed on account of his opinions, even in regard to religion, provided their manifestation does not disturb the public order established by law.

XI. The free communication of thought and opinion is one of the most precious rights of man. Every citizen can then speak, write, and publish freely; but he shall be responsible for the abuse of this liberty in cases determined by law.

XII. The guaranteeing of the rights of man and of the citizen necessitates a public force. This force is, then, instituted for the advantage of all, and not for the special use of those to whom it is confided.

XIII. For the maintenance of the public force and for the expenses of the administration, a common contribution is indispensable. It ought to be equally distributed among all citizens, according to their means.

XIV. All citizens have the right of verifying, themselves or by their representatives, the necessity of the public contribution, of consenting to it without compulsion, of seeing how it is employed, and of determining the quota, assessment, payment, and duration.

XV. Society has the right to demand from every public agent an account of his administration.

XVI. A society in which a guarantee of rights is not assured, nor the separation of powers set forth, has no constitution.

XVII. Property being a sacred and inviolable right, no one can be deprived of it, except when public necessity, lawfully ascertained, evidently demands it, and then only after a previous and just indemnity has been awarded.

NECKER AND THE FINANCES. (*Rabaut Saint-Étienne, 124–125.*)

The National Assembly seemed in one day to have atoned, by the decree abolishing feudalism, for the inaction forced upon it by the terrible crises of state. But now the state was undergoing a new crisis due to lack of money and the disorder existing in the kingdom. M. Necker suggested to the Assembly a loan of thirty millions at five per cent, without stoppage. The Assembly, by not giving any security for this loan, by not fixing any time for redemption, and by reducing the interest to four and a half, presumed too much upon the national credit and the patriotism of the rich. The loan fell through. It is doubtful whether M. Necker's plan would have been any better; but the Assembly was evidently at fault, and M. Necker did not fail to reproach it. When the minister next proposed a new loan of eighty millions (which realized only forty), the Assembly voted it without examination. This experienced no better success and the National Assembly again bore all the blame.

EMBARRASSMENTS OF THE GOVERNMENT. (*Extract from a letter of Jefferson to John Jay, Paris, August 27, 1789.*)

The embarrassments of the government for want of money are extreme. The loan of thirty millions proposed by M. Necker has not succeeded at all. No taxes are paid. A total stoppage of all payment to the creditors of the state is possible every moment. These form a great mass in the city as well as country, and among the lower class of people too, who have been used to carry their little savings of their service into the public funds, upon life rents of five, ten, twenty guineas a year, and many of whom have no other dependence for daily subsistence. A prodigious number of servants are now thrown out of employ by domestic reforms, rendered necessary by the late events. Add to this, the want of bread, which is extreme. For several days past, a considerable proportion of the people have been without bread altogether; for though the new harvest is begun, there is neither water nor wind to grind the grain. For some days past the people have besieged the doors of the bakers, scrambled with one another for bread, collected in squads all over the city, and need only some slight incident to lead them to excesses which may end in nobody can tell what. The danger from want of bread, however, which is most imminent, will certainly lessen in a few days. What turn that may take which arises from the want of money is difficult to be foreseen. M. Necker is totally without influence in the National Assembly, and is, I believe, not satisfied with this want of importance. That Assembly has just finished their bill of rights. The question will then be whether to take up first the constitution or the business of finance.

THE ASSEMBLY SUPPRESSES THE PARLEMENTS. (*Révolutions de Paris, No. 5.*)

One was impatient at seeing the *parlements* still have power over legislation. There were cries of joy and applause from all sides when the suppression of the *parlements* was proposed in the National Assembly. The motion was made by representatives of three great provinces which had provided in their charters for the establishment of *parlements* in their principal cities. The assertion has been in the mouth of all good citizens that there will be "no liberty whatever unless the very name of *parlement* is wiped out." All this proves that public opinion is solidly against these aristocratic bodies which have for so many years impudently called themselves the representatives of the people, desiring to be so only in order to augment their power and bring added misfortunes.

PARIS THE FOCUS OF TROUBLE. (*Fersen, 73–74.*)

Disorder is increasing throughout the country, and God alone knows what will come of it. Paris is the focus of trouble, and nearly everyone is in haste to leave it. Vagabonds and deserters are taking refuge there, and the number of the latter is very considerable. They are received into the militia which is being raised under the command of the Marquis de La Fayette; they have better pay than our regiments and there are no means not employed to entice them. It is said that, according to the report of the regiments rendered to the war office, there have been since July 13, 12,750 deserters, without counting the French guards. The king's authority is totally annihilated, so is that of the *parlements* and the magistrates; the States-General themselves tremble before Paris, and this fear greatly influences their deliberations. There are no longer in this kingdom either laws, order, justice, discipline, or religion; all bonds are broken; and how can they be re-established? That is what I do not know, but these are the effects of the progress of the ideas of Anglomania and philosophy; France is ruined for a long time to come.

THE PARIS COMMUNE DESIRES ORDER. (*Révolutions de Paris, No. 5.*)

The assembly of representatives of the commune of Paris, in order to put an end to the uprisings, mob gatherings, and disorders occasioned by the carrying off of the powder, has decreed that "the commanding general of the Parisian national guard shall take, in conjunction with the commandants of all the districts, the most prompt and sure measures to put a stop to the seditious mob gatherings, which must not be confounded, however, with assemblages of peaceful citizens; forbidding all movements except district assemblages, and seeing to all other disorders of similar nature.

"The assembly has notably enjoined the citizens of Saint-Roch, Saint-Honoré, the Oratoire, the Petits-Pères, the Filles-Saint-Thomas, and all others, to assure the execution of the present decree, maintain efficient police in each district, and lend all necessary assistance to this effect.

BAILLY, Mayor; MOREAU DE SAINT-MÉRY, and DE LA VIGNE, Presidents; BROUSSE DES FAUCHERETS, Secretary."

LETTER OF THE KING TO OFFICERS AND SOLDIERS OF HIS ARMY.

Valiant soldiers, the new obligations which, in concert with the National Assembly, I impose upon you, will not give you noticeable trouble. Your primary duties as citizens will always be in harmony with the obedience you owe me, since it is my wish never to employ my authority except in defense of the laws and the interests of the nation.

The officers who command my troops, and who have my entire confidence, will take the same pleasure as myself in seeing that there is no incertitude when military co-operation is necessary for the maintenance of public order.

The greatest service that I now expect from my army is that it show its zeal in uniting with all good citizens to repulse the brigands who, not content with throwing my kingdom into disorder, are also trying to pervert the minds of my good and faithful subjects in order to involve them in their violences or in their perfidious designs. . . .

You may rely then upon my benevolence, as I shall always rely upon your fidelity.

Louis

OATHS TAKEN BY THE ARMY.

We swear to remain faithful to the nation, the king, and the law, and never employ those under our orders against citizens except when required to do so by civil and municipal officials. (Officer's oath.)

We swear that we will never abandon our colors, will be faithful to the nation, the king, and the law, and will conform to the rules of military discipline. (Soldier's oath.)

DECREE ON THE GRAIN TRADE.

The National Assembly, having heard the report of the committee on subsistence, decrees (1) that throughout the whole kingdom there shall be no restrictions upon the sale and transportation of flour and grain; (2) that the transportation of flour and grain by sea shall be accompanied by exact declarations to the municipalities at places of departure and disembarkation. Certificates to this effect must be presented to the municipalities. Exportation to foreign countries is and will remain provisionally forbidden.

SLOWNESS OF THE ASSEMBLY. (Extract from a letter of Jefferson to John Jay, Paris, September 19, 1789.)

The sloth of the Assembly (unavoidable from their number) has done the most sensible injury to the public cause. The patience of a people who have less of that quality than any other nation in the world is worn threadbare. Time has been given to the aristocrats to recover from their panic, to cabal, to sow dissensions in the Assembly, and distrust out of it. It has been a misfortune that the king and aristocracy together have not been able to make a sufficient resistance, to hoop the patriots in a compact body. Having no common enemy of such force as to render their union necessary, they have suffered themselves to divide. The Assembly now consists of four distinct parties: (1) The aristocrats, comprehending the higher members of the clergy, military, nobility, and the *parlements* of the whole kingdom. This forms a head without a body. (2) The moderate royalists, who wish for a constitution nearly similar to that of England. (3) The republicans, who are willing to let their first magistracy be hereditary, but to make it very subordinate to the legislature, and to have the legislature consist of a single chamber. (4) The faction of Orléans. The second and third descriptions are composed of honest, well-meaning men, differing in opinion only, but both wishing the establishment of as great a degree of liberty as can be preserved. They are considered together as constituting the patriotic part of the Assembly, and they are supported by the soldiery of the army, the soldiery of the clergy, that is to say, the *curés* and monks, the dissenters, and part of the nobility, which is small, and the substantial bourgeois of the whole nation. . . . [A] powerful bond of union between these parties is our friend the Marquis de La Fayette. He left the Assembly while they as yet formed but one party. His attachment to both is equal, and he labors incessantly to keep them together. . . . His command of the armed militia of Paris (thirty thousand in number, and comprehending the French guards, who are five thousand regulars), and his influence with the municipality, would secure their city; and though the armed militia and the municipalities of the other cities are in no wise subordinate to those of Paris, yet they look up to them with respect, and look particularly to the Marquis de La Fayette as leading always to the rights of the people.

TALLEYRAND ADVOCATES AN ANNULLING OF INSTRUCTIONS. (*Malouet, I, 264–265.*)

One will be astonished perhaps to learn that next to Mirabeau I rank Talleyrand, Bishop of Autun. He is not only a man of distinguished mentality, but he has, by a single motion, had the greatest influence upon all operations of the Assembly. I do not know if the idea of annulling our representatives' instructions was exclusively his; but the author of this, whoever it was, made a great step in revolution. Our instructions were the only barrier against disastrous systems and innovations. All instructions, without exception, left to monarchical government its stability and to the king sufficient power. Property, religion, and other essential parts of our ancient institutions were respected. Abuses were pointed out, and there was a desire for reformation, but no one showed any penchant for subversion.

THE QUESTION OF THE ROYAL VETO. (*Bailly, II, 326–328.*)

A certain part of the Assembly, wishing to gain the support of the people, had inflamed their minds and raised the quarrel about the veto. This is still going on in 1792, for the members of this party are indefatigable. The people were told that traitors were desiring an absolute veto, and that France was going to be enslaved. All this agitation had two motives; one, to prevent the National Assembly from giving the king the veto; the other, to protect the life of M. de Mirabeau, which was in danger. I do not give much credit to this pretended danger . . . It is rather queer that people who opposed the absolute veto feared for the life of Mirabeau, who favored it. The people did not yet know their lessons well. And there is nothing so ridiculous as for the confused multitude at the Palais-Royal to want to influence the deliberations of the representatives of the nation, or so unconstitutional and opposed to the validity of the constitution as to suppose for a moment that it had the power. It was being said that fifteen thousand men should march to Versailles and invite the nation to get rid of its unfaithful representatives so that others could be named for their places. And what was most remarkable was that they were going to supplicate the king and M. le Dauphin to come to Paris for safety.

(*Weber, I, 415.*)

The members of the committee on the constitution received every day anonymous letters threatening them with the anger of the people and openly announcing to them that fifteen thousand men were going to march out and light up their châteaux and houses if they persisted in their proposal to give the king a veto which struck at the sovereignty of the people. Such a veto might well be given to twenty-five million people, but never to a sole individual.

Not a single one of these people could have given a definition of the veto which gave them so much uneasiness. But they had been told so often that it was an invention of the aristocrats that they were ready to rise in insurrection against this veto; and since physical objects are more comprehensible to the lower classes than abstractions, the veto was at once personified. Louis XVI and Marie Antoinette were called *Monsieur* and *Madame Veto*.

SIÉYÈS OPPOSES THE VETO. (*Extract from a speech of Siéyès in the National Assembly, September 7, 1789.*)

I define law as the will of the governed; therefore the rulers should have no part in its formation.

The king can be considered a citizen, a king, and a chief executive. His wishes as a citizen have no more weight than those of other citizens. As king, he presides over the different assemblies and proclaims the law made by the nation or its representatives. As chief executive, he is only an agent, and his functions are limited to the execution of the law entrusted to him.

The vote of the king has no more weight than that of a president. Were it otherwise, the will of one man would triumph over the general desire. Lawmaking is, in reality, nothing but the converging of individual desires at a common center, that is to say, the law. If the king could prevent this, his individual wish would triumph over the general will, which cannot and ought not to take place. As chief executive, the king is not an integral part of the law. The execution of the law takes place after its formation; therefore it has nothing to do with the making of law.

Hence, whatever one thinks of the veto, it is always contrary to the principle that the head of the executive power does not form an integral part of the law; for the right of obstructing a law is the same as making a law: there is no difference whatever. The man who says, "I do not wish this done," says in reality, "I wish to prevent you from doing it."

After this preliminary survey, I believe that I may state that the majority of the legislative ought to act independently of the executive power; and that the veto, whether absolute or suspensive, is only a *lettre de cachet* against the general will.

MIRABEAU SUPPORTS THE VETO. (Extract from a speech of Mirabeau in the National Assembly, September 1, 1789.)

To demonstrate by an example that this danger [of thwarting the general will] would exist if the prince were deprived of the veto on all propositions of law presented to him by the National Assembly, I ask that one only suppose a bad choice of representatives and two parliamentary rules which have already been proposed and which have been authorized by the initiative of England. These are the exclusion of the public from the national chamber on the simple demand of a member of the Assembly, and the interdiction of newspaper accounts of its deliberations.

These two regulations once adopted, there would soon be an expulsion of all unwary members. With the fear of the Assembly's despotism acting upon the Assembly itself, there would be needed, under a weak prince, only a little time and address to establish legally the domination of twelve hundred aristocrats. The royal authority would be reduced to a passive instrument in their hands, and the people would be plunged back into the state of debasement which servitude to a prince entails.

The prince is the perpetual representative of the people, as the deputies are its representatives for certain epochs. The rights of the one, like those of the others, are founded only upon their utility to those who established them.

No one objects to the veto of the National Assembly, which is in reality only a right of the people confided to its representatives to oppose all propositions tending to re-establish ministerial despotism. Why then object to the veto of the prince, which is likewise only a right of the people confided specially to the prince? The prince is as interested as the people in preventing the re-establishment of aristocracy.

A SUSPENSIVE VETO ADOPTED. (Extract from a letter of Jefferson to John Jay, Paris, September 19, 1789.)

They have determined that the king shall have a *suspensive and iterative veto*; that is, that after negativing a law, it cannot be presented again until after a new election. If he negatives it then, it cannot be presented a third time till after another new election. If it be then presented, he is obliged to pass it. This is perhaps justly considered as a more useful negative than an absolute one, which a king would be afraid to use. M. Necker's influence with the Assembly is nothing at all. Having written to them, by order of the king, on the subject of the veto before it was decided, they refused to let his letter be read.

IX. *The Mob Goes to Versailles*

DESIRES FOR MOVING THE GOVERNMENT. (*Weber, I, 421.*)

IN THE state of fermentation and uneasiness that existed, each party sought to ensure victory to itself. The members of the committee on the constitution, M. Malouet, and all those who afterwards formed the party of the moderates desired that the king and the assembly be transferred to Tours in order to escape the disastrous influence exerted by the neighborhood of Paris; the revolutionists on their side conceived the project of transferring the National Assembly to Paris, the center of popular agitation. The king, who saw no real friends of royal authority in the party of moderates, rejected the proposal to withdraw made to him by M. Necker and M. Montmorin.

SAINT–HURUGE PROPOSES TO CONDUCT THE POPULACE TO VERSAILLES. (*Mounier, 66–67.*)

All occasions were made use of to excite the people. In the month of September, when the populace was assembled in the Palais-Royal, and when Saint-Huruge proposed to conduct it to Versailles, they were already talking of carrying off the king and the dauphin, and proscribing the members of the Assembly who defended the royal sanction. Horrible designs against the queen were also announced. The execution of this project was deferred; but the attempt was not in vain; for one knew the influence that it had on the most essential prerogative of the throne.

After the imprisonment of Saint-Huruge, they persisted in the design of making an incursion into Versailles. I repeat, without fear of contradiction, that the ministers received every day the most alarming information on this subject. The king's guards were on several occasions obliged to pass the night ready to take horse. At that time they appeared resolved to repulse force with force in any attempt made to violate the king's right to choose his residence.

FEARS OF THE REVOLUTIONISTS AND COUNTER–REVOLUTIONISTS. (*Ferrières, I, 259–263.*)

The two parties, like two strong athletes confronting one another in the arena, awaited only a favorable moment to begin the attack. The court, tired of the endless sacrifices exacted of it, recognized at last the urgent necessity of arresting the enterprises that tended to the complete annihilation of the

monarchy, and perhaps the discarding of the monarch. Necker and his partisans saw their plan of constitution rejected, and the ambitious hopes with
which they had flattered themselves, vanish without return. The nobility,
the clergy, and the *parlements* could no longer doubt that their ruin was sworn.
These three important groups, united by common interest, hated and ought to
have hated the new order of things; and secret manoeuvers and indirect
attacks proved that they were occupying themselves with the means of overthrowing it. The revolutionists realized how important it was to forestall the
attempts which, though several times failing, would perhaps in the end be
crowned with success. Strongly supported by the people whom they directed
at will, informed of the movements of their adversaries, and sure of circumvent-
ing them, they watched for a mistake, an imprudence.

Through vaguely spreading rumors, people were prepared for some extraordinary event. When the Versailles bookseller Blaisot came to see the Comte
de Mirabeau, the count, after a moment's conversation, dismissed the three
secretaries who wrote under his dictation. Carefully closing the door, he said:
"My dear Blaisot, in friendliness to you I want to warn you that within but very
few days you will witness great calamities; horrors even, blood spilled at Versailles. I tell you, in order to dissipate your uneasiness: good citizens like you
have nothing to fear." The skilfully contrived circumstances, and particularly
the false calculations of the minister Necker, still favored the revolutionists in
the execution of their projects.

The scarcity and dearness of grain increased in an alarming manner; the
doors of the bakers were besieged; the people gathered there, and agents,
mingling with the citizens, increased the disorder by increasing the crowd. A
multitude of laborers, obliged to wait a whole day to procure a four-pound loaf,
returned with despair in their hearts, and often without having provided for
the needs of their families. Yet the harvest had been abundant; it was in
October; throughout the provinces the new grain was being eaten. This
factitious famine, instead of diminishing, augmented daily. All parties contributed to maintaining it; for all desired an insurrection, some in the hope of
directing it against the National Assembly, others of directing it against the
court.

To these manoeuvers, already so apt to arouse the people, were added
rumors of civil war and projects of counter-revolution. The rumors were not
entirely without basis: a large number of nobles, priests, and financiers, nursing
the foolish hope of reviving the ancient order of things, formed associations,
gathered signatures, and prepared plans for the withdrawal of the king to
Metz.

*THE REGIMENT OF FLANDERS BROUGHT TO VERSAILLES. (Mme. de Tourzel,
I, 24–25.)*

In the month of September of this year, the king, tired of his position, and
unable to hide from himself the advantage which the rebels derived from his
proximity to Paris, seriously thought of leaving Versailles. He wished, by
withdrawing himself from the city, to remove all possibility of the realization
of the projects which the incendiary proposals of the Jacobins gave him only too

much reason to dread. Their Majesties, ever full of goodness, were kind enough to warn me to be in readiness to depart without any preparation, if circumstances should so require. They were not yet decided as to the place where they would settle, and I never knew it; but they soon changed their minds, and resolved on remaining at Versailles.

Nevertheless, the number of the victims multiplied, and crimes remained unpunished. The populace of Versailles meditated hanging an unfortunate baker, whose only crime in their eyes was that he made two sorts of bread. They pillaged his shop, and he was with difficulty rescued from their hands. Advantage was taken of this circumstance to impress upon the municipality the necessity of increasing the repressive force, and the Comte d'Estaing, commandant of the national guard of Versailles, was consequently authorized to request a reinforcement of 1000 men of the regular army, and the regiment of Flanders was ordered to Versailles.

The spirit of this regiment was at that time excellent, and so was that of the chasseurs of Lorraine, who were then stationed at Meudon. These two corps, together with the *gardes du corps*, were more than enough to enable the king to leave Versailles without the slightest difficulty, and if he had taken that step he might perhaps have avoided all the misfortunes which led him to his ruin.

(*Ferrières, I, 271.*)

As soon as the arrival of the regiment of Flanders was known at Paris, the disquieted revolutionists worked to spread the alarm. Masses of troops, they said, were being brought in around Paris and Versailles; it was planned to carry off the king and conduct him to Metz; the regiment of Flanders was destined to cover his retreat. In order to make the arrival of this regiment appear contrary to the wishes of the inhabitants of Versailles, and even to the wishes of the majority of the bourgeois militia, they began to intrigue among the companies. When the Comte d'Estaing wished to have them ratify the requisition of the staff, twenty-eight companies obstinately refused.

THE ROYALIST BANQUET. (*Weber, I, 422–427.*)

When a new regiment arrived in a city where other troops were stationed, an immemorial custom of the French army required that the officers of the different corps banquet one another. The king's *gardes du corps* were accustomed to offer fêtes to crowned heads, and a few years before had given one of greatest magnificence to the queen. They could not dispense with receiving the officers of the regiment of Flanders in a manner conformable to military etiquette and worthy of their courtesy. The latter had given their first repast in the great stable where they were quartered. When it came to returning the favor, the king permitted his *gardes du corps* to use the beautiful hall of the palace opera, unsurpassed in grandeur and magnificence by any of the theaters of Europe. The number of guests rendered such a large place necessary. The banquet took place the 23rd of September; the health of the king and queen was pledged with enthusiasm, and fervent demonstrations of loyalty burst forth on all sides. . . .

Soon the august family was entreated to descend and make a round of the hall. Marie Antoinette, yielding to an irresistible impulse, imitated her august mother by taking M. le Dauphin by the hand and conducting him around the tables, proud of showing to the defenders of the throne the handsome child who was the heir presumptive. At the sight of so much majesty and grace, of so much beauty and innocence, sentiment and admiration reached the height of intoxication, and all eyes were filled with tears of emotion as the music intoned the touching air of "Richard-Cœur-de-Lion":

"O Richard! ô mon roi!
L'univers t'abandonne."

This air, which made such a striking allusion to the situation of Louis XVI, and which for so long a time has been proscribed in France, was repeated in chorus by all lips. Never had there been a more loyal concert. Never had a purer sentiment stirred a whole assembly. The august faces of the king and queen bore that evening the imprint of contentment and happiness, instead of the melancholy of several months past.

I was present at this fête, and as an eyewitness can give assurance that nothing which occurred exceeded the limits of gaiety or the most scrupulous decency.... The sole irregularity that I noticed was the action of some soldiers of the regiment of Flanders who, finding themselves in the courts when the banquet hall resounded with acclamations, made several efforts to mount the balcony of the palace by climbing up the columns....

In the evening, ladies in service at the court were seen to make, from some pieces of white paper, cockades which they distributed in the apartments of the *gardes du corps* at the palace and to officers they met on the way. All this was very simple and gay and should have been regarded only as a trait of the French character, an expression of great devotion to the king and his family. Ought a demonstration of joy in the royal palace be imputed a crime?

In the crowd of spectators at this banquet there were, as everywhere else, ardent republicans. Furious at a love so true and touching, they immediately published throughout the whole city and in the National Assembly that they had assisted at the banquet of the *gardes du corps*; that they had perceived there plots and conspiracies of the court against the city of Paris; and that similar orgies were held daily. The soldiers had trampled the national cockade underfoot and had put on the black cockade. They had insulted the nation and this insult must be avenged.

PARIS IN INSURRECTION. (*Weber, I, 428–429.*)

On Sunday, October 4, the people resorted to acts of violence in the public promenades against officers of the army and other individuals who were pointed out to them as aristocrats. There was in Paris an extreme agitation. The symptoms of a violent insurrection were alarmingly manifest in the evening. Monday, the 5th, as early as morning, one saw women, a species of furies, running the streets, crying out that there was no bread at the baker's. They were soon joined by a considerable number of men in the Place de l'Hôtel de Ville. Their first operation was to hang on a lamp-post a baker accused of having sold bread under weight. This man was saved by M. de Gouvion, a major of the national guard. These maniacs wanted to get into the town hall; there they turned the papers in some of the offices topsy-turvy, threatening to set fire to them; but they were prevented from executing their project. They loaded the most atrocious insults on MM. Bailly, de La Fayette, and the members of the commune; and this circumstance proves better than any amount of reasoning that the authorities who then governed Paris had no connection with the insurgents who directed this disorder.

(*Maillard; Bailly, III, 406–412.*)

[Maillard] was occupied with a crowd of women ... he took away their torches, and nearly lost his life in thus opposing their project. He told them that they could go in a deputation to the commune to demand justice and present their situation, which was that all demanded bread. But they replied that the commune was made up of bad citizens, all deserving to be hanged to the lamp-post, MM. Bailly and La Fayette first of all ... these women would not listen to reason, and after having put in ruin the Hôtel de Ville, they wanted to go to the National Assembly to find out what had been decreed previous to this day of the 5th of October ... [Maillard secured] a drum at the door of the Hôtel de Ville, where the women had already assembled in great numbers. Detachments of them departed for various districts to recruit other women, to whom they gave rendezvous at the Place Louis XV. Maillard saw several men place themselves at their head, and make to them harangues calculated to excite sedition ... they took the route to Versailles, having before them eight or ten drummers. The women at that time might have numbered six or seven thousand. . . .

LOUIS REFUSES TO STOP THE MARCH ON VERSAILLES. (*Mme. de Tourzel, I, 28.*)

M. de Narbonne Fritzlard, who was at that moment beside the king, begged His Majesty to give him a few troops and some guns, assuring him that he would soon rid him of this band of robbers. "It is necessary," he said, "to hold the bridges of Sèvres and Saint-Cloud. They will either abandon their project or advance by Meudon. Stationed on the heights, I will open fire on them, and I will pursue them with the cavalry in their flight in such a way that not one of them will reach Paris." The king, who always hoped by kindness to recall the wandering spirits to himself, could not make up his mind to adopt a plan which would cause bloodshed among his subjects. and he placed no obstacle in the way of this army of brigands, incapable of any other feeling than that of rage and the hope of plunder.

THE MOB REACHES VERSAILLES. (*Maillard; Bailly, III, 416–417.*)

They [the mob of women] consented to do what he [Maillard] wished. In consequence the cannon were placed behind them and the said women were invited to sing *Vive Henri IV!* while entering Versailles and to cry "Long live the King!" This they ceaselessly did in the midst of the people of this city, who awaited them, crying, "Long live our Parisiennes!" They arrived at the door of the National Assembly. . . .

After some debating among these women, fifteen were found to enter with him to the bar of the National Assembly. . . . he asked the president, M. Mounier, for permission to speak. This being accorded him, he said that two or three persons whom they had encountered on the way, and who were riding in a carriage from the court, had told him that an *abbé* attached to the Assembly had given a miller two hundred livres to stop making flour, and had promised him a like sum every week. The National Assembly vigorously demanded his name, but Maillard was unable to give it . . . The Assembly still persisting in its desire to know the name of the man denounced, M. de Robespierre, deputy from Artois, took the floor and said that . . . the Abbé Grégoire could throw some light on the subject . . . Maillard then asked for the floor and said it was also essential that they end the disorder and uncertainty which had spread through the capital upon the arrival of the regiment of Flanders in Versailles. This regiment should be sent away because the citizens feared that they would start a revolution. M. Mounier replied that they would inform the king of this in the evening when he returned from the hunt, which was where he was said to be.

(*Ferrières, I, 306.*)

Maillard and the women who accompanied him appeared to be drunk. "Where is our Comte de Mirabeau?" these women asked repeatedly. "We want to see our Comte de Mirabeau!" Some of them showed a piece of black and moldy bread and added, "We will make the Austrian [Marie Antoinette] swallow it and we will cut her throat." The number of women gradually increased. They entered pell-mell into the seats of the deputies and carried on loud conversations with those in the tribunes. Some surrounded the desk of the secretaries, others the chair of the president. They obliged the president and several of the deputies to receive their grimy and unpleasant kisses.

THE PALACE INVESTED. (*Weber, I, 431–432.*)

After the return of the king to the palace, several *gardes du corps* and other persons in service at the court, who had been searching for the king in all directions, found themselves in the grand avenue in the midst of these brigands of both sexes, and were assailed with insults and musket shots. Several balls fired at them struck the walls of the hall of the National Assembly.

The insults and indignities, together with the musket shots fired by the first column of brigands, had given just cause for uneasiness at the court. The king's guard, the regiment of Flanders, and the national guard of Versailles were ordered to take to arms. The guards at the gate closed the grills, and the king's guards, stationed outside, received orders not to touch their sabers or pistols, and to avoid everything that might irritate the people. The *gardes du corps* conformed to this order with such resignation that they could have been peaceably massacred one after the other if only their enemies had dared to attempt it.

NEGOTIATIONS WITH THE KING. (*Mme. de Tourzel, I, 29–30.*)

While the palace was invested and the brigands were scouring the town, the Assembly occupied itself in procuring the sanction to its decree of the 30th of September, the acceptation of the first articles of the constitution, and especially [the acceptation of] the declaration of the rights of man. It first of all resolved that the president should go at the head of a deputation to demand from the king the acceptance, pure and simple, of the decree. It would not listen to the representations of the king in regard to the inconvenience of his giving his sanction to isolated decrees without having seen the entire constitution; and although, in order to remove all distrust as to his intentions, he consented to give this sanction, his reservation of keeping the executive power entirely in his own hands and not expressing any opinion about the declaration of the rights of man until the constitution should be completed displeased the Assembly extremely. The latter, more intent on gaining its own ends than on the dangers incurred by the king and the royal family, insisted afresh on the acceptance, pure and simple, of the decree, and requested His Majesty to name the hour for his reception of the deputation which it would send to him on this subject. The king consented to receive it at nine o'clock in the evening.

(*Ferrières, I, 307–309.*)

A deputation of eight women was introduced into the palace. They were conducted to M. de Saint-Priest, the minister of Paris, of whom they demanded bread. "When you had only one king," dryly replied Saint-Priest, "you did not lack for bread; now that you have twelve hundred, go ask them for it." The women were then admitted to the council room; they repeated to the king the request they had proffered to M. de Saint-Priest. "You should know my benevolence," replied the king. "I am going to order that all the bread in Versailles be brought and given to you." This response appeared to satisfy these women. Most of them were there in good faith, knowing nothing of the projects of the conspirators. Forcibly dragged to Versailles, they had had it dinned into their ears that the people were dying of hunger and that the only means of ending the famine was to address themselves to the king and the National Assembly. They believed they were fulfilling the purpose of their expedition in obtaining a decree on sustenance from the Assembly, and having it sanctioned by the king. These women, enchanted with the way they had been received, left the council room, crying, "Long live the King! Long live the *gardes du corps!*"

(*Mounier, 134, 162.*)

It is false to say that I made earnest entreaties in order to obtain a simple declaration of acceptance from the hand of the king. I confined myself to announcing the decree of the National Assembly, giving reasons why one should not wait for a second deputation, and soliciting some reply or other which would allow me to return to the Assembly. I persist in maintaining that this precaution was indispensable for saving the king, and for assuring the success of whatever means might be employed. . . .

At ten o'clock, having received from the king a written agreement using the expressions exacted by the National Assembly relative to what it termed *the acceptance of the constitution*, I returned to the hall of the Assembly, where I was much surprised to see that the session had been adjourned, and that the populace occupied the seats of the deputies. Believing that on this night they ought to be in session, in order to make any decisions circumstances might require, I begged the municipal officers to proclaim by the sound of the drum that all deputies were asked to assemble. Meanwhile, hoping that I could calm the crowd by which I was surrounded, or at least remove pretexts for factiousness, I read the agreement signed by the king. I had a copy carried to M. de La Fayette in order that his army might be informed of it. I will not enter into the details of the scandalous tumult caused by the populace during my absence.[1]

LA FAYETTE COMES TO PROTECT THE KING. (La Fayette, II, 346–347.)

The numerous and armed hordes who quitted Paris on the 5th of October, and who, united with the populace of Versailles, committed the disorders of that day, were totally distinct from the immense assemblage that, blockading themselves and us, made it difficult for the news of that tumultuous departure for Versailles to reach the Hôtel de Ville. I instantly perceived that, whatever might be the consequence of this double movement, the public safety required that I should take part in it, and, after having received from the Hôtel de Ville an order and two commissaries, I hastily provided for the security of Paris, and took the road to Versailles at the head of several battalions. When we approached the hall of the Assembly, the troops renewed their oath. They only advanced after I had offered my respects to the president...

(Dumas, I, 156–157.)

The king gave orders to admit M. de La Fayette.... He was so excessively fatigued that we carried him almost into the apartments. Two commissioners from the commune of Paris, delegated to accompany the general, obtained permission to enter with him, and the king even allowed them to be introduced into the council chamber. As we passed through the Œil-de-bœuf, where a mournful silence prevailed, just as we were going into the levee-room, a knight of Saint-Louis, of tall stature, said in a loud voice, "Behold Cromwell!" La Fayette stopped and, looking at this individual, replied with composure and dignity, "He would not be here alone." We accompanied him to the door of the king's cabinet, and waited in the council chamber with some persons belonging to the palace for the end of this memorable audience.

(La Fayette, II, 347.)

...the king...having heard speeches from the commissaries and me, desired me to occupy the posts of the former French guards... at that time,

---

[1] As a great number of women demanded bread, I sent to the ushers alone an order for them to procure it, but I did not order the tavern-keeper to furnish Bologna sausages, wine, and liquors. (Note by Mounier.)

the pretension of taking possession of the palace would have appeared a most singular one. Not only the *gardes du corps* on service, but the Swiss sentinels stationed in the garden and four hundred *gardes du corps* on horseback on the side towards Trianon were not dependent in the slightest degree on me.

I certainly did not carry terror into the palace; I answered for my own troops; the result proved that I was right in doing so. I was not sufficiently master of the minds of the courtiers to believe that their security depended only on myself; for example, it was not I who sent to their own homes, in Versailles, the greatest number of the officers of the *gardes du corps*; nor was it I who sent to Rambouillet, at two o'clock in the morning (instead of employing them in forming patrols), the four hundred horse-guards placed on the side nearest to the gardens of the Trianon.

LA FAYETTE REASSURES THE KING AND ASSEMBLY. (*Weber, I, 438.*)

My uneasiness, increased by the arrival of these bands, forced me from my home, and made me run in all directions, seeking information. I saw that the multitude remained quiet enough, and I learned that the king and queen had just been reassured by the Marquis de La Fayette, who had said to them that he would answer with his head for the conduct of his soldiers; and that the royal family might consequently give itself over to repose without uneasiness.

(*Mounier, 169.*)

It was three o'clock when M. de La Fayette came to the hall to ask for me. I did not want to leave the Assembly, and begged MM. de Lally-Tollendal and Clermont-Tonnerre to report to me what he had to say. They returned to assure me, at his instance, that the intentions of the Parisian militia were good, and that the posts had been filled in a manner that should leave no inquietude. He would be responsible for everything, was even going to take some rest, and urged me to follow his example. At that I adjourned the sitting. When I had left the hall, I had from his own lips the confirmation of all that had been said to me in his name.

(*Weber, I, 441–442.*)

Leaving the hall of the Assembly, this general went to the king, to whom he said, on entering, that Paris was very quiet and that he and his troop had come to watch over the safety of the royal family and the Assembly. Following this, he conversed privately with His Majesty for a few moments; after which the president of the Assembly arrived at the palace with a cortège of deputies. The king told them that the arrival of M. de La Fayette and the promises he had just made reassured him in regard to the circumstances in which he found himself; that he thanked them for their zeal and urged them to retire. M. de La Fayette placed some soldiers of his militia as sentinels at various posts in the palace; then, having answered for the intentions of his troop and the maintenance of good order, retired towards two o'clock to the Hôtel de Noailles in order to take some repose.

This sleep of M. de La Fayette has been bitterly reproached. If nature, exhausted by the excitement and fatigues of the day, exacted a momentary repose, it was in the antechamber of the king that he should have taken it. And indeed, he should have known that the faction which had that morning put the dregs of the Parisian population on the march would in the darkness of the night attempt to put its secret designs into execution. And with this danger at hand, how could he have deserted the sacred persons of the king and queen?

(*Malouet, II, 2.*)

... it is not fair to incriminate M. de La Fayette as much as has been done. "He slept against his king!" is a cruel and terrible epigram. Twenty-four hours of fatigue and exhaustion excuse an hour of sleep, however unhappy may have been the consequences.

THE MOB IN THE PALACE. (*Mme. de Tourzel, I, 33–34.*)

The brigands did not sleep, but being sure of the national guard of Versailles, they were engaged in carrying out their own designs. A tinge of superstition, intermingled with their barbarity, which one would scarcely credit, led them at six o'clock in the morning to visit the priest of Saint-Louis, in whose parish they had passed the night, to request him to say mass for them. Scarcely was it over than one portion of the horde spread themselves through the town, forced their way into the barracks of the *gardes du corps*, and massacred everybody they found there, except a few whom they took to the palace gates in order to deliberate as to the punishment they should inflict on them. The other portion forced the gates, and rushed through the courtyards and terraces on the side of the garden with the idea of gaining an entrance into the palace. These ruffians, who encountered no obstacle, killed two of the *gardes du corps* who were on guard at the apartments of the king's aunts, and the heads were cut off by a monster in the gang, who called himself Coupe-Tête. They then went up the grand staircase, direct to the apartments of the king. The *gardes du corps*, though few in number, defended the entrance with the greatest bravery; several of them were dangerously wounded, among others MM. de Beaurepaire and de Sainte-Marie, but they had fortunately enough time to shout, "Save the queen!" Mme. Thibaut, her first lady-in-waiting, who luckily had not gone to bed, had only time to give her a dress, and make her take refuge with the king. Hardly had Her Majesty left the room than these wretches forced their way in, and furious at not finding her there, they stabbed the bed with their pikes, so as to leave no room for doubt as to the crime they intended to commit.

LA FAYETTE TO THE RESCUE. (*Mme. de Tourzel, I, 35.*)

The apartments of the king had not yet been broken into. The men of the *gardes du corps* arranged between themselves to defend, one after the other, each room of the suite where a single one of them might be, the others falling back room by room to that where the royal family were; and with the greatest courage they awaited the death which they believed to be inevitable. M. de La Fayette, whom his own neglect had placed in the most fearful position, at this juncture made the greatest efforts to induce the national guard to defend the king and rescue the *gardes du corps*. The grenadiers undertook to do so, and therefore knocked at the door of the room occupied by the *gardes du corps*, calling out that they had come as friends to defend them and save the king.

(*La Fayette, II, 349.*)

I found the apartments occupied by national guards. The king deigned never to forget the scene that ensued, when the grenadiers, with tears in their eyes, promised me to perish to the last man with him. During that time our guards were arriving; the courts were lined with national guards, and filled with a multitude in a high state of excitement. Those who heard me address the king were not dissatisfied with me.

I had long been of the opinion that the Assembly would be more quiet and the king more secure in Paris. I refused, however, to be present at the deliberation (become necessary, I own) in which the departure was decided upon; and as soon as the queen had declared her noble determination of accompanying the king, I did, before thousands of witnesses, all that could be expected from the circumstances and my devotion. It was then that, in the king's cabinet, while embraced by Madame Adelaide, I received from that respectable princess testimonies of approbation that ill prepared me for the abuse from which I have since been obliged to vindicate myself.

(*Weber, I, 450–451.*)

The people, who had given quarter to the *gardes du corps*, did not, for all that, lose sight of the principal object of their enterprise. They demanded, with shrieks, that the king come to Paris; they said that if the royal family would come to Paris to live there would be no lack of provisions. M. de La Fayette seconded this desire with all his might in the council which was then held in the presence of Their Majesties. Finally, the king, fatigued, solicited, and pressed by all, gave his word that he would depart at midday. This promise flew from mouth to mouth; the acclamations of the people and a fusillade of musketry were the results.

His Majesty appeared then for the second time on the balcony to confirm to the people the promise he had just given to M. de La Fayette. At this second appearance, the joy of the populace was unrestrained. A voice demanded "the queen on the balcony." This princess, who was never greater nor more magnanimous than at moments when danger was most imminent, unhesitatingly presented herself on the balcony, holding M. le Dauphin by one hand and Madame Royale by the other. At that a voice cried out, "No children!" The queen, by a backward movement of her arms, pushed the children back into the room, and remained alone on the balcony, folding her hands on her breast, with a countenance showing calmness, nobility, and dignity impossible to describe, and seemed thus to wait for death. This act of resignation astonished the assassins so much and inspired so much admiration in the coarse people that a general clapping of hands and cries of "Bravo! long live the Queen!" repeated on all sides, disconcerted the malevolent. I saw, however, one of these madmen aim at the queen, and his neighbor knock down the barrel of the musket with a blow of his hand, nearly massacring this brigand who was doubtless one of those who had made the irruption of the morning.

THE RETURN TO PARIS. (*Weber, I, 452–455.*)

One saw first the mass of the Parisian troops file by. Each soldier carried a loaf on the end of his bayonet. Then came the fishwives, drunk with fury, joy, and wine, holding branches of trees ornamented with ribbons, sitting astride the cannon, mounted on the horses of the *gardes du corps*, and wearing their hats. Some disported cuirasses before and behind, and others were armed with sabers and muskets. They were accompanied by the multitude of brigands and Paris laborers. . . . They halted from time to time to fire new salvos, while the fishwives descended from their horses and cannon to march around the carriage of the king. They embraced the soldiers and roared out songs to the refrain of "Here is the baker, the baker's wife, and the baker's little boy!" The horror of a cold, somber, rainy day; the infamous militia splattering through the mud; the harpies, monsters with human faces; the captive monarch and his family ignominiously dragged along surrounded by guards; all formed such a frightful spectacle, such a mixture of shame and anguish, that to this very day I cannot think of it without my senses being completely overwhelmed.

At times the queen was in a state of passive endurance difficult to describe. Her son was on her knees; he suffered hunger and asked for food. Unable to fulfill his desires, Marie Antoinette pressed him to her heart, weeping. She exhorted him to suffer in silence. The young prince became resigned.

(*Weber, I, 456–457.*)

As soon as the royal family entered the Hôtel de Ville, the king had to listen to two harangues by M. Bailly, and to denunciations against his ministers. Then an official report of the sitting was drawn up and publicly read by M. Bailly. But as it cited some words of the king's discourse inexactly, the queen interrupted him with that presence of mind which was one of the fine traits of her character. He had forgotten one of the most touching parts of the discourse of the king. The queen recalled to him gracefully that His Majesty had said, "I have relied upon the attachment and fidelity of my people, and have placed myself in the midst of my subjects with complete confidence." . . .

After this the family re-entered the carriage in the midst of acclamations and betook themselves, with a part of the national guard, to the palace of the Tuileries. Monsieur and Madame went to the Luxembourg.

(*Mounier, 193–194.*)

The Comte de Mirabeau announced [to the Assembly] that the king was about to depart for Paris. In eagerness to hold their sessions in the midst of the tumult of the capital, they declared themselves inseparable from the monarch, and carried to him this declaration as a proof of their zeal for his interests. In reality, it was an express approbation of the violation of his liberty.

ACCUSATIONS OF CONSPIRACY. (*Mounier, 329–330.*)

The magistrates of the Châtelet, in judging the information gathered in regard to the assassinations of the 6th of October, declared that the Duc d'Orléans and the Comte de Mirabeau appeared to be open to indictment. At the session of August 7, they presented the case to the National Assembly. They announced that witnesses had brought accusations against some of its members, and that these members would deem it honorable, no doubt, to descend into the arena of justice, there to manifest their innocence. They added that the Assembly had made it impossible to bring them to trial, and that they awaited its decision. [The National Assembly declared that there was no ground for accusation against the Duc d'Orléans or the Comte de Mirabeau.]

(*Paroy, 130–131.*)

M. de La Fayette requested of the Duc d'Orléans a rendezvous at M. de Coigny's and spoke to him thus: "Prince, France and the king have equal need of peace, and your presence here seems to be an obstacle to it; they abuse your name to lead the people astray and excite disorder. You have connections in England; you could there serve your country and immediately remove all pretext from the disturbers of public peace." After this interview, M. le Duc d'Orléans decided to depart, but, to veil the real motive of his departure, the king offered him a special mission. M. le Duc d'Orléans went to take leave of His Majesty, who received him coldly. Mirabeau, having learned of his departure, cried, "He is not worth the trouble taken for him!" This statement was taken up and made public.

THE QUEEN REFUSES TO AID IN THE PROSECUTION. (*Mme. de Tourzel, I, 99–100.*)

Ever great and noble, this princess compelled respect even from those who were most disposed to fail in it. The commune of Paris, when enquiring into the occurrences of the 5th and 6th of October, their instigators and adherents, sent a deputation to the queen to beg her to throw some light upon those fearful days. "No," she replied, "I will never be the accuser of the subjects of the king." Her reply to the deputation from the Châtelet on the same subject was no less noble. "I have seen all, known all, forgotten all." And she confined her reply to these splendid words.

X. The Assembly at Work

THE ASSEMBLY HOLDS ITS SESSIONS IN PARIS. (*Weber, II, 9–10.*)

THE National Assembly removed itself to Paris on the 19th of October. It held its sessions there, for twenty days, at the archiepiscopal palace, until the riding-school of the Tuileries, which it had chosen, should be ready to receive it. (This choice was the object of many pleasantries, and gave rise to several pamphlets, among which there was one in three parts, entitled *The Horses in the Riding School.* . . . Thus Mirabeau, under the name of *Pétulant,* is represented as "vicious and holding nothing sacred"; the Abbé Maury as "disgracefully famous through low complaisance and corrupt favors"; the Abbé M—— as "an ambitious man whose progress was always tortuous and ambiguous"; D'Esprémesnil as a "fanatic"; the Chevalier de Boufflers as a "zero"; and finally Cazalès, to whom his enemies could not deny great talents, offers, according to the author, "an adulterated mixture of philosophy and pusillanimity, of eloquence and garrulity, of rigidity and flexibility of principles, of pride and vulgarity.")

(*Mme. de Staël, 183.*)

The Constituent Assembly had been mistress of the fate of France from the 14th of July to the 5th of October, 1789, but after the latter date was itself controlled by popular violence.

DEPUTIES LEAVE THE ASSEMBLY. (*Weber, II, 3.*)

At this epoch a large number of deputies left the National Assembly and even France. Among the latter were M. Mounier and M. Lally-Tollendal, who subsequently, in a very energetic manner, expressed their indignation in regard to the crimes of the 6th of October. M. Bergasse retired also.

(*Letter of Lally-Tollendal to one of his friends, setting forth the motives for his withdrawal from the Assembly.*)

Let us discuss the decision I have taken. My conscience tells me it is well justified. Neither this reprehensible city, nor this still more culpable Assembly deserves an explanation; but I have set my heart upon preventing you, and people who think as you do, from condemning me. My health, I swear, renders my services impossible; but, even without that, it was beyond my forces to endure the horror caused by the blood, the heads, the queen almost murdered, and the king led into Paris as a slave, surrounded by assassins and preceded by the heads of his unhappy guards. Then there were the perfidious janissaries, the murderers, the cannibal women, and the cry of "All bishops to the lamp-post!" at the moment when the king entered his capital with two bishops of his council in his carriage. I saw the musket-shot fired into one of the queen's carriages. M. Bailly called this a great day; while the Assembly declared coldly that morning that it was not suited to its dignity to go in a body to rally around the king. M. Mirabeau was impudently saying in the Assembly that the ship of state, far from being arrested in its course, would be launched more rapidly than ever towards its regeneration. M. Barnave laughed with him when streams of blood flowed around us, the virtuous Mounier escaping by a miracle from twenty assassins who wanted to make of his head one more trophy.

This is what made me swear never again to put foot into that cavern of anthropophagi (the National Assembly), where I no longer had the strength to lift my voice; where for six weeks I had lifted it in vain, I, Mounier, and all honorable men. A last attempt at right was to leave it. I had no thought of fear; I blush to defend myself from such an accusation. Moreover, from people on the road, less guilty than those who aroused them to fury, I have received acclamations and applause which would have flattered others, but which made me shudder. It was on account of indignation, horror, and physical convulsions at the sight of blood that I yielded. One braves a single death, or braves it a number of times if necessary; but no power under heaven, no sentiment, public or private, had the right to condemn me to suffer uselessly a thousand tortures a minute and perish of rage and despair amidst the triumph of crimes which I could not prevent. They will proscribe me, they will confiscate my goods; I will go back to the soil and see them no more. . . . This is my justification; you may read it, show it, hand out copies; so much the worse for those who cannot understand it; it will be my fault for having given it to them.

THE ELEMENTS OF THE ASSEMBLY. *(Ferrières, II, 122–124; Thiers, I, 122–123.)*

In the National Assembly there were not more than about three hundred really upright men, exempt from party spirit, not belonging to any club, wishing what was right, wishing it for its own sake, independent of the interests of orders or of bodies, always ready to embrace the most just and beneficial proposals, no matter from what quarter they came or by whom they were supported. These were men worthy of the honorable function to which they had been called, and they were the ones who made the few good laws that proceeded from the Constituent Assembly. It was they who prevented all the mischief which it did not do. Invariably adopting what was good and invariably opposing what was bad, they have frequently produced a majority in favor of resolutions which but for them would have been rejected from a spirit of faction; and they have often defeated motions which but for them would have been adopted from a spirit of interest.

While on this subject I cannot abstain from remarking on the impolitic conduct of the nobles and bishops. As they aimed only at dissolving the Assembly and throwing discredit on its operations, instead of opposing mischievous measures, they manifested an indifference on this point which is inconceivable. When the president stated the question they quitted the hall, inviting the deputies of their party to follow them, or, if they stayed, called out to them to take no part in the deliberations. The Clubbists, having a majority in the Assembly through this dereliction, carried whatever resolutions they pleased. The bishops and nobles, firmly believing that the new order of things would not last, hastened with a sort of impatience the ruin of the monarchy and themselves, as if determined to accelerate the downfall. With this senseless conduct they combined an insulting disdain of both the Assembly and the people who attended the sittings. Instead of listening, they laughed and talked aloud, thus confirming the people in the unfavorable opinion which it had conceived of them, and, instead of striving to recover its confidence and its esteem, they strove only to gain its hatred and its contempt. All these follies arose solely from the mistaken notions of the bishops and nobles, who could not persuade themselves that the Revolution had long been effected in the mind and heart of every Frenchman. They hoped, by means of these dikes, to set bounds to a torrent which was daily swelling. All they did served only to produce a greater accumulation of its waters, and occasion greater ravages. They obstinately clung to the old system, which was repudiated by all, as the basis of all their actions and of all their opposition. By this impolitic obstinacy they forced the revolutionists to carry the Revolution beyond the goal which they had set up. The nobles and bishops then exclaimed against injustice and tyranny. They talked of the antiquity and the legitimacy of their rights to men who had sapped the foundation of all rights.

SIÉYÈS THE ORACLE OF THE ASSEMBLY. (Mme. de Staël, 160–161.)

On the first row of the popular side one noticed the Abbé Siéyès, isolated by his character, although surrounded by admirers of his wisdom. He had led, up to the age of forty, a solitary life, reflecting upon political questions, and carrying great proficiency in abstraction into this study; but he was little fitted to communicate with others, being so easily irritated by their peculiarities, and wounding them with his. Yet, as he had a superior mind and laconic and trenchant ways of expressing himself, it was the custom in the Assembly to show him an almost superstitious respect. Mirabeau was willing to give the silence of the Abbé Siéyès precedence over his own eloquence, for this kind of rivalry is not redoubtable. One believed that Siéyès, that man of mystery, knew the secrets of constitutions, from which were expected astonishing effects when he should reveal them. Many young people, even those of mature mind, professed the greatest admiration for him and joined in praising him above all others. This arose from the fact that he never committed himself entirely on any question.

ROBESPIERRE. (Ferrières, I, 342–343.)

This man, who has since played such an important rôle, was then known only for his extravagant opinions and his tendency to exaggerate suspicions, actions, and dangers. He was somber, mournful, suspicious, irascible, vindictive, considering events only in relation to himself. Sober, laborious, and austere in his habits, he nevertheless dressed and powdered with immaculate elegance. His face had something of the cat and of the tiger about it. His movements were uneven and precipitate. He turned furious glances upon those he disliked, but averted his eyes uneasily when someone looked at him. The least danger frightened him, and he would hasten to hide himself. The danger past, he reappeared with insolent assurance, becoming increasingly violent in his discourses in proportion to the cowardliness he had shown in his actions. Jealous of all wealth, elevation, and merit, he represented his hatred of the noble, the wealthy, and the successful as hatred of tyranny and love of equality.

MIRABEAU. (Ferrières, I, 92–93.)

Mirabeau never entirely rid himself of the prejudices and habits of his childhood; he always held for the nobility and the monarchy. "Do you think," said he to some nobles, "that if I had been a deputy for the nobility it would have succumbed so promptly?" Mirabeau showed himself an enemy of the ministers, yet he was the most zealous defender of the ministry! His hatred of despotism did not extend to royalty, for he expected more of kings than he expected of the people; and places in the government did not seem desirable to him unless they conferred great power, and led to great riches.

To the natural talents which make great orators, Mirabeau added a careful study of the art of oratory. He knew that the man of genius appeals more to the feelings than to reason; therefore his gestures, his look, and the sound of his voice were all based upon a profound knowledge of the human heart. His eloquence, rude and savage, but animated and rapid, filled with bold metaphors and striking images, dominated the deliberations of the Assembly. His style was hard and harsh, yet expressive, voluble, and inflated with sonorous words. It resembled a heavy hammer in the hands of a clever artist, and brought beneath his will men whom it was not a question of convincing, but of stunning and subjugating. Mirabeau inspired in them all kinds of ideas, actions, and passions.

(Bailly, I, 303.)

It cannot be denied that Mirabeau was the moving force in the National Assembly.... The principal characteristic of Mirabeau was audacity It reinforced his talents, directed their employment, and developed their force. But whatever may have been his moral character, when he was aroused by some eventuality, his mind became ennobled and refined, and his genius then rose to the heights of courage and virtue.

(*Mme. de Staël, 138.*)

He was more intellectual than talented, and it was only with an effort that he ever improvised at the rostrum. This same inaptness for composition made him have recourse to the aid of his friends in all of his works. Nevertheless, none of them after his death could have written what he had inspired them to write. He said, in speaking of the Abbé Maury, "When he is right, we argue; when he is wrong, I crush him"; but this was because the Abbé Maury often defended even good causes with that kind of facility which does not come from the emotional depths of the soul.

MIRABEAU AND THE MINISTRY. (*Weber, II, 6–7.*)

From this moment [of his departure for England] many friends of the Duc d'Orléans, seeing how little he could be counted upon, desired to turn again towards the court. Mirabeau was not last in expressing a wish to be useful to the king in return for pecuniary and honorary emoluments. This negotiation between Mirabeau and the court would have been concluded much sooner than it was if the National Assembly had not obstinately rejected all measures proposed by Mirabeau when it was suspected that these measures tended to introduce him into the king's council.

The queen, having seen Mirabeau abandon the Duc d'Orléans after the latter's departure for England, thought with reason that nothing should be neglected in making sure of this energetic and influential man and preventing him from going over to the parties which were being formed from the débris of the Orleanist party. M. de La Fayette, who well knew the poor opinion Mirabeau had of him, as well as of M. Necker, opposed him constantly at this epoch. He contented himself with having him given by an intermediary some money under the form of a loan, while he himself retained the functions of principal adviser, governor, and commander-in-chief of the royal family during its sojourn in the Tuileries.

(*Morris, I, 333.*)

La Fayette has committed a great blunder in opening himself to Mirabeau. If he employs him it will be disgraceful; and if he neglects him it will be dangerous, because every conversation gives him rights and means.

(*Ferrières, I, 361–364.*)

The Comte de Mirabeau was, of all the men attached to the Duc d'Orléans, the one that the court was most interested in winning over. It was not enough to cater to his avarice; it was necessary to cater to his ambition. He was promised a place in the ministry. Mirabeau felt that in this precarious position he bore the hate even of those who had called him to the ministry. He would need in the council the influence he derived from being a deputy in the Assembly. He desired, before accepting, to make sure of this influence by retaining the right to take part in the meetings. There he could discuss measures under consideration. He was determined not to sacrifice the established and inviolable position of a deputy to the vainglory and precarious advantage of a post more brilliant than substantial, which had perhaps been offered to him solely to ruin him and strip him of his popularity.

The keeper of the seals, Champion, informed the Lameths of this intrigue. Soon a vague rumor began to spread that Mirabeau was going to be minister. This was equally alarming to aristocrats and revolutionaries. The Lameths, Grillons, and Noailles stirred up the deputies of the commons. They represented to them that if Mirabeau united the position of minister with the ascendancy which his great talent and popularity gave him in parliamentary deliberations he would dominate the Assembly and the most conspicuous deputies would no longer have any influence. "And who knows," added the Lameths, "whether Mirabeau, who is always led by personal interest, will not unite with the nobility and clergy to overthrow the constitution which obstructs his new plans? Not only must Mirabeau not be minister, but none of the ambitious men the court is trying to corrupt must receive the rewards of their treason. Thus only may your purity be conserved and the plots foiled which your enemies are ceaselessly concocting against you."

The Assembly had asked the ministers for information about the state of provisions in Paris, and the best means of putting an end to the factitious famine that worried the people. The ministers replied with vague complainings. They experienced ever-recurring obstacles, the people refused to obey, disorder and anarchy were widespread, royal authority was powerless. The ministry had the complete confidence of the Assembly in the measures they might take to arrest these evils, but it was necessary to discuss with the Assembly the measures as a whole. Mirabeau seized upon this favorable opportunity to obtain the decree he desired. He proposed that ministers be admitted to the Assembly in order to discuss and explain the aims of the administration. A general outcry against this proposition arose, the fight being led by Barnave and Alexandre Lameth. Mirabeau vainly employed all the resources of his eloquence to demonstrate its advantages. It was not a matter of public concern that most of the deputies saw in this important question. They saw only Mirabeau. The nobles attached to the old régime and those attached to the Revolution alike desired his exclusion from the ministry. Adrien Duport reproached the ministers for their ambitious ideas, spoke of the necessity of opposing a law to personal interest, and demanded that no member of that Assembly be allowed to accept any place in the government during the session. This proposition was taken under consideration and the decree to this effect passed almost unanimously.

MIRABEAU'S SPEECH ON EXCLUSION FROM THE MINISTRY.

I can see, gentlemen, how it might be advantageous to exclude a particular member of the Assembly from the ministry.

But since it would be unwise to sacrifice a great principle for this one particular advantage, I propose an amendment which will limit the exclusion from the ministry to the members of the Assembly whom the author of the motion appears to dread, and charge myself with making them known to you.

There are, gentlemen, but two persons in the Assembly against whom this motion could be secretly aimed. The others have given sufficient proofs of liberalism, courage, and public spirit to satisfy the honorable deputy. But there are two members concerning whom he and I can speak more freely, whose exclusion depends upon him and upon me, and his motion must certainly relate to one of the two.

Who are these members? You have already guessed, gentlemen; they are the author of the motion and myself. . . .

Here then, gentlemen, is the motion that I propose: the exclusion demanded shall be limited to M. de Mirabeau, deputy of the commons of the *sénéchaussée* of Aix.

I shall consider myself very fortunate if, as the price of my exclusion, I can conserve to this Assembly the hope of seeing some of its members, worthy of all confidence and respect, become the intimate counsellors of the nation and the king, always regarded by me as indivisible.

NEW CONSTITUTIONAL MEASURES. (*Ferrières, I, 364–365.*)

While engaged in these special proceedings, the revolutionists were making great progress with the new constitution. It was a matter of achieving the destruction of the old government, and to that end abolishing the provincial estates, the corporations, and the tribunals; depriving the monarch of the power of appointment, transmitting it to the people, and excluding the nobles, priests, and men opposed to the Revolution; withdrawing all powers and creating new ones which would have only fictitious and honorary connections with the monarch; pitting these powers against one another, so that through war or anarchy they would be forced to have recourse to the Assembly; arming these powers against the monarch, so that, hemmed in on all sides and enervated in a continual struggle, he could neither direct nor restrain them; and placing the Assembly between the government and the monarch, so that it might use first one and then the other in order to dominate both.

LOUIS MADE KING OF THE FRENCH. (*Paroy, 128.*)

There was a long debate on the title, *King of the French*, because the customary qualification, *King of France*, meant that he could dispose of the territory of France as he wished, and it was therefore thought necessary to follow the ancient formula of *Francorum Rex*. Wild applause resounded through the hall, with repeated acclamations in honor of the King of the French. If I emphasize these details . . . it is because I was a witness when all the royal family and the court were particularly occupied with them.

FRANCE DIVIDED INTO DEPARTMENTS. (*Ferrières, I, 365–366.*)

The Abbé Siéyès conceived a plan which seemed fitted to reconcile the views of the revolutionists. Thouret took charge of presenting it. It was a new divisioning of France, which destroyed the boundaries of the provinces, changed their names, and confounded them in a homogeneous whole. This led without effort to the government of the people which the revolutionists wished to substitute for monarchial government. By this plan France was parcelled into ninety-three departments, about equal in size and population. Each had a separate administration composed of an administrative council of thirty-six members and of a constantly active directory charged with the general administration of the department. The department was divided into districts, each composed of an administrative council of twelve members and of a directory of five charged with the general administration of the district. Decisions, in order to be authentic, had to be approved by the department. Each district was partitioned into cantons of six or seven parishes. The cantons had no jurisdiction, except that in elections they assembled the citizens of the parishes at the headquarters of their districts. Each department had a criminal tribunal, each district a civil tribunal, and each canton a *tribunal de paix*.

COMMUNES ESTABLISHED. (*Ferrières, I, 366–369.*)

The revolutionists established in each parish, to which they gave the name of *commune* (with a view, in changing names, more surely to change things), a municipal body in which they invested great powers. What distinguishes the municipalities from the other constituted authorities is that the people choose the municipal officials directly, while the administrative officials of the department, those of the district, and the judges of the tribunals are named by a certain number of electors chosen for that purpose by the primary assemblies. The reason for this difference is simple. The revolutionists, in desiring to replace the exercise of public authority in the hands of the municipalities, realized that the choosing of municipal officers was the most important. . . .

To these were confided the administration of property and common revenues in cities, towns, parishes, and communities. They were charged with regulating and paying local expenditures, with directing and providing for the execution of public works, with administering the establishments belonging to the commune, with looking after sanitation and health, and with keeping order in the public streets, squares, and buildings. They assessed direct taxes among the people, providing for their collection and their deposit in the treasuries. They were given direct control of enterprises, public investments, general and special police, spectacles, and inspection of the repairing and reconstruction of churches, parsonages, and other religious possessions. But the most important right, and the one that gave it real power, was that of commanding the state forces, thus preventing the national guards and troops of the line from acting except as they desired. In consequence they directed the forces which the Assembly retained in its hands, while paralyzing, when they saw fit, those which the Assembly was constrained to leave at the disposition of the monarch.

THE QUALIFICATIONS OF VOTERS. (*Ferrières, I, 369.*)

The revolutionists classed all Frenchmen as active or inactive citizens. Only active citizens were allowed to take part in the elections. The tax qualification for the exercise of the rights of an active citizen was very low, since it suffered to pay a direct tax equivalent to the sum of three days' wages, estimated at forty-five sols. Nevertheless, many deputies protested against this demarcation as contrary to the equality recognized and proclaimed by the declaration of the rights of man.

ELECTIVE JUDGES. (*Ferrières, II, 45.*)

Should judges be elected by the people or should they be appointed by the king? The election of judges accorded too well with the principles of the Assembly to cause much uncertainty. It was decreed.

SUPPRESSION OF THE PARLEMENTS. (*Ferrières, I, 358–359.*)

A more immediate danger menaced the revolutionists; it was the return of the *parlements*. These bodies, almost as old as the monarchy, continued to receive great consideration, in spite of intrigues and calumnies employed against them. The people were accustomed to respect in them the majesty of the law. They might become a center around which to rally the king, princes, dukes, nobility, clergy, and all Frenchmen who were attached to the monarch and the monarchy. After the *parlements* had once assembled, it would perhaps have been too late to think of attacking them. And with a capricious and changeable people, what might the uniform, wise, and moderate conduct of these magistrates not have accomplished in comparison with the scandalous and turbulent scenes created each day by the deputies of the Assembly?

The revolutionists, according to their practice of using members of the body they wished to destroy to strike that body more telling blows, charged Adrien Duport, a councillor of *parlement*, to demand the dissolution of all the *parlements* of the kingdom. . . . The motion of Duport, supported by the revolutionists and combatted with equal warmth by the opposing party, was decreed.

PROTESTS OF THE CLERGY AND PARLEMENTS. (*Ferrières, I, 370.*)

The bishops, in their mandates, deplored the ruin of religion, thundered against the impious usurpations of the Assembly, and called upon the people to revolt. The estates of Languedoc and Brittany assembled and protested against the division of their provinces into departments. The *parlements* of Rouen, Bordeaux, Metz, and Toulouse drew up resolutions in which they laid before the king their fears in regard to innovations so contrary to the rights of the monarch and his subjects. They declared that they could not obey the decree suppressing the ancient tribunals so essentially connected with the existence of the monarchy. At the same time a multitude of journals and pamphlets subsidized by the ministry exaggerated the inconveniences of the new constitution and the impossibility of making it work.

WEAKNESS OF THE MINISTRY. (*Ferrières, I, 371–372.*)

By their weakness and disunion the ministers contributed to the progress made by the revolutionists. Instead of stemming the torrent which threatened to engulf everything, they waited for it to arrest itself. When they perceived that it was going to overwhelm them as well as the monarch, far from rallying all interests around them and fighting the revolutionists with frankness, courage, and activity, they resorted to the pettiest of means and intrigues. They did not try to rebuild the bases of a government falling to pieces. On the contrary, they fomented disorders and propagated anarchy, believing that the people would through discouragement voluntarily resume their chains.

THE FOUNDING OF THE JACOBIN CLUB. *(Bailly, I, 260–261.)*

An association ... was formed among the deputies of Brittany. It was known at Versailles under the name of the Breton Committee; it became the origin and source of the Jacobins. All those who were not in it at that time disapproved of it. The Bretons were excellent patriots, but ardent and extreme. I do not doubt but that it was here that the desire for liberty brought forth the first projects for a republic and caused their deplorable scission from those who desired the monarchy, a division that has caused so many evils.

(Larevellière-Lépeaux, I, 85–86.)

Before finishing with the Constituent Assembly, I will say two words about the Jacobin Club. This instrument of revolution, terrible in its later actions, owed its origin neither to the Breton Club nor to a particular faction, as is commonly believed. The Breton Club had not survived our removal from Versailles to Paris. But after this epoch the aristocratic party usually named the committees, because they had meetings where they agreed on those they were going to support. It was then that the Franche-Comté deputies, the Angevin deputies like Leclerc, Pilastre, and myself, and several other representatives, upright and well-intentioned men, thought of having meetings on our part to assure the committees to the patriots. They chose for that purpose a low room of the old convent of the Jacobins, Rue Saint-Honoré, in which, it was said, were held the first meetings of the League. Our first meeting took place one Sunday morning. We numbered only fifteen or twenty deputies. At first no strangers were admitted. But soon the Lameths and their friends were there in force and introduced a crowd of intriguers and climbers. The latter were at first their instruments, then, pushing their views still farther, they depopularized them, only to be depopularized in their turn. Finally, in order to remedy such a disappointment as much as possible, they tried to break up the Jacobins by founding another club at the Feuillants, composed, in addition to other elements, of all the members of the Jacobins they could get to desert. It was a man named Gilles, former *chef d'office* of M. de Conti or M. d'Orléans, who had charge of this operation. However, the Feuillant Club did not prosper, and the Jacobins merely became more violent than ever. Their club was soon a den of wild beasts, which ruined the cause of liberty with its frenzies. I attest that long before this happened my friends and I had ceased to put foot in this frightful lair.

(*Ferrières, II, 118.*)

The revolutionists, realizing how advantageously they could use this organization to dominate Paris and the Assembly and extend their influence over the provinces, did not limit their membership to a few constituted authorities. They admitted all sorts of people, exacting no other qualifications than blind submission to the will of the chiefs and entire devotion to revolutionary principles. The new club soon had more than twelve hundred members, among whom were a number of journalists, all agents of the Orléans faction, and a throng of foreigners who had been driven out of their own countries. To these people without principles revolutions were a patrimony.

The Jacobin Club, imitating the overpopulated nations of ancient times, sent out colonies to the principal cities of the kingdom, all in affiliation with Paris.... The Jacobin Club was ruled by Barnave and the two Lameths. Robespierre, Pétion, Antoine, Salle, and Dumets, all heads of factions but following the same interests and acting in concert, supported impatiently the yoke of the Lameths. They were also jealous of the popularity of Barnave, and watched for an occasion to deprive him of it.

THE CLUB OF '89. (Ferrières, II, 119–121.)

The Club of '89, so called from the year of its foundation,[1] was composed of deputies who desired a moderate constitutional monarchy such as that proposed by the Assembly's committee on the constitution. Their efforts were directed only towards the establishment of this constitution, and the protecting of it against the enterprises of the court, the nobles, and the priests. They hoped that Louis XVI, born without ambition, content with the advantages reserved to him by the new government, accustomed to possessing only the shadow of royalty, and used to being led by the queen and his ministers, would unite with them and adopt the constitution in good faith. This hope was founded on their knowledge of the character of Louis XVI; consequently, the members of the Club of '89 did not attribute to this prince the obstacles which they encountered, and they were right. Louis XVI, left to himself, would have yielded to circumstances. This belief, although common to the greater part of the members of the Club of '89, was not, however, general. Some would have preferred a republic; but the fear that the fall of Louis XVI would bring, instead of a republic, anarchy or the Duc d'Orléans kept them attached to the constitutional monarchy.

La Fayette, Bailly, Roederer, Dupont de Nemours, Chapelier, the Duc de La Rochefoucauld, and Siéyès, leaders in the Club of '89, were originally members of the Jacobin Club. They became fatigued by the noise of the sittings, by the irrationality of the orators, and by the necessity of obtaining and holding popular favor, a necessity which forces an honest man to dissimulate his thoughts and, if he wishes to command, to obey all the caprices of an ignorant and uncouth multitude. They ceased little by little to attend the meetings of the Jacobins, and came to establish themselves at the Palais-

---

[1] This club did not open, however, until April 12, 1790. (Berville and Barrière.)

Royal in a superb apartment, with all the pomp and bustle proper for attracting and impressing the multitude.

The Club of '89 had also a great number of champions who were philosophers, academicians, financiers, capitalists, and men of letters. There were Condorcet, Marmontel, Champfort, Clavière, and Duroveray. It counted among its members the principal leaders of the committees and the most' noted men of the majority of the Assembly. . . . They discussed political matters here as they did at the Jacobins'; but they discussed them with decency. Moreover, they gave excellent dinners; papers on public affairs were read. . . . For the rest, they all intrigued for popular favor, and, like the Jacobins, employed speeches and deputations to obtain it. For they also sought to deceive the people and persuade them that they were actuated only by a passion for the public welfare, when in reality they were only animated by a spirit of self-interest and a desire for domination. If the conquerors of the Bastille came to felicitate the Jacobins on their energy, the women of the market-place arrived at the same moment at the Club of '89 and addressed a fine compliment to the genius of M. Bailly. They did not forget the good General La Fayette, the great Mirabeau who said such beautiful things in the Assembly, or M. Chapelier who, without ceasing to be a good Breton, had become a good Parisian.

The Comte de Mirabeau, hated but feared and sought after by the leaders of the two clubs, tipped the balance towards one or the other whenever he united with the Jacobins or with the Club of '89. He did not possess the confidence of any of the leaders, but they employed him to carry out their secret resolutions; for the Jacobins and the Club of '89 had each a committee in which were discussed and decided the different projects relative to the Revolution, before they brought them to the general assembly of the club and thus submitted them to public opinion.

ADMINISTRATION NEGLECTED FOR CONSTITUTIONAL QUESTIONS. (Mme. de Staël, 163–164.)

The functioning of the executive power was impeded by various decrees of the Assembly; the ministers were not allowed to act without first securing its authorization. Taxes were no longer being paid, because the people believed that a revolution so greatly fêted ought at least to bring them the joy of paying nothing. Credit, wiser than public opinion, although appearing to depend upon it, took fright at the faults committed by the Assembly. The Assembly controlled more than sufficient resources to arrange the finances and facilitate the purchase of grain which was becoming necessary on account of the famine which again threatened France. But the Assembly had responded negligently to the reiterated solicitations of M. Necker on this subject, because it did not wish to be considered as having assembled only to consider finances like the old States-General. It was in constitutional discussions that it took the greatest interest. In this it was right; but in neglecting questions of administration it provoked disorder in the kingdom and, through disorder, all the misfortunes which it has experienced.

XI. *Nationalization of the Church*

THE CONFISCATION OF CHURCH PROPERTY PROPOSED. (Ferrières, I, 193–194; 347–348.)

THE Marquis de La Coste affirmed that a people bowed down with poverty could not furnish the succor of which the state had need; but that there was an expedient, and it was for the Assembly to weigh this in its wisdom. "Declare, gentlemen, that ecclesiastical property belongs to the nation; give to the incumbents a revenue for life equal to that which they now enjoy; increase the dotation of the parish priests; fix the incomes of the bishops and destroy the monastic orders: you will immediately find immense sums capable of filling the void in the treasury and fulfilling the engagements of the state." ...

The revolutionists reverted to the great project of despoiling the clergy. The Bishop of Autun [Talleyrand] reproduced the forgotten motion of the Marquis de La Coste. He proposed declaring that all ecclesiastical property belonged to the nation, with the obligation of providing the revenues necessary to the maintenance of the church and the clergy: no priest should receive less than twelve hundred livres above living expenses; the nation should take upon itself the payment of the ecclesiastics, take charge of hospitals and schools, and thus carry out the intentions of the founders. The Bishop of Autun, entering after that into the details of his plan, said that eighty millions would be appropriated to the ministers of the Catholic cult; that the nation would pay the debts of the clergy; that the landed property, put on sale, would produce a capital of two billion one hundred millions; that the public debt being at two hundred and twenty-four millions, one hundred and thirty-one would be reimbursed, and the state would be liquidated.

MIRABEAU SPEAKS IN FAVOR OF CONFISCATING CHURCH PROPERTY.

This will I say: never has the navy appropriated the vessels that the people have constructed for the defense of the state; never, according to our present customs, does an army partition among the soldiers the countries that it has conquered. Shall it be true of the clergy alone, that the conquests of its piety through the devotion of the faithful are to belong to it and remain inviolable, instead of forming a part of the indivisible domain of the state?

Then, if I wished to envisage this important question in its connections with the new constitution of the kingdom, with moral principles, and with those of political economy, I should first determine whether, in the new order of things which we have just established, it is suitable for the government, as distributor of all ecclesiastical wealth through the nomination of incumbents, to perpetuate in that alone countless possibilities for action, corruption, and influence.

I would ask if, in the interests of religion and public morals themselves, those two benefactors of the human race, it is not important that a more equal distribution of the wealth of the church be opposed henceforth to the luxury of those who are only the dispensers of the goods of the poor, and to the license of those whom religion and society hold up to the people as living examples of purity.

My object has not been to show that the clergy ought to be despoiled of its wealth, nor that other persons ought, nor that other possessors should take their place.

What then, gentlemen, have I tried to show? A single thing: that the principle is and ought to be that the entire nation is the sole and veritable owner of the property of the clergy. I have only asked you to consecrate that principle, because there are errors or truths which are the ruin or salvation of nations.

ATTACKS ON THE CLERGY. (*Ferrières, I, 350–351.*)

The calculations had been made; they wanted the property of the clergy at any cost ... they worked to render the priests odious and despicable: they substituted the name *calottin* for that of ecclesiastic: men were hired to spread exaggerations about the riches of the clergy, representing them as the only means of avoiding bankruptcy. They did not forget the morals of the priests, the pomp and pride of the bishops, the incontinency and drunkenness of the monks, the soft and voluptuous lives of the abbots. A multitude of writings and pamphlets succeeded one another. Some, with an appearance of depth and reason, set forth the pretended rights of the nation over the wealth of the clergy; others, savagely ironical, deluged the ecclesiastics with hate and contempt. They played *Charles IX* at the Théâtre Français: everything, in this tragedy, was done in the name of religion, although history teaches us that all was the result of politics.

THE DECREE OF CONFISCATION VOTED. (*Ferrières, I, 354–355.*)

However, opinion fluctuated uncertainly   The Comte de Mirabeau perceived this wavering, and realizing the influence the substitution of a word has upon vacillating minds [spoke as follows]: "M. le Président, I see that this sentence in the decree: *The wealth of the clergy belongs to the nation*, in having different meanings for different minds, retards the discussion. I ask that it read: *The wealth of the clergy is at the disposition of the nation*." The revolutionists and capitalists seized upon this happy amendment with delight, and cried for a vote on the proposition. The bishops and nobles, discerning the perfidious ingenuity of the Comte de Mirabeau, demanded the former wording. This was in vain; the revolutionists sustained the phraseology of Mirabeau. A large number of deputies who were reluctant to dispossess the clergy openly, not seeing or feigning not to see the consequences which would be entailed by the principle that they were about to consecrate, joined the revolutionists. The decree passed by a large majority.

THE ASSIGNATS. (*Ferrières, I, 404–405.*)

Montesquiou proposed not to permit any anticipation, bonding, or transfer of the revenues of 1791; to form a capital of four hundred millions from the domains of the crown and the property of the clergy free from all public service; to order its deposit in a special treasury; to authorize the controller of this to issue assignats for a like sum carrying three per cent interest; to reimburse, with these assignats, the one hundred and seventy millions due to the discounting bank; and to place in the public treasury one hundred and thirty-two millions for use in the current year. The proposal of Montesquiou became the basis of discussion: but a preliminary measure was necessary; it was that of getting from the clergy at least the value of the funds which were to serve as a basis for the four hundred million assignats. They cast their eyes upon the municipalities; and, with the view of engaging them to fulfill promptly the obligations that they wished them to contract, it was decreed that they could subscribe for unlimited amounts, which would be estimated by experts and transferred on the condition that they be resold to individuals. To reimburse the municipalities for the cost of the appraising, they were to be allowed a sixth on the profits of the sale. The municipality of Paris appeared first at the bar, headed by the mayor, Bailly: it subscribed for two hundred millions of the clergy's property, located in the department of Paris. The municipalities of the large cities followed the example of the municipality of Paris.

THE KING ACCEPTS THE CONSTITUTION. (*Weber, II, 19.*)

The king having promised to maintain the constitution, it was decreed forthwith that no one should enter upon a public function without having taken the civic oath, worded as follows: "I swear to be faithful to the nation, the law, and the king, and to maintain with all my power the constitution decreed by the National Assembly and accepted by the king." Then began the long-drawn-out comedy of taking oaths which have been so often renewed and violated since, and which do not yet seem to approach their end. All the members of the National Assembly took this oath one after another, with the exception of the Vicomte de Mirabeau, three other members of the nobility, MM. de Chailloué, de Boinville, and de Belbeuf, and M. Bergasse, deputy of the Third. It was at the end of this session that the Vicomte de Mirabeau broke his sword over his knee, in the corridors of the hall, while pronouncing these celebrated words: "When the king breaks his scepter, his servants should break their swords."

THE ASSEMBLY GROWS UNPOPULAR. (*Fersen, 81–82.*)

The States-General [the Assembly] do what they choose, without the slightest opposition; they reform and destroy everything with the utmost levity;

but they do not create so readily, and what they establish takes root with difficulty. Poverty and discontent are increasing; they are beginning to touch the people, especially the populace of Paris, which now finds itself without resource, owing to the diminution or annihilation of fortunes occasioned by the decrees of the Assembly. There are persons who have lost forty thousand to fifty thousand francs a year, and others their whole revenue, by the abolition of feudal rights. Most of the workmen and artisans have come to beggary. The shopkeepers are earning nothing, for nobody buys. The best workmen are leaving the kingdom, and the streets are full of paupers. One and all they blame the Assembly; they reproach it for the absence of the great world, who were their subsistence, and for the diminution of fortunes which forces everyone to economize. The royal treasury is exhausted; the taxes are very ill paid or not paid at all; there is neither credit nor confidence; money has disappeared, everyone hoards it; nothing is seen but bills on the discounting bank, which lose six per cent in realizing them.

THE FAVRAS CONSPIRACY. (*Weber, II, 10–11.*)

A hot-headed man, M. le Marquis de Favras, imagined at that time that it would be possible to start a counter-revolution. It was only a matter, according to his plan, of carrying off the king, conducting him to Péronne, making sure of the persons of the Marquis de La Fayette and M. Necker, bringing together twelve thousand horsemen in Paris, and supporting them with an army composed of twenty thousand Swiss, twenty thousand Sardinians, and twelve thousand Germans.... the Marquis de Favras having sounded some soldiers of the troop of M. de La Fayette, and having been so venturesome as to cause them to understand that the project had the sanction of important personages, was denounced to the Marquis de La Fayette, then arrested and sent to the Châtelet to be tried....

Favras was hanged in the Place de Grève for having thought to do a good deed.

ATTACKS UPON MIRABEAU. (*Ferrières, II, 48.*)

Mirabeau was particularly concerned about denying the reproach, made by the nobles and bishops in the Assembly, that he was giving the government a strong tendency towards a republic. The bishops and nobles, having nothing reasonable to say in reply, had recourse to insults. "You are a ranter," cried the Comte Faucigny-Lucinge, "and nothing else!" "M. le Président," replied Mirabeau, "restrain the insolence of these people who dare to insult me in the rostrum." The tumult became extreme. The bishops and nobles addressed the grossest insults to Mirabeau, accompanying them with menacing gestures. "A public challenge is not noble enough to merit my reply," Mirabeau coolly returned. The president compelled a return to calmness.

MIRABEAU'S SHIFTING POLICIES. (*Mounier, 323.*)

The 15th of June, 1789, wishing to prevent the commons from naming themselves the *National Assembly*, he [Mirabeau] maintained with reason that it would arouse pretensions, and through absurd systems lead to anarchy. "You will not even have," said he, "the questionable glory of civil war; you will have massacres, pillage, and conflagrations in all parts of the kingdom"; but since that time he has continuously excused the crimes he foresaw. He also maintained, the 15th of June, that the sanction of the king was indispensable for all exterior acts of the Assembly, that the authority of the monarch could never be inactive, and that he would rather live in Constantinople than in France if the king did not have a veto; then, on July 16, he called the National Assembly *the sovereign* and *the representative of the sovereign*, and pretended that the powers of the king were suspended if they were not in accord with it. On August 7, 1789, the ministers, several of whom were members of the National Assembly, came to request a loan of thirty millions. A deputy having proposed voting in their presence, the Comte de Mirabeau cried out, "I demand the proscription of that vile slave"; but in the following month of November, he proposed giving ministers the right to sit in the Assembly and discuss executive measures. On the 7th of August, he combatted the thirty million loan, from respect *for the imperious wording of their instructions*, and maintained that they must have the authority of their constituents. Since then he has shown nothing but disdain for these instructions and those who wished to follow them. On the 7th of August, he defied the most loyal of his colleagues to carry further than he a devout respect for the royal prerogatives; and on the 26th of March, 1790, he did not concede to the king the prerogative even of writing to the Assembly without the countersign of a minister. He called the *personal inviolability of the king a genuinely precarious and ideal privilege*; and in the session of the 20th of May, in discoursing on peace and war, he supposed that a king could *perish on a scaffold*. On the 1st of September, 1789, he defended the royal sanction, and said that in choosing representatives, there would always result *an aristocracy which would desire to render itself equal to the monarch*; and on the 18th of the same month, he maintained that the decrees of the 4th of August had no need of this sanction. On the 22nd of February, 1790, he said that the municipal officers who did not employ with courage and firmness the power confided to them, were committing a great crime, and ought to be held responsible; and on the 12th of May, he said that the municipal officers of Marseille ought to yield to the wishes of the people, and demand the surrender of the forts. He began by refuting the doctrine of national conventions; he ended by vaunting the omnipotence of constituent bodies. He opposed the reading of petitions against assignats, and a few days later spoke of the sacred right of petition.

MIRABEAU ACCUSED OF CONSPIRACY. (*Paroy, 169–170.*)

The two Lameths, long jealous of Mirabeau, whom they regarded as an obstacle to their ascendancy, believed that they had found an occasion to make him unpopular. Charles de Lameth reproached Mirabeau from the tribune in unrestrained terms for betraying the interests of the people, and next day the news-vendors were hawking *The Great Treason of the Comte de Mirabeau*, a libel composed and printed on the very night preceding the discussion, and in which Mirabeau was accused of having received a large sum of money to cause the relegation to the king of the right to declare war. This pamphlet was handed to the Comte de Mirabeau by one of his friends on the next day, May 22, when he entered the hall of the Assembly. He cast his eyes upon the title and said, "I know it well enough; they will carry me from the Assembly in triumph, or to the tomb."

Mirabeau, knowing that in revolutions, where public opinion is a great power, this opinion influences and carries away even those who have contributed most to creating it, applied himself to proving that the debate arising between him, Barnave, and the Lameths was only a selfish combat, a rivalry for glory, and that, agreeing as to principles, they differed only as to the manner of their presentation.

"A clear explanation is necessary," interrupted Duport. "Friendly discussion," replied Mirabeau imperturbably, "brings better understanding than the perfidious insinuations of calumny, than passionate inculpations, rival hatreds, or the machinations of intrigue and malevolence. It has been said for several days that the section of the Assembly which desires the concourse of the royal will in making peace and war, is assassinating popular liberty; there have spread vague rumors of perfidy, of corruption; popular vengeance is invoked to sustain the tyranny of dogmas." Here Mirabeau turned to Barnave: "And as for me, they wished to carry me in triumph, and now they cry in the streets *The Great Conspiracy of the Comte de Mirabeau!* I have no need of that lesson to know that it is but a step from the Capitol to the Tarpeian Rock; but the man who fights for the right and for his country does not allow himself to be so easily vanquished."

ABOLITION OF NOBILITY. (*Mme. de Tourzel, I, 130–132.*)

On the 23rd of June [1790], the Assembly, taking advantage of a limited attendance at the evening sitting, decreed the suppression of the nobility without allowing any discussion on so important a subject. M. de Lameth opened the proceedings by demanding the removal, before the 14th of July, of the statues in chains around that of Louis XIV, as being monuments of slaves which disgraced the Place des Victoires. The Aubusson family in vain laid claim to them as family property, and the artists as masterpieces. The latter, grieved at such destruction, offered to remove the chains. "You cannot remove the attitude of humiliation," said M. Bouche. And M. de Saint-Fargeau added, "We will equal the monuments of the century of Louis XIV, and that grand century will be effaced by the century of a great nation."

M. Lambel, an advocate, the Vicomte de Noailles, and Mathieu de Montmorency demanded the suppression of the nobility, hereditary titles, liveries, and coats of arms; and Charles de Lameth added that all who continued to bear them should be looked upon as enemies of the constitution. "No more highness, excellency, or eminence!" shouted Lanjuinais. "Let all territorial names be suppressed," said M. de Saint-Fargeau, "and let everybody be compelled to resume that of his family."

M. de La Fayette opposed every kind of exception, even in case of princes of the blood. According to him, in the system of equality which was about to rule France there ought only to be active citizens. . . .

M. Landsberg, a deputy of Alsace, spoke with wisdom and moderation, and declared that, as he was certain to be disavowed by his constituents, he would keep his sorrow to himself. "In submission," he said, "to the decrees of the Assembly, they will know that they live with the blood with which they were born, and nothing can prevent them living and dying as gentlemen." "If you destroy the nobility," said M. de Faucigny, "you will have in its place the distinctions of bankers, usurers, stock-jobbers, and proprietors of incomes of three hundred thousand francs, and the love of wealth will replace French honor, the soul of the nobility."

THE DECREE ABOLISHING NOBILITY.

The National Assembly, wishing to found the French constitution upon the principles which it has just recognized and proclaimed, irrevocably abolishes the institutions harmful to liberty and the equality of rights.

There are to be no longer any nobility, peerage, hereditary distinctions, distinctive orders, feudal régime, patrimonial justices, any of the titles, denominations, or prerogatives derived from them, any order of knighthood, any organizations or decorations which require proofs of nobility, or which suppose distinctions of birth, or any other superiority than that of public officials in the exercise of their functions.

There is to be no longer any sale or inheritance of public office.

There is to be no longer, for any part of the nation or for any individual, either privilege or exception under the law common to all the French.

There are to be no longer any wardenships or corporations of professions, arts, and trades.

The law does not henceforth recognize any religious vow or any other engagement which shall be in conflict with natural rights or with the constitution.

NECKER OPPOSED TO THE ABOLITION OF THE NOBILITY. (Mme. de Staël, 193–194.)

In the council of state, M. Necker alone advised the king to refuse his sanction to the decree which annihilated the nobility without establishing the patriciate in its place; and, his ideas not having prevailed, he had the courage to publish them. The king had resolved to sanction indiscriminately all the decrees of the Assembly: his system was to consider himself, dating from the 6th of October, as being in a state of captivity; and it was only on account of his religious scruples that he did not consequently put his name to the decrees which proscribed the priests who submitted to the power of the pope.

THE UNIVERSE COMES TO THE ASSEMBLY. (Ferrières, II, 64–65.)

On June 19, the day definitely decreed for the consummation of this great enterprise, there was arranged an unanticipated spectacle proper to attract the eyes of the multitude; sixty aliens were assembled, men without country living in Paris by swindling and intrigue; they are decorated with the pompous name of envoys of all the peoples of the universe; they are dressed up in borrowed clothes, and induced by the twelve francs promised them, they consent to play the rôle intended for them. One Clootz, Prussian, a species of jester, a subordinate intriguer, one of these men always ready to stir up trouble, because they exist by disorder, put himself at their head and demanded in the name of humankind to present a petition to the National Assembly. Menou, chosen by the Lameths to fill the president's chair on that day, ordered the doorkeeper to introduce the petitioners. Clootz entered, followed by a troop of people who were announced to be Prussians, Dutchmen, English-men, Spaniards, Germans, Turks, Arabs, Indians, Tartars, Persians, Chinese, Mongols, Tripolitans, Swiss, Italians, Americans, and Grisons. They wore the habiliments of these different peoples. The stock of the Opéra had been exhausted.

At the sight of this grotesque masquerade, everyone stared open-eyed and waited in silence for an explanation. The initiated filled the hall with noisy acclamations. The galleries, overcome with joy in seeing the universe in the midst of the National Assembly, clapped their hands and stamped their feet.

MIRABEAU AND THE COURT. (Ferrières, II, 78–79.)

The decree which forbade the members of the Assembly to accept any place at the disposition of the government while it was in session had nullified the agreement between the court and the Comte de Mirabeau. Mirabeau, flattered and paid when urgent circumstances rendered his help necessary, abandoned and persecuted when they believed they could do without him and drag him with the others into a general proscription, realized what little reliance could be placed upon an irresolute king, upon a queen capable of sacrificing her dearest interest to an unwise vengeance, and upon a designing minister who hated and feared him. In truth, despite the advances which the court and ministers continued to make to Mirabeau, everything indicated the design to ruin him, and nothing indicated a design to negotiate with him in good faith. They unleashed the party writers upon him; he was decried in a multitude of libels; they harassed him through the Lameths; they em-ployed the same duplicity with the other leaders of the revolutionary party. The court was so habituated to petty intrigues that it could never go beyond them and rise to greater conceptions.

THE CIVIL CONSTITUTION OF THE CLERGY. (Ferrières, II, 50–51.)

The earlier decrees had dissolved this corps and confiscated its property; it was now a question of determining the relations between the clergy and the constitution, and of placing on a fixed basis the emoluments that would be accorded to the present incumbents and to the ministers of the cult per-forming religious services. . . . These changes consisted in reducing to eighty-three the one hundred and seventeen bishoprics existing in France, in having the bishops and priests named by the electors who were to choose the adminis-trators of the departments and the deputies for the legislature, in suppressing the cathedral chapters, and in replacing them with sixteen priests who performed the functions of vicars, while the bishops performed those of parish priests.[1]

The ecclesiastical committee, author of the project, was dominated by Camus, Fréteau, Treilhard, and Martineau, extreme Jansenists, who wished to realize in the new religious constitution the democratic and popular régime which the Jansenists called the discipline of the primitive church. The persecutions which they had experienced under Louis XIV and Louis XV made them regard this measure as the only guarantee of the liberty of their sect.

OPPOSITION TO THE CIVIL CONSTITUTION. (Révolutions de Paris, No. 73.)

It is the Bishop of Tréguier who has given the signal for the ecclesiastical insurrection which disturbs the kingdom at this moment. After having declared that he would personally regard as intruders the bishops and priests who would be elected according to the new formula, he protested that he would not communicate with them *in divinis*. In another letter to the priests of his diocese, after having set forth his anti-patriotic doctrine, he added: "We must remain united, and our conduct must be uniform."

Several bishops have joined this "holy league." Those of Soissons, Dijon, Verdun, Nantes, and Vienne have protested against the decrees, in declaring that they would delay their decision until the reply of the Roman pontiff to the king's letter was received. The Bishop of Beauvais has filled a curacy in his diocese and refuses to agree to the changing of his cathedral into a parish church. The former Archbishop of Lyon has done the same. Several chapters have protested in the same fashion....

Many fanatical priests have imitated their bishops and their chapters, openly preaching to their parishioners resistance to the decrees of the legislative body.

Finally, as if to crown this sacerdotal delirium, the bishops who are members of the National Assembly have distributed, in the greatest profusion, a species of protestation filled with sophisms and absurd principles... This document ends with the following sentence: "We think that our first duty is to await with confidence the response of the successor of Saint Peter, who, occupying the center of Catholic unity and communion, should be the interpreter and spokesman of the wishes of the universal church."

THE FEDERATION. (Ferrières, II, 76–77.)

The revolutionists did not deny that the National Assembly had gone beyond its powers and established a constitution contrary, in several points, to the instructions given to the deputies. Desiring to reply to the reproaches incessantly addressed to them, they devised a federation of all the French. It was decreed that there should be named in each canton six deputies, to whom should be added representatives of the army and navy. These deputies, furnished with special powers, were to come to accept the new constitution and take oath to it. The revolutionists had another motive which they did not avow; the new constitution, placed, so to speak, in equilibrium between

[1] See the Appendix for the text of the civil constitution.

republican government and absolute monarchical government, threatened to fall into one of these two extremes. In fact, the government could function with only the king and the departments, and there was no need of the Assembly; with the Assembly and the departments, the government would work also, and the king could be dispensed with. It was therefore necessary to rally the discordant parties around a common center (the Assembly), and make it the real sovereign.

THE FESTIVAL OF THE FEDERATION. (*Weber, II, 23–24.*)

The anniversary of July 14, the day of the taking of the Bastille, had, by a decree rendered May 27, been set aside for a general federation of all the French. All national guards of the whole of France and all army corps had been ordered to assist by deputation at this civic festival.

The Duc d'Orléans selected this epoch for his return from England without the king's permission, although he had gone to that country only by His Majesty's order. He used the federation as a pretext for his return to France; his quality of deputy requiring him, he said, to take part in it.

(*Ferrières, II, 93–94; Thiers, I, 156–157.*)

Meanwhile, more than three hundred thousand people of both sexes, from Paris and the environs, had been assembled since six in the morning at the Champ-de-Mars. Sitting on turf seats, which formed an immense circus, drenched, draggled, sheltering themselves with parasols from the torrents of rain which descended upon them, and at the least ray of sunshine adjusting their dresses, they waited, laughing and chatting, for the federates and the National Assembly. A spacious amphitheater had been erected for the king, the royal family, the ambassadors, and the deputies. The federates, who first arrived, began to dance *farandoles*; those who followed joined them, forming a round which soon embraced part of the Champ-de-Mars. A sight worthy of the philosophic observer was that exhibited by this host of men, who had come from the most opposite parts of France, hurried away by the impulse of the national character, banishing all remembrance of the past, all idea of the present, all fear of the future, and indulging in a delicious thoughtlessness. Three hundred thousand spectators, of all ages and of both sexes, followed their motions, beating time with their hands, forgetting the rain, hunger, and the weariness of long waiting. At length, the whole procession having entered the Champ-de-Mars, the dance ceased, each federate repaired to his banner. The Bishop of Autun prepared to perform mass at an altar in the antique style, erected in the center of the Champ-de-Mars. Three hundred priests in white surplices, girt with broad tricolored scarfs, ranged themselves at the four corners of the altar. The Bishop of Autun blessed the oriflamme and the eighty-three banners: he struck up the *Te Deum.* Twelve hundred musicians played that hymn.

THE ROYAL FAMILY ACCLAIMED. (Mme. de Tourzel, I, 161.)

At the elevation of the Host, M. de La Fayette, appointed by the king to be major-general of the federation, gave the signal for the oath, ascended the altar steps, and pronounced it. In a moment every sword was drawn and every head raised. M. de La Fayette then went to the king and informed him that the moment had arrived for him to take the oath. The rain was falling in torrents, and a great number of the spectators, who were being inundated, sought to diminish its effect by opening their umbrellas. As this prevented the king from being seen, the crowd shouted, "Down, down with umbrellas!" M. de La Fayette, who at first only heard the words "down, down," thought that the shout was probably meant for him; he hesitated for a moment, and his ordinary pallor visibly increased, but recovering himself quickly he resumed his progress . . .

(Ferrières, II, 94–95; Thiers, I, 157.)

La Fayette, at the head of the staff of the Parisian militia, and of the deputies of the army and navy, went up to the altar, and swore, in the name of the troops and the federates, to be faithful to the nation, to the law, and to the king. A discharge of four pieces of cannon proclaimed to France this solemn oath. The twelve hundred musicians rent the air with military tunes; the colors, the banners, waved; the drawn sabers glistened. The president of the National Assembly repeated the same oath. The people and the deputies answered with shouts of "I swear it." The king then rose, and in a loud voice said, "I, King of the French, swear to employ the power delegated to me, by the constitutional act of the state, in maintaining the constitution decreed by the National Assembly, and accepted by me." The queen, taking the dauphin in her arms, held him up to the people, and said, "Here is my son; he joins as well as myself in those sentiments." This unexpected movement was repaid by a thousand shouts of "Long live the King! Long live the Queen! Long live M. le Dauphin!" The cannon continued to mingle their majestic voices with the warlike sounds of military instruments, and the acclamations of the people.

LOYALTY TO THE KING AROUSED BY THE FEDERATION. (Ferrières, II, 95–96; Thiers, I, 157.)

The enthusiasm and the festivities were not confined to the day of the federation. During the stay of the federates at Paris, there was one continued series of entertainments, of dances, and of rejoicings. People again went to the Champ-de-Mars, where they drank, sang, and danced. M. de La Fayette reviewed part of the national guard of the departments and the army of the line. The king, queen, and the dauphin were present at this review. They were greeted with acclamations. The queen, with a gracious look, gave the federates her hand to kiss, and showed them the dauphin. The federates, before they quitted the capital, went to pay homage to the king: all of them testified the most profound respect, the warmest attachment. The chief of the Bretons dropped on his knee, and presented his sword to Louis XVI.

"Sire," said he, "I deliver to you, pure and sacred, the sword of the faithful Bretons: it shall never be stained but with the blood of your enemies." "That sword cannot be in better hands than those of my dear Bretons," replied Louis XVI, raising the chief of the Bretons, and returning him his sword. "I have never doubted their affection and fidelity. Assure them that I am the father, the brother, the friend, of all the French." The king, deeply moved, pressed the hand of the chief of the Bretons, and embraced him. A mutual emotion prolonged for some moments this touching scene. The chief of the Bretons was the first to speak. "Sire," said he, "all the French, if I may judge from our hearts, love and will love you, because you are a citizen king."

COUNTER-REVOLUTIONARY PROPAGANDA. (*Ferrières, II, 100–101.*)

They asserted that this order of things was impracticable; that it could not continue; that the king would soon resume his full authority; that the absent princes would re-enter France at the head of a powerful army, augmented by all the dissatisfied element of the interior; that the Assembly would be dissolved; that the insurgents would be delivered up to the rigor of the law; that not only those who had held government positions, but also the ones who had favored the constitution, or at least had not been opposed to it, would be deprived of their places and punished severely. The nobles were reminded incessantly of honor, of courage, of devotion to the monarchy and the king. The bishops reminded the priests and monks of the zeal of the early Christians in maintaining the faith and the sacred authority of the church. They treated the decrees as audacious attempts, impious, and directed against God even. The papers kept up the dissension, revived hates, fed the madness. There arose a thousand individual protestations against the decrees of the thirteenth of April and the nineteenth of June.

Durosoy and Royou put these protests in their journals. The most ignorant *curé*, the least worthy priest, if he avoided the civil constitution of the clergy, became suddenly a Jerome, an Ambroise, an Athanasius. If the smallest country noble, occupied with his daily rabbit chase, rose against the decree which abolished the nobility, he became a Bayard, a Gaston, a La Trémoille.

THE TROOPS AFTER THE FEDERATION. (*Ferrières, II, 99.*)

Thus, while the revolutionists were stirring up trouble in the interior, inciting everywhere license and insurrection, and arousing the soldiers against their officers, the aristocrats were working to increase the disorder and were bringing about the final disintegration of the army. They ordered the officers to show the soldiers at one time criminal indulgence, and at others outrageous severity, in order to disgust them with the service and to cause a general desertion before the establishment of the new military code.

(*Mme. de Tourzel, I, 84–85.*)

The Vivarais regiment in garrison at Béthune... revolted. It refused to accept the Chevalier de Maillier as its lieutenant-colonel, although it had no ground of complaint against him. The king, after having given it time to repent, and being anxious to put an end to so dangerous an example, ordered the regiment away from Béthune, at the same time directing that the loyal soldiers should be separated from those in revolt, and that only those should be kept with the colors who would recognize the authority of the Chevalier de Maillier. This order was read out to the regiment on its arrival at Lens; but the majority of the men, with several non-commissioned officers at their head, refused to obey, seized the colors, chest, and equipment of the regiment, conveyed everything to Béthune, and handed it over to the commandant of the national guard.

MUTINIES WIDESPREAD. (*Mme. de Tourzel, I, 132–133.*)

The army became more and more disorganized day by day. The royal marine regiment, on leaving Marseille for Lambesc, got rid of all its officers, recommending them to the interest of the nation. The municipality vainly endeavored to recall the mutineers to their duty. The Assembly merely testified its satisfaction to the municipality of Lambesc, and threatened the regiment that if it did not return to its duty it should be excluded from the federation.

The minister of war complained in vain of the inconvenience which might result from crimes of so grave a character. Deeply hurt by the carelessness of the Assembly, he submitted to it a memorandum, which forcefully represented that the army threatened to fall into the most violent anarchy. Whole regiments were in revolt, and were violating their most solemn oaths. "Regulations," said he, "are without force, commanding officers without authority, the military chests and the colors carried off, the officers dishonored, despised, and frequently prisoners, commanding officers murdered before the eyes of their own men, and the orders of the king openly defied."

(*Bouillé, 131–134.*)

Everywhere the soldiers formed among themselves in each regiment committees to determine their actions; they chose a small number of deputies who claimed from their superiors, at first with moderation, the retentions which had been made under the old régime of inspectors. Their claims were just; that was recognized. There were corps where they were considerable; others where they had been reduced to little or even nothing. The soldiers, not satisfied with having succeeded in their first demands, formulated others, unjust and exorbitant, which were refused them. They then took to arms, refused admittance to their officers, carried off the flags to their barracks, posted guards at the houses of their leaders and at the regimental treasuries, and had the coffers opened and the money distributed among themselves. . . .

I was with the first regiment which rose in arms to take possession of the military coffer and the flags; I harangued the soldiers who had drawn themselves up in line of battle with loaded weapons, their officers having been ordered to take their usual places in the ranks. I could do nothing with them. . . . I had sent, however, to a regiment of dragoons whose barracks were nearly adjoining, the order to mount and charge the German regiment. The officers obeyed, but the dragoons refused to a man. The commanders of the different corps of the garrison having likewise tried to have them put down this insurrection, the soldiers refused to take up arms, proclaiming loudly that they had promised not to act against the soldiers of this regiment, whose demands were fair and of whose conduct they approved.

INSURRECTION AT NANCY. (*Bouillé, 145–159.*)

Meanwhile, the insurrection at Nancy grew, assuming every day a more frightful character. The garrison was composed of four battalions of the king's regiment, which was one of the best in France; two battalions of Swiss from Geneva, Vaux, and Neuchâtel; and regiments of cavalry. The hope of pillage had brought together four or five thousand men of the city and its environs; they had opened the arsenals and carried off five thousand guns; they had seized the stores; they had taken possession of the powder magazine and charged eighteen pieces of artillery. . . .

On the morning of the 30th, I dispatched a summons to the town, in which I renewed the order for the people and the soldiers to obey the decrees of the Assembly, to return to their duty, and to give up their most mutinous leaders; I gave them twenty-four hours to reply. . . .

It is true that we had taken twelve cannon, killed many of the rebels, and made more than five hundred prisoners among the garrison or the people who were fighting against us. The revolting regiments had fallen back before their barracks with their cannon, and the people had gone back to their houses or had left the city . . .

The 1st of September, the three Swiss battalions asked permission to assemble a council of war to court-martial about twenty-four soldiers of Châteauvieux who had been taken in arms. The Swiss corps in the service of the king had the right, according to the treaty between the Swiss Federation and France, to private and independent judgments. This council of war condemned twenty-two soldiers to death and over fifty to the galleys, sentences which were carried out without my having any right to interfere. About a hundred and eighty soldiers of the king's regiment and three hundred civilians had been taken in active combat: I could not have them court-martialled. They were all released later without having been tried, and no one was punished.

This is what was called the massacre of Nancy.

(*Ferrières, II, 142.*)

The victory of Bouillé threw the Jacobins into consternation. There was a unanimous outcry against the general, against La Fayette, against the ministers. This example of an insurrection repressed by force, and, what caused them the most anxiety, the unexpected collaboration between the troops of the line and the national guard, was going to give strength to the government.

(*Bouillé, 168.*)

I had left Nancy perfectly quiet. The Assembly had sent two commissaries to find out the causes of the insurrection. They did much harm by their extreme leniency and by their efforts to re-establish the patriotic sentiments nearly extinguished in the city after this event.

MIRABEAU AND THE DISTURBANCES. (*Mme. de Tourzel, I, 187–188.*)

M. de Mirabeau spoke strongly in opposition to such disturbances [mutinies and revolts], and declared that he saw no other remedy for so many evils than the disbanding of the army. He proposed to decree it for the 20th of September, to terminate the furlough from the moment when the decrees on the military organization should be passed, and to make every man composing the army take so precise and definite an oath that all diversity of principles and opinions should be excluded. He proposed, moreover, to issue at the same time an address to the army, setting forth the obligations imposed by this oath, which would act as a preservative against such interpretations as ignorant and enthusiastic persons had placed on the declaration of the rights of man. He concluded by avowing that it was time that this declaration should be followed by one setting forth individual obligations. If this declaration, so urgently demanded by the sensible members of the Assembly, and so obstinately refused, had been decreed at once after that of the rights of man, many misfortunes would have been avoided. The proposal of M. de Mirabeau was unfortunately too late; the evil might easily have been prevented in its earliest stages, but it became difficult to remedy later on.

THE RETREAT OF NECKER. (*Mallet du Pan, I, 211.*)

If M. Necker had hoped to save France by ruling its legislators he was promptly undeceived. On the first trial of his power he met with rebuffs; his name and his opposition to the court were no longer needed; his courtiers had become his masters. In vain did he timidly address them; his advances were not responded to; his ascendancy declined from day to day; the deference paid him in matters of finance could not compensate for the discredit attached to his opinions. He lavished them in vain, and, by a remarkable fatality, his political counsels were unsuccessful, except in the memorable discussion on the absolute veto, against which he declared, yet not until he had been convinced by M. Mounier. They worked on his weakness and fears to bring him to a decision.

The same feeling of dread soon carried him into the vortex of the torrent; he swam with the waves, instead of stemming them; he saw the monarchy strike the rocks, without having the power to work at the helm. He withdrew his confidence from the last defenders of royal authority, in the vain hope of subduing its enemies, who took advantage of his illusion.... In vain did he address the Assembly in a tone of submission and flattery, entitling it a galaxy of light, a senate of sages; he met with no response from policy, ambition, or hatred. Complaints at last were made of the continual interference of the minister of finance in the administration of his own department; his office was changed to that of public treasurer at the very moment when he was reproached for not devising general measures. [He resigned on September 4 and retired to Switzerland.]

PEOPLE TIRED OF POLITICS. (Mme. Roland, 243.)

I saw with sadness that public-spiritedness seemed to weaken, even in the capital; I could see it in everything that took place in the Assembly, which would have been more consistent, more firm with the ministers, if public opinion had been sane and powerful, as it always is when justice and universality characterize it. I could see it in the indifference and negligence which was evident in your elections: why did Paris furnish but six thousand voters in the nomination of the procurator of the commune? As long as there is so little interest that the choice of candidates for positions is no longer considered, regardless of what those positions are, the public welfare will suffer.

XII. *Europe and the Revolution*

EUROPEAN POLICY. (Dumouriez, II, 179–180.)

ALL the powers of Europe regarded France as an impotent state on account of its revolution which, instead of progressing towards beneficial and necessary reformation, had turned into the most frightful anarchy. The two departments of government, instead of uniting, had become more widely separated day by day. Every European nation had a more or less direct interest in the prompt cessation of these troubles; but an erroneous point of view and a faulty statecraft misled them all. The complaints of the French fugitives added to the mistaken ideas of the courts which had received them.

They depicted the National Assembly as a group more audacious than powerful. They maintained that their party was still the strongest, that the troops of the line were still with them, or were in any case weakened by the emigration of all the officers. The national guard was nothing but a collection of timid bourgeois, incapable of standing fire. The provinces were merely awaiting their return to destroy the constitution and joyfully reinstate the government under which they had lived for fourteen centuries. The constitution was impracticable and unsuited to the spirit of the nation, accustomed to revere its kings. They cited themselves as examples of this devotion, and yet they had abandoned their king to these very insurgents of whom they spoke so disdainfully.

All the governments of Europe gave credence more or less to these exaggerations. The more distant showed an unforeseeing indifference; those who were nearer indulged in the hope of annexing territory in payment for any active part they themselves might take. The partition of Poland had caused them to adopt the policy of making capital out of the internal troubles of neighboring countries. Louis XIII, Louis XIV, and even Louis XV had added to France Roussillon, Bresse, the Gex country, Alsace, Franche-Comté, Flanders, and Lorraine. This system of partition had succeeded in Poland; the same effects could be produced by inciting civil wars in France. Spain, Italy, and Germany would find opportunity to make up for former dismemberments. England would gain colonies by dividing the French possessions, which would be a fine revenge for the American war.

ENGLAND AND THE REVOLUTION. (Dumouriez, II, 186–187.)

It was to England's interest to remain neutral, and in spite of the king's extreme dislike of the French nation, the court of Saint James conducted itself wisely. The minister had always treated very frankly with Lord Gower, its ambassador. Together they had smoothed out several minor subjects of dissension, and it took all the imprudence of Brissot, all the petulance of the National Convention, and a crime as atrocious and impolitic as the murder of Louis XVI to force the English, in 1793, to depart from their system of neutrality and plunge into a costly war, which gave to the islands momentary advantages, but was offset by great losses and enormous subsidies, without there being any assurance of lasting conquests.

RUSSIA AND THE REVOLUTION. (Besenval, II, 275–276.)

England was thirsting for vengeance on account of the loss of America and the Dutch alliance which France had taken from her. Observing the deplorable state of the royal finances and the internal disorder of the kingdom, she believed that the moment had come for making an important move. In consequence, her minister to the Porte, by force of intrigue, induced the Turks to declare war on Russia at the very moment we were making every effort to guarantee them against the invasion which the Empress of Russia and the [Holy Roman] emperor had planned for a long time.

The Porte, our ally, had been prompted to this action in order to render us suspect to Russia, alienate us anew, and cause us to lose the fruit of the negotiations of the Comte de Ségur, who had brought Russia, by great astuteness, to the point of concluding a commerical treaty with us. It also brought an end to our old alliance with the Turks, thus destroying, or at least greatly hampering, our commerce in the Levant.

(Dumouriez, II, 190.)

Russia exhibited the most violent rancor against the French nation. Perhaps it covered a deep-laid policy. Russia was sure to profit by sending the armies of Prussia and Austria far from her borders to shatter themselves against the strongholds that bristled in France. The second partition of Poland gave an impetus to these views. We shall shortly see, perhaps, the rest of her plan carried out against the unhappy Turks, who since the year 1794 have been menaced by this ambitious power which, under the pretext of attacking the southern coast of France, plans to cover the Black Sea, the Bosporus, and the Ægean with its numerous vessels.

PRUSSIA AND THE REVOLUTION. (Dumouriez, II, 193.)

The court of Berlin, if it had not found itself involved with Russia in the partition of Poland, would have viewed the French Revolution with indifference. Too far off to cause anxiety, it would not have been meddled with. Up to the Congress of Reichenbach, Russia had been hostile to the House of Austria, and in conjunction with The Hague had fomented the Belgian insurrection. Nevertheless, the court of Vienna won it over by its complaisances. The King of Prussia realized that in uniting with Austria, first to put a stop to the troubles in the Low Countries, and then to stifle the French insurrection, he would be given more leeway in carrying out the second partition of Poland, which would pay the expenses of a war against France. This war, it was predicted, would be very short.

INTRIGUES OF FOREIGN COURTS. (*Miles, I, 254.*)

Some of the German courts have emissaries here — all apostles of liberty — preaching equal rights, and assuring the giddy multitude that their example will be followed by the whole world! Prussia for intrigue takes the lead. She pays court to each party as appearances may seem to favor. The Tuileries she disregards. All her agents vociferate against the House of Austria as plotting with the queen for the purpose of destroying the Revolution. The King of Sardinia is also involved in this accusation; and, while the emperor is said to have an army in the Netherlands ready to enter France by Lille and Valenciennes, the court of Turin is reported to have ordered several thousand poignards to be manufactured in Piedmont for the French emigrants on the banks of the Rhine under the Cardinal de Rohan, the younger Mirabeau, and others, and for the aristocrats at Paris in league with them. All these tales, absurd as some of the fabrications are, pass for authentic, and serve no less to bewilder than to inflame the public mind. That the Revolution will have to proceed is a fact as clear as noonday. It is obvious to every man of discernment. But the king, from imbecility, and the queen, blinded by her wishes and her hopes, believe in a counter-revolution, and listen to every designing knave that chants the same tune. Mirabeau, too versatile to be steady to any one object, is already less ardent in the cause of liberty; and yet the Tuileries vainly imagines that, if they can get this man over to their interests, the counter-revolution would be instantly effected.

(*Ferrières, II, 288–289.*)

The French Revolution interested too greatly the kings of Europe for them and their ministers not to keep their eyes continually open to what was happening in France. The Comte d'Artois and the Prince de Condé pointed out the consequences of it to them. But the sort of prison where the king and the royal family found themselves incarcerated in the midst of a people that could so easily be rendered furious, did not permit the emperor, the King of Prussia, and the court of Turin, those most interested in these events, to act before Louis XVI had broken what they called his chains. Meanwhile, they occupied themselves in stirring up discord and encouraging the emigration, not doubting that in adding to the number of malcontents and enemies of the Revolution they would succeed the sooner in re-establishing the old order of things. Thus there departed daily from the kingdom crowds of nobles, officers who were abandoning their corps, rich financiers who were carrying away their fortunes, and ladies of quality trailed by their admirers and their almoners. The men went to join the refugee princes and watch for the moment to enter France at the head of a foreign army, while the women supported intrigues and correspondents in Paris.

THE ÉMIGRÉS. (Ferrières, II, 289–290.)

The majority of these *émigrés*, young, presumptuous, and self-sufficient, delivered themselves up to that national vainglory which brings well-merited ridicule upon the French. They were bored, they said, to death; they found the country stupid, the customs disagreeable: all desired to be colonels, none desired to obey. However, as they had brought a certain amount of money, they were wanted in the inns, where, cheated and badly lodged, they were usuriously despoiled of what they possessed, being charged excessive prices for the things most necessary. Their money and jewels once gone, they were ignominiously driven out, and went somewhere else to weep over their folly. The Prince de Condé, surrounded by brilliant youth, and encouraged in his projects, held his little court at Worms. The *émigrés* exaggerated the number and strength of his army, and boasted of the brilliancy and wisdom of the Comte d'Artois, the friendly attitude of the foreign powers, and their numerous armaments.

DECREE AGAINST ÉMIGRÉS PROPOSED. (Ferrières, II, 294.)

[Chapelier proposed the adoption of the following decree]:
"The National Assembly, in times of trouble, shall name a council of three persons who shall exercise dictatorial power solely in regard to the right of leaving the kingdom and the obligation to re-enter it. This commission shall designate the absent who are to be ordered to return to France, and who must obey under pain of forfeiture of their rights as French citizens and confiscation of their goods and revenues."
I must render justice to the Assembly: it rose almost unanimously. "If you delay an instant in rejecting with horror this infamous project," said M. Dandré, "you will cause the flight of half the kingdom." "This iniquitous law," added Mirabeau, "is more worthy of the Draconian code than of the constitutional code of an Assembly destined to establish national liberty: but what I mean to prove, if need be, is that its barbarity is the highest proof of the impracticability of a law against the *émigrés*."

AVIGNON AND ROME. (Dumouriez, II, 182–183.)

The pope foresaw the diminution of his power and of his revenues. He had lost the Comtat d'Avignon, which had become the scene of atrocious crimes that were only the forerunners of greater ones. This county, formerly usurped from Provence by pious fraud, and held through redeemable engagements, could have been legitimately recovered by France, if she had wished to give the pope a fair return for the redemption of the engagements. It is even believable that he would have consented to the agreement which Dumouriez, acting in the name of justice and for the nation's honor, tried to bring about.
The pope, not being in a position to sustain by force this small remnant of temporal sovereignty surrounded by French territory, would finally have ceded it upon receiving the price. But he had another irreconcilable interest, that of his spiritual authority, which, if diminished in France, would destroy

the famous concordat of Leo X and deprive him of immense revenues. All this, however, would not have hindered negotiations, and the pope would have been obliged to sacrifice that unwarranted source of wealth which his predecessors had enjoyed only through the astuteness of Leo X and the foolishness of Francis I. But the National Assembly spoiled everything by very imprudently alienating all the clergy with an absurd oath.

DECREE ON THE CIVIL OATH OF THE CLERGY.

ARTICLE I. Bishops, former archbishops, and priests retained in office will be required, if they have not done so, to take the oath to which they are subject by article XXXIX of the decree of the 24th of July last, and which is regulated by articles XXI and XXXVIII of that of the 12th of the same month concerning the civil constitution of the clergy; consequently, they will swear, by virtue of this last decree, to watch with care over the faithful of the diocese or of the parish which is confided to them, to be faithful to the nation, to the law, and to the king, and to uphold with all their authority the constitution decreed by the National Assembly and accepted by the king; this to be done by those who are actually in their dioceses or their parishes, within the course of the week; by those who are in foreign countries, within two months; all dating from the publication of the present decree. . . .

V. Those of the said bishops, former archbishops, and other public church officials who shall not have taken the oath within the fixed time limit prescribed for them, respectively, shall be said to have renounced their offices. . . .

VIII. All persons, lay or clerical, who league together to refuse obedience to the decrees of the National Assembly, as accepted or sanctioned by the king, or to arouse any opposition to their execution . . . shall be prosecuted as disturbers of the public order, and punished according to the rigor of the law.

THE CLERGY REFUSE TO TAKE THE OATH. (Rabaut Saint-Étienne, 237-238.)

The Assembly, having . . . organized the clergy according to the principles of the French constitution, required that the priests take the oath to maintain the constitution taken by all citizens; but at the same time required that they swear to maintain the constitution of the clergy. Of all the soldiers that had taken and violated the civic oath, none thought of saying that heaven had been offended by the military organization. Their pretext had been that they had already taken an oath to the king, which rendered the other void. But priests are accustomed to identify themselves with God, and he who offends them, offends heaven. Subtle intellects would discover, therefore, the means of creating a schism by saying that this temporal constitution was a spiritual one, and even another religion; that it would violate consciences, torment priests, and expose them to martyrdom. They even asked for death or torture, being well assured that the National Assembly would do nothing.

(Ferrières, II, 207-210.)

The revolutionists began to repent of a violent, impolitic measure which was practically useless in establishing the civil constitution of the clergy; but the splenetic hate of the Jansenist Camus against the episcopate and the perhaps legitimate desire for vengeance on the part of the Protestants caused both to think less of what was really beneficial than of their pleasure in destroying an organization which during the last century had so greatly abused its immense power....

Only four bishops submitted to the law: the Archbishop of Sens, and the Bishops of Autun, Orléans, and Pamiers. It was found very difficult to replace the others....

The bishops refused to give up their functions; they declared void all baptisms and ordinations performed by the priests who dared to replace them. Sacraments administered by them were not sacraments. They denied them the power of confession and absolution, forbade the faithful to communicate with them under pain of excommunication, and neglected none of the means formerly so effective in dealing with the people, but which had now become impotent since philosophy and knowledge had enlightened their minds.

CONSECRATION OF THE NEW BISHOPS. (Ferrières, II, 214–215.)

One difficulty remained, that of finding canonical bishops who would consent to install the constitutional bishops. The Archbishop of Sens and the Archbishop of Orléans were approached: they refused. The Bishop of Autun [Talleyrand] and the Bishop of Lida proved to be less difficult. They had no longer any cause for circumspection in regard to Rome or the court: they consented to install the new bishops. The ceremony was held in the Church of the Oratoire: the revolutionists neglected nothing that would render it impressive. A throng of people were present. In vain did the aristocrats, in their speeches, papers, and societies, seek to ridicule the consecration and the new bishops. The people, tired of the resistance of the clergy, which had been represented to them as obstructing the constitution, obstinately insisted upon recognizing the new bishops and affirming that the old had been legally removed.

LOUIS CONSENTS TO SIGN THE OATH. (Mme. de Tourzel, I, 235–237.)

A period of eight days was fixed for the acceptance or refusal of the oath, and the king was strenuously urged to sign the decree. The position of His Majesty was frightful. Placed between his conscience and the misfortunes which were pointed out to him as inevitable in the event of his refusal, he requested time to confer with the pope as to the means of conciliation which could be adopted to comply with the wish of the Assembly without wounding the consciences of the bishops and clergy. He sent word to say that he had written to the pope on the subject, and that he wished to wait for his reply....

The king held out for a long time, but, overcome by the fear of bloodshed, he, on the 26th of December, 1790, gave the sanction so longed for by the rebels and so dreaded by the friends of the monarchy.

(*Ferrières, II, 196–198.*)

That evening, between four and five hundred men of the populace gathered under the windows of the king and loudly demanded the sanctioning of the decree. The court was awaiting this move. Next day, the king caused it to be announced to the Assembly that he had just accepted the decree; but that it was his pleasure to explain the motives which had delayed his acceptation. . . .

The ecclesiastics belonging to the revolutionary party in the Assembly would not await the time prescribed for the taking of the oath. The Bishops of Autun and Lida set the example.

THE OATH CONDEMNED BY THE POPE. (*Ferrières, II, 212.*)

The bishops wanted to be authorized by a brief from the pope, hoping that a decision from Rome would give more weight to their intrigues. The pope accorded the brief. He declared that the National Assembly, in making a civil constitution of the clergy, had exceeded its powers, and that those who had taken or should take the oath were schismatic.

The revolutionists turned the pope's brief into ridicule. They had it publicly burned at the Palais-Royal, together with an effigy of the pope himself clothed in pontifical robes. This spectacle greatly amused the populace, who mocked both the pope and his brief.

(*Extract from a letter of Catherine II to Grimm, January 13, 1791.*)

. . . one never knows if you are still alive in the midst of the murders, extirpations, and disorders in the den of brigands who have seized upon the government of France and are going to reproduce a Gaul of the time of Caesar. But Caesar will subdue them! When will Caesar appear? Oh, he will come, never fear. He will force himself to the front. If I were M. d'Artois or M. de Condé I would know what to do with those 300,000 French cavaliers. *Morgué!* they would save the country or I would die, despite all your *comités de recherches.* All these reflections are for you alone; I do not want them to prejudice Paris against the king and queen.

CONFUSION AND DIVISION. (*Extract from a letter of La Fayette to Bouillé, February 7, 1791.*)

Paris has been sundered by factions, and the kingdom torn by anarchy. Inordinate aristocrats dream of counter-revolution, and the priests are in favor of it through fanaticism. The moderate aristocrats, without the courage to act foolishly, talk foolishly. The impartial monarchists and the various groups of the Right are only acting a part, having neither means, power, nor mental faculties, and would be aristocrats if they were able to be anything. On the Left there are a great number of honest men who wait, a Club of 1789 that is lost in philosophical speculation, a Club of Jacobins who in the main have good intentions, but whose leaders make trouble everywhere. All that is multiplied by associates in the capital and in the provinces who unhappily aim more at numbers than at quality and are guided by personal interests and passions. As for the ministers, they are involved in the Revolution and thus have no choice except to yield to the popular party, whose denunciations they fear. The courtiers, as formerly, are exceedingly stupid, despicable, and aristocratic. The queen is resigned to the Revolution, hoping that sentiment will change somewhat, but fearful of war. The king is for the general welfare and for tranquillity, especially his own. I was forgetting to speak of myself. I am violently attacked by all leaders of the various parties, who regard me as an obstacle, incorruptible and impossible to intimidate; and the first aim of every evil project is disorganization. Add to this the well-deserved hatred of me by the aristocrats and the Orléans party, who have more power than they appear to have. Add also the anger of the Lameths, with whom I have been allied, and of Mirabeau, who says I have despised him. Add money and widespread libels, as well as the anger I arouse in those I prevent from plundering Paris, and you should have the sum of all who work against me.

(*Mme. Roland, 250–251.*)

I frequented the meetings; I saw the powerful Mirabeau, the amazing Cazalès, the audacious Maury, the wily Lameths, and the cool Barnave. I noticed with vexation, on the Right, the type of superiority which gives in any gathering ease of presentation, purity of language, and distinguished manners. But logic, courage of conviction, philosophic enlightenment, understanding of cabinet affairs, and knowledge of law should assure victory to the patriots of the Left...

THE COURT SOUNDS MIRABEAU. (*Ferrières, II, 241–242.*)

Laporte, controller of the civil list, was charged to sound him [Mirabeau]. "I am," he said to him, "persuaded that your character, your talents, and your monarchical principles render you the man most fitted to serve the king and the monarchy advantageously. This has been my sole reason for abandoning my resolution to immerse myself in the domestic affairs confided to me by the king. He authorizes me to speak. I think it is superfluous to urge you to employ all your resources; but I beg you to make known just what they are, and to indicate the course the king ought to take."

"I am greatly disposed," said Mirabeau, "to serve the king from attachment to his person and to royalty, and also from self-interest. If I do not serve the monarchy in some way, I shall be, at the end of all this, one of those eight or ten intriguers, who, having thrown the kingdom into a commotion, will be execrated and will come to a shameful end, although they may for a moment have been, or appeared to have been, very successful. I have still to live down the sins of my youth and a reputation perhaps undeserved. I know of no other way of arriving at this and making my name respected than by great services."

MIRABEAU BRIBED BY THE COURT. (*Mme. Campan, 268–269.*)

The private communications which were still kept up between the court and Mirabeau at length procured him an interview with the queen in the gardens of Saint-Cloud. He left Paris on horseback, on pretense of going into the country, to M. de Clavière, one of his friends; but he stopped at one of the gates of the gardens of Saint-Cloud, and was led to a spot situated in the highest part of the private garden, where the queen was waiting for him. She told me she accosted him by saying: "With a common enemy, with a man who had sworn to destroy monarchy without appreciating its utility among a great people, I should at this moment be guilty of a most ill-advised step; but in speaking to a Mirabeau," etc. The poor queen was delighted at having discovered this method of exalting him above all others of his principles; and in imparting the particulars of this interview to me she said, "Do you know that those words, 'a Mirabeau,' appeared to flatter him exceedingly?" On leaving the queen he said to her with warmth, "Madame, the monarchy is saved!" It must have been soon afterwards that Mirabeau received considerable sums of money. He showed it too plainly by the increase of his expenditure. Already did some of his remarks upon the necessity of arresting the progress of the democrats circulate in society. Being once invited to meet a person at dinner who was very much attached to the queen, he learned that that individual withdrew on hearing that he was one of the guests; the person who invited him told him this with some degree of satisfaction; but all were very much astonished when they heard Mirabeau eulogize the absent guest, and declare that in his place he would have done the same; but, he added, they had only to invite that person again in a few months, and he would then dine with the restorer of the monarchy. Mirabeau forgot that it was more easy to do harm than good, and thought himself the political Atlas of the whole world.

PLANS FOR COUNTER-REVOLUTION. (*Mallet du Pan, I, 234.*)

Mirabeau, devoted to the king's interest for a year before his death, had at his command all the money he asked for. "He was not interested," says M. de Montmorin; "I used to give him all he asked for; this has amounted to twelve thousand francs a month." The king had secured to him in bills signed by the royal hand two million five hundred thousand livres, to be paid the moment his plan of counter-revolution was executed. Six months ago M. de Montmorin was still in possession of these ten bills for two hundred and fifty thousand livres each.

This plan of counter-revolution was drawn up at M. de Montmorin's house, in a memorial that still exists, in which the National Assembly is spoken of with horror and with the deepest contempt. Mirabeau proposed instituting: first, a system of corruption in the tribunals, the sections, and the clubs; second, a system of publications; third, inspectors of the registers, to be sent into the departments under pretext of verifying the rolls of taxes, but really to distribute these publications, and so gain over the members of the directories; fourth, to incite the king's departments to send in addresses demanding the dissolution of the Assembly, and the formation of a new legislative body; fifth,

M. de Bouillé and his army were to support these addresses. He forwarded this plan to M. de Bouillé, who still retains it.

MIRABEAU'S ADVICE TO THE COURT. (*Ferrières, II, 242–244.*)

Mirabeau, then going into details concerning the actual conditions in France, added: "It is the Assembly that must be worked upon. Circumstances are favorable because of the excesses of fanatics. The Assembly is composed of three classes of men. The first, small in number, includes at most thirty persons, madmen who, without having any fixed end in view, oppose and always will oppose the royal authority. The second includes about forty-eight persons. These hold principles more in harmony with monarchy, but they are somewhat too imbued with the original doctrines of the Revolution. The third and most numerous class is made up of men who have no opinions of their own and follow the ideas of their guides and oracles. The Right is good for nothing; the awkward, insensate way they conduct themselves in deliberations prevents their being taken into consideration. Three principal factions divide Paris at present: that of the aristocrats, that of five or six Jacobin leaders of the Orléans faction, and that of La Fayette. There is nothing to be said about the first; the second is completely atrocious, and its atrociousness will cause its downfall. Thus there remains only the third. It reveals itself in a succession of manoeuvers which indicate an unchanging plan. The recent occurrence at the palace, with the disarming of the nobles, has a hidden significance. The party proclaims its attachment to the king and to royalty: these sentiments mask republicanism. It adds falseness and intrigue to other means furnished by circumstances. The position of the king is all the more critical in that this prince is betrayed by three-fifths of the people who approach him. This makes dissimulation necessary, not the customary dissimulation of princes, but dissimulation on a grand scale to remove all pretexts from the malevolent and bring the king and queen great popularity. Leaving Paris is imperative. As long as the king remains in the city it will be impossible to establish order. The foolish activity of the nobles has retarded by two months the measures employed to that end. The illness of the king will repair the damage. This last opportunity must be used with dexterity. It would be vexatious if the Assembly should be dissolved. The moment has not yet come, but it must not pass us by." Mirabeau finished by complaining that none of the promises made him had been kept. They had not acted in good faith towards him; Necker had deceived him. He wanted an assured income, either in life annuities from the state treasury, or in real estate.

The court followed the plan of conduct that Mirabeau had outlined for it.

MIRABEAU UNABLE TO HALT THE REVOLUTION. (*Vaublanc, 171–172.*)

When he wished to repair the evil to which he had so greatly contributed, he was not able to do so. He opposed the declaration of the rights of man; he maintained that the king should have the power of absolute veto, and not a ridiculous provisory veto, that acme of human absurdity; he wanted the king to have the right to make peace or war, and the privilege of commanding the army; he opposed the emigration law; he fought against the division of France into departments; and he demanded that most important thing, the freedom of the king to choose his ministers from among the deputies. He was defeated on all these questions and in every case by insignificant rivals. Thus the real glory of Mirabeau lay in having upheld the principles of monarchy; but the written speeches that he read from the tribune were not as effective as the destructive orations which he had at first pronounced.

(*Bouillé, 211.*)

La Fayette had had, at Emery's in Paris, a three-hour conversation with Mirabeau, which he himself had solicited. I was hoping that, knowing Mirabeau's plans or suspecting them, he had perhaps conceived the desire to identify himself with them and help carry them out, and, enlightened at last by reason, had decided it was the only way of extricating himself from the labyrinth in which he was enmeshed. This union of Mirabeau, La Fayette, and myself, had it been possible between three people so different in character and opinions, could have saved the kingdom. Mirabeau disposed in some fashion of the majority of the Assembly and he had a great following among the Jacobins. ·

La Fayette, in the decline of his power, still retained a large following in Paris, and even in the provinces. I had regained great influence over the troops and some of my authority; I even had . . . great prestige among the national guards and among the government authorities of the provinces along the frontier. The support of those two men would have augmented my powers and increased their own: but Mirabeau was attacked a few days later by a violent illness and died . . .

THE DEATH OF MIRABEAU. (*Ferrières, II, 296–300.*)

. . .the Comte de Mirabeau had too greatly abused his youth; he could not hope to realize a long career. His temperament had altered; his physical habits had become languid and heavy. His spirit had of late yielded to melancholy, his mind to discouragement. He was no longer alert: his ideas came with a painful slowness not at all natural. Tormented with nephritic pain which appeared masked under a thousand different forms, he thought to fight it by means of baths charged with corrosive sublimate, a type of treatment which did not interfere with his functions as deputy, but which necessitated a Spartan régime. This Mirabeau neglected to observe. . . .

Mirabeau's illness produced a great sensation in Paris. From the first day on, his door was besieged by crowds of men and women of all classes, parties, and opinions. The numerous groups that gathered habitually in public places talked only of Mirabeau and the hopes or fears inspired by the hourly bulletins. The Jacobin Society, yielding to the force of public opinion, sent a deputation of several of its members. . . .

Mirabeau summoned the Comte de Lamarck and Frojot, with whom he had had a long-established friendship. He made them sit beside him and talked to them a long time of his private affairs and the friends he was leaving. He spoke of the present state of France and the progress of the Revolution; turning over in spirit the leaves of the great book of the future, and seeing as a presentiment all the events which were in a little while to become a reality, he cried with bitter feeling, "I shall take with me in my heart the requiem of the monarchy, whose débris will be the prey of sedition." These were practically his last words. . . .

(*Miles, I, 270.*)

This event may possibly occasion some confusion in the National Assembly, and a momentary surprise to the nation, but the surprise will only be momentary, for the natural vivacity of the French people will prevent its being of longer duration. If Mirabeau had been an honest man, or if he had possessed either virtuous pride or noble sentiments, he might, by his talents and acquired knowledge, have rendered his country most essential service. . . . I knew him personally. You may form some idea of him when I inform you that he was an object of dread and contempt to all parties. The confidence which his countrymen had in his capacity and superior attainments obtained him a degree of influence in the National Assembly; this influence he preserved to the last; and it would be an injustice to his memory to deny that the Revolution owed much to his collected firmness.

XIII. *The Flight to Varennes*

THE KING DECIDES TO FLEE. (Paroy, 238.)

THE king had steadfastly refused to leave Paris despite the oft-repeated instances of his most devoted servants, the obviousness of the arguments used to convince him, and the opportunities which were presented, especially during his prolonged stay at Saint-Cloud during the summer of 1790. The queen had discussed it with him several times, but could never bring him to a decision. Horror of civil war had kept him from leaving the capital. He would never have taken this step if the Assembly had remained within the bounds of moderation, and had not so boldly shown its intention of seizing the executive power and exercising it to the least detail. The dismissal of his ministers to make room for revolutionary ones and the atrocious religious persecution to which the king seemed accessory were the real reasons why the situation became intolerable and why towards the end of 1790 he desired to escape from the Assembly's control. The queen was the first person in whom he confided. Knowing the character of the king, she did not at first dare encourage him in his idea of flight, but seeing him really determined, she began to hasten its execution in all seriousness.

THE KING CLOSELY GUARDED. (Paroy, 238–239.)

One could leave Paris only by artfulness; force would have been useless and even dangerous. Although the Assembly appeared to become furious whenever anyone expressed the least doubt concerning the king's freedom, and had, by decree, declared him free, it was none the less true that the royal family were prisoners in the Tuileries under the strictest surveillance. Six hundred national guards, drawn from all the sections, mounted guard at the Tuileries. Cavalry could be seen at the exterior gates. There were two guardhouses at the Pont-Tournant, sentinels at all gates of the gardens, and the terrace on the riverside was decorated with sentries at every hundred paces. Inside, the sentinels had been multiplied to a greater extent than at Versailles. They had been placed at all the doors that led to the cabinets of the king and queen, and even in the small dark corridor built in the roof timbers, where there were private stairways used for Their Majesties' service or leading to the rooms of their attendants. The officers of the national guard took the place of the *gardes du corps*. Neither the king nor the queen could go out unless accompanied by a certain number of them. Besides this open surveillance, there was another surveillance still more difficult to escape: that of the house-servants, almost all bribed or spying. The king and queen were so convinced of this that out of the entire personnel they relied only upon the king's first four *valets de chambre* and the first *femmes de chambre* of the queen.

(Paroy, 226–228.)

On the morning of February 28, a multitude of people assembled by Santerre, hero of the Faubourg Saint-Antoine, betook themselves to the donjon of Vincennes to destroy it. M. de La Fayette marched at the head of the national guard to disperse them and prevent disorder. There was great uneasiness about the return of these insurgents; at the palace it was believed that a plot was being carried out. Later it was learned that this insurrection, instigated by the Orleanist faction, had no other object than to cause the people to put the brewer Santerre at the head of the national guard in place of La Fayette. In the course of the day more than three hundred noblemen, armed with swords and pistols, assembled at the palace. At eight o'clock in the evening the *garde soldée* returned from Vincennes after having arrested several of the rioters and dispersed the remainder. As all seemed peaceful and the guards in the palace were seen quietly resuming their posts, each of the nobles decided to withdraw; but as fast as they left the apartments they were stopped, searched, disarmed, knocked about, and pushed down the stairs by the grenadiers of the said *garde soldée.* . . .

On his return from Vincennes, General La Fayette was apprized of what had happened, and he addressed the most lively reproaches to those whom he called in his order of the day "head servants." He had the confiscated arms brought to him. These were composed of pistols, swords, and hunting knives, which caused the aforesaid gathering to be called "Knights of the Dagger."

THE TRIP TO SAINT-CLOUD PREVENTED. *(Paroy, 230–232.)*

The court made its plans to repair to Saint-Cloud early in the spring. All the preparations were openly made, but the Jacobin faction, who neglected no occasion for alarming the people and keeping things in a state of fermentation, caused it to be rumored that the trip masked an attempt of the royal family to emigrate. They even maintained that the king's illness was only a ruse to furnish a pretext for a change of air and provide the royal family with the means of escape; that they did not intend to go to Saint-Cloud, but to Metz or some other frontier town; and that, as a precaution, all change of residence on the part of the royal family should be opposed. The Jacobins, informed by bribed officials of the king's kitchen and royal stables as to the hour of the king's departure, stirred up the multitude on the morning of the 18th of April and incited the *garde soldée* to set upon the attendants and prevent the departure. . . .

M. de La Fayette, always timorous and swayed by events, contented himself during this time with haranguing the mob which filled the Carrousel and going to the king for orders to repulse the multitude. He desired to make a semblance of protecting the departure of the court, but the populace, not at all frightened by these preliminaries, reminded him that by his own words "insurrection was the most sacred of duties."

The king, after having been more than an hour in this predicament, finally descended from his carriage and re-entered the palace, heart-broken over the new outrage he had just experienced. He heard a voice cry out, "Veto has had to turn in his thumbs."

He repaired to the Assembly, complained of the opposition that had been made to his trip to Saint-Cloud, and declared that his journey should not be interfered with if they wished to dissipate the rumors which were spreading over Europe about the constraint in which he was kept. At the same time he reiterated his attachment to the constitution and received much applause.

The Assembly took no action on the disturbance which had prevented the king's departure for Saint-Cloud, except that the departmental administration, made up of members of the Assembly, complained in a proclamation of the excessive patriotism of the inhabitants of Paris.

(*Choiseul, 28–29.*)

It is unnecessary to recall here what took place on February 12, when Mesdames took their departure, or the insurrection in which the people rushed to the Luxembourg, aroused by false rumors concerning the emigration of Monsieur [Louis XVIII]; insurrection which Monsieur calmed by his firmness and courageous bearing. The memory of it is too recent to require retelling.

The disarmament on February 28 of all those persons whose zeal for the king brought them constantly to the Tuileries; the insurrection of the 18th of April which obliged the king to descend from his carriage and abandon his projected trip to Saint-Cloud; the futile step taken by the king in complaining to the Assembly of this insult; and, finally, the violation of his conscience by the forced sanctioning of the civil constitution of the clergy, succeeded in resolving the king to a withdrawal from the capital. He had also been forced to make a sort of consecration of the constitutional church by appearing with the queen at Easter Mass in the Church of Saint-Germain-l'Auxerrois, a concession wrung from him by a threat to massacre the dissenting bishops and priests of the Assembly in a popular uprising, in full view of the Tuileries.

PREPARATIONS FOR FLIGHT. (*Choiseul, 27–28.*)

For a long time various plans for departure had been proposed and submitted to the king. The first proposition dates from the month of March, 1790, and had Brussels via Compiègne as its goal. M. d'Angiviller was ordered to procure the plans which were no longer to be found in his offices. Another project more worthy of attention was proposed during October of the same year by M. le Baron de Breteuil. In February, 1791, the Comte Auguste de La Marck, after having conferred with Mirabeau, was at Metz to communicate a plan to M. de Bouillé, and to find out from him to what extent he would be able to co-operate. M. de Biron also made a journey for the same purpose, arousing only distrust. The king, through a secret correspondence with M. de Bouillé, discussed the possibilities of success offered by each of these projects. . . .

The king did not wish to go beyond his own domains, therefore none of the plans for going to Belgium or England suited him. A locality must be chosen in which he would be safe from insurrectionary movements, where he would be surrounded by a loyal armed force, and where in calmness and security it would be possible to make himself (as I have heard him say many times) the mediator between all parties and the arbiter of all claims, making everyone yield to reason and to the public good.

(Bouillé, 221–222.)

I had made the necessary arrangements and preparations for the departure of the king, which was to have taken place during the first days of May. Everything had been arranged at Montmédy for his reception and for the assembling of a small body of troops under the cannon of that fortress, at a mile's distance from the country of Luxembourg. All munitions and provisions had been sent there, but the troops had become so unmanageable that among those who were in Lorraine, the Bishoprics,[1] and Champagne, I had left only eight or ten Swiss and German battalions which I could count upon, all the French infantry being so corrupted that I did not dare to use them near the king.

(Choiseul, 44–75.)

The carriage intended for the departure of the royal family had been ordered a long time before from the saddler Louis by the Comte de Fersen; he had told him its destination was Sweden or Russia . . . consequently this brown-colored carriage was provided with everything necessary for a long journey. . . .

The king had passports which had been demanded by the Russian minister, M. de Simolin, in behalf of a lady, Swedish or Russian, called the Baronne de Korff. . . .

Let us now return to the departure of the king from the Tuileries.

In the Court of the Princes, in the angle at the right of the Pavillon de Flore, is the grand staircase which leads to the queen's apartments. At the left, near two sentinels of the Swiss and national guards, is a small door leading to the apartments of Mme. de Tourzel and to a small interior stairway which gives access to the king's apartments. In the middle of the court is a landing which leads to a glass door . . . It is by that door that the royal family went out, each individual separately and at some distance from each other.

THE DEPARTURE. (Mme. de Tourzel, I, 321–328.)

We went down to the apartments of the queen, where we found the king. Their Majesties told me that they would be followed by three of the *gardes du corps,* one of whom would give his arm to the queen to conduct her on foot to the carriage; and that the two others would conduct the travelling carriage which was to await the king at some distance from the barrier. All the royal family went on foot except Mgr. the Dauphin and Madame. . . .

[1] Toul, Metz, and Verdun.

When the carriage arrived, the queen herself went to see if all was quiet in the courtyard, and not seeing anybody, she embraced me and said, "The king and I, Madame, place in your hands with the utmost confidence all that we hold dear in the world. Everything is ready; go." We went through the apartments of M. de Villequier, where there was no sentry; we passed through a small and little-used doorway, and got into a worn and old-fashioned carriage, like a *fiacre*, which was driven by the Comte de Fersen....

We travelled in a large berlin, very comfortable, but not at all extraordinary in appearance, as has been so often stated since the disastrous issue of this unhappy journey. I had to pass off as the mistress, under the name of the Baronne de Korff; the king was my valet, the queen my maid, and Madame Elizabeth the children's nurse. It was known that the Baronne de Korff, whose name I had assumed, had journeyed express from Paris to Montmédy by the same route that we were taking, in a carriage like ours, with the same number of persons, and that she had nowhere been asked to show her passport. We had been careful enough even to calculate the number of hours which it had taken her to reach Montmédy, and we shall see by and by the sad result of this precaution.

THE JOURNEY. (*Choiseul, 85–86.*)

This journey, save for a few accidents, was made with security; he [the king] had found the route quiet. He reached Châlons at five o'clock, Somme-Vesle at half-past six, Sainte-Menehould at half-past eight, Clermont at ten, and Varennes at eleven-thirty.

Among all these details should be remembered the fermentation which existed at Sainte-Menehould and the uncertainty which reigned there. The courier of the king did not contribute anything, it is said, towards calming them, for being only a little in advance of the carriage, unfamiliar with Sainte-Menehould, and not knowing the post, he made inquiries at several doors, which drew a large number of people into the street. The carriage, arriving a few moments afterward, was encompassed by this crowd....

THE KING RECOGNIZED BY DROUET. (*Rapport du sieur Drouet; Choiseul, 139–141.*)

... The 21st of June, 1791, at a quarter-past seven in the evening, a retinue of two carriages and eleven horses arrived at the gates of Sainte-Menehould; I thought I recognized, in one of the carriages, the face of the queen, which I had seen before; then perceiving a rather stout man on the box, I was struck by his resemblance to the likeness of the king printed on an assignat of fifty livres. The sudden arrival of a detachment of dragoons which had succeeded a detachment of hussars, both destined to guard the passage of a treasure, it was said, confirmed me more and more in my suspicions, especially when I saw the man I believed to be the king talking in an animated manner and in a low voice to the courier who had preceded the equipage. The haste of the couriers to harness the horses, ordered since morning by an aide-de-camp (M. Goguelat), added still more to the evidence. However, fearing to be the author of a false alarm, and being alone at that moment, without having the opportunity to consult anyone (I have the honor to observe to the Assembly that my house is the last one at Sainte-Menehould), I let the carriages depart; but presently seeing the dragoons ready to mount in order to accompany it, I ran to the guardhouse; I had the alarm sounded; the national guard prevented the departure of the dragoons; and being now sufficiently convinced, I went with M. Guillaume in pursuit of the king; and arriving near Clermont, we were informed, by the postilion who had driven the king's coach, that the king had just passed there.

Then we passed behind Clermont and made use of crossroads in such a manner that we arrived at Varennes in sufficient time to be in the king's vicinity before he departed. It was then eleven o'clock in the evening, very dark, and everybody in Varennes had gone to bed. The carriages were lined up in front of the houses and there was a dispute going on between the postilions and the drivers, the master of the post at Clermont having forbidden his postilions to leave Varennes before having rested their horses. The king, fearing that he was pursued, wished to hasten his departure, and would hear nothing of delay, with the result that while the dispute was going on, we ran quickly to the village and put our horses in an inn which we found open. I spoke to the innkeeper, taking him aside because of the many people about by whom I did not want to be overheard. I said to him, "Comrade, are you a good patriot?" "Yes, to be sure," he replied. "Well! my friend, if that is so, go quickly and warn all the honest people you know that the king is on the heights of Varennes, and that he must be stopped." He did in fact go to warn the people; by another route we descended into the village and having reflected that we should not cry "To arms!" or sound the alarm before having barricaded the streets and the bridge by which the king must leave, my friend and I repaired to the neighborhood of the Varennes bridge, next to which was a large van loaded with furniture. We placed it across the bridge; then searched about for other wagons, so that the roads were blocked to the point where it was impossible to pass. Then we ran to the houses of the mayor and the commandant of the national guards. Within a quarter of an hour, we had eight or ten willing men, whose names I shall give in another time and place, and arrived just as the king descended; then the procurator of the commune and the commandant of the national guard approached the coach, and questioned the travellers as to their identity. The queen replied that they were in great haste, and that they prayed to be allowed to pass . . .

THE KING STOPPED AT VARENNES. (*Mme. de Tourzel, I, 336–338.*)

. . . the *gardes du corps* offered to force a passage for the king, but His Majesty declined the offer. Our passports were asked for, and though they were perfectly in order, and the queen asked that no time might be lost, as we were in a hurry to reach our destination, nevertheless, all sorts of difficulties were made, in order to give time for the assembly of the patriots of the town and neighborhood. . . .

The alarm was sounded in Varennes and the entire neighborhood, and it was impossible to conceal from ourselves that we were recognized. The king was resolute for a long time in his refusal to give his name or leave his carriage, but the questions, accompanied by a promise to let us proceed if the examination of our passports was satisfactory, became so pressing that there was no longer any means of resistance. The king went into the house of M. Sauce, procurator of the commune, and was shown into a room, where the children lay down on a bed. . . .

The king, seeing that further dissimulation would be of no avail, confessed that he was the king; that he left Paris to avoid the daily insults with which he had to put up; that he had no intention of leaving the kingdom; that he merely wished to go to Montmédy to be in a better position to watch over the proceedings of foreign powers; and that if the authorities of Varennes doubted the truth of his words, he would consent to be accompanied by such persons as they might select. The king and queen made every possible attempt to touch their hearts, and to revive in them the old love of the French for their king. But theirs were hearts of brass, which fear alone could move. From time to time fears assailed them of the arrival of M. de Bouillé, and then they begged the king to protect them, and hesitated as to allowing him to continue his journey, but this frame of mind altered as soon as he reassured them on this point.

THE ASSEMBLY'S DECREE REACHES VARENNES. (Choiseul, 101–104.)

The hours passed; our astonishment and anxiety increased with every moment. No news of M. de Bouillé, nor of any troops stationed in the neighborhood by his orders. The tocsin continued to sound, the crowd to increase, when finally M. de Romeuf and M. Baillon arrived. It was five o'clock in the morning. . . .

M. Baillon entered alone, his hair in disorder; the fatigue and excitement of the journey had given his face, naturally somber, a still more alarming aspect; his dress coat was open at the neck, his manner and accent betrayed the most violent agitation. "Sire," he said, "you understand . . . All Paris is being butchered . . . our wives, our children are perhaps massacred; you will not go any farther . . . Sire . . . The interest of the state . . . Yes, Sire, our wives, our children!! . . ." At these words the queen seized his hand and showed him the dauphin and Madame [Royale] who, exhausted by fatigue, had fallen asleep on Sauce's bed. "Am I not also a mother?" she asked.

"To come to the point, what do you desire?" asked the king.

"Sire, a decree of the Assembly . . ."

"Where is it?"

"My comrade has it."

The door opened; we saw M. de Romeuf leaning against the window of the front room, greatly agitated, his face covered with tears and holding a paper in his hand. He came forward with lowered eyes. "What! Monsieur, it is you! Oh, I would never have believed it! . . ." said the queen. The king snatched the decree from him, read it, and said, "There is no longer a king in France . . ." This decree was couched in these terms: "The Assembly orders the minister of the interior immediately to despatch couriers to every department, with instructions to all public officials, national guards, and line troops of the realm to stop or have stopped any person leaving the kingdom, no matter whom;

likewise to prevent the departure of goods, arms, munitions, silver or gold money, horses or carriages; and in the event that any of the couriers overtake the king, the members of the royal family, and those who may have aided in their removal, the said public officials, national guards, and troops of the line shall be required to take every measure possible to stop the said removal, prevent them from continuing their route, and afterwards report it to the legislative body."

LA FAYETTE AND THE ASSEMBLY ASSUME AUTHORITY. (Ferrières, II, 331.)

One cannot refuse just praise to the Assembly, merited by the courage and wisdom it displayed in this grave situation. Alexandre Beauharnais, who was presiding at the time, announced the departure of the king. The Assembly showed neither surprise nor fear; animated by a common sentiment, it thought only of the great responsibilities with which it was entrusted.

The ministers were informed; couriers were dispatched to the departments with orders for public officials, national guards, and troops of the line to stop any person leaving the kingdom; and strong detachments were placed around the hall in order to ensure the peaceful procedure of the deliberations.

(Fontanges; Weber, II, 95–96.)

... the populace of Paris had pronounced so strongly against the flight of the king, and upon the necessity of bringing him back to Paris, that, accustomed to letting themselves be dominated by the people, none except those on the Right dared manifest their sentiments nor oppose anything that tended to follow popular movements. ...

At the first news of the king's flight, M. de La Fayette, in concert with the members of the Assembly who had brought him the information, established the fiction that "the king and the royal family had been carried off by enemies of the public welfare." This first point agreed upon, he believed, or appeared to believe, that the king was going to Valenciennes, and he despatched in that direction one of his confidential aides-de-camp, whom he had especially attached to the service of the queen, and whom Her Majesty had loaded with favors. In giving him his orders he said, "They are too far ahead of us to be overtaken, but we must do something." For the rest, the order was couched in these terms: "M. de Romeuf, my aide-de-camp, is charged to make known along his route that enemies of the country have carried off the king, and to order all friends of the public welfare to prevent his passage. I take upon myself all the responsibility for these instructions.

LA FAYETTE."

THE KING DECIDES TO RETURN TO PARIS. (Mme. de Tourzel, I, 342–343.)

The night passed very sadly, the king not daring to employ force to extricate himself from his painful situation, and the officers, who would have obeyed him at the peril of their lives, not considering themselves in a position to take any decisive step without his authority. ...

After waiting at Varennes for eight mortal hours we had neither sign nor news of the arrival of M. de Bouillé. The king, not perceiving any possible means of getting out of the clutches of the mob, which we could see was increasing, came to the conclusion that he could no longer defer his departure, and he made up his mind to return to Paris. . . .

M. de Bouillé reached the high ground overhanging the town just as the king had left it; and he had the unhappiness of seeing the carriage drive away, surrounded by its gruesome escort. The sinister disposition of the district and the troops, added to the fury of the leaders of the mob, made him fear for the lives of the king and the royal family, if he attempted to rescue them. He therefore withdrew, overcome with grief, and he left France at once, having no doubt in his own mind of the fate that was in store for him if he remained.

(Choiseul, 111.)

The causes of the king's arrest were: (1) the lack of precautions at Varennes; (2) the mistake of a detachment which, on leaving Clermont, took the road to Verdun, instead of that to Varennes; (3) the defection of the regiment of Monsieur; and (4) the absence of all help during the eight hours of the king's stay at Varennes, eight leagues from the general's camp! . . .

But among these causes, the first, gravest, and most decisive continues to be the lack of the simplest precautions at Varennes.

The king informed me that he had remained, by his watch, thirty-five minutes on the heights before entering the town, ignorant of where the relays were and with no means of finding out.

I have it on the king's authority that in his last letter M. de Bouillé had written, "The relay will be at Varennes." He had forgotten to tell the name of the inn; it was the Grand-Monarque. If the king had known this, the postilions would have gone there without stopping; and in spite of the lack of precaution and the general inaction of the troops, officers, and everybody, the coach would have arrived and been relayed; M. le Chevalier de Bouillé would have been called, and his hussars warned before Drouet arrived. Proof of this is positive.

THE RETURN. (Pétion, 189–203.)

I was selected by [Latour-] Maubourg and Barnave to go to meet the king and the people who accompanied him. . . .

Passing to the other side of the carriage, I requested silence, obtained it, and read the decree to the citizens. It was applauded. M. Dumas immediately took command of all the guards who until this moment had accompanied the king. There was admirable submission on the part of these guards. It was with joy that they recognized the military chief who placed himself at their head. The Assembly had appointed him; he seemed to be for them a sacred object.

We told the king that it would be in order for us to take places in his carriage. Barnave and I got in. Hardly had we set foot in it than we said to the king, "But, Sire, we are crowding you, disturbing you; it is impossible to find enough room." The king replied, "I desire that none of the persons accompanying me should leave; I beg of you to be seated; we will crowd together and make room for you."

The king, the queen, and the prince royal were on the back seat; Madame Elizabeth, Mme. de Tourzel, and Madame occupied the front seat. The queen took the prince on her lap, Barnave placed himself between the king and queen, Mme. de Tourzel held Madame in front of her, and I sat between Madame Elizabeth and Mme. de Tourzel.

We had not gone ten steps before they renewed their protestations that the king had not wished to leave the kingdom, and testified to us their acute anxiety about the fate of the three *gardes du corps* who were upon the box . . .

The king, appearing greatly affected by it, spoke of an accident which had just happened to a lord who had had his throat cut. The queen repeated that it was abominable, that he had done much good in his parish, and that his own people had assassinated him. . . .

We went slowly along, accompanied by a crowd of people. Madame Elizabeth talked to me about the *gardes du corps* who had accompanied them; she spoke of them with tender interest; her voice held a nuance of flattery. She broke off her words, at times, in a manner that troubled me. I replied with equal gentleness, without weakness, however, and with a sort of austerity that had nothing of fierceness in it. . . .

The windows were always lowered; we were cooked by the sun and stifled by the dust, but the peasants and national guards followed us in a procession; it was impossible to have it otherwise, because they wanted to see the king. . . .

(Mme. de Tourzel, I, 356–357.)

Barnave was silent and respectful during the entire journey. Pétion, garrulous and insolent, asked Madame for something to drink, whenever he was thirsty, with the most revolting familiarity. He was always talking of America, and the happiness of republics. "We well know," said the king to him, "your desire to establish one in France." "France is not yet ripe for that," he replied insolently, "and I shall not be fortunate enough to see one established during my lifetime."

(Mme. de Tourzel, I, 345.)

The people who surrounded the carriage of the king made remarks to Their Majesties with insolent familiarity whenever it pleased them, and replied to their questions with revolting vulgarity. The kindness with which the royal family treated them, and the patience with which they bore the heat and the dust, which were excessive, but only appeared to be felt by them in relation to the sufferings of the young prince and princess, would have made an impression on less hardened hearts; but they had only one feeling — that of rejoicing over the abasement of the royal family, and their own triumph. It was happiness to them to overwhelm their unfortunate sovereign with chagrin.

PARIS RECEIVES BACK ITS KING. (Mme. de Tourzel, I, 360.)

At the barrier of Paris we found an immense crowd assembled on the road along which our unfortunate king had to pass. Everybody had his head covered, by order of M. de La Fayette, who had, moreover, enjoined the most absolute silence, in order, he said, to show the king the sentiments aroused by his journey. His orders were so strictly attended to that several hatless scullions covered their heads with their foul and dirty napkins.

(Pétion, 202–203.)

The concourse of people was immense; it seemed that all Paris and its environs were assembled in the Champs-Élysées. Never had a more imposing spectacle been presented to the eyes of men. The roofs of the houses were covered with men, women, and children; the barriers were loaded down; the trees filled; everyone had his hat on his head; the most majestic silence reigned; the national guard presented itself with arms reversed. This tense quiet was sometimes interrupted by cries of "Long live the Nation!" My own name and Barnave's occasionally intermingled with these cries, which made a most disagreeable impression, especially upon Madame Elizabeth. What was most remarkable was that at no time did I hear a single abusive word directed against the king. They contented themselves with crying, "Long live the Nation!"

THE KING AND QUEEN AT THE TUILERIES. (La Fayette, III, 91–92.)

La Fayette went forward to meet the procession. During his absence an immense crowd had been allowed to approach the Tuileries; and endeavored, as the royal family were alighting, to maltreat the two *gardes du corps* who had served as couriers during the escape, and were then seated on the box of the king's carriage. The commander-in-chief guaranteed them from all violence and placed them himself in security in one of the halls of the palace. The royal family entered without having experienced any insults. The king was apparently calm; La Fayette then, with a feeling of mingled respect and emotion, presented himself at the king's apartment, and said to him: "Sire, Your Majesty knows my attachment to you; but I have not left you in ignorance of the fact that, if you separated your cause from that of the people, I should remain on the side of the people."

"That is true," replied the king; "you have acted according to your principles; it is a question of party. I am now here. I will say to you frankly that until these last events I thought that you had surrounded me by a vortex of people of your opinion, but that such was not the opinion of France; I have really become convinced on this voyage that I have been mistaken and that such was the general opinion."

"Has Your Majesty any orders to give me?"

"It appears to me," replied the king, with a smile, "that I am more under your orders than you are under mine." La Fayette assured him that in everything which was not contrary to liberty and his duty towards the nation, he had always been desirous of seeing him satisfied with his conduct; he then announced to him the decree of the Assembly, at which the king testified no displeasure. The queen betrayed some irritability, and wished to force La Fayette to receive the keys of the desks, which had remained in the carriages. He replied that no person thought, or would think, of opening those desks. The queen then placed the keys on his hat. La Fayette requested her to pardon the trouble he gave her of taking back those keys, and declared that he would not touch them. "Well," said the queen impatiently, "I shall find persons less scrupulous than you are."

(*Ferrières, II, 377.*)

However, the king and the queen were guarded with the most extreme vigilance. Officers watched at night in the anteroom which opened on the bedchambers. The doors remained open, and precautions were pushed to the point of visual assurance that both beds were occupied.

(*Mme. Campan, 297–298.*)

The first time I saw Her Majesty after the unfortunate catastrophe of the Varennes journey, I found her getting out of bed; her features were not very much altered; but after the first kind words she uttered to me she took off her cap and desired me to observe the effect which grief had produced upon her hair. It had become, in one single night, as white as that of a woman of seventy.

XIV. *The King and the Constitution*

THE KING SUSPENDED FROM OFFICE. (*Fontanges; Weber, II, 139–140.*)

DURING this time [of the king's entry into Paris] the Assembly deliberated on what was to be done under the circumstances. That morning a decree had been passed whose first article was couched in the following terms:

"As soon as the king shall have arrived at the Tuileries, he shall be given a temporary guard who, under the orders of the commanding general of the Parisian guard, shall watch over his safety and be responsible for his person."

Two other articles had likewise decreed "a special guard for the heir presumptive, and another for the queen."

The third had decreed that "all those who had accompanied the royal family in its flight be put under arrest and interrogated," and that "the king and the queen be allowed to make declarations; all to be done immediately to allow the Assembly to take the steps thought necessary."

By the fifth and sixth articles, the king had been "provisionally suspended from his royal functions." Finally, the seventh and last article had enjoined the minister of the interior "to have this decree immediately proclaimed, to the sound of the trumpet, in all parts of the capital."

MISTAKE OF THE ASSEMBLY IN ARRESTING THE KING. (*Napoleon, Memoirs; Thiers, I, 179.*)

The National Assembly never committed so great an error as in bringing back the king from Varennes. A fugitive and powerless, he was hastening to the frontier, and in a few hours would have been out of French territory. What should they have done in these circumstances? Clearly they should have facilitated his escape, and thus have avoided the infamy of a regicide government and attained their great object of republican institutions. Instead of which, by bringing him back, they encumbered themselves with a sovereign whom they had no just reason for destroying, and lost the inestimable advantage of getting quit of the royal family without an act of cruelty.

THE REPUBLICAN MOVEMENT. (*Mme. Roland, 255.*)

I had been struck by the terror which seems to have possessed him [Robespierre] on the day of the king's flight to Varennes. I found him that afternoon at Pétion's, where with great disquietude he was maintaining that the royal family had not taken this step without leaving in Paris a faction which would order a Saint Bartholomew of the patriots, and that he was not expecting to live twenty-four hours. Pétion and Brissot maintained, on the contrary, that the flight of the king would ruin him and should be taken advantage of. The people were excellently disposed, and would be more enlightened on the perfidy of the court by this action than they would have been by the most judicious writing. This one action made evident to everyone that the king did not desire the constitution which he had sworn to uphold. It was time to make a more harmonious one, and prepare people for a republic. Robespierre, sneering as usual and biting his nails, asked what a republic was! Plans for a journal called *Le Républicain* (only two numbers appeared) were then conceived. The Genevese Dumont, a man of parts, contributed to it; the military Duchâtelet lent his name, and Condorcet, Brissot, etc., prepared to collaborate.

(*Sergent Marceau, 121–122.*)

After the return of Louis XVI from Varennes, the question was agitated in Paris as to whether, in consequence of the decrees which he had sanctioned, he had not forfeited the throne. The Assembly did not dare to entertain this important question, but it was discussed in the Jacobins. The Cordeliers, more venturesome, resolved to try if the moment were not come to establish the Republic by declaring the deposition of Louis XVI. Already some of the patriots in the National Assembly had been gained over by the court; the people had long watched, and with increasing distrust, subtle disquisitions taking the place of the frank energy which had at first distinguished the Assembly. Suspicion rested chiefly on the minority of the noblesse, with the exception of Beauharnais, who at this time showed both decision and sincerity. The people, divided between the Jacobins and Cordeliers, wished to present a petition to the National Assembly. The republican party in the Cordeliers tried to combine with the Jacobins, in order to make use of the immense popularity of this club, which gave the impetus to the whole nation; but the Cordeliers failed in the attempt. The Jacobins decided upon a petition to be signed by the people at the Champ-de-Mars on Sunday the 17th. Brissot, Danton, Lanthenas, Laclos, and I were chosen to draw up this petition. Laclos and Brissot wished to indicate the House of Orléans as constitutional heirs of the crown. Danton cried, "Either the son of Louis, who alone has any right, or what I should prefer, the Republic."

BARNAVE RALLIES THE ASSEMBLY TO THE MONARCHY. (*Extract from a letter of Gouvernet to Bouillé, August 26, 1791.*)

The return of Barnave, the respect which he had paid to the king and queen while the ferocious Pétion insulted their misfortunes, and the gratitude which Their Majesties testified to Barnave, changed in some measure the heart of that young man, which till then knew no pity. He is, as you know, the ablest and one of the most influential of his party He consequently rallied around him four-fifths of the Left, not only for the purpose of saving the king from the fury·of the Jacobins, but also to restore to him some of his authority, and furnish him with the means of defending himself in the future by keeping in line with the constitution. In regard to the latter part of Barnave's plan, nobody was in the secret but Lameth and Duport; for the constitutional crowd still gave them so much uneasiness that they could not reckon upon a majority of the Assembly without including the Right; and they conceived that they might rely upon it, when, in revising their constitution, they should give greater latitude to the royal authority.

(*Ferrières, II, 395.*)

[A] violent sortie ended the debates; but the Orleanists and the republicans realized by the direction the discussion had taken that the majority of the Assembly desired neither the dethronement of the king nor a republic. The same diversity of opinion reigned among the Jacobins and among the citizens of Paris. The proposals of Brissot had been coldly received. The literature circulated among the people had not produced that enthusiasm which indicates a widespread sentiment and strongly pronounced desires.

THE PETITION AT THE CHAMP-DE-MARS. (*Ferrières, II, 456–457.*)

The petition was posted on all the walls of Paris, and it was announced that all who wished to sign it should betake themselves to the Champ-de-Mars. A crowd of people repaired there early in the morning, some through curiosity, others, emissaries in the pay of the Duc d'Orléans, with the idea of starting a riot. An opportunity presented itself. Two men were found under the nation's altar; one a disabled soldier, the other a wig-maker's apprentice from a neighboring street. . . . This incident, whether prearranged or accidental, was seized upon by the Orleanists; they cried out that there was a diabolic plot, that the aristocrats were planning to blow up the national altar when the people assembled. The two unfortunate individuals were seized and dragged with curses and blows to the Gros-Caillou section. There, without investigation and without a hearing, though there had not been found upon them nor in their hiding-place any indication calculated to give the least appearance of reality to the frightful design attributed to them, they were hanged on the first lamp-post. The Orleanists cut off their heads and put them on the ends of two pikes. They were preparing to parade them in the streets of Paris and carry them to the Palais-Royal, hoping that the populace would rally to this insignia of carnage, when La Fayette and three commissaries of the municipality arrived, supported by a strong detachment of the national guard. The commissaries were received with a shower of stones. They succeeded, however, in taking away the two heads. The instigators of this infamous assassination were arrested; but the people, throwing themselves with fury upon those who guarded them, snatched them away and put them at liberty.

LA FAYETTE FIRES ON THE MOB. (*Ferrières, II, 459–460.*)

The horrors perpetrated in the morning caused it to be feared that still worse were in store for the evening. The most alarming news continued to arrive. The municipality, no longer able to conceal from itself that tragic consequences would follow its negligence, decreed that the red flag be displayed, that martial law be proclaimed, and that the sessions of the municipal corps be transferred to the École Militaire. The municipal corps marched forth in the midst of twelve hundred men of the national guard, preceded by several squadrons of cavalry and three cannon. The people had so often witnessed the mildness displayed towards all insurrections, and seen submission shown to its wishes, that the sight of the red flag and the twelve hundred guards impressed nobody. The Orleanists and the Jacobins cried out, "Down with the red flag!" — "Down with the bayonets!" A hail of stones soon succeeded the hoots and cries. The national guard came to a halt. La Fayette ordered them to fire some muskets into the air, hoping that noise and fright would induce the mutinous to retreat. In fact, a portion of the mob did take flight; but the leaders, recovering from their first shock and seeing that no one was injured, rallied the fugitives and assembled them around the national altar. There, believing themselves strong enough to brave the national guard, cries of "Down with the red flag!" were heard anew and stones began to fly. Some Orleanists, intent upon provoking trouble, drew near the national guards, hurling the coarsest insults and firing several pistol-shots at them. La Fayette ordered a second discharge, this time real. The effect was terrible: more than four hundred people were killed or seriously injured. The terrified crowd precipitated itself towards all the outlets. The national guard fell upon those who still stood their ground, and the cavalry, getting into action at the same time, succeeded in scattering them in flight.

EFFECTS OF THE ACTION ON THE CHAMP-DE-MARS. (Extract from a dispatch of Lord Gower, July 22, 1791.)

As long as the red flag continues to be displayed at the Hôtel de Ville, we may expect to feel the effects of that energy which military law has given to government. A wonderful change has taken place since the disturbances of the 17th compelled the majority of the Assembly to be sensible of its power. It is calculated that two hundred people have been imprisoned since that event, upon suspicion of fomenting sedition by writing or other means. Danton is fled, and M. Robespierre, the great *Dénonciateur* and by office *Accusateur publique*, is about to be *dénoncé* himself.

THE CONSTITUTIONALISTS DO NOT FOLLOW UP THEIR VICTORY. (Ferrières, II, 463.)

If the constitutionalists had known how to profit by the first consternation of the Jacobins, they would have been victors; a decree would have destroyed the clubs. One consideration restrained the constitutionalists: they still feared the nobles and priests more than the Jacobins. They could come to terms with the Jacobins, but they could never come to terms with the nobility or clergy. They still lacked, moreover, a rallying-point of public sentiment, a center from which they could dominate Paris and the departments. A new club appeared to them to be the right agency for rallying to their party the moderates alienated by the extravagances of the Jacobins and the intrigues of the Orleanists. They fixed upon the Church of the Feuillants, situated in the neighborhood where the Assembly held its sessions.

THE KING REPUDIATES FORCE. (*Extract from a letter of Marie Antoinette to Fersen, July 8, 1791.*)

The king thinks that the close imprisonment in which he is held and the state of total degradation to which the National Assembly has reduced royalty, allowing it to exercise no action whatever, is sufficiently known to foreign powers to need no mention here.

The king thinks that it is by negotiations alone that their help can be useful to him and to his kingdom; that all show of force should be secondary, and only in case all means of negotiation be refused here.

The king thinks that open force, even after a first declaration, would be of incalculable danger, not only to him and to his family, but even to all Frenchmen in the interior of the kingdom who do not think in agreement with the Revolution. There is no doubt that a foreign force could enter France, but the people, armed as they are, leaving the frontiers and the foreign troops, would instantly turn their arms against those of their co-citizens whom they have been incessantly taught during the last two years to regard as their enemies. . . .

THE COMTE D'ARTOIS CONTINUES TO AGITATE. (*Fersen, 122.*)

The Comte d'Artois wants no negotiation, only force without regard to dangers. Dissatisfied with the papers [of the king]; wants them suppressed; full powers not necessary. Showed him Breteuil's letter announcing twenty thousand Spaniards, and six millions in Holland for the king at liberty. D'Artois said he knew all that. Monsieur showed signs of feeling; D'Artois talks always and never listens — being sure of everything; wants only force, no negotiations. Monsieur would do better alone, but is entirely subjugated by the other. Calonne is coming from Aix-la-Chapelle; they asked me to wait for him. . . . Condé here, and a number of others. The princes want to dispose of all foreign forces, divide them, and appoint the general officers. They have sent for Broglie and Castries; the former will come; doubtful if the other does, on account of Calonne.

LEOPOLD PREFERS NEGOTIATIONS. (*Ferrières, II, 402–403.*)

Although he was the most interested party, the emperor was awaiting developments. This prince was naturally inclined towards peace. Worn out by the unfortunate war against the Turks, and not at all reassured in regard to the Low Countries, where minor disturbances arose from time to time, he preferred the path of negotiation. He seemed to await some honest way out which would reconcile his honor with what he owed to his brother-in-law and to the German princes with possessions in Alsace. The King of Sweden and the ecclesiastical electors sincerely desired to aid the French princes, but they were not in a condition to arrange alone an enterprise of such magnitude. Therefore, the leaders of the counter-revolutionists, unable to deceive themselves as to the difficulties which opposed the execution of their plans, were ardently employed in removing obstacles.

(Extract from a letter of Edmond Genêt to Montmorin, August 16, 1791.)

... the Austrian courier ... has brought a long memorandum proposing that Russia form a concert with all courts where there are relatives, friends, or allies of the king, even with the court of London, and that this concert be directed against the French nation if it forgets its duty....

(Ferrières, II, 470.)

While the French nation was busying itself with ... stupidities, Calonne, by dint of intrigue and scurryings about, managed to arrange an interview at Pillnitz between the emperor, the King of Prussia, and the Comte d'Artois. The meeting began with fêtes, balls, banquets, and operatic performances. Then attention was turned to business; it was declared that the monarchs of Europe would regard the cause of Louis as their own....

THE DECLARATION OF PILLNITZ.

His Majesty the emperor and His Majesty the King of Prussia, having heard the wishes and representations of Monsieur and of Monseigneur le Comte d'Artois, declare conjointly that they regard the present situation of His Majesty the King of France as an object of interest common to all the sovereigns of Europe.

They hope that that interest cannot fail to be recognized by the powers who are appealed to for assistance, and that in consequence they will not refuse to employ, conjointly with Their Majesties, the most efficacious means within their power in assisting the King of France to establish, in the most perfect liberty, the bases of a monarchical government equally suitable to the rights of sovereigns and the well-being of the French nation. If such should be the case, Their Majesties the emperor and the King of Prussia have decided to act at once, and by mutual agreement, with the forces necessary to realize the common aim proposed. Meanwhile, they will give their troops the proper orders that they may be in a state of readiness.

Pillnitz, August 27, 1791.

LEOPOLD
FREDERICK WILLIAM

AVIGNON UNITED TO FRANCE. *(Mme. de Tourzel, I, 405.)*

The Assembly ... took into consideration the union of the Comtat of Avignon with France. It had resolved upon carrying it out for a long time, and it was proclaimed with the same carelessness as the other decrees. The union was agreed upon in accordance with the so-called wish of the Comtadins

— a wish expressed under the pressure of the terror which had seized upon the majority of the signatories. The only sincere signatures were those of the brigands in harmony with the rebels of the Assembly.

THE ÉMIGRÉS PREPARE TO ATTACK FRANCE. (*Bouillé, 310.*)

I learned that anarchy was growing daily in France, a fact only too well indicated by the crowd of *émigrés* of all ranks seeking refuge across foreign borders. They were given arms and organized into regiments along the banks of the Rhine, forming a small army dangerous to the provinces of Alsace and Lorraine. These activities aroused the fury of the people and favored the destructive aims of the Jacobins and anarchists. The *émigrés* had even wanted to make an attack upon Strasbourg, believing that they had reliable information and friends who would open the gates to them. The king, who was advised of this, employed orders and even prayers in order to stop them and prevent the commission of a hostile act.

THE CONSTITUTION COMPLETED. (*Extract from a letter of Gouvernet to Bouillé, August 26, 1791.*)

I have held out hopes to you which I no longer entertain. That fatal constitution, which was to be revised and amended, will not be touched. It will remain what it is — a code of anarchy, a source of calamities; and owing to our unlucky star, at the moment when the democrats themselves begin to be sensible of some of their errors, it is the aristocrats who, by refusing their support, oppose their reparation.

(*Ferrières, II, 480–481.*)

The constitution having been completed, a solemn reading of it was given. In spite of the patching done by the revisers, the numerous defects of the edifice were evident to everyone. The very rights of man, so foolishly laid down as principles in the first part of the constitution, were a perpetual and ever-fermenting source of disturbances, insurrections, and anarchy; an aliment proper to arouse all sorts of ambitions, desires, and antagonisms; a deadly weapon in the hands of the seditious. The manner of election to office by popular vote was not less vicious, and seemed to predetermine unwise selections, eliminating men who were honest, opposed to intrigue, and scornful of reprehensible popularity. The administrative corps was given an indeterminate position between the legislative body and the king. Not knowing to which of these two it belonged, it was sure to become a subject of continual quarrels and discord. But in justice it must be said that there were excellent things in this same constitution. The rights of the people were definitely established, social equality was wisely delineated, and personal liberty and property rights were guaranteed.

LOUIS XVI ACCEPTS THE CONSTITUTION. (*Mme. de Staël, 213.*)

Louis XVI would have accepted the English constitution in good faith, if it had been presented to him with the respect that was due to the head of the state; but his feelings had been outraged, especially by three decrees more detrimental than useful to the national cause. The right of pardon, a privilege which should exist in every civilized society and which in a monarchy can emanate only from the crown, was abolished; an oath to support the civil constitution of the clergy was exacted from priests under penalty of losing their remunerations; and an attempt was made to take the regency away from the queen.

(*Ferrières, II, 492–493.*)

The ministers bore a letter from the king. This prince, after some reflections on the policies which had guided him since the beginning of his reign, on his love for his people, and on the motives which had determined him to leave Paris and isolate himself from all factions in an endeavor to arrive at a better understanding of the general will, added: "I accept the constitution. I engage to maintain it within the country, defend it from outside attacks, and have it carried out by every means within my power. I declare that being aware of the adhesion of the great majority of the people to the constitution, I renounce my claim to concur in this work; and being responsible to the nation alone, none other, when I renounce it, has the right to complain." At these words the Left and the tribunes echoed with applause and with cries of "Long live the King!" The Right maintained a mournful silence. "Let us agree," continued the king, "to forget the past, so that accusations and prosecutions connected with events of the Revolution may be eliminated in a general reconciliation. I do not speak of those actuated by their attachment to me; can they be regarded as culpable? As for those who have laid themselves open to legal prosecution by excesses which might be considered personal injuries, I will prove to them that I am King of the French." The room resounded with renewed applause and cries of "Long live the King!"

La Fayette asked that all persons under arrest or prosecution relative to the departure of the king, or relative to the Revolution, be immediately set at liberty, with all proceedings against them brought to an end.

Large assemblies are generous and human only in moments of enthusiasm; at other times each individual, isolating his conscience from the law that he makes, regards it, not as his own work, but as the work of all, and does not believe himself personally responsible for any of its effects.

The general rejoicing produced, for the time being, a just and even generous Assembly: the proposal of La Fayette was decreed by acclamation.

THE KING OPPOSED TO FOREIGN INTERFERENCE. (Extract from a letter of Montmorin to the French representative in Russia, September 20, 1791.)

The king having accepted the constitution, His Majesty can no longer be regarded except as enjoying not only full liberty, but also all his authority. Consequently, all attempts that might be made to avenge the royal dignity would henceforth be pointless and would serve to light a flame, the effects of which it would be difficult to foresee.

Such is the veritable sentiment of the king . . .

In this state of affairs, Monsieur, the king has only one desire. . . . We cannot believe, Monsieur, that . . . the emperor . . . has taken upon himself to arouse all the sovereigns of Europe against the French nation in order that all the united sovereigns should come to the aid of a king who has not called upon them. . . .

The king is far from believing, Monsieur, that the empress [Catherine II] will let herself be inveigled into taking part in projects so contrary to the rights of peoples. . . . You must, Monsieur, represent strongly to the Russian ministry that all attempts to change a state of things that the French nation has brought about and the king accepted would be a formal attack upon the independence of France. . . .

THE FESTIVAL OF THE CONSTITUTION. (*Ferrières, II, 494-495.*)

All Paris was filled with joy and celebrated by organizing festivals. This manifestation would not have deceived a judicious observer. The acceptance of the constitution, far from producing a reconciliation, seemed to have intensified hatreds still further; factions were rending each other in the journals, and spared neither intrigue nor slander to cast opprobrium upon their opponents.

A NEW ASSEMBLY TO BE ELECTED. (*Mme. Jullien, 32-36.*)

See how all our legislators are striving to merit our respect. It should be noted that the hall resounded with applause from the tribunes when they revoked the decrees that restricted our electors, and from eighty-three corners of France comes the cry, "A new legislature!" That has the double advantage of making the present one rise to the point to which public opinion is carrying it in spite of itself, and encouraging the coming one to display the real grandeur that we expect. Tell me carefully . . . just what the sentiment is in R——; let me know if the Jacobins have become Feuillants. I am breathless with excitement! . . .

I wish the eighty-three departments were well convinced of the obligations they have towards those who are unjustly designated, even in the capital, as sedition-mongers. Without them and without the courage of our good Parisians, both foolish and wise, you would have received from the painful labors of your Assembly nothing but shackles and affronts.

You are going to elect new legislators, the hope of the country. Everybody is expecting to see arriving from the depths of the provinces Aristides, Fabricius, Cato, Cincinnatus, etc. No priests, above all, and no fine intellects! Virtuous people, who despise wealth.

THE QUESTION OF ELIGIBILITY. (*Ferrières, II, 278-281.*)

Thouret propounded the following question: Should public officials be declared ineligible for the legislature? A multitude of voices cried out from all parts of the chamber, "No re-election!" Robespierre demanded that before discussing this important question the Assembly show itself disinterested, and it was decreed forthwith that the members of one legislature would be ineligible for the next. Aristocrats and Jacobins overwhelmed the proposition of Robespierre with applause. . . .

Neither the Jacobins nor the aristocrats wanted the constitution: the first group desired the establishment of a democratic republic, the second demanded the ancient despotism under whose protection they had lived until now, rich, happy, and respected. The constitution, in spite of all its defects, provided a wise form of government, equally removed from license and despotism. This government would have been gradually established through the lassitude of the people and the inertia of the king, if only the aroused public mind had been allowed to rely upon it. The most effective means of consolidation was, therefore, to accord to the deputies who had made the constitution the privilege of being re-elected to the following legislature. Beyond a doubt the people, having great confidence in them, would have named them in preference to newcomers, and then their influence over their colleagues would have kept the state of things as it was. The Jacobins and the aristocrats realized this perfectly; they foresaw the strengthening of the constitution if a re-election took place; they feared the talents and the popularity of the constitutionalists, and even the customary respect in which they were held; they seemed all the more dangerous to them in that, chastised by experience, they would realize the little stock that could be taken in the people, the necessity of stopping their advance, and of ceasing to regard the monarch as a perpetual enemy, seeing in him instead the support and guarantee of the constitution.

THE PROPERTY QUALIFICATION. (*Mme. de Staël, 222.*)

It was decreed that the payment in taxes of a *marc d'argent*, that is to say, fifty-four livres, would be the necessary qualification for a deputy [to the Legislative Assembly]. This was enough to provoke complaints at the tribune in regard to younger sons and men of genius who would be excluded by their poverty from representing the nation; yet even that was not sufficient to restrict the popular choice to the landholding class.

END OF THE CONSTITUENT ASSEMBLY. (*Ferrières, II, 497–498.*)

The Assembly neared the end of its work. September 30, the day definitely fixed for the close of the session, the king repaired to the hall where the sessions were held. Things had come to the point where the disbanding of the Assembly was a misfortune for the king. Louis XVI felt this perfectly; he said that it would have been better for the Assembly to have continued its sessions for some time in order that it might itself have made some sort of trial of its own work. It could have added to its achievements those things which, already begun, had only needed perfecting and those whose necessity was felt by legislators enlightened by the experience of three years...

(*Bouillé, 306–307.*)

This Assembly had lost its prestige, as well as the esteem and confidence of the nation, and was dominated by the then united Jacobins and Orleanists. It dissolved after having decreed the election of new deputies to form a permanent National Assembly that would henceforth represent the French people, maintain the legislative power, and transmit it successively to other Assemblies which were to be renewed at epochs specified by the constitution.

XV. *The Legislative Assembly*

THE NEW ASSEMBLY GATHERS. (*Vaublanc, 181.*)

THE Legislative Assembly was inaugurated under the most adverse circumstances. Appointed by Seine-et-Marne, I was one of the members of this Assembly and perhaps wielded some influence there. The king, after the return from Varennes, had been kept prisoner in the Tuileries, interrogated by officers of the Constituent Assembly, and re-established upon his throne in swearing to uphold the constitution. The new Assembly was entirely inexperienced, made up of lawyers, procurators, men of letters, and amateur philosophers. It could not produce good; its destiny was to work evil, especially through the crude and ridiculous fundamental principles which it was charged to uphold.

Many members of the Constituent Assembly had come to realize their mistakes. If they had not excluded themselves from the elections, at least two hundred of them would have been returned, and the second Assembly would not have been so foolish and atrocious. There would have been within it elements which would have safeguarded the crown and the royal family.

OPENING OF THE LEGISLATIVE ASSEMBLY. (*Ferrières, III, 6-7.*)

Elected almost entirely by the clubs, the Legislative Assembly opened its sessions amid the acclamations of crowds of club members who came to applaud their selections. Many of these were animated by a violent hatred of the court and the constitutionalists. Brissot, Condorcet, and Fauchet, Bishop of Calvados, had personal grudges to vent. The thirty-three members of the Constituent Assembly attached to the Orléans party were in control of the Jacobins. At first everything seemed to indicate superstitious respect for the constitution. Deputies who were sixty years of age were appointed to go to bring the constitution from the archives. It was decreed that each deputy, with his hand upon this political gospel, should take oath to uphold it and defend it with his life's blood. The document appeared, preceded by the ushers of the Assembly, the archivist Camus marching at the center of the delegation. The deputies, in the silence that attended the reception, rose and removed their hats. The president mounted first to the tribune. The deputies followed and swore to maintain the constitution decreed by the Constituent Assembly.

(*Choudieu, 62–63.*)

The Assembly had begun its sessions on the 1st of October, 1791; on the 4th it decided to send a deputation to the king to announce that it had organized. This deputation having presented itself at the palace on the 5th, the minister of justice brought the information that the king could not receive it until the next day. On the insistence of M. Ducastel, who headed the deputation, the minister returned to the king and brought back word that they would be received that evening at nine o'clock.

This mode of receiving a deputation composed of sixty members of the National Assembly was somewhat cavalier and did not announce a benevolent attitude. Dissatisfaction began to manifest itself in the Assembly, which had been offended, and rightly so.

When the deputation was finally shown into the presence of the king, the leader, M. Ducastel, although he was much devoted to the court, addressed the king with only these few words: "Sire, the Assembly is definitely established; it has deputized us to inform you of this." Louis XVI responded more dryly still, "I cannot meet with you until Friday." This conduct was little calculated to conciliate public opinion in his regard.

THE ASSEMBLY DIVIDES. (*Choudieu, 64–67.*)

A thronelike armchair upholstered in gold and fleurs-de-lis was reserved for the king. Couthon proposed that the king's chair be placed beside that of the president; Grangeneuve demanded that the titles *Sire* and *Majesty*, which had originated in servility, be replaced by the finer and more constitutional *King of the French*.

These two propositions raised a clamor in a part of the hall already occupied by a number of nobles who, upon becoming more numerous, constituted the Right. Among them, I noticed Hérault de Séchelles, former attorney-general of the *parlement* of Paris, the former Marquis de Girardin and de Jaucourt, MM. de Kersaint, Gouvion, Mathieu Dumas, Pozzo di Borgo, Beugnot, Becquet, Vaublanc, Lemontey, etc.

Thus from the very first the Assembly was divided into two parts: the court party, whose principal members I have just named, and the independents, who have since formed what is called the Mountain, and whose most noteworthy adherents were in the beginning Vergniaud, Guadet, Gensonné, Brissot, Couthon, Grangeneuve, the fiery Isnard, etc. . . .

M. Garran-Coulon remarked that, if the Assembly were to conform to article II of the decree which the Constituent Assembly had passed the 29th of the preceding September, and which provided "that the king having arrived at his place, each member can sit down and put on his hat if the king remains sitting with his hat on," it would create confusion, while giving some an opportunity to show idolatry, and others, pride. "So much the better," said another member. "If there are flatterers, it is well to know who they are."

The article adopted seemed directed against the court party. It threw them into a ferment. They hurriedly assembled, as if the country had been in danger, their groups of vassals and sub-vassals, made up of all the weak and easily intimidated. They were persuaded that the king would not present himself if the decree was maintained, and they had the weakness to revoke a measure which had received an immense majority the evening before.

Thus it is that, in deliberative assemblies, a third party forms which properly speaking has no opinions and which in most cases allows itself to be influenced to act without knowing why. These men form a compact body through selfish motives rather than through principle. Without talents and without energy, they feel only the force of inertia. They are a species of amphibious beings, indifferent to all that is not to their personal interest, appearing to be neutral and giving themselves an air of impartiality in the discussions they hardly listen to, but voting selfishly and in obedience to the first signal of their leader.

THE CENTER. (*Vaublanc, 182–184.*)

But what rendered the situation of the Right deplorable from the beginning was the party in the middle called the Plain (*ventre*). This party held the same ideas as ourselves, but did not dare to sit with us. The Left, terminating in the party called the Mountain, was so crowded, and the deputies in the part occupied by the Plain were so closely packed and heaped up, that they had the appearance of regarding us as dangerous men and of taking great care to avoid sitting near us. It is impossible to imagine the consequences of this kind of grouping in an Assembly whose honest and trustworthy members were at the same time incredibly weak in character. The more these incompetents herded together, the more they communicated their weakness to one another; it became contagious. Men of the Plain, who grew pale at roll call when they heard their names pronounced, would have voted differently and with firmness if they had decided to sit with the Right. . . .

[There came to be a group] called the Gluttons (*ventrus*). This title was given them in the Constituent Assembly because the majority were accustomed to leave at dinnertime, although the rest of the Assembly remained in session for the discussion of important affairs. The revolutionaries profited by these absences, and managed the discussions so that the decrees were passed after the departure of a large number of Gluttons, whose main idea was to be on time at the impatiently awaited repast. These people have been responsible for all the disasters of the Revolution.

THE PARTY OF THE LEFT. (*Ferrières, III, 15–17.*)

The republicans included several members of the Constituent Assembly such as Robespierre, Pétion, Antoine, Buzot, Dumets, and Prieur, most of the municipalities of the kingdom, all the popular societies, known under the name of Jacobins, and a throng of ambitious men who were dissatisfied with a revolution from which they had profited little, and who desired to make a second that would be more to their advantage. These men, mingling with the people, intrigued in the sections and aroused the departments. The Orléans faction, joining this party to make it an instrument of its leader's ambitions, lent its influence and its gold. Too weak to act openly, and not daring to make a direct attack upon the king or the constitution, the

Orleanists sowed dissension, and denounced the court and the ministers, representing them as the enemies most dangerous to the constitution. The public, forever duped by the agitators, and failing to find in the new order of things the well-being it had been led to hope for, began to perceive that the constitutionalists had thought more often of their own interests than of the interests of the nation. It gradually cooled towards the constitution, blaming its dissatisfaction now upon the constitution itself, and now upon those who had charged themselves with its execution. The constitutionalists and the counter-revolutionists regarded the republicans as men who pursue a chimera; and instead of uniting against them before they had grown in strength, they fell with fury upon one another, preferring to see republicanism triumph rather than sacrifice their least pretensions. A coalition of some of the most important deputies of the Assembly who seemed to favor the republican party gave it still more consistency. This coalition was known as the Girondins, because Vergniaud, Guadet, Gensonné, Ducos, and Fonfrède, deputies from the department of the Gironde, in directing its course, acquired by their talents, and still more by their intrigues, a great influence over the deliberations of the Assembly and over public opinion. The Girondins were rather indifferent as to the form of government, provided they were in control and could dispose of money and offices. Feeling, however, that the constitutionalists would not give up their prey, they joined the republicans, waiting for events to decide whether it would be to their interest to sell themselves to the court or to the republic.

(*Dumas, I, 217–218.*)

The party formed by the deputation of the Gironde, almost wholly composed of very eloquent young advocates, some of whom, especially Vergniaud and Guadet, had as much natural eloquence as little experience in public affairs, hastened to display great strictness of principles and a lofty republican pride. Theorists, such as Condorcet, Guyton de Morveau, etc., practiced and subtle writers, such as Brissot, joined it. They left the most violent men, the Coryphæi of the Jacobins, to make the first attacks on the majesty of the throne, to sow the seeds of distrust, and to embarrass the government by agitating, from the very beginning of the session, the questions which were most likely to excite popular passions. They kept themselves in reserve behind this vanguard, always ready to support its attacks by profiting by the slightest circumstance to gain ground, sometimes by violent speeches, sometimes by affecting a false moderation. This system of tactics was constantly followed during the whole course of the session, and the constitutionalist party, reduced to act on the defensive, supported itself during the first months only by means of the vacillating neutrality of the greatest number of the members of this Assembly, who, even when throwing much light upon the discussions, always avoided deciding between the two minorities, and ended by forsaking us.

THE PARTY OF THE RIGHT. (*Ferrières, III, 17–18.*)

The counter-revolutionists did not conceal their project of annihilating the constitution and re-establishing the old order of things. The king's two brothers, together with the Prince de Condé, the Duc de Bourbon, and the Duc d'Enghien, had just published a protestation against Louis XVI's having accepted the constitution. They insisted that the acceptation had been forced, and that, had it been voluntary, the king could not have consented to the change from the ancient government. This protestation, carefully spread throughout Paris and the departments, and announced as tacitly endorsed by the king himself, demonstrated to all Frenchmen that the acceptance of Louis XVI had in no way changed the projects of the counter-revolutionists. This party included many members from the Right of the Constituent Assembly, as well as the bishops, the majority of the nobility and higher clergy, the *parlements*, the financiers, and officers of all ranks. The leaders had conceived a most foolish idea. They imagined that by having all the nobles leave the kingdom, they could, by the aid of these nobles and the foreign powers, return sword in hand to re-establish the old order of things, and regain the rights and privileges which had been taken from them by the new constitution.

The nobles were told, then, that they should emigrate and assemble on the frontiers; that they would find there large armies of Austrians, Prussians, Russians, and Spaniards, at the head of which they would return to their country in triumph. The nobles departed from their châteaux in crowds, leaving their wives, children, and property to the mercy of their enemies. They did not even take with them their money, jewels, or arms, and the majority had but one coat and a few shirts. They believed that this voluntary exile, which was to last their whole lives, was only a pleasure trip of five or six weeks.

POLICIES OF THE MINISTRY. (*Ferrières, III, 36–37.*)

... the ministers did not act in good faith towards the Assembly. They all sought to throw upon it the responsibility for the shocks and checks experienced by the constitution, hoping to embarrass the Assembly with details, thinking that it would neglect to use that minute surveillance which is the sole means of forestalling opposition in a new type of government subjected to a thousand cross currents. Thus, by a policy at first appearance adroit, but later proving disastrous to its instigators, the ministers allowed everything to become disorganized, and imputed this disorganization to the constitution itself, insisting that it provided no means for the carrying out of its own laws.

The essential point was to keep the military and naval forces in a state of dilapidation, while appearing to be energetically engaged in putting them on a respectable footing, so that if after internal disturbances there should be an opportunity to enter France, the foreign powers could suddenly appear in a most formidable guise and inspire such terror in the people that, frightened, they would place themselves voluntarily in the hands of the king, begging him to ward off the storm about to burst upon them. It was for this that the minister of war and the minister of marine were working. Thus, while the minister Tarbé exaggerated the financial disorder and complained to the Assembly of the non-collection of taxes, the minister Duportail gave a most satisfactory account of the armies, of army supplies, and of the state of defense along the frontiers.

THE ÉMIGRÉS. (La Fayette, III, 299–300.)

The *émigrés*... were unanimous in their desire for an invasion, and in their exertions at all foreign courts; they were satisfied with having engaged foreign armies in the quarrel, and plunged them into the bosom of their country, for they felt convinced that the counter-revolution would be the certain result of the contest. It was known that M. de Calonne, the principal agent of the princes, had publicly said at Brussels, "If the powers delay making war, we shall know how to make the French declare it." The aristocracy of the court experienced the same feeling. The king and queen hesitated between various parties. The queen especially, who would have consented to owe her deliverance to Austrian or even Prussian arms, was withheld by her reluctance to lay herself under obligations to Monsieur, whom she never liked, and the Comte d'Artois, whom she no longer liked. "The Comte d'Artois will then become a hero!" she exclaimed with bitterness.

LETTER TO THE KING FROM HIS BROTHERS.

I have written to you, but by post and was therefore unable to say anything; we are here, two who think as one; same sentiments, same principles, and same zeal to serve you: we keep silence; in breaking it too soon we would compromise you; but we shall speak as soon as we are sure of being generally supported, and the moment is near. If we are spoken to in the name of those people, we will not listen; if on your part, we will, but we will continue on our way. Thus, if they try to force you to say something to us, do not worry; be at rest concerning your safety; we exist but to serve you; we are working industriously and all goes well; our enemies have too much interest in your conservation to commit a useless crime which would end in ruining them. Adieu.

Louis-Stanislas-Xavier
Charles-Philippe

(Mme. de Tourzel, II, 38–39.)

The Assembly ... by no means paused in its proceedings against the princes, brothers of the king, and M. de Condorcet made a long speech to serve as a preamble to the decree. He stated that the French nation would never take up arms to make new conquests, but simply to secure its liberty and cause its dignity to be respected, and that it would always be able to manage the people of the states with which it might be at war. This speech, interspersed with the ordinary abuse of the princes, the nobility, the priests, and the *émigrés*, might be regarded as an earnest request for the desired treaty. In consequence of it, the Assembly decreed, on the 1st of January, that there were grounds of accusation against Monsieur, Mgr. le Comte d'Artois, Mgr. le Prince de Condé, and MM. de Bouillé, de Calonne, and Mirabeau the younger, whom it described under the name of Riquetti, out of respect to the great man who had borne that of Mirabeau with so much glory; and it directed the united diplomatic and legislative committees to bring forward within three days a draft bill of accusation, adding that the minister of foreign affairs would be held responsible to supply them with all the notes and information he could collect from the agents of the nation in connection with the plans of the *émigrés*, and to denounce all who might assist the latter or neglect to inform the government of the hostile arrangements they might have made or carried out at foreign courts.

DECREES AGAINST THE ÉMIGRÉS AND THE CLERGY. (*Ferrières, III, 30–31, 405.*)

... the Assembly, considering that the heir presumptive to the crown was a minor, and that Louis-Stanislas-Xavier, French prince, adult relative and first in line for the regency, was absent from the kingdom, decreed, in execution of article II of section III of the French constitution, that Louis-Stanislas-Xavier, French prince, be required to enter the kingdom within a period of two months, counting from the day the proclamation of the legislative body should have been published in Paris, the customary place of the sessions; and that, in case Louis-Stanislas-Xavier, French prince, should not have returned within the time decreed, he should be considered to have abdicated his right to the regency, by authority of the article cited in the constitution.

This first decree was followed by two others. One withdrew from the non-juring priests the right of exercising their functions in the parishes where their curacies were situated, and obliged them to leave these parishes and retire to the central town of the district; the other [was as follows]:

The National Assembly, considering that the tranquillity and safety of the kingdom depend upon its taking prompt and efficacious measures against such of the French as, in spite of the amnesty, never cease to plot against the French constitution from beyond the frontiers, and believing that the time has come to punish severely those whom indulgence has not been able to recall to the duties and sentiments of free citizens, has declared the urgent need for a decree, and this having been passed in the form of a resolution, has enacted the following:

ARTICLE I. The French assembled beyond the frontiers of the kingdom are from this moment declared suspect of conspiring against their country.

II. If by the first of January next they are still thus assembled, they shall be declared guilty of conspiracy, prosecuted as such, and punished with death.

III. As for the French princes and public functionaries, both civil and military, who held office at the time of their departure from the realm, their absence on the aforesaid date of January 1, 1792, shall constitute them likewise guilty of the crime of conspiracy against the country, and they shall be punished in the manner prescribed by the preceding article.

(*Ferrières, III, 31.*)

These two decrees made the rupture inevitable. Louis XVI was resolved to refuse his sanction, impelled to this by his individual principles, which did not permit him to ratify, in the name of the law, measures that seemed to him unjust. He was sustained in this resolution by his ministers and even by the constitutionalists, who could not see without pain the frequent inroads upon the constitution made by the Assembly.

THE KING ASKS HIS BROTHER TO RETURN. (*Letter of the king to Louis-Stanislas-Xavier, Paris, November 11, 1791.*)

I wrote to you, my brother, on the 16th of October last, and you ought not to have had any doubt of my real sentiments. I am surprised that my letter has not produced the effect which I had a right to expect from it. In order to recall you to your duty, I have used all the arguments that ought to touch you most. Your absence is a pretext for all the evil-disposed, a sort of excuse for all the deluded French, who imagine that they are serving me by keeping all France in an alarm and an agitation which are the torment of my life. The Revolution is finished; the constitution is completed; France wills it; I will maintain it; upon its consolidation now depends the welfare of the monarchy. The constitution has conferred rights upon you; it has attached to them one condition which you ought to lose no time in fulfilling. Believe me, brother, and repel the doubts which pains are taken to excite in you respecting my liberty. I am going to prove to you by a most solemn act, and in a circumstance which interests you, that I can act freely. Prove to me that you are my brother and a Frenchman, by complying with my entreaties. Your proper place is by my side; your interest, your sentiments alike, urge you to come and resume it; I invite you, and, if I may, I order you, to do so.

LOUIS

(*Louis-Stanislas-Xavier's answer to the king, Coblenz, December 3, 1791.*)

Sire, my Brother and Lord:

The Comte de Vergennes has delivered to me, in the name of Your Majesty, a letter, the address of which, notwithstanding my baptismal names which it contains, is so unlike mine that I had some thoughts of returning it unopened. However, upon his positive assertion that it was for me, I opened it, and the name of brother which I found in it having left me no further doubt, I read it with the respect which I owe to the handwriting and the signature of Your Majesty. The order which it contains to return and resume my place by Your Majesty's person is not the free expression of your will; and my honor, my duty, nay, even my affection, alike forbid me to obey. If Your Majesty wishes to be acquainted with all these motives more in detail, I beg you to refer to my letter of the 10th of September last. I also entreat you to receive with kindness the homage of the sentiments, alike tender and respectful, with which I am, etc., etc., etc.

ATTITUDE OF EUROPE IN REGARD TO AIDING LOUIS. (*Extract from a letter of Fersen to Marie Antoinette, Brussels, October 10, 1791.*)

The Empress of Russia and the Kings of Prussia, Naples, Sardinia, and Spain are very satisfactory, especially the first three; Sweden will sacrifice herself for you. England assures us of her neutrality. The emperor is the least willing: he is weak and indiscreet; he promises all, but his ministry, which fears to compromise itself and wants to avoid interference, holds him back. Hence the contradiction which you notice between his letters and his acts. I was sent to him by the king, with full and unlimited powers, to propose and consent to whatever might serve you. I have been unable to do anything except prevent a few foolish acts of the princes and persuade him to have nothing to do with them.

(Bouillé, 314; Thiers, I, 221.)

It may be inferred . . . that the King of Sweden was quite uncertain respecting the real plans of the emperor and his allies, which ought then to have been not to interfere any more in the affairs of France. The empress (of Russia) was no doubt informed of them, but she had not communicated them to him. I knew that at the moment she was exerting all her influence with the emperor and the King of Prussia to induce them to declare war against France. She had even written a very strong letter to the former of these sovereigns, in which she represented to him that the King of Prussia, for a mere incivility offered to his sister, had sent an army into Holland, while he (the emperor) patiently suffered the insults and affronts heaped upon the Queen of France, the degradation of her rank and dignity, and the overthrow of the throne of a king who was his brother-in-law and ally. The empress acted with like energy towards Spain, which had adopted pacific principles. Meanwhile, the emperor, after the acceptance of the constitution by the king, had received the new ambassador of France, whom he had previously forbidden to appear at his court. He was even the first to admit the national flag into his ports. The courts of Madrid, Petersburg, and Stockholm were the only ones which at this period withdrew their ambassadors from Paris. All these circumstances tend to prove that the views of Leopold were directed towards peace, and that they were the result of the influence of Louis XVI and of the queen.

INTRIGUES OF CATHERINE II. (*Extract from a letter of the minister Lessart to Genêt, Paris, January 1, 1792.*)

It is only necessary to compare the interest with which the empress at first honored the grievances of the *émigrés,* and the indifference with which they are now treated by this princess, to be convinced that her principal aim has always been to involve the King of Prussia and the emperor in a war which might bring diverse fortunes and weaken them both, in order to arrange alone and without contention the fate of Poland, which she has long been accustomed to regard as a dependency of her crown.

In that very logical hypothesis, Austria and Prussia would be dupes, because it is fruitless for their chiefs to think of a new partition. The empress is too clever ever to consent to aggrandize and strengthen such neighbors, and whether she wishes to extend her influence to the north, or whether (as has been always believed) she wishes to create an independent state for Prince Constantine in the neighborhood of ancient Greece, her personal interest is to get rid of the rival powers whose ambitious views she has fathomed.

NEGOTIATIONS WITH VIENNA. (*Dumouriez, II, 134–135.*)

Dumouriez was daily informed through the Girondins, some of whom were members of the diplomatic committee, that this committee, and its leader Brissot in particular, were much displeased by Lessart's negotiations. This was especially true of the negotiations with the court of Vienna, this court having taken advantage of them to make most insulting replies to the nation.

Brissot forced the confidence of Lessart, and informed him of the dangers he ran. The latter, full of confidence, replied that the negotiations were going smoothly, and to prove it showed him a copy of his dispatches to M. de Noailles, the ambassador of France at Vienna, the answers of M. de Noailles, a note forwarded to M. le Prince de Kaunitz, and the reply of that minister. It was of revolting haughtiness; a perfect diatribe against the Jacobins, and a formal refusal to regard the king as a free agent.

LOUIS CONSENTS TO FOREIGN AID. (*Fersen, 245–247.*)

Saw the king at six in the evening. He will not leave, on account of extreme vigilance; but the truth is, he has scruples, having so often promised to remain — for he is an honest man. He has, however, consented that when the armies arrive he will go with smugglers, always through woods, and let himself be met by a detachment of light troops. He wants the congress to concern itself at first solely with his demands, and if they are granted, then to insist that he shall leave Paris for some place chosen for the ratification. If this is refused, he consents that the powers shall act, and he submits to all dangers. He thinks he risks nothing, because the rebels need him to obtain terms of a capitulation.

The king wore the *cordon rouge* [Order of Saint-Louis]. He sees that there is no resource except in force; but in consequence of his feebleness, he thinks it impossible to recover all his authority. I proved to him the contrary; told him it could be done by force and that the powers desired to do it. He agreed. . . .

After a time he said to me: "*Ah ça!* here we are alone and we can speak. I know that I am taxed with weakness and irresolution, but no one was ever in my position. I know that I missed the right moment; it was July 14; I ought to have gone then, and I wished it; but what could I do when Monsieur himself begged me not to go, and the Maréchal de Broglie who commanded said, 'Yes, we can go to Metz, but what shall we do when we get there?' I lost the moment, and since then I have never found it; I have been abandoned by all the world." He begged me to warn the powers that they must not be shocked at anything he was obliged to do, for he was obliged — it was the effect of compulsion. "They must," he said, "put me entirely aside and let me act as I may." He desired also that it should be explained to the powers that he had sanctioned the decree on the sequestration of the property of the *émigrés* solely for the purpose of preserving it; otherwise, it would have been pillaged and burned; but that he would never consent to have it sold as national property. He also wished to veto the decree on passports.

DEATH OF THE EMPEROR LEOPOLD. (*Mme. de Tourzel, II, 73–74.*)

The Emperor Leopold, brother of the queen, was attacked by so severe an illness that it carried him off in three days. The news of his illness and his death arrived simultaneously. The Jacobins, who thought themselves well rid of an enemy, rejoiced over his death, without reflecting that, as the cabinet of Vienna would remain the same and would not change its principles, no alteration would take place in the existing state of things. The queen was of this opinion. She persuaded herself that a prince of the age of Francis II, brought up by the emperor, would infuse greater energy into a war which the arrogance of France in regard to foreign powers made her look upon as inevitable. She was mistaken in this expectation, and the same dilatoriness continued to be conspicuous in the preparations of the court of Vienna.

DESIRE FOR WAR. (*Louvet, 11.*)

Under these circumstances was moved at the Jacobins the grand question whether war ought to be declared against Austria. The Cordeliers were against it because it would give too much power to La Fayette, greatest enemy of Orléans; the Jacobins were for it because a peace of six months would have fixed a despotic crown on the head of Louis, or put a usurped scepter in the hands of Orléans; while war alone, speedy war, could give us a republic. On this occasion burst forth the grand schism between the faction of Robespierre and the party of Brissot.

(*Mme. de Tourzel, II, 29–30.*)

M. Duportail, minister of war, not being able to put up with the insults hurled at him day after day, tendered his resignation, and was replaced by Comte Louis de Narbonne. This individual, full of presumption, and believing himself to be summoned to a great destiny, gladly accepted a ministerial post. The levity of his disposition did not allow of his calculating the obstacles which he must necessarily encounter. Convinced that this post gave him the means of satisfying his ambition, and even placed him in a position to procure for the king more than one happy chance of extricating himself from his cruel position, he set to work to realize the hopes he had conceived. A war was the means he thought most favorable to the end he had in view, and he did his best to persuade the Assembly to undertake one, under the pretext of avenging the nation on foreign powers for the insults paid to it.

NARBONNE'S REPORT. (*Mme. de Tourzel, II, 41–42.*)

M. de Narbonne, who desired no less [than war], made a most satisfactory report on the state of the army and the frontier fortresses. The only thing wanting in his report was the truth; but nobody cared about probing it to the bottom. He assured the Assembly that France was in a position to defend herself against all her enemies; and that by re-establishing order at home, she would become so formidable a power that all the others would seek her. . . .

At the request of the Assembly the king appointed MM. de Rochambeau, de Lückner, and de La Fayette to the command of the three decreed armies, and bestowed the bâtons of marshals of France on the two former, although the constitution limited the number to six. But he undertook not to fill up any vacancies until the number should be reduced to that fixed by law.

FALL OF THE FEUILLANT MINISTERS. (*Ferrières, III, 49–53.*)

The Girondins ... continued energetically in their projects against the ministers. These, by their indiscreet quarrels, furnished them the weapons they needed. The ministers intrigued to supplant one another as in the more peaceful periods of the monarchy. Bertrand de Molleville, minister of marine, was the declared enemy of Narbonne, minister of war. The king dismissed Narbonne, who was thought to be ultra-constitutionalist, because he had the good sense to manage the Girondins. Soon afterwards the king was obliged to sacrifice Bertrand to the protests occasioned by the dismissal of Narbonne. The Girondins were not at all satisfied with the change; they rightly attributed Narbonne's disgrace to Lessart, a tool of Necker and their personal enemy. Lessart had had the imprudence to take charge of the ministry of foreign affairs; a position which was beyond his capacity at any time, and which circumstances had rendered still more difficult. Negotiations with the court of Vienna continued, but with a slowness and carelessness which seemed to indicate little good-will and less good faith. The Girondins complained with reason of the lack of dignity shown by Lessart in these negotiations, reproaching him for lowering the national dignity and letting himself be bandied about by the emperor's council. ...

The ministers of justice and finance, forewarned by the example of Lessart, handed in their resignations. The Girondins, who hated them, were not appeased by this conciliatory act. They had it decreed that no minister might leave Paris, even after resignation, before turning in his reports; and as it was to the Assembly that the ministerial reports were rendered, the Girondins found themselves able to retard acceptance as long as they wished, and keep the ministers that displeased them in danger of being attacked for their administration and brought up before the high court.

XVI. *The Girondins and the War*

THE ROLAND MINISTRY APPOINTED. (*Mme. de Tourzel, II, 60–61.*)

THE king, seeing that it was impossible to retain any minister without exposing him to the persecution of the Jacobins, who were then the masters of all France, resolved upon making trial of a ministry composed of men of that party. He hoped by this step to calm their fury, which increased day by day, to open the eyes of the nation, and to take away from the malevolent all pretext for accusing him of all the disturbances which broke out in every part of the kingdom. He consequently appointed M. Roland de La Platière minister of the interior; M. de Lacoste, of marine; M. Dumouriez, of foreign affairs; and M. Clavière, of taxes. M. Duranthon, a lawyer of Bordeaux, shortly afterwards replaced M. du Tertre; and M. de Grave, who had only been made minister of war a few days previously, remained *ad interim* at that post.

(*Dumouriez, II, 150.*)

There were at first but two members in the ministry who were really Girondins, Clavière and Roland. Afterwards Servan, who took the place of De Grave, was one; but Dumouriez, Lacoste, and even the worthy Duranthon were always independent. Duranthon displeased the faction to such a degree that it forced him to return to Bordeaux whence he had been called. He had, without prejudice to his patriotism, shown some attachment for Louis XVI, who returned his affection.

(*Mme. Roland, 267–268.*)

Dumouriez had more of what is called intellect than any of them, and less moral sense. He was diligent, brave, a good general, and an able courtier. He wrote effectively, conversed easily, and was capable of great things. He only needed more character to complement his mind, or a cooler head to carry out the plans that he had conceived. Pleasing his friends, while ready to deceive them all ... he was made for the ministerial intrigues of a corrupt court. His brilliant qualities and the renown of his glory caused it to be believed that he could be usefully employed in the armies of the Republic; and perhaps he would have behaved well if the Convention had been wise; for he was too clever not to conduct himself as a virtuous man where his reputation and interests were concerned.

DUMOURIEZ'S CONVERSATION WITH THE KING ON BECOMING MINISTER.
(*Dumouriez, II, 140–141.*)

"Sire, your order to accept the place that I have refused persuades me that Your Majesty has recovered from the prejudices aroused against me."

"Yes, entirely so."

"Then, Sire, I pledge myself to your service; but the position of minister is not like that of former times; without ceasing to be the zealous servant of Your Majesty, I belong to the nation. I shall speak to you always in the language of liberty and the constitution. Confining myself to my functions, I shall not play the courtier, and in this respect will break all the rules of etiquette in order to serve you better. I shall work only with you or the council. Nearly all of your diplomatic corps is openly counter-revolutionary. There will be no pressure to make you change it. I shall offend your tastes by my selections; I shall present subjects entirely unknown to you, and others that will displease you. When your repugnance overcomes you, since you are the master, I will obey; but if your decisions are suggested by your *entourage*, and are visibly compromising to you, I shall then entreat you to leave me master, or else give me a successor. . . ."

RELATIONS BETWEEN KING AND MINISTRY. (*Ferrières, III, 53–55.*)

This new ministry of unknown men seemed ridiculous to the courtiers. In derision they called it the *sans-culotte* ministry.

Roland resembled a Quaker in Sunday clothes, with lank gray hair slightly powdered, black costume, and laced shoes. The first time Roland appeared at the council thus arrayed, the master of ceremonies, horrified at this breach of etiquette, drew near Dumouriez with an anxious air. With knitted brows he indicated Roland with a glance, and said in a low, hushed voice, "Eh, Monsieur, not even buckles on his shoes!" "Oh, Monsieur," replied Dumouriez with great *sangfroid*, "all is lost."

Dumouriez went to render homage to the Jacobin Club in return for his nomination. He appeared at the tribune wearing a red cap, at that time a symbol of the Girondin and republican parties. The king forced himself to conceal the disgust that his new ministers inspired in him. He treated them kindly, even showing them that flattering interest which the great know how to use in dealing with their inferiors. He was, however, unable to place any confidence in a ministry made up of men devoted to his enemies, knowing that they faithfully reported to them everything that was done or said in council. He therefore pretended to pay little attention to what took place.

(*Mme. Roland, 262.*)

As for the council, its sessions seemed more like social chats than the deliberations of statesmen. Each minister brought his orders and proclamations to be signed, and the minister of justice presented his decrees to be approved. The king read the papers, asking questions of each one, on such matters as were personal to him, . . . discoursing good-naturedly on affairs in general and reiterating constantly, with an air of frankness, his desire to see the constitution succeed. I have seen Roland and Clavière practically enchanted by the ideas of the king for weeks at a time, believing his every word, and rejoicing like worthy men over the turn which matters seemed bound to take.

THE GIRONDINS IN THE ASSEMBLY. (*Vaublanc, 193.*)

I believe if the lukewarm royalists had sat with us, the Girondins would have pursued a different line of conduct than that which has brought them such unfortunate celebrity. Their position in the Assembly forced them to submit to the domination of the Jacobins. The latter were called Montagnards because they were seated on the top benches at the left end of the hall. From this elevation the Montagnards appeared to dominate their numerous party, hurling down ferocious vociferations from the summit. They spoke loudly and sometimes arrogantly to the Girondins who sat immediately below them. They urged them on to debate certain questions, and baited them in such a fashion as to be heard from the tribunes. The Girondins, who wished above all things to be popular, did not have the strength to resist this sort of summons, supported as it was by the people in the galleries. When a Girondin decided to speak, he went to the tribune accompanied by the acclamations of the people. He would mount the rostrum intoxicated with applause, and this applause seemed a forceful prophecy of the acclaim he was about to win. Declaiming with all the emotional force engendered by this uproar, he often said things he was far from believing, and upon leaving the room would blush at what he had said.

THE GIRONDINS EXCITE THE POPULACE. (*Ferrières, III, 59–60.*)

The queen did not exaggerate: the Orleanists and Girondins never ceased stirring up the people against the king and queen. They no longer called them anything but Monsieur and Madame Veto. A multitude of paid orators retailed daily the slanders that the party had had manufactured. In these, kings were characterized as crowned assassins. Louis XVI was represented to be a Nero, a sanguinary monster breathing murder and carnage, who wished to bring in foreign troops to further his purposes. He was giving Alsace and Lorraine to the emperor, they said, on condition that the emperor would help him to regain his authority and take revenge upon his enemies. The queen was depicted in vile colors as a Messalina devoted to the most shameful dissolution, or as a fury seeking to bathe in French blood. These horrible calumnies were cried through the streets, to be repeated from the tribune of the Jacobins, and at the bar of the Assembly. If some deputy denounced this, showing its guilty intention, the Assembly passed coldly to the order of the day, or referred it to the executive power. The executive power was made up of Girondins, and far from repressing the instigators, it was the first to urge them on.

DUMOURIEZ DESIRES TO SAVE THE QUEEN. (*Mme. Campan, 323–324.*)

All parties were exerting themselves either to ruin or to save the king. One day I found the queen extremely agitated; she told me she no longer knew where she was; that the leaders of the Jacobins offered themselves to her through the medium of Dumouriez; or that Dumouriez, abandoning the Jacobins, had come and offered himself to her; that she had granted him an audience; that when alone with her, he had thrown himself at her feet, and told her that he had drawn the *bonnet rouge* over his head to the very ears; but that he neither was nor could be a Jacobin; that the Revolution had been suffered to extend even to that rabble of destroyers who, thinking of nothing but pillage, were ripe for anything, and might furnish the Assembly with a formidable army, ready to undermine the remains of a throne already too much shaken. While speaking with the utmost ardor he seized the queen's hand and kissed it with transport, exclaiming, "Suffer yourself to be saved!" The queen told me that the protestations of a traitor were not to be relied upon; that the whole of his conduct was so well known that undoubtedly the wisest course was not to trust to it; that, moreover, the princes particularly recommended that no confidence should be placed in any proposition emanating from within the kingdom; that the force without became imposing; and that it was better to rely upon their success, and upon the protection due from heaven to a sovereign so virtuous as Louis XVI and to so just a cause.

THE ÉMIGRÉS PREPARE TO INVADE FRANCE. (*Chateaubriand, Memoirs of the Duc de Berri; Thiers, I, 169.*)

Many of the *émigrés* had joined the army in a state of destitution. Others were spending improvidently the last of their fortunes. Several corps, composed wholly of officers, served as private soldiers. The naval officers were mounted; the country gentlemen formed themselves into companies, distinguished by the names of their native provinces. All were in good spirits, for the camp life was free and joyous. Some became drawers of water, others hewers of wood; others provided and dressed the provisions, and everywhere the inspiring note of the trumpet resounded. The camp, in fact, was a perfect kingdom. There were princes dwelling in wagons; magistrates on horseback; missionaries preaching the Bible and administering justice. The poor nobles conformed with careless philosophy to this altered state of things, cheerfully enduring present privations in the sanguine expectation of speedily regaining all that they had lost. They confidently believed that the end of autumn would find them restored to their splendid homes, to their groves, to their forests, and to their old dove-cotes.

NEGOTIATIONS WITH AUSTRIA. (*Dumouriez, II, 205–206.*)

The French ambassador at Vienna decided to reopen negotiations with the Austrian ministry and exact a categorical response to the definite demands made by the minister of foreign affairs. The reply came in a note from M. de Cobenzl. It was brief, cold, and dry; and imposed conditions upon the French nation. In case the nation could not, or would not, accept these conditions, it was practically a declaration of war. The Austrian ministry was all the more inexcusable in this if the court, as it has since declared, desired the conservation of peace and maintenance of its alliance. The conditions imposed involved the re-establishment of the monarchy on the bases set forth by Louis XVI in the royal session of June 23, 1789, and consequently the re-establishment of the nobility and clergy as orders. There was to be a restitution of property to the clergy, of the Alsatian possessions to the German princes (with all feudal and sovereign rights), and of Avignon and the Comtat Venaissin to the pope.

(*Ferrières, III, 62–63.*)

The Assembly received this menacing reply with indignation, and cried out with one voice that the national honor must be avenged. From that moment the idea of war became general. The Girondins took advantage of this moment of enthusiasm. They sent a deputation to the king to acquaint him with the insult offered to France, and the necessity of anticipating the hostile designs of the emperor. . . .

The negotiations continued; but the court of Vienna, far from facilitating the reconciliation of the interested parties, opposed the reception of the indemnities offered by France to the proprietary princes of Alsace and Lorraine, holding over them the threat of annulling by the diet of Ratisbon the private treaties made in that regard. The electors of Trèves, Cologne, and Mainz, in concert with the emperor, openly favored the levying of troops by the French princes, and were even paying subsidies for their maintenance. They refused to recognize the French ambassadors, although these ambassadors were negotiating in the name of the king, and publicly received the plenipotentiaries of the princes, although these were of unofficial character. Everyone pretended to regard the princes as the real French government and sole representatives of the monarchy. There was even talk of assembling a congress at Aix-la-Chapelle, which would deal with France, as the courts of Berlin and The Hague had dealt with Holland, during its revolution. Dumouriez vigorously pressed the court of Vienna for an explanation; there were affected delays. They seemed to be waiting the news of some approaching event that would change the existing state of affairs in France.

THE GIRONDINS DESIRE WAR. (*La Fayette, III, 301.*)

The Jacobins attached to Robespierre were opposed to war because they feared its being directed by their political rivals, and also because several of them, from pecuniary interests like Danton, or from causes of which they themselves were ignorant, were under the guidance of that small party of the court who, fearing the influence of the princes, were engaged in secret negotiations. It was the Girondins who, at that period, wished for war at any price, in the hope that it would facilitate their vague projects of ambition. . . .

(Ferrières, III, 63–64.)

All the ministers were in favor of war. Louis XVI, committed in spite of himself to a course whose tragic consequences could easily be foreseen, came, in accordance with the constitution, to the Assembly to propose a declaration of war against the emperor. This proposition accorded too well with the secret views of the Girondins to suffer any opposition . . .

LOUIS PROPOSES WAR. *(Mme. de Staël, 249; Thiers, I, 238.)*

I was present at the sitting in which Louis was forced to a measure which was repugnant to him for many reasons. His features were not expressive of his thoughts, but it was not from dissimulation that he concealed them; a mixture of resignation and dignity repressed in him every outward sign of his sentiments. On entering the Assembly, he looked to the right and left, with that kind of vacant curiosity which is not unusual with persons who are so shortsighted that their eyes seem to be of no use to them. He proposed war in the same tone of voice as he might have used in requiring the most indifferent decree possible.

(Barbaroux, 32.)

Defensive war accorded little with French character. Such a war would give the court every means of ruining us by false preparations, and ample time to incite treason on the frontiers and in the interior. Moreover, Brissot wished to profit by the national enthusiasm for war and forestall Austria. One was certain that the court would be forced to reveal the means by which it was deceiving us, and thus expose its perfidies. There was indeed a risk of defeat; but this danger would be obviated by the national indignation, whereas there would be no remedy for the success of the royal conspiracy. These reasons prevailed, and war was unanimously decreed by the legislative body.

THE DECLARATION OF WAR AGAINST AUSTRIA.

. . . The National Assembly proclaims that the French nation, faithful to the principles set forth by the constitution of never making war for the purpose of conquest, and of never using armed force against the liberty of any people, is taking up arms only for the maintenance of its liberty and independence; that the war which she is forced to wage is not a war of nation against nation, but a rightful defense of a free people against the unjust aggression of a king;

That the French will never confound their brothers with their real enemies; that they will neglect nothing to soften the horrors of war, to manage and conserve property, and to cause the misfortunes of war to fall upon those who league themselves against her liberty;

That she adopts in advance all foreigners who, forswearing the cause of her enemies, come to range themselves beneath her flag and consecrate their efforts to the defense of her liberty; that she will even facilitate, by all the means in her power, their establishment in France;

In deliberation upon the formal proposition of the king, and following an urgency resolution, war is hereby declared against the King of Hungary and of Bohemia.

FRANCE AND THE WAR. (Extract from a dispatch of Dumouriez to Genêt, Paris, April 27, 1792.)

Leopold and Gustav, one the supporter, the other the instigator of the coalition against the liberty of the French, no longer exist and France has declared war on the chief of the House of Austria. Our enemies, astonished by our energy, and forestalled by our prompt action, will be some time in agreeing what to do. Time alone can tell what designs will be adopted by the powers of the north. Will Catherine II keep the secret agreements which she made with Gustav and Leopold in regard to affairs in France? Will the regency in Sweden follow the projects of the late king? And will Frederick William believe himself obliged to second Austria?

(Bouillé, 322.)

There were still a few officers who had continued to support the constitution through discontent with the court or through ambition. Among these were Rochambeau, Lückner, La Fayette, and the all too celebrated Dumouriez. These were succeeded by men to whom Nature had given great talents, and whose talents were to be developed by circumstances. The elections allowed by the government in all ranks of the army gave the more capable an opportunity to rise. A staff was formed that was without doubt the most able in Europe.

(La Fayette, III, 294–295.)

Lückner had been the most distinguished partisan of the Seven Years' War. ... After the peace of 1763, the Duc de Choiseul drew him into our service.... He was much attached to the new constitution, but without any understanding of it; and when the Jacobins wished to exalt his liberal opinions to calumniate those of their adversaries, he often embarrassed them by making the most absurd blunders. He had not the power of forming great combinations, but he had a quick eye, the habit of military tactics, and all the activity of youth. Rochambeau, who had made his fortune by arms, had been engaged in the war of Flanders, and distinguished himself also in the Seven Years' War... These two marshals, very dissimilar to one another, had one fault in common — they were too distrustful of their new and inexperienced troops in a struggle against the most renowned troops of Europe. La Fayette did not share this feeling.... He augured better for the enthusiasm for liberty... having been an American general officer at the age of nineteen.... With the exception of these three generals, there was not an officer in the French army who had ever fought at the head of two thousand men.

THE FRENCH ROUTED IN THE FIRST SKIRMISH. (Ferrières, III, 64–65.)

The first assaults did not produce results commensurate with the hopes that had been conceived. General Biron advanced upon Mons at the head of a corps of ten thousand men, arriving at the town of Quiévrain; two regiments fled without even having seen the enemy, crying out that the army was dissevered and that they were betrayed. The infantry became disorganized; six hundred Uhlans sufficed to rout the whole army. The camp and military chest were abandoned. Théobald Dillon, who marched against Tournai with three thousand men, experienced the same fate: a corps of eight hundred men defeated him completely. The French lost their tents, baggage, and artillery. La Fayette, who should have seized Namur, where there were then in garrison only five hundred men, did not even approach the place, and limited himself to fatiguing his army with useless marches. The aristocrats were triumphant and gave themselves over to the most gratifying expectations, as did also the *émigrés*. The constitutionalists raised a hue and cry against Dumouriez, who was known to be the author of the plans of attack; nevertheless these plans were sagely devised, as Dumouriez proves in his *Mémoires*. They were identical with those he used the following December, but a number of unusal factors contributed to the ill-success of this attempt.

(Dumouriez, II, 237.)

The arrival of this news threw Paris and the Assembly into consternation. Dumouriez received it with the greatest calm. He pondered the profound rascality that had frustrated his plan of campaign, and was confirmed in the belief that it was premeditated when he saw the indecent joy manifested by the opposition for several days in the Assembly.

THE ORLEANISTS OPPOSED TO THE WAR. (Ferrières, III, 65.)

The Orleanists did not favor war. They felt that victories would strengthen the constitution. All military positions were controlled by the constitutionalists; generals would be chosen only from among them. The constitutionalists on their side looked with jealousy at the new Girondin ministry; they would have liked to substitute a Feuillant ministry more at their disposition. Both sides co-operated in bringing failure upon Dumouriez's attack upon Austrian Flanders. The emissaries of the Orleanists stirred up the soldiers of Biron by representing their generals as traitors who would deliver them into the hands of the enemy, and by giving the first signal for flight. The constitutionalists contributed to Dumouriez's failure by neglecting to have any general plan of attack or any proper means of making it succeed.

THE KING'S GUARD REMOVED. (Ferrières, III, 75–76.)

The Girondins adroitly profited by the disturbed state of mind. They disbanded the king's guard as unconstitutional. They preferred an indictment against the Duc de Brissac who commanded it, and sent him to Orléans without a hearing, or without wanting to hear him.

The king was much affected by this enactment, and seemed resolved not to obey it. His ministers pointed out to him what would be the consequences of his resistance and, reminding him of the 5th and 6th October, made him fear that similar misfortunes would arise. The king finally acceded to their wishes. With an air of sadness he said to the Duc de Brissac, when that seigneur came to take leave of him: "You are going to a prison. I should be a great deal more distressed were it not for the fact that you are leaving me in one."

THE MINISTRY OF MME. ROLAND. (*Ferrières, III, 77–79.*)

The six ministers had up to that time been on good terms with one another. They dined together on council days, each bringing with him his ministerial report. They decided what things should be presented to the king, discussing them in order to arrive at some common persuasion and avoid disputing before him. But friendship, respect, and confidence did not enter into this union: it did not last. The woman Roland, who really ran the ministry under her husband's name, desired to be present at these discussions. This pretension caused a coolness to arise between the ministers. The entrance of Servan as minister of war finished embroiling them. Servan, uniting with Roland and Clavière, insisted that the conferences between the ministers and the Girondins be held at Mme. Roland's. The Girondins, who had only created a ministry in the hope of making themselves masters of the government, pretended that nothing should be done or even proposed except by them. Dumouriez began to grow tired of this despotism, and impatiently awaited an opportunity to throw off a yoke which galled him all the more in that it hampered the course of his ambitions. He saw with joy that the king displayed less repugnance towards him than towards the other ministers. He was determined to profit by this favorable attitude and get rid of the men who always opposed his plans. But, hated by the court, and even more hated by the constitutionalists, he felt that he needed the Girondins, and particularly the popularity accruing to them. It was this popularity alone that rendered him indispensable to the king and would conserve his prestige in the council. He did not wish to break with them before he was sure of a party strong enough to sustain him against their intrigues.

THE CAMP OF FEDERATES PROPOSED. (*Ferrières, III, 80–81.*)

Louvet's *Sentinelle* and Brissot's *Patriote* reported the discussions in the council, taking it upon themselves to vaunt the patriotic zeal of Roland and the ministers of his party. They censured Dumouriez. They reproached the king for not approving of the constitution and for thwarting the measures taken by the Assembly to put it into effect.

This was but the prelude to a great attack which the three ministers were planning to make against the king and Dumouriez. Servan, following a secret meeting at the house of Mme. Roland, proposed the formation, during the federation, of a camp of twenty thousand men near Paris; to be, he said, a central and permanent army, proper for maintaining the tranquillity of the

capital and assuring the labors of the Assembly. The Girondins and the Orleanists welcomed this proposition with loud applause. The constitutionalists,
who easily discovered the real motive, opposed the decree in vain; the Girondins carried it.

The king in consternation told Dumouriez that he was resolved to veto a
decree so openly aimed at his own ruin and that of the monarchy.

GIRONDIN FEAR OF LA FAYETTE AND THE COURT. (Barbaroux, 34–35.)

La Fayette was at the head of one of our armies; but when he had abandoned
the command at Paris, where he had been so useful to the court, it was hard
to believe that he would do any better at the head of his troops. One was all
the more convinced of this upon seeing him pass from the Moselle to the Nord
(taking with him the army which that of Lückner came to replace) by a cross-
movement until then unprecedented in military tactics and hazardous for
the state, the real purpose of which was to preserve to La Fayette his own
faithful regiments. Neither was anyone deceived in regard to the rout at
Mons, a bloody comedy played to dampen the zeal of patriots and arrest
the formation of new battalions. This was also true in regard to the order to
retreat given Lückner, after the old general had taken possession of Courtrai
in the mistaken belief that a real war was going on. The refusal to sanction
the decree for assembling twenty thousand national guards under the walls
of Paris, the sole means conceived by the genius of Servan to prevent treason
on the frontiers and forestall its effects in the interior, announced all too clearly
the intention of opening the road to Paris to the Austrians. In all parts of the
country, people were rising in indignation against the fanaticism which caused
the royal veto to be placed upon the first decree against nonjuring priests. . . .

(Ferrières, III, 85–86.)

Roland read to the council a long letter that his wife had composed . . . In
this he entered with most abusive and bitter detail into the conduct of the
king during the Revolution. . . .

ROLAND'S LETTER TO THE KING.

Sire:

The present state of France cannot last long. It is a state of crisis, the violence
of which has nearly attained the highest degree; it must terminate in a catastrophe which cannot but interest Your Majesty as deeply as it concerns the
whole empire. . . .

Your Majesty possessed great prerogatives, which you considered as pertaining to royalty. Brought up in the idea of retaining them, you could not
see them taken from you with pleasure. The desire of recovering them was
therefore as natural as regret on seeing them annihilated. These sentiments,
inherent in the nature of the human heart, must have entered into the calculation of the enemies of the Revolution: they reckoned, therefore, upon a

secret favor, till circumstances should admit of a declared protection. This disposition could not escape the nation, nor fail to excite its jealousy.

Your Majesty has therefore been constantly under the alternative of yielding to your first habits, to your private affections, or of making sacrifices dictated by philosophy, and required by necessity; consequently of encouraging rebels by alarming the nation, or of appeasing the latter by uniting yourself with it. Everything has its time, and that of uncertainty has at length arrived.

... two important decrees have been passed. Both essentially concern the public tranquillity and the welfare of the state. The delay in their sanction excites distrust. If it be further prolonged, it will cause discontent; and I am obliged to confess that, in the present effervescence of opinions, discontent may lead to any consequences.

It is too late to recede, and there are no longer any means of temporizing. The Revolution is accomplished in people's minds. It will be consummated at the expense of their blood, and cemented with it, if prudence does not prevent the calamities which it is yet possible to avoid.

... the situation of Paris, and its proximity to the frontiers, have caused the want of a camp in its vicinity to be felt. This measure, the prudence and urgency of which have struck all well-meaning persons, is still waiting only for Your Majesty's sanction....

Already public opinion is compromising the intentions of Your Majesty. A little longer delay, and the disappointed people will imagine that in their king they behold the friend and accomplice of the conspirators.

Gracious Heaven! hast thou stricken with blindness the powers of the earth, and are they never to have any counsels but such as shall lead them to perdition?

I know that the austere language of truth is seldom relished near the throne. I know, too, that it is because it is scarcely ever proclaimed there that revolutions are become necessary; and above all, I know that it is my duty to hold such language to Your Majesty, not only as a citizen subject to the laws, but as a minister honored by your confidence, or clothed with functions which presuppose it; and I know nothing that can prevent me from performing a duty of which I am conscious....

Life is not a consideration with the man who prizes his duties above all things; but next to the happiness of having performed them, the highest satisfaction he can enjoy is that of thinking that he has performed them faithfully; which is an obligation incumbent on the public man.

Paris, June 10, 1792, the fourth year of liberty.

ROLAND

(Ferrières, III, 86–92.)

The king listened to this flow of insults and grossness with admirable patience; he contented himself with saying to Roland, "Monsieur Roland, you sent me that letter three days ago, thus it was useless to read it in council; you agreed that it should remain a private matter between us two." Roland saw that he' was repugnant to the king; he felt that his position was slipping from his grasp. He wished to make of his forced retreat a merit in the eyes of the Girondins and the people, presenting it as the consequence of his principles and his attachment to the constitution. The king, tired of these bickerings, decided to dismiss the three ministers. . . .

Roland, Servan, and Clavière received their dismissal. They hid their rage under a semblance of satisfaction, affecting to congratulate themselves and their friends on leaving a ministry where no good could be accomplished and where one must continuously struggle against the perfidious intentions of a counter-revolutionary court. The king instructed Dumouriez to replace the three ministers that had just been dismissed. Mourgues was given the interior, and Dumouriez continued in control of foreign affairs while awaiting the arrival of the man he had chosen for that place.

Dumouriez had finally arrived at the goal set by his ambition: he saw himself first minister. But the Girondins were furious with him; they treated him as a meddler, traitor, and conspirator, menacing him with their vengeance. Roland and his pamphleteers denounced him at all the clubs.

The three disgraced ministers repaired to the Assembly, and, in the speeches which they made, endeavored to present their expulsion from the ministry as a crime of *lèse-nation*. . . . When Dumouriez then presented himself, hoots and confused cries of "treason" arose on all sides.

DUMOURIEZ RESIGNS FROM THE MINISTRY. (*Ferrières, III, 97–98.*)

Dumouriez, Duranthon, and Lacoste repaired to the king . . . Duranthon said that they came, although with regret, to offer him their resignations. . . . "Well," replied the king with a somber air, "since your mind is made up, I accept your resignation. I will make arrangements." The three ministers departed, affected more by the consequences that the rejection by the king was going to bring than by the regret of losing a place that exposed those who filled it to the hate of all parties.

XVII. *The Girondins and the King*

THE GIRONDINS PLAN TO RE-ESTABLISH THE MINISTRY. (*Ferrières, III, 105.*)

THE Girondins had not in the least abandoned the design of re-establishing the three disgraced ministers; but rightly judging that the king would never voluntarily consent to reinstate them, they resolved that the people should request it, and thus force Louis XVI to recall them. They arranged the instigation of a popular movement; Pétion and Manuel, procurator-general of the commune, undertook its direction.

(*Sergent Marceau, 159.*)

The affair [of the 20th of June, 1792] was invented and arranged in the salon of Mme. Roland; the agents, as was known to a few, were Roland and Clavière. (I did not hear Servan mentioned; the king had dismissed him a short time previously.) Among the deputies who were admitted to this mysterious plot were Brissot, Gensonné, and Guadet; others less notorious were charged with exciting the movement. The general infatuation in favor of Roland served the purpose of the deputies, of Clavière, and of Mme. Roland, who was more of a minister than her husband. I know that in saying this I am attacking an idol before whom the world bows down, because a cruel fate (which I myself lamented at the time) has deified her. But in my opinion (and I had opportunities of judging) this heroine of the Revolution caused more misfortunes than the notorious Théroigne de Méricourt, armed, and followed by a club of women.

(*Dumas, I, 321.*)

... the Assembly adopted the following decree, which was drawn up by Guadet:

"The king's present guard is disbanded; it shall be reconstituted without delay, comformably to the law.

"The duty which the king's constitutional guard has hitherto done shall be performed by the national guard till the new organization shall be completed."

THE INSURRECTION OF JUNE 20. (*Ferrières, III, 105–113.*)

The evening before, a dinner for five hundred people, all Girondins and Orleanists, was given at the Champs-Élysées. The populace came to mingle

with the guests and share the patriotic intoxication of the fête. Couplets
were sung and toasts given. Sauvigny and Laclos repaired to the Faubourg
Saint-Antoine, where Chabot assembled the people in the Church of the
Enfants-Trouvés and openly preached insurrection. . . .

The leaders, sure that no obstacles would be raised by the Assembly,
agreed upon their plan. The Jacobins and Orleanists of forty-eight sections
were called together, the vagabonds and brigands used in important insurrections were sent for, and to these were added the populace of the Faubourgs
Saint-Antoine and Saint-Marceau. This multitude, coalescing with a number
of national guards, took its way towards the Assembly.   The pretext was
that of presenting an address to the king. The procurator-syndic, Roederer,
rushed in to announce that the mob was beginning to gather in spite of the
efforts of the departments to prevent it. He begged the Assembly to take heed
of the consequences, which would be incalculable if, as he had been assured,
the people were going to the palace. Vergniaud and Gensonné replied that
there was nothing to fear; that the civic spirit of the citizens who formed the
gathering was well known; and that it would suffice to send commissioners to
the king in order to avoid any appearance of irregularity in the address that
was to be presented to him. The Assembly, after these observations, passed
to the business of the day and began to listen to a petition from the Jacobins
of Marseille denouncing the executive power. It was decreed that this should
be printed and sent to the eighty-three departments.

. . . preparations were made to repulse the attack of the faubourgs. It was
soon realized that it would be impossible to rely upon the troops that defended
the palace. The gendarmes refused to load their guns. Carl having desired
to make some arrangements, a captain of the Paris militia opposed him and
protested that he would not let him have his cannon, since he was not there
for his benefit.

THE MOB ADMITTED TO THE TUILERIES. (*Deposition of the Sieur Lareynie, Battalion Isle Saint-Louis.*)

. . . the deponent observed that, at this moment, the mob was almost
entirely dispersed, and that it was not till the drums and the music were heard
in the vicinity of the National Assembly that the people, then scattered here
and there, rallied, and joined by the other spectators, filed off quietly three
deep before the legislative body; that he, the deponent, remarked that these
people, in passing into the Tuileries, were guilty of no misdemeanor, and did
not attempt to enter the palace; that even when assembled in the Place du
Carrousel, where they arrived after going round by the Quai du Louvre, they
manifested no intention of penetrating into the courts till the arrival of the
Sieur Santerre, who was at the National Assembly, and did not leave it
before the sitting was over. That then the Sieur Santerre, accompanied by
several persons, among whom he, the deponent, remarked the Sieur Hurugue,
addressed the mob, which at that time was very quiet, and asked *why they
had not entered the palace; that they must go in, and that this was what they had come
for.* That immediately he ordered the gunners of his battalion to follow him
with one piece of cannon, and said that, if he was refused admittance, he must

break open the gate with cannon balls; that afterwards he proceeded in this manner to the gate of the palace, where he met with a faint resistance from the horse gendarmerie, but a firm opposition on the part of the national guard; that this occasioned great noise and agitation, and they would probably have come to blows had not two men, in scarfs of the national colors, one of whom he, the deponent, knew to be the Sieur Boucher-René, and the other was said by the spectators to be the Sieur Sergent, come by way of the courts, and *ordered*, he must say, in a very imperious, not to say insolent tone, at the same time prostituting the sacred name of the law, that *the gates be opened*, adding, *that nobody had a right to close them, but every citizen had a right to enter;* that the gates were accordingly opened by the national guard . . .

THE KING IN THE MIDST OF HIS PEOPLE. (*Weber, II, 172–174.*)

As the doors were opened, the rioters precipitated themselves into the courts, up the staircases, and into the various apartments; the guard-room was invested; the assassins threw themselves against the inner doors which the footmen had closed and locked. . . .

With a calm heart, sole legacy of an irreproachable life, the king, approaching, saw a door-panel yield to the blow of a pike which barely missed wounding him. Seeing a second panel, hacked to pieces, fall at his feet, he quietly ordered the door opened, and appearing before the rebels said: "I am your king. What do you want of me?"

A sudden apparition of divinity in the midst of fire and lightning would not have made a greater impression on this crowd of brigands than that produced by the appearance of the king, alone, without guards and without attendants.

These armed men seemed petrified; a number recoiled in astonishment, and there reigned for a time a profound silence, so much had the serenity and nobility of their king impressed them!

In a few moments the tumult recommenced, and there was heard on all sides cries of "Sanction or death! The camp around Paris! Drive away the priests! Drive out the aristocrats!"

Then a hired brigand from the Faubourg Saint-Antoine, dressed in the uniform of the national guard, was seen to rush forward to bayonet the king, but Providence permitted that Joly [a cannoneer of the national guard of the Section Filles-Saint-Thomas] should dart like lightning upon this madman and fell him; while at the same instant, as a second raised his pike to pierce the king, one Canolle by name had the good fortune to turn aside the fatal blow.

At last the brave Acloque [commander of the battalion from the Faubourg Saint-Marceau] and the grenadiers of the Section Filles-Saint-Thomas seized an opportunity to surround the king and partially separate him from his assailants.

They begged him to mount on a long bench that stood before a casement, and having put a large table before him, grouped themselves around it three deep, in order to make the distance too great for those with the pikes to reach him.

LOUIS WEARS THE BONNET ROUGE. (Ferrières, III, 114.)

Legendre arrives. He presents a red cap to the king. One of the four grenadiers pushes it away. "Let him do what he wants," the king says; "he will offer me some rudeness, what of it?" The king takes the red cap and puts it on his head. The people cheer triumphantly. A man advances holding a bottle, and asks the king to drink the nation's health. They look for a glass but find none. The king takes the bottle and drinks from it. The crowd is increasing, each one wishing to approach the king and speak to him. "Sire," one is saying, "you must be constitutional, or at any rate no more veto." "The king," adds another, "does not want them to exile the priests without trial, but see what that comes to. *Parbleu!* the man is quite bad!" "Bread and meat are too dear," cry a number of workers. "We don't want any more veto."

DEPUTIES GO TO THE TUILERIES. (Ferrières, III, 116–117.)

In spite of murmurs from the tribunes and the efforts of the Orleanists, Dumas, Jaucourt, and Dumolard arranged for the sending of a deputation of twenty-four members to the palace. This was to be renewed hourly in order that the Assembly could be informed as to the state of things. This measure saved the king and disconcerted the Orleanists. "The attempt has failed," said Santerre angrily, on seeing the deputies enter, "but we will come back again." In fact a deputy, seeing some men of ferocious appearance attempting to force their way through the ring surrounding the king, threw himself in front of them and swore that only over his dead body should they reach that prince.

The deputies assured Louis XVI that the Assembly would neglect nothing to maintain his freedom. "You can see that," said Louis gently, showing them the men, the pikes, the guns, the cannon with which he was, so to speak, besieged; and addressing himself to M. Baert [a member of the Assembly]: "You who have travelled much, what do you think they are saying about us in foreign countries?"

PÉTION TO THE RESCUE. (Révolutions de Paris, No. 154.)

MM. Isnard and Vergniaud alternately addressed the people, urging them to disperse. They conveyed to the king the solicitude of the National Assembly, to which he replied *that he was in the midst of the people and undismayed.* Then, taking the hand of a national guard, he laid it upon his heart. "See," he said, "if it palpitates and if I am afraid."

Following this, M. Pétion arrived. He also harangued the people and tried to make them withdraw. The king then had his apartments opened and asked the people to file before him. This was done with the greatest order. At ten o'clock in the evening there was no longer anyone in the Tuileries or in the palace, and one could not see a single group in the streets of the capital.

BONAPARTE WATCHES THE INVASION OF JUNE 20. (Bourrienne, I, 51.)

...We had agreed to meet, for our daily walks, at a restaurant keeper's in the Rue Saint-Honoré, near the Palais-Royal. On going out, we saw arriving from the direction of Les Halles, a mob which Bonaparte computed at five or six thousand men, in rags and grotesquely armed, vociferating and shrieking the grossest abuse, and proceeding rapidly towards the Tuileries. It was the vilest and most abject part of the people of the faubourgs. "Let us follow that rabble," said Bonaparte to me. We got before them, and went to walk on the terrace beside the water. It was there that he saw the disgraceful scenes which took place. I should have difficulty in depicting the feelings of surprise and indignation which these excited in him. He could not comprehend such weakness and forbearance. But when the king showed himself at one of the windows opening on the garden, with the red cap which a man of the people had just placed on his head, Bonaparte could no longer restrain his indignation. "*Che coglione!*" exclaimed he, "how could they have let that rabble enter? They should have swept away four or five hundred with cannon, and the rest would still be running."

LA FAYETTE DEMANDS PUNISHMENT. (Weber, II, 195–196.)

The army showed its discontent; La Fayette ventured to leave it and come to Paris. The war was conducted so languidly along the frontiers that the absence of the general in no way disarranged the unimportant operations that were carried on after the disgraceful skirmishes at Tournai and Mons. When he arrived at Paris, the grenadiers of the national guard came to surround their former chief once more and escort him as a guard of honor to his hotel. He presented himself at the bar of the Assembly. He there denounced the Jacobins, declared himself their enemy, and menaced them with the vengeance of the army....

DISCOURSE OF LA FAYETTE AT THE BAR OF THE ASSEMBLY.

Gentlemen:

I have the honor to speak to you only as a citizen, but the ideas that I express are those of all Frenchmen who love their country, its liberty, its tranquillity, and the laws that it has made; and I have no fear of being disavowed by any of them. It is time to safeguard the constitution from the attacks being made upon it, to insure the liberty of the National Assembly, and to secure the freedom, independence, and dignity of the king. It is time, in short, to put an end to the hopes of unworthy citizens who are waiting for foreigners to establish what they call public order, and which to free men would be shameful and intolerable slavery.

I beg the National Assembly:

1. To order that the instigators and the ringleaders of the disorders committed on June 20 at the Tuileries be arrested and punished as criminals guilty of *lèse-nation;*

2. To destroy a sect that is usurping the national sovereignty, while tyran-

nizing over the citizens, and whose public debates leave no doubt as to the terrible designs of its leaders;

3. Finally, I venture to beg of you in my own name and in the name of all honest people of the realm (murmurs from part of the Assembly) to take such measures as will be effective in inspiring respect for constituted authority, particularly your own and that of the king, and in assuring the army that the constitution will receive no attack from within while brave Frenchmen are shedding their blood in defense of the frontiers.

(*Weber, II, 196.*)

The Jacobins, in their turn, accused him of being the author of the massacre of the Champ-de-Mars, of calumniating the army, of being a member of the Austrian committee that was giving secret advice to the court, and of uniting with the queen to deliver France over to the enemy.

THE COURT REFUSES TO SUPPORT LA FAYETTE. (*La Fayette, III, 336–337.*)

The debate was not closed, when he [La Fayette] repaired to the king. The royal family were assembled together. La Fayette received *de vains remerciements*; and the queen repeated that they were convinced there was no safety for them but in the constitution. Never did Louis appear to express himself with more thorough conviction; he added that he considered it would be very fortunate if the Austrians were defeated as soon as possible. . . . It so happened that the king was next day to review four thousand men of the national guard. La Fayette asked permission to accompany him, apprizing him, at the same time, of his intention, as soon as His Majesty had retired, of addressing the troops and doing what he believed necessary for the service of the constitution and the public order. But the court did everything in its power to thwart La Fayette, and Pétion, the mayor, countermanded the review an hour before daybreak.

(*Mme. Campan, 334.*)

On his [La Fayette's] arrival a plan was presented to the queen, in which it was proposed by a junction between La Fayette's army and the king's party to rescue the royal family and convey them to Rouen. I did not learn the particulars of this plan; the queen only said to me upon the subject that M. de La Fayette was offered to them as a resource; but that it would be better for them to perish than to owe their safety to the men who had done them the most mischief, or to place themselves under the necessity of treating with him.

(*La Fayette, III, 338.*)

"We know that the general will save the king, but he will not save royalty," was the public language of the Tuileries. The queen remembered that Mirabeau, shortly before his death, had predicted to her that, in case of a war, "La Fayette would desire to keep the king a prisoner in his tent." She replied to royalist friends, who however took care to alter it, "It would be too hard upon us to be twice indebted to him for our lives."

(Weber, II, 197.)

La Fayette withdrew the next day to his army. A day longer in Paris and his person would not have been safe, so active and audacious were the Jacobins and Orleanists in their manoeuvers, whether in the Assembly, the clubs, or the faubourgs. His effigy was burned at the Palais-Royal on the afternoon of his departure.

FURY AGAINST THE ROYALIST DEPUTIES. (Vaublanc, 214.)

But Paris was a vast field 'of battle where murder and carnage were brewing. They demanded blood and awaited with barbaric joy the moment it should flow. After the blood of the royal family, what they most desired to shed was the blood of the royalist deputies. The members of the Right were outraged and menaced daily. I never entered the Assembly without passing before a woman whose features, distorted with patriotic rage, were horrible to see. This fury called me by name and proclaimed that she would soon see my head cut off and would drink my blood. When we came forth after a stormy session, we could not pass through the long corridors of the old convent of the Feuillants in the neighborhood of the hall without being surrounded by a furious mob and running the risk of being assassinated. A citizen of Melun, who was tall and strong, one day parried a saber blow aimed at my head. Another time I was indebted to General Bertrand for the same service.

THE GIRONDINS PREPARE FOR ANOTHER ATTACK. (Barbaroux, 39-40.)

We still did not want to abandon Paris and the departments of the north; on the contrary, we resolved to try every means of saving them. The surest was to carry out the decree providing for the camp at Paris in spite of the veto of the king, the petition of the Paris staff, and the opposition of Robespierre, who probably did not expect to find in the departments hired assassins for his conspiracies. I promised to ask Marseille for a battalion and two pieces of artillery. These essentials agreed upon, I quitted Roland, full of respect for him and his wife; I saw him afterwards during his second ministry, as unassuming as in his humble retreat; alone among public officials in opposing his virtue to the machinations of the wicked, and his body to their poignards, never ceasing, in the midst of the tumult, to busy himself with enhancing the national industry and public spirit. . . . Roland is, of all moderns, the one who seems most nearly to approach Cato; but it must be said here that it is to his wife that he owes his courage and his talents.

We did not lose an instant; we wrote to Marseille to send to Paris six hundred men who knew how to die, and Marseille sent them.

(*Mme. de Tourzel, II, 162.*)

The declarations of the deputies, renowned for their violence, were renewed at each sitting. They taxed the king with treason, and accused him of all the evil wrought by their orders and their want of foresight. They pushed their audacity to the extent of demanding his deposition. Vergniaud pretended that he was responsible for the mistakes made by the armies; reproached him with witnessing their triumphs with displeasure, and with sheltering himself under the cloak of inviolability, in order to destroy liberty and to withhold his sanction to the decrees of the Assembly, however useful and necessary they might be. The chamber took into consideration the question of the recall of M. de Lückner, being unable to pardon his adhesion to the sentiments of M. de La Fayette. Everything presaged a crisis, in which it was easy to foresee the danger incurred by the king, the royal family, and even the monarchy.

THE LAMOURETTE RECONCILIATION. (*Ferrières, III, 142–147.*)

In the midst of these agitations and conflicting interests the Abbé Lamourette, constitutional Bishop of Lyon, believed that it would be easy to arbitrate the differences separating men truly attached to the new order of things, and bring about the reconciliation necessary for the welfare of the kingdom. Struck by this idea, simple in itself, Lamourette proclaimed the necessity of rallying to the constitution. He would promote among the deputies a union which circumstances had made more necessary now than ever before. He observed that the main causes of trouble arose from the beliefs that one party of the Assembly desired a republic, while another favored a two-chamber system. "Now is the moment, Messieurs, to condemn with equal execration both republic and chambers. Yes, the time has come for the president of this Assembly to call upon all to rise who are opposed to both republics and double chambers." At these words the deputies arose from their seats, Orleanists, Girondins, constitutionalists, and independents. Stretching their hands to heaven, they swore to repudiate any form of government contrary to the one decreed by the Constituent Assembly. They all began to fraternize, intermingle, and embrace each other, promising to forget the past, and felicitating themselves on this happy reconciliation. . . .

There was no sincerity in this unison, and a new incident soon occurred to furnish a pretext for a rupture. The directory of the department, after examining numerous documents which established that Mayor Pétion and the procurator of the commune, Manuel, were in complicity with the instigators of June 20, suspended them both from their administrative functions.

The king confirmed the department's decree. He well knew that the Assembly would annul this enactment. It owed that service to the department, which had merely acted under its orders. In fact Pétion, sure of his triumph, appeared at the bar, less as an accused man seeking vindication, than as an irreproachable man who has been unjustly outraged in his honor and demands vengeance. The Assembly, after having listened for the sake of form, reinstated him in his functions as mayor.

PROJECT OF A REPUBLIC IN THE SOUTH. (Ferrières, III, 149–150.)

Meanwhile, the Girondins were frightened by the magnitude of their own projects and tormented by the wearing anxiety which always accompanies undertakings of uncertain success. They began to think of constructing a refuge for themselves in the Midi. Barbaroux, an ardent and impetuous young man, arrived at Paris with the Marseillais. Mme. Roland and Servan, the ex-minister of war, were continuously discussing the good will which prevailed in the Midi, and the facilities offered by the provinces for the establishment of a republic. They took maps and traced the lines which were to separate republican France from monarchical France. Servan made a study of this. "We will rely upon the Midi!" cried Barbaroux. "It will be our last resource if the Marseillais I have here are not seconded by the Parisians, and cannot subdue the court; but I hope they will succeed and that we shall have a convention that will make a republic out of all France."

AGITATION FOR THE KING'S DEPOSITION. (Barbaroux, 43–44.)

In Paris, at this time, the abdication of the king was much in question. This, in giving the throne to the dauphin, would give the regency to Philippe d'Orléans, or so his party enthusiastically proclaimed. The duke's creditors, his hirelings, and his satellites; Marat and his Cordeliers; all the swindlers and men overwhelmed with dishonor or with debt, were seen scouring the public haunts to urge this abdication, eager to secure gold and offices under a regent who was their accomplice and their tool. Good patriots were in favor of it also, as the sole means of breaking up the court. The Jacobins, the Paris popular societies, and the forty-eight sections had considered drawing up a petition. A few men of discernment in the legislative body's committee of general defense perceived the snare and attempted to put forward other measures; otherwise, the executive power would pass into the hands of one of the most dissolute of men. The reign of a feeble monarch would be succeeded by a reign of brigandage under the prince's friends, with a regent whose only followers were vile reprobates. It is true that France has not escaped the evils of anarchy, but should the blame fall upon the men who worked sincerely to found the Republic?

MARAT'S IDEAS ON SAVING FRANCE. (Barbaroux, 58–60.)

His journal finished, he talked politics with us. "We were wrong in believing the French should make war with guns; the poignard was the only weapon for free men. With a well-sharpened knife, one can strike down his enemy in a battalion as well as on the corner of the street. The National Assembly," he added, "can still save France by decreeing that all aristocrats wear white ribbons, and that they will be hanged if found in groups of more than three." Then he wanted the royalists and the Feuillants to be ambushed and murdered in the streets. It would be the quickest way, and would really be a humane act, since there was no doubt that they desired to murder us. I observed that in this manner they might kill a great many patriots: feeble objection! "If out of a hundred men killed," said he, "there are ten patriots, what does it matter? Ninety men for ten, and besides there is no danger of mistake. Fall upon those who have carriages, valets, and silk garments, or who are leaving the theaters; you may be sure these are aristocrats." One would never believe that these proposals were made to me by Marat if the same propositions had not been found in his journal.

FEAR OF AN INSURRECTION ON JULY 14. (Mme. de Tourzel, II, 174.)

The moment of the federation approached, and it was feared that advantage might be taken of the opportunity to bring about the movement that the rebels were working to organize. Fortunately the national guard was not disposed to join them, and this compelled them to defer once more the execution of their plans. A large number of the national guard from the provinces, to whom were attached the recruits on their way to defend the frontiers, arrived in Paris to take part in the federation. The majority of the recruits shared the sentiments of the rebels, but the others, indignant at what they saw and at the methods adopted to corrupt their fidelity, made a point of requesting that they should leave Paris and go to join the army.

(Mme. Campan, 330–331.)

At length the king found an opportunity one morning to pull off his coat in the queen's chamber and try on the breastplate.... [He] said to me in a very low tone of voice: "It is to satisfy her that I submit to this inconvenience: they will not assassinate me; their scheme is changed; they will put me to death in another way." The queen heard the king whispering to me, and when he had gone out she asked me what he had said. I hesitated to answer; she insisted that I should, saying that nothing must be concealed from her, and that she was resigned upon every point. When she was informed of the king's remark she told me she had guessed it, that he had long since observed to her that all that was going forward in France was an imitation of the revolution in England in the time of Charles I, and that he was incessantly reading the history of that unfortunate monarch in order that he might act better than Charles had done at a similar crisis.

THE FESTIVAL OF THE FEDERATION. (Weber, II, 207–212.)

It had been announced that the oath would be taken at midday. The king arrived at eleven o'clock. The cortège was very imposing; a detachment of cavalry led the procession, followed by infantry from the line troops.... The king and his family took their places in a balcony covered with rich hangings of crimson velvet embroidered with gold. All those present gathered around him and ranged themselves at his side.

The national cortège entered the Champ-de-Mars by the gate of the Rue de Grenelle. It filed beneath the king's balcony and advanced towards the altar of the country, from both right and left. Behind fifty national gendarmes came a group of men, women, and children armed with pikes, hatchets, and sticks. Harmonious music played the famous air, *Ça ira*; while raga-muffins made insulting gestures and showed insolent placards to the king. The cries of "Long live Pétion! Pétion or death!" began to be heard. These were the dregs of humanity, some beggars and some cutthroats, to judge by their weapons; drunken women crowned with flowers; all the *canaille* of the fau-bourgs, with "Long live Pétion!" inscribed in chalk on the backs of their hats; six Paris legions, dishonored by being there, with a hodgepodge of women and *sans-culottes* in their ranks carrying red caps, loaves of bread, and pieces of meat upon the ends of their guns; chaplains who gambolled at the head of regiments; infamous songs chanted by species of furies who stopped under the king's balcony; placards on the ends of sticks, some atrocious, some stupid, like the one among the drums that announced that they were "drums"; or like the one upon which could be read, "Long live the brave people who died at the siege of the Bastille!" There was a scorn of all goodness, of all prudence, of all reason; a confusion of tongues, men, and things. That was what was presented at this august and solemn occasion! ...

The king could not in fact ascend the altar, because the crowd, and particu-larly some half-naked people, had taken possession of the upper part. There was an alarming movement. The deputy Dumas had the presence of mind to cry out, "Grenadiers! On guard! Ready arms!" The *sans-culottes* stopped and fell back into the crowd. The taking of the oath, accompanied by the thunder of fifty-four cannon ranged on the riverbank, was imposing enough to those who were near the altar.

THE COUNTRY IN DANGER. (*Sergent Marceau, 192–193.*)

The legislative body decreed a levy of volunteers. Paris was to furnish three thousand, and Lajard, the minister of war, had in the king's name ordered registers to be placed in the notaries' offices for the citizens to inscribe them-selves. It was a measure more than ridiculous, and scarcely two hundred volunteers came forward. I pointed out the futility of this royal measure, and proposed the solemn and touching ceremony which was executed by my orders on Sunday the 22nd of July. Early in the morning signal guns an-nounced the fête, and discharges of artillery went on every hour throughout the day. At ten o'clock the municipal officers, mounted on horseback, issued from the Hôtel de Ville bearing a huge tricolor flag with the inscription, "Citizens, the country is in danger." They were followed by artillery and several detachments of the national guard; there were other banners with the legend, "Liberty, Equality, Fraternity, Responsibility." The whole was preceded by solemn music. After the proclamation was read (I chose for this purpose those municipal officers who had the most imposing presence and the most sonorous voices), the enrollings on amphitheaters in the principal public places followed. Tents were erected, covered with garlands of bay and oak leaves, a pike on each side crowned with the *bonnet rouge*, and the flag of each section in front. An imposing group of municipal authorities in full dress sat at a table resting on two drums, and presided over the registers. There were sixty bands of music. A rush of youthful volunteers, generous and ardent, overflowed the square, altogether offering a new and animated spectacle, more curious and interesting than the Revolution had yet afforded. As each volunteer enrolled himself, a venerable officer embraced him, presented him with a laurel wreath, and a roll of drums proclaimed the enlistment. Solemn music was again played while he was leaving the amphitheater. The enrollment went on for two days, and five thousand men were inscribed on the registers amidst the acclamations of the people; the example was followed throughout the country, and gave us those legions which drove the Prussians out of Champagne.

GIRONDIN TEMPORIZING. (Ferrières, III, 166–168.)

The Girondins only wished to frighten the court. Dethronement had not entered their minds at all; it was an extreme measure which had its dangers. They resolved to hazard another attempt and try to bring about the reinstatement of the three disgraced ministers. Guadet read a long address to the king. He reproached him for his lack of frankness, warned him that his present ministers lacked the confidence of the nation, and exhorted him to recall those who, by their brilliant services, had so justly merited that confidence. . . . [In a letter to the king] they promised to rally to him on condition that he would take back the three ministers; but the court, trusting in the promises of foreign powers, and seduced by a false opinion of their strength, preferred to risk whatever eventualities might arise rather than abandon themselves to the Girondins. These, having lost all hope of coming to terms, let the Orleanists act as they wished, and even seconded them with all their power at the risk of seeing themselves dragged down in the general ruin.

XVIII. *The Attack on the Tuileries*

FEARS OF THE COURT. (*Letter of Marie Antoinette to Mercy, July 4, 1792.*)

You already know what happened on June 20; since then our position has become daily more critical. On one side nothing but violence and rage, on the other, feebleness and inertia. Neither the national guard nor the army can be relied upon; one does not know whether to remain in Paris or withdraw to some other place. It is more than time for the powers to speak out forcefully. July 14 and the following days may bring occasion for general mourning in France and cause the powers to regret that they have been too tardy in declaring themselves. All is lost if the seditious are not restrained by fear of impending punishment. They want a republic at any cost, and to gain it have resolved to assassinate the king. The National Assembly and Paris should be held, in a manifesto, responsible for the safety of him and his family. In spite of all danger we shall not change our decisions. You should count upon that as I count upon your devotion. The moment has come to give me signal proof of it, in saving me and mine if there is time.

(*Mme. de Tourzel, II, 195.*)

The emperor and the King of Prussia having given the command of the armies assembled on the frontiers of France to the Duke of Brunswick, the latter wished, before invading France, to announce to its inhabitants the motives which guided the two sovereigns ...

THE BRUNSWICK MANIFESTO.

Their Majesties the emperor and the King of Prussia having entrusted me with the command of the combined armies assembled by their orders on the frontiers of France, I am desirous to acquaint the inhabitants of that kingdom with the motives which have determined the measures of the two sovereigns, and the intentions by which they are guided.

After having arbitrarily suppressed the rights and possessions of the German princes in Alsace and Lorraine; deranged and overthrown good order and the legitimate government in the interior; committed against the sacred person of the king and his august family outrages and attacks of violence which are still continued and renewed from day to day; those who have usurped the reins of the administration have at length filled up the measure by causing an unjust war to be declared against His Majesty the emperor, and attacking his provinces situated in the Netherlands: some of the possessions of the Germanic Empire have been involved in this oppression, and several others have escaped the same danger solely by yielding to the imperative menaces of the predominant party and its emissaries.

His Majesty the King of Prussia, united with His Imperial Majesty by the bonds of a close and defensive alliance, and himself a preponderating member of the Germanic body, has therefore not been able to forbear marching to the aid of his ally and his co-states; and it is in this twofold relation that he takes upon himself the defense of that monarch and of Germany.

With these great interests an object equally important is joined, and which the two sovereigns have deeply at heart; namely, to put an end to the anarchy in the interior of France, to stop the attacks directed against the throne and the altar, to re-establish the legal power, to restore to the king the security and liberty of which he is deprived, and to place him in a condition to exercise the legitimate authority which is his due.

Convinced that the sound part of the French nation abhors the excesses of a faction which domineers over it, and that the majority of the inhabitants await with impatience the moment of succor to declare themselves openly against the odious enterprises of their oppressors, His Majesty the emperor and His Majesty the King of Prussia call upon and invite them to return without delay to the ways of reason and justice, of order and peace. Agreeably to these views, I, the undersigned, commander-in-chief of the two armies, declare:

1. That the two allied courts, forced into the present war by irresistible circumstances, propose to themselves no other aim than the happiness of France, without pretending to enrich themselves by conquests.

2. That they intend not to interfere in the internal government of France, but are solely desirous to deliver the king, the queen, and the royal family from their captivity, and to procure for His Most Christian Majesty the safety necessary to enable him to make without danger, without impediment, such convocations as he shall think proper, and labor to ensure the happiness of his subjects, agreeably to his promises and in so far as it shall depend upon him.

3. That the combined armies will protect the cities, towns, and villages, and the persons and property of all those who shall submit to the king, and that they will concur in the instantaneous re-establishment of order and police throughout France.

4. That the national guards are summoned to watch *ad interim* over the tranquillity of the towns and of the country, and over the safety of the persons and property of all the French, till the arrival of the troops of Their Imperial and Royal Majesties, or till it shall be otherwise ordained, upon penalty of being held personally responsible; that, on the contrary, such of the national guards as shall be taken in arms shall be treated as enemies and punished as rebels to their king, and as disturbers of the public peace.

5. That the generals, officers, subalterns, and soldiers of the French troops of the line are in like manner summoned to return to their ancient fidelity, and to submit forthwith to the king, their legitimate sovereign.

6. That the members of the departments, districts, and municipalities shall, in like manner, be responsible with their lives and property for all misdemeanors, fires, murders, pillage, and acts of violence which they shall suffer to be committed, or which they shall notoriously not strive to prevent in their territory; that they shall, in like manner, be required to continue their functions *ad interim*, till His Most Christian Majesty, restored to full liberty, shall have made ulterior provisions, or till it shall have been otherwise ordained in his name.

7. That in the meantime the inhabitants of the cities, towns, and villages who shall dare to defend themselves against the troops of Their Imperial and Royal Majesties and to fire upon them, either in the open field, or from the windows, doors, and apertures of their houses, shall be instantly punished with all the rigor of the law of war, and their houses demolished or burned. All the inhabitants, on the contrary, of the said cities, towns, and villages, who shall readily submit to their king, by opening the gates to the troops of Their Majesties, shall be from that moment under their immediate safeguard. Their persons, their property, their effects, shall be under the protection of the laws; and provision shall be made for the general safety of all and each of them.

8. The city of Paris and all its inhabitants without distinction are required to submit immediately and without delay to the king, to set that prince at full and entire liberty, and to ensure to him as well as to all the royal personages the inviolability and respect which the law of nature and nations renders obligatory on subjects towards their sovereigns; Their Imperial and Royal Majesties holding personally responsible with their lives for all that may happen, to be tried militarily, and without hope of pardon, all the members of the National Assembly, of the department, of the district, of the municipality, and of the national guard of Paris, the justices of the peace, and all others whom it shall concern; Their Majesties declaring, moreover, on their faith and word as emperor and king, that if the Palace of the Tuileries is forced or insulted, that if the least violence, the least outrage, is offered to Their Majesties the king and queen, and to the royal family, if immediate provision is not made for their safety, their preservation, and their liberty, they will take an exemplary and ever-memorable vengeance by giving up the city of Paris to military execution and total destruction, and the rebels guilty of outrages to the punishments which they shall have deserved. Their Imperial and Royal Majesties on the other hand promise the inhabitants of the city of Paris to employ their good offices with His Most Christian Majesty to obtain pardon of their faults and misdeeds, and to take the most vigorous measures for the security of their persons and property, if they promptly and strictly obey the above injunctions.

Lastly, Their Majesties, unable to recognize as laws in France any but those which shall emanate from the king, enjoying perfect liberty, protest beforehand against the authenticity of all the declarations which may be made in the name of His Most Christian Majesty so long as his sacred person, that of the queen, and of the whole royal family shall not be really in safety; to the effect of which Their Imperial and Royal Majesties invite and solicit His Most Christian Majesty to name the city of his kingdom nearest to its frontiers to which he shall think fit to retire with the queen and his family, under a good and safe escort, which shall be sent to him for this purpose, in order that His Most Christian Majesty may be enabled in complete safety to call around him such ministers and councillors as he shall please to appoint, make such convocations as shall to him appear fitting, provide for the re-establishment of good order, and regulate the administration of his kingdom.

Finally, I again declare and promise in my own private name, and in my aforesaid quality, to make the troops placed under my command observe good and strict discipline, engaging to treat with kindness and moderation those well-disposed subjects who shall show themselves peaceful and submissive, and not to employ force unless against such as shall be guilty of resistance or hostility.

For these reasons, I require and exhort all the inhabitants of the kingdom, in the strongest and the most earnest manner, not to oppose the march and the operations of the troops which I command, but rather to grant them everywhere free entrance and all good will, aid, and assistance that circumstances may require.

Given at the headquarters at Coblentz, the 25th of July, 1792.

CHARLES WILLIAM FERDINAND,
Duke of Brunswick-Lüneburg

THE EFFECT OF THE MANIFESTO. (*Mme. de Tourzel, II, 198.*)

This manifesto exasperated the Assembly, which gave way without restraint to the most violent anger; and as arms were wanting, it proposed to arm the citizens with pikes, lances, axes, and slings. In the height of his anger, Lecointre exclaimed, "Will no man of genius arise to invent a mode in which these free men may make war?"

The manifesto of the Duke of Brunswick compelled the king to make a fresh declaration of his sentiments in order to oppose the invasion of France. He spoke to his erring people as a father who was only anxious for their welfare and their return to their duty, recalling all that he had sacrificed in the hope of making them happy, seeking to prove to them that by union alone and rigid compliance with the constitution they would succeed in avoiding the misfortunes with which they saw themselves threatened.

THE SECTIONS DEMAND THAT THE KING BE DETHRONED. (*Weber, II, 215.*)

However, the appearance of the capital became hourly more turbulent and more alarming. Insolent placards were posted in conspicuous places, even under the very walls of the palace. Marseillais and federates continually milled around it. There could be heard the furious cries of a mutinous populace, summoned from all directions by the sound of the tocsin, and threatening a formidable insurrection unless the National Assembly hastened to fulfill its pledge to the nation by pronouncing the dethronement of the monarch. All this gave announcement that the fatal blow was about to be struck.

(*Ferrières, III, 173–174.*)

... triumphant, and savoring in advance the pleasure of avenging his suspension and satisfying his personal animosity against Louis XVI, Pétion arrived at the head of the forty-eight sections of Paris to demand dethronement and a national convention. "While awaiting, Messieurs, the expression of the will of the people, who are your sovereign and ours, let the Assembly create a solidly responsible ministry appointed from among its members. It is doubtful if the nation retains any confidence in the present dynasty."

AN EXPLOSION PROPHESIED. (*Mme. Jullien, 211–212.*)

At this moment the horizon is dark with clouds that seem to presage a terrible storm. There is lightning in this thunderhead; where will it strike?

The National Assembly seems to me too weak to further the desires of the people, and the people appear to be too strong for it to subjugate them. From this conflict, this battle, should come some result: either the liberty or enslavement of twenty-five million men. My zealous activity has carried me often to the National Assembly, to the Jacobins, or to the public promenades, where resound the news of current happenings.

My observations made in these various places seem to me to be so apt that I see and foresee the future with a prescience that I believe prophetic. The patriot party will prevail, but unfortunately it is almost certain to have its laurels shortly stained with blood.

The dethronement of the king, demanded by the majority, and rejected by the minority that dominates the Assembly, will bring on the dreadful storm that is brewing.

THE SECTIONS TAKE CHARGE OF THE CITY GOVERNMENT. (*Ferrières, III, 180–181.*)

Most [of the sections] placed themselves in a state of insurrection, and declared that they no longer recognized the constituted authorities. Each named six commissioners, who repaired to the municipality, to form there a council general of the commune, saying that, sent by the people and working in unison to preserve the public welfare, they were taking over all powers delegated by the commune. Entering instantly into their new sovereignty, they cashiered the staff of the national guard, asserting that their influence upon the fate of liberty had up to the present day brought nothing but misfortune upon the people. They suspended the municipality under the pretext that it could not function except according to established procedure and could not come to the aid of the people in the present frightful crisis. They kept only Mayor Pétion and the procurator of the commune, Manuel, whom they confined in the Mairie with a guard of four hundred citizens. These were charged to watch over their safety, but in reality they were there to keep the Assembly or the department from requiring them to enforce the law.

(Mme. Jullien, 221.)

The commune has done wonderful things, the details of which I am unable to give. Quickly purged of aristocratic tendencies, it gave itself an organization independent of the department. It has furnished arms and munitions. It has seconded the actions of those citizens who have so completely united against treason that cavalry, grenadiers, chasseurs, and *sans-culottes* are all brothers, serving together the public weal. Pikes and bayonets have joined today in sincere and noble alliance. All the officers are going to be cashiered this evening, Santerre being since midday the commanding general of the national guard. Manuel and Danton have taken charge of the civil government.

LA FAYETTE'S ACCUSATIONS AGAINST DANTON. *(La Fayette, Memoirs; Thiers, I, 175.)*

Danton had sold himself to the court, on condition that they would purchase from him, for one hundred thousand livres, his place of advocate, which, after the suppression, was only worth ten thousand livres. La Fayette met Danton at M. de Montmorin's the same evening that the bargain was concluded. He was a man ready to sell himself to all parties. While he was making incendiary motions in the Jacobins, he was their spy at court, where he regularly reported whatever occurred. On the Friday previous to the 10th of August, fifty thousand crowns were given him, and Madame Elizabeth exclaimed, "We are tranquil, for we may depend on Danton." La Fayette was apprised of the first payment, but not of the ensuing one. Danton spoke of it himself at the Hôtel de Ville, and, endeavoring to justify himself, said, "General, I am a greater monarchist than you are yourself." He was, nevertheless, one of the leaders of the 10th of August.

INTENTIONS OF THE GIRONDINS. *(Ferrières, III, 184–185.)*

The Girondins had not lost hope of gaining control of the insurrection and turning it to their advantage.

Resolved upon sacrificing Louis XVI, they were planning to leave him at the palace, conduct the queen and royal family to the Assembly, proclaim the dauphin king, make Pétion his mentor, and name Roland regent of the realm. It was essential to the execution of this project that Louis XVI should defend himself and that the palace should be forced. That is why the Girondins opposed the sending of a deputation. The Assembly would have made common cause with the king. It would have authorized by its presence the mustering of the Swiss and the resistance to the federates and Marseillais which had already been resolved upon.

THE INSURRECTION BEGINS. *(Cléry, 2–3.)*

Since the morning of the ninth there had been a great deal of agitation. Crowds gathered all over Paris, and the plans of the conspirators became known with certitude at the Tuileries. The tocsin was to be sounded throughout the city at midnight. The Marseillais, in conjunction with the inhabitants of the Faubourg Saint-Antoine, were then to proceed to the attack of the palace. . . .

The courts of the palace were filled with about eight thousand national guards from different sections, ready to defend the king. I went to the Palais-Royal, where I found nearly all the exits closed. There were some national guards under arms ready to march to the Tuileries and reinforce the battalions which had preceded them. A populace aroused by the factious filled the neighboring streets, its clamors re-echoing in all directions.

(*Weber, II, 218–219.*)

Towards five o'clock in the morning, His Majesty appeared on his balcony to show the guard and the reinforcements placed about the courts his appreciation of the zeal they were displaying in his defense. On perceiving him, a nearly unanimous cry of "Long live the King!" rang out. He then descended to the royal courtyard to review the troops that filled it; the acclamations redoubled. It was nevertheless impossible to believe in the sincerity of them all. Since the evening before, many artillerymen had gone so far as to utter, in our presence, frightful menaces against the court. "Tomorrow," they said, pointing with threatening gestures to the balcony of the palace, "tomorrow we will administer justice to all; we will spare the king, perhaps, but the rest, all the rest will be exterminated."

However, we still flattered ourselves that the majority of the national guards would do their duty; and we had taken the precaution to keep the most doubtful under close surveillance. We resolved, in addition, to place four of our grenadiers at every cannon to make sure of its being used. But at the very moment we were putting this measure into effect, we discovered, in the midst of the din of repeated cries of "Long live the King!" a mob of traitors among the gendarmes, and especially among the artillerymen of the different corps. "Long, long live the Nation!" they shouted. "We have, we recognize no other master than the nation." "Yes, *mes enfants*," said the king, with an accent which would have penetrated the most ferocious heart, "yes, the nation and your king are and never can be but one and the same thing."

(*Cléry, 4–6.*)

As the attack on the Tuileries did not appear to be near at hand, I went out a second time, following the quay as far as the Pont-Neuf. I encountered everywhere detachments of armed men, whose evil intentions could not be doubted. They carried pikes, forks, hatchets, and pruning hooks. The battalion of Marseillais advanced in perfect order with their cannon, matches lighted. They invited the people to join them, to help, as they said, dislodge the tyrant and proclaim his dethronement in the National Assembly. Being now quite certain of what was going to happen and thinking only of my duty, I outdistanced the battalion and soon regained the Tuileries. A large body of national guards were leaving in disorder by the gate of the garden fronting the Pont-Royal. Grief was painted on the faces of most of them. Some were saying, "This morning we swore to defend the king, and at the very moment of his greatest danger, we abandon him." Others, belonging to the conspirators, abused and menaced their comrades, forcing them to depart. Thus the loyal let themselves be dominated by the mutinous, and this shameful weakness, accomplice to all the evils of the Revolution, was again responsible for the tragedies of this day. . . .

At seven o'clock, the uneasiness was increased by the cowardliness of several battalions that successively abandoned the Tuileries. Those of the national guards who remained at their posts, four or five hundred in number, showed fidelity and courage. They, with the Swiss, were placed indiscriminately in the interior of the palace, on the different stairways, and at all the exits. . . . The court people and the servants were distributed through the various rooms, after having sworn to give their lives in defending the person of the king. We were in all about three or four hundred, but without other arms than swords or pistols. By eight o'clock the danger became more acute. The Legislative Assembly was holding its sittings in the building of the Manège adjoining the garden of the Tuileries. The king had addressed several communications to it in regard to the position he was in, and asked that a deputation be appointed to aid him with its advice. The Assembly, regardless of the fact that an attack on the palace was being prepared beneath its very eyes, made no reply.

THE KING GOES TO THE ASSEMBLY. (Cléry, 6–7.)

Some moments later, the department of Paris and several municipal officers were seen to enter, having at their head Roederer, at that time procurator-syndic of the department. Roederer, doubtless in accord with the conspirators, urged His Majesty to go with his family to the Assembly. He declared that the king could no longer count upon the national guard, and that if he remained in his palace, neither the department nor the municipality of Paris could be any longer responsible for his safety. The king heard him without emotion. He retired to his chamber with the queen, the ministers, and a few other persons, and soon after left to go with his family to the Assembly. He was protected by a detachment of Swiss and national guards. . . .

The royal family had been in the Assembly a quarter of an hour when I saw on the Terrace of the Feuillants four heads stuck on pikes, having been brought from the direction of the place where the legislative body held its sittings. This was, I think, the signal for the attack on the palace, for at the same moment a terrible cannon and musketry fire broke out. Bullets and cannon shot were riddling the palace. The king being no longer there, each was concerned solely with his own safety; however all the issues were closed and certain death awaited us.

THE ATTACK ON THE TUILERIES. (Pfyffer d'Altishoffen, 357–364.)

Nobles and persons attached to the king had come in great numbers to the palace, armed with swords and pistols. Their intention can only be praised; it was excellent; but one must disapprove of their action and avow that armed as they were they could only embarrass the defense and inspire distrust in the national guard.

At eleven o'clock in the evening, the information was received that the tocsin would sound at midnight. A little later it was known at the palace that the Faubourg Saint-Antoine had passed a resolution of which the principal articles were "to attack the palace; exterminate everybody, with particular attention to the Swiss; force the king to abdicate; and conduct the king, queen, and royal family to Vincennes to serve as hostages in case the foreigners launched themselves upon Paris."

At midnight, the tocsin was heard to sound. . . .

The lugubrious sound of the tocsin, far from discouraging the soldiers, increased their animation. At two in the morning, four battalions from the faubourgs had already arrived on the Place du Carrousel. They were ready to execute their horrible projects and only awaited their comrades.

Between four and five o'clock, M. Mandat received an order to go to the commune. They were waiting to cut his throat on the steps of the Hôtel de Ville. They knew that he had in his pocket an order signed by Pétion authorizing him to repel force with force, and were willing to employ murder to keep this written document from becoming public. . . .

Between eight and nine o'clock, the king decided to repair to the midst of the National Assembly. He was accompanied by all the royal family and some of the nobles. . . .

The army of Santerre put itself into movement, preceded by cannon, and soon was seen advancing towards the gates of the palace.

The brigadier of the day, seeing himself almost alone with the Swiss, judged that he could not hold the courts with so few people. He cried out, "Gentlemen of the Swiss, retire to the palace." They were forced to obey, leaving six pieces of cannon in the hands of the enemy when they abandoned the courts. One should have foreseen that these would have to be retaken or they would be blasted out of the palace; simple soldiers said so loudly. However, they obeyed, and made such dispositions as time and place permitted. They garnished the stairways and windows of the palace with soldiers. The foremost platoon was placed beside the chapel, that is to say, a platoon of Filles-Saint-Thomas grenadiers formed the first line, and the Swiss formed the second. . . .

Here is the state of things at the moment the combat was about to begin. There were seven hundred and fifty Swiss distributed over more than twenty posts, two hundred noblemen without arms, and some national guards who had remained faithful. Without commander-in-chief, without munitions, and without cannon, they were attacked from all sides by nearly a hundred thousand furious people having with them fifty pieces of artillery. This mob felt that it was encouraged by the legislative body, and that it was in control of the municipality.

The troop of Santerre let loose a discharge that wounded several soldiers. The Filles-Saint-Thomas grenadiers replied, followed by the Swiss. . . .

The action became general. It was soon decided in favor of the Swiss; the fire from the windows and that of M. de Durler's reserve had been deadly. In a short time the court found itself evacuated, heaped with dead, dying, and wounded.

MM. de Durler and de Pfyffer made a sortie from the palace with a hundred and twenty men; they took four pieces of cannon, and regained control of the royal gate. . . .

After efforts that were almost disastrous, the Swiss remained masters of the field of battle. The soldiers dragged in the cannon taken from the enemy, aided by the officers; they fought everywhere with equal fury. Everywhere the enemy was repulsed, and the Marseillais, who formed the heads of the attacking columns, suffered prodigiously.

THE MASSACRE OF THE SWISS GUARDS. (*Pfyffer d'Altishoffen, 364–368.*)

But the Swiss saw with anxiety that the moment was approaching when lack of munitions would leave them exposed to the fire of the enemy, without means of responding to it.

At this critical moment, M. d'Hervilly (since dead for the royal cause at Quiberon) arrived without arms, hatless, through musket and cannon fire. They wished to show him the dispositions that had just been made on the side of the garden. "Never mind that," he said. "You have to betake yourselves to the Assembly." . . .

The traversing of the garden was particularly murderous. It was necessary to brave the heavy cannon and musketry fire coming from three different points, the Pont-Royal gate, the gate of the Manège court, and the Terrace of the Feuillants. M. de Gross' thigh was broken by a ball and he fell by the pool near the group of Arria and Pætus.

Finally they arrived in the corridors of the National Assembly. The Baron de Salis, becoming too ardent, entered the hall of the legislative body sword in hand, to the great fright of the Left of the Assembly. The deputies there cried out, "The Swiss, the Swiss!" and several sought to escape through the windows.

A deputy came to order the commander to lay down his arms; he refused to do so. M. de Durler was brought before His Majesty. He said to the king, "Sire, they want us to lay down our arms." The king replied, "Yield them to the national guard; I do not want brave men like you to perish." A moment afterwards, the king sent him a note in his own writing conceived in these terms: "The king orders the Swiss to lay down their arms and retire to the barracks." This order was a thunderbolt to these brave soldiers. They cried out that they could still defend themselves with the bayonet. Several cried with rage, but in this frightful extremity discipline and fidelity prevailed. All obeyed.

This order to abandon their weapons and deliver themselves over defenseless to tigers thirsting for their blood was the final sacrifice demanded of the Swiss. . . .

The palace being no longer defended, the army of Santerre entered it, and began a cowardly massacring of the wounded and those who had lost their way in the immensity of the palace. There were in the apartments a group of Swiss who had not been able to join the detachment that returned to the National Assembly. They descended at the moment the Marseillais entered the palace, and finding the two cannon that M. de Durler had left loaded, fired them, which gave them time to operate their retreat by the garden. With them was Father Second-Lorettan, Capuchin and almoner of the regiment. It was necessary to pass through a hail of musket and cannon shot.... This little troop directed itself first towards the Assembly, but was met with musket fire. They proceeded to the Pont-Tournant and found it closed. Finally, they were able to go out by the garden of the dauphin. Arriving at the Place Louis XV, they were charged by mounted gendarmes and most of them were massacred. Father Second was saved by his disguise. A moment later, Sergent Stofel, from Mels, Canton of Saint-Gall, commanding fifteen men that he had picked up at various posts, made his way to the vestibule where the cannon were that had just been abandoned and which were now being guarded by the Marseillais. He took possession of three, and a fourth was spiked. He defended them for some time, and finally made good his retreat to the Assembly.

Overwhelmed by numbers, the Swiss had left no other trophies than the bodies of their enemies. A thousand deeds of heroism and devotion were submerged in the general glory of the day.

THE VENGEANCE OF THE PEOPLE. (Barbaroux, 73.)

Could one prevent the vengeance of a brother covered with a brother's blood, or the indignation of the people avenging the people? In the midst of massacre none were truly blamable except those cowards who fled during the action, and became assassins after the victory, and those slayers of corpses who pierced the dead bodies with their swords in order to pretend to the honors of the combat. In the apartments, on the roofs, and in the cellars, there took place a massacre of the Swiss armed or unarmed, of nobles, of valets, and all those who inhabited the palace.

(Barras, I, 78.)

The environs of the Rue Saint-Honoré and the Palais-Royal were occupied during the combat by several battalions of the national guard. These were not in sympathy with the sentiments of the majority and had sworn to defend the throne. In fulfillment of their vow, they awaited the outcome of the whole affair. If the court had triumphed, they would not have failed to have espoused its cause, but one does not rally to the vanquished. They dispersed therefore after the victory of the people. Having rearrived at Paris several days before August 10, I saw this decisive battle at close range, just as three years before I had seen the taking of the Bastille on July 14. Although there is no doubt that the people played a great part in these combats, the victory at the Tuileries, as well as at the Bastille, may be attributed to the action of the troops rather than to that of the mob. The Marseillais and Breton battalions played the part at the Tuileries that had been played by the French guards at the Bastille.

THE KING SUSPENDED AND TURNED OVER TO THE COMMUNE. (Barbaroux, 76.)

The legislative body had sat unmoved in the midst of this grand commotion. Saltpeter thundered and cannon balls passed over the hall. The National

Assembly was presided over by Guadet, Vergniaud, and Gensonné in majestic succession while it enacted the most memorable decrees.

Vergniaud left the chair to propose the suspension of the king and the convoking of a convention, in an address that had been ready for several days. This was conclusive proof that the committee of general safety had foreseen what would occur and had found a way to safeguard the people. These decrees were passed unanimously under the eyes of the king, who had been relegated to the stenographer's box. He ate while the combat was going on.

(Ferrières, III, 207–208.)

Louis XVI, seated in the stenographer's box, heard all these debates about himself. He was alive and present, so to speak, at his own obsequies. His pious and courageous resignation supported him in this trying ordeal. The queen was less submissive to the hand that struck her, and suffered infinitely more. Commissioners of the municipality arrived with the information that the Luxembourg had many exits, which would make it easy for the king to be carried off. To arouse this aspiration in the enemies of the public weal would cause fresh disasters. If the Assembly persisted in keeping Louis XVI at the Luxembourg, the municipality refused to answer for his person. They proposed the Temple, smaller and easier to guard. The Girondins realized the danger of this change, but did not dare to oppose it.

(Procès-verbaux de la commune de Paris, 175–176.)

The general assembly decrees that the order of the National Assembly, relative to the arrest of Louis XVI, shall be printed. It decrees further that he shall be placed in the Tower of the Temple, and that M. le Commandant-Général shall be held responsible for the safe conduct and guarding of this hostage.

The general assembly of the commune decrees that the king shall be immediately conveyed to the Temple (preliminary visit made by M. Palloy), and that the guarding of his person shall be committed to the citizens of all the sections.

(Ferrières, III, 208–209.)

This decree was executed on the same evening. Mayor Pétion and two municipal officers came to take Louis XVI from the Assembly to the Temple. There, he was in a state of absolute dependence upon the municipality and the Orleanists. When the decisive moment arrived it would be easy to arrange an uprising of the people in which Louis and his family would naturally be involved.

THE ROLAND MINISTRY RECALLED. (Barbaroux, 78.)

Roland, Clavière, and Servan were recalled to the ministry by the Legislative Assembly. Foreign affairs were confided to Lebrun, a Liége refugee, who had been trained to diplomacy by misfortune and habit. The marine went to Monge, a good marine examiner, but inept as minister. The department of justice fell to Danton, who had been a satellite first of Lameth and then of Orléans, but now no longer wished to serve anything save his own ambition. He was to move towards dictatorship along with Marat and Robespierre. The choosing of Danton was the ruin of France . . .

(Meillan, 2–3.)

Danton had great character. He was hardy in soul, with steadfast courage. He had profound and daring ideas, combined with natural talents. His genius made up for the attainments that he had neglected to acquire. He possessed an unstudied and uncultivated eloquence all his own. He influenced his listeners more by his audacity than by his style or the appropriateness of his ideas. Inexhaustibly resourceful, I have seen him rally his party in the most desperate crises by methods that no one else would have thought of, and all with a prodigious rapidity.

Nevertheless, this Danton, who seemed born to mastery, had much less ambition than he was given credit for. He was lazy and voluptuous. He never acted or worked except when it better assured him of the delights of indolence.

(Ferrières, III, 202–203.)

Inwardly furious that dethronement had not been pronounced, and, above all, that the naming of a governor for the prince royal had been decreed, they [the Orleanists] would have given much to have revoked that part of the decree. They sent a mob of petitioners to complain because the Assembly was content merely to suspend Louis XVI from office, and to demand that it proclaim his dethronement without delay. In this delicate situation, the Girondins had fully made up their minds that if they had to take a stand one way or another, they would consider only their own interests. Vergniaud specified that Paris was only a fraction of the French domains. It was for the sovereign people, in National Convention assembled, to take such measures as they judged proper for the conservation of liberty and equality.

EXIT LA FAYETTE. (Letter of La Fayette to the American minister at The Hague.)

My dear Friend:

You have been acquainted with the atrocious events which have taken place in Paris, when the Jacobin faction on the tenth of August overthrew the constitution, enslaved both the Assembly and king, the one by terror, the other by destitution and confinement, and gave a signal for pillage and massacre.

I could have found a high station in the new order of things, without even having meddled with the plot. But my feelings did not admit of such an idea. I raised an opposition to the Jacobin tyranny; but you know the weakness of our *honnêtes gens.* I was abandoned; the army gave way to clubbish acts. Nothing was left for me but to leave France. We have been stopped on our road and detained by an Austrian detachment, which is absolutely contrary to the *droits des gens*, as may appear from the enclosed declaration, which I request you to have published. You will greatly oblige me, my dear friend, by setting out for Brussels as soon as this reaches you, and insist on seeing me. I am an American citizen, an American officer, no more in the French service. That is your right, and I do not doubt of your urgent and immediate arrival. God bless you . . .

LA FAYETTE

XIX. *The September Massacres*

LONGWY TAKEN BY THE PRUSSIANS. (Mme. Jullien, 264–265.)

LONGWY has been taken; here is a checkmate to our successes. I feel that the taking of this place is but a part of the frustrated plans of the Prussians. We feel distressed, but not discouraged. We will make them retrace every one of their steps. The Poles are in such a rage against the King of Prussia, who has plotted their ruin with that malignant old banshee, Catherine, that I hope they will aid us in his defeat. Mirabeau, a long time ago, said that this king was a fool; but I believe, like many others, that he is really an evil, maleficent beast who devours men as voraciously as Homer's Cyclops.

DANTON AND THE SEARCH FOR ARMS. (Mme. Jullien, 268.)

The minister of justice, Danton, has shown the senate what dangers threaten the country and how important it is that the people should hold themselves in readiness while taking important precautions. He said that while honest people had solicited passports in vain, criminals had been able to buy them. In short, there was decreed what you will find in today's *Moniteur*, the searching of all houses in the name of the law in order to seize unauthorized weapons and find out who has emigrated.

THE DECREE.

The council-general decrees that domiciliary visits shall be announced by the beating of drums. The visits shall be made by the commissaries of the sections, assisted by a sufficient number of armed troops. In the name of the nation they shall demand of each individual an exact declaration of the number of arms in his possession. After the declaration, if the individual is suspect, his home shall be carefully searched. In case the declaration is false, the declarer shall be immediately arrested. Every individual having a domicile in Paris, and who shall be found in the home of another during the domiciliary visit, shall be considered suspect, and as such shall be put under arrest. The commissaries of the sections shall have a register upon which they shall exactly inscribe the names of those individuals visited and the number of arms found. They shall inscribe with the same exactitude the names of persons who are absent from their homes, and affix seals to the doors of their apartments.

Houses in which no one can be found, and which the commissaries are unable to enter, shall be padlocked.

(*Mme. Jullien, 268.*)

At three o'clock, the decree; at six or seven, the drum-beat and the *générale*. All Paris in arms; all Paris on foot: illuminations, patrols, and all the women in the doorways. And now, at midnight, I hear more noise in the streets than at noon on fête days. Sixty thousand Prussians are devastating our frontiers; there are traitors and treason still. That is what should keep us on the alert, until they are vanquished and driven out.

ARREST OF THE PRIESTS. (*Procès-verbaux de la commune de Paris, 232–233.*)

Every nonjuring ecclesiastic in good health and less than sixty years of age who shall be found in Paris fifteen days after his declaration; or any other ecclesiastic of any other department who shall likewise be found in the capital, shall be arrested and conducted to the committee of the section of the *arrondissement* in which he may have been apprehended. The committee shall draft a report on the infraction of the law made by these ecclesiastics. This report shall be sent to the department of police. There, under the terms of article V of the law, and with causes stated, an order shall be drawn up for the confinement of the said ecclesiastics for ten years in a house of detention.

A register shall be kept by each of the forty-eight committees of the sections, upon which shall be inscribed all other nonjuring ecclesiastics, whether secular, regular, simple priests, *pères minorés,* or lay brothers, giving residences and other particulars.

Each time there is a change of residence, the committees of the sections in the *arrondissements* of the old and new residences must be informed of the change.

THE CHURCHES STRIPPED. (*Procès-verbaux de la commune de Paris, 205.*)

The council-general of the commune authorizes the commissaries of the sections to remove from the altars and sacristies of every parish of the capital all objects of silver, even to the chandeliers; this to take place under the surveillance of MM. Charles Jaillant, Monnense, and Venineux.

The Assembly has decided that in vanquishing the enemy metal money must be had for furnishing supplies to the army. The council, after consultation with the procurator of the commune, has decreed that the church bells of every parish shall be taken down and broken up, leaving only two for the use of each parish. M. Monnense is to take charge of this operation.

PROCLAMATION OF THE COUNCIL-GENERAL. (*Sergent Marceau, 227–228.*)

"Citizens, the enemy is at the gates of Paris. Verdun, the only obstacle, cannot hold out more than eight days. All the citizens who are defending the fortress have sworn to die rather than surrender; if they make their bodies your defense, it is your duty to fly to their assistance. Citizens, let all the friends of liberty enlist under the banners this very day. Let us meet at the Champ-de-Mars; let an army of sixty thousand men be raised without delay, and let us march against the enemy, either to fall beneath his blows, or to exterminate him with ours!" Danton, the minister of justice, harangued the people in the Champ-de-Mars, in the most vehement accents. "To arms!" he cried, and the crowd responded; the cannon on the Pont-Neuf sounded an alarm; and the drum was beaten in every section. The federates from Marseille and Brest swarmed in the streets, calling the citizens to the frontier. It was at this moment that the cry arose among the recruits: "There are other Prussians within our walls. When we are gone the prisons will be opened, and they will murder our defenseless wives and children. No quarter for our enemies! To arms, citizens! to arms!"

THE FALL OF VERDUN RUMORED. (*Mme. Roland, 302.*)

The rumor of the fall of Verdun spread abroad on the 1st of September,[1] making a great sensation and causing much fright. Street gossips talked of the enemy's marching on Châlons; within three days they would be in Paris, said these. The people, forgetting that an army on the march with provisions, arms, baggage, and artillery cannot move like an individual, considered only the nearness of the enemy, and were already visualizing foreign troops in the smoking and ravaged capital.

Nothing was neglected that was calculated to inflame the imagination, magnify the facts, and exaggerate the dangers; it was not difficult to obtain measures from the Assembly for this purpose. The domiciliary visits in search of concealed weapons and suspects had been frequent since the 10th of August. These were made general and carried out in the middle of the night, resulting in numerous new arrests and anomalous molestations.

The commune of the 10th was composed for the most part of men who had nothing to lose and everything to gain by revolution. This commune, already guilty of a thousand excesses was forced to commit others, since impunity can be gained only by the commission of additional crimes.

(*Ferrières, III, 224–225.*)

Manuel, procurator-general of the commune, requires that the tocsin be sounded instantly in the forty-eight sections; that citizens able to bear arms assemble in the Champ-de-Mars; that the barriers be closed; and that no one leave Paris unless enrolled in the army. He adds that fine carriage horses must be confiscated for cavalry mounts; the infirm and disabled must serve by giving up their arms; and those who are suspect must be disarmed and shut up for safe keeping.

The commune decrees by unanimous vote these proposals of Manuel. Danton undertakes to support them with a decree from the Assembly. He enters with the fierce look that embodies death. "Messieurs, I take great satisfaction in informing you that France is saved. . . . Yes, at the very moment I am speaking the commune is solemnly proclaiming the country in danger

[1] Verdun did not surrender until September 2.

and the necessity of its salvation. You know that Verdun is not yet in the enemy's power. Our generals are uniting to prevent their advance. The entire people of Paris are rising and dividing themselves into three parts. One division will march to the frontiers, another will work upon fortifications, and the third, armed with pikes, will guard the interior. They are gathering at the Champ-de-Mars. The executive power asks you to name commissaries to work with it in directing the enthusiasm. An important measure has become necessary: the death penalty against anyone who refuses to take the field or give up his arms. The tocsin sounds to begin the work. It is not a cry of alarm; it is a battle cry. Audacity, more audacity, always audacity, and the country is saved!"

(Mme. Roland, 302.)

The misfortunes of the country were solemnly announced. The black flag, the sign of distress, was raised on the towers of the metropolitan church. The alarm gun was fired, and the commune with sounding trumpets proclaimed a general assembly of the citizenry in the Champ-de-Mars on Sunday the 2nd. The purpose of this assembly was to rally to the country's altar the zealous defenders who would march immediately to its defense. In spite of this the barriers were ordered closed and people failed to notice the contradictory orders. They talked instead of conspiracies being hatched by the aristocrats (or the rich) who were confined there in great numbers. There was anxiety among the people, and they were reluctant to abandon their homes to the devouring wolves who would soon be unchained to throw themselves upon the dear ones left behind.

THE COMMUNE FILLS THE PRISONS. *(Pétion in the Moniteur, November 10, 1792.)*

The surveillance committee of the commune filled the prisons: It cannot be denied that, although many of the arrests were just and necessary, others were cursorily haphazard. The leaders were less to blame for this than their assistants. The police were badly organized, and one man whose very name has become a byword, whose name brings terror to the soul of every peaceful citizen, seems to have taken charge of their movements. Assiduous at all conferences, he interfered in everything. He spoke and gave orders as if he were master. I complained loudly to the commune and ended with these words: "Marat is either the maddest or the most rascally of men." Since then I have never mentioned his name.

MARAT DEMANDS THREE HUNDRED THOUSAND HEADS. *(Ferrières, III, 217.)*

Marat never ceased to repeat that the safety of the people demanded the naming of a dictator who should be authorized to arrest and condemn conspirators without appeal. He himself was willing to undertake this task. They could attach a ball and chain to him to make sure of him and his conduct. "Give me three hundred thousand heads; hang above their doors all merchants, bakers, and grocers and I will guarantee that the country is saved."

PREPARATIONS FOR THE MASSACRE. (Ferrières, III, 221–222.)

The commune begins to prepare the vast sepulcher which is to receive the corpses of so many victims . . . a large well that has been filled in for many months is reopened. Seeing that this is not sufficient, they investigate the quarry excavations in the Rue Saint-Jacques, find them suitable for their purpose, and, content on this point . . . repair to the Assembly. Their orator (Tallien) announces that the commune has arrested the subversive priests. "Two days more and the soil of the Republic will be purged of them."

To prepare people for the great movement in question, emissaries are sent to stir up the multitude. They announce new plots and the necessity of preventing them. The conspirators are in prison, it is true; but then, while the people are marching against the foe, is it wise to leave behind so many civic enemies a thousand times more dangerous? Recalcitrants may arm them and use them to murder the wives and children of the country's defenders. "Yes," cries out a Marseillais with oaths, "all traitors must be exterminated. Since I have come a hundred and eighty leagues I might as well hoist a hundred and eighty heads on the end of my pike."

THE SEPTEMBER MASSACRES BEGIN. (Ferrières, III, 226–230.)

While the commissaries of the commune inflame the populace by recitals of imaginary facts, and inspire all hearts with the fury which animates them, two or three hundred scoundrels repair to Les Carmes and to Saint-Germain to murder four hundred priests. They go next to the Abbaye, and soon the cries of the dying, mingled with the shrieks of the people as they call incessantly for new victims, bring terror to the souls of the prisoners. Each awaits in tortured anxiety the instant that is to mark his fate. . . .

The commune, seeking to give this horrible butchery the semblance of popular justice, hastily organizes a tribunal in each prison. He who presides [Maillard] has a long sword at his side; he sits before a table strewn with papers, pipes, and bottles. A dozen men compose the monstrous jury. Some, in workmen's blouses, remain standing. Others lie upon benches, dozing with fatigue and drunkenness. Three cutthroats bring in each prisoner. Their sabers cross his breast and he is warned that at the least movement he will be pierced. Two butchers with naked swords and their sleeves rolled up, their shirts spotted with blood, guard the door. The jailer has his hand on the bolts that secure it. A candle in the middle of the table adds shadowed somberness to the scene. Its wavering light is reflected on the sinister faces of the judges, and reveals their fierce and hideous features. "Your name and your profession," comes in harsh tones from the president. "Take care; a lie will be your ruin."

No plea can save the designated victim. A man of sixty is presented as the president consults his jail-book. Two national guards appear to speak for the accused in the name of the Croix-Rouge section. They insist that he has always been a good citizen. "Recommendations are useless in the case of traitors," says the president shortly. "But that is horrible," the man cries out. "Your trial is an assassination." "My hands have been washed of it," the president .replies. "Please conduct the gentleman." He is hustled out into the court and slaughtered.

SUSPENSE OF THE PRISONERS. (*Jourgniac Saint-Méard; Thiers, I, 360.*)

At half-past two o'clock on Sunday, September 2, we prisoners saw three carriages pass by attended by a crowd of frantic men and women. They went on to the Abbaye cloister, which had been converted into a prison for the clergy. A moment after, we heard that the mob had just butchered all the ecclesiastics, who, they said, had been put into the fold there. — *Near four o'clock,* the piercing cries of a man whom they were hacking to pieces with sabers drew us to the turret window of our prison, whence we saw a mangled corpse on the ground opposite to the door. Another was butchered in the same manner a moment afterwards. — *Near seven o'clock* we saw two men enter our cell with drawn swords in their bloody hands. A turnkey showed the way with a flambeau, and pointed out to them the bed of the unfortunate Swiss soldier, Reding. At this frightful moment, I was clasping his hand, and endeavoring to console him. One of the assassins was going to lift him up, but the poor Swiss stopped him, by saying in a dying tone of voice, "I am not afraid of death; pray, sir, let me be killed here." He was, however, borne away on the men's shoulders, carried into the street, and there murdered. — *Ten o'clock, Monday morning.* The most important matter that now employed our thoughts was to consider what posture we should put ourselves in, when dragged to the place of slaughter, in order to receive death with the least pain. We sent, from time to time, some of our companions to the turret window, to inform us of the attitude of the victims. They brought us back word that those who stretched out their hands suffered the longest, because the blows of the sabers were thereby weakened before they reached the head; that some of the victims lost their hands and arms before their bodies fell, and that such as put their hands behind their backs must have suffered much less pain. We calculated the advantages of this last posture and advised one another to adopt it when it should come to our turn to be butchered. — *One o'clock, Tuesday morning,* after enduring inconceivable tortures of mind, I was brought before my judges, proclaimed innocent, and set free.

UNCERTAINTY OF THE JUDGES. (*Ferrières, III, 230.*)

The principal members of the commune had retired to the Mairie, and from there they directed the assassinations. They permitted the release of several insignificant individuals who had been arrested by mistake, but upon the least doubt they referred it to the Mairie, and the portentous word *release* (agreed to mean *kill*) put an end to the uncertainty of the judges.

(*Sicard, 110–134.*)

The committee of the section was then assembled. They massacred under their very windows in the courts of the Abbaye all the prisoners found in the great prison. The members of the committee deliberated tranquilly upon public affairs without troubling themselves about the cries of the victims whose blood was flowing in the court. Upon the table of the committee were cast jewels, purses, and bloodstained handkerchiefs taken from the pockets of the victims. I was seated at this very table and was seen to shudder at the sight. The president (Citizen Jourdan) showed the same sensibility. One of the commissaries spoke to us. "The blood of the enemy," he said to us, "is a most pleasing thing to the eyes of patriots." President Jourdan and I could not repress a movement of horror. . . .

In the middle of the night, B—— de V—— [Billaud-Varenne] learned that the executioners were robbing the prisoners they had killed. He went to the court of the Abbaye, and there from a landing spoke to his workers, "My friends! my good friends! The commune sends me here to tell you that you are dishonoring this great day. It has been informed that you are robbing these aristocratic scoundrels, after executing justice upon them. Let them alone! Leave all the jewels, all the money, and all the valuables that they have upon them so that they may defray the expenses of the great act of justice that you are executing. Care will be taken to pay you, as you were promised. Be as noble, great, and generous as the business you are performing. Let everything on this great day be worthy of the people's sovereignty, delegated to you."

(Ferrières, III, 230–231.)

The shadows of night added to the horror of these executions. The slayers ran through the galleries, chambers, and dungeons. A jailer, torch in hand, called each prisoner's name in a loud voice, and counted them one by one. With horrible imprecations he threatened that they would all be massacred that very instant if they made any attempt to escape.

THE HEAD OF THE PRINCESSE DE LAMBALLE PARADED. *(Cléry, 18–19.)*

At one o'clock, the king and his family expressed the desire to take a walk; they were refused. At dinner they heard the sound of drums and soon afterward the cries of the people. The royal family left the table in anxiety and assembled in the queen's chamber. I went down to dinner with Tison and his wife, who were on service in the Tower.

We were scarcely seated when a head on the end of a pike appeared at the window. Tison's wife screamed. The assassins thought it was the queen who screamed, and we heard the savage laughter of these barbarians. Believing that Her Majesty was still at table, they had placed their victim where she could not help seeing it. It was the head of the Princesse de Lamballe. Though ensanguined, it was not in any way disfigured; her blonde hair, still in curls, waved about the pike. . . .

However, the cries outside increased in volume; insults to the queen could be distinctly heard. A municipal officer and four men arrived, having been delegated by the people to make sure that the royal family was in the Tower. One of them, in the uniform of a national guard, with epaulets and a large sword, insisted upon the prisoners' showing themselves at the window. The municipal officers opposed him. This man said to the queen in an insulting tone, "They want to keep you from seeing the head of Lamballe, which they have brought to show you how the people take vengeance on tyrants. I advise you to appear if you do not want them to come up here." At this threat the queen fell fainting . . .

THE ASSEMBLY PLAYS PONTIUS PILATE. (*Ferrières, III, 231–233.*)

Meanwhile the commune, pretending not to know what was happening, sent two of its members to demand that the Assembly stop the effusion of human blood, saying that it itself had no means of preventing it. The Assembly limited itself to appointing commissaries to go to the Abbaye. These were to go to the so-called people there and try to stop the carnage by gentleness and persuasion. The commissaries found forty or fifty murderers gathered in a semicircle around the prison doors. Six men in national guard uniforms brought out the prisoners, after having presented them for the sake of form before the tribunal which was to judge them. There was a numerous populace present, and although they took no active part in the murders, they viewed the spectacle unmoved; prolonged cries of "Long live the Nation!" were heard from time to time. A hundred men could have scattered this troop of butchers. Dusaulx, one of the commissaries of the Assembly, spoke of submission to the law, of the taking of the Bastille, and of what he had done for liberty: no one listened. Finally, one of the murderers, tired of these long discourses, said to him with much ingeniousness: "Monsieur, you appear to be a worthy man. Go away, I beg of you; you are keeping me from my work. Since you have been detaining me here my comrades have dispatched more than twenty men."

I shall not enter into the details of the atrocities committed during these forever deplorable days. The people gave themselves over to every excess of which man is capable when his natural ferocity has been inflamed by incendiary discourses and intoxicating drinks. The streets and courts were strewn with heaps of quivering bodies and limbs piled confusedly one upon another. It was before this altar of death that the few prisoners liberated by the commune were conducted. They were there made to swear fidelity to the sovereign people. The massacre continued for four days and nights, and one cannot but wonder at the apathetic insouciance of the Parisians, who looked on with criminal indifference while so many murders were committed before their very eyes. One wonders also at the abjectness of the Assembly, which did not dare to take a single measure to prevent these murders. And then there was the cold-blooded rascality of the commune. It persistently opposed every measure that the minister Roland and some few of the deputies tried to employ to stop the massacres.

PROCLAMATION OF THE COMMUNE REGARDING THE MASSACRES.

The commune of Paris hastens to inform its brethren of all the departments that a part of the ferocious conspirators who are detained in the prisons have been put to death by the people — an act of justice which appeared indispensable in order to restrain by terror the legions of traitors shut up within the walls at the moment when the people are going to march on the enemy; and without doubt the nation, after the long series of treasons which have conducted it to the brink of an abyss, will be eager to adopt these useful and salutary measures, and all the French will say, like the Parisians, "We march against the enemy, and we do not leave behind us brigands to murder our wives and children."

STATEMENT BY PÉTION, MAYOR OF PARIS.

The 2nd of September arrived. Oh, day of horror! The alarm-gun was fired; the tocsin rang. At this doleful and alarming sound, a mob collected, broke into the prisons, murdering and slaughtering. Manuel and several deputies of the National Assembly repaired to these scenes of carnage. Their efforts were useless; the victims were sacrificed in their very arms! I was, meanwhile, in a false security; I was ignorant of these cruelties; for some time past, nothing whatever had been communicated to me. At length I was informed of them, but how? In a vague, indirect, disfigured manner. I was told at the same time that all was over. The most afflicting particulars reached me; but I felt thoroughly convinced that the day which had witnessed such atrocious scenes could never return. They nevertheless continued; I wrote to the commandant-general. I required him to dispatch forces to the prisons; at first he gave me no answer. I wrote again. He told me that he had given his orders; nothing indicated that those orders were attended to. Still they continued: I went to the council of the commune; thence I repaired to the Hôtel de La Force with several of my colleagues. The street leading to that prison was crowded with very peaceful citizens; a weak guard was at the door; I entered.... Never will the spectacle that I there beheld be effaced from my memory. I saw two municipal officers in their scarfs; I saw three men quietly seated at a table, with lists of the prisoners lying open before them; these were calling over the names of the prisoners. Other men were examining them, others performing the office of judges and jurors; a dozen executioners, with bare arms, covered with blood, some with clubs, others with swords and sabers dripping with gore, were executing the sentences forthwith; citizens outside awaiting these sentences — with impatience observing the saddest silence at the decrees of death, and raising shouts of joy at those of acquittal.

The men who sat as judges, and those who acted as executioners, felt the same security as if the law had called them to perform these functions. They boasted to me of their justice, of their carefulness to distinguish the innocent from the guilty, of the services which they had rendered. They demanded — will it be believed? — they demanded payment for the time they had been employed!... I was really confounded to hear them!

I addressed to them the austere language of the law. I spoke to them with the feeling of profound indignation with which I was penetrated. I made them all leave the place before me. No sooner had I gone myself than they returned; I went back to the places to drive them away; but in the night they completed their horrid butchery.

PÉTION AND DANTON DEFENDED. (*Sergent Marceau, 229–230.*)

Six commissaries sent by the Assembly to the prisons were obliged to leave in order to save their lives. All the authorities acted separately. Pétion ran between the prison of La Force and the Assembly. Billaud-Varenne was at the Abbaye, and Manuel at Les Carmes. He was a known enemy of the priests, and could do nothing to save them. The general council, consisting of new men, was presided over by a young painter, a pupil of David, bad as an artist, and worse as an administrator. It was pitiable. I can affirm that the committee of surveillance gave no orders as to the massacres, and that Danton did not appear in it in the first days of September. All I can say of him is that when afterwards someone reproached him in my hearing with having provoked these murders, he replied: "I think with you that such things are distressing, and would take us back to the barbarism of the Middle Ages; but this has perhaps spared us from greater calamities, for it effected the flight of the King of Prussia and his army."

(*Minutes of the Jacobin Club, session of Monday, November 5, 1792.*)

Fabre d'Églantine made some observations on the events of the 2nd of September. He declared that it was the men of the 10th of August who broke into the prisons of the Abbaye, of Orléans, and of Versailles. He said that in these moments of crisis he had seen the same men come to Danton and express their satisfaction by rubbing their hands together: that one of them even desired that Morande might be sacrificed; he added that he had seen in the garden of the minister of foreign affairs, Roland, the minister, pale, dejected, with his head leaning against a tree, demanding the removal of the Convention to Tours or Blois.[1] The speaker added that Danton alone displayed the greatest energy of character that day; that Danton never despaired of the salvation of the country; that by stamping upon the ground he made ten thousand defenders start from it; and that he had sufficient moderation not to make a bad use of the species of dictatorship with which the National Assembly had invested him by decreeing that those who should counteract the ministerial operations should be punished with death.

THE JACOBINS DRAW THE VEIL. (*Mme. Jullien, 287–288.*)

The end requires the means; let us have no false humanity. The people have risen; the people, terrible in their fury, are avenging the crimes of three years of the most cowardly treason... here, with trembling hand, I cast a veil over the crimes that the people have been forced to commit as a result of all those that have been committed against them for the past three years.

VALMY. (*Ferrières, III, 247–248.*)

The King of Prussia had taken possession of Verdun and Longwy. The capture of these two places opened up Champagne to him. General Clerfayt

---

[1] One day Roland told Mme. d'Ayen (mother of Mme. de La Fayette) that the assassinations were organized in the council. (La Fayette, IV, 135.)

at the head of twenty thousand men was besieging Thionville; General Beau-lieu with a like number of Austrians was attacking Lille; and a large corps of *émigrés*, commanded by Monsieur,[1] who had taken the title of lieutenant-general of the kingdom, was advancing towards Châlons. Everything seemed to presage the happiest success; but a single fault, the natural consequence of the confident and unreflective character of the French, destroyed that flatter-ing hope. The King of Prussia and the *émigrés* regarded Paris, reasonably enough, as the sole aim of their advance. They thought to profit by the general indignation following the 10th of August and the detention of Louis in the Temple: with great imprudence they left behind them the strongholds that guarded the frontiers and advanced to offer battle in the ravines of the Argonne and the Clermontois. They were not long in realizing the consequences of this false move; the French generals had transported beyond Châlons all stores that might have aided the enemy. It was late in the season, and the King of Prussia and the *émigrés* were advancing over roads softened by the continuous autumn rains. Obliged to transport their supplies with great difficulty over a long distance, they soon faced a lack of the very necessities of life. Dysentery broke out in the ranks and carried off large numbers of soldiers. A second mistake decided the campaign. The Duke of Brunswick neglected to secure the heights of Bionne, an important post between Sainte-Menehould and Clermont. General Dillon seized it and entrenched himself there. This adroit manoeuver gave Dumouriez and Kellermann time to join forces, and they took up their positions at Valmy.

(*Dumouriez, III, 41–44.*)

[Kellermann] muddled his orders so thoroughly that, taking the battlefield for a camp, he conducted his army, encumbered with baggage, thither and began to deploy. The Prussians, seeing this confused movement on the heights of Valmy, sought to outflank the left. They marched forward in several columns, bombarding all the troops assembled on the heights of Valmy. Kellermann placed practically the whole of his artillery on the plateau by the mill, stopped the advance of the enemy, and began a terrible artillery duel. . . .

As the battle continued, the general [Dumouriez] saw that it would be limited to futile cannonading in that locality and returned to his army. What held the Prussians and prevented them from rapidly attacking the plateau of Valmy was the position of Stengel, who had outflanked them on the left of their line of attack and begun a sharp firing from that direction. With-out him, Kellermann would have been hemmed in and beaten. . . .

Such was the battle of Valmy, where each of the two armies fired over twenty thousand cannon shots and needlessly lost three or four hundred men. It had a good effect upon the French, proving to them that with resolution their firing could stop this formidable enemy.

---

[1] The *émigrés* were really under the command of the Comte d'Artois. (Original editors.)

THE RETREAT OF THE PRUSSIANS. (Ferrières, III, 248–250.)

The position of the King of Prussia became extremely critical. Dysentery continued its ravages, privation became more sensible day by day. To continue towards Paris, leaving Kellermann and Dumouriez behind him, was to invite certain disaster. One could no longer count on the means of information which the *émigrés* boasted they had in that city. The 10th of August had broken up their intrigues; and their partisans, mostly in flight or overwhelmed by terror, dared not show themselves. The public authorities favorable to them had been dismissed and replaced by ardent republicans.

The King of Prussia realized the necessity of falling back before his army was destroyed by sickness and want of provisions. But even retreat became difficult in the presence of an enemy that was daily growing stronger, since the roads were such that artillery and wagons could pass only with great difficulty and slowness. The French generals on their side were somewhat uneasy about the success of another struggle against trained and perfectly disciplined troops commanded by a skilful general. Both sides being in the same state of mind, conferences were arranged under divers pretexts between the French and Prussian generals. As a result of these, positive assurance was given by the French that they would not oppose the Prussian king's retreat. The King of Prussia agreed to give up Longwy and Verdun, entirely evacuating the territory of the Republic.

It is pretended by some that this hasty retreat was the fruit of a Girondin intrigue.

XX. The End of the Monarchy

THE CONVENTION DECLARES FOR A REPUBLIC. (Thibaudeau, I, 8.)

AUGUST 10 had overturned the throne. The Legislative Assembly had suspended the king from his functions. The royal family were prisoners in the Temple. I left for Paris sincerely believing that within six months at the most the National Convention would have decided the fate of the king, that it would have made such modifications in the constitution as the exigencies of the times demanded, and that after having given France internal peace at least, the deputies would return to their departments, there to receive the benedictions of their fellow citizens.

(Ferrières, III, 246–247.)

The Convention opened its sessions. Manuel observed that the first thing to be considered was the abolition of royalty. Collot-d'Herbois maintained that this question was so important that it could not be put off a single day, a single hour, a single minute. Many members begged for more thorough and deliberate discussion. "What is the use of discussion?" cried the constitutional bishop Grégoire. "Kings are in the moral order what monsters are in the physical. Thrones are hotbeds of crime and the sanctuaries of tyrants. The history of kings is the martyrology of nations. Since we are convinced of this truth, what is the need of discussion?"

The Convention was composed of seven hundred and fifty members, but scarcely three hundred were present. One would think that the natural thing for them to have done would have been to await the arrival of the deputies from the outlying departments before deciding such an important question, but the republicans knew that their superiority in numbers was only momentary. The Orléans faction had not expected such immediate action. There was no one who dared to oppose Manuel's motion; royalty was abolished and a republic decreed amidst the acclamations of the deputies and the people in the galleries.

(Durand de Maillane, 45.)

It is evident . . . that before the 10th of August and prior to the forced resolutions that paved the way the party of Pétion had no thought of a republic. The very Girondins who had so strongly opposed La Fayette and his partisans experienced a sort of pain at being forced to abjure the monarchy and abandon the constitution of 1791, which had reconciled the monarchy with the sovereignty and liberty of the people. There is no better proof of this than their letter to the king, whom they would have liked to convert to this first constitution.

THE CONVENTION DIVIDES INTO PARTIES. (Meillan, 11–14.)

[The September] massacres brought men into the Convention who were faced with the alternative of usurping sovereign powers or of going to the scaffold. Closely united, they became the founders of the party known as the *Mountain*. They were soon reinforced by a score of priests, fifteen to eighteen nobles, and all the ambitious and fanatical men from the other deputations.

You first see them endeavoring to pass off the September massacres as an act of popular justice, although in reality the work was done by a hundred subsidized brigands. . . .

The Convention, still powerful and independent, did not allow itself to be imposed upon. Prosecutions were ordered. Garat, as minister of justice, was charged with the execution of this enactment.

Three days had scarcely passed before Garat was able to confide to some deputies that the evidence against some of their colleagues was complete. I have this fact from one of the deputies to whom Garat made the statement. If I remember correctly it was Guadet, who was then a friend of Garat.

The deputies implicated were aware of the danger that threatened them. This danger aroused their anxiety, and served to strengthen the natural alliance between the Mountain and the municipality of Paris. It was then that they essayed the system of terror which subjugated a large number of deputies in the portion of the Assembly known as the *Plain*. These were virtuous and intelligent men, but in their praiseworthy desire for accord, they indulged in an acquiescence which the culpable never ceased to abuse.

The leaders of the sections were put to work stirring up the people. Audacious petitions began to come in. The implicated deputies spoke with arrogance. The Convention weakened, and although it did not revoke the decree, it suspended it indefinitely, which comes to the same thing. This first experience gave the culprits the true measure of the Assembly. From now on they could extort whatever decrees they needed by resorting to these successful methods.

VICTORIES AGAINST THE AUSTRIANS. (Ferrières, III, 252.)

. . . while the Prussians and Austrians were ingloriously evacuating the territory of the Republic, Custine entered the Electorates at the head of ten thousand Frenchmen and took possession of Speyer, Worms, Mainz, and Frankfurt. Dumouriez marched upon Mons, defeated General Beaulieu at Jemappes, and conquered Belgium in less time than it takes a traveller to cross it.

(*Dumouriez, III, 151–181.*)

There was not a corps in the French army that did not take part in the engagement [at Jemappes] and give the enemy the cold steel. The greatest losses occurred among the battalions of the center that had halted for a more accurate fire. Those who rushed on headforemost suffered small loss. In reality, the battle cost only about two thousand men, with six or seven hundred killed. In the artillery, however, a number of men and a good many horses were lost, since this corps, in order to be more effectual, advanced with its usual intrepidity to within musket-shot of the entrenchments. The imperial army lost nearly four thousand men and thirteen pieces of cannon, including seven of large caliber abandoned in the redoubts. But from this moment, desertion and disorder began to appear in their army....

It was during this epoch that he [Dumouriez] wrote to the Convention that on November 15 he would be in Brussels; he entered it the 14th: that he would be at Liége the 30th; he entered it the 28th. His campaign was superiorly calculated like a game of chess, and had it not been for the insurmountable obstacles put in his way by the minister of war, he would have been at Liége on the 20th, and at Cologne on the 30th.

GIRONDINS AND JACOBINS AT ODDS. (*Ferrières, III, 252–253.*)

Up to now a common danger had restrained the different parties that composed the Convention, but since these no longer feared the outcome of a war in which France had every advantage, pronounced dissension was not long in breaking out. The Girondins, reinforced by a number of constitutionalists, began the attack. The Jacobins, sustained by their clubs and the commune of Paris, did not remain long on the defensive. They also made a vigorous attack upon the Girondins. Both sides treated their adversaries as royalists, declaring themselves the only good republicans. They soon perceived that the vague accusation of royalism would be hard to attach to men who had also contributed to the fall of the throne and the maintaining of the Republic. They abandoned the charge and looked for more definite crimes.

The Jacobins accused the Girondins of wanting to establish a federal government. This was a sure means of rendering them odious to the Parisians, who saw in this project nothing but approaching ruin. The Girondins, henceforth working for the good will of the departments, accused the Jacobins of wanting to concentrate the government in the city of Paris. They would accomplish this by making the commune the center of authority and all Frenchmen the subjects of Paris, as all the peoples of Italy had been the subjects of Rome under the Roman Republic. To arrive all the more surely at their goal, they were attempting to disorganize all power and thus win over the worst elements of the populace through the hope of a general division of property.

THE GIRONDINS SEEM MASTERS OF THE SITUATION. (*Dumouriez, III, 314.*)

... this faction ... had long dominated the Assembly and ... made itself master of the ministry ... It had destroyed the Feuillants, moderates, and royalists. It had gained possession of nearly all the journals, such as the Paris *Chronique, Moniteur Patriote, Thermomètre,* and the sheets of Gorsas and Carras. All, in short, which had much publicity or influence were composed, edited, and controlled by members of this faction. The best orators of the Convention — Guadet, Vergniaud, La Source, Brissot, Gensonné, and Condorcet — set forth its opinions. It had taken possession of the principal committees. Siéyès and Condorcet headed the committee on the constitution. Brissot and Gensonné ruled the committee on diplomacy and the one on general defense. The committee on finance was entirely in the hands of Cambon, who was believed to be an ally. With Pétion as mayor, they had long governed Paris.

(Barras, I, 83–84.)

While on mission at Nice, I had corresponded with Roland, minister of the interior; I could render justice to his generous ideas and patriotic views in regard to a reorganization of France favorable to the countries that might soon be included within it. Upon arriving at Paris, I was received by the minister with great cordiality. In his cabinet I silently awaited the departure of his wife in order that we might speak of the most important matters. Roland, comprehending my silence, said, "My wife is not a stranger to the affairs of the ministry." ... I had noticed how imperiously she had greeted me and occupied the cabinet of the minister. I was too little of the gallant to countenance her presence, which I thought unwarranted, and without saying another word, saluted and withdrew. I received next day an invitation to dinner, and refused for the same reason.

THE GIRONDINS ATTACK MARAT. (Meillan, 17.)

Already Marat had spoken of cutting off two hundred and sixty thousand heads. This proposition, which made us recoil in horror, did not disconcert the Mountain. Robespierre had already declared that no Frenchman should possess an income of more than three thousand livres; and although respect for private property was daily proclaimed, it was daily violated, either indirectly by decrees or directly by the use of force. There was an open attack upon business, business men, landed proprietors, farmers, and every class and branch of industry. The tribune resounded with nothing but denunciations of monopoly, and every man was called a monopolist who did not live by the day's work or upon charity.

Already shops had been broken into, in accordance with the formal and public invitation of Marat, who also proposed hanging some of the merchants before their doors. We were forced to summon him before the tribunal. The history of his dishonorable triumph and acquittal without a trial is known to all.

(Marat in L'Ami du peuple, No. 40; Meillan, 27.)

The great weapon of my detractors is the depicting of me as a man of blood who is always preaching murder and assassination. But I defy them to show that I have written about anything except the necessity of striking off a few hundred heads in order to save the heads of three thousand innocent people; and the spilling of a few drops of impure blood to prevent torrents among the blameless, that is to say, the crushing of the principal counter-revolutionists to save our native land. I have never encouraged popular executions except when driven to despair by seeing traitors protected by law, and conspirators escaping justice. I invite my critics to submit what I have said to a tribunal of wise men, and if I do not have their approbation, I consent to pass for a cannibal. Yes, a sincere love of humanity and my reverence for justice caused me to renounce for a time the moderation of philosophy in order to cry out against our implacable enemies. I appeal to all virtuous and benevolent hearts against these cold-blooded men who would watch emotionless and unmoved the extirpation of the human race. The fury I experienced at seeing a handful of scoundrels drag an entire nation down into the abyss constitutes my apology. And that the people have safeguarded the public interests is the reply I make to calumny.

THE ATTACK UPON DANTON. (*Dumouriez, III, 116–117.*)

He [Dumouriez] was greatly disgusted and chagrined by everything he saw during his four days in Paris. When he had left Paris for the army the preceding June there were recalcitrants and intriguers in the Assembly, but there was still some intelligence, talent, and decency to be found there. But now the Assembly was made up of the grossest scoundrels. The Girondins were still masters, but their power was continually undermined by the violence of Marat and the Jacobins. It began to decline, and they maintained themselves only by a policy of feeble Machiavellianism which came to be their ruin.

One man alone could have aided them in saving king and country. They managed to alienate him, although Dumouriez had advised that they treat him with respect and form an alliance with him. That man was Danton. Harsh, ugly, ferocious, common, and ignorant, he had much natural intelligence and an energetic character. When the danger was greatest from the Prussians he alone had maintained his courage. He had not shared the general consternation. He had opposed the transference of king and Convention beyond the Loire, and had forced the Convention and ministers to utilize every national resource. His services were as important in Paris as Dumouriez's in Champagne, and had the Girondins had the good sense to join him, he would have broken up the atrocious Marat faction. He would have controlled or destroyed the Jacobins, and perhaps have saved the life of Louis XVI. But he was provoked beyond all endurance and sacrificed everything to revenge.

(*Ferrières, III, 261–264.*)

The Girondins feared Danton much more than they feared Robespierre and Marat. These were *enfants perdus*, they said, put forward by Danton. Danton, harsh and repulsive in appearance, was simultaneously fierce and sensuous, now sunk in indolence, now strenuous in criminal activity. His policy was coldly calculated destruction, his eloquence an outburst of fury.

Engulfed in debt, he was living in Paris when the Revolution began to take a general trend, and he thought he had found the road to fortune. He threw himself into the movement and forced his way through the rabble horde that obstructed him. On July 14, he became president of the famous Cordeliers district. With extreme audacity, a stentorian voice, and athletic bearing, he soon impressed the multitude and became preponderant in his party. He skilfully made use of this to further his plans. Brought by the Orléans faction to the ministry of justice on August 10, he thus became leader of the mob of brigands that had come to Paris from all parts of France. He knew how to become formidable to his fellow citizens, his fellow ministers, and even the Assembly itself, aided as he was by the commune's committee of surveillance. He planned, ordered, and directed the September massacres, arranging murder and pillage in the departments. The electoral body of Paris was made up of men devoted to him, and this made him master of the elections. He manipulated them for the benefit of his satellites and had himself elected deputy to the Convention.

It was common knowledge that he had embezzled vast sums during his ministry, appropriating the greater part of the funds set aside for government expenses. His plundering was attested by the luxurious way in which he lived. The Girondins thought they could easily ruin him in the popular eye by attacking him on this point. If not, they could at least diminish his influence by presenting him thus as an embezzler. ... Danton emerged victorious from this clumsy intrigue. He jeered at the Girondins and their minister, Roland, speaking disdainfully of him as a weakling who, bewildered by so much destruction, was incapable of ever rising to emergencies.

THE ATTACK UPON ROBESPIERRE. (Louvet, 22.)

On the 21st of September the Convention commenced its sittings, and the very next day Robespierre and Marat went to the Jacobins to preach insurrection against the Convention. A few weeks later, Robespierre dared to complain to the Convention of what he called slanders propagated against him, and challenge an accuser.

(Moore, II, 298.)

"A system of calumny is established," said he with a lofty voice, "and against whom is it directed? Against a zealous patriot. Yet who is there among you who dares rise and accuse me to my face?"

"I," exclaimed a voice from one end of the hall.

There was a profound silence, in the midst of which a thin, lank, pale-faced man stalked along the hall like a specter, and being come directly opposite to the tribune, he fixed Robespierre and said, "Yes, Robespierre, it is I who accuse you."

It was Jean-Baptiste Louvet.

Robespierre was confounded: he stood motionless, and turned pale; he could not have seemed more alarmed had a bleeding head spoken to him from a charger. ...

Danton, perceiving how very much his friend was disconcerted, called out: "Continue, Robespierre. There are many good citizens here to hear you."...

This seemed to be a hint to the people in the galleries that they might show themselves in support of the patriot — but they remained neutral.

(Louvet, 22–23.)

The accusation I preferred against him produced the greatest effect: fifty deputies attested the crimes I announced, the least of which ought to have brought that man to the scaffold. The coward thought that his last hour was arrived, and came to me to solicit grace. If Pétion, who had not then been sufficiently slandered by them to have lost his immense influence, and on whom I had repeatedly called, had thought fit to say openly a quarter of what he knew, Robespierre and his accomplice would have been impeached on the spot. At that time, detested throughout the Republic, and having in Paris a party very inferior to that of the Convention, they would have received the due punishment of their guilt. The infamous Orléans, and a score of subaltern villains, would have returned to their original nothingness: a Barère, a Lacroix, and a multitude of vile intriguers, always ready to drag the car of the reigning party, would have remained Rolandists: the Republic would have been saved.

Pétion, Guadet, and Vergniaud thus committed a fault in not answering my frequent calls on them for their testimony; and another was weak enough to blame me in his paper for bringing forward the accusation.

(Barras, I, 119–120.)

When Louvet attacked Robespierre, Marat stood out before the tribune with crossed arms and defended him with many gesticulations. "I have," said he, "no love for Robespierre; he is an egotist jealous of his power; but he is an untainted republican and on that account I must rally to him. I am no longer a friend of Danton. Republicans should be severe: nothing is being done for the people, and it is the people who must uphold the Revolution. Statesmen are arguing about who shall be leader and forgetting the interests of liberty. They hearken only to passions and interests which are disastrous to the Republic."

SAVOY UNITED TO FRANCE. (Doppet, 61–79.)

It was inevitable that the sun of liberty which shone in France should throw some rays beyond her borders. But it was the soil of Savoy that absorbed them most quickly....

For a long time past the well-to-do Savoyards had been coming to France for instruction and all kinds of knowledge. They had the same language, customs, dress, resources, and even character. All this, added to geographical proximity, made Savoy seem a part of France....

A French army was encamped near Savoy and passed several months in observation. But the French troops were put in motion by insults to the national cockade, repeated outrages against non-royalist French, and an unequivocal appeal from the Savoyard people. Savoy was liberated September 22, 1792....

My compatriots honoring me with their confidence, I departed for Paris in company with three deputies. We were charged by the National Assembly to ask for our union with France....

We presented ourselves before the National Convention at its sitting of the 21st November, 1792. As representatives of a sovereign people we were immediately admitted to the hall, where I spoke forth in the name of the Allobroges....

After the illuminating discourse of the spokesman [for the diplomatic and constitutional committees] the discussion on union began. A number of orators favored it; a single deputy spoke against it. The National Convention unanimously decreed the union of *ci-devant* Savoy with the French Republic....

THE KING'S TRIAL DECREED. (*Dumouriez, III, 316.*)

The Girondin intrigue was quickly unmasked by Danton, Lacroix, Robespierre, and Marat. Impartial men in the Convention believed the Girondin ambition dangerous. The Girondins should now have shown their courage, defended the innocence of the king, and opposed his death. If they had succumbed, it at least would have been with glory. It is quite probable, however, that they would, on the contrary, have succeeded. It is reasonable to believe that the departments would have united with them in saving king and country, and that the destruction of the Jacobins would have been accomplished. They weakly limited themselves to a sort of appeal to the people whereby the fate of Louis XVI was to be decided by primary assemblies. This second measure seemed to be but another signal for civil war.

(*Cléry, 87–88.*)

[The mayor appeared at the king's prison] accompanied by Chaumette, procurator of the commune, and Coulombeau, secretary-recorder. There were a number of municipal officers, and Santerre, commandant of the national guard, had brought his aides-de-camp. The mayor told the king that he had come to conduct him to the Convention by virtue of a decree which the secretary of the commune would now read to him. This decree stated that "Louis Capet would be brought before the bar of the National Convention." "Capet is not my name," said the king; "it is the name of one of my ancestors.... I will go with you, not in obedience to the Convention, but because my enemies employ force." I handed His Majesty his coat and hat, and he followed the mayor of Paris. A numerous escort awaited him at the gate of the Temple.

THE TRIAL OF LOUIS XVI. (*Examination of Louis XVI by the National Convention, December 11, 1792.*)

... The commandant-general of the Parisian guard announces to the Assembly that he has carried out its decree and that Louis is awaiting its orders. "Execute," replies the president, "the decree of the Convention that requires Louis to be brought before the bar." Louis appears at the bar accompanied by the mayor of Paris (Chambon), two municipal officers, and Generals Santerre and Wittengoff. The citizens of the guard remain outside the hall. Profound silence reigns and is not once broken during Louis' presence. It is half-past two o'clock.

The President (Barère): Louis, you are arraigned by the French nation. The National Convention decreed on the 3rd of December that you should be tried before it. On December 6 it decreed that today you should be heard at the bar. You are about to hear the reading of the act stating the case. Louis, be seated.

Louis seats himself. A secretary (Mailhe) reads the act, which the president then proceeds to take up article by article.

The President: Louis, you are to reply to the questions that the National Convention has authorized me to put to you. Louis, the French people accuse you of having committed a multitude of crimes in order to establish your tyranny through the destruction of liberty.

On June 20, 1789, you attacked the sovereignty of the people by suspending the meetings of their representatives and driving them from the place of their sittings by violence. This is attested by the official act which was drawn up by the members of the Constituent Assembly at the Tennis Court of Versailles. What have you to say?

Louis: That at the time there were no existing laws on that subject.

The President: On June 23 you attempted to dictate laws to the nation. You surrounded the representatives with troops, presented two royal declarations subversive of all liberty, and ordered the representatives to separate. Your own declarations and the official minutes of the Assembly attest this. What have you to say?

Louis: The same as before.

The President: You marched an army against the citizens of Paris, your satellites caused their blood to flow, and you recalled this army only when the taking of the Bastille and a general insurrection showed that the people were victorious. The speeches that you made the 9th, 10th, and 14th of July made known your intentions, and the massacres at the Tuileries are charged to you. What have you to say?

Louis: I was the master at that time to call out troops as I wished. It was never my intention to shed blood.

The President: After these events and in spite of the promises made on the 15th at the Constituent Assembly, and on the 17th at the Hôtel de Ville, you persisted in your designs on national liberty. For a long time you evaded the decrees of August 11 which abolished personal servitude, the feudal régime, and the tithe. You long refused to approve the declaration of the rights of man. You doubled your *gardes du corps* and brought the regiment of Flanders to Versailles. You allowed orgies in which the national cockade was trampled underfoot before your very eyes, the white cockade was displayed, and the nation blasphemed. In short, you necessitated a new insurrection and caused the death of several citizens. It was only after the defeat of your guards that you changed your language and renewed your perfidious promises. Proofs of these facts may be found in your observations of September 18 on the decrees of August 11, in the official minutes of the Constituent Assembly, in the events of the 5th and 6th of October at Versailles, and in the speech which you made at that time to a deputation of the Constituent Assembly stating that you wished to avail yourself of its wise advice and never separate from it. What have you to say?

Louis: I made such observations as I thought just and expedient in regard to the decrees which had been presented to me. It is false about the cockade; that never took place in my presence.

The President: At the federation of July 14, you took an oath which you did not keep. Soon after, you tried to undermine public sentiment with the aid of Talon, who operated in Paris, and in conjunction with Mirabeau, who was to start a counter-revolution in the provinces. You distributed millions to effect this perversion, trying to enslave the people by means of the people. These facts are attested by Talon's memoir annotated with your own hand and by a letter written you by Laporte on the 19th of April. Laporte reviewed in this letter a conversation he had had with Rivarol, and told you that the millions you had been induced to distribute had produced no effect. What have you to say?

Louis: I do not remember exactly what took place at that time; but all that was anterior to my acceptance of the constitution.

The President: Was it not in accordance with Talon's plans that you went to the Faubourg Saint-Antoine and there distributed money among the poor workmen, saying that you could not do better? What have you to say?

Louis: There was no greater pleasure to me than in giving to those who were in need. It had nothing to do with any design.

The President: Was it not in accordance with the same plan that you feigned illness in order to sound out public opinion on your withdrawal to Saint-Cloud or Rambouillet for your health? What have you to say?

Louis: The accusation is absurd.

The President: For a long time you meditated flight. On February 23, you were presented with a memoir setting forth the ways and means, and to this you added a postscript. On the 28th, a large number of soldiers and nobles gathered at your apartments in the Tuileries. You tried to leave Paris on the 18th in order to go to Saint-Cloud. The opposition of the citizens showed you that there was great distrust. You tried to dissipate this distrust by communicating to the Constituent Assembly a letter addressed to the representatives of the nation accredited to foreign powers. The letter announced your free acceptance of the constitutional articles which had been presented to you. Yet on the 23rd of June you took flight with a spurious passport, leaving behind you a condemnation of these very articles. You ordered the ministers not to sign any decrees of the National Assembly, and forbade the minister of justice to use the seals of state. The people's money was squandered to assure success to this treason, and national troops were used to protect it. These forces were under the orders of Bouillé, lately charged with the massacres at Nancy. In this connection, you had written to him to guard well his popularity, because it might be useful to you. These facts are attested by the memoir of February 23, which is annotated by your own hand; by your declaration of June 20, which is entirely in your own writing; by your letter of September 4, 1790, to Bouillé; and by a note from the latter accounting for the nine hundred and ninety-three thousand livres furnished by you, and which were used in part to corrupt the troops that were to escort you. What have you to say?

Louis: I have no knowledge of the memoir of February 23. As for the journey that I made to Varennes, I refer you to the statements I made to the Constituent Assembly at the time.

The President: After your apprehension at Varennes, the executive power was for a moment left in your hands. You continued to conspire. On July 17, the blood of the citizens was shed on the Champ-de-Mars. A letter written in your own hand to La Fayette in 1790 proves that a criminal agreement existed between you and La Fayette, to which Mirabeau was accessory. Rehabilitation began under these baneful auspices. Every sort of corruption was tried. You subsidized libels, pamphlets, and newspapers with the intention of perverting public opinion, of discrediting the assignats, and of upholding the cause of the *émigrés*. Septeuil's accounts show what enormous sums were spent upon these machinations against the cause of liberty.

You appeared to have accepted the constitution of the 14th of September and your speeches announced your willingness to support it, but you tried to overthrow it even before it was finished. What have you to say?

Louis: I had no connection with what happened on July 17. As to the rest, I know nothing about it.

The President: An agreement was drawn up at Pillnitz on July 24, between Leopold of Austria and Frederick William of Brandenburg. They engaged themselves to restore absolute monarchy in France. You said nothing about this agreement until it was known to the whole of Europe. What have you to say?

Louis: I made it known as soon as it came to my knowledge. As to the rest, that, according to the constitution, concerned the ministers. . . .

The President: Your brothers, enemies of the state, rallied the *émigrés* to their flag. They raised regiments, made loans, and contracted alliances in your name. You disavowed them only when you were sure it would not interfere with their projects. Your connivance with them is proven by a note from Louis-Stanislas-Xavier, written in his own hand, undersigned by your two brothers, and worded in this wise:

"I have written to you, but by post and was therefore unable to say anything; we are here, two who think as one; same sentiments, same principles, and same zeal to serve you: we keep silence; in breaking it too soon we would compromise you; but we shall speak as soon as we are sure of being generally supported, and the moment is near. If we are spoken to in the name of those people, we will not listen; if on your part, we will, but we will continue on our way. Thus, if they try to force you to say something to us, do not worry; be at rest concerning your safety; we exist but to serve you; we are working industriously and all goes well; our enemies have too much interest in your conservation to commit a useless crime which would end in ruining them. Adieu.

LOUIS-STANISLAS-XAVIER
CHARLES-PHILIPPE"

What have you to say?

Louis: I disavowed my brothers' actions as soon as they came to my knowledge, as the constitution prescribes. This letter gave me no knowledge of them.

The President: The troops of the line, which should have been on a war footing, were at the end of December scarcely a hundred thousand strong. Narbonne, your intermediary, had asked for a levy of fifty thousand men, but he stopped the recruiting at twenty-six thousand, insisting that all was ready: nothing was. Then Servan proposed to establish near Paris a camp of twenty thousand men; the Legislative Assembly decreed this; you refused your sanction. A burst of patriotism caused citizens everywhere to set forth for Paris; you issued a proclamation trying to stop them, although our armies were short of soldiers. The successor of Servan, Dumouriez, had stated that the nation was without arms, munitions, and food supplies, and that the fortresses were in a poor state of defense. What have you to say?

Louis: Since December last I have issued every order that could aid the ministers in increasing the army; the lists were sent to the Assembly. If they were deceived, it was not my fault.

The President: You instructed those in command to disorganize the army, to cause whole regiments to desert, and to have them cross the Rhine to put themselves at the disposal of your brothers and Leopold of Austria. This fact is proved by a letter from Toulongeon, commandant of Franche-Comté. What have you to say?

Louis: There is not a word of truth in the accusation.

The President: You have charged your diplomatic agents to encourage foreign powers to co-operate with your brothers against France, while especially cementing the peace between Turkey and Austria. This would make it unnecessary for the latter to guard its frontiers on the Turkish side, and would free a greater number of troops for use against France. A letter from the former ambassador at Constantinople, Choiseul-Gouffier, establishes this fact. What have you to say?

Louis: M. de Choiseul was not telling the truth. It never happened....

The President: You have brought disgrace upon the French nation by failing to exact reparations from Germany, Italy, and Spain for the bad treatment given the French in those countries. What have you to say?

Louis: The diplomatic correspondence should prove the contrary; besides, that was the business of the ministers.

The President: On August 10, you reviewed the Swiss at five o'clock in the morning, after which the Swiss fired first upon the people. What have you to say?

Louis: I went to see the troops that were assembled at my residence. On that day the constituted authorities were present, the department officials, the mayor of Paris. I even asked the National Assembly for a deputation of its members to advise me what to do. I came myself with my family to the Assembly.

The President: Why did you have the Swiss guard doubled during the early part of August?

Louis: All the authorities had been informed of it, and the palace was menaced with attack. I was a constituted authority; it was my duty to defend it.

The President: Why did you send for the mayor of Paris during the night of August 9?

Louis: Because of rumors that spread abroad.

The President: You have shed the blood of Frenchmen. What have you to say?

Louis: No, Monsieur! it was not I who did it.

The President: Did you not authorize Septeuil to undertake a commerce in grains, coffee, and sugar at Hamburg and other towns? This is proved by Septeuil's letters.

Louis: I have no knowledge of what you say.

The President: Why did you veto the decree providing for a camp at Paris?

Louis: The constitution allowed me to veto at discretion, and at the time I had asked for a camp at Soissons nearer the frontier.

The President: Louis, have you anything else to add?

Louis: I ask for a copy of the act of accusation and the production of the documents; also that counsel be granted me to take charge of my case....

THE CONVENTION DECREES LOUIS' DEATH. (Cléry, 124–125.)

All had spoken, personal enemies, informers, relatives, ecclesiastics, laity, absentee deputies. In spite of this violation of every precedent, those who had voted for death, some as a political measure and others because they believed the king guilty, were but a majority of five votes. Many deputies had voted only for death with reprieve. A second vote by roll call was ordered. It was supposed that the votes of those who wished to delay the regicide would be added to those against the death penalty and form a majority. But at the doors of the Assembly assassins devoted to the Duc d'Orléans and the Paris deputation spread terror with their cries. With poignards they menaced all who refused to be their accomplices, and the capital, either through stupor or indifference, did not want or did not dare to try to save its king.

(Decrees of the National Convention on January 15, 16, 17, 19, and 20.)

ARTICLE I. The National Convention decrees that Louis Capet, late King of the French, is guilty of conspiring against the liberty of the nation and of attempts against the general safety of the state.

II. The National Convention decrees that Louis Capet undergo the penalty of death.

III. The National Convention disallows the *acte* of Louis Capet, brought to the bar by his council, tending to appeal to the nation from the judgment rendered against him by the National Convention. It forbids anyone whatsoever to take any action in regard to this, under penalty of prosecution and punishment as guilty of attempts against the general safety of the Republic.

IV. The provisional executive council shall this day inform Louis Capet of the present decree, and take such police measures and other precautions as will assure execution within twenty-four hours after his notification. An official report of the whole shall be made to the National Convention immediately after the execution.

A DEPUTY RESIGNS AFTER THE KING'S CONDEMNATION. (Letter of Kersaint to the National Convention, January 20, 1793.)

Citizen President, my health has long been impaired. This renders the continuance of life in an assembly as stormy as the Convention impossible. But what is still more insupportable is the shamefulness of sitting there among men of blood whose opinions, heralded by terrorism, take precedence over those of commendable people, as Marat takes precedence over Pétion. If my love for my country has made me support the misfortune of being a colleague of those who promoted and praised the assassinations of September 2, I can at least defend my memory from the reproach of having been their accomplice, and there is only a moment for that; tomorrow will be too late.

I return to the bosom of the people; I strip myself of the inviolability they have given me, ready to render account of all my actions, and, without fear and without reproach, I hereby give my resignation as deputy of the National Convention.

A. GUY KERSAINT

THE TESTAMENT OF LOUIS XVI.

In the name of the Holy Trinity, of the Father, the Son, and the Holy Ghost. Today, the twenty-fifth day of December, one thousand seven hundred and ninety-two, I, Louis, sixteenth of the name, King of France, for four months imprisoned with my family in the Tower of the Temple at Paris by those who were my subjects, and deprived of all communication whatever, even with my family since the eleventh instant; moreover, involved in a trial whose issue it is impossible to foresee by reason of the passions of men, and for which one does not find any pretext or method in any existing law, having only God as witness of my thoughts, and to whom I can address myself, I declare here in His presence, my last wishes and sentiments. . . .

I end in declaring before God, and ready to appear before Him, that I am not guilty of any of the crimes that are advanced against me. Made in duplicate, at the Tower of the Temple, the 25th of December, 1792.

LOUIS

LOUIS ASKS FOR THREE DAYS' GRACE.

I request three days' delay to prepare myself to appear before God; to this end I ask that I may see without constraint the person indicated to the commissaries of the commune, and that this person be protected from all fear and anxiety in performing for me this act of charity.

I ask that I may be freed from the perpetual surveillance established by the council-general the last several days.

I request, during this interval, the privilege of seeing my family when I wish, and without observers; I earnestly desire that the National Convention occupy itself immediately with the fate of my family, and that it permit them to withdraw freely to such a place as the Convention shall deem proper.

I recommend to the benevolence of the nation all those persons attached to my service: there are many among them who have put their whole fortunes into these positions, and when no longer receiving salaries, will be in need; there are likewise those who have lived only upon their salaries; among the pensioned there are many old men, women, and children who have no other means of sustenance.

Done at the Temple, January 20, 1793.

Louis

HUMILIATIONS INFLICTED UPON THE ROYAL FAMILY. (Cléry, 36–37.)

One of the doorkeepers of the Tower, named Rocher, of horrible face, dressed as a sapper, with long moustaches, black fur cap, enormous saber, and a belt from which hung a bunch of heavy keys, appeared at the door as the king wished to leave. He did not open it until His Majesty was quite near him; and under pretext of choosing among his many keys, which he rattled horribly, he ostentatiously made the royal family wait, and drew the bolts with a crash. He then descended precipitately, placed himself beside the last door with a long pipe in his mouth, and as each member of the royal family passed, blew out clouds of tobacco smoke, especially in front of the princesses. A number of national guards, amused by this insolence, gathered about him, guffawing at each puff and making boorish remarks; some even going so far as to bring chairs from the guardhouse in order to regard the spectacle at their ease, remaining seated and obstructing the already narrow passage.

LOUIS XVI GOES TO HIS EXECUTION. (Cléry, 149–150.)

... Santerre, accompanied by seven or eight municipal officers, entered at the head of ten gendarmes and drew them up in two files. Upon this manoeuver the king came out from his chamber. "Have you come for me?" he asked of Santerre.

"Yes."

"I ask for only a minute"; and he withdrew. His Majesty immediately returned, followed by his confessor. The king carried in his hand his will, and said to a municipal officer named Jacques Roux, a constitutional priest, who was a little in advance: "I beg you to deliver this paper to the queen, to my wife."

"That is not my business," replied this priest, refusing to take the document. "I am here to conduct you to the scaffold." His Majesty then addressing Gobeau, another officer, said: "Deliver this paper, I beg of you, to my wife. You may read it; there are in it dispositions that I wish the commune to know."

I was behind the king near the fireplace; he turned to me and I offered him his coat. "I do not need it," said he. "Give me my hat only." I handed it to him. His hand encountered mine, which he pressed for the last time. "Gentlemen," said he, speaking to the municipal officers, "I desire that Cléry continue near my son, who is accustomed to his care; I hope the commune will honor my request." Then looking toward Santerre, he said, "Let us go."

THE EXECUTION. (Edgeworth, 176–179.)

The march lasted nearly two hours. Every street was lined with several ranks of citizens, armed sometimes with pikes and sometimes with muskets. . . .

The carriage arrived . . . in the greatest silence, at the Place Louis XV, and came to a halt in the middle of a large empty space that had been left around the scaffold. This space was bordered with cannon; and beyond, as far as the eye could reach, was a multitude in arms. . . .

As soon as the king descended from the carriage, three executioners surrounded him and wished to take off his coat. He repulsed them with dignity and took it off himself. The executioners, whom the proud bearing of the king had momentarily disconcerted, seemed then to resume their audacity and, surrounding him again, attempted to tie his hands. "What are you trying to do?" asked the king, withdrawing his hands abruptly.

"Tie you," replied one of the executioners.

"Tie me!" returned the king in an indignant tone. "No, I will never consent; do what you are ordered to do, but I will not be tied; renounce that idea." The executioners insisted, they lifted their voices, and seemed about to call for help in order to use force. . . .

"Sire," I said to him with tears, "in this new outrage I see only a final resemblance between Your Majesty and the Savior who is to reward you."

At these words he lifted his eyes to heaven with a sorrowing look that I cannot describe . . . and, turning to the executioners, said: "Do what you wish; I will drain the cup to the dregs."

The steps that led to the scaffold were extremely steep in ascent. The king was obliged to hold to my arm, and by the pains he seemed to take, I feared that his courage had begun to weaken; but what was my astonishment when, upon arriving at the last step, I saw him escape, so to speak, from my hands, cross the length of the scaffold with firm step to impose silence, by a single glance, upon ten or fifteen drummers who were in front of him, and with a voice so strong that it could be heard at the Pont-Tournant, distinctly pronounce these words forever memorable: "I die innocent of all the crimes imputed to me. I pardon the authors of my death, and pray God that the blood you are about to shed will never fall upon France."

(Deux amis de la Liberté, 526–527.)

. . . the executioners seized him, the knife struck him, his head fell at fifteen minutes after ten. The executioners seized it by the hair, and showed it to the multitude, whose cries of "Long live the Republic!" resounded to the very bosom of the Convention, whose place of meeting was only a few steps from the place of execution.

Thus died, at the age of thirty-eight years, four months, and twenty-eight days, Louis, sixteenth of his name, whose ancestors had reigned in France for more than eight hundred years. . . .

Immediately after the execution, the body of Louis was transported to the cemetery of the ancient Church of the Madeleine. It was placed in a pit six feet square, close to the wall of the Rue d'Anjou, and dissolved instantly by a great quantity of quicklime with which they took the precaution to cover it.

(*Mme. Jullien, 337.*)

The death of the king in Paris resembled the banishment of the Tarquins in Rome. The people displayed a calmness and dignity that would have done honor to the greatest days of the Roman Republic.

THE CONVENTION'S BRIDGES BURNED BEHIND IT. (*Barras, I, 86.*)

With this terrible act consummated and its bridges burned behind it, the Convention stood facing its enemies like a centrally placed battery that is powerful enough to fire in all directions. It turned its whole attention to the fabrication of war materials for the universal struggle it had undertaken. The decree which levied three hundred thousand men needed forceful execution. In its first effects, the decree had been used as a pretext for the troubles in the Vendée, which, spreading to the other parts of France, had no other purpose than the lighting up of a general conflagration.

XXI. *Girondins and Jacobins*

ENGLAND SHOCKED AT THE DEATH OF LOUIS XVI. (Malouet, II, 270–276.)

I WAS informed of the king's death by a heart-rending note from Lord Grenville. There was general consternation in London, where the anniversary of the execution of Charles I is still a day of mourning. Those of us who were Frenchmen in exile at this capital scarcely dared show ourselves in the streets; the sorrow and shame caused by this stupendous crime united us all in a common feeling for the first time, for there had been such division among the *émigrés* as to be often a subject of scandal to foreigners. It was equally desired by all of us that the crime be avenged, and that the hateful yoke weighing upon France be broken; but the *émigrés*, like the allied powers, were never able to agree upon the means, so rarely is it that simple good sense, which would be sufficient to direct men's actions, has ever the power to do so . . .

There is no proof that the members of the Convention who desired war with Austria and Prussia would also have desired it with England. They did not fear invasion, but they well knew that they could not employ denunciations of tyranny against the freest people in Europe.

The English constitution was doubtless not in accord with their fierce democracy, but they knew that their doctrines of equality had partisans in England, that Thomas Paine's treatise on the rights of man had seduced a part of the people. Thus they had more reason to conciliate the English nation than to antagonize it, and had they believed that the British cabinet would concern itself actively with the fate of Louis XVI, I do not doubt that a frank and measured statement from this cabinet would have had great consideration.

(Extract from a letter of Lord Grenville to the French ambassador at London, January 24, 1793.)

I am charged to notify you, Sir, that, since the character and functions with which you were invested at this court are today entirely annulled by the death of His Most Christian Majesty, you have no longer any public character here, and His Majesty has judged it proper to order that you quit this kingdom within a week's delay.

FRANCE DECLARES WAR ON ENGLAND AND HOLLAND. (Extract from a letter of Barbaroux to the Municipality of Marseille, February 2, 1793.)

We hasten to inform you that the National Convention at yesterday's session declared war, in the name of the French nation, on the King of England and the Stadtholder of Holland. Dumouriez, who set off three days ago, will, in spite of the destitution of our armies, advance immediately against the United Provinces.

This opens a new career of glory to this general, who has already so well established his fame in the amazing victory of Jemappes, and in defending the defiles of the Argonne where he led seventeen thousand men against twenty-eight thousand.

(*Carnot, 49–50.*)

The ancient and natural limits of France are the Rhine, the Alps, and the Pyrenees. The dismembered parts have been only usurped, and there would be, in ordinary practice, no injustice in retaking them. There would be nothing of ambition in recognizing again as brothers those who were formerly such, or in re-establishing bonds which were broken by ambition.

Moreover, diplomatic claims founded upon long possession are negligible in our eyes when compared with the claims of reason. Each nation has an imprescriptible right to isolate itself if it wishes or to ally itself with others for the common good. We Frenchmen recognize no sovereigns except the people themselves; our policy is not domination but fraternity; for us there are no princes, kings, or masters whatever; we see on the surface of the globe only men like ourselves, beings equal in all political and moral aspects, as they are in talents and virtues....

FRANCE AND THE COALITION. (*Mme. de Staël, 297–298.*)

The coalition of Austria, Prussia, Spain, and England, the civil war in the interior, the hate that the Convention inspired in all honest men still out of prison, none of these diminished the resistance that brought the efforts of the foreigners to naught. This phenomenon can be explained only by the nation's devotion to its cause. A million men took arms to repulse the forces of the allies; the people were animated by a fury which was as deadly inside the country as it was deadly without. Moreover, the factitious but inexhaustible supply of paper money, the low price of commodities, and the humiliation of the property owners, who were reduced to public evidence of their misery, all caused the workers to believe that the incubus of unequal wealth was at last about to be lightened. This fantastic hope doubled the strength given them by nature; and the social order, dependent upon the patience of the masses, appeared suddenly menaced. But the war spirit, whose single aim was to defend the country, restored order in France and covered her with its shield.

THE VENDÉE REVOLTS. (*Mme. de Bonchamps, 21–23.*)

... the Convention ordered the levying of three hundred thousand men, completing the desolation of the inhabitants of our province, that is to say, that portion of the Vendée known as the Bocage. There were almost universal uprisings at two points which were at some distance from each other,

Challans in Bas-Poitou and Saint-Florent on the banks of the Loire. These uprisings, far from being revolts, were a legitimate defense against the most tyrannical persecution. The people, faithful to their religious cult and their ancient race of kings, took up arms only in retaliation for murder and in opposition to the bloodstained barbarians whose sacrilegious and regicidal fury had just immolated the most virtuous of monarchs and overthrown both throne and altar.

At the news of the uprising in our canton, the Convention ordered the troops it sent to the Vendée to exterminate men, women, and children, and even the very animals and vegetation, such was the unheard-of rage inspired by the Vendéen resistance to the military decree. The drawing [of soldiers by lot] had been announced for March 10 at Saint-Florent. All the young men repaired thither, but they were thoroughly determined not to submit. They had to listen to speeches whose purpose was to insult them with expressions full of contempt. To these speeches were added horrible menaces; and then a cannon was bracketed upon them. The piece was fired, but the furious youths threw themselves upon it and carried it off. Everyone scattered before them. The headquarters of the republicans were ransacked, their papers burned, and their strongbox carried off. The money was distributed among the conquerors, paying for the festivities which they instituted in celebration of this initial victory.

They had triumphed over the gendarmerie and had possessed themselves of two culverins and a number of muskets; but they were without leaders, and when the first intoxication of success had worn off, they realized not without alarm that the republicans would return with auxiliary forces, and would embark upon atrocious cruelties, animated by revenge and merciless fury.

THE VENDÉE AND THE REVOLUTION. (Mme. de La Rochejaquelein, 40–48.)

In the year 1789, as soon as the Revolution commenced, the towns showed themselves favorable to it, while the people of the plain were foremost in burning and destroying. Those of the Bocage, on the contrary, saw with dread and regret these excesses and innovations, which, far from adding to, could only disturb their happiness.

When the national guards were formed they begged the seigneur in each parish to take command, and they likewise chose them for mayors. The seigneurial seats were ordered to be removed from the churches; but the order was not executed. In short, the peasants of the Bocage showed themselves uniformly discontented with the new order of things, and devoted to the gentlemen.

The new oath required of the priests added to their discontent. When they saw themselves deprived of their curates, to whom they were accustomed, who understood their manners and their dialect, who almost all belonged to the country, whom they knew and respected, and saw them replaced by strangers, they ceased to attend the mass at their parish. The sworn priests were insulted or abandoned. . . .

It may be seen that this war was not, as has been said, fomented by the nobles and the priests. The unhappy peasants, wounded in everything that was dear to them, subjected to a yoke which the happiness they had formerly enjoyed made them feel still heavier, revolted at last, and chose for their leaders men in whom they had placed their confidence and affection. The gentlemen and the curates, proscribed and persecuted themselves, marched with them, and supported their courage. The insurrection began from the impulse of the moment, without plan, without concert, and almost without hopes; for what could a handful of men, destitute of means of any sort, effect against the forces of all France? Their first successes infinitely surpassed their expectations.

The minds of the people being universally disposed to resistance, the first example was followed generally without previous concert or understanding.

THE VENDÉENS ATTEMPT TO ORGANIZE THEIR TROOPS. (Mme. de Sapinaud, 18–19.)

War in the Vendée began March 12, 1793. The peasants revolted at La Bretière. They afterwards dispersed to the neighboring parishes and came to seek M. Sapinaud de Bois-Huguet, better known under the name of La Verrie. "We are making you our general," they said, "and you are to lead us." Sapinaud tried to make them see the misfortunes they would bring upon themselves and the Vendée. "My friends," he said to them, "it is earthen pot against iron pot, the weak against the strong. What can we do, one department against eighty-two? We shall be crushed." . . . The honest peasants, far from yielding to these reasons, remonstrated that they would never submit to a government that had taken away their priests and imprisoned their king. "We have been imposed upon," they said. "Why have they sent us constitutional priests? These are not the priests who stood at the deathbeds of our fathers, and we do not want them blessing our children." My brother-in-law did not know what to do. He hesitated to expose these good people and himself to what was almost certain death. At last he yielded to their persistence, and placing himself at their head, set forth that very day towards Les Herbiers.

VENDÉEN SUCCESSES. (Mme. de Sapinaud, 23–24, 98.)

At Beaupréau, MM. d'Elbée and Bonchamps had done wonders. They had beaten the republicans at Saint-Florent. The republican general, Gauvillier, having left Chalonne exposed to the enemy with only three thousand national guards to protect it, Bonchamps marched hastily upon the town, and presented the mayor with the following ultimatum:
"People of Chalonne:
The generals of the Roman Catholic army of five thousand men are dispatching to you MM. Rousseau and Lebrun to engage you in the name of God, religion, and the Chalonnais prisoners to give yourselves up; if you resist, your town will be destroyed. If, on the contrary, you surrender, you shall have full pardon; you will give up your arms, and deliver over four of your leading citizens as hostages: we come in the name of humanity."

... In a number of combats, Charette was almost miraculously successful. At the very moment it was announced he had been destroyed, he would most audaciously reappear. His name became a terror to an enemy six times as great. After fatiguing and weakening them, he forced them to withdraw and then retired into the Galins forest.

(Mme. de Bonchamps, 36–37.)

After taking Saumur, the leaders held a council of war. It was decided to advance upon Nantes. Before making this decision, which was far from being unanimous, the Vendéens realized the absolute necessity of having a commander-in-chief. All expressed their preference for M. Cathelineau, to recompense his zeal and amazing courage, as well as to prove their own renunciation of all ambition. M. Cathelineau was therefore elected commander-in-chief without opposition.

WESTERMANN DEFEATED AND REPLACED. *(Mme. de Bonchamps, 38–39.)*

A new army, commanded by the atrocious Westermann, ravaged the Vendéen countryside with fire and sword. MM. de Lescure and La Rochejaquelein vainly attempted to hold out against them; their châteaux were soon in flames. The fright engendered by the rapid progress of Westermann caused them to implore aid from MM. d'Elbée and Bonchamps. The latter, arriving first, proposed to attack the victorious Westermann without delay. This proposal being adopted, the chiefs rushed upon the enemy and overthrew the advance guard posted upon the heights of Moulin-aux-Chèvres. Farther on, however, the Vendéens were stopped by two discharges of grapeshot, and began to waver. My husband ordered his men to crawl along the ground to within musket range, and then shoot the cannoneers at their guns. This order was executed with astonishing rapidity. The whole line fell upon the enemy, and Westermann was forced to abandon his cannon, munitions, and baggage, leaving two-thirds of his force on the field of battle.

After this victory the council assembled to elect a new commander-in-chief in the place of M. Cathelineau.... M. d'Elbée ... was elected and my husband, who had expected this, did not show the least dissatisfaction in regard to the choice which he himself had seconded.

The devastation which Westermann had wrought did not save him from disgrace. The general who replaced him received orders more sanguinary still.

(Turreau, 19–20.)

A method of fighting as yet little understood and perhaps impossible except in this country and with inhabitants such as these; an absolute adherence to their cause; a boundless confidence in their leaders; a fidelity to their promises, which made discipline unnecessary; and an indomitable courage in the face of all sorts of dangers, fatigues, and privations; these are what made the Vendéens such redoubtable enemies and must place them in history as among the greatest of fighting peoples. In short, the Vendéens were Frenchmen animated by the double fanaticism of religion and royalty. Long victorious, they were unconquerable except by French republicans.

THE COMMITTEES. (*Thibaudeau, I, 12–13.*)

Although all powers were vested in the National Convention it remained several months without exercising them. I believed with the majority that concentration of power would mean tyranny. In some regards, however, the separation of powers had been merely illusory, and disappeared entirely when the Convention really took control of the government through the committee of public safety. This was inevitable since it was impossible to have an executive administration which would be above suspicion or which would have any independent existence to give it power. The Convention had had, before this centralization was accomplished, a committee of general defense with the power of constant and active surveillance over the executive council. There was no intention, however, of hindering the actions of the council or destroying its responsibility. Nevertheless, experience soon showed that here were two things impossible to reconcile. The committee of general defense was constantly summoning the ministers and other authorities; members of the Convention could attend its sessions, and a certain number of them were always present. Thus the most secret business was conducted publicly, and the executive council was pulled about in every direction, not knowing whom to answer, whom to obey, nor how to fulfill its duties.

THE COMMITTEE OF GENERAL DEFENSE.

ARTICLE I. The committee of general defense shall be composed of fifteen members; it shall propose all laws and measures necessary for the exterior and interior defense of the Republic.

II. The committee shall summon the ministers composing the executive provisory council to its meetings at least twice a week.

III. The executive council in general, and each minister in particular, shall give the committee all information that it shall desire. They shall report all general enactments within a week's time.

IV. The committee shall report to the Convention each week upon the state of the Republic and upon such of its operations as are proper for publicity.

V. The committee shall each day designate two of its members to give to the Convention any information it may desire upon the state of the Republic.

VI. The committee shall have the floor whenever there is question of a report decreed by the committee.

VII. The committee shall print, when time permits, all tentative decrees presented to the Convention.

THE FIRST COMMITTEE OF PUBLIC SAFETY. (*Durand de Maillane, 102–103.*)

This committee of public safety, without either constitution or laws, concentrated all sovereign powers within itself. The ministers continued as directors of the ordinary routine of their various departments, and did not escape the weight of public responsibility for their acts.

The first committee of public safety was made up of nine members: Barère, Delmas, Bréard, Cambon, Jean de Bry, Danton, Guyton-Morveau, Treilhard, and Lacroix. Jean de Bry resigned and was replaced by Robert Lindet.

This committee, which had been instituted mainly to deal with the armies in the field and important measures of general safety, contributed little to the prevention of warfare among the deputies themselves. The Mountain was supported by the dregs of Paris, whom it had carefully and secretly kept in its train. The new committee of public safety had little to do at first except interpose as mediator between the combatants. Every day new accusations against the Girondins were presented by the sections of Paris. The ministers and the mayor of Paris also presented alarming reports which were the delight of Marat in the tribune.

THE GIRONDINS AND DUMOURIEZ. (Durand de Maillane, 83–84.)

With this situation in the Convention, the generals could not but be disgusted with their toils and labors, and with the daily perils to which they were exposed in leading the armies of a republic whose government was in the hands of a horde of assassins. General Dumouriez separated, from these last, a group of Girondins who had shown themselves favorable to Louis XVI. He had wanted to effect a reconciliation between them and the king, and between the king and the original constitution. These were, in fact, the only means of forestalling the evils of impracticable democracy. Unluckily this group had gone too far in the Legislative Assembly, and political faults are not committed with impunity. Be that as it may, it was thought that Dumouriez had had the idea of enthroning the Duc d'Orléans' eldest son, then doing his first fighting under his command. As a result of all this, Dumouriez wrote on March 12 a remarkably bold letter to the National Convention, and another to the minister of war, in which, threatening to march upon Paris, he spoke of a sane part of the Assembly which he was going to deliver from the yoke of the frightful Mountain.

Much less would have been necessary to stir up trouble. To the Mountain *this sane part* could mean only the Girondins, whom they believed to be plotting with Dumouriez for the downfall of the Republic and the republicans. The Girondins denied this as a calumny; but it would have been better for them, and for France, if Dumouriez had re-established a constitutional monarchy. It was the thing generally desired and needed by the enlightened third estate to extricate itself from the yoke of the lowest pauper elements of the nation! Previously obliged to use these to defend itself, it was now being oppressed by them.

(Thibaudeau, I, 13–15.)

But the Convention in decreeing the union with Belgium destroyed these plans, real or supposed, and sent commissaries to take charge of the organization of the country. Then Dumouriez showed temper, fought openly with the agents, and denounced the minister of war and the commissaries of the treasury with acidity. He made outrageous remarks about the national legislature, thereby confirming the suspicions he had already aroused. He came to Paris under pretext of seeing about army supplies, but really to find out what could be used to further his plans. He found nearly everyone ill-disposed, set off again, reopened his campaign, gained possession of Holland, and was defeated at Neerwinden, March 18.

On the 25th, at a meeting of the committee of general defense, a dispatch from Dumouriez was read which was not thought fit to be made public. In it he complained of the absolute disorganization of his army, of insubordination, cowardliness, desertion, and pillage. He spoke of the bad attitude of the Belgians towards France, of the enemies' superiority, and of the impossibility of resisting them and reorganizing his army in the detestable position at Louvain. He saw no other means of salvation than retreat towards Mons and Tournai. He asked the executive council to make its wishes known to him promptly, saying that he was putting upon it the responsibility.

The minister of war, Beurnonville at that time, said they replied to Dumouriez that he was master to take such measures as he thought proper to save the army and the Republic. . . .

THE TREASON OF DUMOURIEZ. (*Thibaudeau, I, 18–20.*)

On the 29th, Beurnonville presented another letter from Dumouriez, who continued his complaints concerning the cowardliness of the soldiers and the pillaging in which they indulged. He praised the moderation and humanity of the Austrians. According to him, the National Convention had no authority; as long as the government remained in the hands of certain persons, the country would be in the greatest danger; disaster was complete, forts were destitute of garrisons and provisions, and the enemy could easily seize them and march upon Paris. He called France a *kingdom*.

At this recital there was a general outburst of indignation. There was no longer any doubt that Dumouriez was either a traitor or mad, and some thought that he was both; for it was impossible to have conspired against the Convention and the Republic with more indiscretion, levity, and presumption. With a single voice they voted him out of the commandership of the army. . . .

The next day, the 30th, upon the report of Camus, in the name of the committee of general defense, the Convention decreed that Dumouriez be brought before the bar. Four commissaries from the Convention and the minister of war, Beurnonville, were invested with the right to arrest generals who appeared suspect, and were instructed to depart at once for the army of Belgium. Camus was one of the commissaries. He notified the general of the Convention's decree; but Dumouriez was in open revolt. He had the commissaries arrested, handed them over to the Austrians, wrote a threatening letter to the Convention, tried to deliver Condé and surprise Lille, was abandoned by his army, and was obliged, in order to save himself, to go over to the enemy. He wandered about in foreign countries, outlawed by a decree that closed the doors of France forever to this general who had allowed the spirit of ambition and intrigue to lead him from party to party, and finally from the paths of honor.   Treason, which is never under any pretext made honorable by success, becomes all the more odious when it fails.

THE MOUNTAIN AND THE GIRONDE. (*Thibaudeau, I, 22–24.*)

The Paris commune and the Jacobin Society, urged on and supported by the Mountain, became open rivals of the Convention and were loud in their menaces against the Girondins. The military reverses, the audacious conduct of Dumouriez, and even the rejection of Robespierre's motion to expel the Bourbons, aroused cries of treason on all sides. A disarming of suspects and the establishment of the special tribunal were demanded. The section of the Tuileries voted the circulation of a petition among the forty-eight sections in which the Convention was asked if it was in any position to save the country. The commune and all the sections adopted the petition. The fermentation was extreme.

On March 27, the committee of general defense asked the executive council, the municipality, and the department to agree upon some means to forestall the troubles with which they were menaced.

Before the opening of the sitting, Marat made this remarkable statement: "It is false to say that the sovereignty of the people is indivisible. Every commune of the Republic is sovereign in its own territory in times of crisis, and the people can take whatever measures are necessary for their safety."

The mayor and Chaumette, procurator of the commune, accessory to all this agitation, minimized the affair in seeking to lull the suspicions of those it menaced. The Girondins declared that if there was any attack upon the national legislature, the departments would wreak a signal vengeance upon Paris. Gensonné maintained that the deputies were only the agents of their constituents, and not accountable to anyone else until a constitution should make them representatives of the nation as a whole. Such speeches and theories were little calculated to calm the storm.

Next day the mayor came to deliver an address to the Convention. Pétion proposed that the primary assemblies be convoked to recall deputies found unworthy of confidence. Following the suggestion of Boyer-Fonfrède, the Convention decided to answer the petition in saying that they would save the country, but that the commune of Paris would be responsible for the safety of the Convention. This responsibility was not very alarming to those who animated and directed the commune.

(*Mme. de Staël, 292.*)

The only men of this period who were worthy of occupying a place in history were the Girondins. There can be no doubt that at the bottom of their hearts they felt a keen remorse about the means they had employed in overturning the throne; and when these same means were directed against them, causing them to recognize their own weapons in the wounds they received, they must have wondered at the rapid justice of revolutions, where events that would normally take centuries are crowded within a short space of time.

Day by day and hour by hour the Girondins fought with intrepid eloquence against discourses as sharp as poignards, discourses which carried death in every sentence. The deadly entanglements which enveloped the proscribed on all sides did not make them lose that admirable presence of mind which alone can make oratorical talents effective.

ROLAND. (*Meillan, 37–38.*)

Upright, austere, and rigorous in his observance of the law [Roland was] inexorable in the performance of his duty. His downfall was caused by his persistence in demanding an account of what had taken place under the jurisdiction of the municipality on August 10. Practically everybody had done some pillaging. Sergent had worn in the Convention a sparkling agate upon his finger. He confessed that he had taken it, but had promised to pay for it. Panis declared frankly from the tribune that he would give no account of what he had done; they were wrong to ask it of him. Danton did not care to have anyone speak of the sums he had received during his ministry. But Roland, who always came with his accounts under his arm, was a living satire on those who were not so scrupulous. He was an annoying censor; they must get rid of him. Before long he was known as an aristocrat, a Feuillant, a royalist, and a federalist, although these were contradictory things, and finally as a conspirator and counter-revolutionist, entirely deserving of death.

DANTON AND THE GIRONDINS. (*Mme. Roland, 293.*)

Danton let scarcely a day pass without coming to see me ... I looked at that cruel and repulsive face; and although I carefully reminded myself that one ought not to judge without investigation; that I knew nothing certain against him; that even the most upright man might have conflicting reputations in a period of political strife; and finally, that one must distrust appearances, I could not conceive of a virtuous man with a face like that. I have never seen anyone who so perfectly characterized the frenzy of brutal passions. This, in conjunction with an astounding audacity, was partly veiled by an apparent joviality, frankness, and good nature.

(*Miot de Mélito, I, 49–50.*)

He felt profound contempt for the Girondins, regarding them as fools who had recoiled before the logical results of their principles. He made no secret of his love of pleasure and of money, and sneered at vain scruples of conscience and delicacy. Intrenched in the club of the Cordeliers, which he looked upon as a citadel always open to him, he believed himself to be unassailable. The cynicism of his morals exhibited itself in his language, for he despised the hypocrisy of some of his colleagues, and his sarcasms on this vice were principally directed against Robespierre; whom, however, he did not venture to name. Nevertheless, it was easily to be seen that Robespierre was the enemy whom he most dreaded, although he affected to despise his party. "They would not dare," he often said, and this rash confidence was his ruin.

ATTACKS UPON MARAT. (*Durand de Maillane, 81–82.*)

The people's tribunal had just been established. Marat had **advocated** pillage on February 25, 1793, and that same day divers grocers of Paris had been plundered. A hue and cry was raised against him and he was brought before the new tribunal. He had long been inciting murder and assassination in his journal, the *Ami du peuple*. Moreover, he had recently presided over a meeting of the Jacobin Society where a violent address against part of the Convention had been made for the benefit of the affiliated societies in the departments. It was decided to attack him personally, demanding his indictment and detention at the Abbaye. The latter was obtained, but it was stipulated that, before the bill of indictment should be brought, the legislative committee would draw up a report on this subject, and present it to the Convention the following day. On April 14, the Convention, as a result of the findings of this committee, voted Marat's impeachment by a great majority. This decision was obtained, however, only after excessive opposition and numerous insults, following the indecent and abusive methods used by the Mountain against its adversaries.

THE BILL OF INDICTMENT.

As a result of an examination of the various numbers of Marat's journal ... and of an article entitled *Profession de foi de Marat*, Marat is charged with having instigated murder, assassination, and massacre. He has stated that in any country where the rights of the people is not an empty phrase, the pillaging of a few shops and the hanging of the profiteers before their doors would put an end to their evil practices. He has maintained that repressive legal means must be abandoned, since the only effective measures are revolutionary ones. These so-called revolutionary measures have indeed been effective, since on the very day his morning paper counselled pillage, the grocers of Paris were plundered ...

... Marat is charged with having, before the time of the Convention, advocated a government hostile to the sovereignty of the people; that is to say, that of a military tribune, dictator, or triumvir. Posterior to the law of December 4, 1792, which decreed death for advocates of royalty, he stated in No. 80 [of his journal] that he expected nothing good of the lawmakers in France, since most of them were without penetration, talents, reflection, virtue, or public spirit. The Convention, upon which the people had founded their last hopes, could accomplish nothing composed as it was. Afterwards in No. 84 he announced that the nation would be forced to renounce democracy and select a chief, since the Convention could not rise to the heights of its important functions. ... Marat is charged with having vilified the Convention and the constituted authorities, and with having agitated for the dissolution of the Convention in saying that there was in its bosom a criminal faction composed of villains and rascals, atrocious men who were trying to kindle civil war; a faction foreign to the country, enemy of all equality and all liberty, composed of dishonored men who fed their criminal passions, gorging themselves on the property of the people and tyrannizing the nation in the name of the law. . . . The National Convention hereby brings an indictment against Marat, one of its members, before the extraordinary criminal tribunal, as charged with having promoted (1) pillage and murder, (2) a rule hostile to the sovereignty of the people, and (3) the discrediting and dissolution of the Convention. It orders that he be brought before the tribunal to be tried in conformity with the law.

(*Durand de Maillane, 82.*)

In effect, Marat, without ever having put foot in the Abbaye to which he was supposed to have been sent, was acquitted by the revolutionary tribunal and returned with a crown on his head, accompanied by a Jacobin crowd to the very midst of the Convention, where he was received by the acclamations of the Mountain. A voice was heard to cry out that Marat deserved, not condemnation, but a civic decoration.

MARAT BRAVES THE CONVENTION. (*Révolutions de Paris; Saint-Edme, II, 9–10.*)

Who would not have shrugged his shoulders at Marat in the tribune, pulling a pistol from his pocket, as an old-time Capuchin . . . used to draw a *petit bon Dieu* from his sleeve, and jumping about like an Italian clown, saying, "I fear nothing under the sun." (He, Marat, who boasts that he hid in a cellar hole to escape from La Fayette!) "I fear nothing under the sun; but if the Assembly votes against me, I will blow out my brains before you!" Then putting up his instrument of death, which in all probability contained nothing but powder, he continued, "No, I will remain among you to brave your fury." . . . But the Assembly simply passed on to the order of the day, hoping that good citizens would be the first to lament the scandalousness of this sitting. These disgusting scenes must not occur too often; for, as one deputy sensibly expressed it, "The departments know what goes on here. What confidence will they have in our work?"

THE JACOBIN CLUB DENOUNCES THE GIRONDINS. (*Police Report, Schmidt, I, 242–243.*)

. . . a considerable number of people fill the tribunes. Seated in the middle of one of the tribunes at the farthest extremity of the hall, I can turn to the right or left. Motions come from everywhere. They all bear upon the accusations against the Blacks of the Convention, the ministers, etc. "They have plotted the ruin of France; they are doing everything against the people; the people must rise again; there must be another August 10; why not sound the tocsin and fire the alarm gun? Robespierre put his finger on the truth one day when he said that when people are oppressed they should secure justice themselves, and resentment should dictate their conduct. Why didn't he proceed? We were all ready to go. And today they have deliberated for four hours on one individual affair. The Blacks tried to save a counter-revolutionist. The president was obliged to put on his hat four times. Is that the way they spend their time and waste the nation's money? One of the scoundrels has said that luckily the Vendéen troops (the rebels) were advancing on Paris to bring it to reason. Is this proper talk? Are they in league with the rebels?" ...

THE DEMANDS OF ROBESPIERRE. (Extract from the minutes of the Jacobin Club, May 8, 1793.)

I sum up and demand, 1st, that the sections raise an army sufficient to form the nucleus of a revolutionary army that shall collect all the *sans-culottes* of the departments to exterminate the rebels; 2nd, that an army of *sans-culottes* be raised in Paris to overawe the aristocracy; 3rd, that dangerous intriguers and all the aristocrats be put under arrest; that *sans-culottes* be paid at the expense of the public exchequer, which shall be supplied by the rich, and that this measure extend to the whole of the Republic.

I demand that forges be erected in all the public places.

I demand that the commune of Paris maintain with all its power the revolutionary zeal of the people of Paris.

I demand that the revolutionary tribunal make it their business to punish those who have blasphemed the Republic.

I demand that this tribunal bring exemplary punishment upon certain generals without delay. These, taken in the act, ought already to have been tried.

I demand that the sections of Paris unite with the commune of Paris, and counterbalance by their influence the perfidious writings of the journalists in the pay of foreign powers.

By taking these measures and by giving no pretext for saying that you have violated the laws, you will give an impetus to the departments, which will join you in the cause of liberty.

XXII. *The Fall of the Girondins*

STRUGGLE OVER THE COMMISSION OF TWELVE. (Meillan, 38–44.)

THE Right of the Convention resisted energetically the usurpation of the Mountain; but only a twentieth of its members could be relied upon to sustain it with their talents and their courage. Deprived of this support, the Right might perhaps be conquered. For this purpose there would be a passive Convention, a mere machine which would pass decrees to legalize the usurpation and have no power whatever to raise obstacles. Experience has demonstrated how accurate this calculation was. It was only a matter, then, of getting rid of these twenty or twenty-two inconvenient people. . . .

The discovery of this plot aroused the Convention. Becoming courageous through its very cowardice, it ventured to decree the prosecution of the conspirators, and created for this purpose a commission of twelve selected from among its own members. This was a blow to the Mountain and especially grievous in that all Paris approved of it. . . .

The events of May 27 are familiar to everyone. One knows how we were confined to the hall of our sittings, and a decree introduced to abolish the commission of twelve. . . .

[The Mountain] had arranged for the arrival of five or six hundred petitioners, who were nearly all in arms. These spread all over the hall, some mingling with us and audaciously taking part in our deliberations. If a decree was passed, it was they who passed it. I have some reason to believe, however, that they did not even take the trouble to pass it, and I was much surprised to learn that the decree had been passed. Placed immediately in front of the president (Hérault de Séchelles) at ten steps distance and constantly watching his face, since in the midst of the horrible tumult that degraded the Assembly we had no other guide, I can attest that I neither saw nor heard the decree put to a vote.

(Procès-verbaux de la Convention nationale. Séance du 27 mai, l'an II, de la république française.)

. . . A deputation from the section of the Croix-Rouge, in concert with the other sections of Paris, demands the abolition of the commission of twelve, and the release of Hébert and all other patriots.

The petitions from the various sections of Paris are converted by a member into a motion. After some argument the discussion is closed. The president puts the various propositions to a vote.

The National Convention decrees:

1. That those citizens incarcerated by order of the commission of twelve shall immediately be liberated;

2. That the commission of twelve is abolished; the committee of general security is charged to investigate the actions of the members that composed it.

(*Meillan, 44–45.*)

Whether passed or not, it was revoked on the next day (the 28th) by roll call and by a great majority. The Mountain abandoned moderation. It began to prepare for the uprising of May 31, or rather of June 2. The first was, in fact, only a preliminary move, the purpose of which should be explained.

They wished to get rid of the twenty-two already proscribed and take revenge upon the twelve who formed the commission. This could not be done in any legal or legitimate way. Impeachment was impossible since they could not be accused of any crime. There was no longer any hope that the Convention would give them up merely upon the demand of brigands who had usurped the name of the people of Paris. Only insurrection remained. They decided to instigate, or rather to simulate, an insurrection. Never, in fact, had an enterprise shown so few signs of being a popular uprising. It was planned and executed with an art that plainly revealed the manipulations of the ringleaders.

THE FIRST UPRISING FAILS. (*Pétion, 107.*)

The clouds were thickening above our heads and the storm was about to break. May 31 was the day set for the revolt. On that day the Convention would be dissolved and victims would fall beneath assassins' blades. A momentous upheaval was announced by the lugubrious sound of the tocsin. Drums beat the general alarm, barriers were closed, couriers halted, and letters intercepted. Sanguinary proposals were made from the tribunes of the popular societies and repeated by numerous groups, and the hall of the Convention was invaded. There could be no doubt that May 31 was the fatal day fixed by the conspirators, since they had had engraved in advance seals bearing this legend: *The Revolution of May 31.* They had the audacity to open and read letters, which they then stamped and resealed and passed on to the citizens to whom they were addressed.

(*Louvet, 46–48.*)

On the night of the 30th of May, the storm threatened so loudly that we felt the necessity of sleeping from home, perhaps for the fiftieth time. A remote chamber, in which were three wretched beds, but good arms and good accommodations for defense, received Buzot, Barbaroux, Guadet, Bergoeing, Rabaut Saint-Étienne, and me. At three in the morning the sound of the alarm-bell awakened us. At six we quitted our apartment well armed: though distant from the place where the Convention assembled, we resolved to repair thither. Near the Tuileries we passed several knots of rascals, who, having discovered who we were, made as if they would attack us. This they certainly would have done had they not seen our weapons. One of us, I remember, Rabaut Saint-Étienne, was so perturbed that he would have made little resistance. During the whole way he was continually exclaiming, "*Illa suprema dies!* Alas! I shall never behold it more!"

When we entered the hall we found three Montagnards already there. Pointing at one of them, I said to Guadet, "Do you observe what dreadful hopes gleam from that hideous countenance?" "Certainly," replied Guadet. "It is Claudius banishing Cicero." The Montagnard gave us no answer but a horrible smile.

This day, however, their expectations were balked. They were founded chiefly on the projected disarming of the section of the Butte des Moulins, which had long given them some uneasiness. This preliminary operation being accomplished, they would have accused us of having caused it to assume the white cockade, and the decree of impeachment would have been passed. The section, informed of the slanders propagated against it, and of the march of the Faubourg Saint-Antoine, had the good sense to perceive that it was as necessary to retain its arms as its innocence, and that it must seek its justification in victory. It intrenched itself in the Palais-Royal, loaded its guns, pointed its cannon loaded with grapeshot, and lighted its matches. Five adjacent sections prepared to support it. The forty thousand men of the Faubourg Saint-Antoine, when they arrived at the square in front of the Palais-Royal, resolved, notwithstanding all the exertions made to urge them to battle, that it would be proper to send a deputation to verify the fact. The deputies, admitted into the heart of the brave battalion of the Butte des Moulins, found the three-colored cockade in every hat, and the cry of the Republic in every mouth. They united, embraced, danced, and for that evening the plot of the Jacobins failed.

THE DEPARTMENTS DEMAND VENGEANCE. (Thibaudeau, I, 36–37.)

This insurrection [of May 31] aroused the majority of the departmental administrations still composed of honest patriots and landowners. They demanded vengeance for the attack made by the commune of Paris upon the sovereignty of the people in the person of their representatives. The Girondins had already several months before appealed to the departments against the menaces and violence of this commune. The departments had responded to this appeal by addresses; then they had passed condemnatory resolutions in regard to May 31 and had prepared to sustain them by force. Some of the deputies who had fled aroused against the capital an indignation only too well justified. It became a question of nothing less than assembling the departmental deputies at Bourges, organizing a departmental army, and marching on Paris.

THE INSURRECTION OF JUNE 2. (Louvet, 51–52.)

The 2nd of June, however, had been fatal to most of my friends. History, no doubt, will remark that the tumult of that day had taken place for the delivery of Hébert, whom the committee of twenty-one had convicted of endeavoring to dissolve the Convention, and who is now proved to have been an agent of the foreign powers; and of a sort of madman named Varlet, who has since been guillotined as a thief. History will remark that three thousand banditti, destined to go against the Vendée, were a long time quartered within four miles of us, and were brought back at the critical day to besiege us in our hall. History will remark that the revolutionary committee of the commune was almost wholly composed of strangers — Guzmán the Spaniard, Pache the Swiss, Dufourny the Italian, and Marat himself was of Neuchâtel. History will remark that the conspirators were careful to place bands, of which they were sure, close around the hall, so that the battalions of honest citizens could not approach it. . . .

PETITION PRESENTED TO THE CONVENTION BY THE MOB.

Representatives of the people, the forty-eight sections of Paris, which are the constituted corps of the department, have come to solicit a bill of impeachment against the commission of twelve; against the accomplices of Dumouriez; against the men who are setting the inhabitants of the departments upon the people of Paris; against those who slander the citizens of the capital, who won liberty on July 14 and August 10, and still protect it regardless of the number and strength of the enemy; and against those who wish to federalize the departments, when the people want the Republic to be one and indivisible. The people have risen and are in motion. They send us to you, as they once sent us to the Legislative Assembly, to demand the suspension of the tyrant. The revolutions of July 14 and August 10 were bloody because the citizens were divided, particularly the military forces. But the insurrection of May 31 was bloodless because the people and constituted authorities were united in sentiment. The constituted authorities have come to solicit from you a bill of impeachment against the traitors that sit among you. You will be told that we have implored in vain for petitions from the departments. They were also implored on June 20 of last year. Perfidious journals, whose authors sit among you, together with other men of this faction, intrigue with the interior administration to pervert the minds of the people in the departments. What has been done by this faction since it has been in control? It has done nothing except stir up civil war. It has put intriguing ministers into office who have upset everything and driven out patriots and republicans. We demand a bill of impeachment against Pétion, Guadet, Gensonné, Vergniaud, Buzot, Brissot, Barbaroux, Chambon, Biroteau, Raubaut, Gorsas, Fonfrède, Lanthenas, Grangeneuve, Lehardy, Lesage, Dusaulx, Ducos, Louvet, Hardy, Doulcet, Lanjuinais, and Defermon.

Legislators, it must stop; the counter-revolution must end; all conspirators without exception must come beneath the glaive of the law. O patriot saviors of the nation, decree the impeachment of all traitors! Tell us whether you can ensure our liberty; if not, we will ensure it ourselves. These vile conspirators shall bite the dust.

(Durand de Maillane, 125.)

New clamors arose. Several deputies complained of this coercion, and a member of the committee of public safety (Barère), finding himself at the tribune, proposed to end it by having the National Convention advance in a body into the midst of the populace and men in arms that surrounded it, in order to assure them that its members were not afraid, and were willing thus to testify their confidence in the loyalty of the Parisians. It was so arranged in order to palliate the affront the commanding general had just offered to the Convention and its authority by refusing to explain why masses of troops under his orders were surrounding the hall of the Assembly.

(Lanjuinais, 308–309.)

The Convention, in order to issue forth, presented itself at the great gate on the Place du Carrousel. The deputies were bareheaded, except the president, who remained covered to indicate that the country was in danger. Preceded by the attendants of the Convention, he ordered a passage to be opened.

Hanriot came forward on horseback with his aides-de-camp. Pulling his hat down over his eyes and drawing his saber, he refused passage in practically these words: "It is not for you to give orders here. Return to your place and deliver the deputies demanded by the people."

The deputies persisted. Hanriot fell back some fifteen paces and cried, "To arms! ... Gunners, to your guns!" The troop under his command made ready to attack; muskets were aimed at the deputies; cannoneers prepared to fire; hussars drew their sabers.

At the sight of this, the president withdrew and, followed by the Assembly, presented himself in succession to all the troops in the court and garden. Everywhere he found an inflexible resistance.

Meanwhile, the greater part of the armed forces, hats on bayonet points and pikes, cried out: "Long live the Republic! Long live the deputies! Peace, peace, laws, laws, a constitution!" A small number cried: "Long live the Mountain! Long live the worthy deputies!" A still smaller number shouted, "To the guillotine with Brissot, Guadet, Vergniaud, and Gensonné!" and seemed to stop here only through lack of memory. There were others yet who cried, "Purify the Convention! Draw the bad blood!"

ARREST OF THE GIRONDINS VOTED. (Durand de Maillane, 125–127.)

The Convention returned to the hall of the Assembly without having been able to break through the ring of insurgents that surrounded them, and each member resumed his place. One of the deputies (Couthon), after having briefly argued the same bad ideas as the petitioners, concluded that, while they were waiting for the report of the committee of public safety, the deputies denounced by the commune of Paris should be put in a state of arrest. A member of the commission of twelve asked permission to speak in defense of the commission in general, and those members in particular, who had not favored warrants of arrest. Other members spoke generally on the subject of the denunciation, which gave rise to a demand that the discussion be closed. This was decreed....

Isnard... demanded the floor. After forcefully proclaiming his patriotic sentiments, he ended by offering his own suspension as a final sacrifice to the peace and well-being of the state.

Fauchet expressed the same sentiments, and both secured their erasure from the list. It was stipulated, however, that they were to remain prisoners in their Paris residences.

Barbaroux, Lanthenas, and Dusaulx also proclaimed patriotic sentiments, but without offering suspension. After a period of discussion, the decree was passed, in the midst of cries and protests, providing that the members of the Convention... be put under arrest....

(*Larevellière-Lépeaux, I, 152–153.*)

...I was almost alone in energetically protesting against this abominable decree to the very end of the sitting; and yet it did not apply to me.

But it was Lanjuinais who on this day rose to superhuman grandeur. Never were the virtues, reasonableness, and calmness of a noble soul displayed with more force and majesty than by this man surrounded by imminent dangers, overwhelmed with outrages, and threatened with terrible menaces. "Citizens! the ancients also sacrificed human beings; but they covered them with flowers, they did not insult them!" When he pronounced these remarkable words, an aureole of glory seemed to encircle his head, and the monsters who sat among us, or had crowded into the tribunes, fell suddenly silent as if struck by a thunderbolt. Unfortunately the majority of the Assembly, who should have been electrified, had fallen into such stupor, such inconceivable apathy, that they allowed the insurgents time to recover themselves and continue their infamous projects.

THE DECREE OF ARREST.

The National Convention decrees that, from among its members, those deputies named below shall be put under arrest at their homes, there to remain under the safeguard of the French people and the National Convention, as well as under the loyalty of the citizens of Paris.

These deputies are Gensonné, Guadet, Brissot, Gorsas, Pétion, Vergniaud, Salles, Barbaroux, Chambon, Buzot, Biroteau, Lidon, Rabaut Saint-Étienne, La Source, Lanjuinais, Grangeneuve, Lehardy, Lesage (of Eure-et-Loire), Louvet, Valazé, Kervelegan, Gardien, Boileau, Bertrand, Vigée, Mollevault, Henri Larivière, Gomaire, Bergoeing.

Citizens Clavière, minister of public contributions, and Lebrun, minister of foreign affairs, shall also be put under arrest at their homes.

FLIGHT OF THE GIRONDINS. (*Pétion, 109–110.*)

In spite of all our efforts, we could assemble only a twentieth of our members. Of the leaders there were Brissot, Vergniaud, Gensonné, Guadet, and Buzot.

In the discussion that took place, there appeared to be an inclination to repair to the Assembly.

At the same time, we were so convinced of the imminence of danger that we chose two of our group to draw up an address to the French people, exposing our principles, defending our past actions, enlightening the nation in regard to the perils that threatened it, and encouraging a revival of the sacred love of liberty.

At the very moment our representatives were drawing up this address, the brother of Rabaut Saint-Étienne rushed in and exclaimed in frantic accents: "There is no longer any Convention; they have burst into the hall and seized upon the deputies. Make your escape! Everybody for himself!"

We only had time to say, "Let us find refuge at once"; then each departed.

VERGNIAUD DENOUNCES THE JACOBINS. (*Vergniaud to Barère and Lindet of the Committee of Public Safety, Paris, June 28, 1793.*)

Men who are shamefully selling your consciences and the welfare of the Republic for vanishing popularity and uncertain fame!

In your reports, you depict representatives of the people, illegally arrested, as factious men and instigators of civil war.

In exchange, I denounce you to France as impostors and assassins. And this I will prove.

You are impostors; for if you had thought the accused members guilty, you would have reported it at once and demanded a bill of impeachment to satiate your hate and the fury of their enemies.

You are assassins; for, not daring to bring them before the tribunal, where their spectacular justification would have covered you with disgrace, you kept them, by a conspiracy of silence and slander, subjected to the most odious suspicion and in the greatest danger of the people's vengeance.

You are impostors; for if all you say, if all you have to say is true, you would not fear to recall them that they might hear the accusations that concern them, and that you might attack them to their faces.

You are assassins; for you strike them only from behind. You do not bring them before tribunals where they would be allowed to defend themselves. You do not insult them except from the tribune whence they have been violently removed. They can no longer mount this tribune and confound you.

You are impostors; for you accuse them of inciting troubles in the Republic which you and other dominating members of your committee have yourself fomented.

ROBESPIERRE IN POWER. (*Durand de Maillane, 129–130.*)

After the outbreaks of May 31 and June 2, Robespierre attained to power and to the accomplishment of his desires. Having vanquished Pétion and the Girondins, he became master of the Convention, as he had been master first of the mother society of the Jacobins, and then of the assembly of electors in Paris. He had forced the latter to appoint whatever colleagues he designated.

After August 10, in the confusion of an interregnum and the disorder of a bloody anarchy, the idea of dictatorship was put forward. The dictator prescribed was Robespierre. His party had prevailed over the party which desired a triumvirate of Marat, Robespierre, and Danton. Radical though the other two might be, they had no desire for Marat as a colleague. . . .

But this dictatorship, which could not be established legally, existed in actuality and was forcibly exercised by Robespierre. He was like Marius and Sulla, and even more sanguinary, since he proscribed those on both sides. For two whole years his word in France was law. By his command, and before the very statues of liberty, equality, and the Republic, hypocritically invoked by this scoundrel, partisans of his own who had angered him, and those whom he called enemies of the nation, were executed without discrimination. During this period of disaster, he was the nation, and the nation was he. All pretenses to justice were abandoned, and the honor of the Convention was in rags.

(*Barras, I, 154.*)

. . . the Girondins and the Mountain having disputed for power for more than a year, the Girondins were vanquished by the commune of Paris and destroyed by the hate of Robespierre. The permanently established guillotine became a divinity forever requiring new holocausts. "Now it is Danton's turn," ventured some of the ferocious beings who had already committed so many gratuitous crimes. I saw that the idea of destroying this eminent patriot, which would at first have been regarded as inconceivable, had since my return begun to be thought of as a possibility. This was because Danton, the most energetic and model revolutionist of them all, was already being pointed out as a moderate, that is to say, a traitor, because he reproved ultra-revolutionary excesses.

THE CONSTITUTION OF 1793. (*Durand de Maillane, 141–152.*)

This constitution was extremely democratic. The prefatory declaration of rights contained thirty-five articles instead of the seventeen of 1791. Most of these articles invested the people with prerogatives that were extremely far-fetched and dangerous. The last, for example, affirmed the right of insurrection. Thus, under pretext that governments are subversive of rights, they accorded every element of the populace the right to expose the state daily to anarchical upheavals.

As for the constitution, it carried national sovereignty to the length of having the entire people participate in the election of every office-holder and the making of every law. . . .

On June 25 the republican constitution was completed and promulgated by the National Convention. . . .[1]

Robespierre knew how to turn the federates to account. These demanded the prosecution of the arrested deputies. In their own manner they avenged Paris for the insults of the president, Isnard. They proposed the arrest of suspects and the annihilation of all enemies of the Mountain. It was they,

[1] See the Appendix for the text of this constitution.

moreover, who furnished a pretext for suspending the inauguration of the constitution. Seven-eighths of the Republic were waiting for this constitution, whatever it might be like. It would do away with the revolutionary government, that is to say, a government without measure or restraint. After having been well flattered and fêted by the Parisians and leaders of the Convention, the federates returned home, leaving the constitution, just now so solemnly acclaimed, in the ark of the country, whence it never again appeared.

NO DESIRE FOR A REPUBLIC. (Buzot, 32–33.)

... it must be admitted that the majority of the French people were sighing after monarchy and the constitution of 1791. In Paris, especially, this was extremely widespread and was manifested in intimate conversation and private circles. Only a few noble and elevated souls felt worthy of republicanism, desired to see it established in France as it had been in America, and believed in good faith that it could be naturalized in the land of frivolity and inconstance. The rest, except for a mob of wretches without intelligence, education, or ability, who poured insults upon royalty, as in six months they would pour them upon the Republic, and in each case without knowing why, the rest did not desire anything other than the constitution of 1791, and spoke of real republicans as honest men gone mad. Is it possible that the affair of June 2 and the misery, persecution, and assassination that followed have brought a change of sentiment to the majority of Frenchmen? No, but in the cities people must pretend to be *sans-culotte*, because they guillotine those who are not; in the country they must submit to unjust requisitions, because they guillotine those who do not submit; and everywhere young men go forth to the armies, because those who do not go are guillotined. The guillotine, that is the great reason for everything; it is today the main resort of the French government. The people are republican by dint of guillotine.

ATTITUDE OF THE PEOPLE TOWARDS THE REPUBLIC. (Police Report, Schmidt, II, 19.)

Give them pack-saddles, Lord, and you will have asses.

The bourgeois of Paris, the merchants, that is to say, the proprietors in general, persevere in their avarice, their heedlessness, their egotism. They are almost uniformly occupied with their private concerns and seldom take heed of public affairs. There is one thing to be said, and that is that the wine merchants, almost all aristocrats in the present sense of the word, were never as busy or sold as much as they do now in times of revolution and popular insurrection. They may be seen having as many as two, three, or four waiters. "How can I close when I have so much business? People have to be served, who will serve them if my waiters and I go away?" What is going on in one street is going on in every street in Paris. When shall we succeed in doing something with these worthy people? When they have almost exhausted their resources, then, forced to close shop, you will see the whole group *en masse* trying to make the law supply what does not exist....

(Police Report, Schmidt, II, 8.)

...I know Auvergne, having lived there and having travelled through it even since the Revolution. The Revolution has no better supporters than the Auvergnats. They well know from what burdens they were delivered by the abolition of feudal rights; but, if they hated their lords, they loved and still love their priests. Their priests drink with them and vend them absolution... These simple people are divided into two classes, one of which has accepted the juring priests, while the other clings obstinately to the refractory ones, and unfortunately this latter class is the more numerous. I can vouch for it that Spaniards and aristocrats have no enemies more dangerous, nor the land more industrious and indefatigable cultivators; but France will lose these doubly valuable men if she persists in exacting the sacrifice of their priests.

THE DEPARTMENTS AND THE ARREST OF THE GIRONDINS. *(Durand de Maillane, 137–138.)*

It was not the same, however, with the rest of France. General indignation was aroused in the departments by what happened on May 31 and June 2. Everywhere assemblies were formed and took the name of *sections*. They were formed to oppose the deputies of the National Convention, but against these they took no prompt, concerted action. The Girondins, who had taken refuge at Caen, received the approbation of the municipalities and administrations, but obtained little aid. General Wimpfen, ex-member of the Constituent Assembly, and a distinguished officer, was associated with them for a time, but declared that he did not desire to command the troops except in behalf of the son of King Louis XVI. This diversity of interests which existed during the Revolution worked in favor of Robespierre and his followers. I have already had occasion to speak of how all those whom the Revolution had injured had more hope of a change taking place through the excesses of the Mountain than through the moderation and probity of the Plain. A young girl, Charlotte Corday, animated by an entirely different spirit than that which sustained the courage of the deputies, came to Paris to die a useless death after assassinating the practically moribund Marat in his bath.

MARAT ELIMINATED. *(Barras, I, 121.)*

According to his defenders, even the death of Marat was due to generosity. Charlotte Corday presented herself at his home and asked to speak to him. She was told that he was in his bath and ill. She asked them to tell him that an unfortunate lady came to claim his protection and benevolence. It was upon these words being reported to Marat that he ordered her to be admitted. "Misfortune, citizeness," he said when she appeared, "has claims which I have never disregarded. Sit down." Then Charlotte Corday drew her poignard and dispatched him who would perhaps have been dead of disease a few days later. How different things would have been had she accorded the preference to Robespierre!

LETTER OF CHARLOTTE CORDAY TO HER FATHER.

Forgive me, dear Papa, for having disposed of my life without your permission. I have avenged many innocent victims; I have prevented numerous other disasters; the people will some day see this clearly and rejoice at having been delivered from a tyrant. If I tried to make you believe that I had gone to England, it was because I wished to remain unknown, but I see now that it would have been impossible. I hope you will not be persecuted; in any case you will have protectors at Caen. I have retained Gustave Doulcet for my attorney, but only as a matter of form; such a crime as this permits of no defense.

Farewell, dear Papa. Forget me, or what is better, rejoice over my fate; the cause was splendid. You know your daughter; she would not have been influenced by unworthy motives. I embrace my sister, whom I love with all my heart, as I do likewise all my relatives. Farewell, and do not forget the verse of Corneille: "It is crime that is shameful, and not the scaffold."

Tomorrow, at eight o'clock, I shall be judged.

July 16, 1793.

M.-C. Corday

LYON REVOLTS. (*Durand de Maillane, 139–141.*)

The insurrection of the Lyonnais broke out shortly before May 31, and increased the fury of the Montagnards in adding to their dangers.

This city, believing that the Revolution would ruin its commerce and manufacturing, in which it was not greatly mistaken, had early pronounced against it. It had concocted, in the time of the Constituent Assembly, a secret conspiracy, which was strangled in its cradle by the committee of investigation. The conspiracy had been the work of the priests of this populous city and of the nobles of the neighboring provinces. The latter, instead of emigrating, had retired to Lyon, where they were assured of being well received by the Lyonnais on account of their aversion to a government that menaced the luxury which was the source of their riches. The deputies of the commons had been insulted in this city on their return to the Midi. But the sentiments of the Lyonnais were still more openly manifested when the Republic was established and royalty abolished in perpetuity. They assaulted their *sans-culotte* municipality, and put to death a patriot named Chalier. The Mountain laid siege to their city. Dubois de Crancé, sent to take charge of the operations, succeeded in becoming master of the rebellious city only after much destruction in a regular assault. He received no reward for this expedition beyond persecutions engendered by the Mountain. The latter, on account of the resistance of Lyon, abolished its name and called it Commune Affranchie. To it were dispatched Collot-d'Herbois and Couthon, who added grapeshot and demolition to the already deplorable excesses of war. As a result of all this, the Lyonnais after the 9th Thermidor abandoned all restraint and showed themselves as cruel as their adversaries. Irritated because the patriot prisoners incarcerated after the fall of Robespierre were not put to death, they dispatched them themselves without the pretense of a trial and threw them into the Rhône, together with innumerable partisans of the Mountain. Disastrous and unworthy party reprisals!

WIMPFEN THREATENS TO MARCH TOWARDS PARIS.

Félix Wimpfen, commander-in-chief of the army of the Cherbourg coast, and of the departmental forces in the north and west of the French Republic, one and indivisible, to the good citizens of Paris, greetings:

I have once before contributed materially to the saving of the Republic, only to be calumniated and persecuted by the factions. Today I am called upon to save it still more effectively; they proscribe me and put a price upon my head.

The miscreants will tell you, "Félix Wimpfen is marching against Paris." Do not believe it; I am marching towards Paris for the good of Paris and for the safety of the Republic, one and indivisible. I am marching thither by the wishes of the people, not the people of a city faction, but the people of the majority of the departments; the sovereign people, as you yourselves would realize if the inquisitorial commune of Paris allowed the journalists to publish the truth.

Worthy citizens of Paris, let us rally to the common cause. . . . I command the Bretons and Normans.

Brothers, I am willing to fraternize with you; but my orders are to attack all who impede my march. I will attack them, I will conquer them; truth shall be heard and justice done.

GENERAL FÉLIX WIMPFEN

THE BLACK CRIME OF FEDERALISM. (Discourse of Billaud-Varenne, July 15, 1793.)

This black conspiracy is evinced by the uniformity of plans, principles, and impostures which characterize the rebellion of the federalized administrators. At a given moment counter-revolutionary intentions were openly manifested in every part of the Republic. Commissaries sent for this purpose from one department to another were proceeding boldly long before the insurrection of May 31. It is an established fact that Bordeaux deputized them as early as last April. These first attempts must have been hazarded upon the assurance of some of the leaders that their criminal propositions would be well received. There are seditious decrees by these administrators that antedate the insurrection. This, I reiterate, gives an even greater indication of a cause anterior and foreign to the event, as it also indicates the existence of a plot planned and conducted by the leaders that sat on the Right. In short, it is only by bringing together and understanding these circumstances that you have convincing evidence of the crimes you are to punish, and of the authors of these crimes.

(Doppet, 155–156.)

I prefer to think that the majority of the French who leagued together here honestly desired nothing more than the integrity of the Convention and freedom for the imprisoned deputies. Nevertheless, this movement tended to facilitate the conquests made by the enemy. It is a fact that the royalists attached themselves to the federalist coalition, and that the imprudence of the departments in this regard caused the surrender of Toulon to the English, the misfortunes at Lyon, and the death of a large number of republicans. That is an approximate explanation of the war called the war of federalism, but I prefer to call it "a federation against the Convention following May 31."

I know that there are people who say that there was a conspiracy against the unity of the Republic, and that politicians had the intention of dividing France into federated departments and establishing a departmental congress. Without either denying or affirming the existence of this project, I will say that among all these so-called federalists there were a number who honestly believed that they were serving the Republic in marching upon Paris after May 31. But I must also admit that there were many who used this as a pretext for bringing back the old régime. It is clear that to this group belonged those who welcomed the *émigrés* at Marseille and Lyon, proclaimed Louis XVII at Toulon, and assassinated the republicans.

XXIII. *The Beginning of the Terror*

FRANCE IN A SERIOUS PLIGHT. (*Mme. Roland, 67.*)

THE enemy, aided by the internal strife, advances on all sides. The cities of the north are falling into its power; Flanders and Alsace will become its prey. The Spaniard ravages Roussillon. The Savoyards reject an alliance which anarchy renders frightful; they return to a former master whose soldiers are invading our frontiers. The rebels of the Vendée continue to ravage large stretches of territory. The Lyonnais, foolishly antagonized, have increased their resistance. Marseille flies to their aid, and the neighboring departments are on the march. In the midst of all this universal agitation and civil war, nothing is uniform but the march of foreign powers. Our government is a kind of monster, revolting in form and action, which destroys everything it touches and even devours itself. This last is the only thing that consoles its numerous victims.

The armies, poorly equipped and poorly conducted, alternately fight and flee, like people gone mad. Able generals are accused of treason by representatives who know nothing of war. These find fault with what they do not understand, and think that every individual who is more enlightened than themselves is an aristocrat.

(Pache, Mayor, to his Fellow Citizens.)

Paris contains seven hundred thousand inhabitants; the soil of Paris produces nothing for their food, their clothing, their subsistence; it is therefore necessary for Paris to obtain everything from the departments and from abroad.

When provisions and merchandise come to Paris, if the inhabitants rob the owners of them, supplies will cease to be sent.

Paris will then have no food, no clothing, nothing for the subsistence of its numerous inhabitants.

And seven hundred thousand persons, destitute of everything, will devour one another.

(Durand de Maillane, 168–169.)

The lower classes had as yet gained nothing by the Revolution: they had to be given something in order to win their support. The maximum prices fixed on bread and other necessities by the laws of August 17 and September 29 won the people over completely. Danton had supported all this with his customary audacity. "The National Convention," he said, "must choose today between the interests of the monopolists and the interests of the people. Thuriot has explained the vital importance of the project laid before you. If there is anyone here who desires to oppose the *maximum*, let him mount the tribune. We will combat him, and you will give your decision. Nature has not abandoned us; do not abandon the people. Otherwise they will make their own justice, and recognizing the true cause of their misery, will fall upon the aristocrats and tear from them by force what they should have been given by law. Let the law be voted today and executed tomorrow."

ROBESPIERRE ADVOCATES A DESPOTISM OF LIBERTY. (*A kind of catechism by Robespierre written in his own hand.*)

What is our goal? The enforcement of the constitution for the benefit of the people.

Who will our enemies be? The vicious and the rich.

What means will they employ? Slander and hypocrisy.

What things may be favorable for the employment of these? The ignorance of the *sans-culottes*.

The people must therefore be enlightened. But what are the obstacles to the enlightenment of the people? Mercenary writers who daily mislead them with impudent falsehoods.

What conclusions may be drawn from this? 1. These writers must be proscribed as the most dangerous enemies of the people. 2. Right-minded literature must be scattered about in profusion.

What are the other obstacles to the establishment of liberty? Foreign war and civil war.

How can foreign war be ended? By putting republican generals in command of our armies and punishing those who have betrayed us.

How can civil war be ended? By punishing traitors and conspirators, particularly if they are deputies or administrators; by sending loyal troops under patriotic leaders to subdue the aristocrats of Lyon, Marseille, Toulon, the Vendée, the Jura, and all other regions in which the standards of rebellion and royalism have been raised; and by making frightful examples of all scoundrels who have outraged liberty and spilled the blood of patriots.

1. Proscription of perfidious and counter-revolutionary writers and propagation of proper literature.

2. Punishment of traitors and conspirators, particularly deputies and administrators.

3. Appointment of patriotic generals; dismissal and punishment of others.

4. Sustenance and laws for the people.

(Extract from the minutes of the National Convention on the 6th Germinal of the Year III.)

Levasseur de la Sarthe: I was in the committee one day when Carnot had a violent dispute with Robespierre about two clerks of his department who had been ordered arrested by the latter. Carnot said to Robespierre, "Nothing but arbitrary acts are being committed by your police department." Carnot added, in speaking to Robespierre, "You are a dictator." Robespierre called upon those present to witness what Carnot had said to him. The latter looked at him with disdain. . . .

THE LEVÉE EN MASSE.

ARTICLE I. From this moment until that in which our enemies shall have been driven from the territory of the Republic, all Frenchmen are permanently requisitioned for service in the armies.

Young men will go forth to battle; married men will forge weapons and transport munitions; women will make tents and clothing, and serve in hospitals; children will make lint from old linen; and old men will be brought to the public squares to arouse the courage of the soldiers, while preaching the unity of the Republic and hatred against kings.

II. Public buildings shall be converted into barracks, public squares into munition workshops, and the floors of cellars shall be leached to extract saltpeter.

III. Muskets shall be given exclusively to those who march against the enemy; interior service will be done with fowling pieces and side-arms.

IV. Saddle-horses are requisitioned to complete the cavalry corps; draught horses other than those employed in agriculture will be used in the artillery and to haul munitions.

V. The committee of public safety is charged to take all measures necessary for the immediate establishment of a special manufactory of arms of all kinds to correspond to the spirit and energy of the French people. It is, in consequence, authorized to set up all the establishments, manufactories, workshops, and laboratories deemed necessary for the accomplishment of this work, and requisition throughout the whole Republic the craftsmen and workers that can assist in making this a success. There shall be put at the disposition of the minister of war for this purpose thirty millions from the 498,200,000 livres of assignats in special reserve. The central establishment of this manufacturing shall be at Paris.

VI. The representatives of the people sent to execute the present law shall have the power of enforcement in their respective wards in concert with the committee of public safety. They are vested with the same absolute powers given to representatives of the people attached to the armies.

VII. No one will be allowed to furnish a substitute for the place to which he has been requisitioned. Public functionaries will remain at their posts.

VIII. The levy shall be general. Unmarried citizens and childless widowers between the ages of eighteen and thirty-five shall first be called. They shall immediately assemble in the headquarters of their district to be daily exercised in the use of arms until the day of their departure.

IX. The representatives of the people shall so regulate the summons and departures as not to have armed citizens arrive at assembly points unless provisions, munitions, and army supplies exist in sufficient proportions.

X. The places of assembly shall depend upon circumstances, and be designated by the representatives of the people sent to execute the present law, after these shall have received the advice of the generals acting in concert with the committee of public safety and the provisional executive council.

XI. The battalion which is organized in each district shall be assembled beneath a banner bearing this inscription: "The French people risen against tyrants!"

XII. These battalions shall be organized according to the established laws, and their pay shall be the same as that of the battalions on the frontiers.

XIII. In order to gather provisions in sufficient quantity, farmers and managers of national property shall deposit at district headquarters the grain produced from these lands.

XIV. Landowners, farmers, and holders of grain shall be required to pay back taxes in kind, including two-thirds of those of 1793, as listed on the tax records.

XV. The National Convention appoints Citizens Chabot, Tallien, Lecarpentier, Renaud, Dartigoeyte, Laplanche (of the Nièvre), Mallarmé, Legendre (of the Nièvre), Lanot (of the Corrèze), Roux-Fazillac, Paganel, Boisset, Taillefer, Bayle, Pinet, Fayau, Lacroix (of the Marne), and Ingrand as associates of the representatives of the people who are at present with the armies and in the departments. In accordance with the wishes of the envoys of the primary assemblies, they shall execute the present decree and all measures hitherto decreed against enemies in the interior, and against administrators who have conspired against the sovereignty of the people and the unity of the Republic.

The committee of public safety will assign them to their respective districts.

XVI. The envoys of the primary assemblies are urged to return immediately to their various cantons in order to carry out the civic mission relegated to them by the decree of August 14 and to receive the commissions to be given them by the representatives of the people.

XVII. The minister of war is instructed to take all measures necessary for the prompt execution of the present decree. The national treasury shall put at his disposition a sum of fifty millions from the 498,200,000 livres of assignats in special reserve.

XVIII. The present decree shall be sent to the departments by special courier.

THE LAW OF SUSPECTS.

ARTICLE I. Immediately upon the publication of the present decree, all suspect people still at liberty within the boundaries of the Republic shall be put under arrest.

II. Those to be considered suspect include:

1. Those who by their conduct, relations, discourse, or writings have shown themselves to be partisans of tyranny or federalism, and enemies of liberty....

3. Those who cannot after the manner prescribed by the Law of March 21 give an account of their means of existence and their performance of civic duties.

4. Those to whom certificates of civism have been refused.

5. Public functionaries whom the National Convention or its commissaries have suspended or dismissed and not reinstated, notably those who have been dismissed or ought to be dismissed by virtue of the Law of August 14.

6. Those among the former nobles, together with the husbands, wives, fathers, mothers, sons, daughters, brothers, sisters, and agents of *émigrés*, who have not steadfastly manifested their attachment to the Revolution.

7. Those who have emigrated during the period dating from July 1, 1789, to the publication of the Law of April 8, 1792, even if they have returned to France during or previous to the period fixed by this law.

8. The committees of surveillance established by the Law of March 21, or the authorities who have been substituted for them by the representatives of the people with the armies and departments or by special decrees of the National Convention, are enjoined to draw up lists of suspects in their respective districts, issue warrants of arrest, and seal their papers. Commanders of state forces to whom these warrants are remitted are to execute them immediately under pain of dismissal.

9. The members of the committee shall not order the arrest of any individual except by a majority of seven members present.

10. Individuals arrested as suspects shall first be conducted to prison at the place of their detention. If prisons are lacking, they shall be kept under constant guard at their respective dwellings.

11. In the course of a week they shall be transferred to national buildings which the administrators of the departments shall designate and prepare for this purpose immediately after receiving notice of the present decree.

12. Those detained may bring to these buildings the articles of furniture absolutely necessary to them, these remaining in custody there until the end of the war.

13. The prison expenses shall be charged to the prisoners and equally apportioned among them. Guard duties will be given preferably to fathers of families and relatives of citizens who are going to the front. Each guard shall be paid a day and a half's wages.

14. The committees of surveillance shall immediately inform the committee of general security of the National Convention as to the civil status of the persons they have arrested, the reasons for their arrest, and the papers found upon them.

15. If there are sufficient grounds, the civil and military tribunals may keep under arrest, and send to the above-mentioned prisons, those who have not been indicted for want of evidence, and even those who have been acquitted of the accusations made against them.

THE LAW OF FALSE NEWS. (*Durand de Maillane, 166.*)

The National Convention, after hearing the report of its committee of public safety, decreed that "All persons who spread false news or excite terror in the provinces, arouse the citizens, or cause disturbances and trouble, shall be brought before the extraordinary tribunal and punished as counter-revolutionary."

With such laws, what man could flatter himself that he would not be condemned as guilty? It was not necessary that there should be uprisings and disturbances; only news that might lead to these. Moreover, there was nothing definite about the application of the law against suspects. Everybody was at the mercy of men who were blinded by passion, or else depraved and corrupted by selfish ambitions, as was often the case in the revolutionary committees and even in the tribunals. Hence we have masses of guillotined whose memory will forever bring public execration upon the authors of these laws of blood as well as upon the men who executed them.

OTHER DECREES OF THE CONVENTION. (Révolutions de Paris, No. 212.)

Decree according the department of the Vendée a sum of two hundred thousand livres by way of succor. Bill of impeachment against Carra. Decree for the arrest of Rouyer and Brunet, commissaries of the Convention of the Midi. Decree providing that royal assignats be received in selling the personal property of the émigrés. Decree confiscating the property of the former Princesse de Lamballe. Decree authorizing the national treasury to pay fifty millions at the order of members of the committee of public safety. Decree declaring that the garrison at Mainz has served the country well and that the staff shall be liberated. Decree suppressing all the academies. Decree providing for the founding of public institutions where the children of citizens may be brought up and educated. Decree giving envoys of the primary assemblies the right to summon to the army citizens of the first class. Decree declaring that the French nation will not reimburse the sums loaned to Louis Capet nor liquidate the debts of the civil list. Decree upon the national debt, general reorganization of the established debt, inscription upon the national register of all permanent incomes, and the abolition of various contracts. Decree confiscating property in France belonging to Spaniards. Decree declaring that the French people are to rise en masse in defense of their liberty and constitution, and free the territory of all enemies. Decree ordering a general inventory of the Republic's grain. Decree conscripting all Frenchmen for public service. Decree ordering all young men from eighteen to twenty-five to the front, and establishing workshops in the public squares of Paris. Decree suppressing the discounting bank. Decree ordering the coining of new money from copper and bell metal. Decree condemning notaries to ten years of imprisonment if they give attested copies of royal titles to creditors of the state. Decree fixing a limit of one thousand livres to all emoluments on the civil list. Decree declaring France is in a state of revolution until its independence has been recognized. Decree regarding the forced loan. Decree ordering that royal assignats above one hundred livres be considered as negotiable property of the bearer and subject to registration and endorsement.

THE TERROR. (Morellet, II, 10–13.)

The scoundrels who had become masters of France thought the revolutionary tribunals were not active enough in their operations. Until towards the month of September, 1793, it was not often that many of the condemned were executed on the same day, and there were often intervals in between.

But the law of suspects having been adopted from the report of Merlin of Douai and used to throw two hundred thousand citizens into dungeons, these horrible tribunals had plenty of victims.

Towards the end of October, when twenty-one Brissotins were executed on the same day, there began those national butcheries that were soon to extend to all France. These were the sights presented at Paris on almost every day of the last three months of 1793 and of the first seven months of 1794. The executions from now on usually included fifteen, twenty, thirty, or even sixty persons or more; condemned in a few hours and executed on the same day....

Every day was marked by new massacres, the number of murders mounting ceaselessly. Having my lodgings in the Faubourg Saint-Honoré, at a short distance from the place of execution, I could not go to the Champs-Élysées of an afternoon without hearing the cries of a ferocious mob applauding the falling heads. If upon going out I followed my faubourg street to the city, I saw the same crowds running to the Place de la Révolution to feed upon the spectacles there. Sometimes I was unable to avoid meeting the fatal tumbrils. Thus I had the misfortune to happen upon the Comte de Brienne and all his family going to the scaffold along with Madame Elizabeth, a sanguinary picture that haunted my mind for many a day.

DECREE FOR THE SHORTENING OF TRIALS.

The National Convention, seeing that none of the leading conspirators have been brought to trial, and that attempts have been made to raise aristocratic insurrections dangerous to domestic peace; ... that the hand of justice appears to fall only upon obscure offenders while important criminals are, by the law's delay, left free for intrigues, impostures, and counter-revolutionary audacity; and that it is both absurd and contrary to the purpose of the revolutionary tribunal to submit to an endless procession of crimes ... when an entire nation brings accusation and the whole universe may be used as witnesses, does hereby decree the following:

If the trial of a case by the revolutionary tribunal is prolonged to three days, the president will open the next sitting with the inquiry as to whether the jurymen have heard enough.

If the jurymen reply in the affirmative the verdict shall be rendered immediately.

The president shall allow no questions or interruptions contrary to the provisions of the present decree....

TERROR THE ORDER OF THE DAY. (*Révolutions de Paris, No. 212.*)

Yes, terror is the order of the day, and ought to be for the selfish, for the federalists, for the heartless rich, for dishonest opportunists, for shameless intriguers, for unpatriotic cowards, for all who do not feel the dignity of being free men and pure republicans. Rivers of blood have been shed for the gold of Peru and the diamonds of Golconda. Well! Does not liberty, that inestimable blessing which one would surely not tarnish by comparing it with the vile metals of the Indies, have the same right to sacrifice lives, fortunes, and even, for a time, individual liberties? In the thick of battle is there any foolish wailing over the soldiers fallen from the ranks? They are promptly replaced by others, and with the perfidious aggressor replused, one is free to weep over the unfortunate victims mowed down on the field of battle. Is not the French Revolution just such a deadly combat, a war to the death between those who want to be free and those content to be slaves? This is the situation, and the French people have gone too far to retreat with honor and safety. There is no middle ground; France must be entirely free or perish in the attempt, and any means are justifiable in fighting for so fine a cause. But our resources are being exhausted, say some. Well, when the Revolution is finished, they will be replenished by peace. A free people, as long as they have weapons and hands, can fight their enemies and plow their fields.

(*List of those condemned to death by the Revolutionary Tribunal during the first five days of the second month of the Year II.*)

Pierre-François Malangié, age 55, former justice of the peace in the city of Armentières; Pellerin-Gui Jonaire, native of Armentières; Antoine-François-Joseph Delattre, age 65, wholesale merchant of Armentières; and Paul-François Clarisse, hatter, all four arraigned and convicted for having participated in movements and intrigues to deliver the city of Armentières to the enemy, and secure the progress of their armies within the territory of the Republic. Louis-Aimond Pernon, age 53, director of the national lottery, native of Lyon, convicted of criminal correspondence with the rebels of Lyon and participating in the conspiracies and plots hatched in that city. Pierre-Hyppolite Pastourel, age 43, *curé* of Saint-Hilaire in the district of Saumur, convicted of intrigues and plots in connection with the rebels of the Vendée.

Total number of prisoners in Paris, 3098.

THE QUEEN BEFORE THE REVOLUTIONARY TRIBUNAL. (*Madame Royale, 223–236.*)

On August 2, they awakened us, at two o'clock in the morning, to read to my mother a decree of the Convention. Upon the summons of the procurator of the commune, she was to be conducted to the Conciergerie to be tried. . . . When she arrived at the Conciergerie, they placed her in the dirtiest, dampest, and most unhealthful chamber in the whole building. She was under the constant surveillance of a gendarme who did not leave her day or night.

. . . my mother's trial had lasted three days and nights. They expatiated on all the shameful things concerning which Chaumette had questioned us. The very idea of these things would have occurred only to such people. "I appeal to all mothers," was her reply to these infamous accusations. The people were touched. The judges, alarmed, and fearing that sympathy would be aroused by her firmness, dignity, and courage, hastened to send her to death. My mother heard the sentence with great calmness.

(Moniteur, No. 36.)

During her examination, Marie Antoinette nearly always kept a calm and assured countenance. In the first few hours of the questioning, she was seen to move her fingers along the arm of her chair, in apparent abstraction, as if she were playing a pianoforte.

Upon hearing her sentence pronounced, she allowed herself no sign of emotion, and left the courtroom without a word, addressing no discourse to either the judges or the people present.

THE EXECUTION.

In the name of the Republic.

The public prosecutor of the revolutionary criminal tribunal established at Paris by the Law of March 10, 1793, in execution of today's sentence by the tribunal, requires the citizen commander of the military forces of Paris to lend assistance, and put on foot the civic force necessary for the execution of the said judgment rendered against Marie Antoinette Lorraine Autriche, widow of Louis Capet, and condemning her to the punishment of death; which execution shall take place today at ten o'clock in the morning on the public square of the Révolution in this city. The citizen commander is required to dispatch the said civic force to the court of the Palais on the said day at exactly eight o'clock in the morning.

Done at Paris, the 25th of the 1st month of the second year of the French Republic, one and indivisible. (Old style, Wednesday, October 16, at five o'clock in the morning.)

A. Q. FOUQUIER,
Public Prosecutor

(Révolutions de Paris, No. 212.)

The widow Capet, Marie Antoinette d'Autriche, condemned to death by the revolutionary tribunal after an examination lasting three consecutive days, suffered the penalty for her political and personal misdemeanors, at noon [October 16, 1793], upon the Place de la Révolution at the foot of the statue of Liberty....

The executioner, Citizen Sanson, presented himself in her chamber at seven o'clock in the morning.

"You come early, Monsieur," she said to him. "Could you not have delayed?"

"No, Madame; I was ordered to come."

She was already completely prepared; that is to say, dressed in white like her late husband on the day of his execution. This affectation was remarked and caused the people to smile. A color symbolical of innocence was ill-suited to Marie Antoinette. She desired to go to the guillotine without a bonnet on her head, but this was not allowed. She cut off her hair herself with her own hand. Someone came to her prison chamber and said, "There is a Paris priest asking if you want to confess." She was heard to repeat in a

low voice: "A Paris priest! . . . There are hardly any, any more." The confessor advanced and said to her, "Do you wish me to accompany you, Madame?"

"As you like, Monsieur."

But she did not confess, and did not speak a single word along the whole
route.

Upon leaving the Conciergerie, she perceived the tumbril and was seen to
make a gesture of surprise and indignation. She was persuaded that she
would, like her husband, be taken in a carriage. She was forced, however,
to mount into this vehicle that wounded her proud soul; and one may be
assured that her punishment began at that moment, although she made a
pretense of fortitude. It was easy to see that this appearance of firmness
cost her a great deal. Her face from that moment grew wan. Her hands were
tied behind her back, as is usual. (This practice should be abandoned and
criminals allowed the free use of their hands to the very end.) She maintained
the same expression throughout the whole journey, except in front of the
former Palais-Royal. This edifice probably recalled remembrances that
moved her. She cast a fervent glance in that direction. The people watched
her passage peaceably enough. There were clappings of hands at certain
places; but in general they seemed for the moment to forget all the misfortunes
brought upon France by this woman, and think only of her present situation.
Justice was being done, which was all that the people asked.

In mounting the scaffold, Antoinette accidentally stepped upon the foot
of Citizen Sanson; and the executioner felt pain enough to cry, "Oh!" She
turned to him and said, "Monsieur, I beg you to excuse me; it was quite
unpremeditated." She may have arranged this little scene to add interest
to her memory; for some people are vain up to the very moment of death.

TRIAL AND EXECUTION OF GIRONDIN LEADERS. (*Riouffe, 48–51.*)

I was put in another part of the Conciergerie. I left a den of justly enchained criminals to enter the temple of persecuted virtue. Vergniaud,
Gensonné, Brissot, Ducos, Fonfrède, Valazé, Duchâtel, and their colleagues
were the guests I found installed in my new dwelling-place. . . .

There was something of sublimity in the eyes of Valazé. With a sweet,
serene smile upon his lips, he was experiencing the foretaste of his glorious
death. One could see that his spirit was already free, and that by making a
grand resolution, he had found a guarantee of liberty. Sometimes I said to
him: "Valazé, how desirous you are of a beautiful death! The greatest
punishment for you would be an acquittal!" On the last day, before going
up to the tribunal, he retraced his steps to give me a pair of scissors he had
with him, saying, "It is a dangerous weapon and they are afraid we may
attempt suicide." The irony, worthy of a Socrates, with which he pronounced
these words, affected me strangely. When I learned that this modern Cato had
stabbed himself with a poignard which he had hidden under his cloak, I
was not surprised; I must have divined his purpose. He had retained this
poignard against all searchings, for they were overhauled like common criminals before they went up. Vergniaud threw away the poison he had preserved, preferring to die with his colleagues.

(Vilate, 305–306.)

... I was seated with Camille Desmoulins on the bench before the jurors' table. When these returned to render a verdict [upon the Girondins], Camille advanced to speak to Antonelle, one of the last to reappear. Surprised at the latter's altered countenance, he said to him rather loudly, "Ah, *mon Dieu!* I pity you; you have a terrible rôle to play." Then, upon hearing the jury's verdict, he suddenly threw himself into my arms, agonizing and lamenting, "Ah! *mon Dieu, mon Dieu!* it is I who have killed them! My *Brissot Unveiled!* Ah, *mon Dieu!* it is I who have killed them!" As the accused re-entered to hear the verdict, all eyes were turned in their direction; a profound silence fell upon the hall. The public prosecutor brought in the death penalty, and the wretched Camille, annihilated, out of his mind, let fall these words: "I am going, I am going, I want to go!" But he could not do it.

Scarcely was the fatal word *death* pronounced than Brissot let fall his arms; his head sank suddenly upon his breast. Gensonné, pale and trembling, demanded to speak upon the application of the law; no one heard what he said. Boileau, astonished, waved his hat in the air, crying, "I am innocent!" and turning to the people, invoked them vehemently. Spontaneously the accused arose: "People, we are innocent; you are being deceived!" The people remained unmoved; the gendarmes seized the prisoners and made them sit down. Valazé drew a stiletto from his bosom and plunged it into his heart, falling backward dead. Sillery let fall his crutches and cried out, his face full of joy and rubbing his hands: "This is the most wonderful day of my life."

(Extract from a memoir addressed to Louvet; Pétion, 495–502.)

Salles and Guadet ... departed for Saint-Émilion. ...

Jullien ... sent the members of the committees of Bordeaux to apprehend them. ... When he saw they were going to be taken, Guadet tried to blow out his brains, but the pistol hung fire. Shortly afterwards, thirty scoundrels seized upon them and loaded them with irons. ... Lacombe ... sent them to the scaffold to expiate their error in having had more talent than their persecutors. ...

Pétion, Buzot, and Barbaroux were witnesses of the removal of their colleagues ...

DEATHS OF PÉTION, BUZOT, AND BARBAROUX. (*Letter of Guadet, brother of the Girondin leader, Paris, 21st Ventôse, Year III.*)

... Pétion, Buzot, and Barbaroux had hidden themselves in one of the houses. Domiciliary visits were made for the purpose of discovering them, and they were forced to leave the horrible hovel that had saved their lives. Favored by the obscurity, they had the good luck to escape three thousand spies. Still unseparated, they gained the outskirts of Castillon, where they were again pursued. Together they partook of a frugal repast, their last. Barbaroux, believing that further escape was impossible, decided to end his life, and sent a pistol bullet through his head. The pistol was somewhat deflected by the efforts made by Pétion and Buzot to deter him. He was seriously wounded, and the shot attracted some people who recognized him and transported him to Castillon. He was transferred to Bordeaux, where he ended his existence. Shortly afterwards, Pétion and Buzot were driven to extremities and killed themselves to keep from falling alive into the hands of monsters thirsting for their blood. . . .

(*The Popular Republican Society of Castillon to the National Convention.*)

Citizen representatives, we have kept our promises; our searchings have not been in vain. When we announced the capture of the scoundrel Barbaroux, we ventured to assure you that we would soon have, dead or alive, his perfidious accomplices, Pétion and Buzot, in our power.

And they are, citizen representatives, or rather they no longer are.

The punishment provided by law was too mild for these traitors, and a salutary justice provided one more suitable for their crimes. Their bodies have been found . . . the prey of dogs . . . Such was the horrible end of lives more horrible still. People, contemplate this frightful expiation, a terrible memento of vengeance!

Traitors, let this ignominious death, this horrible example, make you recoil in horror and tremble with fear! Such is the terrible fate that sooner or later will be reserved for you.

THE DEATH OF MME. ROLAND. (*Riouffe, 57.*)

On the day of her conviction, she was in white and carefully dressed, with her long black hair falling unconfined to her waist. She would have softened the hardest heart; but did these monsters have any? However, she gave no thought to this; she had chosen her attire as a symbol of the purity of her soul. After her conviction, she repassed the grating with a swiftness that was almost joy. She indicated by an expressive gesture that she had been condemned to death. Associated with a man who awaited the same fate, but whose bravery did not equal hers, she succeeded in arousing his courage, with a gaiety so charming and real, that she caused a smile to rise to his lips on a number of separate occasions.

On the place of execution, she inclined her head before the statue of Liberty, and pronounced these memorable words: "Oh, Liberty! What crimes are committed in thy name!"

She had often said that her husband would not survive her. We learned in our dungeons that her prediction was well founded. The worthy Roland had committed suicide upon the highway, showing that he wished to die irreproachable towards those who had courageously sheltered him.

PROGRESSIVE NATURE OF THE TERROR. (*Thibaudeau, I, 44–47.*)

The Terror began on May 31 and lasted until the 9th Thermidor. It must be said of this epoch, as L'Hôpital said of St. Bartholomew, *Excidat illa dies.* It is perhaps the only epoch where the truth is so frightful that it cannot be exaggerated by partisan writers. One may attempt to explain its causes, but who would have the courage to excuse it? Anyone who lived through it and thinks back on it is frightened by his own memories. The soul is overwhelmed, and the pen refuses, one may say, to retrace them.

In a despotic state, there are at least the ruler, the courtiers, certain classes, and certain individuals who are not affected by the terror they inspire. They are the gods that hurl the thunderbolts without fear of being struck. Under the Reign of Terror no one in France was exempt; it soared above the heads of all and brought them down indiscriminately, arbitrary and swift as the scythe of death. The Convention, as well as the people, furnished its contingent. Danton, Desmoulins, and the Paris municipals perished on the same scaffold to which they had dragged the Girondins, and the people impartially applauded the slaying of both executioners and victims. Marat, apparently unsurpassable in ferocity, and with execrable features horribly symbolizing the Terror, would not himself have escaped had not the poignard of a courageous woman brought him to the Panthéon. Even Robespierre, high priest of all this sanguinary fury, was doomed to be its final victim.

One overestimates human perversity in imagining that certain persons invented the so-called *system of terror.* Had it been suddenly presented in all its horror, there is not a man, however barbarous, who would not have recoiled aghast. Nothing was further from being a system than the Terror. In spite of the rapidity of its development, it advanced by regular steps. People were forced into it little by little, and followed it without knowing where it would end. They pushed it further and further because they dared not draw back and could see no way out of it. Camille Desmoulins and Danton, the one famous for bold ideas and witty pamphlets, the other for his athletic appearance and popular eloquence, were both overthrown for talking of moderation. Robespierre was already preparing, when he was attacked by men much more concerned about their own safety than the safety of France, to throw upon them the crimes of the Terror.

The extension of the Terror was caused by the opposition of internal and external enemies to the Revolution. There was a birth of exaggerated patriotism. It began with the fervid and violent speeches of the upper classes and ended in active atrocities by the lower classes. When the third estate had abolished privileges, it took the place of the aristocracy in the eyes of the people. When the people had finished its war with these defenders of its rights, it sought within its own ranks for obscure victims with which to feed the Terror, just as slaves have been known to break their chains, exterminate their liberators as well as their oppressors, and then fall upon one another, intoxicated with blood and victory. It seemed then that the only way to escape prison or the scaffold was to bring others there. There were people who denounced and proscribed through their hatred and desire for revenge; but most of them thought they were serving their country and performing a laudable act.

IMPORTANCE OF THE COMMITTEES. (Barère, I, 72–73.)

From as early as September 22, 1792, the National Convention had had a committee of general defense. It was composed of twenty-five members, with all the deputies of the Convention having the right to attend its sittings. The northern frontiers were in danger. The King of Prussia had occupied the strongholds of Longwy and Verdun on the east, and was advancing through Champagne. The committee was daily occupied with trying to defend the French territory; but it was quite unfitted for its difficult and honorable mission. A series of unexpected events, together with the heroic courage of the volunteers that flocked from all departments, accomplished more than did the committee of general defense. The committee was made up of party adherents that were animated by hatred and ambition, and so divided among themselves that only the unexpected could save the nation and liberty. One of the things that occurred was the treason of General Dumouriez. After the disaster at Neerwinden, he imagined he could go to Lille, and from Lille to Paris, where he would seize the power of government and establish a monarchy. The blame for this shameful defection fell upon both the parties of the committee of general defense, who were accused of working for their own ends. In consequence of all this, the committee was abolished. To fill its place, the Convention created a committee of public safety, to be made up of nine members chosen by the Convention.

(Mallet du Pan, II, 11.)

All plans and decrees originate from the committee of public safety. It exercises the initiative in legislation; it enjoys, at the same time, the right of decision, from the subjection into which it has brought the National Assembly. This does not contain more than two hundred or two hundred and fifty members: the rest have been guillotined, arrested, or have escaped. The talk is almost exclusively reserved to thirty or forty Montagnards or more. Robespierre, Danton, Couthon, Billaud-Varenne, hold the minds, tongues, and poignards of men in their hands; neither debate nor discussion is permitted; each representative not belonging to that phalanx trembles for his liberty and life, and purchases both by silent submission to the will of the leaders.

To the number of absentees must be added further the commissaries sent with the army and into the departments. The committee can recall them arbitrarily at any moment, and such a recall is the prelude to a sentence of death: these ambulatory deputies have one interest, one desire, one idea: they all agree in showing themselves in their commission as inexorable and furious as those who appoint them, thus proving their unlimited devotion to the latter.

MEMBERS OF THE COMMITTEE SENT ON MISSIONS. (Barère, II, 121–122.)

While the coalition that had congregated in the Netherlands was attacking us along the coasts, the English made demonstrations against the Channel ports. The committee sent Prieur of the Marne to the ocean ports, with headquarters. at Lorient. Jean-Bon Saint-André asked to be sent to Brest, and everything was arranged to protect the arrival of a large quantity of grain and rice which the committee had secured through its alliance with the United States of America.

DICTATORSHIP OF THE COMMITTEE OF PUBLIC SAFETY. (*Thibaudeau, I, 47–49.*)

The National Convention itself was now only nominally a representative body, having become a passive instrument of the Terror. Upon the ruins of its independence rose the monstrous dictatorship of the famous committee of public safety. The Terror isolated and stupefied the representatives as much as it did the ordinary citizens. A member came to the Assembly with misgivings, heedful of his words and actions lest they be made into a crime. In fact, one had to be careful of everything, the place where one sat, one's gestures, murmurs, smiles. The summit of the Mountain being accounted the place of the highest republicanism, all edged in that direction. The Right had been deserted after the expulsion of the Girondins. Either through conscientious scruples or from shame, their companions refused to join the Mountain and took refuge with the Plain. The Plain was always ready to receive those who desired the safety of its complacency and negativeness. The more pusillanimous refused to identify themselves with any group and would change from seat to seat, thinking that they would thus outwit the spies and give themselves a mixed complexion which would offend no one. The most prudent of all did better still. Fearing to be contaminated and especially to be compromised, they never sat down at all. They remained at the foot of the tribune away from the circle of benches. On turbulent occasions when there was danger in voting against the propositions repugnant to them, they slipped furtively out of the hall.

The majority of the Convention did not want the Terror any more than did the majority of the nation. It had ordered neither the *noyades* of Nantes nor the *mitraillades* of Lyon. But through weakness or fear, it showed no open disapproval of what it privately censured, and preserved a mournful silence. The sessions, previously so long and stormy, were now for the most part calm and formal, lasting only an hour or so. What little liberty they had was in regard to things of no importance. The more serious matters they left to the committee of public safety, and acted according to its wishes. Members of the committee or its reporter would keep them waiting as one waits for sovereign powers and heads of states. When members of the committee came to the hall where the sittings were being held, vile courtiers advanced in front of them as if they were announcing the masters of the world. Faces were scrutinized to see whether they were bringing a decree of proscription or the news of a victory. The reporter mounted the tribune amid profound silence, and if any spoke after he had left the floor, it was only to emphasize what he had said. His conclusions were always tacitly adopted without a formal vote. When the triumphs of the armies were announced, his insolent attitude seemed to declare, "It is not you, or the army, or the people that are victorious; it is the committee of public safety." And they had, in fact, taken over all power of legislation and government in both planning and execution. They finally took the power of proscription away from the committee of general security, leaving to it the doubtful privilege of making out the lists.

PLEBEIANS FURNISH MOST OF THE VICTIMS. (*Thibaudeau, I, 50–51.*)

The Terror was more fatal to the friends of liberty than to the enemies of it. The latter had emigrated through mistaken notions of honor, or because they hated the Revolution or were seeking their own safety. Conscientious and patriotic friends of the Revolution remained faithful to the country that was destroying them. There were more plebeians than priests and nobles that perished in this great hecatomb. After the Terror, the nobles and clergy found many eager avengers, but the memory of the others was buried in hidden tears and silent regrets. Patriots who could not be accused of being aristocrats and royalists were proscribed as federalists and moderates. Most of the citizens and officials who disapproved of May 31 paid for their generous attitude with their heads. When the *émigrés* saw the lists of proscribed, they triumphantly rejoiced; the hearts of the royalists were untouched by the plight of their companions in misfortune. In the prisons, where the Terror heaped up all ranks of its victims pell-mell, proud aristocrats were obstinate in making distinctions. On the very scaffold the royalist often worried less about death than about the humiliation of having to die in the company of patriots with whom he had disdained to live.

(*Vaublanc, 234.*)

[There were executed] from December 2, 1793, to January 11, 1794, two shoemakers, a clerk from the ministry of the interior, a doctor, a woman, Kersaint and Rabaut (deputies of the Convention), a brigadier, Mme. Dubarry, a Paris banker and two sons, a deputy of the Convention, a Swiss, two tailors, two persons undescribed, a former page, four women, the Duc de Châtelet, a servant, three men of the household of the Duc de Montmorency, a grocer, a cooper, a wigmaker, a tailor, two nobles, a chief of army *dépôts*, a justice of the peace of the Constituent Assembly, a *curé*, a priest, a justice of the peace, a public prosecutor, one person undescribed, three women, a commissary of marine, a servant, a haberdasher, a shoemaker, a thatcher, two weavers, a wholesale merchant, a captain, a *curé*, a baker, a doctor and his brother, a clerk, a clockmaker, a director of military equipages, Lebrun (minister of foreign affairs under the Convention), the mayor of Strasbourg, the Duc de Biron (member of the Constituent Assembly and lieutenant-general), an excise collector, two more nobles, a woman, a transfer agent, a commissary, two priests, two women, the son of General Custine, a lieutenant-colonel, a substitute of the procurator-general of the *cour des aides*, Marshal Lückner (convicted, according to the sentence, of having delivered several strongholds over to the enemy), a soap manufacturer, a noble, a priest, a sergeant, a substitute in the Convention, a man of letters, a woman, a printer, the former commander of Sainte-Lucie, the president of the revolutionary committee of

Montpellier (an accomplice of the Brissotins, according to the sentence), and Lamourette (constitutional bishop). Total 89, of which thirteen were women.

(Riouffe, 62–63.)

About the same time, they brought in Bailly, the most honored man of the Revolution and the most excruciatingly martyred. He came to know the ferocity of the populace of whom he had been the idol, and was abandoned in a cowardly fashion by people who still esteemed him. He died, like Plato's man of virtue or like Jesus Christ, in ignominy: they spat upon him; they flagged his face with fire; furious men approached to strike him, in spite of executioners indignant at such fury. They covered him with mud. He was three hours upon the place of execution, and his scaffold was erected upon a heap of refuse. A cold rain, falling in torrents, added to the horror of his situation; his hands tied behind his back, ... he asked them several times to put an end to his misery; but he proffered his words with the calmness of one of the greatest philosophers of Europe. He replied to a man who said to him, "You are trembling, Bailly!" — "My friend, it is from cold."

THE ROYALISTS. (Thibaudeau, I, 51.)

Royalism took advantage of the patriotic insurrections at Lyon and Marseille. From that moment, the insurgents' cause was lost. When they were defeated, the royalist chiefs saved themselves by flight, but the citizens who could not or would not emigrate were shot down without any distinction being made as to whether they were the friends of liberty or its enemies. Those who took refuge in foreign countries were furiously repulsed by the *émigrés*, and scarcely tolerated by foreign governments. The *émigrés* were, however, quite as intolerant of one another. Instead of opening their arms to all the unfortunate exiles, they judged them according to when and why they had emigrated.

(Durand de Maillane, 75–76.)

One must distinguish between the different classes of *émigrés*. If confiscation is ever justifiable, it is when a citizen leaves the country to war upon it or stir up its enemies. The very least that can be done is to deprive him of his resources. All those who favored or followed the flag of the army of Condé should fall into this class. No severity was used for a long time against these disloyal emigrants, for the sale of their property was not begun until September, 1793, that is to say, when extensive measures of defense were put into effect ... By that time the June constitution had been set aside, and everything was in revolution; the innocent were confounded with the guilty, and involuntary *émigrés* with the voluntary. Cupidity, moreover, could, under cover of the law, despoil at leisure the families who had left their homes only to escape prison or death. This had lasted so long that, in regard to these unfortunates, the Law of the 22nd Germinal was useless. Almost all of them, upon their return, found that everything had been sold, their property, their houses, and their furniture; I myself was a witness of this while on my mission to the department of the Var.

THE SOLDIERS. (Thibaudeau, I, 51–53.)

Our early victories have been attributed to the Terror. In all times and countries, the military conscript has had to choose between obedience and summary punishment. Thus the Republic was merciless towards the French conscript who refused to heed the call to war. There were probably some who enlisted voluntarily to avoid proscription, seeking peace in war and safety in battle. Fear has made brave soldiers and sometimes heroes. But under the Terror, as well as after that reign of blood, the masses of Frenchmen who rallied to the flag were fighting for liberty and national independence. The people, whether they were the instruments or the victims of the tyranny that was mangling the country, were indignantly opposed to a rule by *émigrés* and foreigners. Believing that they had kept down trouble at home by filling the prisons with suspects, they marched to the frontiers, noble in their devotion. The patriotic songs of youthful warriors resounded through the apprehensive, mournful cities.

This revolutionary government, so terrible to foreign enemies, was not less so to enemies within its borders. The mercenaries of Europe were defied by its citizen armies, and far-famed generals were defeated by men who had risen from the ranks. Both skill and audacity were shown in these campaigns. The Republic was fortunate in having an unusual man in the committee of public safety. Foreign to intrigue and ambition, simple in manners and tastes, disinterested, incorruptible, and learned in the art of war, he was an enthusiastic supporter of the freedom, glory, and independence of the Republic; in a word, he was like a character of antiquity, the glory of his time and country. This man was Carnot, who was given dictatorship over the armies, and justified it with victory.

THE PEOPLE. (Thibaudeau, I, 54–56.)

While some have pictured the misery of the people under the Terror, others have pretended that they were enriched with the spoils.

It is true that there was no luxury to support the arts and industries. But numerous people were employed in making the necessities of war. Agriculture prospered from the suppression of feudal rights and the sale of national property. The depreciation of the assignats worked a hardship upon the great landowners, the annuitants, and the government employees, but agriculturalists and farmers were enriched. A few sacks of wheat would meet their taxes and make the payments upon their farms. Vainly did the law put taxes upon their produce, proscribe the use of gold and silver, and punish violations with death; the needs of the consumer and the avarice of the sellers caused an evasion of the *maximum* and a raising of prices, just as the laws against usury caused interest rates to rise.

The depreciation of paper money made for increased spending and the stimulation of industry. Nobody wanted to hoard money whose value was uncertain. Everybody hastened to invest it in production and properties, or else spend it. So much buying and selling had never been seen before. Every ground floor in Paris was converted into a shop or store. Such a frenzied and disorderly state of affairs could end only in catastrophe, and this was conjectured from afar. Therefore, when the assignats were eventually called in, it caused no trouble whatever. No one complained about losses, so glad were people to abandon their illusions about paper money, and substitute the realities of a metal currency.

There has been much exaggeration in regard to the benefits derived from the seizure of property. If there were any, it was not the people who profited. The sequestered property of the *émigrés* and the guillotined came into their hands; but the proceeds of the sales went into the public treasury. The requisitions were for the benefit of the armies and the public service. The *maximum*, which seemed to be made for the people's benefit, was only a famine measure. A few individuals were enriched, but the masses were living in privation. Their vanity was gratified by ruling amidst blood and débris, and this consoled them to a certain extent. Their power was not illusory. If they took orders from their leaders, their leaders also took orders from them. The calamities of the Terror were to them a retribution, a passing phase, that would lead to better times.

THE TERROR UNNECESSARY. (*Thibaudeau, I, 57–58.*)

Far from being a natural consequence of the Revolution, the Terror of '93 was an unfortunate deviation. It hindered rather than aided the founding of the Republic. Passing all bounds and attacking both friends and enemies, it became so atrocious that it could be defended by none. This led to a reaction which was disastrous not only to the Terrorists, but also to liberty and the defenders of liberty. The Terror was too violent to last; it ended as unexpectedly as it began.

People unaffected by the Terror or blinded by political fanaticism gave little thought as to how or when it would end. Those who meditated upon it, or suffered the weight of oppression, were unable to foresee what would happen. In most political affairs and crises, reversals and changes come unexpectedly. The Terror did not come to an end because its promoters were weary of slaughter, but because they were terrified and divided among themselves. It was a question of who attacked first; he who merely defended himself was lost.

XXIV. *The Terror in the Provinces*

FAILURE OF THE COUNTER-REVOLUTIONARY MOVEMENTS. (*Weber,I, 5–6.*)

THE Prince of Saxony and General Clerfayt had just overthrown the French at Neerwinden. The French, chased from Mainz, the Liége country, and the whole of the Netherlands, were now unable even to defend the frontiers. Dumouriez and his officers had thrown off all restraint and were preparing to turn their weapons against the regicide government. Oppressed peoples were opening their arms to foreigners who were announcing themselves to be their liberators rather than their enemies. The Duke of York had already triumphantly entered into Valenciennes, the Prince of·Württemberg into Condé, and General Clerfayt into Quesnoy. Thirty-two commissaries of the Convention met unexpectedly at Péronne, all in flight from various points of the frontier. Barère was crying out from the tribune, "It is all over with the Republic if you do not send troops into Nord." The Catholic and royalist armies were becoming prodigious in the west. In the Midi, Toulon and Lyon were raising the royal standard. With all this happening within six months' time, one might certainly be led to believe that the scoundrels, as the Comte de Mercy wrote, would be "overcome by the swiftness of it," without time to know where they were, and would have to purchase their lives by offering safety and deliverance to the august victims still alive within their hands.

But the victorious invaders stopped, themselves divided and broken. The illustrious nephew of Marie Antoinette was unable to induce the allies to advance together towards the goal of his desire. The division in the royal armies assured victory to the troops of the Republic. There was no longer any obstacle to that decisive measure, the *levée en masse*, which a child could have foreseen and a grown man stopped, as was said in a memoir addressed to the Comte de Mercy. The Vendée was enclosed by a circle and within this it would wear itself out. Lyon caused as much despair as hope or admiration. The widow of Louis XVI found herself in the hands of a horde of assassins who were just as ferocious as the assassins of her unfortunate husband and more ignoble. January 21 was surpassed in horror by October 16, 1793. Germany was plunged into mourning, and the whole world was full of pity, astonishment, and indignation.

THE REVOLUTIONARY ARMY OF THE INTERIOR. (*Révolutions de Paris, No. 212.*)

Faint-hearted citizens, who avert your eyes from these great movements, convulsive if you like, but regenerative, wake up and take notice. After each of these movements you think the Republic lost. But see how it now makes headway against the whole of Europe, how it organizes in the midst of the tempest, how it recovers from its losses and day after day wins three victories for every defeat. . . .

But what can be done against the armed miscreants and masked patriots who, in understanding with those beyond the borders, are harassing our citizens and seeking to starve or corrupt them? Another great expedient has been proposed and is even now being carried out; a measure which is extraordinary, but worthy of a justice-loving people. There is to be a revolutionary army which will scour France in every sense of the word. With it will go a tribunal and a guillotine. In the public squares of the cities and under the open sky, popular justice will be pronounced. Retribution will no longer be lame, as represented by the ancients. It will follow closely after a crime; so that at least a scoundrel can commit but one.

(Durand de Maillane, 154–155.)

The Convention decreed this army of six thousand men and gave the nation a tribunal and guillotine with which to embellish the march. The decree, dated September 5, 1793, was as follows:

ARTICLE I. An armed force shall be gathered at Paris, composed of six thousand men and twelve hundred cannoneers. It shall be paid from the public treasury and used in suppressing the counter-revolutionists. It shall protect supplies and execute, whenever necessary, the revolutionary laws and measures of public safety that may be decreed by the National Convention.

II. This armed force shall be organized immediately in the manner prescribed by law.

III. The pay shall be the same as that received by the national gendarmerie of Paris.

THE TERROR AT MARSEILLE. (Durand de Maillane, 148–149.)

. . . Robespierre refused to allow any reconciliation with the men who had followed his own principles in rebelling against the violation of their rights in the person of their representatives. A sanguinary tribunal was established at Marseille; this tribunal wrought only revenges, composed as it was of judges chosen from among the patriot extremists imprisoned during the insurrection. All the upright and wealthy people of Marseille took refuge at Toulon; when they encountered the same sort of violence there, they surrendered to the English as a means of escape. The same horrors, with the same reactions towards them, occurred at Nîmes and Toulouse; in fact, they occurred wherever the people had risen against the tyrannical dominators of the National Convention after the insurrections of May 31 and June 2. This new and frightful kind of butchery, performed in the name of the law, and which was contrary to all laws human and divine, caused torrents of blood to flow throughout the whole of France.

(Doppet, 169.)

On August 25, 1793, we entered Marseille without firing a shot. One section (I believe it was No. 11) had attacked the federalist sections, and already on the evening of the 24th most of Marseille had pronounced in our favor. This came ... from the leaders ... having fled to Toulon.

(Letter of Fréron to Moïse Bayle, Marseille, 5th Pluviôse, Year II.)

The military commission which we have established in the place of the revolutionary tribunal proceeds with tremendous speed against the conspirators. Fourteen of these have already paid for their infamous treason; their heads fall like hail beneath the glaive of the law. Sixteen more are to be guillotined tomorrow; almost all of these are army chiefs, notaries, section leaders, members of the popular tribunal, or soldiers of the departmental army. The military commission will do more in one week than the tribunal has done in four months. Three wholesale merchants will also dance the Carmagnole tomorrow; it is they we are interested in. . .

FRÉRON

TOULON SURRENDERS TO THE ENGLISH. (Letter of Barras to the Committee of Public Safety, Marseille, September 6, 1793.)

... Toulon is in the power of the English. The scoundrel Trogoff and a man who calls himself Barras, an artillery commander, should be ranged among the traitors who have delivered this city to the enemy. At the present moment, Carteaux's division is making an attack in the defiles of Ollioules; the division on the left, commanded by Lapoype, is occupying Souliers as far as Hunes, completely cutting off this rebel city from the interior. The English and Spanish appear to have landed three thousand men in Toulon; these, together with the remnants of the Marseille brigands, have occupied the various points of defense that the place offers. . . .

BONAPARTE AT TOULON. (Doppet, 206–207.)

I had brought with me from the army of the Alps a general of artillery, an excellent and experienced officer named Duteil. Together we inspected the batteries established before my arrival, and to my satisfaction and astonishment this ancient artilleryman applauded all the measures taken by the young Bonaparte, then lieutenant-colonel in the artillery. I take pleasure in saying that this young officer, since become the hero of Italy, had not only a great deal of talent, but a rare intrepidity and the most indefatigable activity. Whenever I made an inspection in this army, either before my voyage to Lyon or afterwards, I always found him at his post. If he had need of a moment of repose, he took it upon the ground wrapped in his cloak; he never left the batteries.

(*Barras, I, 131.*)

The capture of General O'Hara, attributed to Bonaparte, the English vessel he was to have sunk, the plan of campaign in which he was to have participated, these are merely fabrications of the inventor of many others, repeated by his flatterers from the day he had the money to reward them. Bonaparte gave some proof of the military talents that were beginning to develop in him; but only as a subordinate. I repeat that the man who took Toulon was Dugommier. . . .

As to Bonaparte, after the siege of Toulon he was named general of brigade with orders to join the army of Italy under General Dumerbion. It was there, as a protégé of Arena, that he formed connections with the younger Robespierre, Ricord, and his wife. These have since become his protectors.

(*Account dictated by Napoleon at St. Helena, Las Cases, I, 76–77; Thiers, II, 323.*)

The commandant of artillery [Napoleon], who, for the space of a month, had been carefully reconnoitering the ground, proposed the plan of attack which occasioned the reduction of Toulon. He declared that it was not necessary to march against the place, but only to occupy a certain position which was to be found at the extreme point of the promontory of Balaguier and l'Éguillette. If the general-in-chief would occupy this position with three battalions, he would take Toulon in four days. In conformity with this proposal, the French raised five or six batteries against the position, which was called "Little Gibraltar," and constructed platforms for fifteen mortars. A battery had also been raised of eight twenty-four pounders, and four mortars against Fort Malbosquet. The enemy were every day receiving reinforcements; and the public watched with anxiety the progress of the siege. They could not conceive why every effort should be directed against Little Gibraltar, quite in an opposite direction to the town. All the popular societies made denunciation after denunciation on this subject . . . the fort was taken. As soon as they were masters of the position, the French turned the cannon against the enemy, and at daybreak marched on Balaguier and l'Éguillette; but the enemy had already evacuated those positions, which Lord Hood was no sooner informed of than he made signal to weigh anchor and get out of the roads.

(*Barras, I, 116.*)

Bonaparte showed me some copies of a pamphlet he had just written and printed at Avignon, asking permission to distribute them among the officers and even the soldiers of the republican army. Loaded with an enormous pack, he said to each while giving them out: "One can see whether I am a patriot! Can a person be revolutionary enough? Marat and Robespierre, those are my saints!" He did not exaggerate in making this profession of faith; it is quite impossible to imagine anything more ultra-Montagnard than the principles set forth in this infernal pamphlet, which is today in the hands of historians.

THE TERROR AT TOULON. (*Letters of Fréron to Moïse Bayle, his colleague.*)

Toulon, 6th Nivôse, Year II of the Republic.

All goes well here: we have requisitioned twelve thousand masons from the neighboring departments to demolish and raze the city. Since we made our entrance, we have caused two hundred heads a day to fall.

FRÉRON

Toulon, 16th Nivôse.

Eight hundred Toulonnais have been shot already.

FRÉRON

Toulon, 19th Nivôse.

At Marseille all the grand plans of Albitte and Carteaux have failed. If, upon the entry of the troops, they had shot eight hundred conspirators, as we did here, and had created a military commission to condemn the rest of the scoundrels, we should not be where we are now.

FRÉRON

THE VENDÉENS CRUSHED. (*Mme. de La Rochejaquelein, 211–212.*)

On the 17th, in the morning, MM. d'Elbée, de Bonchamps, de La Roche-jaquelein, de Royrand, my father, and all the other chiefs marched upon Cholet, at the head of forty thousand men. The republicans had made their junction with the divisions of Bressuire and were forty-five thousand strong. It was upon the ground before Cholet, on the side of Beaupréau, that the armies met. MM. de La Rochejaquelein and Stofflet led on a furious attack. For the first time the Vendéens marched in close columns, like troops of the line. They broke in upon the center of the enemy, and penetrated as far as the faubourgs of Cholet. General Beaupuy, who commanded the republicans, was twice thrown from his horse in endeavoring to rally his soldiers, and was nearly taken. Disorder was spreading among the Blues, when a reserve of Mayençais arrived. The Vendéens supported the first shock, and repulsed them, but by repeated attacks they were at last thrown into disorder. All our chiefs performed prodigies of valor to recover the day, and succeeded in rally-ing some soldiers, who fought with such fury as made the victory very dearly purchased. MM. d'Elbée and Bonchamps were mortally wounded; the rout became general, although protected in their flight by the arrival of M. de Piron, with a great part of M. de Lyrot's division, which allowed them to carry off their wounded. The republicans had also suffered too much to think of pursuing. They returned to Cholet, set fire to the town, and abandoned themselves during the night to all their accustomed atrocities.

(*Letter of Jullien to Robespierre, Vannes, October 22, 1793.*)

The Vendée is destroyed, the rebels dispersed, and the leaders either killed in battle or dead by suicide. There are a few priests left in the countryside; but we have the republicans on their heels, and fanaticism will repent of federalism.

I am sending you the official report of my operations at Quimper. Tell me if the committee of public safety is satisfied . . .

THE TERROR AT NANTES. (*Letter of Jullien to Robespierre, Tours, 16th Pluviôse, Year II.*)

. . . Justice should be rendered Carrier, since, during a definite period of time, he has crushed monopolies and loudly denounced whatever tendencies there are toward mercantilism, federalism, and aristocracy. But, in addition to this, he has used the Terror against the patriots themselves. He is apparently trying to make them fear him. He has a very bad set of associates, having rewarded with offices the knavery of sycophants. He has rebuffed the republicans, rejected their advice, and repressed their outbursts of patriotism. He adjourned for three days, in an arbitrary fashion, the sessions of a Montagnard society. He has had an insolent secretary receive the deputations of the Popular Society. Those who complained of this intermediary between the representative of the people and the people's club, and those who in an outburst of republican frankness demanded the expulsion of Carrier from the society if he refused to fraternize with them, were arrested at night, brought before him, maltreated, struck, and menaced with death. I have witnessed these occurrences in person. There are other acts for which he is reproached; he is accused of having indiscriminately seized upon the people in the prisons of Nantes, placed them in boats, and drowned them in the Loire. . . .

(*Meillan, 96–97.*)

. . . prisoners from the Vendée, and citizens reputed to be their partisans, were shot by the thousands at Nantes. Representative Carrier wrote derisively that he acted from "humane principles" and advised his colleague Francastel to adopt this "quick and salutary method." This is how they played with the lives of unfortunate people condemned by the barbarity of tyrants.

They finally carried their ferocity to the point of shooting or drowning women, and even children, all without motive or pretext, solely to gratify the frightful whims of monsters organized into revolutionary committees by the commissaries of the Convention.

JAVOGUES ON THE LOIRE. (*Administrators of the Department of the Loire to the Convention, Feurs, 7th Messidor, Year III.*)

. . . this monster [Javogues], in imitating Carrier, reddened the sources of the Loire with blood, while his colleague stopped its mouth with corpses. The days of his mission to the department have been marked by the completest immorality, enormous spoliation, and the most horrible cruelty. It would take too long and be too disgusting to retrace here the scenes of infamy and horror of which we are the witnesses and victims. Our three districts are filled with citizens asking for their fathers, brothers, sons, or spouses who have been slaughtered by the tribunal that Carrier calls his, and which seconds to perfection his covetous projects and his love of blood. . . .

(*Letter of Javogues to Dubois de Crancé and Gauthier, September 30, 1793.*)

... I wish to announce to you that many of the *Muscadin* élite have been killed, among others the former Marquis de Vichy, rich to the extent of three hundred thousand crowns income. We have fourteen fashionable *Muscadins* as prisoners. The butchery has been good. We have captured the lieutenant-general of cavalry called Bureau. Please send us the things we ask for, and we will guarantee to give the *Muscadins* a good drubbing. The bridge is cut in such a manner that our troops can enter whenever we like; we have had all the houses burned at the entrance of Saulée de Perrache. I would have written to you sooner, but when one has been fourteen hours in the saddle, one is tired out.

THE TERROR AT ARRAS. (*Horrors of the Prisons of Arras, 289.*)

In the meantime, these daily executions began to weary even that portion of the people who were in the pay of the tyrants, and the effusion of blood began to lose its attractions for them. The theater of his assassinations became deserted, notwithstanding all the efforts of the infamous Lebon to attract a crowd thither — nay, even to constrain them to be present.

Base and hardened as he was, he could not disguise from his own thoughts that the continuation of his atrocities might sooner or later excite a general revolt, of which he would infallibly be the first victim.

In order to avoid the threatening storm, he went to establish a new tribunal at Cambrai; he caused a permanent guillotine to be established there.

DUMONT'S CONCEPTION OF THE TERROR. (*Letter of Dumont to his colleagues, October, 22, 1793.*)

I send you the brother-in-law of George, and the relative of Pitt. Citizens Petit and Gribeauval will file with the office the hidden treasures that I have discovered; they consist of 88,873 livres in gold and silver, 37,070 livres in assignats, 106 dinner sets, 18 teaspoons, 14 gravy ladles, 8 chandeliers, a gold snuff-box, 4 coffee-pots, two knives, a chalice with the paten, a gold-embroidered flag seized at the home of an *émigré*, and other effects equally valuable. ...

I have just brought about the arrest of some priests who took it upon themselves to celebrate holy days and Sunday; I am taking away the crucifixes and crosses, and soon I shall include in the proscription these black animals called priests. Yesterday, the 10th, I dissolved the Popular Society, and named a secret committee to purify the list: this enactment was roundly applauded. I have likewise had it decreed that all drunkards and promoters of drunkenness be put into the lock-up. This will keep idleness and drunkenness from perverting the public welfare, and from depriving the defenders of the country of the brandy and beverages which are of the first necessity.

I am leaving for Beauvais, which I will put on a diet before giving it its medicine. The departments within my territory are going to rise in emulation of one another, and soon the hard-driven aristocrats will no longer know where to hide. The Republic or death.

DECREE FOR THE DESTRUCTION OF LYON.

ARTICLE I. Upon the recommendation of the committee of public safety, the National Convention shall appoint an extraordinary commission of five members for the immediate punishment of the counter-revolutionists of Lyon by military methods.

II. All inhabitants of Lyon shall be disarmed and their weapons immediately distributed to the defenders of the Republic.

III. A portion of these shall be returned to such patriots of Lyon as have been oppressed by the rich and counter-revolutionary.

IV. The city of Lyon shall be destroyed; all dwellings of the rich shall be razed. Nothing shall be left except the houses of the poor, the dwellings of murdered or proscribed patriots, buildings specially devoted to industry, and monuments consecrated to humanity and public enlightenment.

V. The name of Lyon shall be erased from the list of cities of the Republic, and the group of houses remaining shall henceforth be called *Ville Affranchie.*

VI. A column shall be erected upon the ruins of Lyon to acquaint posterity with the crimes and punishment of the royalists of that city. It shall bear the inscription "Lyon made war upon liberty, and has perished. The 18th day of the 1st month of the Year II of the French Republic, one and indivisible."

VII. The people's representatives shall at once name commissaries for the listing of property belonging to the rich and counter-revolutionary of Lyon, so that the National Convention may immediately enact laws for the execution of the decree of July 12, which gives this property over to the indemnification of patriots.

LYON TAKEN. (Doppet, 199.)

I entered Lyon on the morning of the 9th October. I . . . took measures to secure persons and property, had arms and munitions collected, and immediately set about sending aid to the army before Toulon, which needed help. At the same time, I had to arrange to return to the strongholds of the army of the Alps the pieces of ordnance that had been brought to the siege of Lyon.

(Letter of Collot-d'Herbois to Duplay, Commune Affranchie, 15th Frimaire, Year II.)

. . . We have not revived public spirit here; it does not exist. But we have inspired courage and resolution in a few energetic men, and in numbers of patriots who have been too long oppressed. We have cured them of the luke-warmness caused by false principles and ideas of moderation. These ideas might, in truth, be suitable for conspirators, but they would be fatal to the Republic. We have revived republican justice, that is to say, justice as prompt and terrible as the will of the people. It should strike traitors like flashes of lightning and leave nothing but ashes. The destruction of one infamous and rebellious city will hold the others firm. The death of scoundrels will assure life and freedom to future generations. These are our principles. Whenever possible we are demolishing by cannon fire and the explosions of mines. You can well understand, however, how many hindrances there are to these measures in the midst of a population of a hundred thousand people. Although the ax of the people removes the heads of twenty conspirators a day, they still are not terrorized. Précy still lives, and his influence becomes greater day by day. The prisons are bursting with his accomplices. We have created a commission which judges traitors as promptly as would a true republican conscience. Sixty-four conspirators were shot yesterday at the very place they fired upon patriots. Two hundred and thirty will fall today in the execrable redoubts that belched forth death upon the republican army. Such examples will influence the cities that waver....

(*Guillon, II, 414–416.*)

On December 4, as a matter of fact, sixty young men were led in fetters from the prison of Rouane to appear before the fierce revolutionary commission. They had been condemned in advance by order of the temporary commission. They were conducted next to Brotteaux, which for some time past had been the place of execution for the Lyonnais condemned to be shot. They were arranged two by two, tied in files, and placed upon an embankment about three feet wide ... Behind them were two cannons filled with small shot ... they uttered not a single imprecation. As if inspired by a common motive, they began in concert, with a sort of satisfaction, to express their perseverance in the same generous devotion to their country that they had shown during the siege. They resang a song that had inspired them in the midst of battle, and whose refrain was as follows:

"Mourir pour sa patrie
Est le sort le plus doux
Le plus digne d'envie."

While they were singing these lines the cannons were discharged....

JACOBIN SUCCESSES. (*Révolutions de Paris, No. 212.*)

Lyon is no more; Marseille and Bordeaux have returned to the bosom of the Republic. There is no longer a Vendée. Valenciennes and Toulon will soon have their turn. Federalism is dying; morals are improving; fortunes are levelled; equality is no longer a vain word; luxury gives way to labor. Punishment does not give crime time to breathe except in making confessions. Public enlightenment is being constructed from the débris of pedantry. Civic spirit is improving and spreads through all ranks of citizens. The theaters have become schools of patriotism, and mendacious schoolmen have no following. Intelligent interest will bring prosperity. Courage, worthy legislators! Courage and perseverance! Union and perseverance, good *sans-culottes*, for if the Revolution has been made by you, it has also been made for you, it will be you who will gather the first fruits. The daily occurring and signal acts of justice which you see before your eyes will not have been in vain; the masses are being purified and made to assume the imposing appearance of republicans. Become all the more just, as you become the more free. Moderation has never been expedient, it would have caused you to lose the benefits wrested from despotism and would have led you gradually back to where you were before 1789. Continue to show justice as well as severity and close your mind to the treacherous advice. From time to time it will be breathed into your ears to corrupt you, divide you, and urge you on to excess. The broad bases of the civil structure rest upon you. You are no longer a vile people bent and warped to fit the yoke of arbitrary power. But do not cease to be sensible to the restraints of reason; do not cease to sanctify the Revolution with your virtues. You have founded and sustained it with courageous daring. Let other nations, after fearing you at first, be attracted by the wisdom of your conduct and open their arms to you, asking to share the blessings of liberty that you have won for others as well as for yourself. Let there be eternal war against kings, priests, egotists, compromisers, and federalists; world-wide peace with friends of justice; vengeance upon traitors; succor for the oppressed; and hatred against oppressors of all kinds.

THE ATTACK UPON RELIGION. (*Révolutions de Paris, No. 212.*)

Despotism and superstition have appealed to the imagination in order to control people's consciences and command respect. An expert lawmaker should know how to turn everything to profit. When every sign of feudalism and monarchy has been removed, these will lose, so to speak, their corporeal existence and cease to control the senses of people enslaved by custom. Moreover, people who have risen to the level of a republic ought to look only upon things that are uplifting to the soul and which call to mind the sublime principles of equality. That the houses should be purged of all the foolish emblems of servitude and superstition will not seem trivial to those who know the human heart.

The same is true of the new calendar which has been adopted. It has been based upon political considerations as well as upon astronomy. We must (if we may use the expression) do some housecleaning in the temple of prejudices. Prejudices are like parasitic plants that ruin our gardens and which must be annihilated to the last fragment unless one wishes to see them reappear in greater profusion than before.

THE REVOLUTIONARY CALENDAR.

ARTICLE I. The era of the French dates from the foundation of the Republic, which occurred on September 22, 1792, of the common era, the day on which the sun arrived at the true autumnal equinox in entering the Sign of Libra at eighteen minutes and thirty seconds past nine o'clock at the Paris Observatory.

II. The common era is abolished in civil usage.

III. Each year begins at midnight of the day on which the true autumnal equinox falls at the Paris Observatory.

IV. The first year of the French Republic began at midnight, September 22, 1792, and ended at midnight, between the 21st and 22nd of September, 1793.

V. The second year began September 22, 1793, at midnight, the true autumnal equinox having arrived on that day at the Paris Observatory at eleven minutes and thirty-eight seconds after three o'clock in the afternoon.

VI. The decree that fixed the beginning of the second year at January 1, 1793, is revoked; all laws dated *Year II of the Republic*, passed between January 1 and September 21, inclusively, shall be regarded as belonging to the first year of the Republic.

VII. The year is divided into twelve equal months of thirty days each. Following the twelfth month are five days which complete the regular year; these five days shall not be included in any month.

VIII. Each month is divided into three equal parts of ten days each, called *décades*.

IX. The names of the days of the *décade* are: *Primidi, Duodi, Tridi, Quartidi, Quintidi, Sextidi, Septidi, Octidi, Nonidi, Décadi*.

The names of the months are: in autumn, *Vendémiaire, Brumaire*, and *Frimaire*; in winter, *Nivôse, Pluviôse*, and *Ventôse*; in spring, *Germinal, Floréal*, and *Prairial*; and in summer, *Messidor, Thermidor*, and *Fructidor*.

The last five days are called *Sans-culottides*.

X. One day more is to be added to the regular year when the position of the equinox requires it, in order to maintain the coincidence between the civil year and celestial movements. This day, called the *Day of the Revolution*, is placed at the end of the year and forms the sixth of the *Sans-culottides*.

THE WORSHIP OF REASON. (Durand de Maillane, 181–182.)

The changing of the calendar was the prelude to the abolition of Christianity. The commune proposed this impious act to the Convention, and the Convention, becoming a party to it, decreed the replacement of the Catholic cult by the cult of Reason. This deplorable scandal, addresses in honor of atheism, and indecent abjurations, for the most part forced, figured in the official report sent to the authorities and to the armies. The poet Chénier composed a hymn in which, as a faithful disciple of Voltaire, he made open warfare upon the religion of Jesus Christ.

The Convention decreed the singing of Chénier's hymn in the metropolitan church, acclaiming the new Goddess of Reason. The rest of this hymn may be judged by the first strophe:

> "Descends, ô Liberté! fille de la nature.
> Le peuple a reconquis son pouvoir immortel
> Sur les pompeux débris de l'antique imposture;
> Ses mains relèvent ton autel."

I failed to witness the more than scandalous scenes in the Church of Notre Dame, where an actress of the opera was worshipped as a divinity, and I must say that most of the members of the Convention refused to be present at this. A large number even stopped attending the Assembly after the Bishop of Paris was brought to the bar to declare that he was an impostor, that he had never been anything else, and that the people were rejecting Christianity. His example was followed by priests and Protestant ministers in the Convention, who mounted the tribune to abdicate their religious offices. Some of the deputies became so disgusted and indignant that they ceased to appear in this dishonored Convention. The Montagnards perceived their absence, however,

and forced them to return. They were compelled to listen daily to the most
scandalous addresses, and to the recital of profanations committed by the
imitators of the commune in the departments.

CEREMONY FOR THE JACOBIN MAYOR EXECUTED AT LYON. (*Guillon, II, 347–348.*)

The infamous procession, preceded by warlike music, filed through the city
and finally came to a halt at the Place des Terreaux before an altar of turf
that had been prepared. The image and urn of Chalier were respectfully deposited; the audience knelt around about them in a circle; and the three representatives came forward one after another to kneel before the fetish and address
to it in loud tones their individual invocations. Collot-d'Herbois said to it,
"*Dieu Sauveur*, see the nation prostrate at your feet, demanding pardon for
the impious crime which ended the life of the most virtuous of men. Shade of
Chalier, you shall be revenged; we swear it by the Republic!" Fouché was
more fervent. "Chalier," cried he, "thou art no longer! (Loud sigh.) Martyr
of liberty, the scoundrels have immolated you! (Another prolonged sigh.)
The blood of scoundrels is the only ablution that can appease your justly
angered shade. Chalier! Chalier! we swear before your sacred image to
avenge your martyrdom. Yes, the blood of aristocrats shall become your
incense!"

The inept and recondite Laporte could think of nothing to say. He contented himself with humbly kissing the forehead of the statue and crying out
matter-of-factly, "Death to the aristocrats!"

After these three orisons a brazier was lighted; the audience ceremoniously
surrounded it; and the Gospel and crucifix were detached from the donkey's
tail and thrown into the flames. The donkey was then given something to
drink from the chalice, what, I do not know; and the wafers of the Host, which
were said to have been consecrated, were trampled under foot. Other profanations no less horrible were about to be committed, when a sudden storm
burst forth from heaven and brought such a flood of rain upon this horde of
demons that it interrupted their sacrilegious crimes and forced them to disperse.

PROTESTS OF A DEPUTY. (*Sergent Marceau, 301.*)

My opinion of the Catholic religion is that of a free and independent thinker,
but I was the first, the only deputy who objected to letters being read from
priests announcing that they repudiated the functions which they had falsely
professed to hold sacred. ... I protested against the disgusting scenes repeated
at the bar of the Convention when the spoils of the churches were brought in,
and I demanded the arrest of the *curé* Parens, when he drank off the wine with
which he had filled a chalice. I said that he was turning the senate into a
tavern. I also raised my voice against the ridiculous mania of listening for
hours together to the songs of deputations, converting the Convention into a
vaudeville theater.

XXV. *Strife Between the Terrorists*

ROBESPIERRE AND THE FACTIONS. (*Williams, 76.*)

ROBESPIERRE now thought that it was necessary to his safety to be disencumbered of the faction of the commune and the faction of Danton. It was not difficult to bring a thousand charges against them, of which one would have been sufficient to have directed the sword of national vengeance. But as the accusers could proffer none of those charges without incriminating themselves, they had recourse to the expedient of their being accomplices of the faction of foreigners, which was a most inexhaustible source for the fabrication of all indictments and bills for conspiracies.

When the committee of public safety had marked their victims, it was necessary to inform the Convention that they were going to prepare the sacrifice; not that they feared any opposition or remonstrance, but for the sake of regularity. The Convention was therefore instructed by Saint-Just that a conspiracy framed by foreigners was about to commit a number of horrible things — starve, plunder, and murder the good people of the Republic; that this faction had already overthrown religion and morality, and was about to form "a new sect of immorality and the love of sensual enjoyments from which innocence and virtue had everything to dread"; that the great directors of these machinations of the English court were foreigners then at Paris, who had corrupted the agents of government, and that it was necessary they should all be punished together.

The Convention was seized with horror at hearing these things and, with the same unanimity with which they applauded Carrier's revolutionary wit, decreed, as their committee ordered, that whoever by any act whatever should attempt to degrade, destroy, or put obstacles in the way of the National Convention should be punished with death.

ENMITY BETWEEN HÉBERT AND DANTON. (*Police Report, Schmidt, II, 143–144.*)

People say that peace and union are not yet established between our brother Jacobins and Cordeliers. Hébert is said to have declared that either he or the minister of the interior [Danton] shall perish, and that the Cordeliers Club will not stop until it has overthrown the ministers, other than Bouchotte, to make room for men of their own choice. . . .

The general assembly of the French Panthéon section is always filled with unknown people, concerning whose real patriotism true republicans are doubtful. Motions follow one another with such rapidity that they nullify whatever good they might do. It is believed that these individuals are paid to hinder the work of the Republic. The sections are beginning to show party feeling; one is for Hébert, the next is for Danton, this one for the Cordeliers, that one for the Jacobins. In short, there is danger that this division in sentiment may lead to civil war. . . .

Père Duchesne [Hébert] has covered the walls with placards in reply to reproaches about his being a monopolizer. The public has been reading these placards with attention. Men who appear familiar with the language of Père Duchesne have been emphatic in saying that it is unfortunate he does not wish to be minister. If all the executive council were like Hébert, things would improve. All the ministers, except the minister of war, are Philippotins and must be dealt with. A number of women who listened to all this said it was indeed quite true. Apparently they desired to propagate this opinion, since it has been spread about in several places. . . .

THE PARIS COMMUNE. (*Williams, 69–70.*)

The commune of Paris perceived that the committee of public safety had obtained an absolute power over the Convention, and took measures to provide against it by advertising a system directly opposite to that of the committee, which they judged would be more acceptable to the people and establish their own popularity. They, who had been the contrivers of every insurrection; who had prompted to every murder; who had demanded at the bar of the Convention that terror should be the order of the day, that all priests whatever should be dismissed from all functions, civil and military, that the prisoners of the Temple, the children and sister of the late king, should be sent to common prisons on the grounds of equality, and that all persons who had gone to their country-houses should be ordered, on pain of being suspected, to come into town in order probably to be massacred more conveniently, became at once mild and tender-hearted.

THE ATTACK ON HÉBERT. (*Police Report, Schmidt, II, 149–150.*)

. . . At the Jacobin session they proceeded to the vote on expulsion. This was soon abandoned upon the request of Couthon, who desired that Saint-Just be heard. This speaker read his report in regard to the new conspiracy, which had threads running from London to Paris. The discourse was roundly applauded with cries a thousand times repeated of "Long live the Republic!" Saint-Just informed them of the decree that had followed his report, and applause again broke forth.

The decree establishing six commissions for judging prisoners has been greatly applauded in streets and cafés.

Saint-Just's speech about Chabot has made people believe that the crimes of that deputy are no longer in doubt, and that he was really one of the main authors of the conspiracy that has just been discovered. It is also published about that men believed to be good patriots have been unmasked and will soon be known. No one has been named, however. A discussion broke out about the preachers of insurrection among a group of people in the Jardin National. There were loud words about Hébert and others who deserved to appear upon the Place de la Révolution. Their speedy appearance thereupon was not despaired of. It has been perceptible for some time that the stock of Hébert, Ronsin, and Vincent has fallen greatly in the eyes of the people. . . .

ANALYSIS OF HÉBERT'S "PÈRE DUCHESNE" BY THE REVOLUTIONARY TRIBUNAL.

It is found by the analysis of the numbers of *Père Duchesne* that the author was a declared constitutionalist and royalist. The constitution was, according to him, a beautiful edifice with a façade that was magnificent.

. . . later he perceived that the Convention resembled the Tower of Babel. All at once he became republican. . . .

He announces that there are traitors in the Convention who wish to become tribunes and dictators . . . France is in the hands of two bands of rascals: the *maudlins*, putting forward such words as *people*, *liberty*, and *equality*; and the *Cartouches*, in understanding with Brunswick. . . .

He laments our successes in Savoy, at Lille, and against the Prussians. . . .

He reproaches the Convention for concerning itself with the trial of the king, which is not its business. . . .

He proposes to the people that the two little Capets be done away with at all costs; a child is nothing in comparison with the safety of the Republic.

. . . comparing the people to an infirm dotard dependent upon insolent valets who rob and pillage him, he asserts that this is the case in regard to our representatives, whom he represents as brigands.

. . . as long as the Convention chooses the ministers and holds the purse-strings, the people will always be repressed. They will only have changed masters, and instead of having one king, will have seven or eight hundred.

. . . once we were governed by the masters; now the valets have their feet on our necks.

. . . they want us to be *sans-culottes* in reality. He then makes it understood that everything is going to double in price. . . .

He wants us to deplore our victories Instead of making conquests, we should defend our own soil. It is time that fathers of families returned home to console their spouses.

. . . war must be made upon the monopolizers and the rich. . . . The Convention, instead of taking so much trouble to judge a vile scoundrel, ought to have been establishing primary schools.

. . . our soldiers are forced by decrees to perish of cold and misery . . . the Convention is advancing blindly . . . called to save the country, it seems to be trying to destroy it.

. . . the provincial boobies [in the Convention] are good for nothing . . . this Convention which has destroyed the monarchy and decreed the Republic dares not judge the king in four months. . . .

In four years, three National Assemblies have failed to accomplish anything. The words *nobility* and *royalty* have been destroyed, but nothing else. New tyrants have replaced those who were removed. It is our own fault if we have made a mess of our revolutions. . . .

We should take care not to come to blows with the English. Our troops should be withdrawn to France. . . .

Père Duchesne waited for the recruiting for the Vendée to be effected to warn Paris that sixty thousand scoundrels were preparing to start a conflagration and enthrone the little Capet. . . .

What have three National Assemblies accomplished? Nothing. . . . They want to make the people so miserable that they will demand the old régime. . . .

The Mountain and the committees will usurp all the power. We shall never have any government or we shall have a detestable one. . . .

We resemble a starving man who sniffs the odor of a magnificent repast without being able to touch it. Your constitution is excellent, but it is not for us. There must be an end to all this. Distress is at its height; food is in the hands of the counter-revolutionists and farm monopolizers. . . .

Père Duchesne decides to eulogize the Convention. . . .

He defies Chabot to try to bother him, for he is roughshod. They can sift and resift his past, and find out he is a frank republican. . . .

He ends in complaining about monopolizers, large and small. The law of the *maximum* is not being carried out. If want is prevalent, if vegetables are dear, it is because there are so many farmers and wholesalers at the head of municipalities.

Such, citizens, is the tainted mind of Père Duchesne. You have seen him a royalist and a constitutionalist. You have seen him a precocious republican. The idea must have come to you at once that early fruits do not keep, but easily decay. Superb on one side, they hide their decay from view; such is the history of the author of the journal whose analysis we have presented to you. Until now, he has disguised his tortuous course from the eyes of the vulgar, which is all the more perfidious in that frank and simple people would not believe that one could deceive them in a language that was proclaiming loyalty.

Although Père Duchesne says he is roughshod, you must have remarked that he has fallen and broken his mask. He acted in concert with Jacques Roux, author of *Le Publiciste*. Vacillating between diverse and contradictory opinions, they delivered their readers over to discouragement by maliciously putting them in doubt as to whether they should prefer monarchical government or republican. If Père Duchesne has escaped for a longer time from the surveillance of true republicans, it is because, more adroit than his associated competitor, he was prompter in placing himself to the leeward of public opinion, and because two days after he had insulted and reviled the constituted authorities, he made amends for his abusive language by a small bit of eulogy. Resembling an aristocrat who inveighed against the patriots, and fearing that he had been heard, he hastened to cry out louder than all the rest, "Long live the Republic!"

At last he showed himself openly, contrary to his intentions, no doubt. You have been able to see him stripped bare; you should be persuaded now that his manner of writing followed a plan and a combination that was profoundly atrocious.

In overstraining principles; in exaggerating our misfortunes; in groaning over our successes; in proposing ultra-revolutionary measures; in pitying the wives of our volunteers separated from their husbands; in exhorting our recruits for the Vendée not to depart before crushing the imaginary enemies who are going to burn Paris; in arousing fears concerning the horrors of a famine, whose odium he throws upon your committees, reviling them in more than one manner; in representing the revolutionary tribunals as accessible to corruption; and lastly, in outraging the Convention, what can he hope to accomplish, if not to induce a retrograde movement in the progress of Liberty, which he has represented to us as stained with blood and embracing corpses; to divide the patriots; to open the way to thousands of opinions; to amuse himself afterwards in combatting them all; to establish a state of disquiet among all the citizens; to divert the use of the soldiers' courage; and to produce a general effervescence capable of dissolving the Convention?

Such is the spirit of this journal, too well received, since the unsuspecting people allow themselves to be abused. Not perceiving the snare, they believed everything they did not have time to verify. Provided a cause, real or supposititious, is shown to them, they are satisfied, and do not fail to applaud the author. That, citizens, is the source of the inefficacy of the measures of public safety which you have taken after having weighed them in the light of your wisdom.

After the information which you have just received, is it not surprising that this paper was distributed with such profusion among our armies?

Judge and pronounce.

HÉBERT ARRESTED.

In the Name of the Law.
Warrant of arrest.

Antoine Quentin Fouquier, public prosecutor of the revolutionary tribunal established at Paris by the decree of the National Convention of the 10th of March, 1793, Year II of the Republic, with no recourse to the tribunal of cassation, in virtue of the power given him by article two of another decree of the Convention on the 5th of April following, authorizing the public prosecutor of the said tribunal to arrest, prosecute, and pass judgment following accusation by the constituted authorities or by citizens; instructs and orders all executioners of judicial mandates to condemn to the prison of the Conciergerie, Citizen Hébert, residing Rue des Miracles, Section de Bonnes-Nouvelles, No. 1, accused of complicity with others in having promoted the annihilation of the national representation and having conspired against the liberty of the French people.

The guardian of the said prison is ordered to receive him in the manner prescribed by law; and all guardians of public authority who shall be notified of the present warrant are required to aid in its execution should the necessity arise.

Done and delivered at Paris, the 23rd Ventôse, Year II of the French Republic, one and indivisible.

A.-Q. FOUQUIER

(*Police Report, Schmidt, II, 151.*)

The arrest of Hébert, Ronsin, Vincent, and Momoro has become the subject of all conversation in the streets and cafés. The measure has met with universal approval but, as the conspiracy has not become public, they have merely been called intriguers.

The special session of the Jacobins, demanded by Robespierre, was opened by Billaud-Varenne, who made a forceful speech concerning the conspiracy so fortunately discovered. Hébert, Ronsin, Momoro, and Vincent were only subordinate agents in a vast network of treason conceived by Pitt and our coalesced enemies; corruption was employed at first, ambition had done the rest. First a false patrol was to go to the Abbaye, massacre the guard, and liberate all the prisoners. After having armed these, they were to go to all the prisons and lock-ups; here were victims already designated. The rest were to go to the Convention and the Jacobin Club, where they would slaughter all the members. This accomplished, they would pillage the national treasury, distribute the money to the conspirators and the people, and proclaim a regent.

The orator was several times interrupted by wild applause. "Let us swear," said Billaud-Varenne, in conclusion, "that there will be no mercy to conspirators!" Everyone took this solemn oath....

THE CRIMES OF PÈRE DUCHESNE. (*Débats dans l'affaire d'Hébert, de Ronsin, et autres.*)

No. 10. — The woman Dubois, printer.

In January, 1790, Hébert, in distress, came to ask succor of a friend, who received him. He disappeared after having carried off mattresses, shirts, collars, etc. He took them all to the pawnshop. Encountered again by the man he had robbed, he excused himself on the plea of necessity, and handed over the pawnshop tickets.

Hébert denied the mattresses, but admitted having disposed of his friend's shirts on quitting his lodgings.

No. 18. — Brochet, juror at the revolutionary tribunal.

Momoro, Vincent, and Hébert practiced a harsh despotism at the Cordeliers. Those who did not support their opinions were treated as knaves and scoundrels.

Momoro, as president, allowed those of his opinion to speak, and refused it to those who were opposed.

Manoeuvers of Momoro to suppress the drawing up of the minutes and the reading of them in the presence of the deputation of Jacobins.

As archivist of the Cordeliers Society, he had a register which Momoro took from him by subterfuges.

Ronsin proposed the insurrection. Hébert spoke for and against it, and twice demanded the adjournment of the proposition to lift the veil placed over the rights of man.

Ducroquet, author of the motion to veil the declaration of rights and to go *en masse* to the commune to declare that the section had risen.

Great fermentation engendered in their minds, Momoro as president favoring all that tended to insurrection.

The public safety sheet has rendered an account of the sittings.

At the same time, the same motions were made at Nancy and at Commune Affranchie.

No. 24. — Piquet, clothing administrator.

Heard talk of placards provoking the revolt against the Convention.

No. 28. — Jean-Louis Coutin.

On the 12th Ventôse, heard in a crowd some talk of insurrection. Fortin told him it was the 31st of May, not to leave, that they counted upon him, that he could, moreover, be useful everywhere, and that on the 14th he would hear cannon and could arrive on time.

(Comité de surveillance révolutionnaire.)

We, members of the revolutionary committee, attest and certify that, at the time of our visit to citizens who had provisions of salt-pork, we found at the home of Citizen Hébert, editor of the journal entitled *Père Duchesne*, only a quantity of salt-pork weighing twenty-four pounds, he saying that it was his intention to give the product to the poor, in witness of which we have subscribed our names.

Done in the committee, the 18th Ventôse of the Year II of the Republic.

ROUSSEL, President

LAFOLLIE, DUDOUCET, etc.

DEATH OF THE HÉBERTISTS. (Riouffe, 64–70.)

If some of us were strongly drawn to religious ideas, others were fanatically irreligious. All these instruments of Robespierre's villainy, and many were broken at his pleasure, died while vaunting their irreverence and atheism. Thus died the Grammonts, father and son, the Momoros, the Vincents, the Héberts, the Lebourgeois, and the Ronsins, ill-omened members of a party that was forced, terrible as it was, to disavow their greater madness and almost blush for it. . . .

If I say that Hébert was a coward, and called for death when he feared it himself, who will be astonished? This scandalous producer of slimy newspapers, this theater-door robber, this miserable sedition-monger, still base as a magistrate, died like the weakest of women. He fainted a number of times, and was ashamed and humiliated. The judicial inquiry had brought out his early ignominy; it was all about shirts and purloined goods. That was the kind of magistrate chosen by Paris at this epoch. Nevertheless, he died for imaginary crimes, he who had committed so many real ones. Such a tribunal makes all men innocent, even Héberts. The conspiracy built around him was as unreal as all the others imagined by the committee of public safety. When the crime is connected with government, they do not dare to punish it under its real name; and it is by the proceedings of tribunals that one can prove there is tyranny.

DANTON AND ROBESPIERRE RIVALS. (Sergent Marceau, 308.)

This presentiment [that other victims of Robespierre's jealousy would soon follow Hébert] came true, for Danton, the colossus who supported like Atlas the Revolution on his shoulders, who by his energy and eloquence had taken the place of the celebrated Mirabeau, and had been falsely accused of corruption and of greed, became the hated rival of Robespierre.

A short time before his arrest, he said to Robespierre, at a supper given by Panis for the purpose of reconciling them, "Has the revolutionary tribunal been suppressed, that fatal tribunal of blood? Are the scaffolds to be left standing much longer? What do *you* wish, Robespierre?" The latter answered him contemptuously, "Do you think the time has come for removing them?" The act of accusation drawn up by Amar calls him the "Chief of the Indulgents," and this man, who at an earlier epoch was accused of ordering the massacres of September, was now brought before the tribunal as an Indulgent.

(Meillan, 105–106.)

As to those of their accomplices such as Danton, Hérault de Séchelles, and a number of others who were eventually put to death by the usurpers, it was lust for power that dictated their sentence.

Robespierre had always feared Danton, who was, as a matter of fact, the only rival who angered and annoyed him. Over a long period of time there had been regular attempts to bring him under suspicion, and people were prepared for formal accusations. As early as October, 1793, the confederates of Robespierre were loudly maintaining at Bordeaux, where I then was, that Danton would soon be arrested. They seemed to have quietly worked at undermining his popularity, the sole prop and mainstay of a demagogue. His rival, with the ability or luck to preserve his own popularity, seized upon the moment when Danton was defenseless to get rid of him.

DANTON ASKS FOR ROBESPIERRE'S CO-OPERATION. (Barras, I, 155.)

The dictator was making his toilette according to the forms of the old régime and took a great deal of time. Danton, beginning the conversation as soon as he entered, said without preamble: "Let us come to an understanding and work for the safeguarding of liberty; it is attacked by sinister enemies. They vilify and deceive the people, who think they are their friends."

Robespierre, who thee'd and thou'd no one, replied to Danton: "What is it you are trying to say? Are you hinting at something? You can give my speeches any interpretation you like. Perhaps your own mission in Belgium is not beyond criticism. You were badly seconded and badly advised. Lacroix brought odium upon that mission."

Danton then took a very high tone and said to him: "Thou speakest here as do the aristocrats. They are trying to dishonor the Convention and the men who are in it. I will never suffer them to be attacked; the Revolution must not be defamed in slandering those who made it." The voice of Danton weakened. Robespierre, continuing to dress throughout, looked at him with pity.

Then Danton, aroused, set forth the dangers that were menacing liberty: "It will perish if its defenders are attacked and the Terror used against them, instead of against those who conspire, as was its purpose. Before six months, thou too wilt be attacked, Robespierre, if we divide our forces."

The conversation ended with affected politeness. Danton and Laignelot withdrew. They were still in the street talking of this sinister interview when Robespierre passed by them and feigned not to see them.

DESMOULINS ASKS FOR CLEMENCY. (*Miot de Mélito, I, 54–55.*)

Gloomy and silent, his countenance wore an expression of profound melancholy, and it was difficult to recognize the orator of the early days of the Revolution of 1789, the orator who, standing on a chair at the Palais-Royal, had by his stirring speech produced the great popular movement of that famous period. At the time when I was in the habit of seeing him, he was horror-struck at the terrible scenes which passed before his eyes every day, and was endeavoring to arouse a spirit of humanity. In several numbers of a newspaper entitled *Le Vieux Cordelier*, which was edited by him, he ventured (for it was then an act of the greatest courage) to advocate a return to clemency. Danton laughed at him for what he chose to call his weakness, but Camille Desmoulins, who was also excluded by each so-called patriotic society for having advocated these new doctrines, made no reply. His gloom announced that he already saw the fate awaiting him, and the few words that he uttered were always inquiries or observations on the sentences of the revolutionary tribunal, on the kind of death inflicted on the condemned, and on the most dignified and decorous way of preparing for and enduring it.

(*Sergent Marceau, 310.*)

Danton joined Camille Desmoulins in producing *Le Vieux Cordelier*, in which they attacked, with all the wit and power of which Camille was master, the law of suspects. Nothing equal to it had appeared during the whole time of the Revolution. Lastly, the shameful act of accusation drawn up by the ex-ennobled, ex-secretary of the king, Amar, designated Danton as the chief of the Indulgents. If this Danton were such a monster, would he have perished because he wished to abolish the dreadful system of the Terror?

DANTON'S CONTEMPT FOR ROBESPIERRE. (*Thibaudeau, I, 59–60.*)

Danton . . . was always unconstrained and often amiable. His face, so ferocious while he was on the rostrum, was elsewhere calm and even laughing. His principles were incendiary and his speeches violent even to fury; but in private life he was accommodating, loose, and cynical. He was fond of pleasure and contemptuous of life. He possessed feeling and eloquence; he was completely fitted to be a tribune of the people. He was the Mirabeau of the period.

Like most of the Assembly, I was exposed to the thunderbolts, but had no part in throwing them. Thus it mattered little to me whether they were in the hands of Danton or of Robespierre. These combats meant nothing to me except a change in tyrants, with no end to tyranny.

However, if I had had to make a choice, I should have chosen Danton. When he was being threatened, I was further drawn to him by the inclination I have always had for the feeble and oppressed. I noticed he was no longer assiduous at meetings and spoke a great deal less. One would have said that he was becoming extremely indifferent, gradually detaching himself from politics, as an invalid gives up the world before approaching death. I said to him one day: "Your indifference astonishes me; I do not understand your apathy. Can you not see that Robespierre is plotting your downfall? Will you do nothing to forestall him?"

"If I thought," he replied, with a movement of the lips which with him expressed anger and disdain, "he had the slightest idea in that direction, I would tear out his vitals."

Five or six days later, this terrible man allowed himself to be arrested like a child and slaughtered like a sheep. With him perished Hérault de Séchelles, who, in spite of his devotion to the Revolution, had not been forgiven his noble birth, handsome face, and nobly gracious manners. The wife of Camille Desmoulins, resplendent in youth and beauty, was accused of having plotted to save her husband, and followed them to the scaffold.

INDICTMENT OF THE DANTONISTS. (Decree of the National Convention of the eleventh day of Germinal, Year II of the French Republic, one and indivisible, bringing indictment against Camille Desmoulins, Hérault, Danton, Philippeaux, and Lacroix.)

The National Convention, after hearing the report of its committees of general security and public safety, brings indictment against Camille Desmoulins, Hérault, Danton, Philippeaux, and Lacroix, accused of complicity with D'Orléans, Dumouriez, Fabre d'Églantine, and the enemies of the Republic, and with having participated in the conspiracy to re-establish the monarchy by destroying the national legislature and republican government; consequently their arraignment is ordered, together with that of Fabre d'Églantine.

Countersigned by the inspector,

AUGIER

(Coittant, 83.)

The accused exhibited great firmness before the revolutionary tribunal, and defended themselves in a very vigorous manner. A citizen who witnessed the pleading told us that Danton had made judges and jurors tremble, drowning out with his voice the sound of the presiding judge's bell. The latter said to him, "Do you not hear the bell?"

"Mr. Chairman," replied Danton, "the voice of a man who is defending his life and honor ought to ring louder than your bell." In the midst of the pleadings, the people began to murmur. Danton cried out: "When I have said everything I have to say, then you can judge me. My voice should be heard by you and by all France."

DEATH OF THE FACTIONISTS. (Riouffe, 69.)

Fabre d'Églantine, weak and ill, was only concerned about a comedy in five acts which he had left in the hands of the committee of public safety, and which he was afraid Billaud-Varenne would steal.

Clootz, orator of the human race and personal enemy of Jesus Christ, died as he had lived, although with a courage that I should never have thought he possessed. He was with the Hébert group. These wretches were accusing one another of having brought about their deaths. Clootz spoke forth, and in a loud voice recited to the very end these well-known lines:

> "Je revais cette nuit que de mal consumé,
> Côte à côte d'un gueux on m'avait inhumé;
> Est que blessé pour moi d'un pareil voisinage,
> En mort de qualité je lui tins ce language."

The apologue had its effect, they became friends once more, and Clootz, who was dying with fear that someone might believe in God, again took the lead and preached materialism up to the last breath.

(Arnault, II, 96–97.)

In the conviction that, in working for the Revolution, he had worked for a good cause, Camille still clung to his illusion; he believed he was undergoing martyrdom. In allusion to his late writings, he cried out to the crowds, "My crime was in shedding tears!" He was proud to be condemned. Fabre, forced into revolutionary excesses by less worthy sentiments, was overwhelmed by a realization of the truth. All he could see at the end of the road he was travelling was a scaffold.

Still another countenance came to my attention in this tumbril of reprobates, the face of Hérault de Séchelles. The calmness of the handsome face of the former solicitor-general was different from the calmness of Danton, whose visage seemed a caricature of that of Socrates. The calm of Hérault de Séchelles was the calm of indifference; the calm of Danton was that of disdain. There was no pallor upon the forehead of the latter; but the complexion of the other was as ruddy as if he were returning from a banquet instead of going to the scaffold. Hérault de Séchelles appeared, in short, to care little for the life he had preserved at the cost of so many base and atrocious actions. The sight of this egoist astonished everybody; people were interested to know his name, but his name once known, their interest disappeared.

DANTON AT THE PLACE DE LA RÉVOLUTION. (Barras, I, 161–162.)

Danton, while still upon his way [to the scaffold], displayed that fortitude of soul which remained with him to the end. While passing before the house of Robespierre . . . in the Rue Saint-Honoré, facing the Rue Saint-Florentin, Danton, by a sudden movement which alarmed the executioners and gendarmes accompanying the tumbrils, arose from the fatal bench where he was imagined to be bound. Turning to the dwelling of Robespierre, he cried out in powerful tones, "Thou wilt soon follow me: thy house will be razed, and salt sown upon the place!" And soon indeed might one see the accuracy of this terrible prophecy!

The tumbrils arrived at the Place de la Révolution. Danton was kept for the last, and as his unfortunate companions passed by him, they bowed to him in their emotion. Danton with heroic mien sustained their courage. Camille Desmoulins and Hérault de Séchelles, whose hands were bound behind their backs, tried to embrace Danton. The executioner repulsing them roughly, Danton said to him, "Thou art, then, crueler than death; thou canst not keep our heads from kissing at the bottom of the bag."

When his turn arrived, he went up with alacrity. Lifting his eyes to the sky, he cried out with an emotion he could no longer master, "My wife, my children!" but soon regaining his courage: "No weakness, Danton!" Then to the executioner he said, "Thou wilt show my head to the people: it is worth seeing!"

THE COMMITTEES. *(Barras, I, 164.)*

The committee of public safety became the real executive with dictatorial power in regard to the conduct of the war and all political affairs. The committee of general security had, as is shown by its name, the right to dispose of individuals and their liberty. The prisons opened at its orders. The relinquishing of these powers cost the Convention dear; a great assembly which makes such immense concessions will sooner or later be victimized. The least usurpation of its authority, when tolerated, leads to numerous others.

(Mallet du Pan, II, 50–53.)

Instituted on the 2nd of October, 1792, and invested at the time with the widest superintendence of design, discourse, thought, action, correspondence; authorized to invite and receive accusations, and itself to denounce and ordain the arbitrary arrest of citizens, its [the committee of general security's] formidable functions secured to it no less formidable influence.

Even if this power is not actually fused in that of the committee of public safety, it sinks at any rate to a very subordinate sphere: it is the satellite of the planet, the arm which the head moves at will, and a state inquisition directed by the committee of public safety.

... the terrible arm of a judicial power, the most tyrannical, the most irresponsible to all forms, the most independent of all laws, the most general in the exercise of its vengeance, is embodied in the committee of public safety. It paralyzes with terror all citizens in cottages as in mansions, on the benches of the Convention as in the beds of the aristocracy, and in the Jacobin clubs, no less than by the obscure hearths of the royalist bourgeoisie.

In addition to the power bestowed on the committee by this concentration of inquisitorial, denunciatory, and judicial authority, it draws another, no less formidable, from the absolute disposal of the public funds and of private fortunes. . . .

By means of money, denunciations, the prison, and the scaffold, Robespierre and his confederates dispose also of the revolutionary army.

ROBESPIERRE LEFT DICTATOR. (*Barras, I, 144–145.*)

We were then the prey of the Terror, and Robespierre was indisputably the visible and supreme head of this régime, whose system he had proclaimed. In revolution, there is no greater power than that of disinterestedness and honesty; because it appeals to all interests and offers guarantees to all: among the people of ancient times, such power was of first importance. . . .

Robespierre had therefore founded a real dictatorship upon his reputation for honesty and, so to speak, political stability: he never varied in language, manners, or appearance. Forever powdered, at a time when powder was proscribed, splenetically sad, he remained as he had been from the opening of the States-General, and arrived, perhaps unwittingly, at a supremacy which frightened the world and himself, alarmed as he was to possess a power he dared not abdicate.

(*Meillan, 4–5.*)

Robespierre was simple in his habits. He affected a hatred of grandeur and disdain of riches. He seemed to think only of the welfare of the people. All his discourses were filled with such imposing things as *the subsistence of the people, the welfare of the people, the power, the sovereignty of the people.* Fanatical on the subject of equality, he desired it everywhere, in all cases, all circumstances, and by every means. He esteemed only one other virtue, patriotism, and never wondered whether patriotism depended upon other virtues. One day he praised a man named Desfieux, who was noted for his dishonesty, and whom he afterwards sent to the scaffold. "But your Desfieux," I said to him, "is known to be a scoundrel."

"No matter; he is a good patriot."

"A fraudulent bankrupt."

"But a good patriot."

"He is a thief."

"A good patriot."

And I could not drag anything from him except these three words.

Robespierre had none of the higher talents. His eloquence consisted in a jumble of declamations, lacking order, method, and especially conclusions. We had to ask him, every time that he spoke, just what he was trying to convey. He was always complaining, lamenting, and groaning about the country's misfortunes, without ever proposing a single remedy. He left it to others, especially to Danton, to find expedients. He was always crying out against calumny, and never ceased to calumniate. Jealous, proud, and hard, opinionated, violent, and sanguinary, he would have sacrificed three-fourths of the human race to make the other fourth conform to his system of government or further his projects of elevation.

(*Vilate, 183.*)

Robespierre practiced a somber and consistent austerity. He related himself to events and gave to his name of Maximilien a mysterious importance.

He was gloomy, suspicious, and fearful, never leaving the dismal entrance of his lodgings without two or three vigilant guards. He disliked to be looked at and glared furiously at his enemies. He took a two-hour daily walk, marching precipitately, elegantly dressed and powdered.... Sober and laborious, he was irascible, vindictive, and imperious. Barère called him the giant of the Revolution. "My genius is overwhelmed," he said, "and quakes before his."

OTHER MEMBERS OF THE COMMITTEE OF PUBLIC SAFETY. (*Mallet du Pan, II, 40–41.*)

Lindet, deputy of the department of the Eure, was patronized and appointed by Buzot, whom he betrayed: he adheres to Robespierre, through whom he was appointed to the committee, and to whom he would not be more faithful in the first disturbance than he was to Buzot. A second-rate chief, he will never reach the first grade.

(*Vilate, 230.*)

Billaud-Varenne, bilious, uneasy, false, and steeped in monkish hypocrisy, betrays himself through his very efforts to be impenetrable, having all the deliberateness that premeditates crime, and the relentless energy to carry it out. Low, truckling, and implacable, his ambition will not suffer competitors. Mournful and silent, with vacillating, convulsive eyes, there is something stealthy in his walk. His cold, pallid, and sinister face shows the symptoms of a deranged mind.

(*Mallet du Pan, II, 44–45.*)

Couthon, a lawyer of Auvergne, shares with Robespierre and Billaud-Varenne the supremacy of the committee. He has intelligence and some talents. Sanguinary, like so many others, from want of courage, disinterested from an incapability of enjoyment from loss of health, his relative capacity surpasses that of the greater part of his associates; he is not wanting in extended views, nor of ingenuity in the conception and execution of his plans. The audacity of his genius surpasses and supports that of Robespierre.

Prieur, late deputy of the first Convention, an instrument, but an experimental instrument of revolutionary power, a brigand in his conduct as well as in his principles, will always remain a second-rate man.

Carnot, an officer of artillery, a member of the first legislature, is one of the most useful of this committee. Entrusted with the military department, he manages it with activity, intelligence, and application.... Entirely taken up by his special function, he mixes little in party intrigue and will serve all successively.

(*Vilate, 183.*)

Barère was in perfect contrast with Maximilien; buoyant, frank, flattering, fond of society, especially feminine society, seeking luxurious enjoyment, and knowing how to spend. Under the old régime he had desired to pass as a noble. The appellation *de Vieuzac* flattered his vanity not a little. As variable as a chameleon, he changed his opinions as if they were costumes; in turn Feuillant, Jacobin, aristocrat, royalist, moderate revolutionist. He was atrocious and cruel through weakness, and intemperate by habit, according to the state of his digestion. Atheist in the evening, deist in the morning, he was born without character or political views, skimming the surface of everything, with the single talent of being prodigiously facile in the use of words.

(Mallet du Pan, II, 46.)

Jean-Bon Saint-André, Calvinist preacher of Montauban, instigator of the massacre of the Catholics in that town in 1790, an indefatigable firebrand, bearing in his crimes the character of the climate in which he was born. Sent last autumn to Brest, where he established the ascendancy of the Jacobins; a good instrument of tyranny, but by his resolution and audacity, in a position to raise himself to the highest rank.

(Vilate, 230.)

Collot-d'Herbois, sensitive, enthusiastic, and facile, is enamored with ideas that are magnificent and sublime. He is cruel, but believes himself humane. His soul is as variable as his theatrical and oratorical performances. Inclined to debauchery . . . he is violent, choleric, and unmanageable, although apparently sincere. His face is sometimes inflamed and shows the fury of his passions. He might, perhaps, have been a conscientious and agreeable man had bad company not made him more ferocious than a lion or tiger.

XXVI. *The Fall of Robespierre*

ROBESPIERRE IN COMPLETE CONTROL. (Meillan, 109.)

ROBESPIERRE's turn had come at last. By fawning upon the people he had become their idol, and this will happen to any man who declaims against the rich, causing the people to hope for a division of the spoils. Through the populace, he ruled the Jacobin Club; through the Jacobin Club, the Convention; and through the Convention, France. He dictated decrees and directed the administration. Nothing was done except by his orders or with his approval. His caprices were flattered, and his very manias were praised. The tribunal beheaded those he designated without investigation. His power seemed as terrible to his accomplices as it did to his victims. A number had been sacrificed already and others feared the same fate. They banded together to pull down the idol they themselves had set up.

(Fréron, Notes sur Robespierre; Papiers inédits, 157–158.)

He had doubtless committed some indiscretion through his immoderate use of wine and liquors. Fearing that his secret would escape, he made his renunciation and during the last months of his life drank nothing but water.

He never went out without a brace of pistols, and was accompanied everywhere by trusty body-guards. Guards were stationed at regular intervals along the streets through which he passed, ready to aid him promptly in case he were attacked. Towards the end of his career, he practiced pistol-shooting every day in a garden. He is said to have become very skilful at this exercise. This skill he has not had the courage to use in killing himself. . . .

His face greatly resembled that of a cat, and his writing looked like scratchings.

ROBESPIERRE ASPIRES TO BE A PONTIFF. (Thibaudeau, I, 58–59.)

I have never addressed a single word to Robespierre. Leaving aside his words and deeds, his very person seemed to repel me. He was of medium height, with a lean, cold face, sallow complexion, and deceitful look. His manners were curt and affected, his speech imperious and dogmatic, and he possessed a forced, sardonic laugh. Although a leader of the *sans-culottes*, he was meticulous in his dress, continuing to powder after others had ceased to do so. Uncommunicative, he kept even his intimates at a distance, a vainglorious pontiff who delighted in the cult his Janissaries and devotees had built around him. In this man there was something of Mohammed and something of Cromwell, but he lacked their genius.

(*Vilate, 331.*)

Robespierre is gradually acquiring supreme power, pretending to the honor of repairing the misfortunes of France which he himself has helped to bring about. Aided by Couthon and Saint-Just, he has decided the rôles to be played. The junior member terrorizes the public by proposing frightful expedients and by sowing uneasiness, distrust, and despair. Couthon, under cover of his infirmities, appears to authorize them, moved by unavoidable necessity. Robespierre talks philanthropy and rallies to himself the débris of all the parties, arousing their hopes and proscribing his enemies. Since his ambition is not limited to temporal affairs, he has recourse to celestial interventions by the Supreme Being. Eager to carry the censer and affect the authority of an interpreter of the author of nature with its attendant honors, he proposes a religion as beautiful and pure as man has ever conceived. Meanwhile, in order to identify himself with the Divinity in some fashion or other, he manoeuvers in the background with an obscure sect of visionaries, desiring in his superstition to have himself declared the emissary of heaven.

WORSHIP OF THE SUPREME BEING. (*Durand de Maillane, 185–189.*)

Robespierre, rid of nearly all his rivals, aspired to be the founder of a cult. Since he belonged to the philosophical group, he did not restore the Catholic Church; he confined himself to the proscription of atheism and the acceptation of immortality of the soul and the existence of the Supreme Being. He delivered a long and pompous discourse on this subject, and during the session of the 18th Floréal had a festival decreed to celebrate the new religion. This religion was not as profane perhaps as the Worship of Reason, but it was quite as scandalous to Christians.

... the National Convention followed him [Robespierre] to the garden of the Tuileries, where a vast amphitheater had been elevated to serve as an altar for the new cult. Robespierre, after having harangued the people, advanced, flambeau in hand, towards a monument representing atheism, ambition, discord, etc. He set it in flames, and this group, when consumed, left in view a statue of wisdom. The Convention and the people then went in solemn procession to the Champ-de-Mars, where they were to celebrate this great event.

THE DECREE.

ARTICLE I. The French people acknowledges the existence of the Supreme Being and the immortality of the soul.

II. It acknowledges that the worship most worthy of the Supreme Being is the practice of the duties of man.

PROPOSALS ON EDUCATION. (*Thibaudeau, I, 72.*)

They never ceased to talk about bringing man back to a state of nature, as far as that was possible. There was nothing new in the various schemes proposed; models were sought from among the ancient republics. Rome and Athens were of no use to people who wanted only bread and iron; they turned to the rigid laws of Sparta. Even a number of very enlightened men gave their sanction to these chimeras.

Thus Le Pelletier, whether through conviction or otherwise I do not know, proposed a plan for mass education. It found favor among the Spartiates and was adopted by the committee of public safety. Robespierre was entirely in accord with these principles. Speaking from the tribune he said: "You will come some day to see the necessity of equal education for all Frenchmen. It is not a question now of educating gentlemen, but of forming citizens. The state alone should bring up children; it cannot leave this work to family pride and private prejudice, for this is the regimen which produces aristocracy and domestic federalism. Souls become dwarfed by their isolation, and the lack of equality destroys the very bases of the social order."

The Château of Versailles was proving to be an embarrassment. The proposal was made to turn it into an educational institution, in calculating that it would take care of ten thousand children.

FAMINE AND THE MAXIMUM UNDER ROBESPIERRE. (*Williams, 81–82.*)

The tyranny of these monsters was not the only evil with which the people of France had to struggle; famine was pressing on with hasty strides. The law of the *maximum* had not only driven away the foreign merchant, but also kept at a distance the dealer who was accustomed to provide for the daily returning wants of the inhabitants. The grazier no longer drove his oxen to Paris, where the *maximum* on entering the barriers diminished half their value; nor could the butcher furnish meat, when the *maximum* allowed him but half the purchase money of the cattle. *Des Carêmes Civiques* [Patriotic Lents] and other revolutionary measures of the like sort were recommended to the fasting multitude, but one wag more indignant than the rest painted well the state of want and cruelty to which Paris was then abandoned, by writing on the pedestal of the statue which was placed on the spot of the public execution, "Il n'y a de boucherie à Paris que sur cette place!" [There is no butcher shop in Paris except upon this square!]

THE MAXIMUM AND ASSIGNATS. (*Mallet du Pan, II, 14–15.*)

. . . since the law of the *maximum*, which, by its extension to the greater part of commodities and merchandise, embraces all the articles of necessary consumption, depreciation of the assignats is no longer burdensome to the government, except in the purchase of foreign provisions. This law is executed with rigor; no one dares to complain of it any more: it has delivered the Republic from every expense equivalent to the overplus of price which it paid before for its consumption — it is an enormous saving. The Convention could not compel the assignats to be taken at par; but it has attained the same end by submitting the value of commodities and merchandise to an invariable tariff. Having succeeded in forcing the citizen, not only to sell, but also to sell at a price independent of the value which the paper money may lose in exchange, and which, from its very nature as paper money, must always be inferior to cash, it matters very little if the paper has more or less credit. The Convention has, therefore, made at the same time a very economic and very popular operation; for, to the *sans-culottes*, consuming and not possessing, it is very agreeable to buy with paper at a price which injures those only who sell. What is essentially to be considered is that today, in spite of the enormity of the expenses, the new creation of assignats is less necessary, because a less quantity of them is wanted to provide for the necessity of government... Besides, the committee of public safety no longer considers these new issues in any other light than as a subsidiary resource: its efforts tend, on the contrary, to sustain and raise the paper by diminishing its use, to restrict the quantity in circulation, and to raise the exchanges by payments in specie.

PUBLIC OPINION IN FRANCE. (*Mallet du Pan, II, 37.*)

It may be asserted, without fear of error, that a majority of the people in France abhor the Convention, the Jacobins, the rule, and the rulers: this majority comprehends six-eighths of the nobility, the middle classes, and the small proprietors; but among the last there are still many who adhere to the present revolution from the encroachments which they are allowed to make, on very easy terms, upon the domains of the clergy and the *émigrés*. This majority contains further the greater number of money-jobbers, merchants, manufacturers, the heads of industrial establishments, men of business, lawyers, artisans, who were formerly in easy circumstances, the farmers, and people living by their labor, who have preserved some principles of religion and probity, or who are wanting in the activity and effervescence necessary to raise themselves from nothing and to perceive the advantages of the condition of the *sans-culottes*. . . .

If a sense of weariness and the enormities of the Revolution have detached a great number of its adherents, many unite themselves with their enemies from the fear of falling unconditionally under the yoke of the *émigrés*, and all from a distrust and aversion for foreign force. The Jacobins abhor these latter as dangerous ... and as incapable or ill-disposed to aid them.

THE TERROR AUGMENTED. (*Durand de Maillane, 191–196.*)

But the hand of the Supreme Being soon struck down the man who had made sacrilegious use of His name as a mere cover for hypocrisy and numerous assassinations. At the festival Robespierre spoke only of justice, humanity, and sympathy for the unfortunate, yet on the previous day he had forced through a law which added beyond measure to the number of victims, and delivered France over to the most horrible carnage.

This law, which was presented by Couthon on the 21st Prairial, frightened even the most intrepid Montagnards. As soon as the report was over and the law had been read, Ruamps cried out from his seat: "This decree is important; I demand that it be printed, and that we adjourn. Were it adopted without adjournment, I would blow out my brains." . . . But Robespierre was opposed to any delay, and above all to any attempt at independence on the part of the Assembly. He immediately took the floor and violently opposed all ideas of adjournment: " . . . I ask that the proposal to adjourn be ignored, and that the National Convention discuss, until nine o'clock in the evening, if necessary, the proposed law submitted to it." His proposition was decreed with applause, showing the irresistible influence of Robespierre over the Convention. It must be admitted that the women knitting in the galleries were subsidized, and that these provided three-fourths of the applause given to a law whose mere reading had congealed every heart. The execution of this law caused torrents of blood to flow. Fifty or sixty victims a day were sent to death. None could escape from cruel jurists armed with such a law. One may form an estimate of it from the following provisions:

"The revolutionary tribunal is instituted for the punishment of the enemies of the people.

"The enemies of the people are those who seek to destroy public liberty, either by force or by intrigue.

"The following shall be considered enemies of the people:

"Those who shall have promoted the re-establishment of royalty or have sought to discredit or dissolve the National Convention and the revolutionary and republican government, whose nucleus it is;

"Those who shall have betrayed the Republic while in command of fortresses and armies, or while fulfilling any other military function, who shall have held communication with the enemies of the Republic, or who shall have sought to bring about a shortage of supplies or men;

"Those who shall have sought to prevent the provisioning of Paris, or cause famine in the Republic;

"Those who shall have seconded the projects of France's enemies by concealing and sheltering conspirators and aristocrats, by persecuting and slandering the patriots, by corrupting the representatives of the people, or by abusing the principles of the Revolution, the law, and the government through false and perfidious applications;

"Those who shall have deceived the people or the representatives of the people to induce them to actions contrary to the interests of liberty;

"Those who shall have sought to spread discouragement in order to forward the enterprises of the tyrants leagued against the Republic;

"Those who shall have disseminated false news in order to divide and trouble the people;

"Those who shall have sought to mislead public opinion, prevent the enlightenment of the people, deprave morals, corrupt the national conscience, and impair the strength and purity of the revolutionary and republican principles, or arrest their progress, either by insidious, counter-revolutionary writings, or some other machination;

"Those who compromise the safety of the Republic by dishonest contracts and squanderings of the public wealth, other than those comprised in the provisions of the law of the 7th Frimaire;

"Those who, being charged with public functions, abuse them to aid the enemies of the Revolution, annoy the patriots, and oppress the people;

"And, finally, all those who are designated in previous laws relative to the punishment of conspirators and counter-revolutionists, and who by any means or under any guise shall have made attacks against the liberty, unity, or safety of the Republic, or sought to hinder their advancement.

"The penalty for all crimes whose investigation appertains to the revolutionary tribunal is death.

"The proof necessary to condemn the enemies of the people is any kind of document, material, moral, verbal, or written, which would naturally influence any just and reasonable mind. The method of reaching verdicts shall be left to the consciences of the juries guided by their love for their country. Their goal will be the triumph of the Republic and the ruin of their enemies, their procedure the simple methods indicated by good sense in order to arrive at the truth in conformance with the law."

ARREST FOR TRIVIAL CIRCUMSTANCES. (Mme. de Chastenay, I, 245.)

I saw pass by a man in despair. He had sold some powder for the chase at a lower price in silver than he would have obtained in assignats. He was denounced and brought to trial. I learned that he extricated himself, but he had to appear at Dijon ... This poor fellow had seven children and cried out incessantly in tones I still seem to hear, "Will I then be guillotined?"

I saw MM. Gris, a wigmaker, Michâteau, an honest procurator, and another man in prison for a thing of this sort; but it was only a question of powder for hair-powdering, and friends settled the affair. I saw M. Hugenin, a tinman, condemned to ten days' imprisonment for having put on his Sunday coat on Sunday. He was taken to prison in the incriminating garment, a beautiful coat of apple-green cloth, with handsome pearl buttons. "It is not I that is in prison," he said; "it is my coat."

We had a village mayor who, in a moment of delirium ... wished to profane the sacrament. ... This affair would have been most serious, and it seems to have been suppressed. A certain Malgras, a cabaret-keeper at Vaurois, was imprisoned for more than four months as an accomplice of Pitt and Coburg. One day, in front of his door, he had read aloud from a newspaper which contained these words: "An individual has been arrested at the theater for having cried out, 'Long live Pitt! Long live Coburg!'"

FOUQUIER HORRIFIED. (Fouquier-Tinville's speech at his trial.)

On one occasion the committee of public safety ordered me to increase the executions to one hundred and fifty a day; but the proposal filled me with such horror, that, as I returned from the Seine, the river appeared to run red with blood.

REACTION AGAINST ROBESPIERRE. (Durand de Maillane, 198.)

Meanwhile, the Reign of Terror was nearing its end. Robespierre had become insupportable to his own confederates. Members of the committees were his rivals for power, and feared sooner or later to become his victims. In the Convention, everyone bewailed his tyranny, but no one dared to attack it. His speeches and manoeuvers, however, soon aroused the courage of despair in Tallien, Bourdon de l'Oise, Legendre, Lecointre, and others, who were fearing the fate of Danton and Lacroix. Every tyrant who threatens without acting will himself be struck. Tallien, Bourdon, and two or three other Montagnards who were in peril remained quiescent no longer; they conspired to protect themselves. But how could Robespierre be overthrown? He controlled all the authorities of Paris, all the agitators of the clubs, and the commander of the military forces, Hanriot, was among his most devoted partisans. Nothing but a decree of the Convention could bring down this colossus; for in a war of opinion it is moral force that prevails.

FOUCHÉ INTRIGUES AGAINST ROBESPIERRE. (Fouché, I, 20–23.)

He [Robespierre] was only a step from becoming absolute master of the Revolution he audaciously thought to control; but he must have thirty more heads: he had marked them out in the Convention. He knew that I had divined this; I therefore had the honor of being on the death-list inscribed in his tablets.... He had me driven out of the Jacobins, where he was the high priest; and this was for me practically the equivalent of proscription. I began at once to try to save my head, holding in secret some lengthy deliberations with those of my colleagues who were likewise menaced. All that was necessary was to say to these, such as Legendre, Tallien, Dubois de Crancé, Danou, and Chénier: "You are on the list! You are on the list as well as I; I am certain of it!" Tallien, Barras, Bourdon de l'Oise, and Dubois de Crancé began to show some energy. Tallien was fighting to save two people, one of whom was dearer to him than life. He was ready to strike down the future dictator with his poignard in the midst of the whole Convention.... I revealed to Collot-d'Herbois, Carnot, and Billaud-Varenne the designs of the modern Appius. I placed before each of them such strikingly realistic pictures of their plight and stimulated them with such adroitness and success that I instilled in their hearts something more than anxiety; that is, the courage to oppose henceforth the tyrant in any further attempts to decimate the Convention. "Count the votes in your committee," I said to them, "and you will see that if you make an effort he will be reduced to a helpless minority with Couthon and Saint-Just. Refuse to vote and render him helpless by your inertia." But what stratagems and subterfuges undertaken to avoid the anger of the sycophants and fanatics of Robespierre! Sure of having sown to advantage, I was courageous enough to brave him on the 20th Prairial (June 8, 1794), the day on which he carried out the ridiculous idea of solemnly recognizing the existence of the Supreme Being, and dared to proclaim himself His arbiter and intermediary in the presence of a great throng of people assembled at the Tuileries. As he ascended the steps of his aërial platform, whence he was to launch his manifesto in favor of God, I predicted to him aloud (twenty of my colleagues heard it) that his fall was not far off. Five days later, at a meeting of the committee, he demanded my head and those of eight of my friends, reserving for the future some twenty more at least.

(*Barras, I, 179–180.*)

It was his [Fouché's] policy to exaggerate all his sincerely held fears in order to arouse the men he wished to take a stand. He ran about from morning till night, visiting deputies of all opinions and saying to each, "You will perish on the morrow unless he is destroyed." To those mourners of Danton in danger from the resentment of his executioners, Fouché would say, "We can take our vengeance tomorrow, and it is only then that we shall be in safety." Such a feeling of terror had been aroused by Robespierre that a member of the National Convention, believing that the dictator had observed him putting his hand to his forehead with a thoughtful air, quickly removed it, saying, "He will think I was thinking about something." To arouse their stricken spirits it was necessary to show them more than once that the interests of each of them were involved in the general question. It cannot be denied that in consolidating the sentiment against Robespierre by his clever intrigues, Fouché was a real resource to the elements that were there, ready to be formed into a decisive movement against the Convention's oppressors.

ROBESPIERRE ATTACKS BILLAUD–VARENNE AND COLLOT–D'HERBOIS. (*Billaud-Varenne, 422–423.*)

I disregarded the fact that in this rash attack of a pigmy upon a giant my efforts would, in all probability, only hasten my downfall. Robespierre himself was convinced of it even more than I. The same man who a month before had posted two assassins to get rid of Collot-d'Herbois and myself, when he had both of us in his power at the stormy session of the Jacobins on the night of the 8th Thermidor, allowed us to go forth alive and uninjured from among the transports, cries, and menaces of a convulsive agitation! This violent crisis had publicly begun in the morning, in the very bosom of the legislative body, where we had vigorously tested out our united forces. Those acquainted with the despotic vanity of the man know that he was humiliated as well as angered by the defeat he had sustained in this prelude to the combat. Although he was soon reassured by the nocturnal triumph he had won at the Jacobins, he was certain to push his advantage and cap the climax by bringing us under the ax of the law. On the morrow he would take his vengeance with weapons that were more straightforward, and above all more formidable, with time to bring into action all the more crushing levers furnished by his dictatorial power and popular supremacy.

ATTITUDE OF THE CONVENTION. (*Thibaudeau, I, 82.*)

For some time previous there had been clouds that announced a tempest, and we felt that uneasiness and oppression which always precedes a storm. But on the 9th Thermidor the great majority of the Convention was totally unaware of what was coming. It fell like a thunderbolt. There was no reason why they should have attacked Robespierre on that day rather than on any other, or have hoped for an end of his tyranny. For some time past he had been menacing Billaud-Varenne, Collot-d'Herbois, Tallien, etc., his emulators and accomplices. The Convention was as indifferent to the perils of these as it had been to the death of Danton, and had Robespierre demanded their proscription, they probably would have succumbed. But a realization of their own danger gave them the audacity to forestall it, and, as I have already said, victory is always favorable to the one who attacks.

(Procès-verbal de la séance du 9 thermidor.)

All minds were still full of the discourse pronounced by Robespierre at yesterday's session, a discourse intended to discredit and dissolve the government, divide and immolate the national legislature, and lead to a usurpation of power and the domination of the French people. Everyone remembered the discussion which followed this discourse, and which was so illuminating to all the representatives of the people. Several members had been heard to attack Robespierre personally. They reproached him with having placed himself above the public welfare and nullified the decrees of the National Convention by the liberty he took of suspending their execution on his own authority. They reproached the unmeasured pride and ambition which made him a dictator to all beholders, a man aspiring to tyranny. It was recalled that his defense against such grave accusations had been weak, not to say negligible. For the first time, the voice of a guilty conscience was inhibiting the imperious and imposing tone which had so often been effective, and which had screened him from the eyes of the multitude.

They recalled his inexcusable and admitted absences, during four *décadi*, from the functions in the committee of public safety confided to him by the National Convention; the popular agitation that was aroused; and the attempts to direct this against the government action. His procedure and methods of conduct during the past year were particularly brought to mind. They had seen him, after despairing of leading the people back to fanaticism and Catholic rites, substitute a new cult and a new priesthood, forcing a great political assembly and a free republican government to discard the reasons and principles which forbid that any proper government should interfere in religious matters at any time, except to suppress or punish the abuses, disorders, or crimes which may result from them. They had seen him abusing an institution which was severe, but just and beneficial, and substitute a far-reaching law, astute in its combinations, and hypocritical in its development of apparent motives, but invidious and atrocious in execution and result. They had seen him bristling up and roaring out at the men who had discovered his intentions and had demanded adjournment and discussion of the law. He proscribed them by his glances, gestures, and voice, and demanded, in fact, their heads, or had them demanded by his henchmen.

TALLIEN BEGINS THE ATTACK ON ROBESPIERRE. (*Procès-verbal de la séance du 9 thermidor.*)

Such is the state of mind which meets Saint-Just when he arrives at the rostrum. His gloomily sinister air, his hesitant tone of voice, his ferocious glances, the hour at which he appears (twelve o'clock has just struck), his intimacy with Robespierre, the unaccustomed presence of the latter at a session of the National Convention, remembrances of the previous evening — all seem to announce important discoveries, momentous discussions, and signal events.

Silence succeeds at last to the species of tumult which necessarily results from general uneasiness and agitation.

"I belong to no particular faction," says Saint-Just; "I will fight against them all. The course of events has perhaps ordained that this rostrum shall be the Tarpeian Rock for him who has come to tell you that the government has departed from the paths of wisdom."

With these and similar phrases, the intention of the orator is revealed, as is also his culpable understanding with Robespierre; he is interrupted by a motion of order.

"And I likewise," says Tallien, "belong to no faction; but my heart weeps for the evils that menace the country. Yesterday a member isolated himself from the government in order to indict it; today another does the same, and is about to assail it further, aggravating the country's troubles and precipitating it into an abyss. I demand that the veil be entirely torn away."

"It must be! It must be!" is cried from all sides. "Let truth shine forth at last, and traitors stand revealed!"

A moment later, Billaud-Varenne is reminding them of yesterday's events at the Jacobins. "The society," he says, "was filled with assassins; almost none had cards: an intention to slaughter the national legislature was openly manifested. I see even here one of the men who made that threat." (A single cry is heard, "Arrest him!" The attendants seize upon him immediately and conduct him to the committee of general security.)

"The time has come to tell the facts," Billaud-Varenne then continues. "I am astonished to see Saint-Just at the rostrum. He promised the two committees that he would submit his discourse to them before he read it to the National Convention, and would even suppress it, if they considered that it was dangerous. He made this promise as he left us at five o'clock this morning, and with this end in view was to meet us at the committee at eleven o'clock. At the very moment he knew we could not be here, since we were awaiting him at the committee, he came to perjure himself on this rostrum and try out his baneful poisons upon you!

"The Assembly will badly misunderstand these occurrences and its present position, if it dissembles the fact that it is between two shambles. If it is weak, it will perish." ("No weakness, no, no!" cry all the members, rising as one man; and this unanimous movement, which shows the people that its representatives will always know how to overturn tyrants, is received with universal cries of "Long live the Republic! Long live the National Convention!")

BILLAUD-VARENNE CONTINUES THE ATTACK. (*Procès-verbal de la séance du 9 thermidor.*)

Here a member, Lebas, one of the devoted servitors of Robespierre, makes a great deal of noise and after menacing all those about him with voice and gesture precipitates himself furiously upon the rostrum, in demanding to be heard. Vainly is he told that the last speaker has the floor; in vain is he called to order by the house: his violence continues. He finally subsides into silence upon hearing the demand on all sides that he be sent to the Abbaye.

Billaud-Varenne, who had been interrupted by Lebas, continues his speech and sets forth a picture of the position in which the Convention finds itself.

"You will shudder with horror," said he, "when you know that our armed forces are confided to parricidal hands; when you know that the revolutionary tribunal has declared to the committee of public safety that the commandant of the national guard is an infamous conspirator and the accomplice of Hébert.

"You will shudder with horror when you know that those who accuse the government of placing conspirators and nobles in command of armed forces are the very people who have forced us to accept what nobles we have there. Lavalette, the conspirator of Lille, is a living proof of this. You will shudder with horror when you know that he is the man who, when there was a question of sending some of the representatives of the people into the departments, said there were not twenty members of the Convention worthy of this mission.

"I will say even more. The complaint is being made that patriots have been oppressed. This complaint will surely seem quite strange to you when you learn that the person from whom it comes has caused the arrest of the most patriotic revolutionary committee in Paris, that of the Indivisibilité section, and has arrested the whole committee, although only two of its members were denounced."

The murmurs of indignation which have accompanied this recital redouble and for a moment interrupt the orator. He continues as follows:

"When Robespierre told you that he had isolated himself from the committees to escape their oppression, he carefully avoided the whole truth. He did not tell you that the real reason was that, after having had his own way in this committee for six months, he met with resistance when he and he alone wished to have the decree of the 22nd Prairial enacted, a decree which, in the impure hands chosen by him, would be so disastrous to patriots. (All eyes are turned upon Robespierre and reveal to him the horror he inspires. A general groaning sound is heard.)

"Let me inform you, Citizens," continues the speaker, "that yesterday Dumas, the president of the revolutionary tribunal, openly proposed at the Jacobin Club that all impure men be driven out of the Convention, that is to say, those whom his master, Robespierre, wishes to sacrifice. But the people are there, and patriots will die for the defense of liberty. ('Yes, yes!' cry out all the members and spectators, showing clearly by their applause where their disposition lies.) We all, I repeat, will die with honor; for I do not believe there is a single representative here who would want to live under a tyrant."

A single cry is heard: "Death, death to tyrants!" This republican outburst continues for a long time, with everyone on his feet, and everyone's bearing such that the oppressors see that their last hour has come. . . .

"They wanted to mutilate, to destroy the National Convention; and this intention was so real that there was an organized system of spying upon the representatives of the people they wished to slaughter. It is infamous to talk about justice and virtue when one has violated them and appeals to them only when checked or aggrieved."

THE CONVENTION TURNS AGAINST ROBESPIERRE. (Procès-verbal de la séance du 9 thermidor.)

At these words, Robespierre, whose rage may easily be imagined, rushes to the rostrum, thinking to overawe them with the imperious tone that has always been successful. But the charm has been broken; all have been convinced, and from every side they cry at him, "Down with the tyrant!" Overwhelmed by this terrible word, he drops his head, and descends several steps. Still they discuss his crimes, and he begins to suffer torture.

"I asked just now," says Tallien, who interrupted Saint-Just, "that the veil be torn away: it has been raised by a courageous hand. I rejoice at seeing the conspirators unmasked; they will soon be annihilated, and liberty will emerge triumphant from this new ordeal. Everything indicates that the national legislature will overthrow its enemies.

"I have hitherto relegated myself to silence, having learned from one who approached the tyrant of France that there was drawn up a list of proscriptions. I have refrained from recriminations; but at yesterday's session of the Jacobins I trembled for my country. I have seen the army of a new Cromwell forming and have armed myself with a poignard to pierce his breast, should the Convention lack the courage to indict him." (Numerous bursts of applause show the speaker that the Convention will lack neither courage nor firmness.) . . .

The orator, after comparing Robespierre to Catiline, and his followers to Verres, demands that there be no adjournment until the glaive of the law has safeguarded the Revolution by arresting Hanriot. These two propositions are decreed, and acclaimed by the Assembly and the people amidst cries of "Long live the Republic!" . . .

Robespierre attempts to speak; but a member rises and puts forward new grievances, accusing him of supporting Hanriot, who has long been suspect to true republicans, and of having placed with this general men who were all likewise under suspicion. He demands that the adjutants and aides-de-camp of Hanriot be put also under arrest. The proposition is adopted.

A new member convinces them that there is danger in leaving the armed forces of Paris without a head, and proposes that a provisional commandant be named. Another member immediately presents for consideration the Citizen Deymard, commandant of cavalry, guaranteed to be a good citizen. The Convention elects him.

Robespierre once more presents himself at the rostrum, but is met by a unanimous cry of indignation. He persists, acting in a furious fashion. "Down with the tyrant!" re-echoes on all sides. He turns around for a moment towards Saint-Just, whose attitude shows his despair at being unmasked, and is little calculated to encourage him; he obstinately persists in his attempt to speak, but all members cry out at him anew, "Down with the tyrant!" and force him at last into silence.

The reporter then arouses them to the danger of permitting the existence of a military régime in Paris similar to that which existed in monarchical times. When controlled by the people, the national guard had had legion heads who commanded in turn. Why leave a permanent commander and staff in control

of such an immense armed force? He advocates that the democratic organization of the national guard be restored.

He presents the decree to the Convention and it is adopted ...

ROBESPIERRE'S ARREST VOTED. (Procès-verbal de la séance du 9 thermidor.)

Following these preliminary measures of public safety, Vadier (member of
the committee of general security) brings back the discussion to the crimes of
Robespierre.

" ... It is he who tried to bring ridicule upon the Catherine Théot affair
by saying that she was an old lunatic who could not be taken seriously. But
this old lunatic was with the *ci-devant* Duchesse de Bourbon every day. A letter
was found in her mattress, addressed to Robespierre and announcing to him
that his mission was foretold by Ezekiel; the glory of establishing a religion, a
new cult, unencumbered by priests, had been reserved for him. Another letter
written to him by a certain Chenon, Genevese notary and head of the sect of
the Illuminati, proposed a supernatural constitution. ..."

Public indignation broke forth more than once during this discourse. There
were outbursts of horror, such as are inspired in free men and republicans when
they hear of tyrannical crimes. However, as Vadier has merely presented a
few facts without comprehending the general plan of the conspiracy, Tallien
demands the floor in order to bring the discussion back to the real point in
question. "I shall know how to do that," answers Robespierre, in a menacing,
audacious tone that brings new cries and widespread murmurs to which he is
obliged to yield. ...

Robespierre, tortured in conscience, becomes greatly agitated and cries out
that they are bringing his death. "You deserve a thousand deaths," says a
member. The younger Robespierre now joins his brother and asks to share
his fate. With eyes that gleam with frenzy, and in despair of dominating by
affected calm, they reveal the hidden depths of their souls. They abuse the
National Convention; they insult; they menace. A general indignation arises
in reply to the cries of these madmen; the turmoil steadily increases; the
president covers himself. The elder Robespierre, profiting by the moment
of silence which always follows this act, denounces the president and the
members of the Assembly in the most abusive terms. There is a violent hub-
bub of murmurs and the National Convention rises as one man. Members
demand the arrest of this man who dares to attack the majesty of the people in
the person of its representatives. Another cries out that Robespierre has in-
contestably been a tyrant, and for that alone should have his arrest decreed.
All are demanding the arrest of the two brothers, when another member gains
the floor.

"I have," he says, "positive facts which Robespierre dare not deny, and
which will show you what he is. You heard him accuse the committee of trying
to disarm the citizens. Well! it was he alone who sponsored the resolution.

"He accused the committee of effecting the disappearance of all the monuments consecrated to the Supreme Being. Well! it was Couthon who caused
them to disappear."

Couthon admits his part in this. Robespierre threatens and struggles in vain; he tries various points of the chamber; in vain with furious looks he ascends and descends the steps of the rostrum where he has reigned so long as despot. A violent hatred of tyranny is exhaled from every soul, enveloping him in an atmosphere where he can no longer breathe. He falls gasping upon a seat, and there the indignation of republicans holds him as if enchained. His arrest, and that of his brother, are demanded on all sides. This is finally decreed amid numerous and violent bursts of applause.

"The National Convention decrees the immediate arrest of Maximilien Robespierre, one of its members. . . ."

THE COMMUNE RISES FOR ROBESPIERRE. (*Thibaudeau, I, 83-85.*)

Intoxicated by victory, the Convention adjourned its sitting until evening. But the enemy beaten here was not beaten elsewhere. While the representatives of the people were giving themselves over to rejoicing, Robespierre was being snatched from his prison and conducted to the Hôtel de Ville, there to plot his vengeance. The Convention had made a grave mistake; he did not know how to profit by it. A resolute man would have seized their place of meeting, cut off a dozen heads, and been more powerful than ever. Robespierre lacked the audacity which brings a sort of grandeur to crime; he deliberated and failed to act. When the Convention reassembled that evening, the majority of its members were ignorant of what had happened. When the information spread, joy gave way to stupefaction and consternation. What a single man would have feared to do, an assembly was still less capable of doing; they talked; the greatest indecision reigned; they arrived at no result. Thus with two armies face to face, instead of attacking, they wasted their time in useless talk. The contest appeared unequal. The [city] officials and the leaders of the national guard were for Robespierre. They had brought a large part of the people under their flag and could dispose of a considerable force. The Convention, in its isolation, was reduced to a few good citizens who had been rendered courageous by the success of the morning. Others were waiting in silence for the dénouement of the tragedy, and a far greater number knew nothing of what was taking place. The darkness of night added to the horror of the situation. There was the sounding of the tocsin and the general alarm; some were being summoned to the Convention, others to the Hôtel de Ville. The citizen did not know which way to turn or whom to obey, fearing that in the obscurity he would be marching against relatives or friends. Some of the Convention had formed themselves into a committee to deal with the situation; the representatives were waiting in the greatest agitation; the reports that were coming in were not calculated to calm them. At midnight, with no one able to foresee the result of this struggle, Collot-d'Herbois sounded the president's bell and said in his sepulchral voice: "Citizen Representatives, the moment has come when you must die at your post; I learn that Hanriot is investing the National Convention." This terrifying statement precipitated all the curious people out of the tribunes and through the doors, leaving only clouds of dust and a mournful solitude. The members of the Convention, who had been scattered about the hall, all resumed their places with calm and dignity, waiting in their seats for death. This was an action that was imposing and sublime, and I on my part believed that our last hour had come.

ROBESPIERRE OUTLAWED. (*Thibaudeau, I, 85.*)

Hanriot had, in fact, advanced with a troop of hired assassins as his staff into the very court of the Tuileries; but he had retired again almost immediately, after having won over some of the cannoneers and carried off some of the cannon. However, after the first fright had passed, the members of the Convention regained their courage; and, either because things had come to a final crisis, or because the lack of actual forces brought the recklessness of despair, they decided to end this scandalous struggle by outlawing Robespierre and his accomplices. The decree was passed amid cries of "Long live the Republic!" and commissaries of the Convention, lighted by torches, went forth to proclaim it. In proportion as these advanced and people learned of the decree, the latter threw off their hesitation and joined the Convention, while those who had joined the party of Robespierre through fear were now abandoning it. When the decree became known at the Place de l'Hôtel de Ville, the battalions of national guards which were there disbanded; the citizens retired to their homes or went to meet the commissaries of the Convention; and in the Hôtel de Ville even Robespierre's accomplices abandoned him.

THE CAPTURE AND DEATH OF ROBESPIERRE. (*Méda, 384–385.*)

I saw a group of fifty men in great agitation; the noise of my artillery had surprised them. In the midst of them I recognized the elder Robespierre; he was sitting in an armchair, with his left elbow on his knees, and his head leaning on his left hand. I sprang upon him; and presenting the point of my saber at his heart, I said to him, "Surrender, traitor!" He raised his head and said to me, "It is you who are a traitor, and I am going to have you shot!" At these words I took one of my pistols in my left hand, and, making a turn to the right, I fired. I intended to strike him in the breast, but the ball took him on the chin and broke his left lower jaw; he fell from his armchair.[1] The explosion of my pistol surprised his brother, who threw himself out of the window. At this moment a terrible uproar broke out around me; I cried, "Long live the Republic!" my grenadiers heard me and replied: then the confusion reached its limit among the conspirators; they dispersed in all directions, and I remained master of the field of battle.

Robespierre lying at my feet, they came to tell me that Hanriot was escaping by a secret staircase; I still had one loaded pistol; I ran after him. I came upon a fugitive in this stairway; it was Couthon being rescued. The wind having extinguished my light, I fired at him at random; I missed him, but wounded in the leg the one who carried him. I redescended, and sent searchers after Couthon, who was dragged by the heels to the hall of the council-general of the commune; I had them search everywhere for the wretch I had wounded, but he had been taken away immediately.

Robespierre and Couthon were stretched at the foot of the tribune....

The grenadiers threw themselves upon Robespierre and Couthon, whom they believed dead, and dragged them by the feet as far as the Quai Pelletier.

[1] Other sources indicate that Robespierre shot himself.

There they wished to throw them into the water; but I opposed this and put them under the guard of a company of the Gravilliers.

(Durand de Maillane, 202.)

[The committee of general security] ordered that he [Robespierre] be taken to the prison of the Conciergerie. His trial was short. On the following day he was guillotined, together with Saint-Just, Couthon, and his other accomplices. It was quite a distance from the Palais de Justice to the scaffold, and the immensity of the long Rue Saint-Honoré had to be traversed. Along the whole course, the people pursued Robespierre with hoots and maledictions. He had been given a conspicuous place in the tumbril, his face half covered by a dirty, bloodstained cloth which enveloped his jaw. It may be said that this man, who had brought so much anguish to others, suffered during these twenty-four hours all the pain and agony that a mortal can experience.

THE END OF THE TERROR. *(Coittant, 134–135.)*

We learned of the execution of six of our companions in La Bourbe: Saint-Roman, the Montcrifs, father and son, the younger Button, and Lavoisier. The day we parted, the Citizeness Derigny, her son, and De Thiars were brought before the tribunal. Nothing distressed us more than these removals, and it is a consolation no longer to see them.

Although releases have become quite frequent, they have just brought in Lebas, a great and noble-hearted man.

Three liberations today, the 19th Thermidor, Destournelles, Dufourny, and one other.

Among those released today was the Citizeness Beauharnais [afterwards the wife of Bonaparte]. This woman was greatly beloved here. Upon learning that Tallien had just broken her chains and ended her troubles, there were a thousand manifestations of pleasure. She was so affected by this that she began to grow faint. When she regained her composure she made her adieux and departed, followed by the good wishes and benedictions of all the prisoners.

(Barras, I, 206.)

In order to establish their identity, Robespierre and his accomplices had been sent by the committees to the revolutionary tribunal. The tribunal believed it had obtained a new lease upon existence and that its powers would be continued. The executioners held fast to their prey. I was informed that those who had been condemned on the eve of the 10th Thermidor had remained at the Conciergerie and that Fouquier-Tinville, still retaining his authority, was about to send two cartloads of prisoners to the place of execution. I ran to the Palais de Justice ... I ordered four officers to bring Fouquier-Tinville to me. When he appeared, he approached me humbly. "Take off your hat in the presence of the people," I said to him, and added: "I have just now learned that two cartloads of the prisoners are being sent to death and that you are presiding at the trial of others who are destined to the same fate. No execution can take place without my authorization. This I refuse to give, and I order you, your judges, and your juries, to suspend these trials. My orders are to be obeyed under pain of military punishment." Vociferous applause followed my words, giving them the necessary authority. The very people who were going to follow the fatal tumbrils to the scaffold, and perhaps with cries of approval, as on the days preceding, appeared delighted to hear me and seemed to be in sympathy with the humane feeling that was rescuing the victims.

XXVII. *The Thermidorian Reaction*

THE JACOBINS AFTER THERMIDOR. (*Thibaudeau, 1, 88–89.*)

THE leader of the terrorists had disappeared, but the party still remained. The committee of public safety had been delivered of Robespierre, but the Convention had not been delivered of the committee of public safety. If things had been left to the committee, there would have been no change of system, and the only result of the 9th Thermidor would have been the elimination of a few of their number. Men like Collot-d'Herbois and Billaud-Varenne had seized the bloodstained scepter of Robespierre. They regarded it as a legitimate heritage. They had overthrown the tyrant merely to save themselves and reign in his place; not for a single instant had they thought of abolishing tyranny. Before the 9th Thermidor, the factions of Danton and Robespierre had accused one another of wanting to do away with the revolutionary government and establish indulgence. The report made by Barère, in the name of the committees of public safety and general security, imputed no other crime to Robespierre at the moment of his downfall. Billaud-Varenne, who was as somber and splenetic as Robespierre, did himself justice in believing that he might properly replace him. One day when he was interrupted by signs of disapproval, he bent a threatening glance upon the Convention, and said, "I believe someone murmurs!" This bit of eloquence was overlooked by Nero.

These insolent threats no longer imposed upon the Convention. The 9th Thermidor had completely restored its strength. The memory of its recent oppression made it extremely jealous of the independence it had just recovered. And to cleanse itself of the horrors committed in its name, it had to bring them to an end, disavow them, and even punish their authors.

(*Fréron, 16.*)

Everything presaged a despotism as frightful as the one we had just thrown off. What else could be expected from Amar, Collot, or Billaud? The revolutionary tribunal had continued to function, and Fouquier-Tinville had found defenders in the very bosom of the Convention. Bourdon (de l'Oise) and Thibaudeau, defenders and intimate friends of Billaud, had them pass to the order of the day when there was a courageous denunciation by Lecointre (de Versailles). Bourdon even proposed the arrest of Lecointre, and Lecointre was forced out of the office in which he held the position of secretary.

(*Barras, I, 222–223.*)

... Billaud-Varenne and Collot-d'Herbois tried to regain at the Jacobins some of the support which Robespierre had had before the 9th Thermidor. Billaud-Varenne, with the menacing manner formerly employed by Robespierre, said, while shaking his mane, "The lion has been sleeping, but he will rise up and devour his enemies." This clearly expressed a regret that there had been moments of moderation, and announced that new storms were about to burst upon the Convention.

FRANCE DEMANDS AN END OF THE TERROR. (*Thibaudeau, I, 103–105.*)

The accomplices of Robespierre tried to continue their repression of the popular movement, but public opinion and the majority of the Convention strongly opposed them. The impulse had been given, and the movement could no longer be checked. All over France a terrible cry arose, demanding an end of oppression and the punishment of oppressors. Tallien and Fréron became the leaders of a Thermidorian party, if a whole nation can be called a party. The committees of public safety and general security were reconstructed; the representatives of the people on mission were recalled, and new ones sent out; the majority of the public officials were changed. In short, the victorious party drove out the vanquished in order to take their places. This was called *purification*. For once such a purification was necessary; authority remained in the hands that had soiled it, and which were, moreover, incapable. The 9th Thermidor was, in short, a veritable revolution. But how many of the purifications that followed were only tributes to the triumphs of factions, their passions and their avidity! In such a shifting of offices, citizens learned, it is true, not to regard them as their personal property; but they also learned the perfidious art, which was afterwards perfected, of denouncing in order to supplant. They were none the less disastrous to morality in that they changed from black to white. They learned to sacrifice their consciences and the public welfare to the current ideas, however factitious....

After changing men, there were still things to change. Such a reversal was more difficult. Besides the Terrorists, who opposed this with all their forces, there were in the Convention, as I have said, men who honestly believed that it would be dangerous to release the tension too suddenly. They thought it necessary, for the firmer establishment of the Republic, to continue the revolutionary government until peace should be declared. They believed that autocracy was not a bad thing if it were in good hands. This was contrary to my ideas, and without desiring violent changes, I thought that the oppressive laws should be gradually repealed in favor of others more conducive to individual security while we were waiting for the establishment of a constitutional régime.

THE THERMIDORIAN REACTION. (*Durand de Maillane, 254–264.*)

It must not be thought that the authors of the 9th Thermidor wanted the Republic to end when they brought about the death of Robespierre. It was only as a matter of self-defense that the National Convention combined to oppose the ambitious man who was trying to impose his will upon them all. Although its partisans believed it to be indestructible, the republican system could not continue to exist much longer. But there was, in general, a secret feeling of attachment to the Republic, which was felt by all the deputies. They feared that the fruits of their precious victories over the privileged orders might all be lost, and they dreaded the vengeance with which they were constantly menaced after the fall of Robespierre. A common spirit of democracy became noticeable in the Convention. The Mountain continued to rule collectively as Robespierre had ruled alone, but to palliate this exercise of supreme authority, the Assembly issued decrees in conformity with the principles of justice and humanity. They promised never again to depart from these principles. As a result, the revolutionary tribunal began to render justice as it should be rendered, allowing all legitimate means of defense to the accused. The criminal commissions, which had been charged with furnishing daily batches for the scaffold, were quickly suppressed. The guillotine at Orange was eliminated, and the revolutionary committees were reformed and limited to district headquarters or towns of over eight thousand. There were new regulations which were favorable to prisoners and facilitated their release, with consideration given to those accused of emigrating. While waiting for the constitution to go into effect, wise and vigorous police regulations were put into effect....

At the sitting of the 18th Thermidor of the Year II, a decree was rendered in these terms:

"ARTICLE I. The committee of general security is instructed to liberate all citizens who have been detained as suspects for reasons other than those designated by the Law of the 17th of September last.

"II. All committees of surveillance and revolutionary committees of the Republic are instructed to present to those arrested, or to their relatives or friends, copies of the charges brought against them.

"III. The charges brought in each warrant of arrest issued by the representatives of the people or by the committees of public safety and general security shall in like manner be communicated to those arrested or to their relatives or friends."

A decree on the same day provided for the payment of emoluments to priests, monks, and nuns. At a sitting on the following 7th of Fructidor, new regulations for the revolutionary committees were made. They were given a different organization and less extensive powers than those they had so greatly abused....

A decree of the Convention declared that the citizens who had been persecuted and maltreated for federalism after May 31 and June 2 deserved national commendation. Honor was paid to the memory of the sacrificed Girondins. The anniversary of the Amar report of October 3, 1793 [which indicted the Girondins], was to be marked by a memorial service dedicated to these glorious victims.

The involuntary émigrés were allowed to return to their native land. These had been driven from France after the June events by the fear of certain death, and must be distinguished from the voluntary émigrés who had gone forth only for the purpose of instigating war....

But our policy in this regard, just though it was, appeared scandalous to the Montagnards, who had become accustomed to barbarous autocracy. At first, they vaguely denounced us for what they termed our leniency towards the greatest enemies of liberty. Their next charge was that the return of the *émigrés* had undermined the validity of paper money. Finally, they desired to annul all the changes we had made. Such a demand was inimical to public tranquillity and to the new principles of justice and humanity professed at the time by the National Convention. Consequently, the Assembly, now in possession of its full membership, repulsed the suggestion of the Montagnards. All sensible people could easily perceive that it was absurd and even dangerous at a time when all France was basing its hopes upon the new policy adopted by the Convention.

But all the beneficial changes brought about by the suppression of the revolutionary trials, the return to the court procedure of 1791, and the repatriation of those whom the Mountain considered traitors, royalists, and federalists, led to reaction on the one hand, and insurrection on the other.

FRANCE RETURNS TO NORMAL. (*Thibaudeau, I, 124–125.*)

During the first days that followed the 9th Thermidor, all hearts expanded in happy expectation. It was touching to see citizens eagerly searching one another out, in order to recount their good or bad fortunes under the Terror, to felicitate one another, or to console one another. The oppressors no longer wore fierce and menacing expressions, but showed their vexation and shame. Some of these even joined in the general rejoicing, either through cowardliness or honest conviction. The gloomy restraint of the victims gave way to joyous relief. They emerged as if from a tomb and were reborn into life. There was a resumption of the broken social and political bonds. France ceased to be regarded at home and abroad as the frightful object which had been erased, so to speak, from the list of civilized nations, and resumed her rightful place.

THE DEPUTIES ON MISSION BROUGHT TO TRIAL. (*Durand de Maillane, 265–269.*)

All the departments breathed again as a result of the 9th Thermidor. Real liberty was beginning, to the horror of those who had misused the Terror. The oppressed could now raise their voices and bring direct complaint against the deputies on mission who had authorized the evil by their own examples and used their unlimited power to go to the greatest excess. It was a practice of the Assembly to have all communications read from the tribune every morning before the business of the day was taken up. After the fall of Robespierre, there were widespread complaints against the oppressors maintained in the provinces. The Assembly was stunned and at times scandalized by the daily appearance of such serious and well-founded charges. . . .

After I had made my report and the documents had been read, fourteen deputies were put under arrest. . . .

These fourteen deputies were not the only ones who felt the weight of the

Convention's justice after the death of Robespierre. But Lebon and Carrier were the only ones who were tried and put to death. An example had to be made, and these two were atrocious murderers.

Carrier and Lebon defended themselves, fully confident that their cause was good. But in spite of everything the former could say, there was nothing but horror for his drownings and his fusillades, as unjust as they were shameless. Every opinion that was opposed to his own, he denounced as federalism, royalism, and crime, following the custom of the Mountain to treat as rebellion all indignation aroused by its violences. Lebon, in his excessive loyalty to Robespierre, caused torrents of innocent blood to flow. He was, moreover, guilty of dishonesty. After a vain attempt to defend himself on these two points, he was, like Carrier, arraigned and condemned to death by the tribunals to which they were sent.

(*Manuscrit de l'an trois, 66.*)

The Convention itself was mute when Carrier, awakened from his delirium by the impending scaffold, threw a last look at these his colleagues and emitted the farewell cry: "In condemning me, you have condemned all here as guilty, even to the president's bell!"

(*Durand de Maillane, 269.*)

Fouquier-Tinville was not a deputy, and none of the newly established regulations of the Law of the 8th Brumaire of the Year III were observed in his regard. He was brought immediately before the tribunal, where he put forth a closely reasoned defense. He believed, like Lebon and so many others, that he could throw the responsibility upon Robespierre and the committee of public safety, since he had never allowed himself to bring charges against anyone on his own authority. But he was punished for having assisted in the deaths of so many victims who were obviously innocent, and for having, in the long exercise of constant cruelty, shown himself to be the incarnation of an executioner deserving death.

FRÉRON AND THE JEUNESSE. (*Mme. de Chastenay, I, 279–280.*)

The Thermidorian movement was bringing about a decided improvement. With the coming of tolerance the temples reopened, and the children of the condemned, recovering the property which had not been sold, should have been reimbursed for that which was.

Elsewhere I shall give details of what was due to the *Orateur du peuple*, published under the auspices of Fréron, and other political journals of the same type which were widely circulated. To these the representative Legendre had added a more active force. A number of the young men of Paris were not afraid to pass as hotheads and take part in mad, haphazard affairs. They called themselves the *Jeunesse* or the *Army of Legendre and Fréron*, tearing down all the busts of Marat, and effacing the *bonnets rouges* and the word *death* in the inscriptions. A song denouncing the Terrorists, the *Réveil du peuple*, was the *Marseillaise* of this kind of warfare. In the provinces these songs and disorders often caused a renewal of the excesses they were supposed to discredit and punish. A furious reaction seemed to have made persecutors of the persecuted. This was most unfortunate and was a continual source of unhappiness to me. If some of the exploits of Fréron were a useful stimulus to Paris, they soon took a wrong tack and caused extreme confusion . . .

THE MUSCADINS. (Police Report, Schmidt, II, 304–305.)

Yesterday there were large numbers of extremely excited groups in the national buildings and those of the Égalité. The various movements began to take on a serious aspect. A number of citizens dressed as workers had gone to the Jardin National. It is presumable that they had been incited to disorder or had among them individuals in disguise who had such a purpose in view.

They began by making speeches against the government. Some of the *jeunes gens,* small in number at the moment, became indignant at this seditious talk and harangued them in a lively manner. Then some of the men from the groups of workers fell with fury upon the *jeunes gens* and threw several of them into one of the basins, trying to make them cry "Long live the Republic!" Following this preliminary scene, the crowds threw themselves upon the *jeunes gens,* maltreating them and apostrophizing them with epithets of *Muscadins* and *jeunes gens de Fréron.* A number of these had now arrived in order to aid their comrades, and launched themselves impetuously upon one of the groups, laying about them at random. In the combat which took place between the two parties, the *jeunes gens* were worsted; several were dragged off by the hair and beaten with canes, while others were taken to the guardhouse.

In another group, upon the Terrace of the Feuillants, one of the workers, or someone dressed as such, in the heat of the treasonable talk uttered there, declaimed loudly against the Convention. He maintained that it was made up of nothing but scoundrels, and that they should fire upon the hall with grapeshot. An inspector and one of the *jeunes gens* seized upon this agitator, but not being in force, they were nearly assassinated. When they became aware of this mishap, the *jeunes gens* arrived in crowds; but the exponent of counter-revolutionary principles had succeeded in escaping. State forces arrived, however, and put an end to these seditious disturbances. It was noticed that there were a great many women in the crowds who were urging on the citizens and inciting them to revolt; a number of these were disdainfully driven away.

DISORDERS IN THEATERS AND STREETS. (Police Report, Schmidt, II, 368–369.)

Scenes of extreme agitation. At the theater of the Rue Feydeau, couplets of the *Réveil du peuple* were sung and applauded with great fervor, especially where it says that the Jacobins and the Terror must be brought to a halt. The spectators repeated in chorus "We swear it," and when the couplet about the representatives came, they cried out "Curtain!" in such a fashion that it could not be sung.

In the theaters at the Vaudeville and the Opéra Comique, there was the same agitation and the same applauding of the couplets of the *Réveil,* except the last, which they refused to hear. At the performance of *La République*, the *jeunes gens* became impatient because they were not prompt enough in singing the couplets of the *Réveil*, and six of them mounted the stage to take charge of the curtain. A clash took place between the *jeunes gens* and the artist Dugason; the latter started to draw his sword; but the actors came to his aid and separated the champions. Dugason withdrew and there was a call for Dumas to sing the *Réveil*, which he did. He was loudly applauded, beginning with the couplet of the representatives, and some voices exclaimed, "For the good deputies, well and good!"

Towards noon yesterday, at the time of the guard mount, there was a great gathering of the *jeunes gens* in the court of the Louvre. They stopped the troops, as these were entering the court with General Menou at their head, and with loud cries demanded that the band play the *Réveil du peuple*. The general, not desiring to have them order him about, declared he would play the whole series of revolutionary airs, and began with the *Marseillaise*. There were immediate cries of "Down with the *Marseillaise*," and threats of seizing and breaking the musical instruments if they should continue. The general then thought it would be prudent to consult the Convention. The Convention went on, it was said, with the order of business and left the general to use his discretion. Meanwhile, the cries were redoubling and feeling was running high, with proposals being made that they die fighting rather than yield. The general then proposed an expedient which might tend to conciliate everyone. He asked the people, "Have I been deserving of your confidence or not?" All cried out, "Yes!" and said he was a fine general. He continued: "If I have merited your confidence, leave everything to me. I will move the troops forward into two columns and everyone will be given satisfaction." This was agreed to. The troop advanced at the orders of the general, who put himself at their head and immediately had them play the *Réveil du peuple*. Then every man lifted his hat and began to cry out, "Long live the Nation! Long live General Menou! Down with the Terrorists and Jacobins!" and then the gathering dispersed.

SUSPENSION OF THE JACOBIN CLUBS. (*Police Report, Schmidt, II, 244.*)

21st Brumaire of the Year III. Extreme feeling displayed both for and against the Jacobins. . . . A young man is arrested for presuming to say that the Jacobins are blood-drinkers and regicides who desire to assassinate the people. A man is arrested for crying out "Long live the Jacobins. We need a king!" . . . Some of the citizens warmly maintain that the safety of the Republic depends upon this society. . . . The *ci-devant* Marquis Saint-Huruge, who is a well-known frequenter of streets and cafés, seems to have declared himself the deadly enemy of the Jacobins, and proves to all citizens who do not think as he does that they are wrong by caning them and taking them to the guardhouse, where they are arbitrarily confined.

22nd Brumaire of the Year III. Carrier's arrest has caused a great sensation. The public has been following this representative with cries of "Long live the Convention! Down with drowning and shooting! Let us respect the laws! Let us have a change!"

23rd Brumaire of the Year III. If one so much as resembles a Jacobin, he is in danger of being apostrophized, insulted, and even beaten. Most of the citizens applaud the Convention's measures in regard to Carrier and the suspension of the Jacobin meetings.

There are complaints against monopolizers and merchants of all kinds. These have become objects of hatred ... An individual was arrested on the grand Terrace of the Feuillants for saying a million people should be guillotined. ...

AMNESTY TO THE VENDÉENS. (*Mme. de La Rochejaquelein, 337–341.*)

Soon after, we heard of an amnesty being granted to the Vendéens; but it was declared at first to extend only to the common soldiers. But the hopes these reports might create were soon damped when we heard that a man, who had been enquiring for us in the country, had been seized, loaded with irons, and thrown into a dungeon at Blain. ...

Intelligence arrived daily that the persecutions were at an end. The prisons were opened, and a general amnesty was proclaimed. M. de La Bréjolière immediately availed himself of it, and many Vendéens followed his example ...

Nothing could exceed the attention shown to the Vendéens liberated from prison, or applying for the amnesty; and it was even forbidden, on pain of three days' imprisonment, to call them *brigands.* In the quaint language of the day, the representatives ordered that we should be called *frères égarés* [misled brethren].

RETURN OF THE PROSCRIBED DEPUTIES. (*Thibaudeau, I, 107–109.*)

The deputies who were proscribed on the 31st of May, and had become prisoners or fugitives, were not restored to their places in the Convention until the 18th Frimaire. The main reason for their restoration was that the Thermidorians needed their aid. For once policy harmonized with justice. It was a happy occasion when the seventy-three resumed their functions. They received a sympathetic and enthusiastic welcome. As they resumed their former places, one of their number, Lesage of Eure-et-Loir, spoke in the name of all, saying that the misfortunes they had experienced would be regarded as a patriotic sacrifice, and that they would fight both royalism and terror. Not all of them kept this pledge. There were several who afterwards forgot their promises and sacrificed the public welfare to revenge, which gave great hopes to the royalists, to say the least. The Mountain — for this still existed — took no part in the deliberations ...

Thomas Paine was not included in the decree of recall. I spoke for him in these words: "There is still a great act of justice for the Convention to perform. I am pleading the cause of one of the most zealous defenders of liberty, a man who has brought honor upon his century by his energetic defense of the rights of man, and has gloriously distinguished himself by the part he played in the American Revolution. I know of no reproaches against Thomas Paine. The Legislative Assembly made him a naturalized Frenchman, and he was elected a representative of the people. His expulsion from the Convention was nothing but an intrigue. The pretext was that there was a decree excluding foreigners from the national legislature. There were only two of these in the Convention. One of them is dead. But Thomas Paine, who has done so much for the establishment of liberty in a nation that is an ally of this republic, still lives, and lives in destitution. I propose his recall to the Convention." My proposition was adopted without opposition.

For party reasons there had been an attempt to disparage Thomas Paine as an American citizen and to ridicule him as a deputy. It is true that he did not know a word of French and was consequently unable to perform his duties. But his election had been a tribute to the cause of liberty and to a people who had given a glorious example to France.

THE REIGN OF MME. TALLIEN. (Thibaudeau, I, 130–132.)

Paris was again the center of taste and fashion. Two women noted for their beauty set the tone, Mme. Tallien and, later, Mme. Récamier. At this time we have the completion of the revolution in social customs begun in 1789. The classical had already been introduced into the arts by David and his imitators, and it now became evident in women's clothes, the headdresses of both sexes, and even in furniture. It replaced the Gothic, the medieval, and the mixed, bizarre creations invented in the servility of courts. If in furniture usefulness was sometimes sacrificed to purity of design and outward appearance, this was not true in regard to women's costumes. The things in the Greek and Roman heritage which did not harmonize with our customs and climate disappeared. There remained of these imitations, too servile in the beginning, only what was good and reasonable, and Europe has accommodated itself to them as well as France.

Mme. Récamier owed her successes to her personal charms. She had the grace, simplicity, and beauty of one of Raphael's Virgins.

Mme. Tallien, no less beautiful, added an amiable French vivacity to a voluptuousness that was Spanish. She was the daughter of M. Cabarrus, a Madrid banker, and was the wife of a French nobleman, M. de Fontenay. Arrested during the Terror, she owed her safety to Tallien, and paid the debt by giving him her hand. By this union she found herself associated with the Revolution and thrown into politics. There she played the only rôle that was suited to her sex, taking over the department of grace. She was called "Our Lady of Thermidor," for she gave aid to the unfortunates of every party. This did not prevent the royalists, with gratuitous insult and atrocious ingratitude, from naming her "Our Lady of September," alluding to the massacres of the 2nd and 3rd of September, 1792, when Tallien was secretary of the commune of Paris. Mme. Tallien was courted and sought both on her own account and on account of her husband's influence. She was the ornament of all the fêtes and the soul of all diversions. Ruling without the embarrassment of a throne, her reign dried many tears and, as far as I know, gave hurt to no one.

DINNERS, BALLS, AND CONCERTS. (Thibaudeau, I, 128–130.)

Individuals and families that had been isolated by the Terror now began to reassemble; social life was resumed. Dinners, balls, and concerts were given.

Wealth was no longer a crime, and luxuries reappeared little by little, not in monarchical profusion, but enough in the way of the pleasures and conveniences of life. Instead of pomp and splendor there was nicety and elegance....

Noble families who had not emigrated began to have salons as well as the parvenus. With one it was the love of extravagance, with another that need of society which is so imperious in France, especially in Paris. Some sought protection for their enterprises, some aid in recovering their sequestered property, others repatriation of their emigrant relatives or friends. All were ambitious to have the importance in society which is given by relations with the powerful or the talented. The most perfect equality reigned at these gatherings. Since the Revolution had lowered the nobility and raised the bourgeoisie, they were now on the same level. Consequently no one was humiliated or tried to humiliate others, and monarchical refinement and republican roughness tempered one another. The ostentation of the newly rich has been greatly denounced. There has been much ridiculing of their clumsy, embarrassed manners, and the bad taste that reigned in most of the salons under the Republic. It might well seem thus to those of the old régime or to the partisan spirit which transforms and exaggerates everything. The appellation of *citizen* was as good as that of *monsieur*, and in spite of what the critics might say, our *ci-devant* marquises and countesses did not find our revolutionary officers to be too bad, or disdain to become citizenesses in order to please them.

(*Williams, 6–11.*)

Not to have suffered persecution during the tyranny of Robespierre is now to be disgraced; and it is expected of all who have escaped that they should assign some good reason or offer some satisfactory apology for their suspicious exemption from imprisonment. An *écrou* [extract from the jailer's register] is considered a certificate of civism, and is a necessary introduction to good society: but happy, thrice happy, is he who has been immured in a dungeon, and has been unfortunate beyond the common lot! To him the social circle listens with attention, for him await all private and public honors; he may lay claim to the possession of the highest offices of state, and may aspire in proportion as he has suffered....

Paris once more reassumes a gay aspect; the poor again have bread, and the rich display the appendages of wealth. The processions of death which once darkened the streets are now succeeded by carriages, elegant in simplicity, though not decorated with the blazonry of arms or the lace of liveries.... With the careless simplicity of children who after the rigors of school hasten to their sports, the Parisians, shaking off the hideous remembrance of the past, fly to scenes of pleasure.

DESTITUTION OF THE LOWER ORDERS. (*Police Report, Schmidt, II, 258.*)

In the streets and cafés, good citizens are groaning over the state of the Republic as they see our representatives breaking up into groups and denouncing one another. "Where is their fraternity?" they ask. "How can they expect us to be united when we see what is going on in the Convention and in our sections? This is indeed a great achievement on the part of our enemies. In addition to this, there is famine in the country districts. The merchants have gone the limit; they see who can sell the highest. Our assignats have been completely discredited. No one dares to refuse them, but they are taken at such a low rate that they have very little monetary value. The Convention alone could remedy all these evils and rescue us from the consequent dangers. But they no longer seem to consider us."

Complaints about excessive food prices have reached their height and may lead to trouble. The people are suffering in patience, forever relying upon the good intentions of the Convention. . . .

(Police Report, Schmidt, II, 397.)

Agitation is increasing, and people are growing extremely restless. All this proceeds from circumstances that are daily growing worse. As a matter of fact, stock-jobbing of the most unscrupulous sort has now replaced the old commercial dealings. This brigandage continues with unbounded rapidity, and since its ravages affect all classes of society, it results in scandalously high prices and almost worthless assignats. There is still complaint about the constant lack of bread at the bakers while this highly necessary aliment is prodigally distributed in the squares at the most excessive prices. This carelessness on the part of the government provokes ceaseless plaints, mutterings, and the most atrocious clamorings. It is impossible in all this turmoil to determine public sentiment; it can only be said that misery is at its height, and that the bow has been bent too far.

Empty stomachs are everywhere crying out for vengeance; they are beating the *générale*, and tolling the alarm-bell against the Convention. The crowds have added ridicule to their other weapons. The journal of the Bonhomme Richard, they said, "promises always and has nothing to give." To this it was added that the committee of public safety was a mere committee of speculation, and other quips of the same sort were made.

Complaints, jokes, and murmurs against the Convention continue. Everyone says it is impossible for this to go on long without disorder. Individuals, in recounting the daily sacrifices they make to live, say now their only hope is death. . . .

THE CONVENTION BLAMED. *(Police Report, Schmidt, II, 357.)*

25th Prairial of the Year III. People are talking of the abolition of stock-jobbing, of the restoration of the finances, of the return to peace, and lastly of the new government promised to France, four capital points upon which all good patriots agree.

Order to watch a number of individuals, frequenters of the Valois and Jardin Égalité cafés, whose uniform and singular costumes cause them to be regarded as suspects.

Louis are sold as high as a thousand livres; they are principally bought by foreigners. Uneasiness in regard to the assignats has risen to such a point that negotiators are offering to lend considerable sums without interest, payable in two, four, or six years.

At the Café de Valois the Convention is openly criticized. The present régime is detested and constantly compared with the old order of things, which is loudly proclaimed the better of the two.

26th Prairial of the Year III. The head of a family or an unmarried man, even, can no longer exist on an income of twelve hundred livres. If this is paid entirely in assignats, it has an intrinsic value of only eighty livres, at the present price of merchandise....

(*Larevellière-Lépeaux, I, 253–254.*)

It does not astonish me that careless and especially indifferent people should dance on the edge of a gulf that yawns at their feet, probably to be swallowed up on the morrow. And hardy souls may sometimes laugh in the midst of danger. But that the representatives of a nation should indulge in senseless gaiety, in scandalous feasting, completely forgetful of existing conditions, while the unfortunate nation which put them into office to rescue it, overwhelmed by misery, enfeebled by hunger, and torn by civil war, was falling into ruins everywhere, was shiveringly awaiting a catastrophe still more frightful than those preceding, that is what, I avow, I cannot understand.

STATE OF THE FINANCES IN THE YEAR III. (*Larevellière-Lépeaux, I, 317–319.*)

The national treasury was completely empty; not a sou was left. The assignats were practically valueless; what little value remained was daily vanishing at a rapid rate. It was no longer possible to print enough of them during the night to satisfy the more pressing needs of the following day. The private purses of government officials, or mine at least, were as empty as that of the government....

Meanwhile, the state revenues had been annihilated. There was no longer any financial system; the citizens had lost the habit of paying taxes. The Republic could not meet its expenses except by spending its capital, and this resource was as ineffective as disastrous. Public credit was dead and, in consequence, all confidence was extinct. No business was carried on except by individual cash transactions, or at interest rates that rendered all commercial enterprises impracticable or ruinous.

Frenzied speculation had taken the place of honest and productive commerce; it corrupted all classes of society. It was the unfortunate but inevitable result of the decline in currency values, of the multiplicity of stocks and securities, and of the fury with which the revolutionary government proscribed the most useful professions under pretext of extirpating abuses. The consuming plague devoured both public and private fortunes, to the profit of a horde of swindlers who availed themselves of the impotence of the law and the well-deserved contempt into which it had fallen.

The government was obliged to furnish free provisions for the inhabitants of Paris, the refugees of the Vendée, the army of the interior, etc. Meanwhile, there was not a sack of flour in the stores, or even a single grain of wheat. At

Paris it came to the point where the individual was no longer assured of his poor daily pittance of two ounces of bread or a handful of rice. Often a section went a day or two without receiving its allotment, and it was necessary to stand in line for four or five hours at the places where it was given out. Other kinds of provisions were just as difficult to procure. All the more important communes experienced the same privation.

The country districts were not in any better condition. From all the departments, cities, armies, fleets, hospitals, etc., commissaries were scouring the highways and crossing one another in every sense of the word in their search for grain. The distribution of grain was entirely disorganized, and it was only with the aid of armed forces that the commissaries could bring away their purchases. The strongest and most audacious took possession, and in the more productive places fought one another in order to snatch a few measures of grain.

The charitable institutions were left without revenues, resources, or administration; social amelioration of any kind was almost nonexistent.

The canals were ruined, many of the bridges were broken, the roads were impracticable, the post relays were abandoned, and communication of any sort was extremely difficult. The forests were being devastated. The cuttings which had been made regardless of season, need, or common sense had finally achieved their ruin.

FALL OF THE ASSIGNATS. (Larevellière-Lépeaux, I, 320.)

Their alarmingly rapid fall had reduced the salaries of all employees and public office-holders to a purely nominal amount. At first privation, and then habit caused them to practice the most shameful brigandage and the most criminal treacheries. The debtors and farmers on their side abandoned every consideration of honesty and paid off their creditors and landlords in worthless paper money.

MILITARY SUCCESSES. (Manuscrit de l'an trois, 19–35.)

The events of the 9th Thermidor have just removed the hideous mask that the French Revolution has worn too long. At the same moment victory seems to redouble its efforts to give an imposing and glorious aspect to the new republic.

In the north, Jourdan, the victor of Fleurus, has only a step to make in driving the German armies across the Rhine. In the Midi is Dugommier, who drove the English from Toulon. He has arrived at the Pyrenees and is attacking places in the Spanish line of defense. As to the Alps, republican bayonets crown the summits of the last defenses of Italy; in short, at every pass our armies are ready to fall upon Europe....

Jourdan has crossed the Meuse; he has beaten the Austrian army on the fields of Juliers. He has entered Cologne, and the elector has taken refuge at Vienna, preceded by the Elector of Trèves. Lefèvre, Championnet, Kléber, and Bernadotte are distributing their soldiers along this part of the Rhine. The fortresses in the interior of the country are being encompassed by the rapid invasion, and are falling one by one. Juliers, Venlo, Nimwegen, Maas-tricht, and Rheinfels have opened their gates. There are being attached to the vaultings of the hall of the Convention thirty-six flags which have just been presented to it by the adjutant-general Pajol, Kléber's aide-de-camp. The conquest of the whole country between France and the Rhine has been completed, except for the forcing of the gates of Luxembourg and Mainz.

XXVIII. *Jacobin and Royalist Risings*

PUBLIC SENTIMENT AGAINST THE JACOBINS. (Thibaudeau, I, 140.)

WITH the change in power and the increased influence of the Thermidorians, due to the recall of the seventy-three, a serious prosecution of the Terrorist leaders was begun. These had said that in a revolution one should never look backward, but this the nation was doing. Petitions were coming in from every part of the country, and the sections of Paris were daily before the bar demanding punishment. There were members of the Convention who lifted their voices in support of the petitioners. The threatened deputies, their adherents, and the Jacobins were convinced that they were lost if they limited their efforts to justifying and defending themselves. With every force at their command they tried to ward off the storm and forestall their accusers. They combatted the petitions in which, not daring to speak openly, people complained of the persecution of patriots, or of the audacity of royalists, and earnestly implored the establishment of the constitution of 1793.

THE ATTACK ON THE TERRORISTS. (Thibaudeau, I, 140–143.)

The Convention was in an extremely awkward position. If it refused to prosecute the Terrorists, it would seem to associate itself with their crimes and ruin itself in the eyes of the people who held them in horror. Should trials be held, they could expect the accused to say that they were acting only under the orders of the committee of public safety. All their actions had been reported to it and had received its formal or tacit approval. Thus the Convention would in turn become the accused. The royalists would vent their hatred, and the ambitious their jealousy, by bringing this indictment. . . .

To redeem itself in the eyes of France for the excesses of the Terror, the Convention adopted a course which was forced upon it, but which nevertheless harmonized with the principles of justice and the passions of the Revolution's enemies.

As early as the 8th Fructidor, Lecointre of Versailles made a vigorous attack upon Barère, Collot-d'Herbois, Billaud-Varenne, Vadier, Amar, Vouland, and David. His denunciation was declared to be slanderous. It was resumed by Legendre a month later, but only against the first three. This time it was taken under consideration and referred to a committee. The evidence was exactly the same, but time had passed and there had been a forcible expression of public opinion. . . .

The party had been dealt a blow [by the conviction of Carrier]. Wishing to strike it to the heart, they continued the prosecution of the three members of the committee of public safety. But this was a ruder combat, with victory much more difficult. The investigation progressed too slowly to please the prosecutors, but all too swiftly to suit the accused and their many partisans. They thought that by gaining time they might gain everything. It was first decreed that there was sufficient justification for an examination of the conduct of the accused (25th Frimaire). Then came the decree for their indictment (12th Ventôse).

Meanwhile the accused, together with their party, believed that their fall was inevitable and saw no hope of safety except in plotting against the Convention. The Thermidorians were going to be put upon the defensive. Both sides prepared for combat. I was president of the Convention at the time. Addresses and petitions, spontaneous and instigated, were coming daily to the bar. These were long-distance shots, a prelude to blows at closer range. The recall of the deputies who had been sacrificed on May 31 took place precisely at this time. It furnished the Paris sections with a pretext for demanding the punishment of the Terrorist chiefs. And there was no doubt that royalism was trying to use these complications to bring the Republic to account.

FAMINE IN PARIS. (Police Report, Schmidt, II, 308.)

In every gathering, people have been exclaiming against the government on account of the famine ... freedom of commerce, they say, should not mean that merchants may starve the unlucky to death ...

The state forces, in employing all possible means to repress these forerunners of sedition, did not come off free themselves. ... In attempting to disperse the women, the public forces ... met with resistance, which determined them to arrest the more mutinous ... a tumult arose, and the women were torn from the hands of the armed forces.

... These women, returning in rather large numbers from the Convention and going along the quays as far as the Grève, were crying out and trying to induce all they met to follow them. They stopped in front of the cafés and wineshops where they hoped to gain recruits.

... it was being said that the scarcity of bread would bring about a storm sooner than one imagined. ... The disorder around the bakers' doors had caused the people of the Rues Martin and Denis to close their shops.

The citizens of the Gravilliers section were assembled to the sound of a bell in order that they might go *en masse* to the Convention to ask for bread. ...

In the Temple section, young men and laborers, gathering up other laborers, are crying out, "Bread! Bread! and nothing but bread!"

(Manuscrit de l'an trois, 127–128.)

Brought nightly by the famine to the doors of the bakers, the lower classes of Paris are a powerful reinforcement to the discontent of the Jacobins. But the Thermidorians are also supported by a large number of people, the *honnêtes gens.* All the well-to-do classes of society are in this group. The young people form the light troops, having survived the family misfortunes while escaping from military service. Their righteous indignation is such that their disturbances have all the characteristics of popular fury. They are at present backed by the authorities, and the attempts at Jacobin uprisings will only hasten the measures for their complete suppression. The Convention has already been forced to arraign the three most compromised members of the old decemviral government; Collot-d'Herbois, Barère, and Billaud-Varenne have been brought before the Assembly.

THE ATTACKS UPON COLLOT-D'HERBOIS AND BILLAUD-VARENNE. (Durand de Maillane, 269-271.)

The Convention prosecuted all the members of the committees of public safety and general security who had been connected with the tyranny of Robespierre. There were friends of Danton who would never forgive his death. They knew that Robespierre had been forced to sacrifice this victim to the ferocity of Billaud-Varenne who, after the execution of Robespierre, had avowed the fact in open assembly and even appeared to glory in it. Redoubtable enmities were brought down upon him by this imprudent avowal.

He and his friends were first denounced by Lecointre of Versailles. This singular, but honest and upright man seemed an instrument of Providence bent upon punishing all the great criminals of the Convention. Had it not been for Lecointre, no one would have dared to attack such men.

This first and poorly supported denunciation was laid to mental derangement. Lecointre was declared to be mad, his denunciation calumnious; but it was soon revived as true, with extremely serious results. The Convention was becoming more and more aroused against the assassinations, so crudely masked as trials, where the tribunal allowed no defense, counsel, witnesses, or evidence. There were occasional intervals during the sessions when emphatic statements concerning the accomplices of Robespierre could be heard. Legendre, a sincere friend of Danton, showed himself the most open and persevering of their adversaries. Although a Paris butcher, Legendre had acquired a certain standing in the Convention, and I will even say a certain amount of esteem, on account of the uprightness of his sentiments. He soon took the formal rôle of denouncing Billaud-Varenne, Collot-d'Herbois, and Barère, no longer designating them otherwise than as the "three great criminals." His denunciations were supported, and to these three names from the committee of public safety, three were added from the committee of general security: Vadier, Vouland, and Amar. The committee on legislation brought forward on this subject a report which created a great sensation and which alarmed, not without reason, the accused and their supporters.

Billaud-Varenne appealed to his good brothers, the Jacobins, who were still weeping over the death of their chief. He delivered to them a discourse upon the disastrous results of the reaction which were affecting them all alike. The Jacobins and Montagnards seemed to have become simultaneously aroused. They prepared two insurrections, one on the 12th Germinal and one on the 1st Prairial. Saladin brought in the report from the committee on legislation, the committee declaring that there were sufficient grounds for the investigation of Billaud-Varenne, Collot-d'Herbois, Barère, and Vadier. These were given every opportunity to defend themselves from the rostrum of the Convention, but their attempts at justification having failed, they were sent to the criminal tribunal of La Charente-Inférieure.

ROYALIST TROUBLES AID THE JACOBINS. *(Durand de Maillane, 276–278.)*

The various parties continued their agitation while the Convention was preparing a new constitution whose laws were to bring liberty and internal peace to France. This constitution pleased neither those malcontents who had vengeances to wreak, nor the Jacobins who opposed the reign of moderation. The latter rose in insurrection on the 12th Germinal and 1st Prairial of the Year III, to the great satisfaction of the royalists who hoped to profit by these troubles and who, when their hopes were disappointed, revolted themselves. They made their beginning at Lyon. Their subject of complaint was the new jury system to be used in criminal procedure. "What!" they exclaimed. "When our fathers, relatives, and friends were tried by ridiculous methods, or not at all, their executioners are to have long-drawn jury trials!" Directly afterwards they went out from Lyon to the prisons of Roanne, and killed all the prisoners they chose, until they were satiated. This murderous expedition took place on the 16th Floréal. The news arrived at Aix three days later, and the prisoners there were treated in the same fashion, as they were also at Tarascon and Marseille. In the Midi, the so-called aristocrats went to extremes in their reactionary measures against the patriots; they killed patriots as one kills thrushes in the country, wherever they are found. At Lyon, the Rhône was for them what the Loire had been for the Vendéens. In defense of the patriots it must be said that up to the death of Robespierre they had acted under the law. If the laws were wicked and tyrannical, it was the fault of the lawmakers and not of those who might have been guillotined themselves had they resisted. The group of *honnêtes gens* in the party of vengeance executed the bloodiest reprisals without the least remorse. The Convention set forth laws and proclamations in a vain attempt to end these infractions of justice and this massacring of prisoners. What was needed was a constitution, and this was demanded by everyone as the only remedy for all these evils and the only anchor in the storm. Citizen Thibaudeau convinced them of this necessity in a very well-reasoned discourse on the 7th Floréal of the Year III, and from that time on they worked upon it without intermission. The greatest obstacle, however, was in the Convention itself.

The Montagnard minority had seen patriots, both in and out of prison, sacrificed to the vengeance of the aristocrats during the reaction. They were additionally exasperated by having to wear the yoke of a majority they had always despised. They tried to recover from their fall and rise again to power.

THE INSURRECTION OF THE TWELFTH GERMINAL. *(Thibaudeau, I, 152–156.)*

... on the 12th Germinal, a mob, mostly made up of women, invested all the entrances to the hall and burst in, crying out that they wanted bread, the constitution of 1793, and liberty for the patriots. These cries were encouraged and supported by the Mountain. Vainly did the other representatives try to restore order; their voices were drowned in vociferations, their seats were invaded, and they themselves were assailed with imprecations and threats. The tumult and confusion was so great that the insurrectionaries themselves could not hear one another speak. For four hours the disorder continued. Exhausted by the useless struggle and stricken to the soul by such a deplorable scene, I withdrew into the garden, leaving fate to decide the outcome of this catastrophe which would render the strongest impotent. I encountered the Abbé Siéyès, and together we gave ourselves over to the most somber reflections.

The very excess of the evil brought its own remedy. The Convention had, as a matter of fact, been dissolved by the invasion of its meeting place, and the Montagnards, finding themselves too few in numbers, lost their audacity and did not dare to deliberate. Fatigued by the futility of their own excesses, the insurrectionaries gradually faded away and abandoned the field of battle. The Convention resumed its deliberations. Acting in the name of the committee of general security, Ysabeau proposed the following decree: "The National Convention apprises the French people that there was today an assault upon free deliberation, and that the authors of this assault will be brought before the criminal tribunal of Paris. . . ."

The decree was adopted. The Mountain took no part in the deliberation.

Sentiment had become extremely aroused, and the discussion was continued. André Dumont, who had occupied the president's chair at the moment the insurrectionaries invaded the hall, openly attacked the Montagnards for loudly proclaiming that royalism presided over the Convention.

THE JACOBIN LEADERS DEPORTED OR IMPRISONED. (*Manuscrit de l'an trois, 137–139.*)

"Do you know," asked André Dumont, "what is the purpose of today's uprising? It is to save the three accused whom you have to try. Well, we ought to deal with these three men first. I do not propose to close the debate; I do not propose their death without trial; I propose to drive them out of France."

The Convention forthwith decreed that Collot-d'Herbois, Barère, and Billaud-Varenne leave during the night for Rochefort, to be deported from there to Guiana. Someone, I know not who, rose up to accuse Vadier and add his name to the other three. . . .

Finally, the attention of the Assembly was again directed to the representatives who had betrayed their guilt by the way they had received the insurrectionaries. A proscription list was immediately begun, and the most frightened were not slow in naming the most audacious. Duhem, Choudieu, Chasles, Léonard Bourdon, Huguet, Amar, Foussedoire, and Ruamps were condemned to imprisonment in the Château de Ham. Thus the uprising, which had begun like May 31, ended like the 9th Thermidor.

THE JACOBINS ORGANIZE A SECOND UPRISING. (*Thibaudeau, I, 161–162.*)

One might have thought that the Convention's victory over the Mountain on the 12th Germinal would have crushed this party completely; but, on the contrary, it was merely irritated by its defeat and determined upon revenge. Still strong in numbers and full of audacity, it began an open conspiracy. In the public squares and popular gatherings, the proscription of the Thermidorians was loudly discussed. The government committees were paralyzed by their wretched organization and had no forces upon which they could count. They opposed the danger with incoherent and illusory measures. The Convention was unpopular; after the 9th Thermidor all the so-called *sans-culottes* were against it. The famine and high cost of living, endured so patiently while Robespierre flattered them, now served as pretexts for making outcries and taking up arms against a power which even neglected to give out caresses and favors in compensation for bread. The reaction had raised the hopes and facilitated the intrigues of the enemies of the Revolution. They added fuel to the flames and were watching for a chance to take advantage of the disturbances. They aroused the Convention against the Jacobins, and the Jacobins against the Convention, in order to ruin them both. When their fears brought them over to the party of moderation, they exacted, as the price of their services, concessions which further undermined the Republic. The defenders of liberty, divided by recriminations born of the troubles of the times and the spirit of factional rivalry, had trouble in recognizing one another, and drifted about uncertainly. The weary and disgusted nation displayed an almost complete indifference to all this agitation, and seemed blind enough to its true interests to allow itself to be dominated by a party which would have given it tranquillity at the cost of such stormy liberty.

(Police Report, Schmidt, II, 343–344.)

Yesterday morning a pamphlet was read to various gatherings in the Faubourg Saint-Antoine and distributed with profusion, notably in the Rue Saint-Denis, to the number of five hundred copies. It was the program for the insurrection. The title of the pamphlet was *Insurrection of the People for the Purpose of Obtaining Bread and Reconquering Its Rights.* At nine o'clock the tocsin rang in several sections; the general alarm was beaten; a crowd of women flocked to the Convention from all directions. The sections of the Faubourg Saint-Antoine "came down" at two o'clock; all had written upon their hats "Bread and the democratic Constitution of 1793." This was the women's refrain to the Convention; the business of the sections was to support the women. Among the number of women who succeeded in forcing their way into the hall of the Convention, there was one that seized the saber of a gendarme who was trying to drive her back, and was grievously wounded in the hand. In the afternoon a number of deputies were taken into custody by the women and armed citizens; some were maltreated, and all were conducted to the sectional police of the committee of general security.

THE INSURRECTION OF THE FIRST PRAIRIAL. (*Procès-verbal du 1ᵉʳ au 2 prairial, Durand de Maillane, 358–359.*)

Half an hour has passed since the Convention resumed the course of its deliberations, when the tumult breaks out again in the Salon de la Liberté. Cries of "To arms! To arms!" are heard; the armed force rushes thither; it is too weak to oppose the mass of insurrectionaries, who precipitate themselves upon the door they have previously broken down; they fire several musket shots. Their efforts are resisted for a time, but the guard is finally overcome, and the sanctuary of the law violated. The revolutionary mob, composed of a multitude of women and a large number of men armed with muskets, pikes, and sabers, pour into the place where the Convention is sitting, crying out, "Bread and the Constitution of 1793!" The same words are written on their hats. They fill the floor; they force the deputies to yield the nearest seats. Several of these brigands direct themselves towards the president; others aim their muskets at him. An officer, perceiving this, attempts to cover him with his body; he is assaulted and struck. The people's representative, Féraud, flies to the aid of this gallant soldier. With one arm he helps him climb the rostrum, and with the other strives to repulse the assassins. At this moment, one of the madmen fires upon the courageous representative, and hits him. Féraud falls, the scoundrels seize him, finish the murder with blows of the saber, and drag him by the hair from the presence of the Convention.

It is at an assembly of the representatives of the people, it is within the august temple of the law, that this horrible crime is perpetrated. The infamous horde applauded it, and wished, by calumny, even to justify it. Someone cried out that Féraud had just previously lacerated a woman's hand; he who, like a number of his colleagues, had run with the armed force to the door forced by the seditious, merely to prevent the effusion of blood, and implore them not to indulge in the excesses that would make them sin against all France; he who had been seen to throw himself upon the floor, saying, "You shall not enter the room except over my dead body"; he who had been trodden underfoot by this frenzied multitude.

(*Thibaudeau, I, 163–165.*)

Féraud's body was dragged outside; cannibals cut off his head and brought it to carry in triumph before the Assembly. They presented it to the president, threatening him with the same fate. He waved it aside, turning his eyes away from the bloody trophy. It was Boissy d'Anglas who, on this horrible occasion, immortalized his name by the courage and dignity with which he opposed the shameful frenzies of the multitude.

Exhausted by these harrowing experiences, he yielded the chair to Vernier. The circumstances were too difficult for his age and temperament. With the best of intentions, he became the tool of the insurgents; they did not limit themselves, as on the 12th Germinal, to defiling the hall. The remnant of the Mountain, who directed them, had rallied and did not miss an opportunity to take revenge. Men drunk with wine and fury, and women thirsting for blood, rush through the hall, making it resound with their shrieking, mount-

ing upon the seats, and heaping outrages upon the representatives overwhelmed by the crowd. The Montagnards, of whom the foremost are Bourbotte, Goujon, Romme, Duroy, Duquesnoy, and Soubrany, at first applaud
these excesses; then they begin to speak as if in this disorder there were anything left of the Convention; they make motions; the insurrectionaries support them with bravos and cries, take part in the discussions, and outrage the
representatives who try to oppose them. The command of the forces is bestowed upon Bourbotte by acclamation. He is made a member of a special
commission created to replace the committee of general security. He then
decrees the arrest of all the pamphleteers, whose writings, he says, have em-
poisoned the public mind since the 9th Thermidor, and orders the reincar-
ceration of all those liberated as a result of that day. President Vernier puts
to a vote and proclaims the decrees desired by this multitude, which it is impossible to resist. In short, within two hours all that has been done since the
9th Thermidor is swept away. The day itself is put on trial, and proscription
hangs over the heads of its authors and partisans. A little more foresight and
audacity and it would have all been over; the Terror would have rebuilt scaffolds, inundated France once more with blood, and plunged it into mourning.

THE JACOBINS PUT TO FLIGHT. (Thibaudeau, I, 165–166.)

The Montagnards, blinded by their easy success, neglected to do what was
necessary to reap the fruits of it. While they orated and passed decrees, the
government committees, recovering from their surprise, reassembled their
forces. The Thermidorians scurried through the various sections. Honest
republicans, for the love of liberty; propertied people, for fear of pillage; and
even royalists, to save their heads, arrived to succor the Convention. On the
other side, in proportion as the darkness of night increased, the greater number
of the insurgents who were in the court and in the garden of the Tuileries
retired little by little, for the reason that the Parisians, to use the expression of
the Cardinal de Retz, "cannot change their hours." There remained in the
hall and in the galleries only the more rabid. The committees formed a plan
of attack. Four columns arrived at the same instant at the four entrances to
the hall, and came in at the charge. The surprised insurrectionaries essayed
to repulse them, and the representative Kervelegan, who was at the head of
one of the columns, was slightly wounded; but the multitude, whom dismay
rendered incapable of resistance, sought safety in flight. They could find no
points of egress open, for these were filled with the defenders of the Convention.
For some time they remained in a confounded jumble of conquerors and
conquered, until finally, in order to put an end to this disorder, a door was
cleared and two files formed, between which the revolters retired without
receiving any other punishment than a few kicks distributed among them by
the national guard as they passed.

ARREST AND EXECUTION OF THE TERRORISTS. (Thibaudeau, 167–172.)

"... There has never been [said Thibaudeau] a greater crime committed
against the nation and its representatives than the passing of decrees while the

Convention was overwhelmed and slaughtered by scoundrels. I demand that these unfaithful mandatories, who have betrayed the most sacred of duties, be put under arrest; that the government committees, who, in spite of the so-called decrees abolishing them, will no doubt recover their power, present to you just and severe measures against these deputies who have broken their oaths; and that upon the demand to consider decrees that should never have existed the Convention pass to the order of the day, justified by a preamble which will present a historical tableau of this moment of oppression and crime, so that the people and posterity may judge between us and our assassins."

Retreat was impossible. In pardoning them we should have been risking our own heads, those of a large number of Frenchmen, and perhaps the fate of the Republic.

The Convention decreed the arrest of Bourbotte, Duquesnoy, Duroy, Goujon, Romme, and Soubrany. They were arrested....

Barras, invested in these critical circumstances with the command of the public forces, presented himself in company with Tallien before the Faubourg Saint-Antoine, which was then quiet, with an imposing array and everything necessary for laying siege. For a moment they considered whether they should not throw some bombs. They limited themselves, however, to disarming these people whom they themselves had armed in former times.

This measure was imitated in every section, and passions and revenges were covered more than once with the mantle of public welfare....

After the Terrorist party was thought to have been entirely subdued and was no longer to be feared, the accused, transferred on the 2nd Prairial to the Château du Taureau in the department of Finistère, were brought back to Paris, delivered over to a special military commission, and condemned to death (the 26th). The courage which they showed in defending themselves redoubled when they were faced with capital punishment. They resolved to forestall it with death, and stabbed themselves one after another with the same knife. Goujon, Romme, and Duquesnoy died immediately. Duroy, Soubrany, and Bourbotte were less fortunate; grievously wounded, they were dragged dying to the scaffold and executed.

THE RESULTS OF PRAIRIAL. (*Lucien Bonaparte, I, 55–58.*)

The vilest of the populace committed every excess in the fatal days of Prairial (the end of May, 1795). The Convention was at that time truly great. The calm of Boissy d'Anglas, its president, the sublime attitude of that assembly, silently seated upon their benches, distant but two steps from those who came to murder them, equalled all that history offers as the most heroic. The factions of 1793 were repulsed, after repeated attacks. The revolution of Thermidor ended in the month of Prairial. Doubtless it can only be from inadvertence that, in an ably written history of the Revolution, those sanguinary wretches of Prairial are repeatedly called patriots. Patriots! And what, then, were Féraud, Boissy d'Anglas, and their colleagues? ...

The victory of Prairial had completely dispelled the demagogical intoxication. The ideas of justice, of concord, of the division of power, of equilibrium, had replaced the fever of the conventional dictatorship. The enlightened patriots could make themselves heard, and the constitution of the year 1793 made us take a gigantic step towards true republican ideas. Two legislative chambers and an executive directory of five members offered a pledge of stability.

THE ROYALISTS AFTER THERMIDOR. (Barras, I, 220.)

Having been completely overwhelmed since 1792, and subjected to oppression, the aristocrats had the first right of reprisal. It was inevitable that they should profit by the events of Thermidor. They introduced themselves among the authorities and drove out some blameless citizens who had held high offices in the government as Robespierrists, although they had never dreamed of being such. Companies of cutthroats banded together under the most sacred names, especially in the departments in the Midi. Sweeping through the communes, they massacred the more zealous republicans, held up the diligences, and plundered the public coffers. They were powerfully seconded by the *émigrés* beyond the borders, and by those within who had clandestinely returned. Several members of the National Convention seemed to be in collusion with all this, and a number were suspected of having an understanding with England.

THE WHITE TERROR. (Thibaudeau, I, 238–239.)

In several departments, urged and assisted by local authorities and representatives on mission, the reactionaries massacred in the name of humanity and justice. The Midi was the special theater of their sanguinary exploits. Their impious association extended from Lyon as far as Nîmes, Marseille, and Toulon. There they were organized and regimented, so to speak; they were under the command of chiefs, and these were directed by royalist agents established in France or abroad. The assailants took the names of *Companies of Jesus* and *Companies of the Sun.*

In Lyon a man was poignarded in broad daylight because they chose to consider him a Terrorist, and his body was unceremoniously thrown into the Rhône. The police and instruments of justice were either silent or in league with them. Terror closed all mouths and tied all tongues.

In Provence the pious soldiery of the Companies of Jesus massacred in detail and in mass. They had crowded several hundred citizens, described as Terrorists, into the dungeons of Fort Saint-Jean at Marseille, under the pretext that they would bring them before the tribunals. On a concerted day, the butchers went with crucifix and cannon to attack the fort, broke into it, murdered all the prisoners, and in cold blood duplicated the frightful Paris massacres of September, 1792.

Similar massacres took place in the château of Tarascon. From the heights of the towers, the assassins threw the very corpses into the Rhône.

AGITATION FOR A RESTORATION. (Manuscrit de l'an trois, 66–67.)

Meanwhile, information is spreading abroad which makes the royalist party see how much it can profit by the rising indignation, and how far the reaction will go. New rumors are being noised about. Journals are being established to spread these rumors and give their comments upon them. People are beginning to say that the republican government will not last much longer. They discuss the children of Louis XVI, venture insinuations, and challenge the Convention itself with their bold conjectures. "If the Assembly," they say, "persists in keeping the royal offspring near at hand, it may be nourishing a secret intention of restoring the throne!... It is only a step from the Temple prison to the palace of the Tuileries!..." With this talk being circulated about, with these badly disguised insinuations, they succeed in adding a new leaven to the discord. But if royalist sentiment is beginning to dominate the salons, if it is fashionable in certain social circles to confound the Terror with the Republic, and the republicans with fanatics, it is none the less true that a hatred of royalty is instinctive with the people, and is even yet the ruling principle of the more important leaders of the National Convention.

DEATH OF LOUIS XVII. (Huë, Derniers années de Louis XVI; Madame Royale, 222.)

Louis XVII had already been torn from the arms of the queen and imprisoned in the part of the Tower that had been occupied by the king. There the young prince, called the wolf-cub of the Temple by some of the regicides, was abandoned to the brutalities of a monster named Simon, former shoemaker, drunkard, gambler, and debauchee. Innocence, youth, and misfortune; the angelic face, weakness, and tears of the royal child — all were without power to soften the ferocious guardian. One day, when he was drunk, he nearly knocked out an eye of the young prince who, by a refinement of cruelty, was compelled to serve him at table. He beat him without pity.

One day, in an access of rage, he held an andiron over his head and threatened to beat him to death. This descendant of many kings was constantly exposed to coarse expressions and obscene songs.

"Capet," Simon said to him one day, "if these Vendéens rescue you, what will you do?"

"I will pardon you," replied the young king.

(Madame Royale, 254–256.)

During the winter, my brother had several attacks of fever; he was always near the fire. ... He had several deplorable crises. Fever set in, he grew constantly weaker, and expired in agony. Thus on June 9, 1795, at three o'clock in the afternoon, died Louis XVII, aged ten years and two months. ...

I do not believe he was poisoned, as was said at the time, and as it is still rumored. The falsity of this is borne out by the testimony of the doctors who opened his body; they found no traces of poison. The only poison which shortened his days was the bad sanitation added to horrible treatment, cruelty, and unparalleled harshness.

THE FIRST PROCLAMATION OF LOUIS XVIII.

The impenetrable decree of Providence, in calling us to the throne, has created a striking similarity between the beginning of our reign and that of

Henri IV, as though it desired to indicate that this great king is to be our model. We will imitate his noble frankness. . . . Abuses grow up in the most glorious and prosperous empires. . . . Some crept into the government of the French; they bore heavily, not only upon the people, but upon all the orders of the state. The late king, our brother and our sovereign, realized this and gave his whole attention to reform. During his last moments he enjoined his successor to carry out the plans which he had wisely conceived for the happiness of this people, who were allowing him to die upon the scaffold. In descending the throne, from which he was driven by impiety and crime, to ascend the one in heaven reserved to reward his virtue, he indicated our duty to us in his immortal testament, that inexhaustible source of admiration and regret. . . . That which Louis XVI could not do, we will do; but if plans for reform can be made in the midst of disorder, they cannot be executed except in times of peace. . . . The implacable tyrants who hold you beneath their yoke retard this happy moment. . . . They portray us as a man of vengeance, whose only and barbarous aspiration is the pleasure of taking your lives, the only possession they have left you. But learn the heart of your sovereign and allow him to preserve you from the machinations of your enemies. He will not only refuse to consider errors as crimes, but will always be ready to pardon crimes that originated in error. All Frenchmen whose guilt lies only in their having been deceived, far from finding an inflexible judge, will find in us an indulgent father. . . . The triumphs of the army prove that courage lives forever in the hearts of Frenchmen; but this army must not continue to be the enemy of its king. It has preserved its ancient bravery and will resume its ancient virtue, hearkening unto and following after the voice of honor and duty. No, we have no doubts; soon the cry of "Long live the King!" will succeed seditious clamors, and our faithful soldiers will gather around the throne, fighting for its defense, and reading in our paternal regard forgetfulness of the past. . . .

THE CHOUANS. (*Turreau, 13–14.*)

Three brothers by the name of Choin had assembled some men in the neighborhood of Laval and La Gravelle. The spots in which they exercised their brigandage, and such information as could be gathered about them, caused it to be presumed that the leaders were addicted to smuggling as their main occupation. Such was the origin of those rebel bands called *Chouans*. Small at first in numbers, these rebels remained close to the forests of Pertre and La Guerche, their regular haunts. But they were soon reinforced by insurgents from the departments of Calvados, La Manche, and Brittany; by the remains of an army corps which had escaped from the Vendée under the Prince de Talmont after the affair at Cholet, being completely dispersed at Savenay; by a number of struggling malcontents from the neighborhood of Château-Gontier, Sablé, etc., where they had previously started insurrections; and, lastly, by a large number of young men who had fled the first draft.

(*Mme. de La Rochejaquelein, 365–366.*)

After the death of M. de Marigny there were but two armies, for although a third might be said to exist under M. de Royrand, it was very inconsiderable. In this manner the insurrection came to be entirely in the hands of MM. de Charette and Stofflet, who never, in reality, agreed. They were both devoured with jealousy and ambition. The war had no longer that character of union among the chiefs and universal self-devotion, which distinguished the early days of the Vendée. The peasants were disheartened, and severity was become necessary to keep them to their duty, instead of those higher motives by which they were first impelled. No great battles were fought as formerly; it became a war of ruffians, carried on by treachery. The ferocity of the republicans had hardened the most humane, and reprisals were made for the massacring of prisoners, the *noyades* of Nantes, broken promises, villages burnt with all their inhabitants, and all the horrors which posterity will hardly credit! Some republican columns that called themselves the *Infernals* had scoured the country in every direction, massacring men, women, and children. It happened more than once that a republican general, after sending word to the mayor that he would spare the inhabitants of a commune if they would return to their dwellings, had them surrounded and slaughtered to the last man. No faith whatever was kept with these unfortunate peasants.

During this horrible war it must be admitted that M. de Charette acquired immortal glory. The boldness of his measures, his fertility in resources, and his constancy, never subdued in the most desperate situations, mark him a great man. Wounded, pursued from place to place, with scarcely twelve companions left, this general was still such an object of fear to the republicans as to induce them to offer him a million of livres and a free passage to England, which he refused, choosing to persevere in the unequal struggle until he was taken and put to death.

(*The Commander of the Armed Forces to the Committee of Public Safety, Caen, June 27, 1795.*)

The Chouan cause makes renewed progress in the district of Vire. A witness has testified against Doisy that this leader had Louis XVII proclaimed at Beaumont, and that refractory priests, after sermons in favor of the royal family, took with him the white cockade.

The project of the Chouans was to establish relations between Caen, Rouen, and the Vendée, in order that they might control the mouth of the Seine, starve Paris, and receive aid from the English.

ROYALISTS AND ENGLISH DEFEATED AT QUIBERON. (*Henry, Ship-Captain, to Lecoat at Nantes, Lorient, July 1, 1795.*)

The English fleet today numbers thirty-eight vessels. On the 24th, a convoy of sixty sails joined them; the 25th, this convoy entered the Bay of Quiberon; the 26th, the disembarkation began and continued until the 28th, without a blow being struck.

The disembarkation is estimated at around ten thousand men, women, children, and servants, with a great amount of war munitions. The Chouans are assembling in the neighborhood of Carnac. General Hoche is marching against them with three thousand men, which is all we have.

(*General Hoche to the Committee of Public Safety, Vannes, July 22, 1795.*)

The counter-revolutionary army, shut up in the peninsula of Quiberon, was yesterday forced to lay down its arms after Fort Penthièvre and the intrenched camp defended by it were taken by storm. The various attacks, marchings, and manoeuverings were carried on under the eyes of the people's representatives, Blad and Tallien, who never left the column fronts. They will give you the principal details of the affair ...

(*Manuscrit de l'an trois, 306–307.*)

The disaster at Quiberon has not discouraged M. Pitt. "Not a drop of English blood was spilled," he tranquilly announced in parliament. "Yes," M. Sheridan replied, "but honor bled at all its pores." In politics honor is rehabilitated by success, and M. Pitt is ready to try again. "He is going to shower gold upon the coalition," was stated in secret correspondence. But for all that, he does not abandon the franker means of maritime armaments.

The preparations which they have again begun in English ports show that the undertaking momentarily compromised at Quiberon still presents attractive possibilities. A descent upon our western coast is always in question. The leaders of the royal armies of the interior seem to be closely connected with the project. Two divisions of English troops under Generals Doyle and Moyra are designed for the expedition, and M. le Comte d'Artois is already on board one of the vessels.

(*Lucien Bonaparte, I, 57–58.*)

The catastrophe of Quiberon (subject of ineffaceable shame to the English government at that period, if it is true that it abandoned its victims, and for the French government, who had the atrocious courage to immolate them, with or without capitulation) — the catastrophe of Quiberon raised the public indignation. The royalists were equally skilful in appropriating to themselves the fruits of the heroism and the errors of the conventional party. The counter-revolutionary spirit was not calmed.

XXIX. *The End of the Convention*

A NEW CONSTITUTION BEGUN. (*Thibaudeau, I, 177–183.*)

THE commission of eleven, established to formulate the organic laws of the constitution of 1793, began its labors on the 17th Floréal. It was made up of Lesage, Danou, Boissy d'Anglas, Creuzé de La Touche, Berlier, Louvet, Larevellière-Lépeaux, Lanjuinais, Durand de Maillane, Baudin des Ardennes, and myself. Siéyès had been chosen at the outset; he was already a member of the committee of public safety. The Convention ordered that the representatives who were members of both must choose between the government committees and the commission of eleven. Siéyès chose the committee of public safety. In the opinion of France and of Europe, he was the man most capable of constituting a nation. They regarded him as the leading political architect. . . .

The commission decided unanimously to put aside the constitution of 1793. It was used, then, rather as a point of departure than as a basis of operation. A great many publicists, or those who called themselves such, brought forward their ideas and projects. Roederer was distinguished among the crowds and admitted to the conferences. Discussions were amicable and deliberations calm. They were seeking a middle ground between royalty and demagogism. . . .

The word *senate* sounding too aristocratic, the Convention named one of the houses the Council of Five Hundred, on account of the number of its members, and the other the Council of Ancients, on account of the age requirement. All qualifications in regard to property and taxes were rejected; the only requirement was that of age. This was regarded as a sufficient guarantee of maturity and wisdom, for there was, in dividing the legislature, no thought of an aristocracy or ruling class. Baudin said that the chamber of representatives would constitute the *imagination* and the senate the *reason* of the nation. He wanted reason represented by only forty members. This was opposed on the grounds that they would not have sufficient dignity and force. It was decided that the two chambers should be made up of seven hundred and fifty members, in spite of the opposition of Lesage and Lanjuinais who thought the number too large. . . .

Baudin and Danou desired two biennial consuls or supreme magistrates, one to govern the first year, and the other the second. Lesage, Lanjuinais, and Durand de Maillane wanted a one-year president, while the others favored a council of at least three members. In the end, they adopted five. Each had favored a different number in proportion to his fears about recalling monarchy.

The way in which the executive department should be elected was the subject of the most serious consideration. They were practically reduced to two courses, election by the legislature, or direct or indirect election by the people. The former carried the day. Louvet feared that were it otherwise the primary assemblies or their delegates might some day elect a Bourbon.

EXTRACTS FROM THE CONSTITUTION OF 1795.

I. The French Republic is one and indivisible.

II. The generality of French citizens is the sovereign.

XLIV. The legislative body is composed of a Council of Ancients, and a Council of Five Hundred.

LXXVI. The proposing of laws appertains exclusively to the Five Hundred.

LXXXII. The Council of Ancients is composed of two hundred and fifty members.

LXXXIII. No man can be elected a member of the Council of Ancients if he is not forty years of age complete; if he is not married or a widower; and if he has not been domiciled on the territory of the Republic during the fifteen years which immediately preceded the election.

LXXXVI. It appertains exclusively to the Council of Ancients to approve or reject the resolutions of the Council of Five Hundred.

CXXXII. The executive power is delegated to a Directory of five members, nominated by the legislative body, performing the functions of an electoral assembly in the name of the nation.

CXXXV. They cannot be taken but from among the citizens who have been members of the legislative body or ministers.

The disposition of this article shall not be observed until the commencement of the ninth year of the Republic.

CXXXVII. The Directory is partially renewed by the election of a new member every year.

TWO–THIRDS OF THE CONVENTION TO BE RE–ELECTED. (Thibaudeau, I, 187–189.)

An outburst of protest was caused by the preservation of two-thirds of the Convention in the next legislature, as provided in the decrees of the 5th and 13th Fructidor. It was the pretext for violent outbreaks which put France once more in danger of royalism and terror.

The decrees had been almost unanimously adopted. The only important debates in the Convention had been upon the mode of selecting the two-thirds from among its members. Some thought the drawing of names would be the fairest; others, myself included, wanted the Convention to choose them. The majority thought it would be more in harmony with their principles to submit it to the people. The decrees were therefore submitted to them along with the constitution.

They were opposed by the royalists and a number of ambitious men from each of the parties. The royalists, who had been supporting the Convention against Terrorism since the 9th Thermidor, suddenly threw off the mask and declared war upon us. The Jacobins took advantage of this and rallied in their turn to the Convention, which accepted their services. The majority of the nation, which wanted peace and hoped to find it in a constitutional régime, was disposed to accept the constitution and the decrees. Saladin, who from a fiery revolutionist in the Legislative Assembly had become a passionate reactionary in the Convention, denounced these decrees to the people in a printed pamphlet.

The first opposition came from the Paris sections even before they were convoked in primary assemblies for official deliberation. Royalism, meanwhile, had so little confidence in its cause that, instead of nobles whom the people would have rejected, it put forward writers, that is, plebeians who were infatuated with their ability and irritated at being ignored.

SCISSION IN THE CONVENTION. (Durand de Maillane, 289–290.)

... the Convention ... was the prey of an internal scission which threatened a return to terrorism. An animated battle took place between Tallien and Thibaudeau in regard to the measures to be employed until the new constitution was put into literal and active execution. Tallien wanted to annul the work of the electoral commissions and continue the suspension of the constitutional régime. The Convention seemed divided on the question, but fortunately Thibaudeau prevailed. It was decided to uphold the results of the elections and definitely establish the legal system.

THE ROYALISTS BEGIN TO RAISE THEIR HEADS. (Police Report, Schmidt, II, 402.)

... The royalists begin to raise their heads; in the prevailing conversations there is little scruple in talking about a king or even wishing for one. They are tired, they say, of continuing to suffer without any visible end of their misfortunes. In the gatherings on the streets, individuals say that the Convention has no right to conserve two-thirds of its members in the next legislative body. The primary assemblies should pass upon this, and if the people know what is good for them they will open their eyes. Some go so far as to call a group in the national legislature the Chouans of Paris....

(Thibaudeau, I, 194.)

The Convention was forced to resort to violence in order to defend itself against the attacks of the Paris sections. The government committees released the Terrorists they had imprisoned a few months before, and every day proposals were being made to re-establish the revolutionary laws in all the rigor that had lately been abandoned. I was not in sympathy with these ideas. I opposed them vigorously, convinced that they would contribute nothing to the strength of our position.

(Mme. de Staël, 307.)

Those who had taken part in the Terror put forth apologies that were of the most incredible sophistry one could ever hope to find. Some said that they had been forced to do what they had done, yet one could have shown a thousand servile or sanguinary actions that were spontaneous. Others pretended that they had sacrificed themselves to the public good, and one knew that they had thought only of preserving themselves from danger. All put the blame upon a few, and what was singular in a country noted for its martial bravery, several political leaders simply gave fear as a sufficient excuse for their conduct.

THE CONSTITUTION VOTED. (*Thibaudeau, I, 201–202.*)

The sections of Paris were not imitated by the other primary assemblies of the Republic. In spite of the plots and manoeuvers of royalism, no agitation could be noticed other than the agitation which usually accompanies liberty. There were some who rejected the decrees of the 5th and 13th Fructidor, but not a single one revolted. They disbanded after deliberating upon the one subject for which they had been convoked, and their votes resulted in an immense majority for the acceptance of the constitution and the decrees. The Convention had it proclaimed. The sections of Paris had revolted against acceptance, thus opposing the popular will. They maintained that the decrees had not been ratified, and that it was doubtful whether the constitution had been; there had been fraud in the verification of the votes; they had the right to come to verify the official reports, counting, etc. Thus they continued in session, organized their forces, formed coalitions with one another, and deliberated upon all sorts of subjects while under arms. Each of them acted in a dictatorial fashion, and after outraging and menacing the Convention, prepared to attack it.

THE INSURRECTION OF THE THIRTEENTH VENDÉMIAIRE. (*Thibaudeau, I, 210–212.*)

For the defense of the Convention there were several line battalions, three or four thousand strong, and fifteen hundred patriots. They were in possession of cannon, even some presented by the sections themselves, after the events of Prairial, as trophies taken from the Terrorists. The Lepelletier section, now the boldest in revolt, had given the example in this.

Menou, head of the army of the interior, with general headquarters at Paris, found himself put in command. . . .

Barras, Letourneur, and Delmas were the soldier-deputies to whom the Convention confided the burden of its defense at this critical moment. Menou was finally discarded on the eve of battle; and Barras confided, on the 13th Vendémiaire, the command to Bonaparte, who had been cashiered as a Terrorist by Aubry and was vegetating at Paris, poor and unknown. His arrangements brought victory to the national legislature.

BONAPARTE'S STORY OF THE THIRTEENTH VENDÉMIAIRE. (*Account dictated by Napoleon at St. Helena, Las Cases, I, 312–316; Thiers, III, 326.*)

As soon as Napoleon found himself invested with the command of the forces destined to protect the Assembly, he dispatched Murat with three hundred cavalry to Les Sablons to bring off the artillery to the gardens of the Tuileries. A moment afterwards it would have been too late. This officer, on arriving at Les Sablons at two o'clock, fell in with the head of a column of the Lepelletier section, which had come also for the purpose of carrying off the artillery; but his troops being cavalry, and the ground a plain, the section retreated and at six in the morning the forty guns entered the Tuileries. From six o'clock to nine, Napoleon visited all the posts and arranged the positions of his cannon. All the matches were lighted, and the whole of the little army, consisting of only five thousand men, was distributed at the different posts or in reserve at the garden and the Place du Carrousel. The *générale* beat throughout Paris, and the national guards formed at all the debouches, thus surrounding the palace and gardens. The danger was imminent. Forty thousand national guards, well armed and trained, presented themselves as the enemies of the Convention, who, in order to increase its forces, armed fifteen hundred individuals, called the Patriots of 1789. These men fought with the greatest valor, and were of the greatest importance to the success of the day. General Carteaux, who had been stationed at the Pont-Neuf with four hundred men and four pieces of cannon, with orders to defend the two sides of the bridge, abandoned his post and fell back under the wickets. At the same time the national guard occupied the Garden of the Infanta. They professed to be well affected towards the Convention, but nevertheless seized on this post without orders. The sectionaries every moment sent women, or themselves advanced unarmed, and waving their hats over their heads, to fraternize with the troops of the line. On the 13th of Vendémiaire, at three o'clock, Danican, general of the sections, sent a flag of truce to summon the Convention to dismiss the troops and disarm the Terrorists. This messenger traversed the posts blindfolded, with all the forms of war. He was then introduced into the midst of the committee of forty, in which he caused a great sensation by his threats. He was sent back towards four o'clock. About the same time seven hundred muskets were discharged from the Hôtel de Noailles, into which the sectionaries had introduced themselves; the balls reached the steps of the Tuileries. At the same instant Lafond's column debouched by the Quai Voltaire, marching over the Pont-Royal. The batteries were then ordered to fire. After several discharges Saint-Roch was carried, and Lafond's column routed. The Rue Saint-Honoré, the Rue Saint-Florentin, and the adjacent places were swept by the guns. About a hundred men attempted to make a stand at the Théâtre de la République, but a few shells from the howitzers dislodged them in an instant. At six o'clock all was over. There were about two hundred killed and wounded on the part of the sectionaries, and nearly as many on the side of the Convention. The faubourgs, if they did not rise in favor of the Convention, certainly did not act against it. It is untrue that, in the commencement of the action, the troops were ordered to fire with powder only; but it is a fact that when they were engaged, and success had ceased to be doubtful, they fired without ball. On the 14th Vendémiaire some assemblages still continued to take place in the Lepelletier section; they were, however, promptly dislodged, and the rest of the day was employed in going over the city, visiting the chief houses of the sections, gathering in arms, and reading proclamations. In the evening order was completely restored, and Paris once more perfectly quiet.

REASONS FOR THE VICTORY. (*Thibaudeau, I, 212–214.*)

Whatever may have since been said about the ease of the victory, to me it was a veritable miracle; for our aggressors were, after all, men, Frenchmen, and five to one at least. The attack was made in ridiculous fashion; but it might well have happened otherwise. For if the sectionaries had taken advantage of the streets and houses around the Tuileries, those natural entrenchments, they could have riddled the few soldiers who defended the avenues of the palace. Instead of executing a manoeuver so simple and infallible, the sectionaries advanced in close, deep columns which were unable to deploy or execute any movement. This gave an immense advantage to the Convention's sharpshooters and artillery, who were soon able to throw these masses into disorder and confusion. . . .

The leaders had, moreover, persuaded them that the muskets and cartridges were only a matter of form; the troops would fraternize with them as soon as they presented themselves at the Tuileries, and the majority of the Convention would receive them with open arms. Thus, when they heard the musketry and cannonading, most of the sectionaries fled, heaping imprecations upon the intriguers who had deceived them.

THE STEPS OF SAINT-ROCH. (*Duval, 313–314.*)

. . . Bonaparte had just carried the post of Saint-Roch with the bayonet. It was not accomplished without bloody losses on both sides, the post being the point of advantage and defended by the bourgeois troop which showed the most unity, courage, and tenacity. The steps of the church portal, the Rue Saint-Honoré in front of it, and the blind alley Dauphin, which was not yet a street, were heaped with bodies: the church of Saint-Roch was filled with wounded, and blood was flowing in all directions. The steps of Saint-Roch were the first of the steps by which the citizen *sans-culotte* Brutus Bonaparte climbed to the throne a few years later, greatly admired by the Parisians he had so well riddled with cannon and musketry in the Year III of the Republic.

The carrying of Saint-Roch ended the combat and assured the victory to the Convention.

BARRAS DENIES VICTORY DUE TO BONAPARTE. (*Barras, I, 282.*)

Bonaparte exercised on the 13th Vendémiaire no other function than that of my aide-de-camp. He was on foot, while I was mounted, and he could not have followed all my movements. The only commission he received from me was that of going to the Pont-Royal and bringing me an account of what was going on there. He did not give, or have to give, any order, nor did he show himself at any other point of attack than in the Carrousel, whence he never stirred; it was Brune who commanded there.

THE RISE OF BONAPARTE. (Manuscrit de l'an trois, 372–373.)

"Do not forget," said Fréron, "that the artillery general Bonaparte, appointed on the night of the 12th to replace Menou, had only the morning of the 13th in which to make the masterly dispositions of which you have seen the effects!" A few moments later, Barras arrived for the purpose of formally calling the attention of his colleagues to the services of his lieutenant, and to secure the passage of a decree to confirm his appointment as second in command of the army of the interior.

The name of Brigadier-General Bonaparte, passing from the tribune to the newspapers, began from this moment to rise above the obscurity which had hitherto enveloped it.

On the 14th Vendémiaire (October 16, 1795), Bonaparte was promoted to the rank of a general of division; and finally, ten days later (the 4th Brumaire), he received a definite appointment as commander-in-chief of the army of the interior. The great favor which had suddenly fallen on a new man, and the disparity between his youth and high position, caused him to be the center of attention. He was scarcely twenty-six years old; his figure was small and thin; his cheeks hollow and pale; long hair fell on two sides of his forehead, and the rest of his hair, unpowdered, was bound in a queue at the back. The brigadier-general's uniform which he was still wearing had been under fire more than once, and showed the effects of barrack life. The insignia of rank was represented in all military simplicity by a silk stripe called *système*. There was nothing imposing about his appearance, unless it was the pride of his glance!

People demanded of one another whence he came, what he was, and by what previous services he had distinguished himself. No one could say, except his former general Carteaux and the representatives who had been at the siege of Toulon or on the Var line.

BONAPARTE BEFORE THE THIRTEENTH VENDÉMIAIRE. (Manuscrit de l'an trois, 286–289.)

The army … is being reorganized at Nice … the committee wishes to profit by the experience of others as much as possible; it summons the representatives on mission who have been with this army. All concur in pointing out a young brigadier-general, who is in Paris at that moment, "as the man who has the best knowledge of localities, and the most definite ideas concerning the war."

"He began," they said, "to distinguish himself at the siege of Toulon, where he was yet only a captain in the artillery; it was to him they owed the idea of the excellent battery emplacement which brought a total evacuation within twenty-four hours! He afterwards organized the batteries on the Var front with the same success, and has more recently had command of the artillery in the very mountains where it is thought of placing him today. He ought to be well known in the war offices, where he has been petitioning for the last two months."

They did know him there, as a matter of fact. Aubry had removed him from the artillery. Not only had this all too young general been wrong, in his eyes, in having had for several years such protectors as Gasparin, Salicetti, Ricord, Robespierre the younger, Carteaux, Dumerbion, etc., but his rapid advancement was stained by a gross irregularity: he had been promoted from major to brigadier-general without ever having passed through the intermediary grade of colonel. It was in vain that he hastened to Paris, arriving towards the end of Prairial, and continuing to petition from that time on. All that Aubry would consent to do for him was to give him the same rank in the infantry, on condition that he serve in the Vendée. The general refused to subscribe to such an arrangement and, mortified at being so despised, formed the idea of carrying his talents as an artilleryman to Constantinople.

Aubry, however, is no longer on the committee. Doulcet de Pontécoulant and Letourneur of La Manche, who are in charge of these particulars, are tolerant men; in their eyes "youthful services age quickly on the field of battle." Moreover, while on a recent mission to the Mediterranean fleet, Letourneur heard them talking of the artillery commander of the army of the Var; finding him again at Paris, he is disposed to listen to him and has him summoned. Scarcely has the young general been admitted to the topographical cabinet than, seizing upon the government pen as if he were already used to it, he sets forth with a single stroke (1) a plan of campaign; (2) instructions to the general; (3) the letter to be written to the representatives of the people on mission with the general-in-chief; (4) supplementary orders to the artillery generals and the commander-in-chief; and (5) various orders necessary for the co-ordination of those who participate in this great operation ... The committee signs everything.

AFTER VENDÉMIAIRE. (*Lucien Bonaparte, I, 59–60.*)

And the 13th Vendémiaire (October, 1795) could not, unfortunately, assure the triumph of the patriot party except at the price of the blood of too many Frenchmen. ...

General Bonaparte was promoted to the command of Paris. Named commissary of war, I departed for the capital to rejoin my brother. It will naturally be imagined how much I reflected at that moment upon what he had said to me at Antibes, scarcely two years before: "Have patience: in a little time I shall command Paris."

THE END OF THE CONVENTION. (*Duval, 321–322.*)

The cannon of Vendémiaire had ceased to thunder, the portal steps of Saint-Roch, immaculately laved, no longer left the least trace of blood to be seen: the streets had been swept, the gutters cleansed, the dead translated from the field of battle to sleep eternally in the cemeteries, and the wounded ministered to in their homes. With tranquillity thus happily restored, and the sections reduced to impotence, the Convention, victorious over its enemies, proceeded with complete serenity to the nomination of the citizen-directors who were to be charged with the manipulation of the new governmental mechanism called the constitution of the Year III. This done, it adjourned with cries of "Long live the Nation!" and thereby ended its reign.

(*Thibaudeau, I, 264–265.*)

On the 4th [Brumaire], Baudin had the commission of eleven adopt a decree concerning the means of terminating the Revolution. As one of these means, amnesty was to be granted in all cases related solely to the Revolution, excepting only the conspiracy of the 13th Vendémiaire.

The president simply declared that the session was at an end. I urged him to declare at least that the National Convention had fulfilled its mission, and that for this reason its sessions were at an end. He gave utterance to a declaration of this sort.

The Convention had been convoked amid the cannon of August 10; the cannon of the 13th Vendémiaire announced its adjournment.

During a three-year session it had contended against Europe, vanquished its enemies, dictated peace, established the Republic, forced recognition and treaties from the allied monarchs, annexed Belgium, raised France to a high rank among the nations, triumphed over its civic enemies, and pacified the Vendée.

It had established a uniformity of weights and measures, promoted legal equality, laid the foundations of a civil code, and constituted the national debt in inscribing it in the register.

It had legislated codes for all branches of the military service.

It had founded the national museum of arts, and schools for science, letters, and all kinds of public instruction.

It bequeathed to the future abundant resources, terrible lessons, and grand examples.

The good that it had done, or paved the way for, was its own work; the calamities which had afflicted the country during its reign were the result of circumstances.

THE DIRECTORY ESTABLISHED. (*Duval, 332.*)

After the cannon of Vendémiaire had brought dignity to the closing sessions of this Assembly whose marvels I have just described, the Directory was organized. Five regicides composed it. We had, besides that, two legislative corps, that of the Ancients and that of the Five Hundred. I will say nothing of the Ancients; I have only a word to say about the Five Hundred, in which a large part of the Left of the Convention, transfused by violence, formed the nucleus of a new Left, which, feeble, timid, and uncertain in the beginning, became gradually predominant, and ended, as had the preceding Lefts, in leading the Assembly into the same anarchical and revolutionary paths traversed by the former ones. It had already recreated the Jacobin Club, under the name of the Panthéon Club. To this the old *bonnets rouges* repaired *en masse*, and, with their threats, were soon intimidating the capital anew. They had already bestowed upon us the law of the forced loan and the law of hostages, and proposed to lead us gradually back to the régime of '93, when a lightning flash from the Orient announced to us the arrival of a liberator: it was Bonaparte. He did not hesitate; he transferred the nest of anarchists to Saint-Cloud, followed closely after, and seeing them ready to mutiny, made them leap through the windows of the Orangerie, whence these heroes of verbosity fled at top speed, leaving on the bushes, to escape recognition during their flight, their insignia of office, made inglorious by a fortunate soldier. When the reign of this fortunate soldier began, that of the revolutionary orators ended.

Appendix

Appendix

THE CIVIL CONSTITUTION OF THE CLERGY

The National Assembly, after having heard the report of its ecclesiastical committee, has decreed and decrees the following as constitutional articles:

TITLE I

ECCLESIASTICAL OFFICES

ARTICLE I. Each department shall form a single diocese, and each diocese shall have the same extent and the same limits as the department.

II. The seats of the bishoprics of the eighty-three departments of the kingdom shall be located as follows: [Here follows the location of all the bishoprics, etc.]

III. The metropolitan district of the Channel Coasts shall comprise the bishoprics of the departments of [Here follows the composition of this and other metropolitan districts.]

IV. All churches and parishes in France, and all French citizens are forbidden to recognize, in any case or under any pretext whatever, the authority of an ordinary bishop or archbishop whose see is established in the name of a foreign power or that of its representatives residing in France or elsewhere; all this without prejudice to the unity of faith and the communion which shall be held with the visible head of the universal Church, as shall hereafter be prescribed.

V. When the bishop of the diocese shall have pronounced in his synod upon matters within his jurisdiction, recourse may be had to the archbishop, and decision pronounced in the metropolitan synod.

VI. There shall immediately take place, in concert with the bishops of the diocese and the district administration, a recreating and delimiting of all the parishes of the kingdom; the number and extent to be determined according to the rules that will be established.

VII. The cathedral church of each diocese shall be restored to its primitive state, to be at the same time a parish church and an episcopal church, through the suppression of the parishes, and by the dismemberment of the habitations which it may be thought suitable to bring together there.

VIII. The episcopal parish shall have no other immediate pastor than the bishop. All the priests that shall be established there shall be vicars and perform their functions as such.

IX. There shall be sixteen vicars of the cathedral church in cities of more than ten thousand souls, and only twelve where the population is less than ten thousand.

X. There shall be continued or established in each diocese a single seminary to prepare for the taking of orders, without prejudice, for the present, to the other institutions of instruction and education.

XI. The seminary shall be established, when circumstances permit, near the cathedral church, and even within the buildings intended for the habitation of the bishop.

XII. For the management and instruction of the young pupils received into the seminary, there shall be a head vicar and three directing vicars, subordinate to the bishop.

XIII. The head vicar and the directing vicar are to assist, in conjunction with the young ecclesiastics of the seminary, at all the offices of the episcopal parish, and there perform all the functions which the bishop, or his principal vicar, shall think proper to give over to them.

XIV. The vicars of the cathedral churches, the head vicars, and the directing vicars of the seminary shall constitute the ordinary and permanent council of the bishop, who shall not perform any act of jurisdiction that concerns the government of the diocese or seminary without having first deliberated with them. The bishop may, however, in the course of his visits, institute such provisional regulations as come within his office.

XV. In all cities and towns containing not more than six thousand people, there shall be but a single parish; the other parishes shall be suppressed, and united to the principal church.

XVI. In cities in which there are more than six thousand people, each parish may contain a larger number of parishioners, and it shall be retained or established as the needs of the people and localities may require.

XVII. The administrative assemblies, in concert with the bishop of the diocese, shall designate to the next legislature the parishes, annexes, or auxiliaries in city or country that may properly be reserved or extended, established or suppressed; and they shall indicate the districts that are suitable to the needs of the people, the dignity of the cult, and the different localities.

XVIII. The administrative assemblies and the bishop of the diocese may even, after having resolved upon the suppression and readdition of a parish, agree that, in places which are isolated, or which, during part of the year, would find difficulty in communicating with the parish church, a chapel shall be established or retained to which the parish priest shall send, on holidays and Sunday, a vicar to say mass, and to give the people the necessary instruction.

XIX. The addition that may be made of one parish to another shall always bring with it the belongings of the suppressed church to be added to the belongings of the other church.

XX. All titles and offices, other than those mentioned in the present constitution, all dignities, canonries, prebends, half prebends, chapels, chaplainships, either in cathedral churches or in collegiate churches, and all regular and secular chapters, of either sex, abbacies and priorships, both regular and *in commendam*, of either sex, together with all other benefices and prestimonies in general, of whatever nature and denomination they may be, are, from the day of the proclamation of the present decree, suppressed and extinguished with nothing of the kind ever to be re-established.

XXI. All benefices of lay association are subject to all the provisions of the decree relating to the benefices of full advowson-gift or of ecclesiastical association.

XXII. Likewise comprised in the said provisions are all titles and foundations of full advowson-gift, excepting chapels within the precincts of private dwellings, where at present officiates a chaplain or officiating minister, at the sole disposition of the proprietor.

XXIII. The provisions of the preceding articles shall be carried out in spite of all stipulations, even of reversion, inserted in the acts of foundation.

XXIV. Foundations for masses and other services, now acquitted in parish churches by the parish priests and by the priests attached to them, without their places in regard to the benefice being perpetual titles, shall continue temporarily to be acquitted and paid as in the past; without, however, replacing those who die or retire in the churches where are established communities of priests not holding perpetual titles in connection with benefices, and known under the various names of godsons, assistants, familiars, communalists, *mépartistes*, chaplains, etc.

XXV. The foundations made to provide for the education of relatives of the founders shall continue to be executed in conformity with the provisions set forth in the foundation titles; and in regard to all other pious foundations, the interested shall present their memorials to the department assemblies, in order that, upon their advice or that of the bishop of the diocese, laws may be made by the legislative body upon their conservation or replacement.

TITLE II

ELECTION TO OFFICE

ARTICLE I. From the day of the publication of the present decree there shall be only one manner of selecting bishops and parish priests, namely, by election.

II. All elections shall be carried on by means of balloting and an absolute majority of votes.

III. The election of bishops shall be carried on according to the prescribed forms by the electoral body designated in the decree of December 22, 1789, for the naming of members of the department assembly.

IV. As soon as the *procureur-général-syndic* of the department receives the news of a vacancy in an episcopal see through death, resignation, or some other cause, he shall notify the *procureurs-syndics* of the districts to convoke the electors who have taken part in the last election of the members of the administrative assembly; and at the same time shall indicate the day on which the election of the bishop shall take place, which shall be, at the latest, on the third Sunday after the letter of notification which he has written.

V. If the vacancy in the episcopal see comes in the last four months of the year in which the election of the members of the administration of the department takes place, the election of the bishop shall be deferred and carried over to the next assembly of electors.

VI. The election of the bishop shall not take place or begin except on Sunday, in the principal church of the headquarters of the department, following the parish mass, which all the electors shall be required to attend.

VII. To be eligible for bishop, it shall be necessary to have fulfilled, for fifteen years at least, the functions of ecclesiastical ministration in the diocese, in the quality of parish priest, curate, vicar, head vicar, or directing vicar of the seminary.

VIII. The bishops whose sees are suppressed by the present decree may be elected to the bishoprics now vacant, and also to those which shall become vacant afterwards, or which may be erected in some departments, even if they have not had fifteen years' experience.

IX. The parish priests and other ecclesiastics who, through the new delineation of dioceses, find themselves in a diocese different from that in which they were exercising their functions shall be considered to have exercised them in their new diocese, and shall consequently be considered eligible there, provided they have elsewhere had the experience required.

X. Present parish priests may also be elected who shall have had ten years' experience in a parish or diocese, even though they have not hitherto fulfilled the functions of vicar.

XI. It shall be the same with the parish priests whose parishes have been suppressed by virtue of the present decree, and there shall be counted towards their experience the time that shall have passed since the suppression of their parishes.

XII. Missionaries, vicar-generals of bishoprics, and ecclesiastics officiating in hospitals, or in charge of public education, shall likewise be eligible when they shall have fulfilled their functions for fifteen years, counting from their promotion to the priesthood.

XIII. Likewise eligible are all dignitaries, canons, or all incumbents and titularies in general who were obligated residents or exercised ecclesiastical functions, and whose benefices, titles, offices, or employment were suppressed by the present decree, when they shall have had fifteen years' experience, counted as for parish priests in article XI.

XIV. The elect shall be proclaimed by the president of the electoral assembly, in the church where the election was held, in the presence of the people and the clergy, and before beginning the solemn mass that shall be celebrated in connection with this event.

XV. The official report of the election and of the proclamation shall be sent to the king by the president of the assembly of electors, to inform His Majesty of the choice that has been made.

XVI. Not later than the month following his election, he who shall have been elected bishop shall present himself in person to his archbishop, and if elected to the metropolitan see, to the oldest bishop of the district, bearing the official report of the election and proclamation, and request the accordance of canonical confirmation.

XVII. The archbishop or oldest bishop shall have the right to examine the elect, in the presence of his council, upon his doctrine and habits: if he judges him capable, he shall give him the canonical institution; if he believes he ought to reject him, the causes of the rejection shall be given in writing, signed by the archbishop and his council, excepting that the interested parties may appeal against injustice, as shall be set forth later.

XVIII. The bishop of whom confirmation is asked shall exact no other oath of the elect than that he professes the Apostolic Roman Catholic Religion.

XIX. The new bishop cannot address himself to the pope to receive any confirmation whatever; but shall write to him as the visible head of the universal Church, as a sign of the unity of faith and of the communion he should maintain with him.

XX. The consecration of the bishop shall not take place elsewhere than in his cathedral church and by his archbishop, or in the latter's default, by the oldest bishop of the metropolitan district, assisted by the bishops of the two nearest dioceses, and on Sunday, during the parish mass, in presence of the people and the clergy.

XXI. Before the ceremony of consecration begins, the elect shall take, in the presence of the municipal officers, people, and clergy, the solemn oath to watch with care over the faithful of the diocese confided to him, to be faithful to the nation, the law, and the king, and to maintain with all his power the constitution decreed by the National Assembly and accepted by the king.

XXII. The bishop shall have the liberty of choosing the vicars of his cathedral church from among all the clergy in his diocese, provided that he name only priests who have exercised ecclesiastical functions for ten years. He may not remove them except upon the advice of his council, and through a resolution taken by majority vote after investigation of the case.

XXIII. Priests now established in any cathedral church, as well as those from suppressed parishes that are to be added to the cathedral church and form part of its territory, shall have the full right, if they desire it, to become the first vicars of the bishop, each according to seniority rank in pastoral functions.

XXIV. The head vicars and directing vicars of the seminary shall be named by the bishop and his council, and may not be removed save as in the same manner as the vicars of the cathedral church.

XXV. The election of parish priests shall be made according to the forms prescribed and by the electors indicated in the decree of December 22, 1789, for the choosing of members of the administrative assembly of the district.

XXVI. The assembly of electors shall meet for parish elections each year at the time of the meeting of district assemblies, even when there is only a single parish vacancy in the district; consequently, the municipalities shall inform the *procureur-syndic* of the district of all parish vacancies that happen in the district through death, resignation, or other means.

XXVII. In convoking the assembly of electors, the *procureur-syndic* shall send to each municipality a list of all the parishes in which elections must be made.

XXVIII. The election of parish priests shall be carried on by means of a separate ballot for each parish vacancy.

XXIX. Each elector, before placing his ballot in the urn, shall take oath to vote only for him whom he would have chosen, on his soul and conscience, as the most worthy, without being influenced by gifts, promises, solicitations, or menaces. This oath shall be taken at the election of bishops as well as that of parish priests.

XXX. The election of parish priests cannot be begun or carried out upon any other day than Sunday, in the principal church of the headquarters of the district, following the parish mass, which all the electors shall be required to attend.

XXXI. The proclamation of those elected shall be made by the president of the electoral body in the principal church, before the solemn mass which shall celebrate this result, and in presence of the people and the clergy.

XXXII. To be eligible for parish priest, it shall be necessary to have fulfilled the functions of vicar in a parish, hospital, or other charitable institution of the diocese, for at least five years.

XXXIII. The parish priests whose parishes shall have been suppressed through execution of the present decree may be elected, even though they may not have had five years' experience in the diocese.

XXXIV. Likewise eligible as parish priests are all those who have been declared, as above, eligible to bishoprics, provided they shall also have had five years' experience.

XXXV. He who shall have been proclaimed elected to a parish shall present himself in person to the bishop, with the official report of his election and proclamation, in order to receive from him the canonical institution.

XXXVI. The bishop shall have the right to examine the elect, in presence of his council, upon his doctrine and habits: if he judges him capable, he shall give him the canonical institution; if he believes he ought to reject him, the causes of the rejection shall be given in writing, signed by the bishop and his council, but recourse may be had to civil authorities, as shall be set forth later.

XXXVII. In examining the elect who shall have demanded of him canonical institution, the bishop may not exact of him any other oath than that he professes the Apostolic Roman Catholic Religion.

XXXVIII. The parish priests elected and instituted shall take the same oath as the bishops in their church, on Sunday, before the parish mass, in presence of the people, the clergy, and the municipal officers of the place. Until then they can perform no parish functions.

XXXIX. There shall be in the cathedral church, as well as in each parish church, an individual register upon which the recording secretary of the municipality of the place shall write, without charge, the official report of the taking of the oath by the bishop or by the parish priest, and there shall be no other act of induction than this official report.

XL. The positions of bishops and parish priests shall be reputed vacant until the elected shall have taken the oath mentioned above.

XLI. During the vacancy in a bishopric, the first, and, in his default, the second vicar of the cathedral church, shall replace the bishop in regard to pastoral functions as well as acts of jurisdiction which do not exact the episcopal quality; but in all this he shall be bound to conduct himself according to the advice of the council.

XLII. During the vacancy in a parish church, the administration of the parish shall be confided to the first vicar, unless the municipality requires an additional vicar; and in case there is no vicar in the parish, an officiating minister shall be placed in charge by the bishop.

XLIII. Each parish priest shall have the right to choose his vicars; but he may not fix his choice except upon priests ordained or admitted to the diocese by the bishop.

XLIV. No parish priest can dismiss his vicars except for legitimate causes passed upon by the bishop and his council.

TITLE III

EMOLUMENTS OF MINISTERS OF THE RELIGION

ARTICLE I. Ministers of the religion, exercising the first and most important functions of society, and obliged to reside continually in the place of service to which the confidence of the people has called them, shall be paid by the nation.

II. Each bishop, parish priest, and officiating minister in annexes and chapels of ease shall be furnished a suitable lodging, on condition that he make all the repairs, without any changes being made at present in parishes where the lodging of parish priests is furnished in money, subject to the departments taking cognizance of the demands formulated by the parishes and parish priests; moreover, emoluments will be assigned to all in the regulations which follow.

III. The emoluments of bishops shall be as follows: the bishop of Paris, fifty thousand livres; bishops of cities of fifty thousand population or above, twenty thousand livres; other bishops, twelve thousand livres.

IV. The emoluments of vicars of cathedral churches shall be as follows: at Paris, the first vicar, three thousand livres; in cities of fifty thousand population or above, the first vicar, four thousand livres, the second, three thousand livres, and all others, two thousand four hundred livres; in cities of less than fifty thousand population, the first vicar, three thousand livres, the second, two thousand four hundred livres, and all others, two thousand livres.

V. The emoluments of parish priests shall be as follows: at Paris, six thousand livres; in cities of fifty thousand population or above, four thousand livres; in those of less than fifty thousand population and more than ten thousand, three thousand livres; in cities and towns of less than ten thousand population and more than three thousand, two thousand four hundred livres; in all other cities, towns, and villages where the parish shall have three thousand population or less, as low as two thousand five hundred, two thousand livres; when between two thousand five hundred and two thousand, eighteen hundred livres; when between two thousand and one thousand, fifteen hundred livres; and when one thousand or less, twelve hundred livres.

VI. The emoluments of vicars shall be as follows: at Paris, the first vicar, two thousand four hundred livres; the second, fifteen hundred livres; and all others, one thousand livres.

In cities of fifty thousand population or above, the first vicar shall receive twelve hundred livres; the second, one thousand livres; and all others, eight hundred livres.

In all other cities and towns of more than three thousand population, the first two vicars shall receive eight hundred livres, and all others, seven hundred livres.

VII. The emoluments *in money* of ministers of the religion shall be paid them in advance, every three months, by the treasurer of the district, under penalty of his being arrested for debt by a simple summons; and in case the bishop, parish priest, or vicar shall happen to die or give his resignation before the end of the last quarter, no recovery of money may be made from him or his heirs.

VIII. During vacancies in bishoprics, parishes, and other ecclesiastical offices supported by the nation, the accumulation of emoluments in these places shall be deposited in the district funds to provide for the expenditures hereinafter mentioned.

IX. The parish priests who, on account of their great age or infirmities, can no longer discharge their functions, shall inform the directory of the department, which, upon instructions from the municipality and the district administration, shall allow them the choice, if possible, of taking another vicar, who shall be paid by the nation upon the same footing as the others, or of retiring upon a pension equal to the emoluments that would have been bestowed upon the vicar.

X. Vicars, almoners of hospitals, seminary superiors, and others exercising public functions may, upon establishing their circumstances according to the manner just prescribed, retire upon a pension equal to their emoluments, provided that it does not exceed the sum of eight hundred livres.

XI. The arrangement here set forth in regard to the emoluments of ministers of the religion shall go into effect upon the day of the publication of the present decree, but only in regard to those that shall be afterwards provided with ecclesiastical offices. As regards the present incumbents, whether their offices have been suppressed or conserved, their emoluments shall be fixed by a special decree.

XII. On account of the emoluments assured them by the present constitution, bishops, parish priests, and their vicars shall perform the episcopal and parish functions gratuitously.

TITLE IV

THE LAW ON RESIDENCE

ARTICLE I. The law on residence shall be strictly observed, and all those invested with an office or ecclesiastical function shall be subject to it without exception or distinction.

II. No bishop may absent himself from his diocese for more than fifteen consecutive days during the year, except in case of veritable necessity, and with the consent of the directory of the department in which his see is established.

III. Likewise parish priests and vicars may not absent themselves from the place of their functions beyond the term just fixed, except for grave reasons; and even in that case must the parish priests obtain the consent of their bishop as well as that of the directory of their district; and vicars the permission of their parish priests.

IV. If a bishop or a parish priest violate the law on residence, the municipality of the place shall inform the *procureur-général-syndic* of the department, who shall command him in writing to return to his duties, and, after a second monition, shall bring suit to deprive him of his emoluments during the full time of his absence.

V. Bishops, parish priests, and vicars may not accept charges, employs, or commissions which will oblige them to leave their dioceses or parishes, or which will take them from their ministerial functions; and those who are at present so encumbered shall be required to make their option within three months from the notification which shall be made to them of the present decree by the *procureur-général-syndic* of their department; otherwise, after the expiration of this term, their office shall be declared vacant, and their successor shall be appointed according to the forms prescribed above.

VI. Bishops, parish priests, and vicars may, as active citizens, assist in the primary and electoral assemblies, be named electors and deputies in the legislatures, or be elected members of the general council of the commune or the councils of district administration and departments; but their functions are declared incompatible with those of mayor, other municipal officers, and members of the district and departmental directories; and if they are elected, they must make an option.

VII. The incompatibility mentioned in article VI shall not have retroactive effect; and if any of the bishops, parish priests, or vicars have been called by the wishes of their fellow citizens to the office of mayor, or other municipal office, or named members of district or departmental directories, they may continue to exercise their functions.

THE CONSTITUTION OF 1791

DECLARATION OF THE RIGHTS OF MAN AND OF THE CITIZEN

The representatives of the French people, constituted as a National Assembly, considering that ignorance, forgetfulness, or contempt of the rights of man are the sole causes of public misfortunes and the corruption of governments, have resolved to set forth in a solemn declaration the natural, inalienable, and sacred rights of man, in order that this declaration, constantly before all members of the social body, may recall to them at all times their rights and duties; in order that the acts of the legislative power and of the executive power, being at each instant open to comparison with the aims of all political institutions, may be more respected; and in order that the demands of citizens, founded henceforth on simple and incontestable principles, shall tend always to the maintenance of the constitution and the happiness of all.

Accordingly, the National Assembly accepts and declares, in the presence and under the auspices of the Supreme Being, the following rights of man and of the citizen:

ARTICLE I. Men are born and remain free and equal in rights. Social distinctions can be founded only upon common utility.

II. The purpose of all political association is the safeguarding of the natural and imprescriptible rights of man. These rights are liberty, property, security, and resistance to oppression.

III. The principle of all sovereignty resides essentially in the nation. No body, no individual, can exercise any authority which does not expressly emanate from it.

IV. Liberty consists in freedom to do all that does not harm others. Thus the exercise of the natural rights of each man has no other limits than those which assure other members of society the enjoyment of these same rights. These limits can be determined only by law.

V. The law has the right to forbid only those actions which are harmful to society. All that is not forbidden by law cannot be prevented; and no one can be constrained to do what it does not command.

VI. The law is the expression of the general will. All citizens have the right to assist personally, or through their representatives, in its formation. It ought to be the same for all, whether it protects or whether it punishes. All citizens, being equal in its eyes, are equally admissible to all dignities, places, and public positions according to their capacity, and without other distinctions than those of their virtues and talents.

VII. No man can be accused, arrested, or detained except in cases determined by the law, and according to the forms that it has prescribed. Those who solicit, expedite, or execute arbitrary orders, or have them executed, should be punished; but every citizen, summoned or seized by virtue of the law, ought to obey instantly. He renders himself culpable by resistance.

VIII. The law should establish only those punishments which are strictly and evidently necessary; and no one can be punished except by virtue of a law established and promulgated previous to the offense and legally applied.

IX. As every man is presumed innocent until he has been declared guilty, when it is deemed indispensable to make an arrest, all severity not necessary for making sure of the person should be rigorously repressed by law.

X. No one should be disturbed on account of his opinions, even in regard to religion, provided their manifestation does not disturb the public order established by law.

XI. The free communication of thought and opinion is one of the most precious rights of man. Every citizen can then speak, write, and publish freely; but he shall be responsible for the abuse of this liberty in cases determined by law.

XII. The guaranteeing of the rights of man and of the citizen necessitates a public force. This force is, then, instituted for the advantage of all, and not for the special use of those to whom it is confided.

XIII. For the maintenance of the public force and for the expenses of the administration, a common contribution is indispensable. It ought to be equally distributed among all citizens, according to their means.

XIV. All citizens have the right of verifying, themselves, or through their representatives, the necessity of the public contribution, of consenting to it without compulsion, of seeing how it is employed, and of determining the quota, assessment, payment, and duration.

XV. Society has the right to demand from every public agent an account of his administration.

XVI. A society in which a guarantee of rights is not assured, nor the separation of powers set forth, has no constitution.

XVII. Property being a sacred and inviolable right, no one can be deprived of it, except when public necessity, lawfully ascertained, evidently demands it, and then only after a previous and just indemnity has been awarded.

THE NATIONAL ASSEMBLY, wishing to found the French constitution upon the principles which it has just recognized and proclaimed, irrevocably abolishes the institutions harmful to liberty and the equality of rights.

There is to be no longer any nobility, peerage, hereditary distinctions, distinctive orders, feudal régime, patrimonial justices, any of the titles, denominations, or prerogatives derived from them, any order of knighthood, any organizations or decorations which require proofs of nobility, or which presuppose distinctions of birth, or any other superiority than that of public officials in the exercise of their functions.

There is to be no longer any sale or inheritance of public offices.

There is to be no longer, for any part of the nation or for any individual, either privilege or exception under the law common to all the French.

There are to be no longer any wardenships or corporations of professions, arts, and trades.

The law does not henceforth recognize any religious vow or any other engagement which shall be in conflict with natural rights or with the constitution.

TITLE I

FUNDAMENTAL REGULATIONS GUARANTEED BY THE CONSTITUTION

The constitution guarantees, as natural and civil rights,

1. That all the citizens are admissible to places and employments, without any other distinction than that of virtue and talents.

2. That all taxes shall be equally divided among all the citizens, in proportion to their abilities.

3. That the same crimes shall be subject to the same punishments, without any distinction of persons.

The constitution in like manner guarantees, as natural and civil rights, liberty to every man to go, stay, or depart, without being arrested or detained, except according to the forms of the constitution.

Liberty to every man to speak, write, print, and publish his thoughts, without the writings being subjected to censure or inspection before their publication, and to exercise the religious worship to which he is attached.

Liberty to address, to the constituted authorities, petitions signed by individuals.

The legislative power can make no law which would attack, or impede, the exercise of the natural and civil rights expressed in the present title, and guaranteed by the constitution; but as liberty consists only in the power of doing whatever neither injures the rights of another, nor the public safety, the law may establish penalties against acts, which, attacking either the rights of others, or the public safety, would be injurious to society.

The constitution guarantees the inviolability of property, or a just and previous indemnity for that of which public necessity, legally proved, shall require the sacrifice.

Property destined to the expense of worship, and to all services of public utility, belongs to the nation, and shall at all times be at its disposal.

The constitution guarantees all the alienations which have been, or which shall be made according to the forms established by the law.

The citizens have a right to elect and choose the ministers of their religions.

There shall be created and organized a general establishment of *public aid* for the education of deserted children, to relieve the infirm poor, and to procure work for the healthy poor who have not been able to find it for themselves.

There shall be created and organized a *public instruction*, common to all citizens, gratuitous with regard to those parts of instruction indispensable for all men, and of which the establishments shall be gradually distributed, in a proportion combined with the division of the kingdom.

There shall be established national festivals, to preserve the remembrance of the French Revolution, to keep up fraternal affection amongst the citizens and attachment to the constitution, the country, and the laws.

There shall be drawn up a code of civil laws, common to all the kingdom.

TITLE II

Of the Division of the Kingdom, and the State of the Citizens

I. The kingdom is one and indivisible; its territory is divided into eighty-three departments; every department into districts; each district into cantons.

II. Those are French citizens who are born in France of a French father; who, having been born in France of a foreign father, have fixed their residence in the kingdom; who, having been born in a foreign country of a French father, have returned to settle in France, and have taken the civic oath; in fine, who, having been born in a foreign country, being descended, in whatever degree, from a French man or a French woman who have left their country from religious motives, come to reside in France, and take the civil oath.

III. Those who, having been born out of the kingdom of foreign parents, but reside in France, become French citizens, after five years of continued residence in the kingdom; if, besides, they have acquired immovable property, or married a French woman, or formed an establishment of agriculture or commerce, and if they have taken the civic oath.

IV. The legislative power may, upon important considerations, naturalize a foreigner, upon no other condition than that of residing in France and taking the civic oath.

V. The civic oath is: *I swear to be faithful to the nation, the law, and the king; and to maintain, with all my power, the constitution of the kingdom decreed by the National Constituent Assembly in the years 1789, 1790, and 1791.*

VI. The quality of a French citizen is lost: 1st, by naturalization in a foreign country; 2nd, by being condemned to penalties which involve civic degradation, provided the person condemned be not reinstated; 3rd, by a sentence of contumacy, provided the sentence be not annulled; 4th, by an association with any foreign order of chivalry, or any foreign body, which shall suppose either proofs of nobility, or distinction of birth, or require religious vows.

VII. The law regards marriage solely as a civil contract. The legislative power shall establish for all the inhabitants, without distinction, the mode by which births, marriages, and deaths shall be ascertained, and shall appoint the public officers, who shall receive and preserve the certificates of them.

VIII. French citizens, considered with respect to those local relations which arise out of their association in cities and in certain divisions of territories in the country, form the *communes*.

The legislative power may fix the extent and boundary of each commune.

IX. The citizens who compose each commune have a right of choosing, for a time, according to the forms prescribed by law, those among them who, under the name of *municipal officers*, are charged with the management of the particular affairs of the commune.

To the municipal officers may be delegated certain functions relative to the general interest of the state.

TITLE III

OF THE PUBLIC POWERS

I. The sovereignty is one, indivisible, inalienable, and imprescriptible; it belongs to the nation; no section of the people, nor any individual, can assume to itself the exercise of it.

II. The nation, from which alone flow all the powers, cannot exercise them but by delegation.

The French constitution is representative; the representatives are the legislative body and the king.

III. The legislative power is delegated to a national assembly, composed of temporary representatives freely chosen by the people, to be exercised by this assembly, with the sanction of the king, in manner afterwards determined.

IV. The government is monarchical; the executive power is delegated to the king, to be exercised under his authority, by ministers and other responsible agents, in manner afterwards determined.

V. The judicial power is delegated to judges chosen for a time by the people.

CHAPTER I

OF THE LEGISLATIVE ASSEMBLY

I. The National Assembly, forming the legislative body, is permanent, and consists of one chamber only.

II. It shall be formed by new elections every two years. Each period of two years shall form one legislature.

III. The dispositions of the preceding articles shall not take place with respect to the ensuing legislative body, whose powers shall cease the last day of April, 1793.

IV. The renewal of the legislative body shall be matter of full right.

V. The legislative body cannot be dissolved by the king.

SECTION I

Number of Representatives — Bases of Representation

I. The number of representatives in the legislative body is seven hundred and forty-five, on account of the eighty-three departments of which the kingdom is composed, and independent of those that may be granted to the colonies.

II. The representatives shall be distributed among the eighty-three departments, according to the three proportions of territory, of population, and of direct contribution.

III. Of the seven hundred and forty-five representatives, two hundred and forty-seven are distributed according to territory.

Of these·each department shall nominate three, except the department of Paris, which shall only nominate one.

IV. Two hundred and forty-nine representatives are attributed to the population.

The total mass of the active population of the kingdom is divided into two hundred and forty-nine parts, and each department nominates as many of the deputies as it contains parts of the population.

V. The sum total of the direct contribution of the kingdom is likewise divided into two hundred and forty-nine parts; and each department nominates as many deputies as it pays parts of the contribution.

SECTION II

Primary Assemblies — Nomination of Electors

I. In order to form a National Legislative Assembly, the active citizens shall meet every two years, in primary assemblies, in the towns and cantons.

The primary assemblies shall form themselves, of full right, the second Sunday of March, if they have not been convoked sooner by the public officers established by law.

II. To be an active citizen it is necessary,

To be born, or to have become, a Frenchman;

To be twenty-five years of age complete;

To have resided in the city or canton during the time determined by the law;

To pay, in any part of the kingdom, a direct contribution, at least equal to the value of three days' labor, and to produce the acquittance;

Not to be in a menial capacity; namely, that of a servant receiving wages;

To be inscribed, in the municipality of the place of residence, in the list of the national guards;

To have taken the civic oath.

III. Every six years the legislative body shall fix the *minimum* and the *maximum* of the value of a day's labor, and the administrators of the departments shall determine the rate for every district.

IV. None shall exercise the rights of an active citizen in more than one place, nor employ another as his substitute.

V. Those shall be excluded from the rights of an active citizen,

Who are in a state of accusation;

Who, after having been constituted in a state of failure, or insolvency, proved by authentic documents, shall not produce a general discharge from their creditors.

VI. The primary assemblies shall name electors in proportion to the number of active citizens residing in the town or canton.

There shall be named one elector for a hundred active citizens present, or not, in the assembly.

There shall be named two for one hundred and fifty-one to two hundred and fifty; and so on in this proportion.

VII. No man can be named elector, if to the conditions necessary in order to be an active citizen, he does not join the following: In towns of more than six thousand inhabitants, that of being proprietor or life-renter of a property valued, on the rolls of the contribution, at a revenue equal to the local value of one hundred and fifty days labor.

VIII. In towns below six thousand inhabitants, that of being proprietor or life-renter of a property valued, on the rolls of contribution, at a revenue equal to the local value of one hundred and fifty days' labor; or of renting a house, valued on the same rolls, at a revenue equal to the value of one hundred days' labor.

And, in the country, that of being proprietor or life-renter of a property valued, on the rolls of contribution, at a revenue equal to the local value of one hundred and fifty days' labor, or of being a farmer of lands, valued on the same rolls, at the value of four hundred days' labor.

With respect to those who shall be at the same time proprietors or life-renters on one hand, and taxpayers or farmers on the other, their powers on these different accounts shall be added together, to establish their eligibility.

SECTION III

Electoral Assemblies — Nomination of Representatives

I. The electors named in each department shall convene in order to choose that number of representatives whose nomination shall belong to their department, and a number of substitutes equal to a third of the representatives.

The electoral assemblies shall form themselves, of full right, the last Sunday of March, if they have not been convoked sooner by the public officers appointed by law.

II. The representatives and substitutes shall be chosen by an absolute majority of votes, and cannot be chosen but from amongst the active citizens in the department.

III. All the active citizens, whatever be their condition, possession, or contribution, may be chosen representatives of the nation.

IV. Those, however, shall be obliged to decide between one or other situation — ministers, and other agents of the executive power, removable at pleasure; commissioners of the national treasury; collectors and receivers of direct contributions; superintendents of the collection or management of indirect contributions and national domains; and those who, under any denomination whatever, are attached to the employ of the military or civil household of the king.

The administrators, sub-administrators, municipal officers, and commandants of the national guards shall also be obliged to make a choice.

V. The exercise of judiciary functions shall be incompatible with those of a representative of the nation, during all the continuance of the legislature.

The judges shall be replaced by their substitutes, and the king shall provide, by briefs of commission, for the replacing of his commissaries at the tribunals.

VI. The members of the legislative body may be re-elected to the next legislature; but not afterwards, until after an interval of one legislature.

VII. The representatives named in the departments shall not be representatives of a particular department, but of the whole nation, and no mandate can be given them.

SECTION IV

Session and Regulation of the Primary and Electoral Assemblies

I. The functions of the primary and electoral assemblies are limited to the right of electing; and as soon as elections are over, they shall separate, and shall not form themselves anew until they shall be convoked, except in the case of section II, article I, and of section III, article I, above.

II. No active citizen can enter or vote in an assembly if he is armed.

III. Armed force cannot be introduced in the meeting, except at the express desire of the assembly, unless in the case of actual violence, when the order of the president shall be sufficient to call in the aid of public force.

IV. Every two years there shall be drawn up, in each district, lists by cantons of the active citizens; and the list of each canton shall be published and posted up two months before the meeting of the primary assembly. The protests which shall be made either in regard to the qualifications of the citizens named in the list, or on the part of those who shall affirm that they are unjustly omitted, shall be carried to the tribunals, to be there summarily decided upon.

The list shall serve to regulate the admission of citizens in the next primary assembly, in every point that shall not have been ascertained by judgments pronounced before the sitting of the assembly.

V. The electoral assemblies have the right of verifying the qualifications and powers of those who shall present themselves there; and their decisions shall be provisionally executed, with a reserve for judgments of the legislative body at the time of the verification of the powers of deputies.

VI. In no case, and under no pretext, shall the king, or any agents named by him, interfere in the questions relative to the regularity of the convocations, the sitting of assemblies, the form of elections, or the political rights of the citizens, without prejudice, however, to the functions of the commissaries of the king, in the cases determined by law, where questions relative to the political rights of citizens ought to be carried to the tribunals.

SECTION V

Meeting of the Representatives of the National Legislative Assembly

I. The representatives shall assemble on the first Monday of May, in the place of the meeting of the last legislature.

II. They shall form themselves, provisionally, into an assembly, under the presidence of the eldest, to verify the powers of the representatives present.

III. As soon as those shall have been verified, to the number of three hundred and seventy-three members, they shall constitute themselves under the title of the *National Legislative Assembly*; they shall name a president, vice-president, and secretaries, and enter upon the exercise of their functions.

IV. During the whole of the month of May, if the number of representatives present falls short of three hundred and seventy-three, the Assembly shall not perform any legislative act. They may issue an arrest, enjoining the absent members to attend to their functions within fifteen days at farthest, under a penalty of three thousand livres, if they do not produce any excuse which will be deemed lawful by the legislative body.

V. On the last day of May, whatever be the number of members present, they shall constitute themselves a National Legislative Assembly.

VI. The representatives shall pronounce in a body, in the name of the French people, the oath *to live free, or die*.

They shall then individually take the oath *to maintain, with all their power, the constitution of the kingdom, decreed by the National Constituent Assembly during the years 1789, 1790, and 1791; to propose or assent to nothing, in the course of the legislature, which may at all tend to infringe it; and to be, in every respect, faithful to the nation, the law, and the king.*

VII. The representatives of the nation are inviolable; they cannot be examined, accused, or judged at any time with respect to what they have said, written, or done, in the exercise of their functions of representatives.

VIII. They may, for a crime, be seized in the act, or in virtue of an order of arrest; but notice shall be given of it, without delay, to the legislative body; and the prosecution shall not be continued, until after the legislative body shall have decided that there is ground for accusation.

CHAPTER II

OF THE ROYALTY AND OF THE MINISTERS

SECTION I

Of the Royalty and the King

I. The royalty is indivisible, and delegated hereditarily to the race on the throne, from male to male, by order of primogeniture, to the perpetual exclusion of women and their descendants.

Nothing is prejudged respecting the effect of renunciations, in the race on the throne.

II. The person of the king is sacred and inviolable; his only title is *King of the French*.

III. There is no authority in France superior to that of the law. The king reigns only by it, and it is only in the name of the law that he can require obedience.

IV. The king, on his accession to the throne, or at the period of his majority, shall take to the nation, in the presence of the legislative body, the oath *to be faithful to the nation, and to the law; to employ all the power delegated to him to maintain the constitution decreed by the National Constituent Assembly in the years 1789, 1790, and 1791, and to cause the laws to be executed.*

If the legislative body shall not be assembled, the king shall cause a proclamation to be issued, in which shall be expressed this oath, and a promise to repeat it as soon as the legislative body shall assemble.

V. If, one month after an investigation by the legislative body, the king has not taken this oath, or if after taking it he shall retract, he shall be deemed to have abdicated the royalty.

VI. If the king should put himself at the head of an army, and direct the forces of it against the nation; or if he should not oppose, by a formal act, any such enterprise undertaken in his name, he shall be deemed to have abdicated.

VII. If the king, having gone out of the kingdom, does not return, on the invitation of the legislative body, and within the delay fixed by the proclamation, which cannot be less than two months, he shall be deemed to have abdicated.

The delay shall commence from the day when the proclamation of the legislative body shall have been published in the place of its sitting; and the ministers shall be obliged, under their responsibility, to perform all the acts of the executive power, the exercise of which shall be suspended in the hands of the absent king.

VIII. After abdication, express and legal, the king shall be in the class of citizens, and may be accused and tried, like them, for acts posterior to his abdication.

IX. The particular effects which the king possesses at his accession to the throne are irrevocably united to the domain of the nation; he has the disposition of those which he acquires on his own private account; if he has not disposed of them, they are in like manner united at the end of the reign.

X. The nation makes provision for the splendor of the throne by a civil list, of which the legislative body shall fix the sum, at the commencement of each reign, for the whole duration of that reign.

XI. The king shall appoint an administrator of the civil list, who shall institute all suits for the king, and against whom all actions for debts of the king shall be carried on, and judgments given and executed. Sentences of condemnation, obtained by creditors of the civil list, shall be executed against the administrator personally and his private fortune.

XII. The king shall have, independent of the honorary guard which shall be furnished him by the citizen national guards of the place of his residence, a guard paid from the funds of the civil list. It shall not exceed one thousand two hundred foot, and six thousand horse.

The degrees and rules of advancement shall be the same in it as among the troops of the line. But those who compose the king's guards shall pass through all the degrees exclusively among themselves, and cannot obtain any in the army of the line.

The king cannot choose his guards but among those who are present in active service in the troops of the line, or among the citizens who have served a year in the national guards, provided they are residents in the kingdom, and that they have previously taken the civic oath.

The king's guards cannot be ordered or required for any other public service.

SECTION II

Of the Regency

I. The king is a minor until the age of eighteen complete; and during his minority there shall be a regent of the kingdom.

II. The regency belongs to the relative of the king who is the next in degree according to the order of succession to the throne, and who has attained the age of twenty-five, provided he is a Frenchman resident in the kingdom, and not presumptive heir to any other crown, and has taken the civic oath.

Women are excluded from the regency.

III. If a minor king has no relatives who unite the above qualities, the regent of the kingdom shall be elected as is directed in the following articles:

IV. The legislative body shall not elect the regent.

V. The electors of each district shall assemble in the chief place of their district, after a proclamation, which shall be issued in the first week of the new reign, by the legislative body, if convened; and if separated, the minister of justice shall be bound to make that proclamation in the same week.

VI. The electors shall name in every district, by individual scrutiny, and absolute plurality of votes, a citizen eligible, and resident in the district, to whom they shall give, by the *procès-verbal* of the election, a special mandate, limited to the sole function of electing the citizen whom he shall judge, in his heart and his conscience, the most worthy of being regent of the kingdom.

VII. The citizens elected in the districts, having these mandates, shall be bound to assemble in the town where the legislative body holds its seat, the fortieth day at farthest, counting from that of the advancement of the minor king to the throne; and they shall form there the electoral assembly, who shall proceed to the nomination of the regent.

VIII. The election of the regent shall be made by individual scrutiny and an absolute plurality of votes.

IX. The electoral assembly cannot employ itself but relative to this election, and shall separate as soon as the election is finished. Every other act which it shall attempt is declared unconstitutional, and of no effect.

X. The electoral assembly shall make its president present the *procès-verbal* of the election to the legislative body, which, after having verified the regularity of the election, shall make it public over all the kingdom by a proclamation.

XI. The regent exercises, until the king's majority, all the functions of royalty, and is not personally responsible for the acts of his administration.

XII. The regent cannot begin the exercise of his functions until after taking to the nation, in the presence of the legislative body, an oath *to be faithful to the nation, the law, and the king; and to employ all the power delegated to the king, and of which the exercise is confided to him during the minority of the king, to maintain the constitution decreed by the National Constituent Assembly in the years 1789, 1790, and 1791, and to cause the laws to be executed.*

If the legislative body is not assembled, the regent shall cause a proclamation to be issued, in which shall be expressed this oath, and a promise to repeat it as soon as the legislative body shall be met.

XIII. As long as the regent is not entered on the exercise of his functions, the sanction of the laws remains suspended; the ministers continue to perform, under their responsibility, all the acts of the executive power.

XIV. As soon as the regent shall have taken the oath, the legislative body shall fix his allowance, which shall not be altered during his regency.

XV. If, on account of the minority of the relative called to the regency, it has devolved to a more distant relative, or been settled by election, the regent who shall have entered on the exercise of it shall continue his functions until the majority of the king.

XVI. The regency of the kingdom confers no right over the person of the minor king.

XVII. The care of the minor king shall be confided to his mother; and if he has no mother, or if she be married again at the time of her son's accession to the throne, or if she marry again during the minority, the care of him shall be delegated by the legislative body.

Neither the regent, nor his descendants, nor a woman, can be chosen as guardian of the minor king.

XVIII. In case of the king's insanity, notoriously admitted, legally proved, and declared by the legislative body, after three successive deliberations held monthly, there shall be a regency, as long as such incapacity continues.

SECTION III

Of the Royal Family

I. The presumptive heir shall bear the name of *Prince Royal.* He cannot go out of the kingdom, without a decree of the legislative body, and the king's consent.

If he is gone out of it, and if, being arrived at eighteen years of age, he does not return to France, after being required by a proclamation of the legislative body, he is held to have abdicated the right of succession to the throne.

II. If the presumptive heir be a minor, the relative of full age, and next in order to the regency, is bound to reside within the kingdom. In case of his going out of it, and not returning on the requisition of the legislative body, he shall be declared to have abdicated his right to the regency.

III. The guardian elected, or the mother having the care of the minor king, forfeit their charge if they go out of the kingdom.

If the mother of the presumptive heir, a minor, goes out of the kingdom, she cannot, even after her return, have the care of her minor son, become king, but by decree of the legislative body.

IV. A law shall be made to regulate the education of the minor king, and that of the heir presumptive.

V. The members of the royal family, called to the eventual succession to the throne, enjoy the rights of an active citizen, but are not eligible to any places, employs, or functions in the nomination of the people.

Excepting the places of ministers, they are capable of offices and employs in the nomination of the king; however, they cannot be commanders-in-chief of any army or fleet, nor fulfill the functions of ambassadors, without the consent of the legislative body, granted on the proposition of the king.

VI. The members of the royal family, called to the eventual succession to the throne, shall add the denomination of *French Prince* to the name which shall have been given them in the civil act stating their birth; and this name can neither be patronymic, nor formed of any of the qualifications abolished by the present constitution.

The denomination of *Prince* cannot be given to any other individual, and shall convey no privilege, nor any exception, to the common rights of all Frenchmen.

VII. The acts by which shall be legally stated the births, marriages, and deaths of the French princes shall be presented to the legislative body, which shall command deposit of them in their archives.

VIII. No real appanage (in land) shall be granted to the members of the royal family.

The younger sons of the king shall receive at the age of twenty-five, or on their marriage, an annuity, the amount of which shall be fixed by the legislative body, and which shall terminate with the extinction of their male heirs.

SECTION IV

Of Ministers

I. To the king alone belongs the choice and revocation of ministers.

II. The members of the present National Assembly, and succeeding legislatures, the members of the tribunal of annulment, and those who shall serve in the high jury, cannot be advanced to the ministry, nor receive any offices, gifts, pensions, salaries, or commissions from the executive power, or its agents, during the continuance of their functions, nor during the two years after having finished the exercise of them.

The same shall be the case with respect to those who shall be only inscribed in the list of the high jury, during all the time that their inscription shall continue.

III. No one can enter upon the exercise of any employ, either in the bureaux of ministers, or in those of the administrations of public power, without having taken the civic oath, and having verified his having taken it.

IV. No order of the king can be executed if it is not signed by him and counter-signed by the minister or controller of the department.

V. The ministers are responsible for all the offenses committed by them against the national safety and the constitution;

For every attack on individual property and liberty;

For every waste of the money allotted for the expenses of their department.

VI. In no case can the written or verbal order of a king shelter a minister from responsibility.

VII. The ministers are bound to present every year to the legislative body, at the opening of the session, the state of the expenses of their department; to give an account of the employment of the sums destined for that purpose; and to mention the abuses which may have crept into the different parts of the government.

VIII. No minister in or out of place can be criminally prosecuted for any transaction of his administration, without a decree of the legislative body.

CHAPTER III

OF THE EXERCISE OF THE LEGISLATIVE POWER

SECTION I

Powers and Functions of the National Legislative Assembly

I. The constitution delegates exclusively to the legislative body the powers and functions following:

1. To propose and decree laws: the king can only invite the legislative body to take an object into consideration.

2. To fix the public expenses.

3. To establish the public contributions — to determine their nature, quantity, duration, and mode of collection.

4. To divide the direct contribution among the departments of the kingdom — to superintend the employ of all the public revenue, and to demand an account of it.

5. To decree the creation or suppression of public offices.

6. To determine the quality, weight, impression, and name of the coin.

7. To permit or prohibit the introduction of foreign troops into the French territories, and of foreign naval forces into the ports of the kingdom.

8. To fix annually, after the proposition of the king, the number of men and ships of which the land and naval armies shall be composed; the pay and number of individuals of each rank; the rules of admission and promotion; the forms of enrollment and discharge; the formation of naval equipments; the admission of foreign troops, or naval forces, into the service of France; and the pay of troops, in case of their being disbanded.

9. To regulate the administrative government, and the alienation of the national domains.

10. To prosecute before the high national court the ministers and principal agents of the executive power, in what relates to their responsibility.

To accuse and prosecute before the same court those who shall be charged with any attack or conspiracy against the general safety of the state, or against the constitution.

11. To establish the laws according to which marks of honor or decoration, purely personal, shall be granted to those who have rendered services to the state.

12. The legislative body has the right to decree public honors to the memory of great men.

II. War cannot be determined on but by a decree of the legislative body, passed on the formal and necessary proposition of the king, and sanctioned by him.

In the case of imminent or commenced hostilities, of an ally to be supported, or of a right to be preserved by force of arms, the king shall notify the same without delay to the legislative body, and shall declare the reasons of it.

If the legislative body be not sitting, the king shall assemble it immediately.

If the legislative body decides that war ought not to be made, the king shall immediately take measures to stop or prevent all hostilities, the ministers being responsible for delays.

If the legislative body finds that the hostilities commenced are a palpable aggression on the part of the ministers, or any other agent of the executive power, the author of the aggression shall be prosecuted criminally.

During the whole course of the war, the legislative body may require the king to negotiate peace, and the king is bound to yield to the requisition.

On the immediate conclusion of war, the legislative body shall fix the time within which the troops levied above the peace establishment shall be discharged, and the army reduced to its ordinary state.

III. It belongs to the legislative body to ratify treaties of peace, alliance, and commerce; and no treaty shall have effect but by this ratification.

IV. The legislative body has the right of determining the place of its sittings, of continuing them as long as it shall think necessary, and of adjourning; at the commencement of each reign, if it be not sitting, it shall be bound to meet without delay.

It has the right of police in the place of its sittings, and to such extent around it as shall be determined.

It has the right of discipline over its members; but it can pronounce no heavier punishment than censure, arrest for eight days, or imprisonment for three.

It has the right of disposing, for its safety, and the respect that is due to it, of the forces which shall be placed, by its consent, in the city where it shall hold its sittings.

V. The executive power cannot march, or quarter, or station any troops of the line within thirty thousand *toises* [1] of the legislative body, except on its requisition, or by its authority.

SECTION II

Holding of the Sittings, and Form of Deliberating

I. The deliberations of the legislative body shall be public, and the proceedings of its sittings shall be printed.

II. The legislative body may, however, on any occasion, form itself into a *general committee*.

Fifty members shall have a right to demand this.

During the continuance of the general committee, the assistants shall retire, the

---

[1] About thirty-six miles.

chair of the president shall be vacant, and order shall be maintained by the vice-president.

III. No legislative act can be debated and decreed except in the following form:

IV. The plan of the decree shall be read thrice, at three intervals, the shortest of which cannot be less than eight days.

V. The discussion shall be open after every reading; nevertheless, after the first and second reading, the legislative body may declare that there is reason for adjournment, or that there is no need for deliberation; in this last case, the plan of the decree may be introduced again in the same session.

Every plan of a decree shall be printed and distributed before the second reading of it can be commenced.

VI. After the third reading, the president shall be bound to propose its deliberation; and the legislative body shall decide whether they are qualified to pass a definitive decree, or would rather choose to postpone their decision, in order to gather more ample information on the subject.

VII. The legislative body cannot deliberate if the meeting does not consist of at least two hundred members; and no decree shall be made except by the absolute majority of votes.

VIII. No plan of a law, which, after having been submitted to discussion, shall have been rejected after the third reading, can again be introduced the same session.

IX. The preamble of every definitive decree shall announce, first, the dates of those sittings at which the three readings of the plan of the decree were made; second, the enactment by which it shall have been resolved, after the third reading, to decide definitively.

X. The king shall refuse his sanction to the decrees whose preamble shall not attest the observance of the above forms; if any of those decrees be sanctioned, the ministers shall neither put to it the seal, nor promulgate it, and their responsibility in this respect shall continue six years.

XI. Exempt from these regulations are decrees recognized and declared urgent by a previous deliberation of the legislative body; but they may be modified, or revoked, in the course of the same session.

The decree by which a matter shall have been declared urgent shall announce the reasons of it, and there shall be mention made of this previous decree in the preamble of the definitive decree.

SECTION III

Of the Royal Sanction

I. The decrees of the legislative body are presented to the king, who may refuse his assent to them.

II. In the case of a refusal of the royal assent, that refusal is only suspensive.

When the two legislatures which shall follow that in which the decree was presented shall successively represent the same decree in the same terms in which it was as originally conceived, the king shall be deemed to have given his sanction.

III. The assent of the king is expressed to each decree by the following formula, signed by the king: *The king consents and will cause to be executed.*

The suspensive refusal is thus expressed: *The king will examine.*

IV. The king is bound to express his assent or refusal, to each decree, within two months after it shall have been presented.

V. No decree to which the king has refused his assent can be presented to him by the same legislature.

VI. The decrees sanctioned by the king, and those presented to him by three successive legislatures, alone have the force of a law, and bear the name and title of *laws*.

VII. There shall be, however, executed as laws, without being subjected to sanction, those acts of the legislative body which relate to its constitution as a deliberating assembly;

Its interior police, and that which it may exercise in the exterior places, which it shall have determined;

The verification of the powers of the members present;

The injunctions to absent members;

The convocation of the primary assemblies in case of delay;

The exercise of constitutional superintendence over the administrators and municipal officers;

Questions of eligibility, or the validity of elections;

Exempted likewise from sanction are acts relative to the responsibility of ministers, and all decrees importing that there is ground of accusation.

VIII. The decrees of the legislative body, concerning the establishment, prorogation, and collection of public contributions, shall bear the name and title of laws; they shall be promulgated and executed without being subject to sanction, except with respect to those dispositions which should establish other penalties than pecuniary fines and constraints.

These decrees cannot be passed except after the observation of the formalities prescribed by articles IV, V, VI, VII, VIII, and IX of section II of the present chapter; and the legislative body shall not insert in them any dispositions foreign to their object.

SECTION IV

Connection of the Legislative Body with the King

I. When the legislative body is definitively constituted, it shall send a deputation to inform the king. The king may every year open the session, and propose the objects, which, during its continuance, he thinks ought to be taken into consideration: this form, however, is not to be considered as *necessary* to the activity of the legislative body.

II. When the legislative body wishes to adjourn longer than fifteen days, it is bound to inform the king by a deputation, at least eight days previous.

III. A week, at least, before the end of each session, the legislative body shall send a deputation to the king, to announce to him the day on which it proposes to terminate its sittings. The king may come, in order to close the session.

IV. If the king find it of importance to the welfare of the state that the session be continued, or that the adjournment be put off, or take place only for a shorter time, he may send a message to this effect, on which the legislative body is bound to deliberate.

V. The king shall convoke the legislative body, during the interval of its session, at all times when the interest of the state shall appear to him to require it, as well as in those cases which the legislative body shall have foreseen and determined, previous to their adjournment.

VI. Whenever the king shall visit the place of meeting of the legislative body, he shall be received and conducted back by a deputation; he cannot be accompanied into the inner parts of the hall by any except the prince royal and the ministers.

VII. The president can in no case form part of a deputation.

VIII. The legislative body shall cease to be a deliberating body while the king shall be present.

IX. The acts of correspondence of the king with the legislative body shall be always countersigned by a minister.

X. The ministers of the king shall have admission into the National Legislative Assembly; they shall have a place assigned to them; they shall be heard always, when they demand it, on objects relative to their administration, or when they shall be required to give information. They shall also be heard on objects foreign to their administration, when the National Assembly shall grant them liberty to speak.

CHAPTER IV

Of the Exercise of the Executive Power

I. The supreme executive power resides exclusively in the hands of the king.

The king is the supreme head of the general administration of the kingdom: the care of watching over the maintenance of public order and tranquillity is entrusted to him.

The king is the supreme head of the land and sea forces.

To the king is delegated the care of watching over the exterior security of the kingdom, and of maintaining its rights and possessions.

II. The king names ambassadors, and the other agents of political negotiations.

He bestows the command of armies and fleets, and the ranks of marshal of France and admiral.

He names two-thirds of the rear-admirals, and one-half of the lieutenant-generals, camp-marshals, captains of ships, and colonels of the national gendarmerie.

He names a third of the colonels and lieutenant-colonels, and a sixth of the lieutenants of ships — the whole in conformity to the laws with respect to promotion.

He appoints, in the civil administration of the marine, the directors, the controllers, the treasurers of the arsenals, the masters of the works, the under-masters of civil buildings, half of the masters of administration, and of the under-masters of construction.

He appoints the commissaries of the tribunals.

He appoints the chief superintendents of the administration of indirect contributions, and the administration of national domains.

He superintends the coinage of money, and appoints the officers entrusted with this superintendence in the general commission and the mints.

The effigy of the king is struck on all the coinage of the kingdom.

III. The king orders letters patent, brevets, and commissions to be delivered to all the public officers that ought to receive them.

IV. The king orders a list of pensions and gratifications to be made out, for the purpose of being presented to the legislative body each session, and decreed, if there is reason for it.

SECTION I

Of the Promulgation of Laws

I. The executive power is charged with ordering the seal of state to be put to laws, and causing them to be promulgated.

It is equally charged with causing to be promulgated and executed those acts of the legislative body which have no need of the sanction of the king.

II. Two copies of each law shall be made, both signed by the king, countersigned by the minister of justice, and sealed with the seal of state. The one shall be deposited in the archives of the seal, and the other shall be sent to the archives of the legislative body.

III. The promulgation of the laws shall be thus expressed:

"N. (the king's name) by the grace of God and the constitutional law of the state, King of the French, to all present and to come, greeting. The National Assembly has decreed, and we will and ordain as follows:"

(Here a literal copy of the decree shall be inserted without any variation.)

"We command and ordain to all administrative bodies and courts of justice to cause these presents to be transcribed on their registers, read and published, and posted up in their departments and respective places of resort, and executed as a law of the realm; in witness of which we have signed these presents, to which we have caused the seal of the state to be put."

IV. If the king be a minor, laws, proclamations, and other acts proceeding from the royal authority during the regency shall be conceived in these terms:

"N. (the name of the regent) Regent of the Kingdom, in the name of N. (the king's name) by the grace of God and the constitutional law of the state, King of the French, etc."

V. The executive power is bound to send the laws to the administrative bodies and courts of justice, to have it certified that they are so sent, and to answer for it to the legislative body.

VI. The executive power cannot make any law, not even provisional, but merely proclamations conformable to the laws, to ordain or enforce the execution.

SECTION II

Of the Interior Administration

I. There is in each department a superior administration, and in each district a subordinate administration.

II. The administrators have no character of representation.

They are agents, chosen for a time by the people, to exercise, under the superintendence and the authority of the king, the administrative functions.

III. They can neither intermeddle in the exercise of the legislative power, nor suspend the execution of the laws, nor assume any authority over judicial proceedings, nor over military regulations or operations.

IV. The administrators are essentially charged with the repartition of the direct taxes, and with the superintendence of the funds arising from all the contributions and public revenues in their territory.

It belongs to the legislative power to determine the rules and mode of their functions, with respect to the objects above mentioned, as well as with respect to all the other parts of the interior administration.

V. The king has a right of annulling such acts of the administrators of department as are contrary to the law, or the orders he has transmitted to them.

He may in case of obstinate disobedience, or of their endangering, by their acts, the safety or peace of the public, suspend them from their functions.

VI. The administrators of department have also the right of annulling the acts of the sub-administrators of department contrary to the laws or to the decisions of administrators of departments, or to the orders which the latter shall have given or transmitted.

They may likewise, in case of an obstinate disobedience on the part of sub-administrators, or if the latter endanger, by their acts, the public safety or tranquillity, suspend them from their functions, with the reserve of informing the king, who may remove or confirm the suspension.

VII. The king, if the administrators of department shall not use the power which is delegated to them in the article above, may directly annul the acts of sub-administrators, and suspend them in the same cases.

VIII. Whenever the king shall pronounce or confirm the suspension of administrators, or sub-administrators, he shall inform the legislative body. This body may either remove or confirm the suspension, or even dissolve the culpable administration; and, if there be ground, remit all the administrators, or some of them, to the criminal tribunals, or enforce against them the decree of accusation.

SECTION III

Of External Connections

I. The king alone can keep up foreign political connections, conduct negotiations, make preparations of war proportional to those of neighboring states, distribute the land and sea forces as he shall judge most suitable, and regulate their direction in case of war.

II. Every declaration of war shall be made in these terms: *By the King of the French, in the name of the nation.*

III. It belongs to the king to resolve and sign, with all foreign powers, all treaties of peace, alliance, and commerce, and other conventions which he shall judge necessary for the welfare of the state, with a reserve for the ratification of the legislative body.

CHAPTER V

OF THE JUDICIAL POWER

I. The judicial power can in no case be exercised either by the legislative body or the king.

II. Justice shall be gratuitously rendered by judges chosen for a time by the people, and instituted by letters patent of the king, who cannot refuse to grant them. They cannot be deposed, but for forfeiture duly judged; nor suspended, but for an accusation admitted.

The public accuser shall be named by the people.

III. The tribunals cannot either interfere in the exercise of the legislative power, or suspend the execution of the laws, or undertake the administrative functions, or cite before them the administrators on account of their functions.

IV. The citizens cannot be withdrawn from the judges whom the law assigns to them, by any commission, or by any other attributions or evocations than those which are determined by the laws.

V. The right of the citizens to terminate definitively their disputes by way of arbitration shall receive no infringement from the acts of the legislative power.

VI. The ordinary courts of justice cannot receive any civil action, until it be certified to them that the parties have appeared, or that the pursuer has cited the opposite party to appear before mediators, to endeavor to bring about a reconciliation.

VII. There shall be one or more judges of peace in the cantons and in the towns. The number of them shall be determined by the legislative power.

VIII. It belongs to the legislative power to regulate the number, and extent of jurisdiction, of the tribunals, and the number of judges of which each tribunal shall be composed.

IX. In criminal matters, no citizen can be tried but on an accusation received by a jury, or decreed by the legislative body, in the cases where it belongs to it to pursue the accusation.

After the admission of the accusation, the fact shall be recognized and declared by a jury.

The accused shall have a right to refuse as many as twenty jurors, without assigning reasons.

The jury which declares the fact cannot be of fewer than twelve members.

The application of the law shall be made by judges.

The examinations during the process shall be public, and assistance of counsel cannot be refused to the accused.

No man acquitted by a lawful jury can be retaken or accused on account of the same fact.

X. No man can be seized upon but in order to be conducted before an officer of the police; and no man can be arrested or detained but in virtue of a mandate of the officers of police, of an order for personal arrest by a tribunal, of a decree of accusation of the legislative body in cases where it belongs to it to pronounce, or in a sentence of imprisonment or detention for the sake of correction.

XI. Every man seized upon and conducted before an officer of police shall be examined immediately, or at latest, in twenty-four hours.

If it results from the examination that there be no ground for blame against him, he shall be directly set at liberty; or if there be ground to send him to a house of arrest, he shall be conducted there with the least delay possible, and that in any case cannot exceed three days.

XII. No man arrested can be detained if he give sufficient bail, in all cases where the law permits a man to remain free under bail.

XIII. No man, in the cases when detention is authorized by the law, can be conducted or detained anywhere but in those places legally and publicly marked out as houses of arrest, of justice, or of imprisonment.

XIV. No guard or jailor can receive or detain any man but in virtue of a mandate, order of arrest, decree of accusation, or sentence, mentioned in the tenth article above, nor without transcribing them to his own register.

XV. Every guard or jailor is bound, and no order can release him from the obligation, to produce the person detained to the civil officer who superintends the police of the house of arrest, as often as it shall be required of him.

The production of the person detained also cannot be refused to his relatives and friends who bring an order from a civil officer, who shall be bound always to grant it, unless the guard or jailor produce an order from a judge, transcribed in his register, to keep the person arrested secret.

XVI. Every man, whatever his place or occupation, except those to whom the law confides the right of arrest, who shall give, sign, execute, or cause to be executed an order to arrest a citizen; or whoever, even in the cases of arrest authorized by law, shall conduct, receive, or retain a citizen in a place of detention not publicly and legally marked out; and every guard or jailor who shall act in opposition to the dispositions of articles XIV and XV above shall be culpable of the crime of arbitrary detention.

XVII. No man shall be taken up or prosecuted on account of the writings which he has caused to be printed or published, whatever be their subjects, if he has not designedly provoked disobedience to the law, outrage to the established powers, and resistance to their acts, or any of the actions declared crimes or offenses by the law.

The censure of all the acts of the established powers is permitted; but voluntary calumnies against the probity of public officers, and against the rectitude of their intentions in the exercise of their functions, may be prosecuted by those who are the subjects of them.

Calumnies or injurious sayings against any kind of persons, relative to the actions of their private life, shall be punished by prosecution.

XVIII. No man can be judged, either civilly or criminally, for acts of writing, printing, or publishing, except it has been recognized and declared by a jury, 1st, that there is an offense in the writing denounced; 2nd, that the person prosecuted is guilty of it.

XIX. There shall be, for the whole kingdom, a single tribunal of annulment, established near the legislative body. Its function shall be to pronounce,

On demands of annulment of judgments given in the last resort by the tribunals;

On demands of being remitted from one tribunal to another, for lawful causes of suspicion;

On regulations respecting judges, and suits against a whole tribunal.

XX. In questions of annulment, the tribunal of annulment shall never take cognizance of the affair itself; but after having annulled the sentence which shall have been pronounced in a process, and in which the forms have been violated, or which shall contain an express contradiction to the law, it shall remit the original affair to the tribunals which ought to decide on it.

XXI. When, after being twice annulled, a sentence pronounced by a third tribunal shall be attacked on the same grounds as at first, the question shall no more be judged by the tribunal of annulment, without having been submitted to the legislative body, which shall pass a decree declarative of the law, to which the tribunal of annulment shall be bound to conform.

XXII. Every year, the tribunal of annulment shall be bound to send to the bar of the legislative body a deputation of eight of its members, to present a statement of the decisions passed, on the margin of each of which shall be placed a short account of the affair, and the text of the law which shall have determined the decision.

XXIII. A high national court, formed of the members of the tribunal of annulment, and of high jurors, shall take cognizance of offenses committed by the ministers and principal agents of the executive power, and of those crimes which attack the general safety of the state, after the legislative body shall have passed a decree for accusation.

It shall not be assembled but at the proclamation of the legislative body, and at the distance of thirty thousand *toises* at least from the place where the legislative body holds its meetings.

XXIV. The orders issued for executing the judgment of the tribunals shall be conceived in these terms:

"N. (the name of the king) by the grace of God, and by the constitutional law of the state, King of the French, to all present and to come, greeting. The tribunal of —— has passed the following judgment:" (Here shall follow a copy of the judgment, in which shall be mentioned the names of the judges.)

"We charge and enjoin all officers, upon the present demand, to put the said judgment into execution, our commissaries of the tribunals to enforce the same, and all the commanders and officers of the public force to be assisting with their force, when it shall be legally required: in witness of which, the present judgment has been signed by the president of the tribunal, and by the register."

XXV. The functions of the king's commissaries in the tribunals shall be to require the observance of the laws in the judgments to be given, and to cause them to be executed after they are passed.

They shall not be public accusers; but they shall be heard on all accusations, and shall require, during process, regularity of forms, and, before judgment, application of the law.

XXVI. The king's commissaries in the tribunals shall denounce to the director of the jury, either officially, or according to orders given them by the king,

Offenses against the individual liberty of citizens, against free circulation of provisions and other objects of commerce, and against the collection of contributions;

Offenses by which the execution of orders given by the king, in the exercise of the functions delegated to him, shall be disturbed or impeded;

Infringements of the laws of nations;

And opposition to the execution of judgments, and to all executive acts proceeding from established powers.

XXVII. The minister of justice shall denounce to the tribunal of appeal, by means of the king's commissary, and without prejudice to the rights of the parties interested, the acts in which the judges have exceeded the bounds of their power.

The tribunal shall annul these acts; and if they give ground for forfeiture, the fact shall be represented to the legislative body, which shall pass the decree of accusation if there be ground, and refer the parties informed against to the high national court.

TITLE IV

Of the Public Force

I. The public force is instituted to defend the state against external enemies, and to maintain internal order and the execution of the laws.

II. It is composed,

Of the land and sea armies;

Of the troops specially destined for home service;

And, subsidiarily, of the active citizens, and their children of age to bear arms, registered in the roll of national guards.

III. The national guards do not form a military body, or an institution of state; they are the citizens themselves, called to assist the public force.

IV. The citizens can never embody themselves, or act as national guards, but by virtue of a legal requisition or authority.

V. They are subject, in this quality, to an organization to be determined by law.

They shall be distinguished in the whole kingdom by only one form of discipline, and one uniform.

Distinctions of rank and subordination exist only relatively to the service, and during its continuance.

VI. Officers are chosen for a time, and cannot again be chosen until after a certain interval of service as soldiers.

None shall command the national guard of more than one district.

VII. All the parts of the public force employed for the safety of the state from foreign enemies shall act under the command of the king.

VIII. No body or detachment of troops of the line can act in the internal part of the kingdom without a legal order.

IX. No agent of the public force can enter the house of a citizen if it be not on purpose to execute the orders of police and of justice, or in cases formally provided for by the law.

X. The requisition of the public force, in the internal part of the kingdom, belongs to the civil officers, according to the regulations provided by the legislative power.

XI. When any department is throughout in a state of commotion, the king shall issue, under the responsibility of his ministers, the necessary orders for the execution of laws, and the re-establishment of order; but with the reserve of informing the legislative body if it be assembled, and of convoking it if it be not sitting.

XII. The public force is *essentially obedient*; no armed body can deliberate.

XIII. The land and sea armies, and the troops destined to preserve internal security, are subjected to particular laws, both for the maintenance and discipline, and for the manner of judgments, and nature of punishments, on occasion of military offenses.

TITLE V

OF PUBLIC CONTRIBUTIONS

I. Public contributions shall be debated and fixed every year by the legislative body, and cannot continue in force longer than the last day of the following session, if they are not expressly renewed.

II. The funds necessary to the discharge of the national debt, and the payment of the civil list, can, under no pretext, be refused or suspended.

The salaries of the ministers of the Catholic religion who are paid, preserved, elected, or named in virtue of the decrees of the National Constituent Assembly form a part of the national debt.

The legislative body cannot, in any case, charge the nation with the payment of the debts of any individual.

III. The accounts at full length of the ministerial department, signed and certified by the ministers or commissaries, shall be rendered public by being printed at the commencement of the session of each legislature.

So shall also the state of receipts of the different taxes, and all the public revenues.

The state of receipt and expenditure shall be distinguished according to their nature, and shall express the sums received and disbursed, year by year, in each district.

The private expenses of each department, and those relative to the tribunals, the administrative bodies, and other establishments, shall also be rendered public.

IV. The administrators of department, and sub-administrators, can neither establish any public contribution, nor make any distribution beyond the time and sums fixed by the legislative body; nor deliberate, or permit, without being authorized by it, any local loan to be charged to the citizens of the department.

V. The executive power directs and superintends the collection and paying in of contributions, and gives all the necessary orders to this effect.

TITLE VI

OF THE CONNECTION OF THE FRENCH NATION WITH OTHER NATIONS

The French nation renounces the undertaking of any war with a view to making conquests, and will never employ its forces against the liberty of any people.

The constitution no longer admits the right of escheat.

Foreigners, whether settled in France or not, inherit the property of their parents, whether foreigners or Frenchmen.

They can contract, acquire, and receive property situated in France, and dispose of it, as well as any French citizen, in every mode authorized by the laws.

Foreigners in France are subject to the same criminal laws and regulations of police as French citizens, with a reserve for conventions agreed on with foreign powers. Their persons, effects, industry, and religion are equally protected by the law.

TITLE VII

OF THE REVISION OF CONSTITUTIONAL DECREES

I. The National Constituent Assembly declares that the nation has an imprescriptible right to change its constitution; and nevertheless, considering that it is most suitable to the national interest to make use of the right of reforming those articles which experience shall demonstrate the inconvenience of only by means appointed by the constitution itself, decrees that the assembly of revision shall proceed in the following manner:

II. When three successive legislatures shall have declared an uniform wish for the change of any constitutional article, the revision demanded shall take place.

III. The ensuing legislature (that commencing in 1791) cannot propose the reform of any constitutional article.

IV. Of the three legislatures which shall successively propose any changes, the first two shall not occupy themselves relative to that object but in the last two months of their last session, and the third at the end of its first annual session, or at the beginning of the second.

Their deliberations on that matter shall be subjected to the same forms as the legislative acts; but the decrees by which they shall have expressed their desires shall not be subjected to the sanction of the king.

V. The fourth legislature, augmented by two hundred and forty-nine members chosen in each department, by doubling the ordinary number which it furnishes for its population, shall constitute the assembly of revision.

These two hundred and forty-nine members shall be elected after the nomination of representatives to the legislative body shall have been terminated, and there shall be formed a separate official report of it.

The assembly of revision shall not be composed of more than one chamber.

VI. The members of the third legislature which shall have demanded a change cannot be elected in the assembly of revision.

VII. The members of the assembly of revision, after having pronounced together the oath *to live free or die,* shall individually swear *to confine themselves to deciding on the objects which shall have been submitted to them by the unanimous wish of three preceding legislatures; and to maintain, in other respects, with all their power, the constitution of the kingdom decreed by the National Constituent Assembly in the years 1789, 1790, and 1791; and to be in all faithful to the nation, to the law, and to the king.*

VIII. The assembly of revision shall be bound to occupy itself afterwards, and without delay, with the objects which shall have been submitted to its examination; and as soon as this task is finished, the two hundred and forty-nine new members, named over and above, shall retire, without taking a part, in any case, in the legislative acts.

The French colonies and possessions in Asia, Africa, and America, although they make a part of the French empire, are not included in the present constitution.

None of the powers instituted by the constitution have a right to change it in its whole, or in its parts, excepting the reforms which may be made in it by the mode of revision, conformably to the regulations of title VII, above.

The National Constituent Assembly commits the deposit of it to the fidelity of the legislative body, of the king, and of the judges, to the vigilance of fathers of families, to wives and to mothers, to the attachment of young citizens, to the courage of all Frenchmen.

The decrees passed by the National Assembly, which are not included in the act of constitution, shall be executed as laws; and those anterior laws which it has not altered shall also be observed so long as they shall not be revoked or modified by the legislative power.

VERNIER,
President
POUGEARD
COUPPÉ
MAILLY-CHÂTEAURENAUD
CHAILLON
AUBRY,
Bishop of Department of the Meuse
DARCHE
Secretaries

THE CONSTITUTION OF 1793

The French people, convinced that forgetfulness of, and contempt for, the natural rights of man are the only causes of the misfortunes of the world, have resolved to expose, in a declaration, their sacred and inalienable rights, in order that all citizens, being able always to compare the acts of the government with the end of every social institution, may never suffer themselves to be oppressed and degraded by tyranny; and that the people may always have before their eyes the basis of their liberty and happiness; the magistrates the rule of their duty; and the legislature the object of their mission.

They acknowledge therefore and proclaim, in the presence of the Supreme Being, the following

DECLARATION OF THE RIGHTS OF MAN AND OF THE CITIZEN

ARTICLE I. The end of society is common happiness. Government is instituted to secure to man the enjoyment of his natural and imprescriptible rights.

II. These rights are equality, liberty, safety, and property.

III. All men are equal by nature, and before the law.

IV. The law is the free and solemn expression of the general will. It ought to be the same for all, whether it protects or punishes. It cannot order but what is just and useful to society. It cannot forbid but what is hurtful.

V. All citizens are equally admissible to public employments. Free people avow no other motives of preference in their elections than virtues and talents.

VI. Liberty is that power which belongs to a man of doing everything that does not hurt the rights of another: its principle is nature; its rule is justice; its protection the law; and its moral limits are defined by the maxim, "Do not to another what you would not wish done to yourself."

VII. The right of manifesting one's thoughts and opinions, either by the press, or in any other manner; the right of assembling peaceably; and the free exercise of religious worship cannot be forbidden. The necessity of announcing these rights supposes either the presence or the recent remembrance of despotism.

VIII. Whatever is not forbidden by law cannot be prevented. No one can be forced to do what it does not order.

IX. Safety consists in the protection granted by society to each citizen for the preservation of his person, his rights, and his property.

X. The law avenges public and individual liberty of the abuses committed against them by power.

XI. No person can be accused, arrested, or confined but in cases determined by the law, and according to the forms which it prescribes. Every citizen summoned or seized by the authority of the law ought immediately to obey; he renders himself culpable by resistance.

XII. Every act exercised against a man to which the cases in the law do not apply, and in which its forms are not observed, is arbitrary and tyrannical. Respect for the law forbids him to submit to such acts; and if attempts are made to execute them by violence, he has a right to repel force by force.

XIII. Those who shall solicit, dispatch, sign, execute, or cause to be executed, arbitrary acts, are culpable, and ought to be punished.

XIV. Every man being supposed innocent until he has been declared guilty, if it is judged indispensable to arrest him, all severity not necessary to secure his person ought to be strictly repressed by law.

XV. No one ought to be tried and punished until he has been legally summoned, and in virtue of a law published previous to the commission of the crime. A law

APPENDIX 433

which should punish crimes committed before it existed would be tyrannical. The retroactive effect given to a law would be a crime.

XVI. The law ought not to decree any punishments but such as are strictly and evidently necessary; punishment ought to be proportioned to the crime, and useful to society.

XVII. The right of property is that right which belongs to every citizen to enjoy and dispose of according to his pleasure his property, revenues, labor, and industry.

XVIII. No kind of labor, culture, or commerce can be forbidden to the industrious citizen.

XIX. Every man may engage his services and his time, but he cannot sell himself — his person is not alienable property. The law does not acknowledge servitude — there can exist only an engagement of care and acknowledgment between the man who labors and the man who employs him.

XX. No one can be deprived of the smallest portion of his property without his consent, except when the public necessity, legally ascertained, evidently requires it, and on condition of a just and previous indemnification.

XXI. No contribution can be established but for general utility, and to relieve the public wants. Every citizen has the right to concur in the establishment of contributions, to watch over the use made of them, and to call for a statement of their expenditure.

XXII. Public aids are a sacred debt. Society is obliged to provide for the subsistence of the unfortunate, either by procuring them work, or by securing the means of existence to those who are unable to labor.

XXIII. Instruction is the want of all, and society ought to favor, with all its power, the progress of public reason; and to place instruction within the reach of every citizen.

XXIV. The social guarantee consists in the actions of all to secure to each the enjoyment and preservation of his rights. This guarantee rests on the national sovereignty.

XXV. The social guarantee cannot exist if the limits of public functions are not clearly defined by the law, and if the responsibility of all public functionaries is not secured.

XXVI. The sovereignty resides in the people. It is one and indivisible, imprescriptible and inalienable.

XXVII. No portion of the people can exercise the power of the whole, but each section of the sovereign assembled ought to enjoy the right of expressing its will in perfect liberty. Every individual who arrogates to himself the sovereignty, or who usurps the exercise of it, ought to be put to death by free men.

XXVIII. A people have always the right of revising, amending, and changing their constitution. One generation cannot subject to its laws future generations.

XXIX. Every citizen has an equal right of concurring in the formation of the law, and in the nomination of his mandatories or agents.

XXX. Public functions cannot be considered as distinctions or rewards, but as duties.

XXXI. Crimes committed by the mandatories of the people and their agents ought never to remain unpunished. No one has a right to pretend to be more inviolable than other citizens.

XXXII. The right of presenting petitions to the depositories of public authority belongs to every individual. The exercise of this right cannot, in any case, be forbidden, suspended, or limited.

XXXIII. Resistance to oppression is the consequence of the other rights of man.

XXXIV. Oppression is exercised against the social body when even one of its members is oppressed. Oppression is exercised against each member when the social body is oppressed.

XXXV. When the government violates the rights of the people, insurrection becomes to the people, and to every portion of the people, the most sacred, and the most indispensable of duties.

CONSTITUTIONAL ACT OF THE REPUBLIC

ARTICLE I. The French Republic is one and indivisible.

OF THE DIVISION OF THE PEOPLE

II. The French people are divided, for the exercise of the sovereignty, into primary assemblies of cantons.

III. For the administration of justice they are divided into departments, districts, and municipalities.

OF THE STATE OF CITIZENS

IV. Every man born and resident in France of the age of twenty-one years complete, every foreigner aged twenty-one years complete who has resided a year in France, who has acquired property, married a French woman, adopted a child, or maintained an aged person; in short, every foreigner who shall be judged by the legislative body to have deserved well by his humanity shall be admitted to exercise the rights of a French citizen.

V. The exercise of the rights of citizens shall be lost by being naturalized in a foreign country, by accepting functions or favors from a government not popular, and by condemnation to disgraceful or penal punishments.

VI. The exercise of the rights of citizens shall be suspended by a state of accusation; and by being declared contumacious, as long as the sentence is not reversed.

OF THE SOVEREIGNTY OF THE PEOPLE

VII. The sovereign people are the generality of the French citizens.

VIII. They shall immediately name the deputies.

IX. They shall delegate to electors the choice of administrators, public arbitrators, criminal judges, and judges of repeal.

X. They shall deliberate on laws.

OF PRIMARY ASSEMBLIES

XI. Primary assemblies shall be composed of citizens who have resided six months in each canton.

XII. They shall consist of two hundred citizens at least, or six hundred at most, called to vote.

XIII. They shall be constituted by the nomination of a president, secretaries, and scrutineers.

XIV. Their police shall belong to them.

XV. No person can appear there with arms.

XVI. The elections shall be made by scrutiny, or openly by the voice of each voter.

XVII. A primary assembly cannot in any case prescribe a uniform mode of voting.

XVIII. The scrutineers shall certify the vote of citizens who, not being able to write, prefer voting by scrutiny.

XIX. The suffrages on laws shall be given by *yes* or *no*.

XX. The will of the primary assembly shall be proclaimed as follows: *The citizens united in the primary assembly of —— to the number of —— voters vote (for or against) by a majority of ——.*

OF THE NATIONAL REPRESENTATION

XXI. Population is the only basis of national representation.

XXII. There shall be a deputy for every 40,000 inhabitants.

XXIII. When primary assemblies unite, so as to form a population of from 39,000 to 41,000 souls, they shall immediately choose a deputy.

XXIV. The nomination shall be by an absolute majority of votes.

XXV. Each assembly shall count the suffrages, and send a commissioner to the general verification, in the place marked out as the most central.

XXVI. If the first verification does not give an absolute majority, recourse shall be had to a second appeal, and the contest shall lie between the two citizens who have the most votes.

XXVII. In case the votes are equal, the oldest shall have the preference, either to be balloted for, or to be elected. In case of equality of age, chance shall decide.

XXVIII. Every Frenchman exercising the rights of citizen is eligible throughout the whole extent of the Republic.

XXIX. Each deputy belongs to the nation.

XXX. In case of the refusal, resignation, suspension, or death of a deputy, his place shall be supplied by the primary assemblies who elected him.

XXXI. A deputy who submits his resignation cannot quit his post until his successor shall have been admitted.

XXXII. The French people shall assemble every year, on the 1st of May, for elections.

XXXIII. They shall proceed to them whatever may be the number of citizens who have the right to vote.

XXXIV. The primary assemblies shall form themselves extraordinarily on a request by the fifth part of the citizens who have a right to vote.

XXXV. The convocation shall be made, in this case, by the municipality of the usual place of meeting.

XXXVI. These extraordinary assemblies shall not deliberate unless half of the citizens, plus one, who have a right to vote there, are present.

Of Electoral Assemblies

XXXVII. The citizens united in primary assemblies shall name an elector for every 200 citizens, present or not; two for from 201 to 400, and three for from 401 to 600.

XXXVIII. The holding of the electoral assemblies, and the mode of election, shall be the same as for the primary assemblies.

Of the Legislative Body

XXXIX. The legislative body is one, indivisible, and permanent.

XL. Its time of sitting shall be one year.

XLI. It shall meet on the 1st of July.

XLII. The National Assembly cannot constitute itself unless it be composed of half the deputies, plus one, at least.

XLIII. The deputies cannot be seized, accused, nor tried at any time for the opinions which they express in the legislative body.

XLIV. For criminal acts, they may be seized in cases where the fact is notorious, but neither a mandate of arrest, nor a mandate for trying them, can be decreed but by authority of the legislative body.

Holding of the Sittings of the Legislative Body

XLV. The sittings of the National Assembly shall be public.

XLVI. The minutes of the sittings shall be published.

XLVII. It cannot deliberate unless it consists of more than 200 members at least.

XLVIII. It cannot refuse to hear its members when they wish to speak, in the order they demand.

XLIX. It shall decide by a majority of those present.

L. Fifty members have the right to require a roll call.

LI. It has a right to censure the conduct of its members within the place of sitting.

LII. The police belongs to it in the place of its sittings, and within a certain district which it shall determine.

OF THE FUNCTIONS OF THE LEGISLATIVE BODY

LIII. The legislative body shall propose laws and pass decrees.

LIV. Under the general name of *laws* are comprehended acts of the legislative body concerning civil and criminal legislation; the general administration of the revenues and ordinary expenses of the Republic; the nature, amount, and collecting of the contributions; the declaring of war; every new division of the French territories; public instruction; and the public honors granted to the memory of great men.

LV. Under the particular name of *decrees* are comprehended acts of the legislative body concerning the annual establishment of the sea and land forces; permitting or prohibiting the passage of foreign troops through the French territories; the introduction of foreign naval forces into parts of the Republic; measures of general safety and tranquillity; the annual and temporary distribution of aids and public labors; orders for the coining of money of every kind; unforeseen and extraordinary expenses; measures peculiar and local to one administration, commune, or kind of public works; the defense of territory; the ratification of treaties; the nomination and suspensions of commanders-in-chief of the armies; the prosecuting and responsibility of members of the council, or public functionaries; the accusing of persons guilty of forming plots against the general safety of the Republic; every change in the partial division of the French territory; and national rewards.

ON THE FORMATION OF A LAW

LVI. Every plan of a law shall be preceded by a report.

LVII. The discussion cannot be continued, nor the law provisionally decreed, longer than fifteen days after the report.

LVIII. The plan shall be printed and sent to all the communes of the Republic, under the title of *a law proposed*.

LIX. Forty days after the plan has been published and distributed, if in one-half of the departments, plus one, a tenth part of the primary assemblies of each of them, regularly formed, have not remonstrated against the plan, it shall be considered as accepted, and shall become a *law*.

LX. If there be a remonstrance, the legislative body shall convoke the primary assemblies.

OF THE TITLE OF LAWS AND DECREES

LXI. Laws, decrees, sentences, and all public acts shall be entitled: *In the name of the French People, the —— year of the French Republic.*

OF THE EXECUTIVE COUNCIL

LXII. There shall be an executive council composed of twenty-four members.

LXIII. The electoral assembly of each department shall name a candidate, and the legislative body shall from the general list choose the members of the council.

LXIV. One-half of the members shall be renewed each legislature, in the last months of the session.

LXV. The council is charged with the direction and inspection of the general administration. It cannot act but to execute laws and decrees of the legislative body.

LXVI. It shall appoint, but not from among its own members, the chief agents of the general administration of the Republic.

LXVII. The legislative body shall determine the number and functions of these agents.

LXVIII. These agents shall not form a council. They are separate, without any immediate connection among themselves. They shall exercise no personal authority.

LXIX. The council shall appoint, but not from among its own members, the external agents of the Republic.

LXX. It shall negotiate treaties.

LXXI. The members of the council, in case of misconduct, shall be accused by the legislative body.

LXXII. The council shall be responsible for the non-execution of laws and decrees, and for abuses which it does not denounce.

LXXIII. It shall have the power of displacing agents whom it has appointed.

LXXIV. It is bound to denounce them, if there be occasion for it, before the judicial authorities.

Of the Relations of the Executive Council with the Legislative Body

LXXV. The executive council shall reside near the legislative body. It shall have admission to its sittings, and a distinct place in the hall where it meets.

LXXVI. It shall be heard whenever it has a report to give in.

LXXVII. The legislative body shall have the power of calling before it the whole, or any part, of its members, whenever it thinks proper.

Of Administrative and Municipal Bodies

LXXVIII. There shall be in each commune of the Republic a municipal administration; in each district an intermediate administration; and in each department a central administration.

LXXIX. Municipal officers shall be elected by the assemblies of the communes.

LXXX. The administrators shall be chosen by the electoral assemblies of departments and districts.

LXXXI. Municipalities and administrations shall be half renewed every year.

LXXXII. Administrators and municipal officers have no character of representation. They can in no case modify the acts of the legislative body, nor suspend the execution of them.

LXXXIII. The legislative body shall determine the functions of municipal officers and administrators, rules for their subordination, and the punishments they shall incur.

LXXXIV. The sittings of municipalities and administrations shall be public.

Of Civil Justice

LXXXV. The code of civil and criminal laws shall be uniform for the whole Republic.

LXXXVI. No infringement shall be made in the right which citizens have of deciding their differences by arbitrators chosen by themselves.

LXXXVII. The decision of these arbitrators shall be definitive if the citizens have not reserved to themselves the right of appealing.

LXXXVIII. There shall be justices of peace, chosen by the citizens of certain districts determined on by the law.

LXXXIX. These shall settle differences, and judge respecting disputes, without occasioning any expense to the parties.

XC. Their number and competence shall be regulated by the legislative body.

XCI. There shall be public arbitrators chosen by the electoral assemblies.

XCII. Their number and the extent of their districts shall be fixed by the legislative body.

XCIII. They shall take cognizance of disputes which have not been definitely terminated by private arbitrators, or by justices of peace.

XCIV. They shall deliberate in public; they shall give their opinion openly; they shall determine in the last instance on verbal defenses or simple memorials without a long process, and without expense to the parties; and they shall assign a reason for their decisions.

XCV. Justices of peace, and these public arbitrators, shall be chosen annually.

Of Criminal Justice

XCVI. In criminal affairs no citizen can be tried but on an accusation received by a jury, or decreed by the legislative body. The accused shall be allowed counsel, chosen by themselves, or officially named; the prosecution shall be carried on publicly; the fact and intention shall be declared by a jury of judgment; and the punishment shall be applied by a criminal tribunal.

XCVII. The criminal judges shall be elected annually by the electoral assemblies.

Of the Tribunal of Appeal

XCVIII. There shall be for the whole Republic a tribunal of repeal.

XCIX. This tribunal shall not enquire into the merits of cases; it shall decide only on violations of form, and express contradictions to the law.

C. The members of this tribunal shall be chosen annually by the electoral assemblies.

Of Public Contributions

CI. No citizen is exempted from the honorable obligation of contributing to public charges.

Of the National Treasury

CII. The national treasury is the central point of the receipts and expenditures of the Republic.

CIII. It shall be managed by accountable agents appointed by the executive council.

CIV. These agents shall be under the inspection of commissioners chosen by the legislative body, but not from among their number, and responsible for abuses which they do not denounce.

Of Responsibility

CV. The accounts of the agents of the national treasury, and administrators of the public money, shall be laid annually before responsible commissioners appointed by the executive council.

CVI. These auditors shall be under the inspection of commissioners named by the legislative body, but not from among their own members, and responsible for abuses and errors which they do not denounce. The legislative body shall balance their accounts.

Of the Forces of the Republic

CVII. The general force of the Republic consists of the whole people.

CVIII. The Republic shall keep in its pay, even in times of peace, a naval and armed force.

CIX. All Frenchmen are soldiers; they shall all be exercised in the use of arms.

CX. There shall be no generalissimo.

CXI. Differences of rank, its distinguishing marks, and subordination exist only in respect to service, and while it continues.

CXII. The public force employed to maintain peace and good order in the interior shall not act but on a requisition in writing from the constituted authorities.

CXIII. The public forces employed against internal enemies shall act only under the orders of the executive council.

CXIV. No armed body can deliberate.

Of National Conventions

CXV. If in the half of the departments, plus one, the tenth part of the primary assemblies of each of them, regularly formed, shall demand a revision of the constitutional code, or the alteration of any of its articles, the legislative body is bound to convoke all the primary assemblies of the Republic to know whether there be occasion for a national convention.

CXVI. The national convention shall be formed in the same manner as the legislative, and possess all its powers.

CXVII. It shall not occupy itself in regard to the constitution, but on those subjects which have given occasion for its being convened.

Of the Connection of the French Republic with Foreign Nations

CXVIII. The French people are the friends and natural allies of free peoples.

CXIX. They will not interfere in the government of other nations. They will not suffer other nations to interfere with theirs.

CXX. They will grant asylum to foreigners banished from their country for the cause of liberty. They will refuse it to tyrants.

CXXI. They will not make peace with an enemy who occupies their territories.

Of the Guarantee of Rights

CXXII. The constitution guarantees to all the French equality, liberty, safety, property, the public debt, the free exercise of worship, a common instruction, public succor, unlimited liberty of the press, the right of petition, the right of meeting in popular societies, the enjoyment of the rights of man.

CXXIII. The French Republic honors loyalty, courage, filial piety, and misfortune. It puts the deposit of its constitution under the guard of all the virtues.

CXXIV. The Declaration of Rights and the Constitutional Act are engraven on tables, in the bosom of the legislative body, and in the public places.

COLLOT-D'HERBOIS,
President
DURAND-MAILLANE
DUCOS
MÉAULLE
CH. DELACROIX
GOSSUIN
P. A. LALOY
Secretaries

Concordance of Dates

in the Years I, II, III, and IV for Immediate Reference

YEAR I

1st   Vendémiaire — September 22, 1792
10th Vendémiaire — October 1
1st   Brumaire — October 22
11th Brumaire — November 1
1st   Frimaire — November 21
11th Frimaire — December 1
1st   Nivôse — December 21
12th Nivôse — January 1, 1793
1st   Pluviôse — January 20
13th Pluviôse — February 1
1st   Ventôse — February 19
11th Ventôse — March 1
1st   Germinal — March 21
12th Germinal — April 1
1st   Floréal — April 20
12th Floréal — May 1
1st   Prairial — May 20
13th Prairial — June 1
1st   Messidor — June 19
13th Messidor — July 1
1st   Thermidor — July 19
14th Thermidor — August 1
1st   Fructidor — August 18
15th Fructidor — September 1
1st   Sans-culottide — September 17
5th   Sans-culottide — September 21

YEAR II

1st   Vendémiaire — September 22, 1793
10th Vendémiaire — October 1
1st   Brumaire — October 22
11th Brumaire — November 1
1st   Frimaire — November 21
11th Frimaire — December 1
1st   Nivôse — December 21
12th Nivôse — January 1, 1794
1st   Pluviôse — January 20
13th Pluviôse — February 1
1st   Ventôse — February 19
11th Ventôse — March 1
1st   Germinal — March 21
12th Germinal — April 1
1st   Floréal — April 20
12th Floréal — May 1
1st   Prairial — May 20
13th Prairial — June 1
1st   Messidor — June 19
13th Messidor — July 1
1st   Thermidor — July 19
14th Thermidor — August 1
1st   Fructidor — August 18
15th Fructidor — September 1
1st   Sans-culottide — September 17
5th   Sans-culottide — September 21

YEAR III

1st   Vendémiaire — September 22, 1794
10th Vendémiaire — October 1
1st   Brumaire — October 22
11th Brumaire — November 1
1st   Frimaire — November 21
11th Frimaire — December 1
1st   Nivôse — December 21
12th Nivôse — January 1, 1795
1st   Pluviôse — January 20
13th Pluviôse — February 1
1st   Ventôse — February 19
11th Ventôse — March 1
1st   Germinal — March 21
12th Germinal — April 1
1st   Floréal — April 20
12th Floréal — May 1
1st   Prairial — May 20
13th Prairial — June 1
1st   Messidor — June 19
13th Messidor — July 1
1st   Thermidor — July 19
14th Thermidor — August 1
1st   Fructidor — August 18
15th Fructidor — September 1
1st   Sans-culottide — September 17
6th   Sans-culottide — September 22

YEAR IV

1st   Vendémiaire — September 23, 1795
9th   Vendémiaire — October 1
1st   Brumaire — October 23
10th Brumaire — November 1
1st   Frimaire — November 22
10th Frimaire — December 1
1st   Nivôse — December 22
11th Nivôse — January 1, 1796
1st   Pluviôse — January 21
12th Pluviôse — February 1
1st   Ventôse — February 20
11th Ventôse — March 1
1st   Germinal — March 21
12th Germinal — April 1
1st   Floréal — April 20
12th Floréal — May 1
1st   Prairial — May 20
13th Prairial — June 1
1st   Messidor — June 19
13th Messidor — July 1
1st   Thermidor — July 19
14th Thermidor — August 1
1st   Fructidor — August 18
15th Fructidor — September 1
1st   Sans-culottide — September 17
5th   Sans-culottide — September 21

Bibliography

Argenson, *Mémoires et journal inédit*, 5 vols., Paris, 1857. René-Louis de Voyer, Marquis d'Argenson (1694–1757), minister of foreign affairs under Louis XV, an ambitious noble who "loved both royalty and the people," is unsparing in his criticism of pre-revolutionary France.

Arnault, *Souvenirs d'un sexagénaire*, 4 vols., Paris, 1833. Antoine-Vincent Arnault (1766–1834), a poet and writer of fables, was a member of the *entourage* of Monsieur. He was imprisoned in the Abbaye, but was released and went to England.

Bailly, *Mémoires*, 3 vols., Paris, 1821–1822. Jean-Sylvain Bailly (1736–1793) was one of the leaders of the third estate. He became president of the Constituent Assembly and mayor of Paris after the fall of the Bastille. He lost his popularity in the massacre of the Champ-de-Mars and was executed in 1793.

Barbaroux, *Mémoires*, Paris, 1822. Charles-Jean-Marie Barbaroux (1767–1794), deputy of the National Convention, belonged to the Girondin party. He brought the Marseillais to Paris, took part in the conspiracy of August 10, shot himself when outlawed and pursued in 1794, and was taken dying to the scaffold.

Barère, *Mémoires*, 4 vols., Brussels, 1842. Bertrand Barère de Vieuzac (1755–1841), a member of the National Convention, presided at the trial of the king, became a member of the committee of public safety, helped overthrow the Girondins, and advocated the Terror. He was one of the Jacobins who helped overthrow Robespierre. He was saved from transportation by the amnesty after the 18th Brumaire.

Barras, *Mémoires*, 3 vols., Paris, 1895. Paul-François-Jean-Nicolas, Comte de Barras (1755–1829), took part in the storming of the Bastille and of the Tuileries. He became a member of the Convention, and commanded the troops on the 9th Thermidor and the 13th Vendémiaire. He aided Bonaparte to rise and arranged his marriage with Josephine. He was the most influential member of the Directory. His *Mémoires* are often untruthful.

Besenval, *Mémoires*, 2 vols., Paris, 1821. Baron Pierre-Victor de Besenval (1722–1791), a Swiss officer at the French court during the reigns of Louis XV and Louis XVI, commanded the troops in Paris immediately preceding the fall of the Bastille, for which he was arrested and tried. During the trial he was attacked by a malady of which he died, as he had predicted.

Billaud-Varenne, *Mémoires inédits et correspondance*, Paris, 1893. Jean-Nicolas Billaud-Varenne (1756–1819), member of the Convention and of the committee of public safety, was one of the Jacobin Terrorists. He aided in the plot to overthrow Robespierre and attacked him in the Convention. Arrested during the Thermidorian reaction and deported, he died in Haiti.

Bonaparte, *Memoirs*, 3 vols., London, 1836. Lucien Bonaparte (1775–1840), brother of Napoleon, was a witness to the disturbances of Prairial and throws some light upon Napoleon's attitude at this period. He later became president of the Five Hundred and Prince of Canino.

Bonchamps, Mme. de, *Mémoires*, Paris, 1823. Madame de Bonchamps was the wife of Charles-Melchior-Artus, Marquis de Bonchamps, one of the foremost leaders of the Vendéens, whose revolt she describes in her memoirs.

Bouillé, *Mémoires*, Paris, 1822. François-Claude-Amour, Marquis de Bouillé (1739–1800), lieutenant-general of the king's armies, chevalier of his orders, governor of Douai, member of the Assembly of Notables, and general-in-chief of the army of the Meuse, Sarre, and Moselle, witnessed the last years of the reign of Louis XV and played an important part in the reign of Louis XVI. He was entrusted with the suppression of the revolt at Nancy and with safeguarding the flight of the king to Varennes. He was a cousin of La Fayette.

Bourrienne, *Mémoires sur Napoléon, le Directoire, le Consulat, l'Empire, et la Restauration*, 11 vols., Stuttgart, 1829–1830. Louis-Antoine Fauvelet de Bourrienne (1769–1834), minister of state, and secretary to Napoleon, gave details of Napoleon's actions during the Revolution.

Buchez, P. J. B., and Roux, P. C., *Histoire parlementaire de la Révolution française ou Journal des Assemblées nationales depuis 1789 jusqu'en 1815, contenant la Narration des événemens; les Débats des Assemblées; les Discussions des principales Sociétés populaires, et particulièrement de la Société des Jacobins; les procès-verbaux de la commune de Paris; les Séances du Tribunal révolutionnaire; le Compte-rendu des principaux procès politiques; les détails des budgets annuels; le Tableau du mouvement moral extrait des journaux de chaque époque, etc.; précédée d'une Introduction sur l'histoire de France jusqu'à la convocation des États-généraux*, 40 vols., Paris, 1834–1838.

Buzot, *Mémoires*, in *Mémoires inédits de Pétion et Mémoires de Buzot et de Barbaroux*, Paris, 1866. François-Léonard-Nicolas Buzot (1760–1794), member of the Constituent Assembly and deputy of the National Convention from the department of the Eure, was one of the Girondin leaders. Pursued after June 2, he committed suicide and was found half devoured by dogs or wolves.

Campan, Mme., *Memoirs of Marie Antoinette, Queen of France and Wife of Louis XVI (Memoirs of the Courts of Europe)*, New York, 1910. Used by permission of P. F. Collier and Son Company. Jeanne-Louise-Henriette Campan, *née* Genêt (1752–1822), lady-in-waiting to Marie Antoinette, devoted her memoirs to defending the queen and describing the events in which both took part. She was the sister of Edmond Genêt, envoy to the United States.

Carnot, *Mémoires historiques et militaires sur Carnot, rédigés d'après ses manuscrits, sa correspondance inédite et ses écrits*, Paris, 1824. Lazare-Nicolas-Marguerite Carnot (1753–1823), a member of the National Convention, and of the committee of public safety, organized and disciplined the fourteen armies of the Republic. He saved France from invasion and made possible the victories of Napoleon.

Chastenay, Mme. de, *Mémoires*, 2 vols., Paris, 1896. Louise-Marie-Victoire (Victorine), Comtesse de Chastenay-Lantry (1771–1855), was elected Canoness of Épinal at the age of fourteen. Her father was a member of the Constituent Assembly. Her preoccupation with her family in trouble brought her in touch with many political leaders. She was imprisoned during the Terror. She was one of the first to discover the genius of Bonaparte.

Choiseul, *Relation du départ de Louis XVI le 20 juin 1791*, Paris, 1822. Claude-Antoine-Gabriel, Duc de Choiseul-Stainville (1760–1838), a peer of France, took part in the arrangements made by Bouillé to protect the king's flight to Varennes. These memoirs were published to defend himself against the implication in the memoirs of Bouillé that he allowed the arrest of the king by withdrawing from Châlons and Somme-Vesle when the people became suspicious.

Choudieu, *Mémoires et notes*, Paris, 1897. Pierre-René Choudieu (1761–1838) was a representative of the people in the Legislative Assembly, the Convention, and with the armies of the Vendée and the north. He was imprisoned for opposing the Thermidorians and lived in exile during the Empire and the Restoration, returning after the Revolution of 1830.

Cléry, *Journal*, Paris, 1825. Jean-Baptiste Cant Hanet Cléry (1759–1809) served Louis XVI for five months as *valet de chambre* in the Temple, and was able to give a detailed account of the life of the royal family during that period.

Coittant, *Journal des événemens arrivés à Port-Libre depuis mon entrée dans cette maison*, in *Mémoires sur les prisons*, 2 vols., Paris, 1823.

Courtois, see *Papiers inédits*.

D'Argenson, see Argenson.

Desmoulins, *Le Vieux Cordelier*, in Berville and Barrière, *Collection des mémoires relatifs à la Révolution française*, 68 vols., Paris, 1821–1828. Lucie-Simplice-Camille-Benoist Desmoulins (1760–1794), journalist-revolutionist, aroused the mob that attacked the Bastille, was elected to the National Convention, supported Danton against Robespierre, and because of this and his attack upon the Terror, was sent to the guillotine.

Deux amis de la Liberté, *Histoire de la Révolution par deux amis de la Liberté*, in Ferrières, *Mémoires*, 3 vols., Paris, 1821–1822.

Doppet, *Mémoires politiques et militaires*, Paris, 1824. General François-Amédée Doppet (1753–1800) was physician, author, and general. He figured in the affair of August 10, in the uniting of Savoy to France, and in the war of federalism.

Dumas, *Memoirs of His Own Time including the Revolution and the Restoration*, 2 vols., London, 1839. Lieutenant-General Count Guillaume-Mathieu Dumas (1753–1837) entered the service as sub-lieutenant in 1773 and took part in the American war. He served on La Fayette's staff in the national guard and accompanied him to Versailles on the 5th October. He became a member of the Legislative Assembly.

Dumont, *Recollections of Mirabeau and of the First Two Assemblies*, Philadelphia, 1833. Pierre-Étienne-Louis Dumont (1759–1829), a Genevese political writer, aided Mirabeau with the *Courier de Provence*, and helped write his speeches for the National Assembly.

Dumouriez, *La vie et les mémoires*, 4 vols., Paris, 1822–1823. Charles-François Dumouriez (1739–1823) became Louis XVI's minister under the constitution of 1791, having charge of foreign affairs in the so-called Roland ministry. After his resignation he was made commander of the armies, winning the famous battles of Valmy and Jemappes, and conquering Belgium. Summoned to appear before the Assembly, he deserted to the enemy.

Durand de Maillane, *Histoire de la Convention nationale*, Paris, 1825. Pierre-Toussaint Durand de Maillane (1729–1814) helped draw up the cahiers at Arles, was elected deputy of the third estate, and in the Convention voted for the banishment of Louis XVI. He denounced Robespierre on the 8th Thermidor. Accused of royalism and of entering into relations with the *émigrés*, he was put under arrest, but later released.

Dusaulx, *De l'insurrection parisienne et de la prise de la Bastille*, Paris, 1822. Jean-Joseph Dusaulx (1728–1799) was a member of the committee of the Bastille. As elector he defended Flesselles and deplored the fate of De Launay.

Duval, *Souvenirs thermidoriens*, Paris, 1844. Georges-Louis-Jacques Duval (1772–1853), dramatic author and man of letters, in his *Souvenirs* tells of personal observations after the fall of Robespierre, giving free reign to his hatred of the Revolution.

Edgeworth, *Les dernières heures de Louis Seize*, in Cléry, *Journal*, Paris, 1825. Henry Essex Edgeworth de Firmont (1745–1807) was the last confessor of Louis XVI and accompanied the king to the scaffold. He was later the chaplain of Louis XVIII.

Ferrières, *Mémoires*, 3 vols., Paris, 1821–1822. Charles-Élie, Marquis de Ferrières de Marsay (1741–1804), deputy of the nobility in the States-General, was identified with the party of the Right in the National Assembly, having opposed the union of his order with the third estate. He was a severe critic of the king and the nobles as well as of the revolutionists.

Fersen, *Diary and Correspondence Relating to the Court of France (Versailles Memoirs)*, New York, 1902. Used by permission of P. F. Collier and Son Company. Count Hans

BIBLIOGRAPHY

Axel Fersen (1755–1810) was made a colonel in the French army for his services, in America under Rochambeau. Residing at the French court, he became devoted to Marie Antoinette and assisted in arranging the flight to Varennes, afterwards negotiating with the powers in behalf of the king and queen.

Fontanges, *Relation du voyage de Varennes, addressée par un prélat, membre de l'Assemblée constituante, à un ministre en pays étranger*, in Weber, *Mémoires*, 2 vols., Paris, 1822. The prelate is, to all appearances, M. de Fontanges, Archbishop of Toulouse.

Fouché, *Mémoires*, 2 vols., Paris, 1824. Joseph Fouché (1759–1820), a Terrorist and Montagnard, took a leading part in arousing the Convention against Robespierre. He was made minister of police and Duke of Otranto by Napoleon, and betrayed him after the Hundred Days.

Fournier, *Mémoires secrets*, Paris, 1890. Claude Fournier l'Héritier (1745–1825), called *l'Américain* from having lived in Santo Domingo, took part in the events of the 5th and 6th October, June 20, and August 10. He was in charge of the Orléans prisoners massacred at Versailles, September 8, 1792.

Fréron, *Mémoire historique sur la Réaction royale et sur les massacres du Midi*, Paris, 1824. Louis-Marie-Stanislas Fréron (1754–1802), ex-deputy to the National Convention and commissary of the government in the southern departments, was noted for his fusillades at Marseille and Toulon. He was one of the leaders of the Thermidorian reaction.

Gower, *Despatches*, Cambridge, 1885. George Granville Leveson, Earl Gower (1758–1833), was the English ambassador in France from 1790 to 1792. His dispatches to his government constitute reliable sources. He afterwards became Duke of Sutherland.

Guerres des Vendéens et des Chouans contre la République française ou annales des départmens de l'ouest pendant ces guerres, d'après les Actes et la Correspondance du comité de Salut public, des Ministres, des Représentans du peuple en mission, des Agens du gouvernement, des Autorités constituées, des généraux Berruyer, Biron, Canclaux, Rossignol, Santerre, L'Échelle, Kléber, Marceau, Turreau, Moulin, Hoche, etc., et d'après les Règlemens, Proclamations et Bulletins du conseil supérieur et des chefs des Vendéens et des Chouans; par un officier supérieur des Armées de la République, habitant dans la Vendée avant les troubles, 6 vols., Paris, 1824–1827.

Guillon, *Mémoires pour servir à l'histoire de la ville de Lyon pendant la Révolution*, 3 vols., Paris, 1824. L'Abbé Aimé Guillon de Montléon (1758–1842), placed in the midst of the events of which Lyon was the center, became the historian of that unfortunate city's rebellion against the Republic.

Horrors of the Prisons of Arras; or, the Crimes of Joseph Lebon, and his Agents, in the Reign of Terror, London, 1826.

Impartial History of the Late Revolution in France from its Commencement to the Death of the Queen and the Execution of the Deputies of the Girondin Party, Boston, 1794.

Jefferson, *Writings*, 9 vols., New York, 1854–1856. Thomas Jefferson (1743–1826), American ambassador to France, witnessed the opening of the States-General. He found much prosperity in rural France in spite of the heavy taxes and feudal dues. He was succeeded by Gouverneur Morris in 1789 and returned to the United States.

Jullien, Mme., *Journal d'une bourgeoise pendant la Révolution, 1791–1793*, Paris, 1881. Mme. Jullien (de la Drôme), wife of a member of the Constituent Assembly, remained in Paris after the dissolution of this Assembly, becoming a partisan of the Jacobins and the Republic. She was influenced by her study of Rousseau and the classics.

Lacroix, Camille, *Chefs-d'œuvres de l'éloquence parlementaire*, 4 vols., Paris, 1893.

La Fayette, *Mémoires, correspondance, et manuscrits*, 6 vols., Paris and London, 1837. Marie-Joseph-Paul-Yves-Roch-Gilbert Motier, Marquis de La Fayette (1757–1834), served under Washington in America, became a member of the States-General and commandant of the national guard, brought back the king from Versailles and Varennes, opposed the Jacobins as a constitutional monarchist, and failing in this, fled across the border. Arrested by the Austrians, he remained a prisoner until 1797. He afterwards took part in the Revolution of 1830.

La Motte, Mme. de, *Mémoires justificatifs, écrits par elle-même*, London, 1789. Jeanne de Luz de Saint-Rémy de Valois, Comtesse de La Motte (1756–1791), claimed descent from the Valois line of kings, and gaining access to Marie Antoinette through this claim, became involved in the diamond necklace affair. In her memoirs she alleges that the queen asked Rohan to buy the necklace, suggested the forged signature, and kept the necklace. This affair tended to discredit the queen in the eyes of the people.

Lanjuinais, *Les 31 mai, 1er et 2 juin, 1793, Fragment*, Paris, 1825. Jean-Denis, Comte Lanjuinais (1753–1827), was active in the Constituent Assembly and in the Convention. He brought forward the motion excluding Mirabeau from the ministry, and tried to secure the abandonment of the king's trial. Allied with the Girondin group, he played a noble part on June 2. He was recalled to the Convention in 1795 and became a peer of France under the Restoration.

Larevellière-Lépeaux, *Mémoires*, 3 vols., Paris, 1895. Louis-Marie Larevellière-Lépeaux (1753–1824), member of the States-General, the National Convention, and the Directory, refused to ally himself to any party. He was proscribed after the affair of June 2, but returned to the Convention after the 9th Thermidor.

La Rochejaquelein, Mme. de, *Memoirs*, Philadelphia, 1816. Marie-Louise-Victoire de Donissan, Marquise de La Rochejaquelein (1772–1857), observed the struggles of the Vendéens under the leadership of her husband, Henri de La Rochejaquelein, one of the celebrated chiefs of the revolt.

Las Cases, *Mémorial de Sainte-Hélène*, 3 vols., Paris, 1842. Emmanuel, Comte de Las Cases (1766–1842), accompanied Napoleon to St. Helena and kept a faithful account of what he did and said, taking down verbatim dictations.

Louvet, *Narrative of the Dangers to which I Have Been Exposed, since the 31st of May, 1793, with Historical Memorandums*, London, 1795. Jean-Baptiste Louvet de Couvray (1760–1797), author and publisher of *La Sentinelle*, was one of the Girondin leaders who combatted Robespierre and the commune. Proscribed on May 31, he retired to Calvados. Readmitted to the Convention after Thermidor, he became a member of the Five Hundred.

Madame Royale, *Récit des événements arrivés au Temple*, in Cléry, *Journal*, Paris, 1825. Marie-Thérèse-Charlotte, Duchesse d'Angoulême (1778–1851), daughter of Louis XVI, was known as Madame Royale at the time of the imprisonment of the royal family in the Temple. She later exercised great influence over Louis XVIII and Charles X. Napoleon called her the "only man in the family."

Mallet du Pan, *Memoirs and Correspondence*, 2 vols., London, 1852. Jacques Mallet du Pan (1749–1800), a Swiss, became editor of the *Mercure de France*. He was outspoken in his criticism of Necker and the Constituent Assembly, raising his voice in defense of the ill-treated Catholic clergy. He defended the royalist cause and was exiled in 1792.

Malouet, *Mémoires*, 2 vols., Paris, 1874. Pierre-Victor, Baron Malouet (1740–1814), a member of the Constituent Assembly, was a constitutional monarchist who favored reform, but opposed extremes. Denounced after August 10, he escaped to England. He became a member of the council of state under the Empire and minister of marine under the Restoration.

Manuscrit de l'an trois (1794–1795), contenant les premières transactions des puissances de l'Europe avec la république française, et le tableau des derniers événemens du régime conventionnel, pour servir à l'histoire de cette époque, par le baron Fain, alors secrétaire au comité militaire de la Convention nationale, Paris, 1828. Agathon-Jean-François, Baron Fain (1788–1837), secretary to the military committee of the National Convention and to Napoleon I at a later date, is known as a French historian.

Marmontel, *Memoirs*, 4 vols., London, 1805. Jean-François Marmontel (1723–1799) was a man of letters in close touch with the Revolution. He was an elector for the section of the Feuillants and one of the commissioners charged with drawing up the *cahiers*.

Méda, *Précis historique inédit des événemens de la soirée du 9 Thermidor An II*, in Berville and Barrière, *Collection des Mémoires relatifs à la Révolution française*, 68 vols., Paris, 1821–1828. Charles-André Méda (1775–1812) was a gendarme who was charged with arresting Robespierre. He died a baron and general of brigade.

Meillan, *Mémoires*, Paris, 1823. Arnaud Meillan (1748–1809) was a member of the National Convention, representing the department of the Basses-Pyrénées. An adherent of the Girondins, he participated in their downfall.

Mémoires sur les prisons, contenant les Mémoires d'un détenu, par Riouffe; l'Humanité méconnue, par J. Paris de l'Épinard; l'incarceration de Beaumarchais; le tableau historique de la prison de Saint-Lazare, 2 vols., Paris, 1823.

Mercy-Argenteau, *Correspondance secrète du comte de Mercy-Argenteau avec l'empereur Joseph II et le prince de Kaunitz*, 2 vols., Paris, 1889–1891. François, Comte de Mercy-Argenteau (1727–1794), Austrian ambassador at Paris, and confidant of Marie Antoinette, supported first Brienne, then Necker. He advised the flight of the royal family in 1791.

Miles, *Correspondence on the French Revolution, 1789–1817*, 2 vols., London and New York, 1890. Used by permission of Longmans, Green, and Company. William Augustus Miles (1754–1817), an English diplomatic agent in close connection with Pitt, described the events of the Revolution in letters from Paris to various English friends and statesmen.

Minutes of the Jacobin Club, in Thiers, *History of the French Revolution*, 4 vols., Philadelphia, 1848.

Miot de Mélito, *Memoirs*, 2 vols., London, 1881. Comte André-François Miot de Mélito (1762–1841), minister, ambassador, councillor of state, and member of the Institute of France, was present at the opening of the States-General, the events of the 5th and 6th October, the 10th of August, etc.

Mirecourt, Eugène, *Avant, pendant, et après la Terreur, Échos des gazettes françaises, publiées à l'étranger de 1788 à 1794*, 3 vols., Paris, 1865.

Moniteur, Réimpression de l'ancien Moniteur depuis la Réunion des États-Généraux jusqu'au Consulat, 31 vols., Paris, 1840–1845.

Montesquieu, *The Spirit of the Laws*, 2 vols., London, 1758. Charles de Secondat, Baron de La Brède et de Montesquieu (1689–1755), contributed to the Revolution in criticizing government. His great principle was separation of the powers.

Moore, *Journal*, 2 vols., London, 1793. John Moore (1729–1802), a British physician and author, kept a journal of the events which he witnessed in France in 1792.

Morellet, *Mémoires*, 2 vols., Paris, 1823. The Abbé André Morellet (1727–1819) was a priest of such liberal views that they savored of heresy. He consorted with Mirabeau, Necker, Siéyès, Turgot, Condorcet, D'Alembert, Holbach, Diderot, Voltaire, Rousseau, Helvétius, and Raynal. He became a member of the *corps législatif* and the chamber of deputies. He was a writer of some note.

Morris, *Diary*, in Jared Sparks, *Life of Gouverneur Morris, with Selections from his Correspondence and Miscellaneous Papers*, 3 vols., Boston, 1832. Gouverneur Morris (1752–1816), the American ambassador to France, witnessed the progress of the Revolution after he succeeded Jefferson in 1789. He was unfriendly to the Revolution.

Mounier, *Appel au tribunal de l'opinion publique, du Rapport de M. Chabroud, et du Décret rendu par l'Assemblée nationale le 2 Octobre 1790. Examen du Mémoire du Duc d'Orléans, et du Plaidoyer du Comte de Mirabeau, et nouveaux Éclaircissemens sur les crimes du 5 et du 6 Octobre 1789*, Geneva, 1791. Jean-Joseph Mounier (1758–1806), a deputy in the States-General, was president of the Assembly when the mob arrived on the 5th of October. After this he tried to induce the moderates to imitate him in resigning from the Assembly. He raised a revolt in Dauphiné, and ended by emigrating.

Papiers inédits trouvés chez Robespierre, Saint-Just, Payan, etc., supprimés ou omis par Courtois; précédés du rapport de ce deputé à la Convention nationale, 3 vols., Paris, 1828.

Paroy, *Mémoires*, Paris, 1895. Jean-Philippe-Gui le Gentil, Comte de Paroy (1750–1824), was one of the most active supporters of the royal family. He defended the Tuileries on June 20 and August 10, and thenceforth a refugee, continued to support the royal cause. He remained unrewarded during the Restoration.

Pétion, *Mémoires,* in *Mémoires inédits de Pétion et Mémoires de Buzot et de Barbaroux,* Paris, 1866. Jérôme Pétion de Villeneuve (1756–1794), a deputy in the Constituent Assembly, mayor of Paris, and finally a deputy in the National Convention, was a prominent Girondin. He was for a time the idol of Paris. Proscribed on May 31, he committed suicide in company with Buzot.

Pfyffer d'Altishoffen, *Récit de la conduite du régiment des gardes-suisses à la journée du 10 août 1792, par M. le colonel Pfyffer d'Altishoffen, chevalier des ordres militaires de Saint-Louis, de Saint-Maurice, et de Saint-Lazare; publié à Lucerne en 1819,* in Weber, *Mémoires,* 2 vols., Paris, 1822.

Political State of Europe, Containing an Authentic and Impartial Narrative of the Operations of the Present Belligerent Powers, and a Correct Copy of Every State Paper, Declaration, Manifesto, etc., that has been and may be issued during the present War upon the Continent. Likewise a considerable number of Original Papers, Facts, and other Elucidations. A Correct Translation of the Debates and Proceedings of the National Assembly of France, upon all Points relative to the War and Government, will also be given, from the best accounts published at Paris; together with a complete and accurate Survey of the Politics and Conduct of the Neutral Powers, at this very critical and interesting Period, 10 vols., London, 1792–1795.

Procès-verbal de l'Assemblée nationale, imprimé par son ordre, 75 vols., Paris, 1789–1791.

Procès-verbal de la séance du 9 thermidor, in Durand de Maillane, *Histoire de la Convention nationale,* Paris, 1825.

Procès-verbal des conférences sur la vérification des pouvoirs, tenues par MM. les Commissaires du Clergé, de la Noblesse, et des Communes, tant en la Salle du Comité des États-Généraux, qu'en présence de MM. les Commissaires du Roi, conformement au désir de Sa Majesté, Paris, 1789.

Procès-verbal des Électeurs, in Bailly, *Mémoires,* 3 vols., Paris, 1821–1822.

Procès-verbaux de la commune de Paris. Extraits des séances de la municipalité qui s'installa de vive force à l'Hôtel-de-Ville dans la nuit du 10 août 1792, in *Mémoires sur les journées de Septembre 1792,* Paris, 1823.

Rabaut Saint-Étienne, *Précis historique de la Révolution françoise, suivi de l'Acte constitutionnel des François. Seconde édition, augmentée de Réflexions politiques sur les circonstances présentes, par le même auteur,* Paris, 1792. Jean-Paul Rabaut Saint-Étienne (1743–1793), a Protestant pastor elected to the States-General and later to the Convention, was an ardent patriot, delighting in the civil constitution of the clergy and the constitution of 1791. He died on the guillotine.

Reign of Terror, The; a Collection of Authentic Narratives of the Horrors committed by the Revolutionary Government of France under Marat and Robespierre, written by eye-witnesses of the scenes, 2 vols., London, 1826.

Révolutions de Paris. Dédiées à la Nation et au district des Petits Augustins. Publié par le sieur Prudhomme, Paris, 1789–1794.

Riouffe, *Mémoires d'un détenu,* in *Mémoires sur les Prisons,* Paris, 1823. Honoré-Jean, Baron Riouffe (1764–1813), a revolutionist of Girondin sympathies, described the prison experiences of himself and others.

Rivarol, *Mémoires,* Paris, 1824. Antoine Rivaroli, who called himself the Comte de Rivarol (1753–1801), after having won a name in the literary world, ranged himself among the enemies of the Revolution, and attacked it in the *Journal politique et national* and in the *Actes des Apôtres,* the latter being directed against the Constituent Assembly. Unsuccessful in his attempts, he emigrated in 1792.

Roland, Mme., *Mémoires,* Paris, 1863. Marie-Jeanne (Manon) Phlipon (1754–1793), wife of the minister Roland, was the guiding spirit of the Girondins, with her salon their favorite meeting place. When the Girondins were overthrown, she was imprisoned and sent to the guillotine. She died after the manner of the classic heroes she admired.

Rousseau, *Œuvres*, 24 vols., Geneva, 1782. Jean-Jacques Rousseau (1712–1778), whose philosophy dealt with a return to nature, the goodness of man, and the social contract, contributed largely to the French Revolution with his radical doctrines.

Saint-Edme, *Répertoire général des Causes célèbres anciennes et modernes, rédigés par une société d'hommes de lettres sous la direction de B. de Saint-Edme, auteur du dictionnaire de la pénalité, etc., etc., Membre de la Société française de Statistique universelle, de l'Académie de l'Industrie, etc.*, 2e série, 5 vols., Paris, 1834–1835.

Sapinaud, Mme. de, *Mémoires historiques sur La Vendée*, in *Mémoires sur La Vendée*, Paris, 1823. Mme. de Sapinaud de Bois-Huguet described the revolt of the Vendée, in which her relatives took a leading part.

Sbornik Imperatorskago Russkago Istoritcheskago Obshtchestva, St. Petersburg, 1878. Correspondence of Catherine II with Grimm.

Schmidt, Adolph, *Tableaux de la Révolution française publiés sur les papiers inédits du départment et de la police secrète de Paris*, 3 vols., Leipzig, 1867–1871.

Ségur, *Mémoires, ou souvenirs et anecdotes*, 3 vols., Paris, 1827. Louis-Philippe, Comte de Ségur (1753–1830), son of a marshal of France, himself member of the Academy, peer, diplomatist, and historian, was one of the liberal nobles who followed La Fayette to America. He was in favor at the French court and became ambassador to Russia.

Sergent Marceau, *Reminiscences of a Regicide*, London, 1889. Antoine-François Sergent (1751–1847), member of the National Convention and administrator of police, was a Jacobin who sat with the Mountain and voted for the death of Louis XVI. He went into exile after the 1st Prairial, and again in 1800. He took the name Marceau in honor of his brother-in-law, a distinguished general.

Sicard, *Relation adressé à un de ses amis sur les dangers qu'il a courus les 2 et 3 septembre 1792*, in *Mémoires sur les journées de septembre 1792*, Paris, 1823. The Abbé Roche-Ambroise Cucurron Sicard (1742–1822) was one of the priests confined in the Abbaye during the September massacres.

Staël, Mme. de, *Considérations sur les Principaux Evénéments de la Révolution française*, Paris, 1843. Anne-Louise-Germaine, Baronne de Staël-Holstein (1766–1817), was the daughter of Necker. An authoress and a liberal, she was interested in political affairs and took some part in them. Napoleon held her in particular aversion.

Ternaux, Mortimer, *Histoire de la Terreur, 1792–1794*, 6 vols., Paris, 1863–1881.

Thibaudeau, *Mémoires sur la Convention et le Directoire*, 2 vols., Paris, 1824. Antoine-Claire Thibaudeau (1765–1854) was a member of the National Convention and president of that body during some of its most important sessions.

Thiers, M. A., *History of the French Revolution*, 4 vols., Philadelphia, 1848.

Tourzel, Mme. de, *Memoirs*, 2 vols., London, 1886. Louise-Elizabeth-Felicité-Armande-Anne-Marie-Jeanne-Josephine de Croÿ-d'Havré, Duchesse de Tourzel (1749–1832), was governess of the king's children from 1789 to 1793, witnessing the insurrection of the 5th and 6th October and the attacks upon the Tuileries. She accompanied the royal family on the flight to Varennes. She was made a duchess by Louis XVIII.

Turreau, *Mémoires pour servir à l'histoire de la guerre de La Vendée*, Paris, 1824. General Baron Louis-Marie Turreau de Linières (1756–1816) commanded a brigade in the war against the Vendéens. Arrested after Thermidor on charges of cruelty, he was acquitted. He wrote his memoirs in prison.

Vaublanc, *Mémoires*, Paris, 1857. Vincent-Marie, Comte de Vaublanc (1756–1845), was born in Santo Domingo, came to Paris in 1782, and as a royalist member sat on the Right of the Legislative Assembly. He was outlawed in 1792 and again under the Directory. He became minister of the interior under the Restoration. He was also a writer of note.

Vilate, *Causes secrètes de la Journée du 9 au 10 Thermidor An II, suivies des Mystères de la Mère de Dieu dévoilés*, in Berville and Barrière, *Collection des Mémoires relatifs à la Révolution française*, 68 vols., Paris, 1821–1828. Joachim Vilate (1768–1795) was connected with the revolutionary tribunal. He had been an ardent leader in the insurrection of August 10 and a follower of Robespierre. Imprisoned on the 2nd Thermidor, he wrote the above accusation of Robespierre in order to justify himself. He was nevertheless condemned and executed.

Voltaire, *Œuvres*, 56 vols., Paris, 1817–1821. François-Marie Arouet (1694–1778), who took the name of Voltaire, contributed to the revolutionary outbreak by his attacks upon church, state, and society.

Weber, *Mémoires*, 2 vols., Paris, 1822. Joseph Weber (1755–   ) was the foster brother of Marie Antoinette. Living at the French court, he witnessed many of the events of the Revolution such as those of the 5th and 6th of October, and the attack on the Tuileries. The date and place of his death are unknown.

Williams, *Letters Containing a Sketch of the Scenes which Passed in the Various Departments of France during the Tyranny of Robespierre, and of the Events which Took Place in Paris on the Tenth of Thermidor*, London, 1795. Helen Maria Williams (1762–1827), an English authoress, resided in France after 1788. She adopted the ideas of the Revolution, was acquainted with the Girondins, and became intimate with Mme. Roland. She was imprisoned by Robespierre. Before and after her arrest she wrote freely her impressions of the events she witnessed or of which she was informed.

Young, *Travels in France during the Years 1787, 1788, 1789*, London, 1890. Arthur Young (1741–1820) was an English writer on agricultural subjects who travelled through France before and during the Revolution, later publishing his observations and investigations.

Index